WEIMAR PUBLICS/WEIMAR SUBJECTS

SPEKTRUM: *Publications of the German Studies Association*

Series editor: David M. Luebke, University of Oregon

Published under the auspices of the German Studies Association, *Spektrum* offers current perspectives on culture, society, and political life in the German-speaking lands of central Europe—Austria, Switzerland, and the Federal Republic—from the late Middle Ages to the present day. Its titles and themes reflect the composition of the GSA and the work of its members within and across the disciplines to which they belong—literary criticism, history, cultural studies, political science, and anthropology.

Volume 1
The Holy Roman Empire, Reconsidered
Edited by Jason Philip Coy, Benjamin Marschke, and David Warren Sabean

Volume 2
Weimar Publics/Weimar Subjects
Rethinking the Political Culture of Germany in the 1920s
Edited by Kathleen Canning, Kerstin Barndt, and Kristin McGuire

Volume 3
Conversion and the Politics of Religion in Early Modern Germany
Edited by David M. Luebke, Jared Poley, Daniel C. Ryan, and David Warren Sabean

Volume 4
Walls, Borders, Boundaries: Spatial and Cultural Practices in Europe
Edited by Marc Silberman, Karen E. Till, and Janet Ward

Volume 5
After The History of Sexuality: German Genealogies With and Beyond Foucault
Edited by Scott Spector, Helmut Puff, and Dagmar Herzog

Volume 6
Becoming East German: Socialist Structures and Sensibilities after Hitler
Edited by Mary Fulbrook and Andrew I. Port

Weimar Publics/Weimar Subjects

Rethinking the Political Culture
of Germany in the 1920s

~:~

Edited by

KATHLEEN CANNING

KERSTIN BARNDT & KRISTIN MCGUIRE

berghahn
NEW YORK · OXFORD
www.berghahnbooks.com

First published in 2010 by

Berghahn Books

www.berghahnbooks.com

Library of Congress Cataloging-in-Publication Data

Weimar publics/Weimar subjects : rethinking the political culture of Germany in the
1920s / edited by Kathleen Canning, Kerstin Barndt & Kristin McGuire.
    p. cm.
    Includes bibliographical references and index.
ISBN 978-1-84545-689-4 (hardback) -- ISBN 978-1-84545-846-1 (institutional ebook)
ISBN 978-1-78238-107-5 (paperback) -- ISBN 978-1-78238-108-2 (retail ebook)
    1. Political culture—Germany—History—20th century. 2. Popular culture—
Germany—History—20th century. 3. Germany—Politics and government—
1918–1933. 4. Germany—Intellectual life—20th century. 5. Germany—Social
conditions—1918–1933. 6. Social conflict—Germany—History—20th century.
7. Social change—Germany—History—20th century. I. Canning, Kathleen. II. Barndt,
Kerstin. III. McGuire, Kristin.
    DD240.W3925 2010
    943.085—dc22

    2009042366

British Library Cataloguing in Publication Data

A catalogue record for this book is available from the British Library

Printed in the United States on acid-free paper.

ISBN: 978-1-78238-107-5 paperback   ISBN: 978-1-78238-108-2 retail ebook

❧ CONTENTS ❧

~: ILLUSTRATIONS :~

❧ PREFACE ❧

The essays in this volume reflect a longer-term conversation that began among several of us at a kitchen table in Ann Arbor and quickly widened to include colleagues at other institutions in the United States, Great Britain, and Germany. From the outset our discussions were interdisciplinary, conjoining inquiries in history and German studies, art history, film studies, and gender studies. We wish to thank those institutions which provided generous financial support for our initial meetings and workshops, including the "Rethinking Weimar" conference, which we organized at the University of Michigan: the German Academic Exchange Service (DAAD), the Max Kade Foundation, the University of Michigan's Office of the Vice-President for Research, Rackham Graduate School, the Center for European Studies, and the Departments of History and Germanic Languages and Literatures.

We would also like to thank colleagues at Michigan and elsewhere who participated in spirited exchanges that shaped this volume, including those who provided incisive comments on the essays featured here: Matthew Biro, Tina Campt, David Crew, Edward Dimendberg, Geoff Eley, Michael Geyer, Elizabeth Goodstein, Atina Grossmann, Julia Hell, Sabine Kienitz, Paul Lerner, Vernon L. Lidtke, Mary Nolan, Patrice Petro, Helmut Puff, Julie Sneeringer, Scott Spector, James Steakley, Dennis Sweeney, Cornelia Usborne, Janet Ward, Meike Werner, and Benjamin Ziemann. In addition, we would like to thank the anonymous reviewers of this volume whose insights and suggestions certainly enriched the individual essays and the collection as a whole. The publication of this volume has been made possible by the generous support of the Office of the Vice-President for Research (OVPR), the Department of History, and the Department of Germanic Languages and Literatures at the University of Michigan.

Finally, the editors would like to dedicate this volume to Mary O'Reilly, our colleague, friend, and PhD candidate at Michigan whose own promising dissertation on new women, fashion, and advertising was cut short by her death in April 2009 of cancer. Mary worked with us in preparing these essays for publication and each of its essays bears traces of her expertise. With this dedication we honor her contributions to this volume and to the broader field of politics and culture in Weimar Germany.

Kerstin Barndt, Kathleen Canning, Kristin McGuire
Ann Arbor, July 2009

∽: CONTRIBUTORS :∾

Manuela Achilles is Lecturer of History and Germanic Languages and Literatures and Program Director of the Center for German Studies at the University of Virginia. Her articles include "Nationalist Violence and Republican Identity in Weimar Germany," in David Midgley and Christian Emden, *German Literature, History and the Nation* (Oxford, 2004) and "With a Passion for Reason: Celebrating the Constitution in Germany," *Central European History* 43 (2010), forthcoming. Currently, she is revising her manuscript *Democratic Culture in Weimar Germany. Beyond the Failure Paradigm.*

Kerstin Barndt is Associate Professor of German Studies at the University of Michigan, where she is also affiliated with the Museum Studies Program. She is the author of *Sentiment und Sachlichkeit. Der Roman der Neuen Frau in der Weimarer Republik* (Cologne, 2004) and is currently completing a book manuscript on shifting representations of temporality in museum culture entitled *Non/Simultaneities. Exhibiting Time and History in Contemporary Germany.*

Kathleen Canning is Sonya O. Rose Collegiate Professor of History and Arthur F. Thurnau Professor of History, Women's Studies, and German at the University of Michigan. She is the author of *Languages of Labor and Gender: Female Factory Work in Germany, 1850-1914* (2nd ed., Ann Arbor, MI, 2002) and *Gender History in Practice: Historical Perspectives on Bodies, Class, and Citizenship* (Ithaca, NY, 2006). Her current book project is entitled *Citizenship Effects: Gender and Sexual Crisis in the Aftermath of War and Revolution in Germany, 1916-1930.*

Brigid Doherty is Associate Professor of German and Art and Archeology at Princeton University. She has published widely on Weimar avant-garde art and is the coeditor of *Walter Benjamin: The Work of Art in the Age of Its Technological Reproducibility and other Writings on Media* (Cambridge, MA, 2008). Her current book project, "Homesickness for Things," situates the work of writers and artists, including Rainer Maria Rilke and Hanne Darboven, in relation to theories of "projective identification" and related phenomena of thinking, feeling, and intersubjectivity in psychoanalysis.

Peter Fritzsche is Professor of History at the University of Illinois at Urbana-Champaign. His most recent publications include *Life and Death in the Third Reich* (Cambridge, MA, 2008), *Nietzsche and the Death of God* (Boston, 2007), *Stranded in the Present: Modern Time and the Melancholy of History* (Cambridge, MA, 2004), and *Germans into Nazis* (Cambridge, MA, 1998). His current research focuses on comparative questions of memory and identity and vernacular uses of the past in modern Europe.

Martin Geyer is Professor of Modern History at the Ludwig-Maximilians-Universität München. He was Acting Director of the German Historical Institute in Washington, DC, from 1995–1997. His most recent publications include *Verkehrte Welt. Revolution, Inflation und Moderne, München 1914–1924* (Göttingen, 1998) as well as two coedited volumes, *The Mechanics of Internationalism in the Nineteenth Century* with Johannes Paulmann (Oxford, 2001) and *Two Cultures of Rights: Germany and the United States* with Manfred Berg (Cambridge, 2002). His current book project is entitled "Die Bundesrepublik 1974 bis 1982: Der Sozialstaat im Zeichen wirtschaftlicher Rezession (Bd. 6, Geschichte der Sozialpolitik in Deutschland seit 1945)."

Sharon Gillerman is Associate Professor of Jewish History at the Hebrew Union College—Jewish Institute for Religion in Los Angeles. Her most recent publication includes *German into Jews. Remaking the Jewish Social Body in the Weimar Republic* (Stanford, 2009). Presently she is writing a book on the performances and reception of Zishe Breithaupt.

Miriam Hansen is Ferdinand Schevill Distinguished Service Professor in the Humanities at the University of Chicago. She is a coeditor of *New German Critique* and the author of *Babel and Babylon: Spectatorship in American Silent Film* (Cambridge, MA, 1991). Her most recent book, *Kracauer, Benjamin, Adorno on Cinema, Mass Culture and Modernity*, is forthcoming with the University of California Press.

Stefan Jonsson is Associate Professor of Aesthetics at Södertörn University and Associate Professor of Ethnic Studies at the University of Linköping. His book, *Subject Without Nation: Robert Musil and the History of Modern Identity*, appeared with Duke University Press in 2000. He is also the author of *A Brief History of the Masses: Three Revolutions* (New York, 2008), and he is just completing *Cultures of the Crowd*, a book on the masses in interwar Europe.

Anton Kaes is Class of 1939 Professor of German and Film Studies at the University of California, Berkeley. He is the coeditor of the book series *Weimar and Now: German Cultural Criticism* at the University of California Press.

His book publications include *From Hitler to Heimat. The Return of History as Film* (Cambridge, 1989); *The Weimar Republic Sourcebook*, coedited with Martin Jay and Edward Dimendberg (Berkeley, 1994); and a contextual analysis of Fritz Lang's famous film *M* (London, 2000). His most recent book is *Shell Shock Cinema: Weimar Culture and the Wounds of War* (Princeton, 2009).

Kristin McGuire is a Research Fellow at the Institute for Research on Women and Gender at the University of Michigan and co-Director of the Global Feminisms Project based at the University of Michigan. She is the co-author of *Global Feminisms through a Virtual Archive* (Chicago, 2010). She is currently working on a comparative historical analysis of women activists in Germany and Poland from 1890–1918. She teaches Women's Studies and History at the University of Michigan and Eastern Michigan University

Thomas Mergel is Professor of Twentieth-Century European History at the Humboldt University Berlin. His most recent publications include *Propaganda nach Hitler. Eine Kulturgeschichte des Wahlkampfs in der Bundesrepublik 1949–1990* (Göttingen, 2010), *Grossbritannien seit 1945* (Göttingen, 2005), *European Political History (1870–1913)*, coedited with Benjamin Ziemann (Aldershot, UK, 2007), and *Parlamentarische Kultur in der Weimarer Republik. Politische Kommunikation, symbolische Politik und Öffentlichkeit im Reichstag 1919–1933* (Düsseldorf, 2002).

Elizabeth Otto is Assistant Professor of modern art in the Department of Visual Studies at the State University of New York at Buffalo. She is the author of *Tempo, Tempo! The Bauhaus Photomontages of Marianne Brandt* (Berlin, 2005), a catalogue that accompanied an exhibition of Marianne Brandt's works that Otto also curated. The exhibition was shown at the Bauhaus Archive in Berlin, Harvard's Busch-Reisinger Museum, and the International Center of Photography in New York.

Annemarie Sammartino is Assistant Professor at the Department of History at Oberlin College. She has recently completed her book, *The Impossible Border: Germany and the East, 1914–1922*, which will be published by Cornell University Press in 2010. Her next project is entitled: "Freedomland: Modernity and Mass Housing in New York City and East Berlin, 1965–2000."

Dirk Schumann is Christian-Gottlob-Heyne-Professor of Modern History at the Georg-August-Universität in Göttingen. He is the author of *Bayerns Unternehmer in Gesellschaft und Staat, 1834–1914* (Göttingen, 1992), *Political Violence in the Weimar Republic, 1918–1933: Battle for the Streets and Fears of Civil War* (New York, 2009; German edition, Essen, 2001), and *Raising Citi-*

zens in the "*Century of the Child.*" *The United States and German Central Europe in Comparative Perspective* (New York, 2010).With Richard Bessel, he coedited an essay collection on *Life after Death. Violence, Normality and the Construction of Postwar Europe* (Cambridge, 2003).

Bernd Widdig is Director of the Office of International Programs at Boston College. He was formerly Associate Director of the MIT International Science and Technology Initiative (MISTI) and Director of the MIT-Germany Program. He is also an affiliate of the Center for European Studies at Harvard University. He is the author of *Culture and Inflation in Weimar Germany* (Berkeley, 2001) and *Männerbünde und Massen. Zur Krise männlicher Identität in der Monderne* (Opladen, 1992).

Lora Wildenthal is Associate Professor of History at Rice University. She is the author of *German Women for Empire, 1884–1945* (Durham, 2001), and coeditor of *Germany's Colonial Pasts* (Lincoln, 2005). Currently she is working on a book project entitled "The Language of Human Rights in West Germany." Some of this research has appeared in "Human Rights Activism in Occupied and Early West Germany: The Case of the German League for Human Rights," *Journal of Modern History*, vol. 80, no. 3 (September 2008).

INTRODUCTION

Weimar Subjects/Weimar Publics
Rethinking the Political Culture of Germany in the 1920s

KATHLEEN CANNING

The place of the Weimar Republic in Germany's twentieth century has been defined by its catastrophic beginnings and end—Germany's defeat in 1918 and the Nazi seizure of power in 1933. Weimar's history has, until recently, been preoccupied with politics as an arena of flawed decisions and failed compromises. The fault lines in Weimar politics have been exhaustively analyzed and debated in the search for answers to the question, both political and moral, of how those fissures enabled the Nazis to rise to power, more or less legally, in 1933. Weimar culture was characterized by its own contradictions—"exuberant creativity and experimentation" in contrast to "anxiety, fear, and a rising sense of doom"—and each of these impulses was deeply imbricated in politics, in the struggles of republic against nation, of Left versus Right, of revolutionaries against reform.[1] The high drama of the republic's struggle to survive—from its birth "with a hole in its heart" through the intertwined crises of inflation, occupation, and parliamentary politics, to the political violence and economic despair of its last years—means that its collapse in 1933 usually overshadows even its most illustrious social experiments or cultural accomplishments.[2]

The republic's own ability to break effectively with the past, to innovate and renovate institutions and ideologies, has been a measure of its longer-term chances for success. German histories of the 1970s and 1980s traced Germany's "special path" from the Bismarckian nation-state to National Socialism, noting the republic's inability to cast off the heritage of the Kaiserreich, its authoritarian structures and mentalities, its dissonant and reluctant modernity. The debates about the German *Sonderweg* centered mainly on the nineteenth century, especially the period from the 1848 revolutions through the First World War. British critics of the "special path" delivered empirically grounded studies of popular nationalism, Catholicism, and liberalism, highlighting the capacity of the Kaiserreich to mobilize economic impulses and social formations "from below" and arguing for a more fluid and dynamic view of the connections between and among state, public sphere, and civil society in Imperial Germany.[3] Scholars critical of the *Sonderweg* shed light on Wilhelmine Germany's highly modern economy and class structure, on state welfare and social reform as well as on the new sciences of society, which clearly had implications for the Weimar period, although Weimar was seldom at the center of these scholarly disputes.[4]

The contradictory impulses of the republic—its authorization and celebration of invention in some arenas, its repeated recurrence to the Wilhelmine past in others—constitute a paradox of Weimar's particular "modernity." In Detlef J. K. Peukert's still-influential study, *The Weimar Republic*, the German defeat, revolution, and founding of democracy effected an abrupt and distinct rupture with its nineteenth-century past, creating the impetus, even the necessity, for experiments with modernity. In Peukert's terms the Weimar Republic represented a "critical phase in the era of 'classical modernity,'" one characterized by endemic crisis in which "teetering over the abyss was the norm and the resolution of conflict was the exception."[5] Its experiment in modernity "took place under the least propitious circumstances," including recurrent crises of "economics, politics, high culture and mass consumption, science and technology, architecture and city planning, the family and gender relations." Its "charged atmosphere of social and cultural innovation," its "dreams of reason" and the opposition they engendered, constituted the crisis of classical modernity that ultimately left the republic vulnerable to the Nazi assault.[6] Despite the vast expansion of scholarship on the Weimar period in the fields of cultural studies, film, history, art history, and gender studies, Peukert's notion of a "crisis of classical modernity" has remained remarkably tenacious across fields.

Although Peukert approached Weimar's crisis as emblematic of more general processes of modernization, the collapse of the Weimar Republic remains a crucial history lesson of the twentieth century. Given the consequences of that collapse—the dictatorship, war, and genocide that followed—it is easy to discount the significance of its "charged atmosphere of social and cultural innovation," its bold embrace of living in the future tense, when we consider the consequences of the republic's end. Certainly little of Weimar's newness was left to inspire the next German democracy, founded under American tutelage after 1945. If Peter Gay is right to note that the Weimar spirit found its true home in exile, then it is also true that, like its émigrés, Weimar never quite found its place in postwar Germany.[7] Rather, Weimar's history is one of recurrent "shattering" that can neither be forgotten nor assigned significance in shaping the history that followed it.[8] Its trajectory seems peculiarly one-way, its collapse the first act in the Nazi seizure of power, its republican heritage claimed by neither of the two Germanies after 1945.

In a masterful review essay of 1996, Peter Fritzsche surveyed the state of the field of Weimar history, beginning with Peukert and including synthetic political histories by Hans Mommsen and Heinrich August Winkler; a broad range of culturally inflected political and local histories; studies of everyday life, gender, and bodies; and finally, *The Weimar Republic Sourcebook*, which assembled a wide variety of original documents on everyday life, social thought, politics, philosophy, and culture of the period.[9] The crucial question of this essay, "Did Weimar Fail?" is one that historians have seldom posed. Fritzsche draws on both Peukert and the *The Weimar Republic Sourcebook* in his exploration of the republic's "blueprints, cultural experiments, and social initiatives on the Left and Right." Drawing a sharp line between the failure of political democracy and "the destruction of the laboratory" in which Weimar's "eclectic experimentalism" took shape, Fritzsche questions the causal association of modernity and crisis with the republic's eventual failure. Boldly suggesting that "much more than parliamentary democracy was at stake" in the republic's struggle to survive, Fritzsche shifts the terms in which we might understand the relationship between culture and politics.[10] Fritzsche's essays from the mid-1990s suggest that both Weimar politics and culture constituted "landscapes of danger and design," which were deeply embedded in one another. His call to "enlarge the gallery of modernism" points to deeper reconsiderations of the relationships between culture and politics, not the mere insertion of Weimar culture into narrative accounts of Weimar politics. Eric Weitz's study of Weimar's "promise and tragedy," published in 2007, fulfills this call in many respects. Weitz takes the reader on a stroll through Berlin, masterfully analyzing the visual and tactile experiences that comprised everyday lived cultures across class milieus, offering insightful explorations of the realms of film, photography, and photomontage, of both stage and street theater, highbrow and popular literature, cabarets and nightclubs, of sex reform and new politics of the body, thus reaching far beyond the realms of high culture at the heart of Peter Gay's classic study of *Weimar Culture*.[11] Weitz's study certainly offers an excellent road map for grasping the ways in which "renovation and crisis went hand in hand."[12] As Fritzsche argues, the "consciousness of crisis" that characterized the 1920s produced both disorientation and a sense of "exuberant possibility."[13]

If this "consciousness of crisis" has usually been associated with anxiety, uncertainty, resentment, and trepidation about the future and longing for the past, or for the arrival of a strong leader, recent research by German cultural historians advances a new interpretation. Authors of the essays collected in the volume *Die "Krise" der Weimarer Republik* (2005) emphasize the positive and productive associations with a consciousness of crisis, the embrace of optimism and possibility on the part of Weimar subjects, including their confidence in their own capacity to change, innovate, and even surmount crisis.[14] Crisis, in the view of coeditors Moritz Föllmer and Rüdiger Graf, has figured for too long as a "quasi-magical concept" that too easily stands in as a causal factor and an explanation for the rise of Nazism.[15] Föllmer and Graf also sharply question the presumptive normality that underpins the notion of crisis in the Weimar Republic, suggesting instead that crisis is more aptly understood as a rhetorical standpoint, one that had different (and not always negative) resonances across distinct cultural, intellectual, or political milieus. An understanding of crisis as a rhetoric or political language illuminates the differences between those historical actors who embraced the productive possibilities of crisis and those who worked to foreclose such possibilities.[16]

Our own original quest to "rethink Weimar" shared a starting point with Föllmer and Graf, in that we also began our "Weimar group" with a critical engagement of Peukert's notion of a crisis of classical modernity. We were certain that the congealing of interdisciplinary scholarship around topics like consumption and popular culture, film and visual studies, citizenship and minority cultures, gender and sexuality, political symbolism and political violence, and empire and colonialism would necessitate redefinition of Peukert's key terms of *modernity* and *crisis*. Of particular interest to our early Weimar group was the question of how new cultural studies of film, visual culture, literature, mass culture, and body politics might create new temporal and spatial frameworks for understanding the political and cultural visions of Weimar subjects and for analyzing how they remained entangled in the experiences of war, defeat, and revolution long after 1918. In proposing to rethink the visions and sentiments that fostered Weimar democracy, we explored the formation of new publics, not only of voters and activists, propelled into politics by the defeat, revolution, and subsequent civil strife, but also publics that formed in the realms of consumption, popular culture, and mass entertainment and that were intensely politicized in the course of the 1920s. Finally, we contemplated the new subjectivities that became possible under the conditions of this fragile democracy, as individual and mass, public and subject acquired new meanings and as new women, new men, and new citizens claimed their place in the material and visual landscapes of the republic.

Rather than proposing a new paradigm or interpretive grid for understanding the political culture of the Weimar Republic, the essays in this volume probe the political languages and cultural categories of public and subject that changed as the republic contended with the aftermath of war, fought to anchor democracy, mobilized citizens, and demobilized soldiers. Addressing both the aestheticization of politics and the politics of aesthetics, the essays featured here offer case studies rather than comprehensive coverage of visual culture and the memory of war (section 1); the convening of citizens and the complex sites at which citizenship became meaningful beyond parliaments and parties (section 2); the symbolic contests over democracy and public space from constitutions and parliaments to courtrooms and street battles (section 3); the emergent dichotomy of mass and individual, fragment and whole, that preoccupied intellectuals and cultural critics, sharpened by the sense of cultural decline following the inflation and crisis of 1922–23 (section 4); and finally the imaginaries of space and time, nation and republic, citizen and immigrant, homeland and borderland, and past and future that changed as Germans absorbed the shocks of war and peace that would refigure its borders, both real and imaginary (section 5).

Defeat and the Legacy of War

In the first section and running throughout several of the essays in the other sections is an exploration of the war's end as the republic's actual beginning and as its longer-term unconscious. Conceiving of the end of the war as a rupture, these essays take up Peter Fritzsche's suggestion that the war was "at once the site of the invalidation of the past and the point of departure for the future."[17] They address the abrupt experiences of defamiliarization, disorientation, and trauma of defeat and revolution at the beginning of the republic, which ripped open the fabrics of possibility and required that they be stitched together again and again throughout the 1920s. For Anton Kaes the "return of the undead" was a recurring theme in Weimar cinema throughout the 1920s. His article in this volume suggests that the rupture of the war transformed not only politics but also representations of past and future experience and that the death and devastation of the First World War persisted in haunting the republic into its final years. German cinema, he contends, became a crucial space for mourning the mass death and transformations of everyday life, both that which was tangible or transparent and those memories that remained suppressed or hidden from view. The war dead reappeared "as moving images and phantoms" as cinema became the "ultimate realm of the undead."[18] Kaes' reading of Murnau's film *Nosferatu* "as ghost and phantom residing in the shadow realm of the dead" is suggestive of the ways in which the war loomed over Weimar society in the guise of the cinematic "living dead," which symbolized the millions of soldiers left unburied in the trenches. The drama of Nosferatu's murderous return from the land of the phantoms to the land of the living and his subsequent annihilation are suggestive of the anxious desire for closure and its ultimate impossibility in the aftermath of war.[19]

Kaes's study of *Nosferatu* underscores the importance of resituating Germany's defeat as the opening act of the Weimar Republic. In a now classic study of visions of insurrectionary warfare in October 1918, Michael Geyer uncovers the politics and the emotions surrounding the "impending defeat and the way it was negotiated."[20] Geyer's remarkable reinterpretation of the fantasies of "insurrectionary war" examines the "tortured and terrified reasoning" that led German authorities to call for an armistice while simultaneously considering the prospects for resuming hostilities in the form of a levée en masse. Ending the war, as Geyer shows, unleashed a "deep emotional crisis that ran through German society" and fueled calls for "popular insurrection" that continued to "gain momentum and national stature after the war." Geyer thus offers an exemplary case study of a rupture that must be understood on different temporal planes, for the shock of Germany's defeat and the imagination of insurrection it fostered lived on in the "deep memory" of the Weimar Republic, fueling notions of people's war and national redemption that would ultimately "set the agenda for a war of annihilation to come."[21] In this sense Kaes and Geyer offer different kinds of evidence for the rupture represented by the German defeat and for the impossibility of German history simply "being restarted in November 1918" with the founding of the republic.[22]

In Brigid Doherty's study of "The Work of Art and the Problem of Politics in Berlin Dada" the aftermath of war, revolution, and the near civil war between Socialists and Communists form the backdrop for the contests over the "preservation of cultural heritage" in the republic and the place of artists in the new collectives it convened. Refusing the political settlement of Social Democratic rule and the "eternal value" of works of art, Doherty's Dadaists call for cultural vandalism. To artists Georg Grosz and John Heartfield, political violence against artistic and political party compromise figure as parallel "aesthetic experiments." In their essay, "Art Scoundrel" ("Der Kunstlump"), Grosz and Heartfield offered a sardonic denial of art's ability to transcend the "unbearable circumstances of life on earth."[23] They cast postwar Dadaism as a "breakout" from an aesthetics that "hovered in the air between the classes" and failed to recognize "any shared responsibility for the collective."[24] This refusal took the form in 1920 of a sculptural montage, "Der wildgewordene Spießer," an artwork that denied the prospect of escaping the miseries and strife of postwar everyday life. The sculpture represented the forcible, violent return of the petit-bourgeois (*Spießer*) to social and artistic control: his body in parts was comprised of artifacts, a lightbulb replacing his head, a metal rod replacing his one leg, his arms with a doorbell and a revolver. The impossibility of art as a *Flucht*, an escape, and its entrapment in the artifacts of everyday technologies, left the *Spießer* a ruin, reminiscent of the war, with its missing leg, its "replacement parts of memorials to its fruitless revolt."[25]

At the heart of Elizabeth Otto's "secret history of photomontage" are two subjects: the male soldier or militarist and the female viewer, both of whom were marked by the transformations of war and defeat. Weimar photomontage artists rendered the violence of the trenches and the impossibility of reassembling either social or individual bodies in the aftermath of war as they cut up and recombined "mass-produced photographic images of landscapes and human figures."[26] In her critical representations of war and militarism Weimar artist Marianne Brandt departed from prewar montaged soldier portraits, which Otto examines in the first part of her essay. In Brandt's montages soldiers are "situated in sterile scenes where they march aimlessly or struggle helplessly." Spatial and temporal disjunctures are reflected in landscapes composed of fragments that are global rather than national, encompassing images of Asian rice fields, volcanoes erupting, and "soldiers and other human figures run riot in a disjointed, composite countryside."[27] Gazing coolly over these landscapes in several of Brandt's photomontages are female figures, featuring the short hair and cigarettes marking them as new women.[28]

These studies of the "undead" who continued to haunt the republic in Kaes's study of cinema; the reassembled and enraged *Spießer*, trapped in a body of parts in Doherty's portrayal of Dada; and the female figure in Brandt's photomontages, poised to assemble the fragments of war, peace, and faraway catastrophes, each offer evidence of the visualization of memory and mourning, ideology and identity, in the aftermath of war and revolution. The postwar explosion of the "visual material available to the public"[29] bespeaks of a different arena of democratization, one that complicated the assembly and articulation of the new democratic subjects of the Weimar Republic. The transformations of subjectivities—of soldiers and men broken by war—and of women who were left to reassemble the pieces—seldom found expression in the formal sphere of politics, where the reordering of gender and family life became a crucial task of the new republic.

New Citizens/New Subjectivities

The essays collected in the second section of this volume explore new collectivities and subjectivities that took shape in the expanding publics of the new republic. Certainly not all of these new collectivities embraced the republic or the democratic citizenship it proffered. Indeed, the nationalists and militarists who belonged to the Freikorps, the Stahlhelm, and the associational networks surrounding the DNVP, including many nationalist women, mobilized in fierce opposition to democracy and must also be counted as citizens.[30] The founding of the republic, the prevalence of the secular Social Democrats at its helm, and the widening scope of the welfare state challenged both churches and religious parties, which were often ambivalent about the republic, even as they fought to protect it against militarist assault.[31] The Catholic Center Party, of course, shared not only the burden of republican governance with the Social Democrats, but also its commitment to social reform and *Volkswohl* (the peoples' well-being). As Peter Gay has noted, the Weimar Republic "gave Jews unprecedented prominence" in both the realms of culture and politics. In fact, those who hated the republic rallied against it as a so-called Jewish republic.[32] Civic life among secular or assimilated Jews flourished during the Weimar years, while a new wave of migration of "*Ostjuden*" (Jews from the East) from

Russia and Poland during and after the war tested the boundaries of republican citizenship and prompted outbursts of anti-Semitic violence in Berlin.[33] As Sharon Gillerman's article makes clear, distinctions of class and religiosity divided the largely assimilated German Jews from the *Ostjuden*, even in the face of growing anti-Semitism.

In addition to collectivities and publics, each of these essays explores citizenship as a new language of democratic participation that called up new subjectivities, especially for those who were first named citizens in 1918. The traumatic losses of war, the trepidation about the postwar *Frauenüberschuss* (female excess), and the new burdens placed upon the welfare state form a crucial backdrop for understandings of citizenship, ideologies of gender, and the social body in need of repair. As these essays make clear, the participatory rights of women constituted only one aspect of citizenship, which was newly embodied as reproduction and sexuality became matters of state and social, moral, and hygienic reform. Until now the history of women and gender in Weimar politics has turned around the discrepancy between the politicizing effects of war, revolution, and the declaration of suffrage, which drew unprecedented numbers of women into party and union politics, and the purported disappointment and disappearance of women from those same formal arenas of politics after 1920. The essays in this section take a wider view of politics and citizenship to encompass consumption, mass culture, and popular entertainment, along with reproductive and sexual politics as the arenas in which Weimar subjects conceived of themselves as citizens.

In Kristin McGuire's study of "Feminist Politics Beyond the Reichstag," the end of the war, the revolutionary proclamation of female suffrage, and the founding of the republic alter the terms of both citizenship and subjectivity for long-time feminist activist and sexual reformer Helene Stöcker. Challenging the terms of Weimar democracy from its inception, Stöcker called upon its founders to break with the legacy of violent war and to commit the new republic to a pacifist standpoint.[34] Although the revolution and the writing of the constitution convened a new collectivity of female citizens, Stöcker refused to regard the vote as the fulfillment of citizenship. Instead, she insisted that equality in the civil and political realms would be meaningful only if both sexes had equal rights to sexual expression and sexual pleasure. Stöcker emphasized the "revitalization of sexuality" and the "desire for life and procreation" as life forces of the new system of governance.[35] In this she proposed radical new connections between citizenship and the work of reproduction, conceived not as the actual act of childbearing but as the release of "life-affirming sexual energy that guaranteed an embrace of the next generation."[36]

Even as political parties and revolutionary actors spoke in the name of new collectivities in the early republic, Stöcker always posited the individual as the starting point for the moral and political transformations she advocated. She acknowledged the interest of the state in regulating the collective reproduction of the populace, while nonetheless insisting that love and sexuality constitute the most private of realms that should be shielded from the state. McGuire's analysis of these contradictory standpoints points to an interesting disjuncture between reproduction and sexuality in Stöcker's notions of individual and collectivity, state and citizen, as illustrated in her advocacy of both free love and eugenics. In Stöcker's view the new republic of Weimar required not only new forms of governance and an ethical mobilization of civil society but also a newly conscious sexual subject as citizen.

Like Kristin McGuire, my own essay also begins with the new imaginary of female citizenship that took shape on the German home front during the war and culminated in the declaration of suffrage in November 1918. The surprising conferral of voting rights to women sparked an extraordinary campaign of political agitation and mobilization, as each of the new or reconstituted political parties sought to win the loyalties of new female voters. Regardless of their political affiliations, suffrage rights created the legal framework for a new self-consciousness on the part of women voters who were eager to prove themselves citizens and who viewed themselves as holding "Germany's future in their hands."[37] The revolutionary declaration of female suffrage unleashed a process of politicization, drawing women into the project of republic building and schooling them in matters of state and in the meaningful exercise of their new rights on the eve of the first elections.

While its legal inscription represents a crucial framework for women's citizenship, my essay also argues that the real work of defining citizenship had only just begun in 1918. The implications of women's new political citizenship rights for their economic rights (the right to work) and rights within the civil spheres of family and property ownership would remain a topic of vigorous debate as Germany's first democratically elected parliamentary body convened to draft the Weimar constitution. In months of deliberations, the assembly ascribed new rights to explicitly gendered (embodied) citizens, and sought to anchor the legitimacy of the new state in a reinvigorated family and a sexual division of labor that crisscrossed the private-public divide (home/workplace/welfare state/ public sphere). Thus the spaces for citizenship in the formal realm of politics narrowed after 1920 as parliaments and political parties moved to subordinate the concerns of female voters into their broader party political goals.

Despite the reconciliatory impulses that underpinned the writing of citizenship in 1919—the compromises between capital and labor, republic and nation—some of the outcomes of war were less reparable than others. Indeed, the naming of women as citizens set into motion processes that neither law nor realms of formal politics could ultimately contain. For even if women did not achieve *equality* in 1918, they retained the capacity to conceive of themselves as citizens and to reimagine the political. Moreover, competing notions of citizenship jockeyed to the fill the unprecedented vacuum of political power created through defeat and revolution. The fact that an underlying sense of gender crisis persisted throughout the history of the republic makes clear that neither masculinity nor femininity could simply be restored or returned to an idealized prewar era. Despite persistent efforts on the part of state and social reform to reconcile the sexes and repair the social body, a sense of crisis surrounding family, gender, and sexuality percolated through the republic, often undetectable in the realms of formal politics.

In fact, the arenas of popular culture, consumption, and informal politics offer many examples of the ways in which contemporaries represented, puzzled through, and played with the instabilities of femininity and masculinity, from the novels and reading publics in Kerstin Barndt's essay to the photomontages of Marianne Brandt analyzed by Elizabeth Otto. The preoccupation of social and cultural reform institutions during the mid- to late 1920s with governing and disciplining sex, consumption, and women's participation in mass culture, including the self-fashioning embodied in the figure of the new woman, offers further evidence of this continued preoccupation with gender order/disorder. The prolonged battle over birth control and abortion at the height of economic and political crisis represents another example of the continued efforts of the state, courts, churches, and social reform agencies to anchor the social order in governance of sexuality, body, and gender.

New women and class-laden discourses of moral reform are also at work in Kerstin Barndt's analysis of the new collectivities of female cultural consumers. A female reading public became visible in the course of the *"Bücherkrise"* (book crisis) of the mid-1920s. At stake in the book crisis were the habits of taste and consumption of female readers who fostered a new market for *Unterhaltungsliteratur* (entertainment literature) that came under scrutiny of politicians, pedagogues, and moral reformers.[38] The attempts of both Social Democrats and bourgeois feminists to guide and prescribe young women's tastes for literature offers evidence of the unease in both milieus about the unpredictability and ungovernability of young women's habits of consumption, whether of fashion, entertainment, or literature. The entwined discourses of "consumption, femininity, and mass culture," in fact, formed "a tight conceptual interrelation" that often figured "low-brow literature as 'trash,'" in contrast with "male-inflected notion of bourgeois high culture."[39] The "new interpretive communities" of female readers were viewed with suspicion as potential sites of female agency, pleasure, and self-representation.

The contests over female readers attest to the ways in which gender relations had changed in the aftermath of war. If the war years and the granting of female suffrage represented an apparent *"Umbruch,"* or rupture, the worry about female readership, consumption, and citizenship suggest that this rupture, too, lived on into the late republic, fostering the multiple and contradictory subject positions that comprised "the new woman."[40] Publishers, pedagogues, and political journals competed for the attention and allegiance not only of the female reader and cinema-goer but also of the female voter, an increasingly unreadable and inscrutable phenomenon after Weimar's first elections. The fear of the "roaming female subject," whether reader, voter, or fashion-conscious "new woman," suggests intriguing connections between reading publics and voting publics and establishes mass culture as a site of citizenship.[41]

Sharon Gillerman's analysis of German Jews as empowered subjects, with the capacity to contest and transform the discourses that excluded them, shares a notion of subjectivity with the other essays in this section. As Gillerman shows, Jewish social and sexual reformers selected and adopted mainstream reform initiatives and ultimately "produced a new ideal for an embodied Jewish collectivity."[42] The embodied politics of both Jewish belonging and Jewish difference reflected not only the desire of German Jews to reimagine the Jewish social body, but also to situate themselves as citizens within the expanding welfare state and fields of medical and hygienic reform. The central goals of their campaign were not only the general promotion of population growth and protection of the family, but the "fitness and viability of Jews as a group," the rescue of the "sick and ailing Jewish *Volkskörper* from the stifling effects of decades of infertility."

In Gillerman's study the female body "symbolized the nation's challenge and its future capacity as a vital and productive organism." Her intriguing analysis of the "embodied politics" of reproduction emphasizes the place of Jewish women in reimagining the Jewish social body in the new republic. She is also interested in the ways in which Jewish policy-makers constituted their own historically contingent subjectivities, asserting their capacity for "prudent management" of Jewish reproductive "wealth" within the refashioned arenas of Weimar medical and social hygienic reform, population policy, and reproductive politics. Jewish social policy reform experts identified two groups that held the keys to regenerating both the Jewish population and social order. First, they took aim at Jewish "new women," whose work outside of the home and low birth rates seemed to suggest a conscious "birth strike."[43] Second, because of their high birth rates, Eastern European Jews gradually came to represent a solution to the problem of German-Jewish intermarriage and depopulation. Coded as external to the German Jewish community, East European Jewish women would require tutelage in matters of household and social hygiene, marriage, and child rearing, if the Jewish population was to flourish.[44] In the view of Jewish population experts, "disciplining the female body" came to represent the "last best hope for securing a viable Jewish future in post-Emancipation Germany."[45] Gillerman points to the fields of moral and hygienic reform as important sites for a new kind of custodial citizenship, whether of German Jews over *Ostjuden,* or elite educated women over unschooled citizens.[46]

Symbols, Rituals, and Discourses of Democracy

Each of the authors in the third section of this volume takes a cultural history approach to a terrain of politics, examining how new publics and subjects were mobilized. Their essays explore the mentalities and sentiments, symbols and rituals that welded democracy together at crucial points or galvanized disaffection and protest at other points. These essays offer insights into the emotional underside of citizenship, into the affinities and desire for democracy, as Manuela Achilles terms it, as well as into the codes of ethics that shaped citizens' expectations of those who governed them, explicated by Thomas Mergel. Dirk Schumann probes the performative realms of the streets and citizens' militias where conceptions of democratic space, order, and comportment were continually tested and redefined. In attending to the significance of languages and emotions, symbols and rituals in forging and dissolving consent, these essays make clear the benefit of a cultural approach to the history of politics. They also offer interesting perspectives on the republic's chances to survive and the ways in which everyday battles over symbols, scandals, and street corners contributed to its collapse.

Schumann's essay explores the place of political violence in the new public spaces of the Weimar Republic. He takes a critical view of the thesis most frequently associated with the work of historian George Mosse that the brutalization of war left former soldiers prone to postwar violence.[47] The street violence that "pervaded and helped destroy Weimar Germany," was not a continuation of the violence learned in the trenches, Schumann argues, but took shape in the "political laboratory" of the early republic, amidst the conjuncture of defeat, revolution, the negotiation of peace, and the struggles over the forms of governance between 1918 and 1921.[48] The fact that the "severe violence of the postwar period" came to an end in 1921 leads Schumann to conclude that "political violence did not doom the Weimar Republic from the beginning."[49]

The violence that ensued after 1921 was new, Schumann contends, involving more specific and localized clashes between right- and left-wing militias over streets and squares. Such public spaces became new sites of a militarized mass politics in which citizenship often meant the conquest or defense of marked public spaces but seldom involved attempts to kill or maim opponents. Violence is understood here in performative terms: it was embodied in the militias' ritualized display of "hardened" masculinity adorned with uniforms and flags. Moreover some of the republic's militias—most notably the *Einwohnerwehren* (civil guards)—actually armed to protect local authorities and interests and were staffed by local residents who feared revolution but who remained largely on the peripheries of contests over public space.[50]

In Schumann's estimation the systemic or spectacular sorts of violence contributed less to the demise of Weimar democracy than the low-level, spontaneous incidents of political violence that undermined the republic slowly, eroding the spaces for compromise that the republic had successfully created in its early years.[51] While offering a view of the republic that had succeeded in garnering public loyalty for a time and that "actually had a chance to survive," Schumann sheds light on the struggles over public space as a site of an increasingly militarized and masculinized citizenship. By contrast with the feminized publics of reading, cinema, and consumption, he claims that the battles of the streets and militias not only implicitly disqualified women from this terrain of citizenship but sought to reclaim public space as masculine despite—or perhaps in response to—women's new political rights.[52] If tensions between the masses and individuality form a thread that runs through the political culture of the republic, Schumann points out that "the shaky balance between emotionality and its rational control" was a crucial part of the debate about "reconstructing the subject" that intensified as politics spilled into the streets.[53]

Manuela Achilles' essay examines the symbols and rituals that allowed democracy to "emerge as a force" during the early 1920s, defending and buttressing the republic against nationalism. Her aim is to counter the long-standing view that the republic lacked the symbolic appeal to unify collective sentiment or to win the support of the populace. In her analysis the "republican martyrdom" of Walter Rathenau—his murder, funeral, and public mourning in 1922—marks a defining moment for the republic, prompting an outpouring of antinationalist fervor and rousing a positive desire for democracy.[54] The symbol of Rathenau's body, representing the "assaulted body politic," galvanized and localized the republicans' claims to the body politic.[55] The widespread mourning for Rathenau, which crossed class and regional boundaries, offers insight into a different economy of emotion than the performative passions of street fighting that Schumann analyzes. The passage of the "Law for the Protection of the Republic" marked a turning point in the symbolic reordering of the republic. So, for example, black-red-golden flags were distributed widely and Friedrich Ebert decreed von Fallersleben's "Deutschlandlied" the national anthem. Commitment to the democratic nation, Achilles notes, became "an absolute value that transcended the confines of class, faith, ethnicity or race."[56] The murder of Rathenau, Achilles concludes, did not succeed in destabilizing the republic; instead it "allowed the democrats to seize the ethico-political initiative from the political Right."[57]

Achilles also offers less spectacular examples of the affinities for democracy than the public mourning of Rathenau. For example, "Constitution Day" was instituted amidst controversy in 1921 and gained new meaning in the aftermath of Rathenau's murder, culminating in a festive ten-year jubilee in 1929.[58] Despite a fundamental ambivalence about symbols of the imperial past, Achilles musters persuasive evidence of Weimar republicans' new vision of "a pluralist society in which different ethnic, religious, or cultural groups could coexist peacefully within one democratic nation." This, she contends, represents "an alternative route that Weimar Germany might have taken."[59]

Thomas Mergel explores the web of expectations and disappointment that bound those in possession of citizenship and voting rights to both nation and republic. As such, his study of the public perceptions of politics portrays the publics of Weimar democracy as more fragmented than their nineteenth-century counterparts. For one, the revolution and founding of the republic represented an upheaval that had "changed the parameters of the political system, but not, as in Russia one year earlier, those of the social order."[60] German citizens' expectations of their representatives were both "unrealistically high" and "intensely moral," Mergel argues, a fact he traces back to the experiences of wartime and the longing for social harmony. The crucial problem the Reichstag thus faced was how to "represent the people in its entirety," while engaging in the often divisive work of governing. Mergel analyzes the rise of a new subjective concept of representation, one grounded in direct and palpable experience, in the life of the people. This meant not only that critics sometimes questioned the life experience of their elected officials, but that they also generated a "shared semantic" of antiparliamentarism, aimed against "partyism," politics as a "machine," or the "soullessness of politics."[61] Politics, Mergel asserts, increasingly "became invested with a compensatory function for the country's failed social integration."[62]

Mergel's analysis of citizens' expectations and disappointments reaches deeply into the mentalities of citizens who sought not only tangible change and material benefits from state and parliament but also the performance of leadership, which itself was continually challenged and redefined as coalitions formed and dissolved and repeated crises threatened the stability of the republic.[63] He traces the emergence of a vocabulary of "*Volk*," a concept that "promised integration and unity" and that was soon embraced by every party but the Communists.[64] The fact that the German citizenry, increasingly congealed into the entity of *Volk*, failed to recognize itself in the Reichstag, prompted a growing desire for "decisive elites who stood out from the amorphous mass," for a Führer, "a man who cannot be a party" and who thus had the potential to overcome the political paralysis of the republic.[65] Mergel concludes that the Nazis were ultimately able to capitalize on citizens' high expectations, to seize the language of morality and to "represent the people in a much more direct way than did the other parties."[66]

Martin Geyer's examination of the "Kutisker-Barmat" corruption scandal of the mid-1920s focuses on the politics of scandal—a realm of "spectacular" rather than symbolic politics. Like Mergel, Geyer is interested in the relationship between the public and its perceptions of its political representatives, but draws quite different conclusions. The stakes of the scandal surrounding government loans to Jewish financiers, Iwan Kutisker and the Barmat brothers,

represented in the sensationalist press as corrupt *Ostjuden* and Jewish profiteers, was "no less than the political and moral order of the Republic."[67] The
vision of a government that was both corruptible and beholden to capitalism
was particularly volatile in the aftermath of the inflation. Reading Geyer's case
study against the backdrop of the migration crisis analyzed in Annemarie
Sammartino's essay underscores the brisance of the figure of the *Ostjuden*, alleged in this case first to have acquired German assets and property during the
inflation and then to have bilked the Prussian State Bank and the *Reichspost*
out of millions.[68] If the mass press appears in Geyer's analysis as a corrosive
force, one that fueled an ethnicization of politics through its "surplus of narratives and rumors" about "Jewish profiteers," the organs of the republic proved
responsive to the pressure to purge corruption from its ranks. In this Geyer and
Achilles share a more positive assessment of the republic's capacity to defend
itself against vicious attacks—from both the Right and the Communist Left.
The successful prosecution of this case in the courts constituted "a republican
success story," Geyer concludes, one in which "reason prevailed over emotion."[69]
The essays by Schumann, Achilles, Mergel, and Geyer explicate the emotions,
affinities, desires, and expectations that characterized citizens' encounters with
the republic and its key sites of governance—the Reichstag, the courts, the
streets. Linking these essays is their shared interest in the politics of representation. The essays in this section suggest that the fate of Weimar democracy
depended not only upon the capacity of governments to form coalitions or to
quell crisis but also on the mediation and mobilization of political symbols in
ever-widening publics, on the suturing of the stirred up emotions and identifications of the postwar period to the republic.

Publics, Publicity, and Mass Culture

If the essays by Achilles, Geyer, Mergel, and Schumann in the previous section
are concerned mainly with crises of representation, the essays in this fourth section of the volume explore the preoccupation of Weimar cultural theorists with
the refigured phenomenon of the mass/the masses and mass culture. As the essays by Miriam Hansen, Stefan Jonsson, and Bernd Widdig show, debates about
mass culture/the masses also involved dilemmas about "how society ought to be
represented and by whom."[70] If the nineteenth century saw a sharpened distinction between individuals as citizens in possession of rational capacities and the
"masses," presumably driven by their passions and in need of strong leadership,
the epoch after the First World War was marked by the expansion of citizenship
and mass politics and hence by a merging of citizens and masses. In Miriam
Hansen's analysis "the masses"—at least those who interested cultural critic
Siegfried Kracauer—became a target of both cultural analysis and social reform.

In the aftermath of war, revolution, and the founding of democracy, Hansen suggests, the masses came to figure as objects of violence and disease and as powerful agents of those revolutions and mobilizations. In a similar vein, Stefan Jonsson emphasizes the ways in which wartime patriotism, the politicization of labor and the women's movements during the war, and the inception of universal suffrage at its end, imparted new meanings to the "masses."[71] Yet these meanings shifted as the republic endured civil war, inflation, and occupation. By the period of so-called stabilization (1924–1929), preoccupation with the mass/masses centered less on citizens' material or political circumstances and more directly on mass culture, which encompassed the expanding sphere of consumption—"cheap, mass-produced material goods as well as sites of cultural encounter, from book clubs to dance halls and cinemas."[72] As the spheres of popular culture and consumption widened their scope in the course of the 1920s, Germans discovered new possibilities for self-representation beyond the realms of formal politics.

Reading the essays by Hansen and Jonsson together makes clear that Weimar cultural theories of the mass/mass culture involved society in its totality, encompassing, as Jonsson notes, "all branches of knowledge from criminology and pedagogy to demography and theology."[73] Both Hansen and Jonsson understand the mass in terms of its potential to represent a new, modern social formation of actors imbued with agency—even citizens—and of "mass culture" as a potential site of democracy. Hansen explores Siegfried Kracauer's "Americanism"—his refusal to regard the "massification of culture" as a symptom of decline and his attempt to discern the possibilities for a "democratic mass culture under the conditions of advanced capitalism" that America seemed to represent. In his view, entertainment culture, "crystallized around America and American style," presented "a new aesthetic configuration that at once spawns and responds to a new type of collective." Newly congealed collectives and "alternative public spaces," especially that of cinema, held out the promise of new modes of "sociation" (in Jonsson's terms) and new possibilities for mobility, for transcendence of class and gender hierarchies, and for self-representation, both aesthetic and political.[74] In fact, Jonsson contends that the "presence and pressure of 'the masses' ... determined the very forms of artistic and intellectual labor" in the Weimar era.[75]

Following Kracauer's rendering of "the mass ornament," both authors seek to complicate or even to dissolve the binary between masses and individuality. Jonsson critiques the idealized notion of individuality, situated outside of the collective, and turns instead to Kracauer's observation that during the 1920s the "*Vollindividuum*" has transformed into a partial self, a "*Teil-Ich*" within the collective. As both Hansen and Jonsson suggest, Weimar society was "no longer a society of individuals, but of partial-selves, swinging legs, heads and arms without bodies, a mass of passions and interests."[76] Individuality, in turn, figures as a subject position not external but intrinsic to the masses. Kracauer's focus on the *Angestellten*—"a group that at once personified the structural transformation of subjectivity and engaged in a massive effort at denial" in Hansen's terms—highlights the changing tensions between individual and mass, production and consumption, capitalism and leisure culture, as Weimar tipped towards its final crisis. Kracauer's insistence that the masses would "come to their senses" or to self-consciousness fueled his eloquent critiques of ideology that sought to invigorate and empower the capacity of citizens/subjects/masses for self-representation in culture and politics.[77] Yet as Hansen notes, by the turn to the 1930s Kracauer's hopeful ambivalence towards the "mass ornament" had "all but disappeared form his writings."[78]

Bernd Widdig's study of "Cultural Capital in Decline" examines the traumatic rupture that ran through Weimar politics and culture as a result of the inflation of 1922–23, noting its repercussions far beyond the economic sphere. Widdig's focus is not the mass subject that preoccupied Hansen and Jonsson but the changing place of the German intelligentsia in the aftermath of the inflation. As Germany succumbed to an era of the "limitless reign of the economic," the cultural capital of intellectuals declined.[79] If the cultural goods they had once produced were not calculable in monetary terms, the inflation turned social relations and notions of social value upside down, threatening to render culture an appendage of the economic sphere. Widdig explores German intellectuals' own responses to their situation, most notably, Alfred Weber's treatise on the plight of the *"geistige Arbeiter"* (intellectual workers) from 1922. Weber, whose own scholarly interests encompassed economics and cultural sociology, viewed *geistige Arbeiter* as the occupants of "the last independent island outside strict class interests," as representing "an asylum for ideas and arguments that were not linked to the economic."[80]

Widdig posits an intriguing relationship between the diminished status of German intellectuals and the "massification" and commodification of cultural production as evidenced in the rapid proliferation of penny novels, movie houses, dance revues, and sporting spectacles. Widdig argues that the pace of cultural production and circulation paralleled the inflation in its uncontainability. Indulgent and unreflected consumption provided a distraction from economic and social realities, fostering a cultural economy that eschewed a sense of saving or investment in the future. These features of mass consumption stood in stark contrast with the practices of *Sammlung und Bildung* (collecting and educating) associated with high culture, which represented a "savings account of national culture."[81] Widdig suggests an intriguing analogy between inflation and mass culture, viewing the uncontrollability and unpredictability of economic life as a backdrop for heated debates about the proliferation and circulation of mass cultural goods. He argues that the inflation prompted a deep questioning of the "fundamental character of reproduction," noting that this issue also preoccupied Walter Benjamin in his essay, "The Work of Art in the Age of Mechanical Reproduction."[82] The inflation represented a particularly acute crisis for German intellectuals not only because it had diminished their own social position but also because in the course of the inflation, reproduction had come to figure as a "limitless, out of control process that utterly devalued the product."[83]

The essays in this section each examine the ways in which "massification"—whether of culture or political subjects—preoccupied Weimar intellectuals, social reformers, and cultural theorists. The debates about mass make clear that the fields of aesthetics and politics were deeply enmeshed with one another during the 1920s. In fact, the aestheticization of politics and the politicization of aesthetics, as mutual processes, were crucial hallmarks of Weimar's modernity. Indeed, "the masses" form a linchpin for the formation and transformations of both publics and subjects/subjectivities during the Weimar Republic.

Weimar Topographies

The essays in the fifth and final section of this volume contend with the changing notions of space and time that underwrote both politics and culture during the Weimar Republic. As Peter Fritzsche's essay suggests, the remapping of the postwar world involved replacing older cognitive templates with new ones. The ruptures in governance and German nationhood that occurred at the end of the war were both political and geographic, imparting new cartographical meanings to the political ideologies of democracy, socialism, and nationalism. These essays offer abundant evidence of the ways in which these ideologies became charged with new notions of past and future, borders and boundaries, as Germans came to terms with the loss of colonies (Lora Wildenthal) and as they sought to define the limits of citizenship in all of its dimensions—national belonging, social and participatory rights (Annemarie Sammartino).

Germany's defeat forms the starting point of Fritzsche's analysis, for it is the defeated subject that was to be "rebuilt and reactivated." This rebuilding of subjects—and the formation of entirely new kinds of subjects (such as veterans, war widows, welfare experts, etc.)—aspired to a "new regime of necessity and possibility" rather than to a restoration of the postwar world to its prewar state.[84] Fritzsche's economy of experience presumes that a rupture of "epochal nature" took place as the war ended and the republic was founded. The "crisis of inheritance" that resulted from this temporal break unleashed a sensibility of living in the present, which became a hallmark of Weimar cultural and intellectual production. Drawing upon Kracauer, Fritzsche views mass culture as emblematic of the new economy of experience, encompassing the "nonstop production of the new" that was cast in the "unconditional form of the future tense."[85]

Peter Fritzsche's analysis of the "economy of experience" points to the efface-ment of the "memory of what had been" in the space of the Kurfürstendamm, which Siegfried Kracauer deemed the "street without memory," where shops and fashions were "eternally new," changing, replacing and displacing one an-other.[86] Miriam Hansen's exploration of Kracauer's "Americanism," a lens through which he sought to read the emergence of mass consumption and lei-sure culture in Germany, highlights the fascination with rationalization, in its essence also a new mode of partitioning and measuring time.[87] In other words, the unconditional embrace of the future tense that is at the heart of Fritzsche's argument may be thinkable only in the aftermath of ruptures like those Ger-many experienced in 1918–19.

The image that best characterizes Fritzsche's notion of the economy of ex-perience is that of the surveyor, whose "tap, tap, tap … on uncertain ground" constitutes the work of "interpretive innovation or interpolation," the search for a new, active historical subjectivity, individual and collective. Weimar subjects reflected critically on the "alterity of the present" in order to "envision and initi-ate radical and social political departures," a process that also involved imagin-ing new temporalities and topographies of the German nation. The techniques of mobility, learned in war and curtailed so abruptly by the Versailles Treaty, imparted new meanings to the German borderlands and lost territories and reconstituted Germany's "national form."[88]

Literal and figurative, "remapping" in Peter Fritzsche's terms means refigur-ing the relationship between urban and rural, city and nation, each as different kinds of "living communities."[89] The idealized landscape of Weimar modernity was indisputably the city: the calibration of everyday life "to a regime of constant movement" and the immersion in a "mass culture that was relentlessly 'modern, ahistorical, respectless,'"[90] was thinkable only in a city like Berlin. In this sense the consciousness of modernity changed the cartography of Germany, assign-ing home towns and rural regions, where *Heimat* and nation had flourished during the prewar period, an ambiguous place in postwar modernity. Another distinguishing feature of Weimar's topography was the fascination with the dichotomy of surface and depth as a visual code of urban modernity. As Janet Ward has argued, "façade culture," "glamour," "asphalt," and "surface" were the keywords in debates about the modern, urban, commercial experience in which "high and low culture become almost seamlessly enmeshed."[91]

The articles by Annemarie Sammartino and Lora Wildenthal highlight the spatial tenuousness of the nation once Germany became a republic. In Sam-martino's case the arrival of immigrants pushed at the borders of Germany from the East during the early republic, while Wildenthal analyzes the reinvig-oration of colonial activism among new female citizens in the face of Germany's postwar decolonization. These two case studies make clear that the new codes of citizenship that anchored the republic were strikingly porous and subject to petition in the face of mass migrations or colonial "mixed" marriages.[92] Sammartino takes up the contingency of citizenship at both national and provincial levels during the early 1920s. The debates and deliberation of German citizenship took place, she notes, at an ironic conjuncture of the postwar peace settlement when nationalism was enshrined as an organizing principle in Europe at the very same time that its meaning, through the redrawing of borders and movement of peoples, "was thrown into crisis."[93] Sammartino illustrates the expanding terrain of citizenship during the early years of the republic, when some one million *Auslandsdeutsche* (ethnic Germans from abroad) crossed the border into Germany, along with a half million non-German, non-Jewish Russians, and another seventy thousand Russian Jews. Amidst the mounting refugee crises of the early 1920s, when petitions for German citizenship increased by 250 percent, citizenship came to represent a "battleground upon which German officials debated the meaning of the German nation."[94]

The refugee crisis highlighted the ambiguity of German citizenship laws, confounding both the 1913 law, with its "fragile equation of ethnicity and culture," and the new participatory and social rights of citizenship elaborated in the Weimar constitution.[95] Sammartino notes that refugees who could prove their ethnic German identity were viewed as eligible for German citizenship by all but the extreme Left. Yet the suitability of non-Germans for citizenship was determined by cultural criteria, such as their capacity for assimilation, the possession of particular socially valuable skills or talents or their "firm inner connection to Germany."[96] Even as nationalists clamored to close off the nation to immigrants, Sammartino makes clear that the republic's restrictive citizenship policies were unable to contain the influx of immigrants.[97] So for example, no fundamental ban was issued against the immigration of Eastern European or Russian Jews despite the circulation of ominous imagery of the Reich's inundation with *Ostjuden*. While the republic's refugee crisis tested the boundaries of Weimar citizenships, Sammartino's evidence suggests that Germany's borders remained permeable and that citizenship cases continued to constitute a field of negotiation between the Reich and the states into the late republic. The ethnic and cultural meanings of German citizenship continued to be tested throughout the republic, she argues, and citizenship ultimately became entangled in the "same dynamic of extremism and paralysis that so poisoned the life of the republic."[98]

Notions of national belonging, imperial domination, and individual rights underpinned the citizenship claims of the nationalist and colonialist women's associations, which Lora Wildenthal examines. Female colonial activists embraced women's new political rights in order to defend the memory and the hope for future reinvigoration of Germany's dismantled empire. Imagining a sphere of liminal citizenship in which "cultural public enactments" defined belonging, female colonial activists sought to defy Germany's new borders in different ways than the migrants and refugees Sammartino studies, asserting new citizenship claims for ethnic Germans "trapped" within the new boundaries of Poland, Czechoslovakia, and Southwest Africa. Although figured in some nationalist narratives as victims of the German defeat and the new republic, female colonial activists were active agents, launching agitation for renewed engagement in Germany's former colonies on a "household by household, community by community" basis.[99] They called for an intensely domestic and "depoliticized" colonial engagement with families, youth, and schools in the former colonies. Upholding the "quiet, unobtrusive work" of the "German wife and mother," female colonial activists stepped in to claim a role for female experts as more fitting arbiters of colonies than "governments and peoples."[100] The energetic commitment of nationalist female activists to a renewed colonial politics also fueled the campaign against the "black shame on the Rhine" during the early 1920s, in which German women were widely viewed as victims of sexual coercion or rape by African soldiers stationed with French troops in the Rhineland.

At the same time, however, female colonialists represented a stance that seems very close to that of Weimar "new womanhood," embracing a kind of jaunty independence, adventuring alone to the former colonies, traversing Africa by plane or automobile, and narrating their journeys much like the male explorers of the previous century. Wildenthal's analysis suggests that the colonial female activist of the Weimar era represented a new subject position—fashioned in a setting far from Germany—of independent women who aspired to reassert German influence in the colonies and to reverse the peace settlement of Versailles. In fact, colonialist female activists offer an intriguing example of the new Weimar subject—"a traveler, an explorer, a metropolitan,"[101] whose individuality was embedded in the new mass culture of the 1920s.

Conclusion

The perspectives of different disciplines represented in this volume complicate the causal links between the two moments of rupture at the beginning and the end of the republic—between the republic's birth trauma and its disintegration in 1931–1933. In loosening these causal links to probe the meanings of these initial shocks and ruptures into the later republic in the work of intellectuals and cultural theorists (Hansen, Jonsson, Doherty, Fritzsche, McGuire); in the realms of parliaments, parties, and the politics of the everyday (Mergel, Achilles, Geyer, Sammartino, Schumann, Canning); and in the spheres of consumption, leisure, and mass culture (Barndt, Kaes, Otto, Doherty, Widdig), this volume takes seriously the landscapes of ambition and hope, promise and disappointment that galvanized new publics during the Weimar era. As studies in political culture, the essays in this volume focus on the political languages and cultural categories that emerged from the ruptures of the German defeat, revolution, and the founding of democracy. The terms *citizen* and *subject, public* and *mass*, were part of the changing languages of politics and social identities. But they were also more than discursive categories, for they also encompassed practices that forged new connections between culture and politics. The essays featured here suggest that the efforts and imaginations of Weimar intellectuals and cultural producers, as well as those of politicians and social analysts, converged around the same phenomena—the mobilization of new publics and the articulations and claims of the new subjects they fostered. The issue of the mass/masses as a newly volatile formation in a postwar democracy involved Weimar "society in its totality" and preoccupied experts in "all branches of knowledge," from politics to social science and cultural theory.[102]

The lingering of the "undead" of World War I had undeniable consequences for both culture and politics in Weimar Germany. In fact, artistic, filmic, and literary representations of the dead and maimed intruded continuously upon the state's attempts to achieve a postwar settlement. Berlin Dadaists inveighed against compromise, both artistic and political; their calls for cultural vandalism made clear that art could never serve as an escape from politics or the lingering destruction of the war. The attempts of cultural theorists to discern and prescribe the tastes of female readers or film-goers coincided with broader campaigns of the conservative parties to prohibit the dissemination of "trash and filth" literature, especially to youth. If the cultural milieus of film, literature, and visual arts became political battlegrounds in their own right, Weimar politics were increasingly reliant upon cultural mediation. From the republic's first election campaign the iconography of female voters in the posters of the Socialist and Democratic parties complicated the new landscape of citizenship, even suggesting a place for "new women" in politics. In the photomontages of Bauhaus artist Marianne Brandt, for example, figures of new women were placed at the center of landscapes that fused politics and popular culture (bombs and circuses, marching soldiers and balloons), while Gilgi, the quintessential new woman in Irmgard Keun's novel of the same name, became a topic of intensive political debate among Social Democrats on the eve of the Nazi rise to power. Against the backdrop of fears about female emancipation and female excess as outcomes of the war, female sexuality acquired a new volatility during the 1920s. The expanded visibility of women in public, both as cultural consumers and citizens, along with postwar anxieties about the German birth rate fueled a continued preoccupation with sex and reproduction through the late years of the republic. The battles over abortion centered on paragraph 218 of the German criminal code, spanning the arenas of legislature and popular culture, including film, novels, and political art. The female body, whether sexual or maternal, came to symbolize the capacity and fitness of the social and national body.

These essays furthermore suggest that the work of building and defending democracy involved not only the arduous negotiations of constitutions and assemblies but also the initiation of new symbols and rituals that fostered new affinities between citizens and state. The performative aspects of politics, of parliamentary representation, even of armed conflicts over street corners and squares helped to cultivate those emotions and affinities—for and against democracy. A more drastic example of culture's inextricability from politics is the inflation of 1922–23, which resulted not only in a massive realignment of affinities between voters and parties but more fundamentally in a "radical transvaluation" of all that was familiar and established. The collective memory and trauma of the inflation was reproduced and recast through the mass press, through fiction and popular narratives, and fostered a new politics of resentment that would echo into the final years of the republic.[103] The boundaries that were drawn and then challenged in the Weimar years, whether of citizenship or social body, religion, ethnicity, or race, relied upon compromises of law and politics, but also mobilized cultural norms and moral-ethical visions. Mass migrations from Russia and the newly formed nations in Eastern Europe tested the limits of German citizenship laws, while the arrival of *Ostjuden* in Germany gave rise to new restrictive codes of belonging among German Jews. Both the courtroom and the mass sensationalist press arbitrated the government corruption scandal involving Jewish financiers from the East in which not only politics but the moral order of the republic was at stake. Contests over the politics of representation—the question of how the interests of German citizens should be represented and by whom—were central to both the founding and the collapse of the Weimar Republic. Understanding the dilemmas of representation in performative terms reveals the significance of culture in the mediation of politics—through visual and textual media, symbols and rituals, parades and assemblies, uniforms and insignias, body languages and rhetorics of resentment.

The essays collected here assert that Weimar democracy was defined by both the politics and the aesthetics of representation. In the same vein the efforts to destroy the republic required new languages and forms of politics as well as a thoroughgoing transformation of aesthetics. The founding of the republic authorized the formation of new publics while innovations in visual and popular culture changed the very meanings of publicness, rendering politics visible and tangible in new ways. Of course, the proliferation of publics also widened the potential arenas for conflict in times of crisis: our approach here acknowledges both the volatility of new publics and their capacity for innovation. Finally, the transformations of publics authorized new forms of consciousness and belonging, of identifying and displaying the self, encompassed in the term *subjectivity*. In some cases here the term *Weimar subjects* denotes new designations of actors, new forms of collectivity and individuality; in others it highlights the ways in which certain groups became new subjects of expertise, discipline, fantasy, and cultural representation. Hallmarks of the new Weimar subjects—whether salaried masses or sex reformers, street fighters, film-goers, or female readers—was their willingness to abrogate the "traces of the past" and to embrace of the "radical possibilities of the present."[104]

Notes

1. Peter Gay, *Weimar Culture* (Middlesex, UK, 1968), xi–xiii; Walter Laqueur, *Weimar: A Cultural History* (London, 1974); and John Willett, *Art and Politics in the Weimar Period: The New Sobriety 1917–1933* (New York, 1978).
2. The term "born with a hole in its heart" is from Arthur Rosenberg's *Entstehung der Weimarer Republik* and *Geschichte der Weimarer Republik* (Frankfurt a.M., 1955).
3. The German "special path" is best presented by Hans-Ulich Wehler, *Das deutsche Kaiserreich* (Göttingen, 1973), and Ralf Dahrendorf, *Society and Democracy in Germany* (Garden City, NY, 1967). The first collection of studies critical of Wehler's argument was published in the essay collection edited by Richard J. Evans, *Society and Politics in Wilhelmine Germany* (London, 1978). Influential monographs that followed include: Geoff Eley, *Reshaping the German Right: Radical Nationalism and Political Change after Bismarck* (New Haven, CT, 1980), and David Blackbourn, *Class, Religion, and Local Politics in Wilhelmine Germany: The Centre Party in Württemberg Before 1914* (New Haven, CT, 1980).
4. Also see David Blackbourn and Geoff Eley, *The Peculiarities of German History: Bourgeois Society and Politics in Nineteenth-Century Germany* (Oxford, 1984).
5. Detlef J. K. Peukert, *The Weimar Republic*, trans. Richard Deveson (New York, 1989), xiii. Peukert's study was published in German in 1987. For an excellent essay on Peukert's notions of both modernity and crisis, see David F. Crew, "The Pathologies of Modernity: Detlev Peukert on Germany's Twentieth Century," *Social History* 17, no. 2 (May 1992): 319–28.
6. Peukert, *Weimar Republic*, 273–82.
7. Peter Gay, *Weimar Culture: The Outsider as Insider* (New York, 2001 [1968]).
8. On the place of the Weimar Republic in Germany's twentieth century, see Michael Geyer and Konrad Jarausch, *Shattered Past: Reconstructing German Histories* (Princeton, NJ, 2003), 16–17, 89–90, 290–93.
9. Peter Fritzsche, "Did Weimar Fail?" *Journal of Modern History* 68, no. 3 (September 1996): 629–56; Anton Kaes, Martin Jay, and Edward Dimendberg, *The Weimar Republic Sourcebook* (Berkeley, CA, 1994), Preface, xviii.
10. Fritzsche, "Did Weimar Fail? 630–31.
11. Erik D. Weitz, *Weimar Germany. Promise and Tragedy* (Princeton, NJ, 2007).
12. Peter Fritzsche, "Landscape of Danger, Landscape of Design: Crisis and Modernism in Weimar Germany," in *Dancing on the Volcano: Essays on the Culture of the Weimar Republic*, ed. Thomas W. Kniesche and Stephen Brockmann (New York, 1994), 44–45.
13. Fritzsche, "Landscape of Danger," 40–45, and "Did Weimar Fail?" 654.
14. Moritz Föllmer and Rüdiger Graf, *Die "Krise" der Weimarer Republik. Zur Kritik eines Deutungsmusters* (Frankfurt/New York, 2005), see Vorwort, 7, and "Einleitung: Die

Kultur der Krise in der Weimarer Republik," 10–11, 21. Also see the helpful review by Ofer Ashkenazi, "A Constructive Use of the 'Magical Concept': Discourses and Experiences of 'Crisis' in the Weimar Republic," H-Net German, June 21, 2006.

15. Ashkenazi, "A Constructive Use of the 'Magical Concept,'" 1.

16. Föllmer and Graf, "Einleitung," 24–25; see also in the same volume: Michael Makropoulos, "Krise und Kontingenz: Zwei Kategorien im Modernitätsdiskurs der Klassischen Moderne," 45–76; Wolfgang Hardtwig, ed., *Ordnungen in der Krise: Zur politischen Kulturgeschichte Deutschlands 1900–1933*, (Munich, 2007); Rüdiger Graf: *Die Zukunft der Weimarer Republik. Krisen und Zukunftsaneignungen in Deutschland 1918–1933*, (Oldenbourg, 2008).

17. Fritzsche, "The Economy of Experience," this volume.

18. Kaes, "The Return of the Undead," this volume.

19. Ibid.

20. Michael Geyer, "Insurrectionary Warfare: The German Debate about a Levée en Masse in October, 1918," *Journal of Modern History* 73 (September 2001): 462–63.

21. Geyer, "Insurrectionary Warfare," 463–64, 514, 526–27. See also Jörg Duppler and Gerhard P. Groß, eds., *Kriegsende 1918. Ereignis, Wirkung, Nachwirkung* (Munich, 1999), and Jost Düffler and Gerd Krumeich, eds., *Der verlorene Friede. Politik und Kriegskultur nach 1918* (Essen, 2002).

22. Geyer, "Insurrectionary Warfare," 462–63; also see Richard Bessel's study of Germany as a *Nachkriegsgesellschaft: Germany after the First World War* (Oxford, 1993), and Bessel, "Was bleibt vom Krieg? Deutsche Nachkriegsgeschichte(n) aus geschlechtergeschichtlicher Perspektive," *Militärgeschichtliche Mitteilungen* 60, no. 2 (2001): 297–305.

23. Doherty, "The Work of Art," this volume.

24. Ibid.

25. Ibid.

26. Elizabeth Otto, "The Secret History of Photomontage: On the Origins of the Composite Form and the Weimar Photomontages of Marianne Brandt," this volume.

27. Ibid.

28. Elizabeth Otto, *Tempo, Tempo! The Bauhaus Photomontages of Marianne Brandt* (Berlin, 2005).

29. Otto, "The Secret History."

30. Elizabeth Harvey, *Women and the Nazi East: Agents and Witnesses of Germanization* (New Haven, CT, 2003), and Raffael Scheck, *Mothers of the Nation: Right–Wing Women in Weimar Germany* (New York, 2003).

31. Margaret Stieg Dalton, *Catholicism, Popular Culture, and the Arts in Germany, 1880–1933* (Notre Dame, IN, 2005); Jonathan Wright, *Above Parties: The Political Attitudes of the German Protestant Church Leadership 1918–1933* (Oxford, 1974); W. Reginald Ward, *Theology, Sociology, and Politics: The German Protestant Social Conscience 1890–1933* (Bern, 1979).

32. Peter Gay, *Weimar Culture: The Outsider as Insider* (New York, 2001). See "Introduction to the Norton Paperback Edition," vi. Also see Wolfgang Benz, Arnold Paucker and Peter Pulzer, eds. *Jüdisches Leben in der Weimarer Republik* (Tübingen, 1998); Michael Brenner, *The Renaissance of Jewish Culture in Weimar Germany* (New Haven, CT, 1996).

33. David Clay Large, "'Out with the *Ostjuden*': The Schenuneviertel Riots in Berlin, November 1923," in *Exclusionary Violence: Anti-Semitic Riots in Modern Germany History*,

ed. Christhard Hoffmann, Werner Bergmannm and Helmut Walser Smith (Ann Arbor, MI), 123–40.

34. Kristin McGuire, "Feminist Politics beyond the Reichstag: Helene Stöcker and Visions of Reform," this volume.
35. Ibid.
36. Ibid.
37. Kathleen Canning, "Claiming Citizenship: Suffrage and Subjectivity in Germany after the First World War," this volume.
38. Brigid Doherty, "The Work of Art and the Problem of Politics in Berlin Dada," and Kerstin Barndt, "Mothers, Citizens, and Consumers: Female Readers in Weimar Germany," this volume.
39. Barndt, "Mothers, Citizens, and Consumers."
40. Ibid.
41. Ibid.
42. Sharon Gillerman, "Producing Jews: Maternity, Eugenics, and the Embodiment of the Jewish Subject," this volume.
43. Ibid. See Claudia Prestel, "The 'New Jewish Woman' in Weimar Germany," *Jüdisches Leben in der Weimarer Republik*, eds. Wolfgang Benz, Arnold Paucker, and Peter Pulzer (Tübingen, 1998, 135–56).
44. Gillerman, "Producing Jews."
45. Ibid.
46. Other recent studies that offer new perspectives on Helene Stöcker include: Tracie Matysik, *Reforming the Moral Subject: Ethics and Sexuality in Central Europe, 1890–1930* (Ithaca, NY, 2008), and Edward Ross Dickinson, "Reflections on Feminism and Monism in the Kaiserreich, 1900–1913," *Central European History* 34, no. 4 (2001): 191–230.
47. George L. Mosse, *Fallen Soldiers: Reshaping the Memory of the World Wars* (New York, 1990). See especially "The Brutalization of German Politics," 159–81.
48. Dirk Schumann, "Political Violence, Contested Public Space, and Reasserted Masculinity in Weimar Germany," this volume.
49. Ibid.
50. Ibid.
51. Ibid.
52. Ibid.
53. Ibid.
54. Manuela Achilles, "Reforming the Reich: Democratic Symbols and Rituals in the Weimar Republic," this volume.
55. Ibid.
56. Ibid.
57. Ibid.
58. Ibid.
59. Ibid. For an analysis of republican readings of Rathenau's Jewishness, see Manuela Achilles, "Nationalist Violence and Republican Identity in Weimar Germany: The Murder of Walther Rathenau," in *German Literature, History and the Nation*. Papers from the conference "The Fragile Tradition," Cambridge, 2002, ed. David Midgley and Christian Emden, Oxford, 2004, 305–28.
60. Thomas Mergel, "High Expectations—Deep Disappointment: Structures of the Public Perception of Politics in the Weimar Republic," this volume.

61. Ibid.
62. Ibid.
63. Ibid.
64. Ibid. On this point also see Fritzsche, "The Economy of Experience."
65. Mergel, "High Expectations—Deep Disappointment."
66. Ibid.
67. Martin Geyer, "Contested Narratives of the Weimar Republic: The Case of the 'Kutisker-Barmat Scandal,'" this volume.
68. Ibid.
69. Ibid.
70. Stefan Jonsson, "Neither Masses nor Individuals: Representations of the Collective in Inter-War German Culture," this volume.
71. Miriam Hansen, "'A Self-Representation of the Masses': Siegfried Kracauer's Curious Americanism," this volume and ibid.
72. Hansen, "'A Self-Representation of the Masses.'"
73. Jonsson, "Neither Masses nor Individuals."
74. Hansen, "'A Self-Representation of the Masses'"; ibid.
75. Jonsson, "Neither Masses nor Individuals."
76. Ibid.
77. Hansen, "'A Self-Representation of the Masses.'"
78. Ibid.
79. Bernd Widdig, "Cultural Capital in Decline: Inflation and the Distress of Intellectuals," this volume. See also Bernd Widdig, *Culture and Inflation in Weimar Germany* (Berkeley, CA, 1999).
80. Widdig, "Cultural Capital in Decline." Weber's text entitled *"Die Not des geistigen Arbeiters"* was a keynote address at the yearly convention of the Verein für Sozialpolitik in Eisenach. It was published in 1923.
81. Widdig, "Cultural Capital in Decline."
82. Ibid.
83. Ibid.
84. Fritzsche, "The Economy of Experience."
85. Ibid.
86. Ibid.
87. Hansen, "'A Self-Representation of the Masses.'"
88. Fritzsche, "Economy of Experience."
89. Ibid.
90. Ibid.
91. Janet Ward, *Weimar Surfaces: Urban Visual Culture in 1920s Germany* (Berkeley, CA, 2001), 9–11.
92. Lora Wildenthal, "Gender and Colonial Politics after the Versailles Treaty," and Annemarie Sammartino, "Defining the Nation in Crisis: Citizenship Policy in the Early Weimar Republic," this volume.
93. Sammartino, "Defining the Nation in Crisis."
94. Ibid
95. Ibid.
96. Ibid.
97. Ibid.
98. Ibid.

99. Wildenthal, "Gender and Colonial Politics after the Versailles Treaty."
100. Ibid.
101. Fritzsche, "The Economy of Experience"; Hansen, "'A Self-Representation of the Masses,'" and Jonsson, "Neither Masses nor Individuals."
102. Jonsson, "Neither Masses nor Individuals."
103. Widdig, *Culture and Inflation*, 7, 12.
104. Fritzsche, "Economy of Experience."

PART I

❧ ✦ ❧

Defeat and
the Legacy of War

CHAPTER 1

~:~

The Return of the Undead
Weimar Cinema and the Great War

ANTON KAES

> It's not enough to die; you still have to disappear.
> —Jean Baudrillard

German cinema in the wake of the First World War is haunted by images of ghosts, monsters, and comatose creatures. It appears as if the movies themselves are looking for ways to cope with the experience of death on a massive scale—the central experience of the First World War when two million young German men were killed in the span of four years. The trauma of "accelerated dying," as Rilke put it in 1914, had a profound impact on all cultural production after the war, but especially on cinema, which, barely twenty years old, was still in the process of legitimizing itself as an art form. Could the movies, long criticized for their mindless and immoral fare, gain respectability by depicting such serious subject matter as death and dying? Could films perhaps even provide a space for mourning? I would like to argue that a number of films in the Weimar Republic aspired to engage with the traumatic experience of the First World War. They did so, however, not as war films with heroic soldiers in trenches, special-effects bombardment, and folkloric humor and melodrama of "men under stress"—the domain of films like *Westfront 1918* (1930) and *All Quiet on the Western Front* (1930).

The shock experienced in the immediate postwar years did not lend itself to noisy mimicking of men fighting. Instead, the films of the early Weimar period tend to focus on the victims of war on the home front or on more abstract scenarios involving madness and murder. Such was the psychological toll of those who did return from the battlefield that they fell silent, as Walter Benjamin famously observed. Their experience of killing and facing death was so horrific that words could not express it. I claim that the suppressed memories of this experience instead reemerged in the dark space of the movie theater. Film's uncertain status between documenting and inventing reality made it especially suitable for the task of revisiting the traumatic event. Mute madmen and monsters, barren settings and stories of fatal encounters restaged the unspoken and unspeakable trauma. The very technology of film projection allowed the dead to reappear as moving images and phantoms, thus rendering cinema the ultimate realm of the undead, the privileged site of what can be *imagined* but has no life outside of film. Cinema itself created a realm of phantoms where the boundaries between life and death are unstable.

I would like to use Friedrich Wilhelm Murnau's *Nosferatu, eine Symphonie des Grauens* (Nosferatu, a Symphony of Horror) to help think through these issues. The first filmic adaptation of *Dracula*,[1] Bram Stoker's popular novel of 1897, *Nosferatu* opened in Berlin on 5 March 1922. I argue that Murnau's film represents a radical reworking of Stoker's novel through the lens of World War I.

Overwhelming Death

Let me begin by introducing some statistics to convey a sense of the enormity of the war's human cost. Nine million young men from France, England, Russia, Germany, and many other countries were killed, and about six million more were maimed and wounded. Over 13 million German men had been called up for military service—all of them potential victims. In the first major battle in September 1914, half a million men were killed within five days. The Battle of the Marne wiped out most of the German Youth Movement, whose members had been especially enthusiastic about enlisting and going to the front. In 1916, in the Battle of Verdun, 700,000 soldiers died. In the Battle of the Somme, which lasted five months, over 1 million fell, 200,000 casualties each month. In addition, hundreds of thousands more died in the civil and ethnic wars and revolutions that grew out of the World War and infected all combatant countries.

There were few families in Europe that did not suffer the loss of a father, son, husband, or brother. Reacting to the first bloody battles, Sigmund Freud published his essay "Thoughts for the Times on War and Death" in the journal *Imago* in 1915. He speaks of a "disturbance that has taken place in the attitude which we have hitherto adopted towards death."[2] This new awareness of death and dying, writes Freud, "strips us of the later accretions of civilization, and lays bare the primal man in each of us" (299). Freud is deeply pessimistic about the chances of eliminating war and poses the rhetorical question, "Would it not be better to give death the place in reality and in our thoughts which is its due, and to give a little more prominence to the unconscious attitude towards death which we have hitherto so carefully suppressed?" (299) I claim that Murnau's film *Nosferatu* answers Freud's question. Cinema in the early Weimar period gave death its due.

There is no better space than the movie theater to confront death because it lets us—vicariously and therefore safely—experience the unimaginable: one's own death. In his "Thoughts on War and Death," Freud maintains that the world of fiction—that of literature, theater, and, we might add, cinema—provides compensation for the impoverishment of life. Life without the risk of death becomes, in his words, "flat, superficial, and boring. Thus we are torn: while we crave security for ourselves and our loved ones and forego many things simply because they are too dangerous, we are secretly fascinated by what we have suppressed: adventure, risk, death" (290). Here, according to Freud, fiction acts as a substitute for life-threatening dangers:

> There [in fiction] we still find people who know how to die—who, indeed, even manage to kill someone else. There alone, too, the condition can be fulfilled which makes it possible for us to reconcile ourselves with death: namely, that behind all the vicissitudes of life we should still be able to preserve a life intact. For it is really too sad that in life it should be as it is in chess, where one false move may force us to resign the game, but with the difference that we can start no second game, no return-match. In the realm of fiction we find the plurality of lives which we need. We die with the hero with whom we have identified ourselves; yet we survive him, and are ready to die again just as safely with another hero. (291)

Freud offers here a theory of the status and function of fiction in the modern age that is characterized by increased security, monotony, and predictability, an age in which death is banned from sight and safety is preferred to risk taking. "How can you write a tragedy in the age of life insurance?" Ivan Goll asked in 1920. It is fiction—literature and, even more so, the movies—that provides the ultimate thrill of confronting death and dying without consequences. However, in Freud's view of 1915, the war has changed all that:

> It is evident that the war is bound to sweep away this conventional treatment of death. Death will no longer be denied; we are forced to believe in it. People really die; and no longer one by one, but many, often tens of thousands, in a single day. And death is no longer a chance event. To be sure, it still seems a matter of chance whether a bullet hits this man or that; but a second bullet may well hit the survivor; and the accumulation of deaths puts an end to the impression of chance. Life has, indeed, become interesting again; it has recovered its full content. (291)

In this remarkable passage, Freud captured the duality of danger and risk taking, as it no doubt pertained to the mindset of millions of young Germans in August 1914. No longer dependent upon literary and filmic simulations of an exciting life, they had a chance to experience it firsthand in a war that involved millions and expanded across continents. They became soldiers not necessarily because of their patriotic and nationalistic beliefs but because of the war's promise of adventure. War seemed the surest way to escape the staid and secure life that had become unbearable for German youth. Georg Heym confides in a diary entry, dated 6 July 1910: "I'd wish something were to happen. If only barricades would again be built, I would be the first one to stand on them and, with a bullet in my heart, feel the delirium of enthusiasm. If only a war broke out, even an unjust one. This peace is so foul, greasy and dull as polish on old furniture."[3]

The common experience of summer 1914—leaving home to experience adventure and risk death—has inscribed itself in Murnau's *Nosferatu*. Young Hutter, a real estate agent, is eager to travel to the East to do business with Count Orlok, aka the mythical figure Nosferatu, the Undead. Hutter's rushed leave-taking is encoded as the scene of a young man leaving his fiancée and his friends behind to head to the Eastern Front. In an earlier scene replete with forebodings, he is told that the visit will yield a nice sum of money but also a bit of sweat—and a little bit of blood. It is an allusion innocent Hutter does not understand, but it was not lost on the spectator in 1922. Millions went to the Eastern or Western Front as if embarking on a mere journey. Many did not come back from this journey, and those who did were changed for life. Murnau's film is a record of such a journey.

The Shadow of Life

Nosferatu begins with three title cards that mimic a handwritten diary by an anonymous author (identified by three crosses). The first title gives the exact location and date—"Account of the great death in Wisborg in the year 1838"—while the third reads:

> I have thought long about the beginning and the end of the great death [das grosse Sterben] in my hometown Wisborg. Here is its history: There lived in Wisborg Hutter and his young wife Ellen.

As in *The Cabinet of Dr. Caligari*, the story is set in the past, at the height of the sedate Biedermeier era and the dawn of industry, technology, and modernity. Its enunciative stance, however, is not a subjective flashback (as in *Caligari*) but a written account of a survivor of the "great death." In the tradition of the historical novel, the embedding of the story in an overtly sober and authoritative report lends the uncanny events an air of legitimacy and authenticity. Ostensibly perturbed by the massive dying (*das grosse Sterben*), the chronicler and diarist promises to tell a story *and* reflect on it—"I have thought long about the beginning and the end of the great death"—again gesturing toward his bewilderment and lending the subsequent film the form of an essayistic attempt to come to grips with the "grosse Sterben." To have a sympathetic narrator present a complex story is a narrative trope often used in Romantic literature: it mediates between the insane world of fiction and the sane world of the audience, providing a degree of normalcy against which the bizarre characters and their strange experiences are thrown into stark relief. The narrative voice accompanies the film and appropriately provides a comprehensible conclusion at the end.

The film uses its mock documentary style to elicit a surge of associations and possible meanings from the spectator. A case in point is the year 1838, which, according to the first intertitle, is the year in which the story takes place. It evokes the cholera outbreak in the early 1830s that killed hundreds of thousands in Europe (including Hegel and Clausewitz). Understood as the return of the infamous bubonic plague or Black Death of fourteenth-century Europe that had killed 20 million people (a quarter of the population) in just four years, cholera returned time and again throughout the nineteenth century with death tolls of over a million in Europe alone. While tuberculosis and other diseases had claimed even more victims, the psychological impact of cholera was unprecedented, as the cholera bacillus produced violent symptoms—with death occurring often within a few hours. At the very end of the war in 1918, a global influenza epidemic, the Spanish flu, spread like the plague had in prior centuries. The epidemic that came on top of defeat and starvation produced indelible images of the transmissibility of death. Death itself became contagious. Long lines of hearses filed out of towns to the cemeteries, an image that also appears in *Nosferatu*. Images of the cholera epidemic are a visually potent substitution for the experience of death in World War I; they serve as a mask that hides the traumatic experience of mass killing that could not yet be visually articulated. Representations of plagues of previous centuries provide a language with which Murnau could symbolize the "Great Death" of only a few years before.

While the first and third title cards record the place and time in a pseudo-documentary style, the second title card foregrounds the very constitution of the film as a highly problematic and paradoxical representation:

Nosferatu. Doesn't this name sound like the very midnight call of Death? Speak it not aloud, or life's pictures will turn to shadows, and phantom-like dreams will rise up to feed on your blood.

The rhetorical question and the warning not to name what should remain hidden invoke an image of Nosferatu as a harbinger of death that is located in the subconscious: the vampire's manifestations are "shadows" and "phantom-like dreams" (*spukhafte Träume*)—properties at the time associated just as much with film as with the occult. The very warning results in a contradiction: as the danger of naming is spelled out, the phantom is named and what ensues is exactly what the warning said would happen—the film turns life's pictures into shadows and summons ghosts in dreams. The film itself doubles the unspoken, unspeakable vampiric thoughts of death; it gives them a body, bringing them into representation in the form of a monster. The textual tease (it's there but cannot be revealed) foreshadows Ellen's irresistible temptation to read the *Book of Vampires*, something that she was expressly forbidden to do. She hesitates and wavers, but as she furtively glances at the book, she commits an act of transgression: by opening the book she literally opens herself to vampiric possession. The film displaces its own hypnotic effect onto an earlier medium, the printed page. Forbidden knowledge is thereby associated with secret writings whether they are banned books or encoded letters. The *Book of Vampires* introduces her to the supernatural world of phantoms.

It has often been reported that soldiers living in the trenches for weeks experienced an eerie state between life and death that made them susceptible to superstition and the occult.[4] The extremely restricted vision in the trenches gave rise to hallucinations and apparitions. How can silent film articulate these liminal experiences? How can it show what cannot be seen? How can it bring the immaterial and phantasmic into representation? Film itself, based on the interplay between light and shadow, has a precarious status: its elusive materiality (it comes to life only thanks to electricity and a complex apparatus) is most radically foregrounded through its conscious use of shadows. As E. H. Gombrich argues in his study of the depiction of the shadow in Western art,

> shadows are part of our environment but they ... are fugitive and changeable. ...
> Shadows are not part of the real world. We cannot touch them or grasp them. ...
> It was believed by the ancient Greeks that when we take leave of the real world,
> we survive only as shades among shades.[5]

Adalbert von Chamisso's Peter Schlemihl sells his shadow to the devil but soon realizes that, because he casts no shadow, he has no place in the real world. It is in the Expressionist cinema of the postwar period where shadows again assert an independent existence, exemplifying the degree to which the solidity of the self had been shattered and the unconscious had seized power. Paul Wegener's film *The Student of Prague* (1913) and Artur Robison's *Schatten* (Shadows, 1923), based incidentally on an idea of Albin Grau, the set designer of *Nosferatu*, thematize the imbrication of film and shadows, their common unstable materiality and precarious referentiality. A long tradition of precinematic entertainment, ranging from Plato's cave to the phantasmagoria shows of Philodor and Robertson in the nineteenth century, had used shadows to experiment with the representation of the invisible, unrepresentable, or merely imagined. In a strange amalgam of science and the occult, magic lanterns invoked the illusion of the supernatural by projecting images of spirits of the dead on a screen. The spectral images seemed both real and unreal, exciting and alienating. The predilection for ghosts reappeared in Melies's phantasmagoric illusions, and to this day, cinema has shown unusual fascination with specters and other phantoms of the imagination that foreground film's spectral origins and nature.

"Yesterday I was in the kingdom of shadows," wrote Maxim Gorky about his first visit to the movie house in 1895. "If only you knew how strange it felt. There were no sounds and no colors. ... This is not life but the shadow of life, and this is not movement but the soundless shadow of movement."[6] The narrative of *Nosferatu* unfolds by posing fundamental questions of cinematic representation. For Murnau, film is "not life but the shadow of life," just as it is for Gorky, who must be taken literally: film may very well have become the "shadow of life," a phantom that mimics and distorts but always accompanies and "shadows," spectralizes and "ghosts" our lives. Nosferatu, a purely cinematic creature (with no life outside the movies), rules as a phantom in the kingdom of shadows. As he approaches Ellen's bedroom, he is lit from below by footlights that elongate and enlarge his shadow to such an extreme that we see only the shadow. The figure that throws the shadow is invisible: it is there only by implication, thus underscoring Nosferatu's phantom-like quality.

Along similar lines, practices of spirit photography, which claimed to capture images of the dead and thus make the invisible visible, have inscribed themselves into the film. The supposedly hyperrealistic medium of photography turned out to be (like film) an uncanny phenomenon that not only created a parallel world of spectral doubles but also was put into the service of the supernatural and occult. Seen by the spiritualists in the mid-nineteenth century as a means of reanimating and capturing the dead spirit, photography flourished during times of war. The hope was that the technical apparatus would also see what the naked eye could not and uncover images of the deceased from another realm. Using the latest scientific discoveries in electrical engineering and photographic techniques to produce optical illusions and phantasms, spirit photographers became popular after the Civil War, and again in the aftermath of World War I, when they promised to include images of a recently fallen son or father in family pictures.[7] They added the missing person by double exposure, superimposition, or by manipulating the negative, while claiming that it was the sensitivity of the photo plate that allowed people to see invisible phenomena, including members of the family after their death. (The ghost is often seen hovering above the person photographed.) *Nosferatu* thus partakes of the cult of the undead and is imbricated in the transparency and immateriality of spirit photography.

The vampire—a spirit with a material body that is rendered immaterial qua film—is seen moving about in town without being seen by anyone except the camera. There is a scene in which Nosferatu, instead of entering a building through the door, dissolves into thin air. He simply becomes transparent, implying that he is both substantial and insubstantial, visible and invisible. The film uses its technology (stop motion and double exposure) to foreground the insubstantiality of phantoms. It is film (like photography sixty years earlier) that was able to seize, or more precisely, animate and give life to, the ghosts of the dead.

Likewise, the extreme close-ups of a translucent polyp, seen through a microscope, remind the viewer of the existence of another visible realm that cannot be seen with normal vision. The diaphanous quality of the polyp radiates a spectral, unearthly quality that relates to the image of Nosferatu as phantom. Viewers recognized what they saw but it was unreal—not because it was imagined but because it was scientifically all too real—and simultaneously made unfamiliar. Murnau included these scenes of scientific observation (like fragments of a UFA *Kulturfilm*) to blur the boundaries between science and uncanny wonderment—although the confluence of science and magic has been the very essence of filmmaking since its beginning.

The transition from the realm of the living to that of the phantoms gave Murnau the opportunity to constitute a filmic realm all of its own. The scene where Hutter is trapped on a hair-raising coach ride to the castle reenacts the train journey of the nineteenth century—thrilling, but also risky and dangerous. The spectacular coach scene is full of technical tricks, including a reversal of positive and negative film (made to look eerie because the coach remained black—Murnau had it painted white to achieve this effect), as well as time-lapse photography that imitates the time-motion experiments by Etienne Jules Marey and Eadward Muybridge in the earliest days of film. These experiments have the effect of foregrounding the spasmodic, disjointed, and choppy quality of early cinema. The entire coach trip is reminiscent of the harrowing experience of early train rides that used to lead to traumatic neuroses (called *railway spine*) and that in the early days of cinema was closely associated with the experience of watching moving pictures. Film also allowed images from another realm to emerge—the realm of phantoms, i.e., the realm of film that is constituted by technology, without outside referent and without regard to time and place. In its diegetic construction, Murnau's film appropriates the rules that operate in the film universe; the figure of Nosferatu exists not as a representation of anything outside of film, but as an enactment of the filmic process itself. It is only logical that this phantom simply disappears (as do unprocessed film images) when exposed to sunlight.

The Undead as Phantoms

The figure of Nosferatu has often been read as a representative, even caricature, of Eastern Jews who had emigrated in masses from Transylvania (after it was occupied by Romania in 1916) to Berlin, swelling the population around the Scheunenviertel to 45,000. Nosferatu's heavily coded appearance signified an ultimate "otherness" that made use of freely circulating images from anti-Semitic iconography.[8] Without discounting this interpretation, I want to propose another reading of Nosferatu as ghost and phantom residing in the shadow realm of the dead. It is a fact that during the mass killings of World War I, tens of thousands of fallen soldiers were never properly buried and mourned. Corpses were strewn over the battlefields or dumped into mass graves—the trenches themselves often served as graves where soldiers were buried alive after a shell explosion. Thus there was widespread fear that the ghosts of the unburied (and thus undead) soldiers would roam the earth in search of a final resting place. A large spiritist and occultist movement sprang up in Germany in the immediate postwar years because it held out the promise of contacting the spirits of relatives killed in battle.[9]

The fear of ghosts has deep roots in folkloric myths and primitive religions, with ritual burial of the dead being one way to protect the living from vengeful spirits. In his study *Vampires, Burial and Death*, Paul Barber states, "There are such creatures, it seems, in a variety of disparate cultures: dead people who, having died before their time not only refuse to remain dead but return to bring death to their friends and neighbors."[10] Because, according to these myths, ghosts of unburied dead soldiers frequently appear on battlefields, corpses of military personnel were often maimed to prevent the dead from walking. Consequently burial and mourning rites began as acts of self-preservation rather than altruism and respect for the dead.

In this reading, Nosferatu, the Undead, returns from the land of the phantoms to the land of the living, killing and contaminating everything in his path. As a mythical figure, he resonated more deeply than an invented, fictional character, and at the same time allowed the spectator the pleasure of distance. The annihilation of Nosferatu at the end of the film adds closure to the period of anxiety and horror directly following the war. Symbolically representing millions of unburied soldiers, the threat of the living dead is eliminated thanks to the selfless sacrifice of an innocent woman. (In Abel Gance's film *J'Accuse* of 1919, soldiers rise from their graves to march in protest—a motif that recurs in horror film classics like *Night of the Living Dead*.)

"What haunts," writes Nicolas Abraham in his essay on the Phantom, "are not the dead, but the gaps left within us by the secrets of others."[11] For Abraham, the phantom is a figure of speech that objectifies a gap in knowledge transmitted to the subject; it encodes what cannot be known and articulated. The phantom in its shadow-like elusiveness thus allegorizes what cannot be grasped in a subject's unconscious; it is a foreign body lodged within the subject, causing traumatic impressions that find expression in unconscious impulses. The phantom is the embodiment and enactment of what cannot be said, of what cannot be represented—except by translation into film-specific terms such as manipulation of light and shadow, film stock, speed, stop-action photography, and other tricks.

To Ellen, whose body language is modeled after Jean-Martin Charcot's female hysterics, Nosferatu appears as a phantom, as something deep inside her that pulls her against her will. This can be seen in her nocturnal sleepwalking, her reaching her arms out to him, and her final submission to him. Nosferatu is thus a hallucinatory effect of Ellen's death wish (the death wish of the home front). Her death is at once a redemptive gesture towards the war dead (inasmuch as she sacrificed herself in a momentous displacement of all the young men), as well as an act for the good of the community. The film explicitly and repeatedly asserts that only if she gives in to the vampire can the town be saved. It is no coincidence that around the time of *Nosferatu*, many war memorials were erected with the explicit purpose to honor those who gave their life for the country.

Let me conclude by taking the cinematic trope of the return of the vampiric phantom into the present. In a contemporary rereading of the vampire myth, Abel Ferrara's cult film *The Addiction* (1995) translates the Return of the Undead into an exploration of self-perpetuating evil and violence. The film begins with graphic slide images of the My Lai massacre during the Vietnam War; later we see photographs from a Holocaust exhibition and a Holocaust documentary video. These images invade the world of an impressionable young film student at New York University. She is haunted by the dead she sees portrayed in photographic and filmic images and is deeply disturbed by the violence to which they testify—these phantom-like images of the dead return to infect the living. She claims that there is no past. In her opinion the past is always part of the present—one cannot escape the past because media technology has made historical atrocities part of the present at all times. The images of past horrific violence contaminate new generations, leading to new violence and bloodshed. Drug addiction is merely a code word that stands for the addiction to violence that, vampire-like, forever needs new blood.

By using black and white photography in both the war documentary and the scripted shots, Ferrara suggests a link and continuation between the photographic images of atrocities and those images shot outside in New York's Greenwich Village. It is a hybrid film mixing of the horror genre with documentary, destabilizing the boundaries of both: the documentary images of corpses have become phantoms that—as the embodiments of the inexpressible—have entered the student's mind and made her susceptible to vampirism that feeds on violence. The traumata of war and genocide of the twentieth century are, the film suggests, far from over. They have produced new aggression, evil, death—from World War I to World War II, the Holocaust, the massacres at Vietnam and too many other places in a vampiric process that finds no end. But it is the filmic images themselves that haunt the living—these phantoms of the past do not have to return; they are always already with us.

Notes

The argument laid out in this essay partly overlaps with chapter 3 of my book *Shell Shock Cinema. Weimar Culture and the Wounds of War* (Princeton, 2009). I thank Princeton University Press for permission to reprint.

1. There is also a legal dimension to the changes made in title and characters' names from *Dracula* to *Nosferatu*. Murnau and the production company failed to acquire the rights from the Stoker estate for their remake and were therefore sued by a British court, which (unsuccessfully) ordered the destruction of all prints. On the twisted history of the film's production, see David J. Skal, *Hollywood Gothic: The Tangled Web of Dracula from Novel to Stage to Screen* (New York, 1990), 43–63.
2. Sigmund Freud, "Thoughts for the Times on War and Death," in *The Standard Edition of the Complete Psychological Works of Sigmund Freud*, ed. James Strachey (London, 1957), vol. 16, 273–300; here 289. Further references to page numbers from this text are given in parentheses.
3. Georg Heym, "Aus den Tagebüchern," in *Georg Heym*, ed. K. L. Schneider (Munich, 1971), 240 (my translation).
4. See Eric J. Leed, *No Man's Land: Combat and Identity in World War I* (Cambridge, 1979).
5. E. H. Gombrich, *Shadows: The Depiction of Cast Shadows in Western Art* (New Haven, CT, 1995), 55.
6. Maxim Gorky, "The Lumière Cinematograph," in *The Film Factory*, ed. Richard Taylor (Cambridge, MA, 1988), 25. See also Tom Gunning, "Animated Pictures: Tales of Cinema's Forgotten Future," in *Michigan Quarterly Review* 34 (Fall 1995): 465–85.
7. On spirit photography, see Rolf H. Krauss, *Beyond Light and Shadow: The Role of Photography in Certain Paranormal Phenomena. An Historical Survey* (Tucson, AZ, 1995). See also Tom Gunning, "Phantom Images and Modern Manifestations: Spirit Photography, Magic Theater, Trick Films and Photography's Uncanny," in *Fugitive Images from Photography to Video*, ed. Patrice Petro (Bloomington, IN, 1995), 42–71.
8. Nosferatu is associated with rats, an anti-Semitic symbol for Jews as shown in the 1940 Nazi film, *Der ewige Jude* (The Eternal Jew). See Régine Mihal Friedman, "Juden-Ratten. Von der rassistischen Metonymie zur tierischen Metapher in Fritz Hipplers 'Der ewige Jude,'" *Frauen und Film* 47 (September 1989): 24–35. See also Jürgen Müller, "Der Vampir als Volksfeind: F.W. Murnau's 'Nosferatu': ein Beitrag zur politischen Ikonografie der Weimarer Zeit," in *Fotogeschichte* 72 (1999): 39–58.
9. Even Thomas Mann went to one of these séances and wrote about it in "Occulte Erlebnisse" (Occult Experiences) in 1923.
10. Paul Barber, *Vampires, Burial, and Death* (New Haven, CT, 1988), 68.
11. Nicolas Abraham, "Aufzeichnungen über das Phantom," in *Psyche* 45 (August 1991): 692.

CHAPTER 2

~:~

The Work of Art and the Problem of Politics in Berlin Dada

BRIGID DOHERTY

"Der Kunstlump" [The Art Scoundrel] is a diatribe by Berlin Dadaists George Grosz and John Heartfield that appeared in the journal *Der Gegner* [The Opponent] in April 1920. Notorious for its "anti-art" stance, "Der Kunstlump" was written in response to an appeal by Oskar Kokoschka in which the Expressionist painter and playwright had beseeched the German public to take measures to ensure the preservation of the cultural heritage under conditions of civic unrest. In a statement that ran in more than forty German newspapers in March 1920, Kokoschka implored those involved in violent political conflict to avoid damaging works of art. He was responding to the events of 15 March 1920, in Dresden, where, in the wake of the counterrevolutionary Kapp-Lüttwitz Putsch that had overthrown the constitutional government in Berlin on 12 March, fighting had erupted between *Reichswehr* troops loyal to the "national dictatorship" of the putschists and workers demonstrating in connection with the general strike that would bring about the demise of the Kapp government on 17 March. Fifty-nine persons were killed and 150 wounded during that day's clash on Dresden's Postplatz; the battle also sent a stray bullet into Peter Paul Rubens's *Bathsheba* in the nearby Zwinger picture gallery. In his statement, Kokoschka, who had been appointed professor at the Dresden academy of art in 1919, pleads with people of all political persuasions to do their street fighting at a safe distance from any place where "human culture might come into danger."[1]

"Der Kunstlump" dismisses Kokoschka's plea and urges "vigorous resistance" to the Expressionist's position on the part of all those "who, knowing that bullets tear human beings to pieces, feel it a trivial matter when bullets damage paintings."[2] Indeed "Der Kunstlump" takes its disagreement with Kokoschka a step further, as Grosz and Heartfield announce: "We greet with pleasure the fact that bullets whiz into the galleries and palaces, into the masterpieces of Rubens, instead of into the homes of the poor in the workers' districts."[3] A 1920 montage painting by the Dresden-based artist and close associate of the Berlin Dadaists, Otto Dix, shows an actual copy of Kokoschka's published plea lying in a gutter not far from a blind and limbless World War I veteran attempting to sell matches on a Dresden sidewalk as the legs of indifferent middle-class citizens wearing seamed stockings and spotless button-up spats hurry past. (Figure 2.1) With its paper torn and its text truncated, Kokoschka's appeal as pasted into the painting echoes the damaged condition of the match-selling veteran's body; and vice-versa: a dachshund raises his leg before the mutilated match seller, sprinkling him with piss as the gutter's filthy puddles soak the paper of Kokoschka's statement. Dix's display of contempt for Kokoschka's appeal responds to the Expressionist's plea for the protection of works of art as if that plea implied a corollary disregard for the situation of human beings. Understood in the terms of Dix's crude and vivid critique, it is as though Kokoschka was asking to see works of art treated as if they were persons, and was doing so, moreover, in a context in which human beings—for example, the workers who had demonstrated on Dresden's Postplatz—felt compelled to risk their lives in demanding recognition of their own personhood and the rights it was said to entail in the representational democracy of a federal republic. Confronted with a situation in which the collective demands of human beings for self-determination faced military suppression and in turn themselves sometimes took the form of violent resistance, Kokoschka called for the protection of works of art as objects of a shared heritage at risk of destruction in a dangerous public sphere. The Dadaists, by contrast, demanded the transformation of the social and political conditions against which the workers were originally demonstrating and of which they took Kokoschka's text itself to be symptomatic, not because Kokoschka lent his support to the radical, antidemocratic right (he did nothing of the kind), but because instead of standing on the side of demonstrating workers, he spoke up on behalf of masterpieces. That the realization of demands such as those voiced by the workers on Dresden's Postplatz might happen occasionally to involve the destruction of works of art did not concern the Dadaists, except insofar as they were pleased to see bullets fired in the midst of monuments and museums rather than in neighborhoods where workers make their homes.

Many contemporary readers of "Der Kunstlump" understood the text as a call to cultural vandalism, and it was widely condemned on those grounds, including in the Communist press. In a reply to Grosz and Heartfield published in the German Communist Party organ, *Die Rote Fahne*, in early June 1920, the newspaper's cultural editor, Gertrud Alexander, characterized Kokoschka's

Figure 2.1. Otto Dix, "The Matchseller I" (1920). Oil on canvas with collage. Staatsgalerie Stuttgart. © 2009 Artists Rights Society (ARS), New York/VG Bild-Kunst, Bonn. Photograph courtesy Erich Lessing/Art Resource, NY

original plea as typical of the cynicism of modern artists, agreeing with the Dadaists that it was in principle preferable that a precious painting rather than a human life should be damaged or destroyed by a bullet, stray or otherwise. But to greet the destruction of art with pleasure was another matter, and the bulk of Alexander's response was taken up with refuting the Dadaists' declaration to that effect. Culture, for Alexander, was made up of things of eternal value, things that in a revolutionary society would represent nothing less than the cultural patrimony of the proletariat as it came to power, a "past beauty" that would have to be (and deserved to be) maintained to serve as a source of pleasure and edification for the "new human being" in advance of the production of a postrevolutionary and properly proletarian culture.[4]

Grosz and Heartfield did not value "past beauty." Instead they wrote derisively of how "sculptures preach the flight of feelings and thoughts, away from the unbearable circumstances of life on earth, to the moon and the stars, to the sky." The work of art that provided an occasion for such flight was, to the Dadaists, a tendentious work, grounded in a theory of art that they linked to their present historical moment, which they believed to be ruled by a cynical and violent politics: "The machine guns of Social Democracy have their way as they aim to transport the disenfranchised to a better afterlife."[5] In other words, the way the work of art transports its viewer to a place apart from the everyday world (to the moon and the stars, to the sky) provides an aesthetic counterpart to the way the fledgling Social Democracy of the early Weimar Republic suppressed left-wing political activity with military power and thereby, as if beneficently, transported its victims to a better world beyond [*ein reineres Jenseits*]. The Dadaists have in mind the various and prolonged states of emergency enacted by the Social Democratic administration of President Friedrich Ebert in response to perceived threats of uprisings on the Left, along with the deployment of troops against the Left, including not only the *Reichswehr* but also right-wing paramilitary outfits and the infamous *Freikorps*. It is almost as though the Dadaists' scenario of political violence as salvation should itself be seen as an aesthetic experiment, a travesty of the aestheticization of social problems elsewhere in modernism. Indeed the next line of "Der Kunstlump" asserts the tendentiousness at work when "a weakling like Rainer Maria Rilke, himself propped up by the perfumed leisure class, writes: 'Poverty is a great glow from within' ['*Armut ist ein großer Glanz von innen*' (*Stundenbuch/The Book of Hours*)]."[6]

"What did the Dadaists do?" ask Grosz and Wieland Herzfelde in their 1925 pamphlet "Die Kunst ist in Gefahr!" [Art is in Danger!]. "They said, it does not matter whether one lets loose some gasping and panting—or a sonnet by Petrarch, Shakespeare or Rilke, whether one gilds boot heels or carves madonnas: there will still be shooting, there will still be profiteering, there will still be starvation, there will still be lying; to what end the entire enterprise of art?" The Dadaists' only mistake, they say, "was involving ourselves seriously with so-called art in the first place. Dadaism, carried out with caterwauling and derisive laughter, was a breakout from a narrow, arrogant, overrated milieu that, hovering in the air between the classes, did not recognize any shared responsibility for the life of the collective."[7] Five years earlier, in "Der Kunstlump," Grosz and Heartfield had repudiated works of art that "preach the flight of feelings and thoughts, away from the unbearable circumstances of life on earth, to the moon and the stars, to the sky." In "Die Kunst ist in Gefahr!" Grosz and Heartfield's younger brother Herzfelde, poet, founder of the Malik-Verlag, and author of the "Introduction to the First International Dada Fair" (1920), explained that what Berlin Dada accomplished amounted to an assertion of the effective equivalence—in the face of violence, exploitation, hunger, and hypocrisy—of lyric poetry and the mere breath that constitutes the bodily medium of its speaking. Which is to say that, as far as engagement in the contemporary world was concerned, giving voice to a sonnet by Rilke was no different from letting one's panting respiration be heard. (The em-dash that separates the gasping and panting from the sonnets dramatizes typographically the Dadaists' claim of equivalence between those two effects of breath.) "Die Kunst ist in Gefahr!" goes on to acknowledge that the Dadaists' repudiations and assertions, and their breaking out of a milieu that Herzfelde, in his "Introduction to the First International Dada Fair," called "the clique of trendsetters,"[8] were part of an earnest involvement with art—or, rather, "so-called art." Made to the accompaniment of the Dadaists' own howling and sneering, the "products"[9] of Berlin Dada critiqued that involvement by enacting allegorically, in works that often include reproductions of masterpieces, the destruction of objects of "so-called art," things belonging to a category whose meaningfulness and actuality the Dadaists believed had been vitiated under the particular conditions of their historical moment. As Grosz and Herzfelde make clear, the Dadaists dissatisfaction with works of "so-called art"—with sculptures, for example, that "preach the flight of feelings and thoughts, away from the unbearable circumstances of life on earth, to the moon and the stars, to the sky"—was ethical in origin. It represented their abhorrence, first, of the indifference of artists to the situation of human beings in the surrounding social world and, second, of the hypocrisy of those artists who depicted aspects of that social world with a pathos that—in the view of the Dadaists—could not fail to be empty. Indeed, this pathos was ethically fraudulent, despite, or rather as a consequence of, its potential aesthetic effects, which for the Dadaists were predicated on, and served further to reproduce, an abdication of shared social responsibility. In each case, artists were described as lacking a stable place among the social classes: in "Der Kunstlump," the Dadaist's repudiation of Rilke's mystification of poverty was made vivid in their description of the poet as himself "propped up by the perfumed leisure classes," while in "Die Kunst ist in Gefahr!," contemporary artists were described as "hovering in the air between the classes."

Gertrud Alexander's critique of "Der Kunstlump" in *Die Rote Fahne* provoked a defense of Grosz and Heartfield from Julian Gumperz, coeditor (with Herzfelde) of *Der Gegner* and future member of the Frankfurt Institut für Sozialforschung. Alexander responded in turn with an article published in two installments on 23 and 24 June 1920, just days before the opening of the First International Dada Fair in Berlin.[10] In this second round of criticism, Alexander described bourgeois society as forever subject to an impulse towards "flight from reality" [*Wirklichkeitsflucht*], a phenomenon exemplified by bourgeois responses to works of art.[11] In Alexander's estimation, the proletariat, unlike the bourgeoisie, did not readily give itself over to *Wirklichkeitsflucht*, above all because proletarians lacked the leisure to devote themselves to fanciful contemplation. Nonetheless, she writes that "it is our responsibility [that is, the responsibility of the vanguard Communist intelligentsia] to insure that the proletarian does not become captive to flights from reality," and to do so not by destroying the works of art that so often played a part in scenarios of *Wirklich-*

keitsflucht, but by "eradicating bourgeois society," that is, by radically transforming social relations and thereby (necessarily) altering relations between human beings and works of art.[12] "When comrades Heartfield and Grosz get agitated [about Kokoschka's plea for the protection of works of art], that is itself merely the fear of the bourgeois gone wild [*die Angst des wild gewordenen Bürgers*], the fear of that impulse, that *Wirklichkeitsflucht*, to which the bourgeois always falls victim."[13] Thus in her condemnation of Grosz and Heartfield, the Communist Party newspaper's cultural editor anticipated—indeed I think she perhaps provided—the language of the title of Grosz's and Heartfield's 1920 sculptural montage, *Der wildgewordene Spießer Heartfield* [The Middle-Class Philistine Heartfield Gone Wild], a title that would appear in Herzfelde's catalogue to the Dada Fair when it was published nineteen days later, on 14 July 1920. (Figure 2.2) As my translation of the title indicates, the Dadaists used the word *Spießer* to name a middle-class philistine, a person of petit-bourgeois sensibility. But the word *Spießer* has other, older meanings that the Dadaists' invocation also calls up. In Germany in the seventeenth century, a *Spießer* or *Spießbürger* was an upstanding member of a civilian militia, armed with a pike and ready to march.[14] The *Spießer*, then, was a paramilitary man, a figure of habitually upright posture, something like a knight. That is a connection subsequently stressed in the writings of Adolf Behne, a prominent German critic and theorist of art and architecture who reviewed the Dada Fair and knew the Berlin Dadaists and their work well. Pointing to a

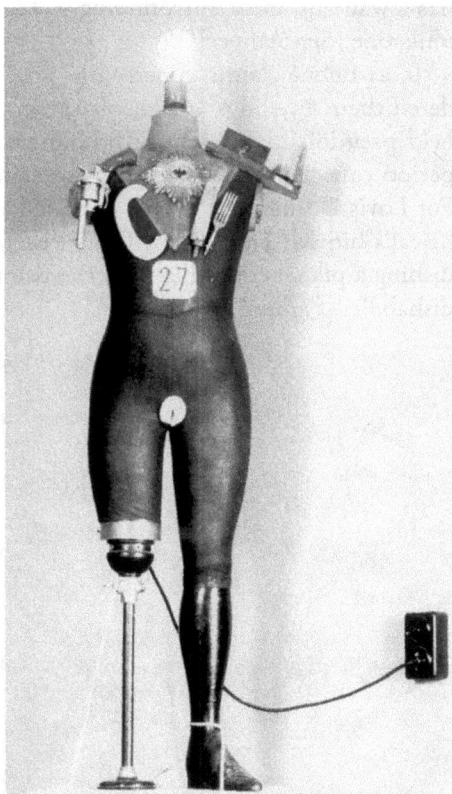

Figure 2.2. George Grosz and John Heartfield, "The Middle-Class Philistine Heartfield Gone Wild" (1920). Tailor's dummy, revolver, doorbell, knife, fork, letter "C" and number "27" signs, plaster dentures, embroidered insignia for the Black Eagle Order on horse blanket, Osram light bulb, Iron Cross, stand, and other objects. Reconstruction, 1988. Berlinische Galerie, Landesmuseum für Moderne Kunst, Photographie, und Architektur, Berlin. © 2009 Artists Rights Society (ARS), New York/VG Bild-Kunst, Bonn, and Estate of George Grosz/ Licensed by VAGA, New York, NY.

tendency among Germans of all classes to arrange the décor of their domestic spaces along diagonals, Behne argued that the "deeper cause" of that inclination lay in the "unconscious retention of a posture of struggle and defense. ... Just as the knight, suspecting an attack, positions himself crosswise to guard both left and right, so the peace-loving burgher, several centuries later, orders his art objects in such a way that each one, if only by standing apart from all the rest, has a wall and moat surrounding it. He is thus truly a militant, middle-class philistine [*Spießbürger*]."[15]

If, as Behne claims, nineteenth- and early twentieth-century Germans ordered their dwellings and displayed works of art according to unconsciously held pseudofeudal postures, prominent artists working in Germany in that period consciously took up the pose and put on the costume of the knight. For Lovis Corinth the knight provided a figure of positive identification; here he calls himself *Der Sieger* [The Victor], and stands, clad in armor and brandishing a pike, behind his wife, the painter Charlotte Berend-Corinth, she in dishabille. (Figure 2.3)

Figure 2.3. Lovis Corinth, "The Victor" (1910). Oil on canvas. Present location unknown.

For Kokoschka, in whose work the knight also often appears and who painted himself as an errant one in his eponymous self-portrait of 1914–15, the type of the *Irrender Ritter* (Knight Errant) underwrote an allegory of the artist's undoing, depicted here in the knight's collapse across a craggy outcropping with his back to a temperamental sea. (Figure 2.4) "It is not my trade to unmask society," Kokoschka explained in his autobiography, "but to seek in the portrait of an individual his inner life."[16] Hence this self-portrait has been seen to display the painter's own "inner life" in a grouping of allegorical figurations of his relationships and experiences around the time of its production.[17] Both the reclining knight and the winged figure hovering in the dark sky above him resemble the painter as he portrayed himself in other works of the period. The winged figure has been identified as the angel of death, and the knight has been likened to a wounded Christ: "*Eloi, Eloi, lama sabachthani?* [My God, my God, why hast Thou forsaken me?]," the knight may be asking in the shorthand "ES" inscribed above his left arm, which he lifts across the blustery horizon in a dramatic demonstration of frailty. Or, the winged figure may represent the child never to be born to Kokoschka and his lover Alma Mahler, who had broken off their relationship and ended a pregnancy shortly before Kokoschka set to work on this picture in the second half of 1914 (the kneeling naked woman hunched head-in-hand among the green, black, and white swirls of the middleground's blasted landscape has been seen as a portrait of Mahler). It seems Kokoschka finished *Self-Portrait (Knight Errant)* either just prior to his departure for military service in March 1915, or just after his return to Vienna some seven months later. This uncertainty concerning the date of the work's completion leaves open the question of whether the painting might further re-

Figure 2.4. Oskar Kokoschka, "Self-Portrait (Knight Errant)" (1914–15). Oil on canvas. Solomon R. Guggenheim Museum, New York. © 2009 Foundation Oskar Kokoschka / Artists Rights Society (ARS), New York/Pro Litteris, Zurich.

late to Kokoschka's experiences in World War I, during which he was wounded in combat. When Kokoschka mentioned the painting in a letter of 27 December 1915 to Herwarth Walden, impresario of the Berlin art gallery *Der Sturm*, he called it "Knight in a Magical Landscape."[18]

No matter which, if any, the picture's particular points of reference may be, the place where Kokoschka's self-representation appears is meant to seem enchanted. For Kokoschka, plying the painter's "trade" is like taking up the quest of a knight errant whose charge is "to seek in the portrait of an individual his inner life." It is as if in this instance the painter's pursuit of the inner life of his portrait subject involved making the artist's trade itself magical, conjuring emblems and allegories (miniature winged figures with plaintive faces, tiny naked melancholy women, scrawny leafless trees, portentous tides and skies, tender seashells) to render visible the sitter's intimate, internal preoccupations. The painter as maker of magical landscapes appears here as himself captive to that magic, such that the self-portrait as a presentation of Kokoschka's inner life in allegorical figures becomes an allegory of the painter's fate as subject to art's effects of enchantment. Shown nearly life-sized, Kokoschka as knight errant has the vacant face and lumbering gestures of a somnambulist, here tipped to recline open-eyed and stiff on the ground plane of the picture's narrow horizontal.

Made in the wake of Grosz and Heartfield's critique of Kokoschka in the so-called Kunstlump-Debatte [Art-Scoundrel Debate], *Der wildgewordene Spießer Heartfield* embodies something like the conditions of possibility for getting the contemporary artist back up on his feet.[19] In place of the work of art as a means of seeking the inner lives of individuals, the Dadaists' collaborative product insists on the exteriority of the object and its subject: the artwork is a thing mounted with devices and artifacts of everyday life, not a magical landscape into which we gaze, not a sacred sculpture that promises to transport us to a better world; and the *Spießer* himself is oriented outward, knight-like in the disposition of his defensiveness, but bereft of a quest. Postured and outfitted for present-day life, *Der wildgewordene Spießer Heartfield* stands for the disenchantment of the work of art.[20]

I want now to return to the place of "der wildgewordene Spießer" in the political discourse of the Berlin Dada period, and specifically in a vitriolic attack on anarchist radicalism and petit-bourgeois revolutionism launched in a speech delivered by Lenin in Moscow on 27 April 1920. Appendices were added to the text of that speech on 12 May, and it was published in Russian in pamphlet form on 20 June. Soon after, the brochure was issued simultaneously in English, German, and French translations. Published in German under the title *Der "Radikalismus" die Kinderkrankheit des Kommunismus*, Lenin's text was translated by the Executive Committee of the Communist International in 1920 as *The Infantile Sickness of "Leftism" in Communism*, but it is now more commonly known by the title under which it appeared in New York in 1934,

"Left-Wing" Communism: An Infantile Disorder. Der *"Radikalismus"* was widely available to the German public by mid-July 1920, at which time advertisements for its publication in pamphlet form were appearing in the Communist press.[21] Moreover, the effects of Lenin's condemnation of Left extremism and petit-bourgeois revolutionism were quickly felt in Germany. Members of the Communist Party (KPD)—especially those based in Berlin and including Franz Jung, a writer closely associated with Grosz and Heartfield, who were also founding members of the KPD—left the party in large numbers starting in April 1920, when many joined in launching the German Communist Workers' Party (KAPD). As Barbara McCloskey has noted, the KAPD monthly, *Proletarier* [The Proletarian], criticized Lenin for having the "bureaucratic mentality of an arrogant leader who thinks the revolution is his monopoly," and the KAPD actively sought the engagement of avant-garde artists and writers who were likely to feel less welcome in the KPD as it began to articulate a cultural politics along the lines of Alexander's critique of the Dadaists.[22] Grosz, for example, mentions his regular attendance at KAPD meetings in a 1921 letter to fellow Dadaist Raoul Hausmann. The letter's sardonic tone suggests, however, that Grosz was no more at home in the KAPD than in the KPD, to which he continued to belong.[23] When we compare the militant, middle-class philistine bearing Heartfield's name to the proletarian drawn by Hans Baluschek for the cover of the October 1920 edition of the KAPD's eponymous journal, it is not hard to see why a Dadaist might have felt out of place at that party's gatherings. (Figure 2.5) Not that the Dadaist's self-identification as *wildgewordener Spießer* should be understood as other than ironical. What remains to be explained is the connection of that ironical identification to a particular work of art, and to the problem of politics in Berlin Dada.

As published that summer of 1920, Lenin's *"Der Radikalismus"* contains the following passage:

> The experience of all European revolutions and revolutionary movements fully confirms … that the small proprietor … who under capitalism is constantly oppressed and suffering, and whose conditions of life often take a sharp and rapid turn for the worse, when faced with ruin moves easily to extreme revolutionism, but is incapable of displaying any stability, organization, discipline and firmness. The petit-bourgeois who is beside himself with rage as a consequence of the horrors of capitalism [*der infolge der Schrecken des Kapitalismus "außer sich geratene" Kleinbürger*] is a social phenomenon which, like anarchism, is peculiar to all capitalist countries. The weakness of such revolutionism, its futility, its very nature enables it to transform itself into obedience, apathy, phantasy and even into a "mad" infatuation with some bourgeois "fashionable" tendency—all this is common knowledge.[24]

Subsequent German translations of Lenin's text would rephrase the line *"der infolge der Schrecken des Kapitalismus 'außer sich geratene' Kleinbürger"* as *"der*

JAHRGANG 1   HEFT 1   OKTOBER 1920

PROLETARIER
MONATSSCHRIFT FÜR KOMMUNISMUS

PREIS   1,50 M.

Figure 2.5. Hans Baluschek, cover of *Proletarier* (October 1920). Hannah Höch Archive, Berlinische Galerie, Landesmuseum für Moderne Kunst, Photographie und Architektur, Berlin. © 2010 Artists Rights Society (ARS), New York/VG Bild-Kunst, Bonn.

durch die Schrecken des Kapitalismus 'wild gewordene' Kleinbürger,"[25] a formulation that is clearly very close to the title *Der wildgewordene Spießer Heartfield.* I am not claiming that the Dadaists themselves necessarily had read and were responding directly to Lenin's polemic. It is my sense, however, that through her association with *Die Rote Fahne,* Alexander could have read or otherwise come to know something of the vocabulary and tone of Lenin's pamphlet in advance of its official publication in Germany, and could thus have adopted Lenin's terms when she referred to Grosz and Heartfield as seized by the "fear of the bourgeois gone wild" [*die Angst des wild gewordenen Bürgers*] on 24 June. And I do not think it is impossible that by the time the title of *Der wildgewordene Spießer Heartfield* was set for printing shortly before 14 July, Grosz, Heartfield, and Herzfelde—all members of the Communist Party, well-connected in left-wing publishing circles, and affiliated with *Der Gegner*, which was paying a great deal of attention to Lenin in the spring and summer of 1920[26]—could have come to recognize the phrase as part of Lenin's larger argument. The Berlin Dadaist Hannah Höch was in possession of a copy of what she describes in a notebook as "Lenin, *Der Radikalismus*," as well as his *State and Revolution*, when she catalogued her books some years later.[27] I stress these connections—which I acknowledge to be speculative—because I believe the Bolshevik leader's rhetoric is particularly apposite to the works that were on view at the Dada Fair, and to the politics those works were meant to manifest. "Dada is a German Bolshevist affair," proclaimed Richard Hülsenbeck in his history of the Dada movement published in July 1920.[28] *Der wildgewordene Spießer Heartfield* makes clear how idiosyncratic Berlin Dada's "German Bolshevism" was.

Tendentious from head to toe, *Der wildgewordene Spießer Heartfield* is a sculpture that offers no escape from the conditions of life in the modern world. No religious stupefaction. No moon and stars. And the glow comes from its glaring lightbulb head, not from a grand and luminous poverty deep inside. The photograph of Grosz and Heartfield holding their "Art is Dead" placard[29] as they stand in front of *Der wildgewordene Spießer* at the Dada Fair gives a sense of the apparently improvised nature of the work's original display, with a glimpse of anchoring twine and of the makeshift slate-topped table that was the sculpture's pedestal. (Figure 2.6) Pulled tight, the narrow cords attached to the joint at the knee of the peg leg and looped around the boot-like mannequin ankle seem indeed to be keeping the figure down, holding *Der wildgewordene Spießer* in place as if in accordance with the chalk lines mapped on the slate. I have suggested elsewhere that the chalk markings might be associated with military drills performed on the Tempelhof field in Berlin—a site invoked in related works on display at the Dada Fair, and the place where Grosz, Heartfield, and Herzfelde took part in training exercises during World War I—but there is something about the way the figure is tied that also suggests primitive imprisonment, ad hoc court martial, or facing the firing squad.[30] It is as if the *Spießer* had gone wild, and then, forcibly, violently, had been brought back under control. He stands erect and still, subdued and frozen in a dignified pose. But it is as though the going wild had transformed his body, replacing his head with a lightbulb, his leg with a metal rod, his arms with a doorbell and a revolver, his penis with a plaster impression of a human mouth. The *Spießer*, we might say, attempted escape, but got caught, or stayed caught. Now the figure embodies both the attempt (the going wild) and the failure (the getting or remaining captured) in the form of the mechanisms that make up his body, mechanisms that announce his enforced rootedness in the world, and his endless experience of the rage the world inspires. That rage, once manic, is now suppressed, but the body bears replacement parts as memorials to its fruitless revolt.

We know from "Der Kunstlump" that Grosz and Heartfield had Rilke in mind during the spring of 1920. The fact that they misquote him there—the line from the *Stundenbuch* is more dramatic, more Rilkean, than the Dadaists indicate, and actually reads, "*Denn Armut ist ein großer Glanz aus Innen. ...*" —only underscores how readily his poetry could be summoned. Massively popular, Rilke's works did not require looking up in print; they could be recited—or at least fairly well paraphrased—straight from memory. *Der wildgewordene Spießer* stands like a fragment of an ancient statue arranged for display, and in other ways suggests a travesty of Rilke's 1908 sonnet "Archaïscher Torso Apollos" [Archaic Torso of Apollo]. (Figure 2.7) This is not the place for an interpretation of Rilke's poem. Given, however, that Grosz and Herzfelde put lyric poetry and its recitation at the crux of what the Dadaists did ("They said, it does not matter whether one lets out some gasping and panting—or a sonnet by Petrarch, Shakespeare, or Rilke") it will be worth exploring how *Der wildgewordene Spießer* might be seen to operate in relation to Rilke's rendering of an encounter with the "meaningful fragment" of an ancient work of art.[31]

> We did not know his stupendous head
> in which the eyeball-apples ripened. But
> his torso still glows like a gas lamp
> in which his gaze, just turned to low,

Figure 2.6. George Grosz and John Heartfield at the *First International Dada Fair*, Berlin, 1920, photograph in Richard Huelsenbeck, *Dada Almanach* (Berlin: Erich Reiss Verlag, 1920).

abides and gleams. Otherwise the curve
of his breast could not blind you, nor the gentle turn
of his loins send forth a smile
to the center that once procreation bore.

Otherwise this stone would stand disfigured, short
beneath the shoulders' transparent drop
and would not shimmer like a wild beast's fur:

and not burst out of all its contours
like a star: for here there is no place,
that does not see you. You must change your life.[32]

Der wildgewordene Spießer has a head we do not know; we can hardly bear to look at it—it is blinding. And like Rilke's Apollo, Dada's *Spießer* is lamp-like at the site of his gaze—in the most literal and up-to-date way. Where the gaze of Rilke's Apollo was *zurückgeschraubt*, turned down low as though by means of a mechanism like those on modern, gas-powered cande-labra,[33] the illuminated gaze of Dada's *Spießer* has a brand name: bulb by Osram™. The breast of the *Spießer* curves outward with the mannequin's built-in upright stance, and that stance, mounted on a metal leg that resembles a support to stabilize an ancient statue on display though it is in actuality a component borrowed from a gas lamp (the twine that holds the sculpture in place is tied alongside the mechanism with which a functioning lamp would be *zurückgeschraubt*), now gestures towards an antique allusion. In the poem, we have reached the midpoint of the Apollonian body and of the Rilkean sonnet, where the smile resides, the point at which Dada's travesty hits its mark, with stunning, ridiculous force, confronting metaphor with the literalness of matter, and rendering the *Spießer*'s body gro-

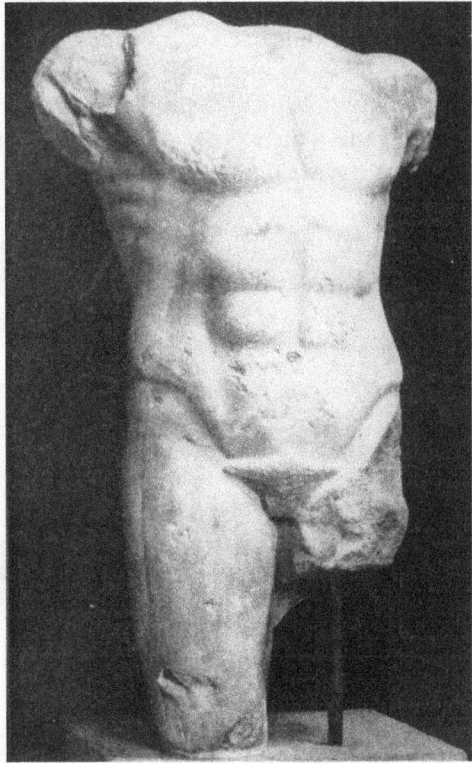

Figure 2.7. Male torso, called the "Miletus Torso," Louvre Ma2792 (ca. 480–470 BC). Island marble (from Paros?), sculpted in the round. Musée du Louvre, Paris.

tesque, even obscene: "nor the gentle turn / of his loins send forth a smile / to the center that once procreation bore." The place of procreation on the *Spießer* might gape, chew, laugh, nip, chomp, chatter—it might do the common jobs of the mouth, but that plaster cast of lips and teeth, itself a miniature sculpture, cannot smile like the face of an ancient statue. Inverted to vertical, the displaced mouth cannot smile at all, unless the *Spießer* finds a way to recline like Kokoschka's knight, to lie down and let himself be seen horizontally, propped up on a doorbell- or revolver-arm, like a vanquished mechanical Mars, or a very modern Venus, on whose pudenda the plaster mouth would then appear as if the seashell resting before the hips of Kokoschka's knight had moved up the picture plane and attached itself to his crotch. (Among the works Grosz exhibited at the Dada Fair was one called *Mißachtung eines Meisterwerkes von Botticelli (Primavera)* [Contempt for a Masterpiece by Botticelli (Primavera)], in which the Dadaist registers his contempt in an "X" taped across the glass of a framed reproduction of the painting; here I juxtapose to the *Spießer* another masterpiece by Botticelli, namely, *Venus and Mars*.) (Figure 2.8) The *Spießer's* mouth is barren. It opens onto shallow blackness backed up against a mannequin's crotch of cloth and wood. Central to Rilke's sonnet is the statue's "visible-invisible phallus," marked as missing by the displaced smile that travels through the loins to that center which once gave rise to procreation, which once was the site of Apollonian genitals.[34] In Berlin Dada's *Spießer*, a boy-sized

tailor's dummy presents a center that cannot yet have given rise to procreation; with a reproduction of a mouth in place of genitals, his middle now never will. A statue but not of stone, the *Spießer* stands disfigured, short, peg-legged, and plaster-crotched, beneath the glow of his incandescent electrified head. His shoulders support a doorbell and a gun, but from them nothing plunges. If, in addition to a see-through drop, a translucent fall from noble shoulders to the gentle torsion of smiling loins, Rilke's choice of the word *Sturz* summons at once both the ruin of an antique torso itself and the protective glass cover that separates a work of art from its modern museum audience,[35] the *Spießer* incorporates its own status as a ruin on display in the metal support that stands in for a missing leg. Around that support the *Spießer* has been tied down, as if to emphasize that he can no longer (or could not ever have) burst forth from his own contours, that he cannot (or never could) explode like a star to accost his beholder with an ethical exhortation: "You must change your life."

The *Spießer* wears his light on the outside, in the form of a bright transparent bulb; nothing glows within him any longer. He has gone wild, and the energy of what might have been (or might have become) his own attempt at life-changing has been spent. All that remains incandescent is that electric lamp, which keeps him close to the wall, near the outlet into which he must be plugged. Rilke figures as a ruin, in fragments reconstituted as a sonnet, what the Dadaists, in montage, aimed to actualize, in order thereby to disfigure it

Figure 2.8. Sandro Botticelli, "Venus and Mars" (ca. 1485). Egg tempera and oil on poplar. National Gallery, London. Photograph courtesy Alinari/Art Resource, NY.

even further: the work of art as an object of contemplation that does not so much tell us, let alone show us, how to live, but that how we are living must change. Dada's *Spießer* does not admonish us; it cannot bring itself, cannot hold itself together, to tell us: "You must change your life." But the Dadaist work of art registers, in its travesty, the relinquishing of the wish, or the loss of the hope, to do so.[36]

A 1919 pen and ink drawing that was published with the title *Nachkriegsidyll* [Postwar Idyll] in Grosz's 1921 book *Das Gesicht der herrschenden Klasse: 57 politische Zeichnungen* [The Face of the Ruling Class: 57 Political Drawings], prefigures the appearance of the *Spießer* at the Dada Fair.[37] (Figure 2.9) Calling the picture an idyll and thus situating it in relation to lyric poetry, Grosz shows a blind veteran propped against a wall, wearing a uniform with patches at the elbow, steadying himself with a cane, and proffering a box of matches from a carton that hangs around his neck. Tucked in behind the carton is a sign on the match seller's chest that bears the word "blind," and dangling over the top of that sign is a military medal, an Iron Cross. The face of a raging Prussian officer occupies the extreme foreground of the drawing, while just behind the officer at left a one-legged veteran, also still in uniform, labors to walk on crutches and casts a bitter sidewise glance in the direction of his superior. A fat man in fancy clothes strolls toward the middle of the picture, enjoying a cigar and taking notice neither of the figures he is approaching (the three men in uniform) nor of the ones behind him (an aristocratic couple on horseback, a hapless bourgeois carrying an umbrella and a cigar in a holder, and, at the back, a unit of steel-helmeted soldiers marching in formation and bearing the German national flag). The fat man's indifference to the match seller, the figure nearest to him and one who might be expected to arouse his passing interest, if not his sympathy, represents an extreme case of the failure or refusal to "recognize any shared responsibility for the life of the collective" that Grosz and Herzfelde criticized in "Die Kunst ist in Gefahr!" and that characterizes the behavior of all the figures in Grosz's 1919 drawing. The one-legged veteran and the blind match seller differ from the others in that they display a kind of agonizing incapacity for recognition that registers around their eyes, which in the match seller appear as dense ink hatchings that may stand for the shadow cast by the man's visor or for the cavernous absence of an eyeball, while in the one-legged veteran the eye exposed in profile rolls back into his head at the outside corner where its lids meet, as if the man's desperate effort to apprehend the world and the others in it could only end in extreme dissatisfaction and discomfort, with the man now turning his frustrated gaze back in upon himself, or rather upon the corner of his own eye.[38] Like the blind match seller, the fat man has a wooden cane; smoothly finished and fitted with metal details, it gets put to fashionable instead of practical use, hanging from the crook of the stroller's elbow rather than helping him to stay up on his feet. Along with the others on the page, the fat man—a familiar type in Grosz's drawings of the period—is a profiteer, a man grown rich in the war economy and now taking pleasure in his postwar station. As if in recognition of the source of that on which he has grown fat, an Iron Cross hangs like a charm from the substantial watch-chain at his middle. An oversized diamond tie-pin gives off rays of light that spread across the profiteer's chest, and we are bound to notice how both the diamond and the flimsy, store-bought Iron Cross have been aligned along diagonals with the blind match seller's medal, which is meant to look as though its bearer earned it (the drawing gives no indication that the match seller might be a fraud—that is, not blind, not a decorated veteran, or neither.) *Nachkriegsidyll* is typical of Grosz's caricatures of the period, which perform a kind of comparative anatomy of the cast of characters they represent (in that sense the match seller's authenticity hardly matters: the fraud would be an equally salient type).

Figure 2.9. George Grosz, "Postwar Idyll" (1919). As reproduced in George Grosz, *Das Gesicht der Herrschenden Klasse* (Berlin: Malik-Verlag, 1921). © 2009 Estate of George Grosz/Licensed by VAGA, New York, NY.

Der wildgewordene Spießer Heartfield, which bears an Iron Cross of its own on its buttocks, does something different. It is as if that montage-sculpture subsumed the types depicted in the drawing in a new composite body, a figure of absolute actuality and infinite contradiction, with the posture of a soldier trained to march; the slender, stiff-backed haughtiness of a monocled count; the fraught bemusement of the middle-class intellectual; the vulgarity of the profiteer; the missing limbs and blinded eyes of wounded veterans; and the rage of the ranting officer. It is worth the risk of taking this too far to make the point visually: the *Spießer's* breast gleams as though the profiteer's diamond had been fused with the blind veteran's medal to form the gilded imperial eagle medallion that is displayed, as if proudly, upon the mannequin's velvet chest.

Nachkriegsidyll is a "political drawing," and *Der wildgewordene Spießer Heartfield* might be called the embodiment of politics in Berlin Dada, an ironical identification with a figure of militant, middle-class philistinism and petit-bourgeois
revolutionism, and a corollary to the Dadaists' positive self-definition as "the
vanguard of dilettantism." The latter was a position that envisioned a democratization of the making and viewing of works of art that would follow upon
the destruction of the cult of art.[39] In this regard, the placard that announces
"Die Kunst ist tot" does not so much articulate an "anti-art" stance as present the Dadaists' appraisal of the situation of the work of art in the contem-

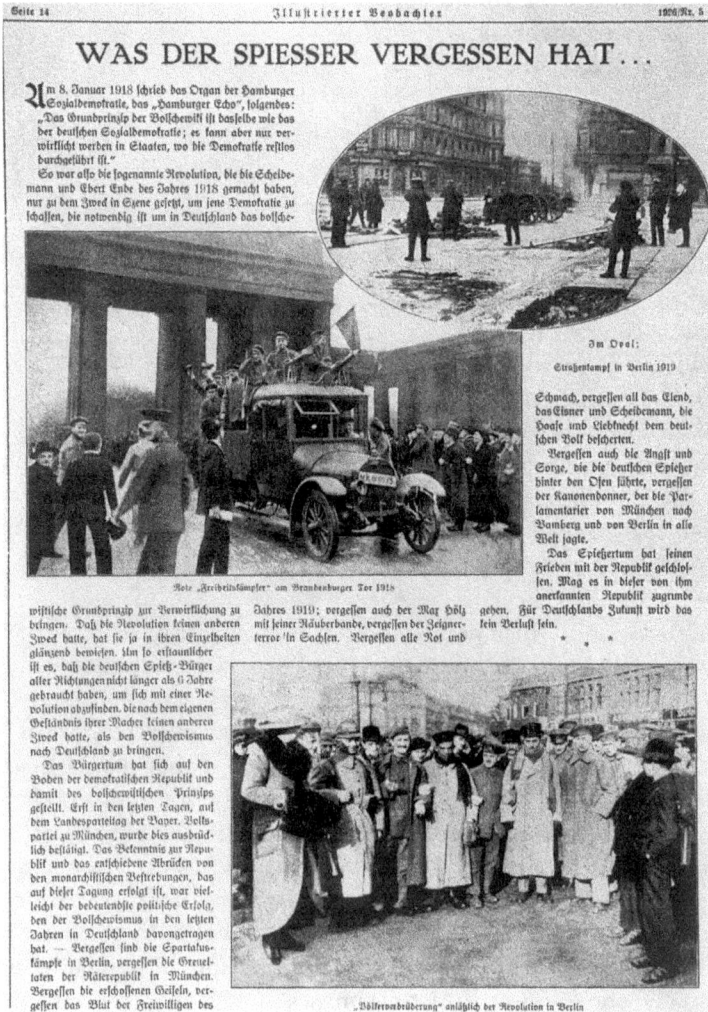

Figure 2.10. "What the Militant Middle-Class Philistine Forgot...,"
Illustrierter Beobachter (1926).

porary world. "Art is not alive," the placard might be saying, with the implied ethical position that human beings ought not to treat works of art as if they were persons when they do not treat other human beings that way. The Dadaists' position is ethical, and, finally, political: *"All indifference is counterrevolutionary!"* declared Grosz and Heartfield in "Der Kunstlump."[40] Berlin Dada produced an art of failed revolution, in which the destructive energy as well as the actual collapse of revolutionary politics in Germany circa 1919–20 are figured in the destruction of the traditional work of art as a component of the work of Dada montage. The medium of that destruction, montage, embodies the energy as well as the collapse, and the Dadaists' technique keeps both in play.

With the publication of "Die Kunst ist in Gefahr!" in 1925, Grosz and Herzfelde repudiated the Dadaists' earnest involvement with art, pointing to what they saw as the unresolved problem of politics in Berlin Dada: the hazard of embodying politics in works built up around figures of absolute actuality and infinite contradiction. That hazard has another aspect, to which an article published in 1926 in the far-right weekly the *Illustrierter Beobachter* points. Called "Was der Spiesser vergessen hat …" [What the middle-class philistine forgot …], the article, which is illustrated with photographs of the November Revolution, had made its peace with the republic that right-wing radicals, like their counterparts on the left—the Dadaists among the latter—despised: "May the *Spießertum* find its own demise in the republic whose legitimacy it has recognized. For Germany's future there would be no loss in that."[41] (Figure 2.10) The *Illustrierter Beobachter* inverts the extremism of Lenin's *Der "Radikalismus"* in conflating Social Democracy, seen as the politics of the German *Bürgertum*, with Bolshevism. But common to this article and Berlin Dada's self-ironizing identification with the *wildgewordener Spießer* was an attempt to glimpse a future politics in a critique of the German *Spießertum*. The problem is, the future belonged to the *Illustrierter Beobachter*.

Notes

Thanks are due to the editors of *October* and to MIT Press for permission to reprint, with minor revisions, this essay, which originally appeared in *October* 105 (Summer 2003): 73–92.

1. Oskar Kokoschka, cited in George Grosz and John Heartfield, "Der Kunstlump," *Der Gegner*, no. 10–12 (n.d. [April 1920]; Reprint, 1979), 53. On the subject of what came to be called the *"Kunstlump-Debatte,"* see Walter Fähnders and Martin Rector, eds, *Literatur im Klassenkampf. Zur proletarisch-revolutionären Literaturtheorie 1919–1923: Eine Dokumentation* (Munich, 1971), 43–50; Barbara McCloskey, *George Grosz and the Communist Party: Art and Radicalism in Crisis* (Princeton, NJ, 1997), 65–69; Beth Irwin Lewis, *George Grosz: Art and Politics in the Weimar Republic* (Princeton, NJ, 1991), 93–95; Roland März, ed., *John Heartfield: Der Schnitt entlang der Zeit* (Dresden, 1981), 102–28; Joan Weinstein, *The End of Expressionism* (Chicago, 1990), 240–

41; Hubert van den Berg, *Avantgarde und Anarchismus: Dada in Zurich und Berlin* (Heidelberg, 1999), 390–98.

2. Grosz and Heartfield, "Der Kunstlump," 53. Unless otherwise noted, all translations are mine.

3. Ibid., 55. Italics in original.

4. G. G. L. [Gertrud Alexander], "Herrn John Heartfield und George Grosz," *Die Rote Fahne*, no. 99 (9 June 1920). Reprinted in Manfred Brauneck, ed., *Die Rote Fahne: Kritik, Theorie, Feuilleton, 1918–1933*, Munich, 1973), 65.

5. Grosz and Heartfield, "Der Kunstlump," 51.

6. Ibid.

7. George Grosz and Wieland Herzfelde, *Die Kunst ist in Gefahr!* (Berlin, 1925), 23–24.

8. See Wieland Herzfelde, "Introduction to the First International Dada Fair," trans. Brigid Doherty, *October* 105 (Summer 2003): 100–104.

9. On the Dadaists' use of the term *products*, see Brigid Doherty, introduction to Herzfelde, "Introduction to the First International Dada Fair," *October* 105 (Summer 2003): 93.

10. See ibid., 93–99.

11. Alexander, "Kunst, Vandalismus und Proletariat," *Die Rote Fahne* 112 (24 June 1920). Reprinted in Brauneck, *Die Rote Fahne*, 73.

12. Ibid.

13. Ibid.

14. The following description of the seventeenth-century German *Spießer's* French counterpart appears in the opening paragraph of the chapter "Docile Bodies" in "Part Three: Discipline" of Michel Foucault's *Discipline and Punish*, trans. Alan Sheridan (New York, 1979), 135:

> Let us take the ideal figure of the soldier as it was still seen in the early seventeenth century. To begin with, the soldier was someone who could be recognized from afar; he bore certain signs: the natural signs of his strength and his courage, the marks, too, of his pride; his body was the blazon of his strength and valour; and although it is true that he had to learn the profession of arms little by little—generally in actual fighting—movements like marching and attitudes like the bearing of the head belonged for the most part to a bodily rhetoric of honour; "The signs for recognizing those most suited to this profession are a lively, alert manner, an erect head, a taut stomach, broad shoulders, long arms, strong fingers, a small belly, thick thighs, slender legs and dry feet, because a man of such a figure could not fail to be agile and strong"; when he becomes a pike-bearer, the soldier "will have to march in step in order to have as much grace and gravity as possible, for the pike is an honourable weapon, worthy to be borne with gravity and boldness" (Montgommery, 6 and 7).

15. Adolf Behne, *Neues Wohnen, Neues Bauen* (1927), cited in Walter Benjamin, *The Arcades Project*, trans. Howard Eiland and Kevin McLaughlin (Cambridge, MA, 1999), 215. Translation slightly modified.

16. Kokoschka, cited in Claude Cernuschi, *Re/Casting Kokoschka: Ethics and Aesthetics, Epistemology and Politics in Fin-de-Siècle Vienna* (London, 2002), 55.

17. See, for example, Jaroslaw Leshko, "Kokoschka's *Knight Errant*," *Arts Magazine* (January 1982): 126–33; Thomas M. Messer, "Der irrende Ritter," in *Oskar Kokoschka* (Vienna, 1986), 183–86; and Werner Hofmann, "Der irrende Ritter," in *Oskar Kokoschka*, 265–78.

18. See Tobias G. Natter, ed., *Oskar Kokoschka: Early Portraits from Vienna and Berlin, 1909–1914* (New York, 2002), 180.

19. See Herzfelde's "Introduction to the First International Dada Fair" for a gloss on another 1920 work by Grosz that purports to represent his friend and collaborator Heartfield: *'Der Sträfling': Monteur John Heartfield nach Franz Jungs Versuch, ihn auf die Beine zu stellen* ['The Convict': Monteur John Heartfield after Franz Jung's Attempt to Get Him Up on His Feet]. On *'Der Sträfling'* as a Groszian self-portrait, see Brigid Doherty, "'See: We are all Neurasthenics!' or, The Trauma of Dada Montage," *Critical Inquiry* 24, no. 1 (Fall 1997): 104–18.

20. On modernism and disenchantment, see T. J. Clark, *Farewell to an Idea: Episodes from a History of Modernism* (New Haven, CT, 1999), 7, passim. On modernist disenchantment and reenchantment in the art of Adolf Menzel, see Michael Fried, *Menzel's Realism: Art and Embodiment in Nineteenth-Century Berlin* (New Haven, CT, 2002), 231–46.

21. See, for example, *Die Rote Fahne* 134 (20 July 1920).

22. See McCloskey, *George Grosz and the Communist Party,* 68.

23. See Grosz, letter to Raoul Hausmann, 13 December 1921, in *Hannah Höch: Eine Lebenscollage, 1921–1945,* ed. Ralf Burmeister and Eckhard Fürlus, (Ostfildern-Ruit, 1995), 2:34–35.

24. W. I. Lenin, *Der "Radikalismus," die Kinderkrankheit des Kommunismus* (Leipzig, 1920), 13–14.

25. W. I. Lenin, *Werke* (Berlin [GDR], 1970), 31:161.

26. For example, an installment of Gregorij Sinowjew's *Lenin: Sein Leben und Seine Tätigkeit* [Lenin: His Life and Work] was published in the same issue of *Der Gegner* as "Der Kunstlump."

27. See BG HHC H346/79, Hannah Höch Archive, Berlinische Galerie, Berlin.

28. Richard Hülsenbeck, *En Avant Dada: Die Geschichte des Dadaismus,* 1920; reprint, (Hamburg, 1984), 39.

29. The placard's complete text reads: "Art is dead / Long live the new / machine art / of Tatlin." Those lines paraphrase a sentence from a 1920 article on the Russian artist Vladimir Tatlin by Konstantin Umanski. In that article, the first in a four-part report on contemporary art in Russia, Umanski writes: "Die Kunst ist tot—es lebe die Kunst, die Kunst der Maschine mit ihrer Konstruktion und Logik, ihrem Rhythmus, ihrem Bestandteile, ihrem Material, ihrem metaphysischen Geist,—die Kunst des 'Kontrereliefs' [Art is dead—long live art, the art of the machine with its construction and logic, its rhythm, its components, its material, its metaphysical spirit—the art of the counter-relief]." See Umanski, "Neue Kunstrichtungen in Rußland. I. Der Tatlinismus oder die Maschinenkunst," *Der Ararat* 1, no. 4 (January 1920): 12. On the Dadaists' knowledge and reception of Tatlin's art, see Helen Adkins, "Erste Internationale Dada-Messe," in *Stationen der Moderne: Die bedeutenden Kunstausstellungen des 20. Jahrhunderts in Deutschland* (Berlin, 1988), 159; and Eva Züchner, "Die Erste Internationale Dada-Messe in Berlin: Eine meta-mechanische Liebeserklärung an Tatlins Maschinenkunst," *Berlin-Moskau. Moskau-Berlin* (Berlin, 1995), 118–24. On the relationship of the Dadaists' (mis)understanding of Tatlin's art to their conception of politics, see Samantha Kate Winskell, "Between Mass Culture and Proletkult, the Death of Art and Utopia: Berlin Dada and the Soviet Cultural Model," chapter four of her "Dada, Russia and Modernity, 1915–1922" (PhD diss., Courtauld Institute of Art, London, 1995).

30. *Preußischer Erzengel* [Prussian Archangel], a collaborative sculptural construction attributed to Heartfield and Rudolf Schlichter that hung from the gallery's ceiling at the Dada Fair, consisted of a plaster pig's head attached to a stuffed German military

officer's uniform to which was clipped a sign that read: "To grasp entirely the meaning of this work of art, one must, while completely outfitted for battle and carrying a fully-loaded knapsack, perform daily twelve-hour drills on the Tempelhof field." See Doherty, "The Trauma of Dada Montage," 118–21.

31. I borrow this phrase from Judith Ryan, *Rilke, Modernism, and Poetic Tradition* (Cambridge, 1999), 80.

32.
> Wir kannten nicht sein unerhörtes Haupt,
> darin die Augenäpfel reiften. Aber
> sein Torso glüht noch wie ein Kandelaber,
> in dem sein Schauen, nur zurückgeschraubt,
>
> sich hält und glänzt. Sonst könnte nicht der Bug
> der Brust dich blenden, und im leisen Drehen
> der Lenden könnte nicht ein Lächeln gehen
> zu jener Mitte, die die Zeugung trug.
>
> Sonst stünde dieser Stein entstellt und kurz
> unter der Schultern durchsichtigem Sturz
> und flimmerte nicht so wie Raubtierfelle;
>
> und bräche nicht aus allen seinen Rändern
> aus wie ein Stern: denn da ist keine Stelle,
> die dich nicht sieht. Du mußt dein Leben ändern.

Rainer Maria Rilke, "Archaïscher Torso Apollos" (1908), in *Werke. Gedichte 1895 bis 1910*, vol. 1 of 4, ed. Manfred Engel and Ulrich Fülleborn (Frankfurt a. M., 1996), 513.

In the course of attempting a translation of "Archaïscher Torso Apollos" that would be apposite to the claims of this essay, I have consulted and sometimes borrowed from the following bilingual editions and translations of Rilke's sonnet: Rilke, *New Poems*, revised bilingual edition, ed. and trans. Edward Snow (New York, 2001), 182–83; *The Essential Rilke*, bilingual edition, ed. and trans. Galway Kinnell and Hannah Liebmann (Hopewell, NJ, 1999), 32–33; Rilke, *Neue Gedichte/New Poems*, ed. and trans. Stephen Cohn, (Evanston, IL, 1998), 142–43; *The Selected Poetry of Rainer Maria Rilke*, bilingual edition, ed. and trans. Stephen Mitchell, intro. Robert Hass, (New York, 1982), 60–61; *Possibility of Being: A Selection of Poems by Rainer Maria Rilke*, ed. and trans. J. B. Leishman (New York, 1977), 53; *Selected Poems*, ed. and trans. C. F. MacIntyre (Berkeley, CA, 1940), 92–93; *Selections from the Poetry of Rainer Maria Rilke*, ed. and trans. M. D. Herder Norton (New York, 1938), 180–81. I am also indebted to Ryan's translation and analysis of "Archaïscher Torso Apollos" in *Rilke, Modernism, and Poetic Tradition*, 80–89. Wolfram Groddeck's essay "Blendung: Betrachtung an Rilkes zweitem Apollo-Sonett," in *Interpretationen: Gedichte von Rainer Maria Rilke*, ed. Wolfram Groddeck (Stuttgart, 1999), 87–103, has been helpful to my reading of "Archaïscher Torso Apollos" and its interpretations. I share Groddeck's skepticism regarding efforts to locate and name the sculptural "sources" of Rilke's Apollo sonnets. Let me therefore mention that the question of whether the Miletus Torso (ca. 480–470 BC; Musée du Louvre, Paris), illustrated here as reproduced in Ulrich Hausmann, *Die Apollosonette Rilkes und ihre plastischen Urbilder* (Berlin, 1947), or indeed any other individual work of art can properly be described as an immediate source for Rilke's "Archaic Torso" is irrelevant to my juxtaposition of that work and its apparatus of museum display with *Der wildgewordene Spießer Heartfield*. Here the Miletus Torso stands for antique sculpture in general, and for the specific conditions of its visibility in modernity. In *Montage und Metamechanik* (Berlin, 2000), Hanne Bergius proposes that the works produced by the Berlin Dadaists beginning in late 1919 and designated as "metamechanical"—of which *Der wildgewordene Spießer* would be a key example, though it is not the object of a sustained analysis by Bergius (she discusses it briefly on 281)—represent the introduction into Dada montage of an "Apollonian" principle opposed to the "Dionysian" one that had governed the production of earlier works (9). While I agree with Bergius that the terms of Nietzsche's *The Birth of Tragedy from the Spirit of Music* (1872) are pertinent to Berlin Dada in general, I see the connections differently, as my claims in this essay should suggest. My remarks on *Der wildgewordene Spießer* in relation to Rilke's "Archaic Torso of Apollo" are indebted to a conversation with Michael Fried that began at Johns Hopkins in December 1995, and that since then has meant more to me than a footnote can convey.

33. See Ryan, *Rilke, Modernism and Poetic Tradition*, 88.
34. On "der sichtbar-unsichtbare Phallus" in "Archaïscher Torso Apollos," see Groddeck, "Blendung," 98–99.
35. On the definition of *Glassturz* as "a protective glass cover for an art object," see Ryan, *Rilke, Modernism and Poetic Tradition*, 236, n. 70; see also Groddeck, "Blendung," 98, n. 8.
36. I have more to say about this aspect of Berlin Dada, specifically in relation to the aesthetic theories of Walter Benjamin and Theodor Adorno, in *Montage: The Body and the Work of Art in Dada, Brecht, and Benjami,* (Berkeley, CA, forthcoming).
37. See Grosz, *Das Gesicht der herrschenden Klasse: 57 politische Zeichnungen,* 3rd expanded edition, vol. 4 of Kleine Revolutionäre Bibliothek, ed. Julian Gumperz (Berlin, 1921), 16.
38. The profile and eye of the one-legged veteran strongly resemble those in a number of Grosz's self-portraits of the period, for example '*Der Sträfling,*' discussed in Doherty, "The Trauma of Dada Montage," 104, passim. See also note 19.
39. See Herzfelde, "Introduction to the First International Dada Fair."
40. Grosz and Heartfield, "Der Kunstlump," 56. In *Montage*, I locate the Dadaists' position within a larger problematic of modernism to which the following passage from a 1967 essay by Stanley Cavell points. Cavell's specific subject is "contemporary music," but his claims speak to modernism in general. What responses to contemporary music suggest, he writes:

> is that the possibility of fraudulence, and the experience of fraudulence, is endemic in the experience of contemporary music; that its full impact, even its immediate relevance, depends upon a willingness to trust the object, knowing that the time spent with its difficulties may be betrayed. I do not see how anyone who has experienced modern art can have avoided such experiences, and not just in the case of music. ... [T]he dangers of fraudulence, and of trust, are essential to the experience of art. ... Contemporary music is only the clearest case of something common to modernism as a whole, and modernism only makes explicit and bare what has always been true of art. (That is almost a definition of modernism, not to say its purpose.) Aesthetics has so far been the aesthetics of the classics, which is as if we investigated the problem of other minds by using as our examples our experience of *great* men or *dead* men. In emphasizing the experiences of fraudulence and trust as essential to the experience of art, I am in effect claiming that the answer to the question "What is art?" will in part be an answer which explains why it is we treat certain objects, or how we *can* treat certain objects, in ways normally reserved for treating persons.

See Cavell, "Music Discomposed," in *Must We Mean What We Say? A Book of Essays* (Cambridge, 1969), 188–89. Italics in original.
41. Anonymous, "Was der Spiesser vergessen hat ... ," *Illustrierter Beobachter* 5 (1926): 5, 14.

CHAPTER 3

~:~

The Secret History
of Photomontage
On the Origins of the Composite Form and
the Weimar Photomontages of Marianne Brandt

ELIZABETH OTTO

Faced with an explosion of photographically based, printed mass-media during the period of the Weimar Republic, a number of avant-garde artists turned images from illustrated papers into ready-mades for the medium of photomontage. By cutting up and repositioning the illustrated press's pictures from everyday experience and political events, photomonteurs created often playful works that also functioned as a sophisticated mode of imbedded cultural critique. While a number of artists would later claim to have invented the medium of montage, it is clear that all were inspired by earlier forms of popular and private imagery, including advertising, postcards, and scrapbooks. Yet there is a dearth of analysis of the interrelationship between mass-produced and avant-garde forms of composite imagery. By tracing a particularly contested element in montage iconography—the figure of the soldier—from the late nineteenth century through the Weimar period, this essay seeks to explore the productive relationships between images produced in these different historical contexts and to investigate varied modes of historical viewership in the construction and critique of military masculinity.

Photomontage and the Engaged Viewer

In the spring of 1917, a Frau Anna Westal was one of many women in Germany to receive a picture postcard from the field entitled *Stolzenfels am Rhein* (Figure 3.1). The two lines of a little couplet provide a frame for the card's

Figure 3.1. Artist unknown, *Stolzenfelz am Rhein* (n.d., sent in 1917), postcard, lithographic print of photomontage, and painting, 9 x 13.5 cm. Courtesy of Altonaer Museum, Hamburg – Norddeutsches Landesmuseum.

scene: "The musketeer looks back to his love one more time. / He sends her a thousand greetings; what does his last look say?"[1] Any German soldier of the First World War could have purchased this postcard, the very title of which evoked a romantic vision of Germany's past by referring to the historic castle on the Rhein.[2] He could then have turned the card over and, on its back, written the words that he had been too shy to speak aloud when bidding his beloved farewell.

Parallel to the two kinds of texts on the postcard, printed and hand-written, *Stolzenfels am Rhein* is a composite of two media, painting and photography, which have been combined and reprinted through the halftone process. The rolling hills of western Germany provide a painted backdrop for groups of figures in the print's foreground. On the left, a waving mother and her two children are rendered in a flat, self-consciously naïve style that nostalgically recalls the folk art traditions and imagery of small-town life. While painting provides a good deal of the print's background and peripheral elements, the center of the composition is dominated by a group of photographed soldiers who jauntily shoulder their muskets. All but one of these men have turned their backs on the small family and are ready to march off to war.

There is a disturbing similarity to the appearances of the eight men. As closer inspection reveals, this group has been created by double and triple printing three photographed figures. While the montage is clumsily executed—a soldier in the middle is stepping on his neighbor's foot, for example—it is precisely this repetition through composite photographic imagery that gives members of the group an overall unity in their heights, stances, and general appearance. But one man is unique among his fellows: the soldier furthest to the left appears only once. He has turned his back to us and faces his family to point commandingly towards the village in the shadow of the Stolzenfels castle, where he intends for them to stay in safety. This soldier's gaze and gesture connect him to the family group and, through them, to peacetime domestic life. Yet the fact that he is rendered photographically rather than in paint separates him irrevocably from his loved ones and situates him firmly in the group of battle-ready conscripts. Dressed in the uniform worn by thousands and with his face hidden from view, this figure's identity remains open to adoption by any soldier who might purchase this card and sign his name to it. As she held this postcard in her hands and read the awkward rhyme on its front, Anna Westal might have found that it expressed a question she was left with upon parting from her musketeer: what was he thinking as he went off to war? What, indeed, did his last look say? Despite the advanced technology of halftone color printing used to create this layered image and to show detail and specificity in the reproduced photograph of this soldier, his facial expression remains beyond the scope of pictorial representation.

In the following pages I tease out a link between two groups of fragmentary, photography-based representations of the male soldier's body that span both sides of World War I—the moment of the composite Stolzenfels postcard—and that chart shifts in gendered experiences of military culture. As I will show, examination of montage and other composite photographic forms highlights the ways in which these media produce meaning and create particular understandings.[3] I first investigate the forms and reception of a subgenre of composite soldier portraiture that arose concurrently with the founding of the German nation and was developed by later nineteenth- and early twentieth-century professional photographers. Along with examining these portraits as avant-garde precedent—the "secret history" of this essay's title—my close analysis of the soldier portraits provides a model for addressing a form of popular imagery that was both mass produced and intensely personal. In the second half of this essay, I follow the fragmented representation of the soldier into a group of works made nearly a decade after the war, the photomontages of Marianne Brandt from the late 1920s and early 1930s. The turn to montage on the part of avant-garde artists was not only a move to deskill art by creating images from preexisting elements; the use of such fragmentary ready-mades also provided a way of denaturalizing conventional representations of men by creating visual breaks within imaged bodies or by highlighting a gap between a body and its setting. In following the historical trajectory of the pairing of composite media and the image of the soldier, my investigation reveals how historical and avant-garde composite forms were implicated in the creation and undoing of ideals of masculinity.

While the potential for experiences of war and military culture to cultivate specific forms of masculinity is well known, the role that pictorial representation played in shaping soldiers' identities has rarely been investigated.[4] Mass-produced postcards and keepsake images created a space for conversation about and interpretation of experiences of war. While composite photographic images and avant-garde montage have begun to receive more scholarly attention in recent years, among the areas that remain to be explored are those that pull at the temporal margins of the early Weimar moment of Berlin Dada: composite images made prior to and during the First World War as well as montages from the later 1920s and 1930s. Further, German avant-garde montages created outside of the Dada context have yet to be interrogated for what they reveal of the relationship between the war's profound violence and the interwar explosion of a similarly violent medium that involved cutting up and recombining mass-produced photographic images of landscapes and human figures.

As I examine fragmentary representations of militarized male bodies, I am interested in the ways in which Weimar avant-garde montages were, in part, enacting an archaeology of their own past by drawing on the imagery of the still-recent war. The tradition of allegory—an interpretive mode familiar to viewers from such diverse sources as public statuary and Renaissance painting—was substantively investigated and reconceived by a number of cultural theorists during the interwar period, most notably Walter Benjamin. In *The Origin of German Tragic Drama*, written during the middle years of the Weimar Republic, Benjamin describes allegory as a complex form of expression that he likens to speech and writing in that it can communicate multiple levels of information to a receptive reader or viewer.[5] The term "allegory" comes from the Greek *allêgoría*, which means literally to speak otherwise than one seems to speak.[6] Allegories therefore differ from symbols, for the significance of fragments in allegorical works is not immediately apparent and always remains ambiguous.

In Benjamin's understanding of allegorical representation, the spectator encounters such devices as repetition and elements of what he calls "the art of interruption"—fragmented or nonsequential images—that create meaning through interaction. Crucial to representations that function allegorically are their obviously constructed nature. Benjamin's analysis of tendencies in Baroque drama applies equally well to his contemporaries in the visual avant-gardes of Weimar: "[t]he writer must not conceal the fact that his activity is one of arranging, since it was not so much the mere whole as its obviously constructed quality that was the principal impression which was aimed at. Hence the display of the craftsmanship, which ... shows through like the masonry in a building whose rendering has broken away."[7] Through its use of breaks and blank spaces that interrupt the flow of representation by calling attention to the pictorial surface and creating moments of abstraction, the allegorical work of art defies direct, symbolic interpretation. It thus remains open and allows its pictorial elements to play off of and contradict one other.

Avant-garde photomontage, with its awkward cuts and unexpected juxtapositions, excels at showing itself as pieced and cobbled together. It is also an ideal medium for combining traditional and modern imagery. Rather than referring exclusively to the Christian, mythological, or astrological traditions that formed the basis of conventional allegory, avant-garde allegorical montages also draw much of their meaning from modern life, including newspapers and popular entertainment.[8] At the same time, conventional allegories may also be read in many of these works. Benjamin's allegory provides an interwar methodology that aids in interpreting the cut-up and reassembled imagery of avant-garde montage, in which jolting and awkward combinations, unexpected interruptions, and empty pictorial spaces are as central to compositions as pictorial representations.

While they do not lend themselves as easily to allegorical interpretation, the pre–avant-garde soldier portraits are also created out of fragments; they present an invitation to viewers to see an individual person in relation to historical events. My exploration will reveal how, in its early forms, the medium of photomontage was employed to create and support particular myths of masculinity and that these images also required viewer participation in order to be complete. While such images encouraged viewers to piece together a particular understanding of the scene before them, these viewers could accept or decline this offer. And, as we shall also see, avant-garde photomontage subsequently became a tool for unpacking these myths of masculinity. Through its own juxtapositions, this essay ultimately shows how avant-garde montage practice was, in part, rooted in propagandistic soldier portraiture and was in conversation with traditional representations of militarized manhood.

Manhood Multiplied

That so little has been written about the soldier portraits is due in part to the fact that, as a vernacular form, they have rarely been collected or exhibited by museums.[9] Yet in recent years, many in the field of art history have shown an increased interest in the forms of visual culture—both popular and avant-garde—that could be made cheaply and quickly and thus respond to political and cultural events. From the earliest examples of this form of portraiture, made during the 1870s, printed settings and landscapes formed the basis of the image. These prepared backgrounds set their subjects into pastoral or genre scenes rather than representations of the battles that were usually seen to define military experience.

In a double portrait by an unknown photographer from approximately 1890, Lance-Corporals Wilhelm Bode and Wilhelm Kelterborn appear on a lithographic background showing a scenic old village in which soldiers chat and laugh with the friendly locals (Figure 3.2). While the image appears informal,

Figure 3.2. Artist and photographer unknown, *Gefreiter Wilhelm Bode, Gefreiter Wilhelm Kelterborn, 11 Compagnie des 3. Hannoverschen Infantrie Regiments No. 79* (1890), lithograph, hand-colored albumen print, and montage, 32 x 24 cm. Museum Folkwang, Essen.

its caption gives it an official note by identifying the men's regiment and rank. In its representation of quaint town life and its reliance on narrative details to create atmosphere, this portrait draws on forms of representation typical of genre painting and commemorative group portraiture in Dutch Baroque art. In Bode and Kelterborn's portrait, military conflict is reduced to a reprimand from a charming female baker who holds out an unpaid bill to the two men. She embodies contradictions by smiling even as she chides; and the iconography of her comely outfit pairs her severely corseted, hourglass figure with the apron and rolled-up sleeves of a laboring baker. Her clothing also suggests a sexual invitation. The open purse that hangs at this young baker's side evokes the money that she is owed, and it references a bawdy pun in traditional German slang in which a woman's genitals can be referred to as her *Börse* or "purse." Thus the baker's need to balance her books also marks her as potentially sexually available.

To create this portrait, Bode and Kelterborn each sat for the photographer who then cut the resulting pictures of helmeted heads out and glued them to the print's surface. Only once these photographed heads had been glued on did the reproduced genre scene become an individuated double portrait. Similar images provided many soldiers with mementos of their time in the service (*Dienstzeit*); these portraits were colorful, idealized, and accurate likenesses that were still affordable to most lower-ranking soldiers. Like the *Stolzenfels am Rhein* postcard—which was created through montage and represents a soldier whose identity can be taken on by anyone buying the image—so these portraits' printed backgrounds offer one or more soldier bodies that are waiting to be adopted by a specific purchaser. None of these background prints would have been complete until it had been selected by a man who would give it his face in the form of photographed image.

While these portraits were primarily sold to ordinary soldiers rather than officers, the makers of these images often went to great lengths to create fictionalized representations of the glory of a man's military service. Such practices reached their height in the genre of the triple portrait (*Dreifachporträt*), as we see in the commemorative image of the *Grenadier* or Private Selten made by M. Hirschfeld from 1899 (Figure 3.3). With its heavy frame of classical columns, shields for Germany's various regions, and images of royalty, Selten's portrait is situated in a crowded vision of his time as a private. The background landscape features an awkwardly compressed scene of German Romantic highlights; a majestic home, a dramatically pointed hill topped with romantic ruins, and an imposing castle appear together as symbols of personal and national pride that require the protection of such a soldier as Selten. Perhaps the most surprising feature of this portrait is the fact that its subject's head and body appear three times in a variety of poses and uniforms, each with its attendant accoutrements. On the far right he is shown with rifle and helmet, ready for

Figure 3.3. M. Hirschfeld and Hannah Höch, *Portrait of Grenadier Selten bei der 6. Companie / Der Anfang der Photomontage*, (1899 and after 1919), steel plate print, colored and collaged, 42.5 x 51.7 cm. Courtesy of Berlinische Galerie, Landesmuseum für Moderne Kunst, Fotografie und Architektur, Hannah-Höch-Archiv.

battle; in the center Selten is in his full dress uniform; and at the left he appears as a casual gentleman-soldier, his hat off and a beer mug at his side. Selten's portrait is awkwardly executed, and his three heads appear too small for his bodies, rendering him not only as multiple, but as massive and powerful, a capable soldier who can follow the real thinkers behind military strategy. And indeed, such military heads are shown directly above the private's tripled image, with Kaiser Wilhelm II most prominent among them.

Traditions of soldierly portraiture kept pace with printing technologies during the later nineteenth century, and printed scenes became increasingly photographic in their detail around 1910. In the First World War, established conventions provided a popular iconographic tradition for the romantic ideal of the soldier male in which the figure—often multiple—was set into a full-color, nationalized landscape. In a portrait by photographer Albert Pfeiffer made in 1915, shortly after the start of World War I, a colored print forms the ground for the visages of Musketeer Podolski and his two comrades (Figure 3.4). This

Figure 3.4. Albert Pfeifer, *Portrait of Musketier Podolski, 7. Companie, 2. Unter Elsässer Infantrie-Regiment Nr. 137, Hagenau* (1915), gelatin silver bromide print, multicolored lithograph, and montage, 45 x 32 cm. Museum Folkwang, Essen.

image of three men in a forest carries on established traditions of soldier portraiture such as the mixing of photographic with lithographic elements and the
combining of pastoral and military imagery.

Pfeiffer locates his subjects in a peaceful, agrarian landscape that is dap-
pled with villages and church spires and that features the single, ruin-crowned
hill that viewers had come to expect from earlier, less naturalistic portraits of
Selten's type. Pfeiffer creates a timeless scene but for a few specific references
to the war including the soldiers' uniforms and, guarding the heavens behind
them, a zeppelin, one of the most significant tactical and symbolic additions
to warfare at this time.[10] In contrast to the heavy framing of Selten's portrait,
Podolski's has almost no frame at all; it allows the foliage of the Alsatian forest—that hotly disputed terrain—to come right up to the picture plane.

The updated military technology of the First World War brought other
changes to the tradition of soldier portraiture that are evident in Pfeiffer's image. In Bode and Kelterborn's double portrait, the two men are heavily armed,
but their weapons seem to be incidental decoration. Their swords are sheathed
and their rifles appear only casually: slung over the shoulder of the man at the
left and used as a walking stick on the right. In contrast, Podolski's commemorative image emphasizes weaponry and technology to highlight his possession
of up-to-date equipment for war. Field glasses hang from his neck; in his left
hand is a pistol and his right arm holds a modernized rifle so that it dominates his
presence. The zeppelin floats directly above Podolski's head, showing further
evidence of his mastery of modern military technology to a loved one viewing
this picture. "He will triumph," these machines reassure us. Somewhat out of
place in this romanticized setting, the presence of these modern weapons in
Podolski's portrait emphasizes the ideological importance of technology in the
First World War. Yet this technology served to harm many more people than it
protected. The use of such advanced weapons became one of the defining features
of a war that historian Deborah Cohen has called "murderous without precedent" and that took an average of 5,600 lives for every day that it continued.[11]

The deployment of technological imagery in Podolski's portrait parallels the
production of the portrait itself. The introduction of the halftone process in the
1880s and the subsequent development of offset printing made the creation of
mass-produced combinatory images possible in the early years of the twentieth
century. True to the format of such portraits, a photograph of Podolski's head
has been glued onto the printed composition. But this image has an added
advantage over earlier forms of portraiture: photographer Pfeiffer has utilized
photolithography to reproduce setting, comrades, and even a body for his sitter. These photographic elements were combined with color and reproduced
directly as a part of the print itself. Thus these scenes had a further element of
photographic credibility, even though all elements but the sitter's face would
still have been identical in every portrait made with this background. Through

his skill with the modern machines of image making, Pfeiffer has created an appropriately heroic and technically advanced representation, one that could be used again for any other man who might request it.

However, as with earlier forms of composite soldier portraiture, the technique was not perfect; Podolski's head is slightly too large for his body and has had to be trimmed at the neck to provide a credible fit. This slight disproportion makes him appear child-like, as if his shoulders were too narrow for his heavy pack and his hands too small for his rifle; these elements, while surely unintended by the photographer, cast doubt upon whether or not Podolski is man enough for his military role. For any viewer who looked closely at this portrait, the glued-on head would stand out from the rest of the image, forcing a break between Podolski's face and his body as well as with the landscape around him. The very detail that gives this portrait its specificity reveals itself as a foreign body, as separate from the rest of the portrait.

Because of their mode of manufacture, soldier portraits were based on an incomplete illusion. The combination of landscape, military machinery, and soldier's body forms the core of these pictures, and yet these images' narrative flow is interrupted by the introduction of the most important element of the portrait: the individual soldier's face. Thus these portraits present viewers with an awkward choice: should they believe in these visions of the war's glories shown either in overwhelming detail, as in Selten's picture, or imaged as romantic naturalism, as we see in Podolski's portrait? The works also offer viewers an invitation to recognize the face of a family member or loved one, to overlook disjuncture, and to mentally combine the best of various media: color and idealized landscapes provided by reproduced painting and the perceived truthfulness of photography.[12] Such portraits encourage viewers to participate actively as they bridge these gaps in order for the image to work. But instead of the politically critical stance invited through allegorical viewing, activation in this manner might encourage feelings of patriotism or belief in the war effort, ideas caught up in the construction of a national narrative. The fictions perpetuated by this form of composite portraiture were imbedded in the medium itself, and this layer of montage history was subsequently available for avant-garde artists to draw upon when they turned to montage in the wake of the war's loss.

However, given the choices with which viewers were presented in these portraits, we should also consider the fact that it was possible for them to opt for a resistant reading. There is evidence of one such reading in Selten's triple portrait. While it was completed in 1899, it did not reach its present state until about twenty years later when Dadaist Hannah Höch obtained it, pasted the title "The Beginning of Photomontage" ("Der Anfang der Fotomontage") onto its lower right corner, and signed it as an artist would her own work. Höch's gesture undermines the original artist's intent; it also gives credit to the genre that both she and Raoul Hausmann stated was the source of their inspiration for first creating photomontages. According to both accounts, it was during Hausmann and Höch's own escape into another ideal landscape—a seaside vacation town on the Baltic—that they discovered montage and brought it back to the metropolis of Berlin.[13] Höch's retitling is also mocking, as if to draw a line between the real photomontage and its humble origins seen here. In the 1960s, when she recounted her version of the discovery of the medium, she suggested the distaste with which most members of the Weimar avant-garde would have remembered such images by referring to them as "naïve kitschy."[14] Yet this kitsch from a previous era still held strong associations with the recently deposed monarchy and the First World War and thus provided powerful imagery for artists to draw upon.

By echoing this earlier form of montaged portraiture that had come abruptly to an end with the loss of the war, members of the Weimar avant-garde ironically recalled the glory that this pictorial tradition had promised. What is most proper to allegory is, according to Craig Owens, "its capacity to rescue from historical oblivion that which threatens to disappear."[15] It was by taking up the tools of democratized military portraiture and by further fragmenting the imagery of these tentatively assembled pictures that avant-garde artists could most effectively expose the myths behind the militarism of a previous age. For whereas the postcard and portraits that I have discussed here provided one well-proportioned, strong, and able body to fit all men, the veterans who managed to survive the war were often left with bodies and psyches that were severely damaged and scarred, each in their own unique ways. Interwar photomontage would continuously problematize images of masculinity from the past in a manner that also evoked the broken bodies of the Weimar Republic's present. Evocations of dismemberment and decapitation are clearest in the fragmentary images produced in the early Weimar moment of Berlin Dada.[16] But, as I will show, representations of soldiers who were in danger or dead were a constant presence in the later Weimar works of many photomonteurs, Brandt central among them. The word *monteur* originally entered the German language through military terminology and subsequently was a part of the vocabulary of productive labor and work with machinery; thus, through the images they produced and even the etymology of their trade, *monteurs* were performing an immanent critique of militarist trends that would continue throughout the period of the Weimar Republic.

Manhood Recontextualized

During the middle years of the Weimar period, Bauhaus artist Marianne Brandt turned to the medium of photomontage to explore constructions of gender in which she often focused on the representation of the militarized male body. Like the soldier portraits, Brandt's montages have only recently been the subject of scholarly investigation.[17] Brandt studied with László Moholy-Nagy at the Bauhaus, and she is primarily known as one of the school's most successful metal designers. Parallel to creating her sleek, practical, metal objects, Brandt made complex photomontages that engage and critique the culture of later Weimar. While for most of these photomontages, there is no clear record that she exhibited them at the time, she most likely shared them with friends and colleagues at the Bauhaus where she lived and worked. In this manner too Brandt's montages are similar to the soldier portraits, for they were originally only viewed in the context of an intimate circle.[18]

Full of references to contemporaneous culture and politics, the imagery of some of Brandt's photomontages also echoes the older composite form of soldier portraiture. In implying such connections, Brandt's images raise critical questions about the enthusiasm for technology at the Bauhaus and the quest for rearmament—expressly forbidden by the terms of the Treaty of Versailles—by many in the late 1920s. Instead of perpetuating notions of a reproducible, standardized male body or the timeless landscape that should be fought for, Brandt situates soldiers in sterile scenes where they march aimlessly or struggle helplessly. Instead of imaging a nationalized countryside, her landscapes reveal their devastation, argue for historical contingency, and highlight the consequences of war.

Such consequences are played out in a work known as *Untitled (Airplane, Soldiers, and Military Cemetery)* (*o.T. [Flugzeug, Soldaten, und Soldatenfriedhof]*) from approximately 1930 (Figure 3.5), which presents three male figures in a landscape, just as we saw in Pfeiffer's portrait of Musketeer Podolski. As in the portrait, the composition of Brandt's montage is given a specifically military context by two uniformed men who accompany a central heroic figure and by an aircraft in the sky; this time we see the enormous, looming form of an airplane instead of a distant zeppelin floating peacefully. But rather than showing a scenic forest and a calming, symbol-laden landscape to justify the war, Brandt has situated these men in a bare, snow-covered field of grave markers with names partially visible on them. Whereas Podolski's comrades appear calm and poised in battle, one standing at the ready, the other kneeling and prepared to shoot, in Brandt's montage the two soldiers accompanying the central figure strike agitated poses that evoke panic and defeat. The soldier at the upper right of Brandt's composition gesticulates wildly, as if he is attempting to signal for help to the airplane above. In the composition's lower left corner, a small figure crawls through the mud, dirtying his elaborate, old-fashioned uniform. His epaulet is torn, and he wears a scull and crossbones on his sleeve, a symbol that brings to mind the right-wing, paramilitary *Freikorps* groups that continued to roam city streets and engage in low-level warfare during much of the Weimar Republic. Yet this figure's outdated uniform could also refer back to that marker's origin with the Prussian cavalry.[19] Were it not for his position on the ground, he could be an image from a soldier portrait.

In Podolski's portrait, his two comrades stand in for the larger troop of which he was an integral part; in Brandt's montage the accompanying men appear to have lost the military groups to which they belong. They are vulnerable

Figure 3.5. Marianne Brandt, untitled (c. 1930), photomontage on cardboard, 65 x 50 cm. Dresden, Kupferstichkabinnett. © 2010 Artists Rights Society (ARS), New York/VG Bild-Kunst, Bonn.

in the harsh landscape, and their uniforms serve less as reminders of their status than as evidence of a breakdown of order. The largest figure of this composition smiles like a modern hero, but Brandt's montage suggests his cruel nature by positioning him so that he is grinding one of his comrades into the dirt with the ball he holds in his hand.

Landscapes are deployed to create particular arguments in both of these composite images. In the case of Pfeiffer's 1915 portrait, with its evocative forest of oak trees—Germany's national symbol—and a winding path leading to the homes of a scenic village in the distance, the promise that this war will bring a lasting peace in Germany's favor is made in the landscape. The scenery argues that these three men have only taken up arms to defend their way of life and the land that they love. And this portrait invites us to imagine that, when the war is over, these same men will leave their modern weapons and their clear photographic identities behind to melt into the hazy distance with its pleasant village. In contrast, Brandt's landscape is devoid of romanticizing details; instead of a bountiful harvest, this cold landscape yields only the markers of a massive graveyard. Her work strategically employs the sleek visual language of New Objectivity by utilizing few elements and strong contrasts.[20] The field of graves is tilted dangerously to one side; they stretch to the horizon, in rows that angle off at the sides in a manner suggestive of the curve of the earth's surface. It is as if this is all that is left of the world.

Images of modern technology are also included in both of these pictures. These elements lend a sense of dynamism to composite soldier portraits such as Podolski's, in which, as we have seen, weapons and fighting techniques play an essential part. In Brandt's montage, by contrast, up-to-date technology appears, but it is shown without any sense of heroism. Looming over the entire composition is the world-famous, German-made Do X airplane, photographed here shortly before its first flight across the Atlantic. This powerful aircraft, with its twelve motors and an unprecedented forty-eight-meter wing-span, promised the first affordable and regular transatlantic flights.[21] Set into the context of Brandt's work, photomontage retools the Do X as a military vehicle, one that might even increase the range and scale on which future wars could be carried out. Brandt's untitled montage seems to systematically counter the Romantic traditions of soldier portraiture. She brings together images of failing, panicked, and cruel men and sets them in an endless graveyard, a strong answer to the convention of visualizing landscape as the homeland to be fought for. And, in this montage, Brandt presents technologically advanced machines not as positive symbols of military superiority but as threatening and dangerous.

In contrast to the lifeless fields of Brandt's untitled montage with the Do X, the photographic elements of *On the March* (*Es wird marschiert*) (Figure 3.6), from 1928, create a work teeming with the ebb and flow of crowds of people who demonstrate and march through this densely packed landscape.

Figure 3.6. Marianne Brandt, *Es wird marschiert* (1928), montage of newspaper and magazine photographs, 50.2 x 65.5 cm. Militärhistorisches Museum der Bundeswehr, Dresden. © 2010 Artists Rights Society (ARS), New York/VG Bild-Kunst, Bonn.

Freed from the original contexts in which they were printed, soldiers and other human figures run riot in a disjointed, composite countryside. Visual elements such as buildings, rowboats, and raised hats and arms echo one another, swarming and crowding throughout the picture plane of this complex photomontage and challenging our perception of scale.

Brandt has repositioned montage elements culled from documentary and literary journals into a composition that offers spectators the chance to come to grips with an array of scenes of the day. The year that this work was created, 1928, was a time of widespread labor unrest including the lockout of several hundred thousand workers in the Ruhr iron and steel dispute.[22] In the lower right quarter of Brandt's montage are scenes of fighting police and protesters, which seem to address this clash of union politics and big business that posed a serious challenge to the authority of the young democratic government of the republic. In *On the March*, Brandt has extended the crowd's image by utilizing a technique that we first saw in the *Stolzenfels am Rhein* postcard: parts of the same photographic image appear twice. In *On the March*, the doubling gives a sense of the enormity of the group of protesters. It also gives a temporal element to the work by suggesting repeated gestures of police pushing back the crowd. These doubled photographic images even evoke the frames of a newsreel film, the medium through which many would have learned of this story.

Images of soldiers and men in uniform appear at several points in this work. To the left is one of the most dynamic groups, a marching army of Asian men in military greatcoats and traditional hats. In 1928, they could have brought to mind the contemporary struggles against colonial rule in Asia or the ongoing unrest in China, both of which were frequently represented in the illustrated newspapers.[23] These soldiers appear to be marching right out of the composition of On the March, as the doubled columns of their ranks recede dramatically into the distance. In the work's foreground a portly officer barks orders and appears as a caricature of the military disciplinarian. This figure was clearly recognizable as Otto Hörsing, a leader in the Reichsbanner Schwarz-Rot-Gold, a center-leftist paramilitary organization, one of the Freikorps associated with the Social Democrats. This passage thus functions as a representation of both local and worldwide militarization, and it reveals embedded layers of allegorical meaning at play in Brandt's work. Other references to war appear throughout the photomontage. In the upper left corner, the looming figure of an oversized baby in a sailor suit stands with toy boats at his feet. These boats reveal themselves to be enormous warships going up in flames, a disorienting reversal of scale and a startling mixture of domestic and military imagery. By removing groups of soldiers and demonstrators from their newspaper contexts and the historical narratives in which their mobilization would have occurred, On the March places them into a setting in which their actions are without provocation and appear as senseless, overwhelming pattern.

In the examples of earlier composite images that I have discussed, women are present at times, but they tend to stand in as representations of a longed-for domestic space, as we saw in Stolzenfels am Rhein, or as flirtatious admirers who are happy to have soldiers visiting their towns, as in the double portrait of Lance-Corporals Bode and Kelterborn. In On the March, Brandt's pairing of montage and images of soldiers enacts a further, more fundamental change by placing a modern woman at its center. Dominating and observing the crowded landscape around her is the figure of a fashionable Garçonne, a boyish and sexy female type who was often discussed by her contemporaries for her glamour, frivolity, and preoccupation with passing fashion.[24] This figure appeared in a photograph by Umbo entitled Gaby Meyer in the Bar at Mali und Igor (Gaby Meyer in der Bar bei Mali und Igor) (Figure 3.7). Like Brandt, Umbo had also trained in the Bauhaus metal workshop, and she appears to have had an interest in his photographs.[25] Brandt cut the reproduction from the literary and culture magazine Uhu, where it was framed by a poem called "the Dance-Hall Girl," a superficial rhyme about the reminiscences of a fashionable, made-up young woman who makes her living by selling dances.[26]

In On the March, the worries of this female figure go far beyond the personal intrigues and fixation on appearance associated with popular perceptions of the Garçonne. Instead Brandt presents her as a model reader whose critical, assessing gaze is turned on the events of the day. Items from the contemporary illustrated press are spilled out before the *Garçonne* as if they have come to life during her perusal of the pages of a copy of the *Berliner Illustrirte Zeitung* or another of the sixty dailies and weeklies produced in Berlin alone during the Weimar period. This *Garçonne* absorbs the vast amount of visual material available to the public, synthesizes it and appears to have mentally repositioned the images that she has seen into the photomontage that appears before us. She is conversant in current politics, and sweeps her gaze from Europe to Asia; she turns an analytical gaze on the swarms of men before her

Figure 3.7. Umbo (Otto Umbehr), *Gaby Meyer in der Bar bei Mali und Igor* (1927/28), gelatin silver print, 15.9 x 12 cm. © Phyllis Umbehr/Galerie Kicken Berlin.

who are demonstrating or on the march. By cutting into Umbo's photograph and resituating its protagonist, Brandt's photomontage activates this *Garçonne* and gives historical relevance to her thoughtful gaze.

The concerned and contemplative attitude of the New Woman at the heart of *On the March* evokes a well-known image from the German context: Albrecht Dürer's sixteenth-century *Melancholia I* (Figure 3.8). In *the Origin of German Tragic Drama*, completed the same year as *On the March*, Benjamin made use of Dürer's print to flesh out his discussion of allegorical interpretation. According to Benjamin, Melancholia, the central figure in this work, conveys meaning on a number of different levels.[27] She represents a melancholic mental state, for her slightly slumped pose, her position on the ground despite her wings, and her discarded tools reveal her depressed condition. Significant emblems—objects that must be decoded by the viewer, often in accordance with a textual tradition—allow us to discover further meanings associated with the figure. In Dürer's representation, emblems such as keys (which suggest power), a purse (indicating wealth), and various carved objects (forms of sculpture) evoke the figure's artistic and visionary character. In reading this image, Ben-

Figure 3.8. Albrecht Dürer, *Melancolia I* (1514), engraving, 31 x 26 cm.

jamin also shows how allegorical emblems could signify in multiple and even contradictory ways. Melancholia's dog, for example, through its connection to rabies, evokes the darker side of the melancholic personality and its potential for madness. But Benjamin also points out that the animal is known for its "shrewdness and tenacity," and thus it calls to mind the melancholic as a tireless investigator and thinker.[28]

Brandt's *On the March* presents a modern version of *Melancholia I*, a parallel that seems intentional on Brandt's part, for this was a well-known work by an artist that Brandt favored.[29] Both compositions feature a central female figure who holds her head in her hands and gazes into the distance in an attitude that suggests contemplation mixed with despair. A large body of water stretches towards the horizon in the upper left portion of both etching and photomontage; and the downward-gazing baby in the modern version echoes the equally melancholic cupid seated at the shoulder of Melancholia. Yet within this structure of resonance with Dürer's etching, Brandt's montage introduces key differences that emphasize the limitations on the New Woman's ability to act. Melancholia has a selection of tools at hand for measuring and calculating (compass, hourglass, balance, and magic square), signaling (bell), and creating (saw, wood, and nails). These tools empower her and evince her artistic skills. In contrast, Brandt's figure holds only a cigarette, and she is surrounded by teeming masses upon which she is unable to exert any influence. The significant blankness behind her may suggest the possibility of New Womanhood as a chance to remake art and life on the tabula rasa that many perceived in the break with the prewar past. However, viewed in relation to the dangers of war and riots that surround this figure, the blank space may also emphasize the absence of any appropriate tools to solve these growing problems. Brandt's *Garçonne*, bedecked with emblems of change—bobbed hair, revealing clothing, and cigarettes among them—is ultimately in a situation much like that of Dürer's Melancholia, who has wings yet cannot fly.

Seen in historical context, Brandt's imagery engages viewers and encourages a critical response to the militarism of the later Weimar Republic. With hindsight, however, viewers might fault her approach in *On the March* for its tendency to generalize mass movements and to abstract them into the mass ornaments of which Siegfried Kracauer had written the previous year.[30] But rather than offering Weimar viewers an array of moving patterns of human forms as mere distraction, the images of the mass in *On the March* leave viewers with questions about the variety of scenes before them. Further, a mode of critical and active viewing is modeled by the contemplating New Woman shown at the center of this work. In Kracauer's writings from the Weimar period and even those composed after his 1933 flight from Nazi Germany, he was also highly critical of attempts to make art reflect too directly on contemporary life and politics. Kracauer insisted on representative modes that did not direct viewers but rather engaged their critical faculties through dialectics.[31] Such a dialectical approach is at work in Brandt's photomontage recontextualizations, which raise many questions but provide no answers.

A number of Brandt's works show broken and montaged landscapes that are watched warily by women and that play out the interaction of an aggressive, modern masculinity with the increasingly destructive nature of contemporary warfare. Her 1926 *Help Out! (The Liberated Woman) (Helfen Sie mit! [die Frauenbewegte])* (Figure 3.9) places the striking figure of a New Woman in broader historical perspective. This montage more clearly addresses tensions

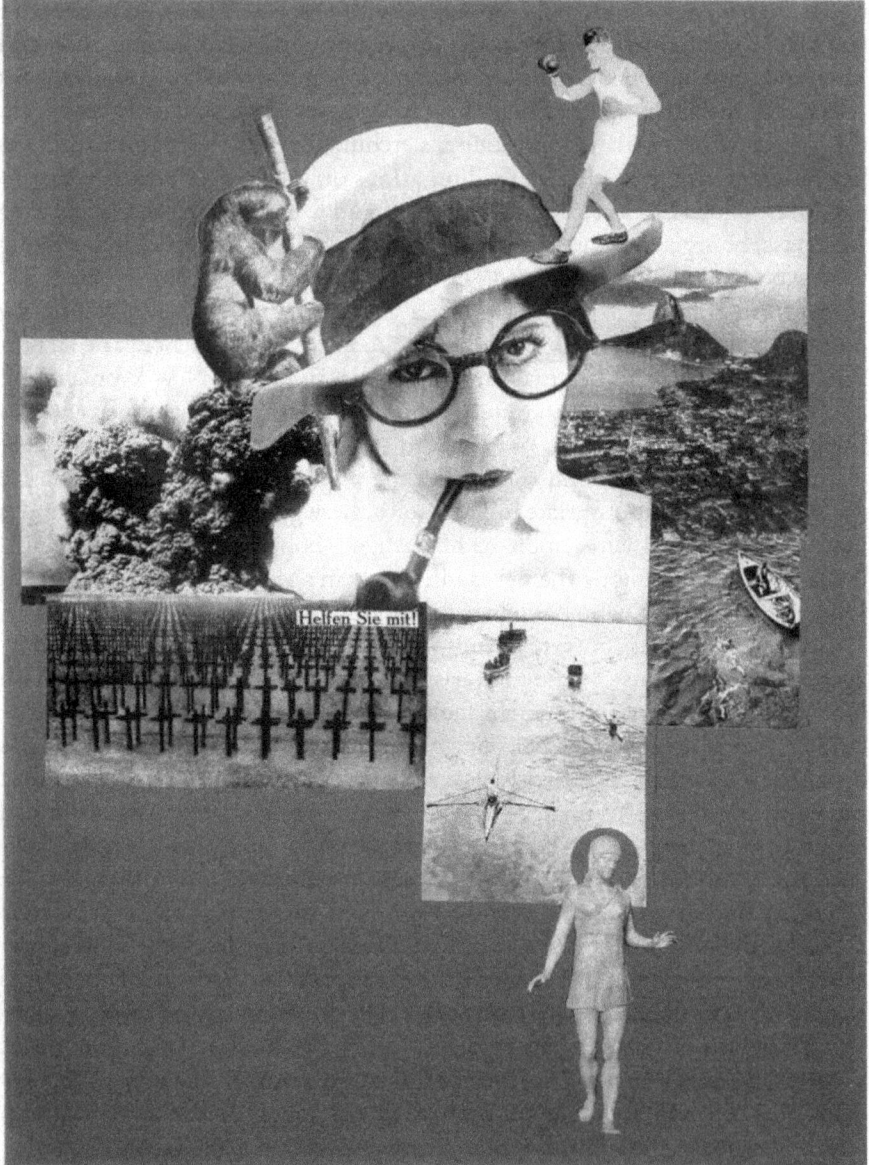

Figure 3.9. Marianne Brandt, *Helfen Sie mit! (die Frauenbewegte)*, photomontage (1926), 68.3 x 50.3 cm. Kupferstichkabinett, Dresden. @2010 Artists Rights Society (ARS), New York, VG Bild-Kunst, Bonn/

between, on the one hand, the hope of enacting political change, and, on the other, the potential for melancholic, contemplative inaction in the face of a complex and often unstable cultural and political landscape. The work is structured around rectangular photographs showing a series of landscapes, each with a strong depth of field. River flows into city and a field of crosses for war dead extends to a horizon where a massive explosion takes place. Paired on the work's right side are images of boating and swimming that flow into a peaceful vision of the city of Rio de Janeiro. This disjointed combination of half-toned prints could be a collection of aerial surveillance photographs, a technology that was used on a large scale and to devastating effect for the first time in World War I.[32] On this background of destruction and dynamically shifting terrain, the head of a pipe-smoking New Woman floats in the clouds. Her skeptical gaze engages that of the viewer, and she combines traits associated with masculinity—including her pipe, short hair, and heavy-rimmed spectacles—with such accoutrements of modern femininity as eye makeup and lipstick.

Not only does this New Woman unite masculinity and femininity, the whole of this photomontage turns on the play of perceived opposites. In this work, Brandt shows us a New Woman surrounded on one side by scenes of the conflicts—great and small, cataclysmic and intimate—that shaped her emergence. On the other side, images of leisure and world travel suggest the freedoms and global perspectives that such New Women enjoyed. On the brow of the New Woman's hat, a boxing champion stands poised to meet his opponent who faces him and mirrors his pose. But rather than pairing him with another boxer, Brandt has given this man a sparring partner who is actually a sloth. Here activity is pitted against laziness; as in English, the German *Faultier,* or the animal sloth, would evoke laziness or the sin of sloth, *Faulheit* in the German. This mismatched boxing pair encapsulates a tension between action and immobility within the montage, one that is also evident in the work's title. The phrase *"Helfen Sie mit!"* or "Help Out!" appears to emanate from the New Woman's pipe like a speech bubble. While her call sounds like a slogan from a political poster, this snippet of text is contradicted by the scenes that surround it. It lies over the field of crosses and just below the explosion, thus calling into question the efficacy of political demonstrations and the justification of mass mobilization by a promise of resulting peace. A certain refusal to help may be seen in the classical statue of a short-skirted and seemingly modern huntress at the bottom of the composition. Though she is given a halo through negative montage, she is no saint. This Diana-like figure has turned her back on the troubled landscapes behind her, declining to be a part of the physical or political movements that seek to pull her in.

The work's subtitle, *die Frauenbewegte,* which Brandt wrote onto the back of the image, brings further ambiguity to the fore. This is a term that, by 1926, would already have sounded a bit tired; it designates the "liberated women" who participated in the celebrated movement for universal suffrage in Germany, a goal that had been achieved seven years earlier with the founding of the Weimar Republic. The phrase also refers to people or things moved by women, a wordplay that suggests women's ability to inspire onlookers through their beauty and charm, but that downplays women's own political powers. *Help Out!* moves between poles of action and inaction in a manner that seems to respond to the unstable and frustrating political situation of the young democracy of the Weimar Republic itself. In thematizing the complex nature of contemporary gender relations and politics, Brandt's montage asks us to reflect upon the limited potential for effective political organization in the wake of the First World War. This work allows for the possibility of redemption and the chance that we might really be able to "Help Out!" But within the scope of images that Brandt montaged into this work, such chances seem to be slim.

In Brandt's works that I have discussed in this essay—the untitled photomontage with an airplane and soldiers, *On the March*, and *Help Out!*—her landscapes visualize the consequences of war for male bodies and convey alarm at the enthusiasm for rearmament that persisted and grew during the course of the interwar period. Brandt's works do this most effectively by drawing on the photographic imagery of her own day. This occurs nowhere more pointedly than in the fields of crosses that appear in two of the montages I have discussed. Because of the massive casualties that resulted from new technologies of the First World War, large numbers of bodies often had to be buried quickly. In death soldiers were once again represented by a standard marker, the crosses upon which their names were printed, if indeed the bodies could be identified. Functioning as a traditional Christian symbol of sacrifice for others, these crosses are also an allegory of the cost of settling political conflict on the battleground. Montaged photographs of such fields stand out amidst Brandt's repeated use of swarming crowds of people, buildings, and objects; they suggest that a new modular unit for the soldier's body has replaced the printed postcard or portrait background. While the graves mark the resting places of men of the past, the futuristic airplanes and explosions in Brandt's works seem to warn of the potential of a similar fate for the men of her day. But rather than preaching or propagandizing, these works ask viewers to engage with and draw meaning from a range of fragmented images. They thus offer viewers the possibility of developing an active, critical gaze that could be turned on the political and cultural world around them.

Juxtapositions

Bringing together these two distinct but related forms of composite images allows us to excavate a significant continuity in montage history and to explore representations of military masculinity. Investigating the forms of address in these two groups of photomontages permits us to complicate notions of active spectatorship, for, though they function in different ways, they both require viewer participation in order to be complete. Further, my comparison between composite soldier portraits and Brandt's representations of militarized masculinity reveals her tactic of foregrounding images of women as active participants in politics and the making of history. In recasting the image of the soldier and showing him as struggling, victimized, or callous, or by creating images of male conflict, Brandt's later Weimar montages perform one of allegory's significant alchemical conversions. As Owens has commented, "allegory becomes the model of all commentary, all critique, insofar as these are involved in rewriting a primary text in terms of its figural meaning."[33] This rewriting asks us to ponder accepted traits of masculinity and femininity and to think about the life and death consequences of politics. Photomontage provided a precisely blunt tool to combat the increasing militarism of the later Weimar years; for, in its lack of specificity, montage forces viewers to become activated and to draw their own conclusions. Brandt's most effective montages do not convey a specific message, for that would simply have yielded further propaganda. Instead, they seek to awaken viewers' own melancholic and allegorical gazes by asking them to contemplate and engage the juxtaposed images and the iconography of contemporaneous society and politics.

Read in relation to the earlier soldier portraits, the three montages by Brandt that I have discussed here each play upon the conventions of soldier portraiture and pick up on its imagery, only to further fragment its surface. In the nineteenth- and early twentieth-century portraits, the disjuncture between photographic head and lithographically reproduced body meant that a space for potential critique was embedded within the work itself, because such works were structured around a flaw. What made these representations compelling to later avant-garde artists was the potential to imagine prying open these representations that had glorified the war and celebrated Wilhelmine greatness and thus to move beyond the flow of propagandistic narrative that such images sought to create. It was through this seam in the composite portraits that Brandt could enter the pictorial landscape to rework and challenge its mythic status and the masculinities it had attempted to represent. Brandt's photomontages reveal a sense of imperative in undermining the imaged fictions of masculinity that had been essential to the creation and maintenance of a militaristic culture. It seems as if Brandt suspected that again convincing the public of the glory of militarized manhood would be an essential prerequisite for undertaking another World War. Brandt's foregrounding of modern women's active, skeptical, or melancholic gazes suggests a powerful intervention at this moment during the middle and later years of the Weimar Republic, when the darkest moments of Germany's history had not yet been determined.

Notes

I am very grateful to Kerstin Barndt, Matthew Biro, Kathleen Canning, Kristin McGuire, Helmut Puff, and Rebecca Zurier for their comments on earlier versions of this essay. My thanks go to the following museums and institutions that allowed me to reproduce the text's images: the Altonaer Museum, Hamburg; the Bauhaus-Archiv, Berlin; the Berlinische Galerie; Galerie Kicken; the Kupferstich-Kabinett, Staatliche Kunstsammlungen Dresden; the Militärhistorisches Museum der Bundeswehr, Dresden; and the Museum Folkwang, Essen.

1. "Noch einmal schaut der Musketier nach seinem Lieb zurück. / Und tausend Grüsse schickt er ihr, was sagt sein letzter Blick?"
2. The castle of Stolzenfels, erected by Karl Friedrich Schinkel during the years 1836–1842 on the site of a thirteenth-century ruin, had been a touchstone of Romantic nationalism since the nineteenth century.
3. An analysis of the production of knowledge itself is what historian Joan Scott calls for as a critical balance to our understanding of the term *experience*. Joan W. Scott, "The Evidence of Experience," *Critical Inquiry* 17, no. 4 (1991): 797.
4. In "Uniform: On Constructions of Soldierly Masculinity in Early Twentieth-Century Visual Culture," I analyze humorous and commemorative representations of uniformed men and women as creating and reinforcing gender norms in relation to German military culture. In *Künstlermythen und Männlichkeitsbilder: Geschlechterentwürfe in der Kunst des Kaiserreiches und der Weimarer Republik*, ed. Martina Kessel (Cologne, 2005), 17–42. Karen Hagemann and Stefanie Schuler-Springorum's excellent collection of essays, *Home/Front: The Military, War and Gender in Twentieth-Century Germany* (New York, 2003), also explores gender constructions in relation to war.
5. Walter Benjamin, *The Origin of German Tragic Drama*, trans. J. Osborne (London, 1977), 159–67. Benjamin submitted this text as his *Habilitationsschrift* to the University of Frankfurt in 1925, but it was rejected. He published in 1928.
6. Angus Fletcher, *Allegory: the Theory of a Symbolic Mode* (Ithaca, NY, 1964), 2.
7. Benjamin, *Origin*, 179.
8. Matthew Biro discusses Benjamin's work on Baroque allegory as strongly informed by "the fundamental experiences of modernity in his own time." "Allegorical Modernism: Carl Einstein on Otto Dix," *Art Criticism* 15, no. 1 (2000): 50.
9. The best collection of portraits is held in the Museum Folkwang in Essen; a selection of these are reproduced in Robert Bosshard, Ute Eskildsen, and Robert Knodt, *Erinnerung an die Dienstzeit: Fotografien der Jahrhundertwende* (Essen, 1993).
10. Count Ferdinand von Zeppelin tested the rigid airship in 1900. In World War I zeppelins were first deployed in military surveillance. See Leslie Bryan, et al., *Fundamentals of Aviation and Space Technology* (Urbana, IL, 1959), 1986.
11. According to Cohen, "more than 9.5 million soldiers died over a period of fifty-two months. … Twenty million men were severely wounded; 8 million veterans returned home permanently disabled. They had suffered the worst injuries ever seen." Deborah Cohen, *The War Come Home: Disabled Veterans in Britain and Germany, 1914–1939* (Berkeley, CA 2001), 1.
12. There are many studies on the perceived scientific accuracy of photographic systems of representation. See, for example, Allan Sekula, "The Body and the Archive," in *The Contest of Meaning: Critical Histories of Photography*, ed. Richard Bolton (Cambridge, MA, 1990), 343–89.
13. Both Höch and Hausmann would later speak of their "discovery" of photomontage through a soldier portrait while on vacation in a small fishing village in the summer of

1918 (Raoul Hausmann, *Courrier Dada* [Paris, 1992 (1958)], 44–45; Hannah Höch, "Erinnerungen an Dada: ein Vortrag 1966," in *Hannah Höch, 1889–1978. Ihr Werk, ihr Leben, ihre Freunde* [Berlin, 1989], 208). Of course, many artists claim to have originated the medium; more significant in this context are the images that Hausmann and Höch claim were their inspiration.

14. Höch, "Erinnerungen," 208.

15. Craig Owens, "The Allegorical Impulse: Toward a Theory of Postmodernism," *Art After Modernism: Rethinking Representation*, ed. Brian Wallis (New York, 1984), 203.

16. Consider as examples the left side of Höch's 1919 *Dada- Rundschau* (*Dada Panorama*), in which a row of pointy-helmeted officers are literally losing their heads; Höch's *Und wenn du denkst, der Mond geht unter* (*And When You Think the Moon Is Setting*) of 1921 in which three male, female, and animal bodies are montaged together (both reproduced in Maria Makela and Peter Boswell, eds. *The Photomontages of Hannah Höch* [Minneapolis, 1996], 26 and 40); or how the legs of both male and female figures appear cut off at the knees or held together by strips of cloth in Rudolf Schlichter's 1919–20 *Phänomen-Werke* (*Phenomenon Works*) (reproduced in Götz Adriani, ed. *Rudolf Schlichter: Gemälde, Aquarelle, Zeichnungen* [Berlin, 1997], 93).

17. For more information on the complete oeuvre of Brandt's forty-five photomontages, see my recent volume, *Tempo, Tempo! The Bauhaus Photomontages of Marianne Brandt* (Berlin, 2005) and my essay "A 'Schooling of the Senses': Post-Dada Visual Experiments in the Bauhaus Photomontages of László Moholy-Nagy and Marianne Brandt," *New German Critique* 107 (Summer 2009): 89–131. Earlier publications on Brandt's montages include: Hanne Bergius, "Fotomontage im Vergleich: Hannah Höch, Marianne Brandt, Alice Lex-Nerlinger," *Fotografieren hieß teilnehmen: Fotografinnen der Weimarer Republik*, ed. Ute Eskildsen (Düsseldorf, 1994), 42–50.

18. For more on Brandt's montage practices, see Otto, "On Photomontage, Tempo, and Marianne Brandt," *Tempo, Tempo!* 8–13. One montage that we know was shown at the time it was made is a commemorative portrait of the metal workshop entitled *ME* from 1928. This was a going-away present for Walter Gropius (Otto, *Tempo, Tempo!* 80–83).

19. In "Advertising Seizes Control of Life: Berlin Dada and the Power of Advertising," Sherwin Simmons points out that the death's head was first worn by members of the Prussian cavalry and adopted for elite storm troops in WWI before it became a sort of trademark for the *Freikorps* during the interwar period (*Oxford Art Journal* 22, no. 1 [1999]: 119–46).

20. For more on the New Objectivity's engagement with visualizations of technology, see Herbert Molderings, "Urbanism and Technological Utopianism: Thoughts on the Photography of Neue Sachlichkeit and the Bauhaus," in *Germany: The New Photography, 1927–1933*, ed. David Mellor (London, 1978), 87–94.

21. The photograph of the Do X appeared on the cover of the *Arbeiter Illustrirte Zeitung* in November 1930 (9, no. 47). This plane was designed in 1926 and had its first flight in July 1929. During the course of its building and early flights, there was frequent coverage of this aircraft's unprecedented size, speed, and international reputation.

22. During the fall of 1928, arbitration failed during wage negotiations in the Ruhr iron and steel dispute; subsequently the employers locked out about 220,000 metal workers—practitioners of the trade that Brandt herself had learned—for several weeks. Detlev Peukert sees the Ruhr iron and steel dispute as an attack on the Trade Union State and a "key test" of an anti-Weimar strategy on the part of employers. Detlev J. K. Peukert, *The Weimar Republic: The Crisis of Classical Modernity*, trans. Richard Deveson (New York, 1992), 126.

23. This image of Asian soldiers comes from the *Berliner Illustrirte Zeitung* 36, no. 15 (10 April 1927): 571. The caption reads: "In Schanghai: Anamitische Soldaten auf dem Marsch durch die französische Niederlassung" ("In Shanghai: Anamitish Soldiers on the March through the French Base").

24. The essential superficiality of the *Garçonne* type is emphasized in almost all accounts of her. Peukert calls her a "glamour girl, a bit too independent to be true, armed with bobbed hair and made-up face, fashionable clothes and cigarette, working by day in a typing pool or behind the sales counter in some dreamland of consumerism, frittering away the night dancing the Charleston or watching UFA and Hollywood films" (*Weimar Republic*, 99). See Lynne Frame's exploration of typologies of New Womanhood in the Weimar press: "Gretchen, Girl, Garçonne? Weimar Science and Popular Culture in Search of the Ideal New Woman," in *Women in the Metropolis*, ed. Katherina von Ankum (Berkeley, CA, 1997), 12–40.

25. Brandt and Umbo would surely have known each other from the metal workshop. However, they were at the Bauhaus together for only for a short period of time. She started there in January of 1924, and he left some time during that same year. In addition to her use of the *Gaby Meyer* image, there are two reproductions of his works in a stash of clippings that she presumably kept for making montages (collection of Bernd Freese, Frankfurt am Main).

26. Joe Lederer, "Die Parkett-Tänzerin," *Uhu* 4, no. 3 (Dec. 1927): 112–13. Umbo himself clearly saw this woman as a *Garçonne* figure; he published another, very similar image of her from this shoot under the title *Die Garçonne im Café*.

27. Benjamin, *Origin*, 149–52.

28. Benjamin, *Origin*, 152. Peter Bürger's later discussion of allegorical processes is a significant elaboration on Benjamin's assertion of the potentially productive nature of melancholy. For Bürger, melancholic contemplation yields a sense of historical loss in both allegorical and avant-garde works (*Theory of the Avant-Garde*, trans. Michael Schaw (Minneapolis, 1984), 71). The deeper understanding enabled by a melancholic state had also been investigated by Sigmund Freud in his 1915 "Mourning and Melancholia" (in *On Metapsychology: The Theory of Psychoanalysis*, Penguin Freud Library, vol. 11, ed. James Strachey and Angela Richards [London, 1984], 251–68).

29. In a letter from her husband, Erik Brandt, from the early 1920s, he mentions a Dürer reproduction as one of two images belonging to both of them—along with a Rembrandt portrait—that he has hung on the walls of their new atelier apartment (Erik Brandt to Marianne Brandt, n.d. [c. 1920/21]; collection of the Bauhaus-Archiv, Berlin).

30. Siegfried Kracauer, "Das Ornament der Masse," *Frankfurter Zeitung*, June 1927; reprinted in Siegfried Kracauer, *The Mass Ornament: Weimar Essays*, ed. and trans. Thomas Levin (Cambridge, MA, 1995), 75–89.

31. See Kracauer's 1932 review of the "Revolutionäre Bildmontage" exhibition in Berlin (*Frankfurter Zeitung*, Feb. 1932; reprinted in Siegfried Kracauer, *Schriften* 5:3. *Aufsätze, 1932–1965*, ed. Inka Mülder-Bach [Frankfurt am Main, 1990], 30–33) and his discussion of the Cross-Section Film (*Querschnittfilm*) in his essay "Montage," in *From Caligari to Hitler: A Psychological History of the German Film* (Princeton, NJ, 1947), 181–89.

32. While Nadar first took aerial photographs of Paris from his hot-air balloon in the 1850s and manned balloons were used for military surveillance as early as the American Civil War, it was only during WWI that photographs taken from aircraft became a regular element of reconnaissance.

33. Owens, "Allegorical Impulse," 205.

PART II

New Citizens/
New Subjectivities

CHAPTER 4

~:~

Mothers, Citizens, and Consumers
Female Readers in Weimar Germany

KERSTIN BARNDT

"Women need books, and books need women." For a particular moment in 1931, the circular logic of this slogan captured the spirit of a heated debate about reading, gender, and culture in the late Weimar Republic. In a massive stream of publications, lectures, advertising campaigns, and other public interventions, publishers, politicians, and feminists probed the relationship of women and books as seldom before. While these groups tried to understand and shape contemporary shifts between gendered acts of reading and the public acts of publishing, selling, and politicking, women readers themselves also raised their voices, clamoring for inclusion as equal partners in the public debate. By investigating this debate, we can gain crucial insights into the self-positioning and self-constructions of Weimar's "new" women, as they negotiated an expanded set of demands and roles in a public arena where battles for cultural and political hegemony raged over matters of literary authority, taste, and censorship.

During the Weimar republic, consumption, femininity, and mass culture had formed a tight conceptual interrelation that often functioned synonymously with the proscription of low-brow literature as "trash," and in strict opposition to a male inflected notion of bourgeois high culture.[1] The central significance of women took shape in the popular figure of the "New Woman"—most visibly, perhaps, in advertising. Accordingly, advertising specialists pointed to the importance of female consumers early on. Writing in the trade magazine, *Die Reklame*, the designer Hanns Korpf—who had created one of the most successful advertising motifs of the Weimar Republic with his "Elida Girl"—pointed out, that "75 percent of all items are bought by women. Women buy for themselves, for their children, their homes, and often also for their husbands. Most money is spent by the hands of women. You, too, should consider carefully whether your goods aren't bought by women."[2]

While businesses began to take women seriously as purchasers and target them with advertising campaigns, the cultural establishment used woman's role as consumer to discredit female reading habits. Behind this attitude stood the long-lived prejudice against women's cultural tastes, continually expanded ever since the pathologizing discourse on female reading addiction as *Lesesucht* around 1800. According to the logic of this prejudice, women "consume" culture, surrendering their subjectivity in identification with their reading or with the images on the screen. In other words, women are said to prefer an emotional experience of cultural artifacts that precludes a cognitive, objective processing of literature and culture. With regard to female readers, the metaphor of consumption was taken literally, in order to differentiate the instrumental-rational (male) reader from the woman's sensual reception: "If it is a real woman and a real book, then she does not read it, but eats it. Perhaps she'll smell it at first, like an apple; then she takes a big bite, without bothering to peel it. Of course it is said that the best vitamins are right under the skin."[3]

But then, there are always good and bad apples. Since the responsibility of selecting good apples could not be left to women alone, political initiatives undertook comprehensive campaigns so as not to lose influence over female tastes and changing conceptions of femininity. My essay explores such state-sponsored mediations of gendered reading practices within wider discourses of cultural crisis, authority, and subjectivity. While Weimar intellectuals and bourgeois educators struggled to claim an autonomous sphere of "high" culture, elevated above mere needs and economic necessities, women gained social, economic, and sexual independence on the grounds of the dialectics between culture and capital. By closely observing the literary and theoretical interventions concerning the female reader and women's own self-production through cultural participation, we will come to understand women as key figures in a historic sea-change. As imperial notions of national culture wedded to high bourgeois culture and colonial visions underwent a fundamental reconfiguration, the popular culture of the masses, male and female, advanced to shape and partly dominate the national cultural norm.

A review of the literature on reading culture in Weimar Germany reveals two insights. First, despite some pathbreaking works, this research field remains a desideratum: what is needed is interdisciplinary inquiry transcending the limits of historical *and* aesthetic analysis.[4] Second, we can observe the striking absence of considerations of *female* readership. As is so often the case, the specificities of gender disappear for the sake of describing a general development. Along with workers and youth, however, women have been at the center of a debate about their roles as gendered consumers, and cultural mediators ever since the dawn of mass culture. As the single largest demographic group, women have enlarged and structurally altered the educated middle classes since the nineteenth century.

During the Weimar Republic, with its burgeoning mass culture and women's enfranchisement, this development became particularly evident. It occurred parallel to a deep transformation of the bourgeoisie from an economic class to "a system of values and a lifestyle."[5] In the literary field, this transformation found its expression in discourses on the "crisis of the book" (*Bücherkrise*), a term coined by concerned critics and commentators. Economically, this crisis spoke to postwar changes in the book trade that pushed for more profitable ways to sell books. The trade adapted to the differentiated tastes of the new middle class(es) by addressing specialized readers as well as a mass audience. New bookstores opened, publishing houses were founded, and book clubs expanded. In 1927, the *Literarische Welt* introduced the first bestseller list with Hermann Hesse's *Steppenwolf* leading the pack.

While the literary merit of the latter novel was little debated, contemporary observers nevertheless expressed concern about the overall emphasis on quantity at the expense of quality. According to the most outspoken contributors to the *Bücherkrise* discourse then, a spiritual crisis lurked behind the economic pressure to modernize the book trade. S. Fischer articulated the logic of this momentous transition from his own position as the leading *Kulturverleger* (publisher of culture), when he lamented, "The book that bears the power and mission of an inner bind has today been abandoned, without any leadership, to the great, anonymous, and nonorganic masses."[6] Implicitly drawing on contemporary discourses of decline, social fragmentation, and a general modern malaise, Fischer's rhetoric is representative of a broader cultural pessimism that befell the bourgeois elite of the Weimar Republic in the face of ongoing changes within the literary field and society at large. Moreover, Fischer points to the question of leadership, echoing Wilhelminian reformist ideas that put much emphasis on the power of culture to enlighten, ennoble, and unite the German nation.[7]

During the Weimar years, however, readers called this power and its underlying gender as well as class biases into question as they relied more and more on their own choices. With its focus on female readers, this essay traces this particular power struggle between ideological positions asserting cultural hegemony and independent women readers.

Spiritual Diet

In 1931, the third year of the newly instituted "*Tag des Buches*" (Day of the Book), women were the focus of national celebration—proof of the central importance attained by women within Weimar culture. Countless women's organizations were involved in planning the day's activities, and its leading participants included prominent figures such as the politician and feminist Gertrud Bäumer, and authors like Ina Seidel, Clara Viebig, or Richarda Huch, the first woman to have been selected to membership in the literary section of the Prussian Academy of Arts.[8]

Yet, rather than addressing women as authors or readers, organizers emphasized their educational function as mothers whose duties included monitoring and guiding their children's reading materials. In other words, while the patriarchal power of bourgeois educators was waning, the organizers of the German book day called upon women to fill the gap. In their collective call published in the book trade paper *Börsenblatt für den Deutschen Buchhandel*, the "rainbow" coalition of women's organizations blended mellow feminist appeals with national-conservative sentiments. By no means, however, was the day meant to address the self-conscious culture of the New Woman. Women were spoken of, rather, as the biological and "spiritual" mothers of the German nation whose "role in the home and in the family" qualified them as "mediators between the book and the people [*Volk*]."[9] Women's intuitive sense for "good" literature should guide the search for children's reading material and the struggle to defend them from "trash." In pushing this pedagogical project, even the metaphor of consumption could take on a positive connotation, given the responsibility of woman-as-mother for the child's nourishment in both the biological and the spiritual sense. "Books are spiritual nourishment," claimed one commentator, advocating the book day's mission, "and mothers only want to give their children those kernels of wheat that have been separated from their hulls."[10]

The organizers of the book festivity eagerly stressed women's role as "formative force in German culture."[11] The language of the manifesto thus reiterated the concept of gender-specific spheres by which women conservatively insure the culture of the nation against the civilizing influence of modern working life to which primarily men are exposed. Rather than adapting to change, the day of the book once again endowed women with the task of preserving culture amidst change. Clearly, this logic collided with Weimar's culture of the New Woman, a culture that to some extent embraced modern tempo, lingo, consumerism, cinema, and pulp fiction. It is telling in this respect that contemporary authors of popular New Woman novels such as Irmgard Keun, Vicki Baum, Marieluise Fleißer, or Joe Lederer did not weigh in on the Day of the Book.

The discourse on women's relationship to books and their reading habits, culminating in the event of the German Day of the Book in 1931, suggests a growing ideological gap between the organized women's movement and women as self-conscious but rather nonpolitical cultural participants. This gap concerned divergent understandings of culture with the women's organizations' nationally inflected notion of culture as collective good (and thus politically more assertive) battling the complexities of popular culture. Questions of leadership and authority again constitute focal points in this battle. Who spoke on whose behalf? While the old bourgeoisie mourned its loss of leadership function with regard to the new middle classes, the women's movement lost its hold on questions of individual emancipation. Women who achieved voting age after 1919 took suffrage, as well as employment in white-collar professions, for granted and no longer attributed these achievements—let alone their new self-confidence—to the efforts of the women's movement.[12] Consequently, the bourgeois women's movement competed with the culture of the New Woman. It saw its political self-concept as well as its cultural mandate threatened by the New Woman's individualization of the claim to emancipation. In agreement with the old cultural elite of the bourgeoisie, these feminists also perceived the book crisis as spiritual crisis, triggered by the arrival of white-collar, middle-class culture. The female white-collar worker, went the complaint, does not avail herself of good books for the purpose of spiritual advancement, but is satisfied with simple "wish-fulfillment literature."[13] Such epithets repeated and compounded the structure of prejudice that has burdened women's literature since the eighteenth century. The author of the contribution in which it appears arrogantly mocked the reading habits of white-collar female readers, to whom the novels of the New Woman were addressed, and who would prefer to read for entertainment: "The little shop girl, the delivery girl for the upscale hat salon, the female secretary—they all need the entertainment book (*Unterhaltungsbuch*) to complement their everyday lives."[14]

What type of book thus presented an alternative to the discredited light entertainment? What were women in fact supposed to read? Book announcements in the *Börsenblatt* delineate a rift between novels of the New Woman and edifying women's literature. In preparation of the Day of the Book, the *Börsenblatt* advertised in high style for a number of books written by and for women.[15] Monographs about "important women" such as Hildegard von Bingen, Christine von Schweden, Niddy Impekoven, or Mary Wigman dominated. Next to these stood mothering guidebooks like *Mutter sein heißt ...* (To Be a Mother Means ...) by Ilse Meister or Dorothea Hofer-Dernburg's humorous essay, *Babys Welt als Wille und Vorstellung* (Baby's World as Will and Representation). Finally, we find Ina Seidel's novel *Das Wunschkind* (The Desired Child, 1930) advertised as "the crowning achievement of all recent German women's books."[16] Seidel's novel tells the story of a mother-son relationship played out against the background of the Napoleonic wars, with an unmistakable national subtext.[17] Due to the novel's success with the public and contemporary literary critics, Seidel's voice gained power with regard to contemporary women's questions; in the end, Seidel was as influential in organizing and implementing the Day of the Book as Ricarda Huch and Clara Viebig. In her contributions, Seidel yet again invoked women as mothers and providers, in both the physical and spiritual sense. Their special duty was to care for the *"Diätetik des Geistes,"* or spiritual diet, of the people:

> Woman is charged with the responsibility of nutrition, which is the basis for the daily regeneration of the body. But how many women are there who are not merely adept at overseeing their households' pantries and kitchen, but who are also versed in the diet of the spirit, and who can always serve their growing children the most nutritional, appropriate, and stimulating foods at the right moment?[18]

In the conservative cultural criticism of her time, Seidel's stories and novels were regarded as positive examples of "female prose," supposedly free of the decadence of the contemporary "mannish" literature of the New Woman. Seidel was not only celebrated by the women's movement, her work was also launched in the *Börsenblatt* at the expense of novels of the New Woman, for which one finds no advertisements at all. The national-conservative attitude of the *Börsenblatt* undeniably influenced the selection of its advertisers.

And yet, the Day of the Book also prompted some surprising encounters. At an event in Berlin, a reading by Else Lasker-Schüler apparently received a warm welcome with the anti-Semitic Seidel also on the podium. A starker artistic contrast is barely imaginable. As early as 1920, Lasker-Schüler had criticized the warmongering of other artists with her stage work *Der Malik*, and she had begun experimenting with self-reflexive writing techniques that were aesthetically in tune with the contemporary avant-garde and in stark contrast to Seidel's *Blut-und-Boden* imagery. In its discussion of the event, the liberal daily *Berliner Tageblatt* did not underline these incongruities, but rather accentuated Lasker-Schüler's "religious fervor and oriental palette." The article stylized the celebrated Jewish author as extravagant, exotic, but nevertheless *religious*, and on this latter premise it was possible to incorporate Lasker-Schüler into the canon of women's edification literature.[19]

Public comments prompted by the book day unambiguously favored a normative concept of women's literature that addressed woman in her care-giving function. The nation's women were entrusted with the duty of educating the family, to which spiritual values, and thus especially religious values, were essential. This rhetoric is clearly aimed against the experiments of the 1920s, whose new female life scripts consciously strove to abandon assumed-to-be-eternal feminine values. The conservative tenor of the book event supports the hypothesis that at the end of the Weimar Republic the culture of the New Woman had to battle nationalistic and reactionary tendencies more intensively. Fashion once again turned to a more feminine line, and magazine articles addressed New Women as new mothers.[20]

Nonetheless, even as this investigation shows that the voices and works of *völkisch*-national writers like Ina Seidel, Agnes Miegel, and Lulu von Strauß und Torney were well represented in the publications of the Day of the Book, we should not overestimate their influence. They constitute only one group within a politically and aesthetically highly differentiated scene of female authors and readers. By and large, that scene showed itself resistant to the normative conception of women's literature. From the beginning, the Day of the Book was conceived as a day of battle against the influence of mass culture. It aimed to elevate the cultural currents of the German nation and to stem the dangerous tide of cultural "trash." The established bourgeois women's movement, which understood the women's question as one of bourgeois education, could easily identify with this mandate.[21] However, it did not escape the notice of the book event's organizers that girls and women did not restrict themselves to reading only what was dictated to them by their mothers or other national pedagogues, including the women's movement. Another interest, thoroughly economic and practical, was concealed behind the official rhetoric of the woman "as mediator between book and the people." Consequently, another series of publications and speeches prompted by the event focused on the empirical question of what women actually read.

Gender Trouble

Two months before the book day event, a vocational college that trained future booksellers in Leipzig had organized a symposium on the topic of "woman as reader." The event drew a sizeable audience, to which Professor Gerhard Menz addressed his opening remarks:

> Today, the sharp dividing lines that separated male from female worlds until well into the nineteenth century have become blurred. The general access to education, and not least the increasingly cheap reading material have led to a situation in which female readers are no longer to be found especially in the upper classes: the woman as reader has become a mass problem today.[22]

First to take up the "problem" identified by Menz's opening remarks was Walter Hofmann, whose study on *Die Lektüre der Frau* (Woman's Reading Matter, 1931) offers a divergent perspective, one that holds on to the separation of gendered spheres and identities. Within the chorus of interventions on the subject of the female reader, Hofmann's voice is particularly important. As a proponent of public education that reaches out to all strata of society while remaining bound to a particular German idea of culture, Hofmann took an ideological stance in line with the overall aim of the Day of the Book. Since the 1910s he had contributed significantly to the construction of the German public library system. Hofmann stressed the authority of the librarian to guide the reader's exposure to literature, and opposed a more open and pluralistic Anglo-American model of the public library.[23] In his writings on the topic of *Volksbildung*, the education of the people, Hofmann emphasized both meanings of the German word *Bildung* as "education" and "formation". Hence, he stressed shaping ethnic identity and national unification through guided reading. As a result, his patronizing and anti-Semitic concept of valuable national literature not only excluded light entertainment fiction but also important modern contemporary literature. In Hofmann's canon of German authors (*Deutsche Erzähler*) the reader looks in vain for established contemporary writers such as Heinrich and Thomas Mann, Franz Kafka, Robert Musil, Alfred Döblin, Anna Seghers, Irmgard Keun, Hans Fallada, Erich Kästner, or Vicki Baum.[24] Hofmann's literary and national politics thus supported the pedagogical goal of the 1931 book day: to utilize literature as a vehicle to establish moral and national consensus. Moreover, the author's research on gendered reading practices supported the Day of the Book's claim to women's unique way with books.

Hofmann vehemently denied the thesis put forth by Menz, according to which previously separate spheres of male and female had blurred together. Based on an evaluation of library cards from Leipzig's public libraries, his research indicated that even at the present time the sexes differed fundamentally in their reading preferences. "Significantly, men prefer educational literature to fictional texts, whereas in women's reading, fiction accounts for more than twice as much as educational literature."[25] Within the category of fiction, women especially valued biographical novels, i.e., those that invited identification. In his study, Hofmann explicitly held that women "seek out figures, women with whom they can identify," and he stressed that these gendered reading patterns transcended class lines. Thus, Hofmann thought it noteworthy that the literary tastes of both proletarian and bourgeois housewives, despite the disparity in education, bore a strong similarity. "Typical female interests are identical in both cases: a rejection of the abstract [coupled with] a need for imaginary expansion of the life sphere, for plasticity and life." When working with female library patrons, Hofmann urged, one should be sensitive to these gendered reading preferences that transcended class. Hofmann takes an undifferentiated group of housewives as the prototype of femininity, "because the living conditions of these women are most intimately tied to the 'female sphere' and have had the least exposure to the inimical impact of modern life, which tends to cover up the feminine."[26]

The more librarians learned about the needs of female readers from studies like Hofmann's, the better they could nobly guide the reading preferences of their female clientele according to the concept of *Volksbildung* described above. By Hofmann's own declaration, his study served the establishment of a special women's catalog that accommodated the needs of female library users and facilitated their selection of books. In order to win over new readers, Hofmann endeavored to fashion libraries friendly to female users. He could vouch for the fact that every book borrowed by a woman from his libraries corresponded to his standard of good literature.

Through those books he designated as valuable, Hofmann aimed to create an elite that spanned class boundaries. The extent to which Hofmann incorporated women into this aspect of his cultural-pedagogical project, however, remains unclear. His study is strongly positivistic and, aside from the prospect of a women's catalog, offers few practical conclusions. The fact that, as before, women's literature differed fundamentally from that of men was itself satisfactory, and was noted with relief. Here, finally, was proof that the "boundaries between male and female spheres"—despite a few unsettling indications—were still operative in certain cognitive and emotional zones, legible in distinctive reading preferences. It is therefore to be assumed that the library policies of Hofmann and other cultural pedagogues were meant to attend to and amplify gender differences. A woman's reading should encourage her to adhere to feminine virtues like providence and motherliness in times of insecure gender boundaries.

Still considered a milestone of German book market research today,[27] Hofmann's analysis of gender-specific reading preferences clearly resonated with contemporaries, as suggested by many of the essays that accompanied the Day of the Book. A recurring theme among these contributions is the special relationship between woman and book. To the woman, the book is a "surrogate for the real world;" in books, she seeks "life," and "everything true, good, beautiful, weighty and fateful that was ever said and crafted in the written word."[28] Woman "generally wants much from a book that she does not receive from men: she wants it to be permanently available, ever present, constantly waiting for her. [...] In a word, woman needs the book and the book needs woman."[29]

Although the predominantly female authors of these essays agree with the diagnosis of their female comrades' overwhelmingly bad taste, and condemn their inclination toward "surrogate literature," a tone distinct from Hofmann's prose predominates. Writing about their own reading experiences, and those of others, they formulate an implicit social critique. The descriptions postulate a relation between women and the literary medium differing from that of men, as even at that time women were denied unrestricted access to many areas of public life. "Alongside their deficient reality, there exists this enchanting world of the novel, in which they blissfully indulge their feelings."[30] These commentators understood reading as an experience revolving around knowledge, ideals, emotions, and unfulfilled desires. Here, in contrast to Hofmann, one senses a historicizing tendency that does not want to commit women's literature to the practice of eternally feminine values. Female reading selections respond to individual and very contemporary problems.

Yet, there is only one voice that criticizes Hofmann unambiguously. Writing in the journal *Die Frau*, Dr. Margarethe Kupfer not only named the women who actually implemented some of Hofmann's projects (such as the women's catalog); she also defended certain elements of progressive women's education against Hofmann's attacks:

It would be dangerous to formulate a basic directive for women's education from the characteristics [Hofmann] attributes to today's housewives. The author invites misreadings of his results when he notes that the "doctrinary desires" of the women's movement have to capitulate to traits of "the eternal feminine." ... It would be dangerous for the spiritual development of women if the educational system that creates the basis for character later in life were to draw its guiding principles from such premature fixations.[31]

Kupfer resisted renewed attempts to hold women to their traditional duties within society. She warned against drawing conclusions from "current types of behavior" about the potential character (*Seinsmöglichkeiten*) of women, and sharply dismissed the claim of men like Hofmann to be "responsible for the formation of feminine essence"—whether through reading or other means. "Nobody can help today's women to solve their problems," Kupfer insisted, "except for the women themselves."

"What We Expect from Books"

Hofmann and his reactionary image of women were granted a prominent position in the context of the Day of the Book. However, one initiative, of which Kupfer would have approved, addressed female readers directly. The Börsenverein Deutscher Buchhändler and the Reichsverband des Deutschen Schrifttums held an essay contest on the subject: "*Was wir vom Buch erwarten!*" (What We Expect from Books). The organizers were interested in hearing about reading preferences and particularly beloved books from female readers themselves—particularly from girls and young women.[32] By March 1931, a jury including both Walter Hofmann and Ricarda Huch, among others, had chosen 443 prize-worthy essays out of 1,900 submissions from all over Germany. The prizes, book gift certificates worth between 3 and 30 Reichsmarks, could be redeemed in time for the Day of the Book at the bookstore. Furthermore, a small selection of entries appeared as an independent publication, which I will briefly address here.[33]

It is noteworthy that Huch, who held a prominent position on the Day of the Book's organizing committee, made her voice heard only in the context of her role on the contest jury.[34] She enumerated the titles and names that were mentioned most often—among them Wassermann's *Der Fall Mauritius*, *Die Buddenbrooks* by Thomas Mann, titles by Rudolf Herzog, or *Der Wanderer zwischen zwei Welten* by Walter Flex. Huch was positively astounded by the excitement with which young women spoke of their reading. Only the classics rated poorly. In addition, Huch observed—like others before her—an inclination toward characters that invite identification. "Many [contributors] express the desire to read life stories by women who had to struggle hard and finally emerge as victors of all adversity." She also identified a desire for "useful, educational" books that, rather than indoctrinating with an "admonishing tone," matter-of-factly reported on "the social question and the political parties."

The selection of published essays confirms Huch's observation that female readers search for both emotional and cognitive orientation. Readers sought enlightenment regarding issues of politics and sex, preparation for an occupation, and "clear knowledge of the problems of our times and of how to find ourselves by overcoming them. That is what I look for in every book, this help in coming to terms with myself, this help and guidance in finding my way out of everything that holds back my real life and determines all my actions."[35] Young women sought books as companions and guides during adolescence; they desired self-knowledge through emotional catharsis. A high school senior wrote: "Now we are struggling to shape our personalities as women. We are forced to struggle because today, there is no ideal woman. The old ideal no longer exists, and the new one has not yet been discovered."[36] This statement betrays an awareness of the transitory character of the concept of femininity that I take to be one of the defining aspects of the discourse of the New Woman.[37] As early as 1902 feminist author Hedwig Dohm had designated the characters in her novel *Christa Ruland*, like the women of her generation, "transitory creatures" (*Übergangs-Geschöpfe*), noting that "we still have the old generation's nerves and the intelligence and will of the new." The fact that this rhetoric of transition remained influential throughout the Weimar Republic and still defined Alice Rühle-Gerstel's 1932 resume of *Woman and Capitalism*,[38] allows us to see a constitutive trait of the New Woman in Dohm's notion of a "permanent revolution" (*Umbruch in Permanenz*). In accordance with theorists of modernity from Charles Baudelaire onward, this view of the New Woman stresses modernity's temporality as contingent and transient.[39] Eager to find a language in which to grasp present change with regard to sexuality and gender, feminists concentrated on the open space left by the erosion of past traditions and rules of conduct. While they remained keenly aware of the binding force of tradition in Wilhelmine and Weimar culture, contemporary theorists of the New Woman like Dohm, Rühle-Gerstel, or Luise Scheffen-Döring proposed a view of femininity as a "gender between the times," a transient set of identifications that resonated with contemporary views of what it meant to be modern.[40]

As we have seen, the relative openness of gender categories fueled both the conservative attempts by educators like Hofmann to reinscribe traditional notions of gender, and women's own attempts to come to terms with divergent norms of femininity. By discussing and writing about their reading experiences with other women, female *readers* also participated in the reinvention of the collective identity of "women."[41] The self-reflexivity of female readers suggests that historicity and plurality of femininity was not only a lived but also a reflexive experience for many women in the Weimar Republic.

This essay's focus on the contemporary discourses prompted by the 1931 Day of the Book brings to light the intuition of female readers: women's literature was a debated category because it investigated and tested the possible collective identities of a gender. Despite intensive efforts at strict definition, of which the conservative gender politics of the national Day of the Book were an example, the category of "women" was more open than ever before, and literature contributed to this state of affairs. Indeed, not only conservative-national forces were attempting to constrict the openness of concepts of femininity—social democratic and communist women's policies were also interested in constraint: for them, literature (not just women's literature) was to depict reality according to the premises of class struggle as defined by social democratic cultural politics. As we will see in the example of the protagonist of Irmgard Keun's novel *Gilgi—eine von uns*—female heroines were to subordinate themselves to these premises. The central question of the broadly public debate on *Gilgi* was how political, or rather, how Social Democratic or bourgeois the character is. The novel's female readers, like those of the social democratic journal *Vorwärts*, were to be educated through their fascination with this character, both with regard to literature and to their own reality. This aspect of education links the *Gilgi* debate with the barely veiled pedagogical subtext of the *Buchtag*'s mission. However, here economic concerns were compounded by the goal of achieving political influence: *Vorwärts* wanted to win not only female subscribers but women voters. To this end women were again addressed as "mothers"—though now with an eye toward their votes.

Gilgi—One of Us ?

Irmgard Keun's first novel, *Gilgi—eine von uns* (Gilgi—One of Us), appeared in the fall of 1931, six months after the celebrations of the Day of the Book events. It tells the story of Gilgi, a female white-collar worker in a contemporary urban setting. The novel introduces its protagonist as an everyday hero, who in her normality appears to be a model of the Weimar New Woman. Through its use of cliché and recognizable fragments of contemporary discourse—which I have described elsewhere as the novel's "jargon of the typical"[42]—the novel produces and interacts with a series of discourses about femininity. However, in the context of its realist ambitions, the novel attempts to authenticate this jargon performatively. Through the gradual transition from an omniscient narrator to an increasingly dialogically organized narration, Keun generates a form of immediacy that emphasizes the everydayness—and thus the typicality—of her protagonist. The novel negotiates conflicts between I and we, individual and collective, romantic ideal and professional identity, between one's own language and the shared "jargon of the typical."

The title of the novel, *Gilgi—eine von uns*, already refers to a collective that asserts a claim to Gilgi's person. Collective demands on the nonpolitical, white-collar Gilgi were the subject of the controversy surrounding the novel, ignited in connection with its publication in the social democratic daily *Vorwärts* at the end of 1932. Gilgi's "type" is in question: at the end of the novel she too wants "to belong again—integrated into obligation and a functioning appara-tus—one will be protected again by the force of daily labor, in the desired law of one's own work."[43] The authenticity effects of Keun's contemporary novel were a decisive factor in its explosive reception. As a result the author and her protagonist were drawn into the political battles of the late Weimar Republic. At the same time, the novel's serialization in *Vorwärts* reached new readers and raised the young author's public profile. In addition to improving *Gilgi*'s circu-lation, the debate also helped the sales of her second novel, *Das kunstseidene Mädchen* (The Artificial Silk Girl, 1932).[44]

By reprinting Keun's novel beginning in August 1932, the editors of *Vor-wärts* hoped to gain subscribers among female typists, office workers, and sales clerks. At the beginning of October, this clientele was targeted explicitly with the announcement of a contest: "The great success enjoyed among female white-collar workers by the recent reprinting of Irmgard Keun's *Gilgi—eine von uns* has led the *Vorwärts* to launch a special contest for its female read-ership."[45] Every female professional who purchased a short-term subscription could participate. They were even offered the previous installments of the novel for free by mail. For the contest itself, the daily paper invited its female readers to describe their own experiences. In three to five pages, they were to depict a "scene from life and work." Subjects pertaining to the "hardships of our times" were explicitly preferred. Prizes included money and attractive items of white-collar culture such as radios, typewriters, or bicycles. In addition to the repre-sentatives of *Vorwärts*, the jury featured Irmgard Keun herself, as well as her publisher at Universitas, Theodor Glocke, and the head publicist for Para-mount Film, E. G. Techow.

With this contest the journal's Social Democratic cultural policy followed in the tradition of the communist League of Proletarian-Revolutionary Writers (BPRS). Among other things, the BPRS aimed to motivate workers "to put pen to paper and publish their experiences in factories and daily work life in their own words. This was intended to break down barriers between producers and consumers of culture, between writing and reading. ... Every reader was also addressed as a potential author."[46] The fact that the Social Democrats, whose cultural policies until that point had proven resistant to experimentation, were beginning to adopt strategies from the BPRS triggered an aggressive, polemical response in communist journalism. Bernard von Brentano addressed the issue in the BPRS's cultural journal *Die Linkskurve*, associating the author Keun, as well as the Social Democrats, with the bourgeoisie as class enemies. According to Brentano, *Gilgi—eine von uns* had all the characteristics of "cheap but effective narcotics": it turned away from "real" life, and weakened resistance to capitalism.[47] In the same vein, the communist women's magazine *Weg der Frau* sided with all the "Gilgis of reality" against the "mass influence" of the novel, whose hero had long come to stand metonymically for all female white-collar workers: "Real Gilgis have completely different concerns than worrying about true love. They, too, lack work and bread—things one does not get through connections, but by a collective struggle of all Gilgis against current conditions."[48]

The pathos underlying this appeal for political solidarity was the last weapon in a struggle for political hegemony that had long been lost. The vehemence with which the Communist press attacked the new initiative of the *Vorwärts* indicates the fatal shift in the lines of conflict at the close of the Weimar Republic. Rather than building a common *Volksfront* to resist the rise of National Socialism, the KPD and SPD battled independently for female votes over issues such as Keun's book and its protagonist. As female voter participation was indicative of societal uncertainty—significantly lower than that of men in times of stabilization, but rising strongly in the time of crisis between 1930 and 1933—every party saw female votes as a potential worth mobilizing.

The reprinting of *Gilgi* in *Vorwärts* concluded just before the election of 6 November 1932, the importance of which was the subject of numerous appeals and contributions in daily papers. Franz von Papen was governing alongside a presidential cabinet. His authoritarian rule met parliamentary and popular resistance which led to the dissolution of parliament and new elections. A series of electoral appeals addressed themselves explicitly to female voters: "To the union members! Men and Women Workers in Germany!" (29 October 1932), "To all Employees! Male and Female Colleagues!" (30 October 1932), "Women, November 6 is calling! Appeal!" (1 November 1932), "Women, Mothers, Girls! A Few More Words with You!" (5 November 1932). These increasingly direct programmatic appeals were framed by the discussion surrounding the reprinting of *Gilgi*, which linked the question of political motivation with the ambitions of Social Democratic cultural policy in the realm of public education. The way in which the editors framed this debate is worth quoting at length for what it reveals about the high stakes of the debate:

> Gilgi's attitude, as well as that of the novel as a whole, has been the object of severe, sometimes passionate, criticism. In this way, the novel by a young female author, whose social perspective is not entirely secure, becomes an *educator*: it demands criticism, it incites us to think through a problem that is relevant to all of us, and thereby it becomes a creative force. But this creative critique must not remain the concern of one individual. It should occupy the public, it should be brought to the attention of the author and thus create a link between the artist and the audience, as befits a democratic age—the forces of cultural reaction

notwithstanding. This critique shall help to create that intimate relationship between artists and audiences that is being prepared by the proletarian, socialist cultural endeavors.[49]

A didactic zeal is evident in the editors' desire to act as "links between artist and audience." Publisher S. Fischer believed himself a mediator between his authors and the public; Hofmann, the *volks*-librarian, hoped to lead female readers to good literature so that they may, as mothers, assume the duty of mediating between *Volk und Buch*; in a similar manner, *Vorwärts* now wished to place itself between author Irmgard Keun and her readers. Common to all these efforts at mediation was a resistance to allowing the relationship between books and female readers to be determined solely by commercial interests. Moreover, editorial attempts at intervention in the case of *Vorwärts* were not only directed at readers, but explicitly incorporated the author herself: as much as Gilgi's, Keun's political standpoint was up for debate.

In the debate over *Gilgi—eine von uns*, Gilgi is figured as the author's stand-in, a young woman whose political standpoint remained too ambiguous for many Social Democrats. In published commentary, both male and female readers wrangle over what is "typical" about the Gilgi character. In one of the earliest comments, Hanna Herz quickly relegates Gilgi to the bourgeois faction. The novel, she argues, is a trendy adaptation of "Krakauer's (sic) sociological studies," a half-hearted attempt to modernize the bourgeois *Mädchenroman*. Too trapped in the narrow horizon of individual needs, Gilgi cannot bring herself to acknowledge the Socialist collective: "For us, Gilgi is *not one of us*, not one of the millions who valiantly struggle for the rise of their class and for the creation of a new society."[50] Indeed, some readers simply refused to discuss the protagonist of "such a novel," which they considered "worthless in literary concerns or in any other respect, for that matter." A contributor by the name of Emma Langhaus judged the novel on a moral basis; arguing that it represents "an insult to any real working girl," she consigns it to the reviled *Schundliteratur*. A couple signing as "Friedrich Huth and wife" joined Langhaus in this opinion two days later, terming the novel *Kitsch*. In a condescending gesture that reveals their *bildungsbürgerlich* bias, the couple writes, "If we nonetheless read the new installments of the novel every morning, it was only because we found all the contradictions in plot and character amusing."[51]

The greater Berlin chapter of the Zentralverband der deutschen Angestellten, a white-collar union sympathetic to the SPD, was united in its opposition to the novel. On 20 October 1932, no fewer then 150 female functionaries and colleagues met to articulate a position that would be passed along to *Vorwärts*. The resulting document criticized Gilgi's unrealistic spending habits and indicted her "struggles with life and love" for being "determined by purely bourgeois-individualist factors."[52] The literary "projection" was sharply contrasted with the reality of white-collar life—hence the female white-collar worker's response to the novel should be one of refusal. From these workers, one hears a moral defense of realism: if literature, in this instance the contemporary novel *Gilgi—eine von uns,* is to relate explicitly to the current reality of female white-collar workers, it must portray its subject according to their own self-understanding (defined here by the Zentralverband der Angestellten). Such an argument implies that readers cannot differentiate between literature and real life; it does not allow for the fact that conceptions of reality are very much a matter of interpretation (or ideological standpoint, as the case may be). Any heteronomous or subjective readers who were not ready to subordinate what they read to a "higher" purpose—the party, class struggle—were indirectly discredited. Supposedly, reading (and writing) makes sense only from a definite political standpoint.

This rather restrictive view of the novel, and of reading more generally, stood in contrast to another position that quickly emerged in the debate. In keeping with the editors' desire for democratic exchange, Dr. Else Möbus put forth the opposing side's thesis in the second published article of the contest: for her, Gilgi is exemplary of "the immediate present, one of today's countless working young women and girls." Möbus chooses to analyze the novel "not from a literary point of view, but as a document of our times," the case history of one girl. "Without roots," Gilgi strives for a life better than that offered her by her traditional, bourgeois (adoptive) parents or the degrading conditions in which she works. Möbus registers with benevolence Gilgi's "honesty toward herself" that prevents her from judging herself according to "false" values or others' opinions. "She knows that her inner law demands equally that she shape her own life and that she find a complement."[53]

While she subordinates the secondary contradiction (of gender) to the central one (of ownership structure), Möbus's essay culminates in praise of the bourgeois theory that man and woman complement each other. The juxtaposition of varying conceptions of women, their divergences and points of contact, is spoken of openly in the debate over *Gilgi,* and linked with the question of mobilization. From these letters one sees an acute desire for political mobilization, and contention over whether Gilgi, the politically indifferent white-collar worker and New Woman, is a potential Socialist.

A typist who signs as "E. Th." speaks out against subsuming the novel and its protagonist under a preconceived notion of collectivity. In a self-assured gesture, she confronts the "censors" in her own party: "Why don't you, dear censors, take a moment to consider how many emotions have found expression in Irmgard Keun's [novel]!"[54] This reader-turned-author seeks the truthfulness of Keun's work not in the reflection of material reality, but in its *emotional* structure. She invokes literature's affective aspect, which in the *Gilgi* debate—as in the *volksbildnerischen* debates over female readers in general—were systematically repressed or discredited under the rubrics of trash literature. The typist's comments reveal that precisely the character's *emotional* conflicts were what she and her colleagues found to be most relevant, and what initiated the novel's singular success as a public and private topic of conversation. Without this affective force, she muses,

> Would such a discussion ever have arisen? Would one spend this much time at the office, at home, and among friends fighting with such verve about all the problems broached in *Gilgi*? And if people are led to reflect on things, is that not meaningful? I had not read the novel, had until recently resisted the piecemeal ingestion of any serialized novels, even those by recognized novelists. But when my [female] colleagues at the office virtually accosted me for not having read this novel, which they thought was something for me, and when I then heard that the seamstress comrades at the worker's welfare were doubly hurt by the censorship of *Vorwärts* because they had to do without *Gilgi* for three days—that is when I delved into *Gilgi* and let myself be carried away.

Motivated by her enthusiastic coworkers, E. Th. begins reading. The text captures her, she "delves" into the book, lets herself "be carried away." At this juncture, the critique that equates female reading with (externally determined) consumption would hold that the female reader is here lost in absorption through the apparently involuntary abandonment of her self to the world of the novel. Yet the secretary's reflections on her own passionate reading encompasses discussions within the social cohort of female coworkers. What had been created here was an interpretive community, whose participants, beyond their predetermined roles as voters, consumers, and mediators, attested to empowering experiences of reading.

The case studies presented in this essay indicate that the efforts of cultural politics and political parties, including the organized women's movement, strove to discipline the obstinate ways in which women might—and often did—read. They viewed with suspicion the emergence of an interpretive community of female readers that was not identical with, or subsumable under, one of the traditional political institutions. What I have described above as so many attempts to assimilate female readers into a political program were symptoms of contemporary changes within the literary field that found expression in widespread talk of a "crisis of the book." Under new economic and political pressures, the relationship between book, reader, and market had to be renegotiated. In this charged historical context, the few remaining accounts by female readers—be they informal interpretive communities of students, groups of blue- or white-collar employees, or participants in metropolitan reading circles—bear witness to a highly differentiated and contradictory public sphere. As political subjects with notable economic power, female readers achieved public recognition as voters, mediators, and consumers. Female readers at the end of the Weimar Republic became roaming subjects, occupying multiple subject positions simultaneously and assuming responsibility for their own emotional and cognitive development. In this process, books became a privileged medium for the articulation of a gendered self "between the times," fueling women's power to insert their voices into the cacophony of the public sphere in the late Weimar Republic.

Notes

This article draws on research first presented in Kerstin Barndt, *Sentiment und Sachlichkeit. Der Roman der Neuen Frau in der Weimarer Republik* (Cologne, 2003). My thanks go to Paul Dobryden for translation support, and to Kathleen Canning and Johannes von Moltke for inspiring discussions that helped me to sharpen my argument.

1. See Eve Rosenhaft, "Lesewut, Kinosucht, Radiotismus: Zur (geschlechter)politischen Relevanz neuer Massenmedien in den 1920er Jahren," in *Amerikanisierung: Traum und Alptraum in Deutschland des 20. Jahrhunderts*, ed. Alf Lüdtke, Inge Marßolek, Adelheid von Saldern (Stuttgart, 1996), 126–27; and Andreas Huyssen, "Mass Culture as Woman: Modernism's Other," in Huyssen, *After the Great Divide. Modernism, Mass Culture, Postmodernism* (Bloomington, IL, 1986), 44–62.

2. Hanns Korpf, "Frauen als Käuferinnen," *Die Reklame* 19 (1926): 649. On the Elida Girl motif, see Susanne Meyer-Büser, "Frauenbildnisse aus den 20er und frühen 30er Jahren. Film- und Werbeplakate," in *Bubikopf und Gretchenzopf—Die Frau der zwanziger Jahre*, ed. Susanne Meyer-Büser, Exhibition Catalogue, Hamburg, Museum für Kunst und Gewerbe, 1995, 156.

3. Dr. Annie Jacker, "Das Verhältnis der Frau zum Buch," *Börsenblatt für den deutschen Buchhandel* 98, no. 50 (1931): 181. For a critique of the eating metaphor as it is applied to female readers, see Janice A. Radway, "Reading Is Not Eating: Mass-Produced Literature and the Theoretical, Methodological, and Political Consequences of a Metaphor," *Book Research Quarterly* 38 (1986): 7–29.

4. Most recently, historian Gideon Reuveni addressed this desideratum in *Reading Germany: Literature and Consumer Culture in Germany before 1933* (London, 2006). Literary and film scholar Anton Kaes provided important context and an incentive for further research on Weimar reading culture in his "Schreiben und Lesen in der Weimarer Republik," in *Literatur der Weimarer Republik 1918–1933*, ed. Bernhard Weyergraf (München, 1995), 38–64. On Wilhelmine book culture see Gangolf Hübinger, "Politik mit Büchern und kulturelle Fragmentierung im Deutschen Kaiserreich," *Germanic Review* 76, no. 4 (2001): 290–307; and Alberto Martino, *Die deutsche Leihbibliothek. Geschichte einer literarischen Institution 1756–1914* (Wiesbaden, 1990). See also Georg Jäger, "Der Kampf gegen Schmutz und Schund. Die Reaktion der Gebildeten auf die Unterhaltungsindustrie," *Archiv für Geschichte des Buchwesens* 31 (1988): 163–91; and Günter Kosch and Manfred Nagl, *Der Kolportageroman. Bibliographie 1850–1960* (Stuttgart, 1993).

5. Reuveni, *Reading Germany*, 460.

6. S. Fischer, "Bemerkungen zur Bücherkrise," *Die literarische Welt* 2, no. 43 (1926), quoted from *Weimarer Republik. Manifeste und Dokumente zur deutschen Literatur 1918–1933*, ed. Anton Kaes (Stuttgart, 1983), 277. On Fischer's changing self-conceptions as publisher from Wilhelmine Germany to Weimar, see Kerstin Barndt, "Railroads for Locomotives of the Mind: Tracking Culture and Crisis in the S. Fischer Verlag" *Germanic Review* 76, no. 4 (2001): 335–48.

7. Dieter Langewiesche, "'Volksbildung' und 'Leserlenkung' in Deutschland von der wilhelminischen Ära bis zur nationalsozialistischen Diktatur," *Internationales Archiv zur Sozialgeschichte der Literatur* 14, no. 1 (1989): 108. Beyond the existing ideological differences both from the cultural elites and among each other, workers' and women's educational associations, as well as Catholic and middle-class liberal educational institutions, agreed on the idea that the masses must be led on the path toward cultivation and culture. On the critique of mass culture during the Weimar Republic, see also Adelheid von Saldern, "Massenfreizeit im Visier. Ein Beitrag zu den Deutungs- und Einwirkungsversuchen während der Weimarer Republik," *Archiv für Sozialgeschichte* 33 (1993): 21–58.

8. The announcement for the *Day of the Book* lists more than fifty women's organizations, from teachers' associations to the Jewish women's union, from the women's committee of the federation of labor unions to an association of female civil servants and the union of national women economists. See "Tag des Buches 1931. 22. März. Frau und Buch," *Börsenblatt für den Deutschen Buchhandel* 98 (1931): 129–32. On the history of the German book day, cf. Reuveni, *Reading Germany*, 195–96.

9. *Börsenblatt für den Deutschen Buchhandel* 98 (1931): 130. On the prewar history of the concept of spiritual motherhood, see Ann Taylor Allen, *Feminism and Motherhood in Germany, 1800–1914* (New Brunswick, NJ, 1991) and Thomas Sandkühler and Hans-Günter Schmidt, "'Geistige Mütterlichkeit' als nationaler Mythos im Deutschen Kaiserreich," in *Nationale Mythen und Symbole in der zweiten Hälfte des 19. Jahrhunderts: Strukturen und Funktionen von Konzepten nationaler Identität*, ed. Jürgen Link and Wulf Wülfing (Stuttgart, 1991), 237–55.

10. Dora Hansen-Blancke, "Frau und Buch. Zum 22. März 1931," *Nachrichtenblatt des Bundes Deutscher Frauenvereine* 11, no. 3 (1931): 16.

11. "Tag des Buches 1931," 130.

12. See Irene Stoehr, "Staatsfeminismus und Lebensform. Frauenpolitik im Generationenkonflikt der Weimarer Republik," in *Rationale Beziehungen? Geschlechterverhältnisse im Rationalisierungsprozeß*, ed. Dagmar Reese, Eve Rosenhaft, Carola Sachsee, and Tilla Siegel (Frankfurt am Main, 1993), 105–41.

13. Jacker, "Das Verhältnis der Frau zum Buch."

14. Ibid.

15. For the following, see the advertising section of the *Börsenblatt*, "Zum Tag des Buches. Frau und Buch," 89, no. 50 (1931): 1330–50.

16. Advertisement in *Börsenblatt* 90, no. 150 (1932): 2929.

17. Cf. Agnès Cardinal, "Ina Seidel: From Das Wunschkind to Lenmacker. Strategies of Dissimulation," in *Travellers in Time and Space*, ed. Osman Durrani and Julian Preece (Amsterdam, 2001), 371–82.

18. Ina Seidel, "Können wir heute noch lesen? Gedanken zum 'Tag des Buches,'" *Blätter für Bücherfreunde* 31, no. 2 (1931): 2. Seidel is adept at shifting her tone. While this article invokes the figure of the motherly woman with much pathos, Seidel uses a different rhetoric in a contribution to the *Nachrichtenblatt des Bundes Deutscher Frauenvereine*. Here, she claims the role of the true artist who "serves all of humanity with his efforts." This artist would transcend the gendered organization of society. See Ina Seidel, "Tag des Buches," *Nachrichtenblatt des Bundes Deutscher Frauenvereine* 11, no. 3 (1931): 16.

19. A. S., "Der Tag des Buches. Die Berliner Veranstaltung," *Berliner Tageblatt*, 23 March 1931, evening edition, 3.

20. See Patrice Petro, *Joyless Streets. Women and Melodramatic Representation in Weimar Germany* (Princeton, 1989).

21. "Ever since the woman's movement began to found educational associations for women, the woman question has become a question of cultivation [*Bildungsfrage*]. Today, women take for granted the notion that all educational means are available to her and that she can satisfy her educational desires. ... One of the most important paths towards cultivation is the book because it is also the easiest." R. von Carlowitz, "Die Frau als Leserin," *Die Frau* 38 (1930/31): 358.

22. Quoted from the summary of the speech in Schönfelder, "Die Frau als Leserin," *Börsenblatt* 98, no. 34 (1931): 115. On Gerhard Menz, who became Leipzig's first Professor for Economics of Book Trade (*Buchhandelsbetriebslehre*) in 1925, cf. Reuveni, *Reading Germany*, 156; and Hans Altenheim, "Gerhard Menz als Autor. Zur Funktion des Buch- und Zeitschriftenwesens im 20. Jahrhundert," *Leipziger Jahrbuch für Buchgeschichte* 14 (2006): 153–87.

23. On the ideological dispute among public librarians cf. Reuveni, *Reading Germany*, 158–62; and Jürgen Eyssen, "Bildung durch Bücher? Volksbüchereien während der Weimarer Republik," *Das Buch in den zwanziger Jahre: Vorträge des 2. Jahrestreffenss Wolfenbütteler Arbeitskreises für Geschichte des Buchwesens*, ed. Paul Raabe (Hamburg, 1978), 77.

24. Eyssen, "Bildung durch Bücher?" 81. Despite his nationalistic leanings, Hofmann would not sympathize with the Nazis, and resisted pressure to integrate NS party poets into his catalog of German authors.

25. Walter Hofmann, *Die Lektüre der Frau. Ein Beitrag zur Leserkunde und Leserführung* (Leipzig, 1931), 29–30. Hofmann published his study in time for the 1931 Day of the Book.

26. Dr. Margarethe Kupfer, "Frauenlektüre als Spiegel weiblichen Seins," *Die Frau* 38 (1930/31): 717.

27. See for example Langewiesche, "'Volksbildung' und 'Leserlenkung,'" 116.

28. Cf. Gabriele Reuter's and Lulu v. Strauß u. Torney's contributions, "Frau und Buch. Zum 22. März 1931," *Nachrichtenblatt des Bundes Deutscher Frauenvereine* 11, no. 3 (1931): 17.

29. Jacker, "Das Verhältnis der Frau zum Buch," 182.

30. Reuter in "Frau und Buch. Zum 22. März 1931," 17.

31. Kupfer, "Frauenlektüre," 718–19.

32. The call went out to fifteen- to twenty-year-old female readers, whose reading preferences were little known (allegedly in contrast to those of boys and young men, who were "clear and unmistakable" in this area). See Börsenverein des Deutschen Buchhandels, ed., *Was wir vom Buch erwarten! Antworten der 15- bis 20jährigen Mädchen. Vorberichte über das Ergebnis eines Preisausschreibens, erlassen vom Börsenverein der Deutschen Buchhändler zu Leipzig und vom Reichsverband des Deutschen Schrifttums* (Leipzig, 1931). The call for responses was circulated through bookstores.

33. Ibid.

34. For the following quotes, see Ricarda Huch, "Das junge Mädchen heute. Bemerkungen anlässlich eines Preisausschreibens," *Die Literarische Welt*, Sonderausgabe zum "Tag des Buches," Frau und Buch, 7, no. 12 (1931): 1.

35. Angestellte, 20 Jahre, o.T., in *Was wir vom Buch erwarten*, 24.

36. Primanerin 17 1/2 Jahre, o.T., in *Was wir vom Buch erwarten*, 19.

37. See Barndt, *Sentiment und Sachlichkeit: Schreib- und Leseweisen der neuen Frau am Ende der Weimarer Republik* (Köln, 2002).

38. "Heute steht das weibliche Geschlecht an einer Umbruchstelle seiner Entwicklung. Der Übergang von der alten zur neuen Weiblichkeit vollzieht sich nicht geradlinig und scheitert zuweilen an den Klippen der Männlichkeit. Zieht man einen provisorischen Schlußstrich, dann kann man die Situation der gegenwärtigen Weiblichkeit wie in einer Abschlußrechnung mit Aktiven und Passiven, mit Gewinn und Verlust vor sich sehen." Alice Rühle-Gerstel, *Die Frau und der Kapitalismus. Eine psychologische Bilanz* (Frankfurt am Main, 1972 [1932]), 409.

39. Charles Baudelaire, "The Painter of Modern Life," in *The Painter of Modern Life and Other Essays*, ed. and trans. Jonathan Mayne (London, 1995), 1–40.

40. Luise Scheffen-Döring, *Frauen von heute* (Leipzig, 1929), vii.

41. I am placing "women" in quotation marks here in order to remain conscious of Denise Riley's argument that "women," as a collective of a certain gender, are a historical construction that is continually redefined. Riley, *"Am I That Name?" Feminism and the Category of "Women" in History* (Minneapolis, 1988), 5.

42. Cf. Barndt, *Sentiment und Sachlichkeit. Der Roman der Neuen Frau in der Weimarer Republik*, 158f.

43. Irmgard Keun, *Gilgi—eine von uns* (München, 1989), 172.

44. *Gilgi* was already in its fifth printing (for a total run of 25,000) by September of 1932. By the same time, and only a few months after its appearance, *Das kunstseidene Mädchen* had reached similar figures (24,000).

45. See announcement in *Vorwärts*, 2 October 1932. Paramount produced a screen version of the novel in the same year, under the tile *Eine von uns* (dir. Johannes Meyer).

46. Kaes, "Schreiben und Lesen," 46.

47. Bernhard Brentano, "Keine von uns. Ein Wort an die Leser des 'Vorwärts,'" *Die Linkskurve* 4, no. 10 (1932): 28.

48. Ingeborg Franke, "Gilgi—Film, Roman und Wirklichkeit," *Der Weg der Frau* 3, no. 2 (1933): 6. See also Marianne Gundermann: "Gilgi—eine vom 'Vorwärts,'" *Weg der Frau* 3, no. 2 (1933): 7.

49. "Eine von uns? Wir diskutieren über Gilgi," *Vorwärts*, 18 October 1932. My emphasis.

50. Hanna Herz, "Keine von den Millionen … ," *Vorwärts*, 18 October 1932.

51. Friedrich Huth und Frau, "Dank an Frau Langhaus," *Vorwärts*, 25 October 1932.

52. Hans Gottfurcht, Gertrud Ellert (writing on behalf of the Zentralverband der Angestellten, Ortsgruppe Groß-Berlin), " … nie und nimmer," *Vorwärts*, 25 October 1932 (evening edition).

53. Dr. Else Möbus, "Einzelfall … ," *Vorwärts*, 18 October 1932.

54. E. Th. "Kunst/Kitsch/Leben? Die Diskussion um 'Gilgi,'" *Vorwärts*, 28 October 1932.

CHAPTER 5

❧ ❦ ❧

Claiming Citizenship
Suffrage and Subjectivity in Germany after the First World War

KATHLEEN CANNING

In the aftermath of war and revolution in Germany, citizenship emerged as a new political imaginary. In this essay I analyze through the lens of citizenship a prolonged moment of crisis and transformation in German history, in which a war was lost, an empire crumbled, and a revolution ushered in a decade of experiments in democracy unprecedented in German history. I am concerned here with the rhetorical and legal processes that framed, instituted, and embodied women's citizenship during the early years of the Weimar Republic. I argue here that gender inflected both the symbolics and subjectivities of this citizenship, which was imagined, desired, and claimed in new ways, particularly by those who lacked some of the most fundamental citizenship rights, such as the right to vote. The catastrophic conditions on the German home front and the deepening divide between militarized state and civic public opened spaces for citizenship claims that would have been unthinkable before the war. This work of envisioning and articulating new claims of citizenship began in the popular protests against expansionist war aims, for peace, bread, and suffrage during the last two years of the war. Its fulfillment became the task of the revolutionary councils and assemblies that took power in November 1918, and then the foremost aim of the first democratically elected parliament in February 1919.

Charting the place of citizenship in the history of the transformations of war, revolution, and the founding of democracy requires, first, a brief assessment of definitions and historical placements of citizenship. I am particularly interested in the arenas beyond the juridical and formal prescriptions of citizenship and the ways in which citizenship was cast, redefined, and contested at different points in these years of crisis and change. One key question is how citizenship acquired a distinctive voice among several political languages and social identities that were jostled about during the ruptures in relations of state and society, women and men. If a vocabulary of class characterized the political language of protest during the *Kaiserreich*, how did spaces for citizenship, both linguistic and social, coalesce amidst the collapse of the *Kaiserreich* and the German defeat? I hypothesize that the years from 1917 through 1924 marked the period of citizenship's greatest resonance and promise, at least for the period of German history from 1848 through 1933. It might be said that citizenship became a new object of desire, a social identity Germans *wanted* or aspired to fulfill, while class and perhaps *Stand* were social identities Germans already *had*, to paraphrase social theorist David Held.[1] In this essay I am particularly interested in those languages of citizenship spoken by and about women, in how old and new ideologies of sexual difference inflected the ascription of citizenship rights to men and women, who were always implicitly embodied. This essay also pursues a historiographical point: namely, to explore the reasons why the turning point in German history at which women became citizens has served as such a dead end in German gender history. Finally, the questions I pursue here about gender and citizenship should shed light on the resonances citizenship gained and lost in the course of founding and then defending democracy.

Citizenship in German History

The specificities of German history, along with the fact that citizenship translates only awkwardly into German—its meaning in English is captured neither by *Staatsangehörigkeit* nor *Staatsbürgerschaft*—may explain the relative absence of the term in most German historiography. Certainly the publication of Rogers Brubaker's *Citizenship and Nationhood in France and Germany* revitalized the interest in the history of German citizenships during the last decade. Yet his study has generated new interest mainly in ethnicity and citizenship law, fostering studies of citizenship in terms of its national boundedness rather than as a realm of experience or a form of social identity within civil societies.[2] In this study I understand citizenship as something transcending the terms of its containment within the strictures of formal, territorially grounded rights of *Staatsangehörigkeit* or *Staatsbürgerschaft*, which functioned not least to delineate national boundaries and national belonging. Taking citizenship in Bryan Turner's terms as a "set of practices—juridical, political, economic and cultural—which define a person or through which persons define themselves as competent members of society," helps to make a bit more concrete a term that is more contingent and indeterminate than class.[3] As a trope in a wide range of national or ethnic conflicts, in struggles for the rights of women, minorities, workers, or welfare recipients, contemporary uses of the term *citizenship* invoke distinct, even discordant catalogs of rights and claims. Narratives of citizenship can serve at times to buttress the integrative practices of states, while in other instances they might enunciate claims of those seeking access to citizenship rights.

If citizenship is understood more broadly as a political language that seeks to define the terms of political participation *within* nations and civil societies, the rhetorics or "narrative identities" of citizenship are also relevant for those on the margins of these formal rights.[4] So, for example, citizenship might have figured as a subversive discourse in Catholic and Social Democratic milieus, both in the wake of persecution by the Bismarckian state and later as the cornerstone of the campaigns of workers' parties in Wilhelmine Prussia to repeal the three-class suffrage system, which remained a volatile issue during most of the Kaiserreich and gained new brisance on the eve of the First World War. German women's movements, both middle class and Social Democratic, also asserted citizenship claims in their prewar campaigns for women's suffrage and their mobilizations against the German Civil Code at the turn of the century, which granted husbands extensive and explicitly patriarchal rights over their wives on matters of child rearing, employment, and property.[5]

Yet citizenship has had only a marginal place in the historiography of the Weimar Republic. It has also been relatively insignificant in the by now abundant historiography on women and gender in Weimar Germany, on family and welfare policies, of labor and/or body politics.[6] The absence of citizenship in feminist histories of Weimar Germany is symptomatic of the demarcations between gender and the study of politics, by which gender is relevant mainly in those realms remote from high politics, such as popular culture, consumption, or sexual reform. Eve Rosenhaft's contention of the mid-1990s that "it is still possible to write [or rewrite] a general account of German history that excludes women" has been reaffirmed in recent years as innovative new studies of Weimar political culture have remained impervious to the impulses of gender.[7] The persistence of these boundaries suggests a puzzling unevenness in the dissemination and reception of gender history across the more specialized thematic fields of modern German history. While scholarship on women and gender during the long nineteenth century has significantly revised understandings of civil society and public sphere, social discipline and social welfare, working-class and middle-class formation, German colonialism and imperialism, gender scholarship on the high-stakes histories of Weimar and Nazi Germany has not fundamentally challenged categories or temporalities. Few would dispute that contests over masculinities and femininities form a crucial part of the post–World War I "crisis of bourgeois Europe," but the work of making these links to the postwar period remains incomplete.[8] My exploration of the links between citizenship and gender, citizenship and bodies, is meant to challenge these historiographical borders and boundaries.

The citizenship that has been most salient to historical study of the democratic experiment of Weimar is typically encompassed in the rights of social citizenship located within the Weimar welfare state.[9] Despite the revolutionary proclamation of new suffrage laws in 1918 and the drafting of the first democratic constitution in 1919, the power of nationalism in the "spirit of August 1914," its resurgence in response to the "dictated peace" of Versailles, and the protracted civil strife between Socialists and Communists in the early years of the republic leaves little space for citizenship in the narratives of Weimar. The Nazi *Volksgemeinschaft* usurped and racialized the civic spaces in which citizenship flourished during Weimar, so that the notions of claims and rights central to the practice of citizenship were silenced during the Third Reich. In modern German history, then, citizenship has been relevant mainly for the study of the Federal Republic since 1949, when democracy was sustained over a longer historical time span and consumption, along with the successful postwar welfare state, expanded the terms of citizenship.

The Specificity of Citizenships: The War and Its Aftermath

In considering *citizenship* a critically important term for the period after the First World War, I understand it as a new legal or social identity that became fixed in political culture as it was embraced by those who had long desired expanded legal and political rights. Moreover, in the volatile political culture of Weimar Germany, citizenship also meant the emergence of new subjectivities within "a new language of democratic participation."[10] The citizenship I am interested in here is thus quite specific—it was born of not only of war but also of defeat, not only of revolution but also of the disintegration of the militarized state from within, torn apart by its relentless drive to both fulfill expansive war aims and provide for the population on the home front. This citizenship took shape precisely in the protests of women and youths on the home front against these contradictory goals of German total war. Second, this is citizenship in a different temporality than Brubaker's jus sanguinis: it was inflected by struggles over rights and respectability in the last decades of the *Kaiserreich*, but its declaration in a moment of rupture suggests that it was not necessarily predetermined by earlier articulations of citizenship. In fact, no neat lines of continuity connect the prewar politics of class or *Stand* in the respective Social Democratic, Catholic, or liberal milieus, and the visions of citizenship that flourished in the streets, pubs, and on the strike lines of the German home front during the war. The sudden inception rather than the continuity or endurance of this citizenship over time is of primary interest here. The citizenship of Weimar was defined not only in different temporal but also spatial terms, as the borders of Germany were redrawn during the very years in which citizenship rights were written into law, so German citizenship of the interwar period was inscribed with loss of territory and longing for restitution of the borders of 1914.

Citizenship was a new juridical and legal status, first declared and then delimited at the highest levels of law and state, at a considerable distance from the realms in which it was imagined and fought over during the last years of the war. Citizenship on the German home front became a language in which new social groups mobilized and staked new claims upon the militarized state—the women of lesser means who feature in Belinda Davis's book, for example, or the war widows and veterans who bore in their respective ways the "bitter wounds" of war.[11] Robert Whalen's estimate that some 6 million Germans belonged to the groups of war wounded, widows, or children orphaned by war points to the potential for new mobilizations and new claims upon an expanded welfare state.[12] That newly congealed social groups held the state accountable for the human costs of the war and articulated claims to this effect (bread, suffrage, peace without annexations) meant that the political language of citizenship was distinct in important respects from prewar languages of class. Citizenship, at the time of its greatest resonance in the early years of the republic prior to the crisis of inflation in 1923–24, was a broader and more porous social identity than class, which remained anchored to notions of labor and skill that were themselves transformed by the militarization of the economy during the war. Indeed, four years of total war had cut a swath through an imagined working-class cohesion, dividing producers from consumers, soldiers from striking workers, veterans from war widows, those with work from the unemployed, those bearing the scars of war from those who survived unscathed. The declaration of citizenship rights—new suffrage rights for women over age twenty and the abolition of the Prussian three-class suffrage system thus convened new communities, national and civic, in November 1918. The turning point I am most interested in here was the naming of women as members of this new civil community that was just taking shape. The conferral of suffrage to women on 12 November 1918 stunned many suffrage advocates, not least because both civilian and military authorities had categorically rejected women's demands for the vote up to the very eve of the outbreak of revolution on 9 November, notably a petition for suffrage submitted jointly by Social Democratic and liberal women's groups to the Reichstag on 8 November.[13]

The proclamation of the democratic rights of citizenship for women, and the subsequent debates about its implications, drew unprecedented numbers of women into the realms of formal and informal politics between 1918 and 1921.[14] The particular power of citizenship rights to propel unprecedented levels of political participation and identification must be understood in the context of the profound reconfiguration of political space that took place as the militarized state disintegrated and the work of imagining and enacting the new

"Reich as republic" began. Yet the desires and disorientations of this turbulent time at the end of the war, in which nearly every aspect of daily life and high politics was uncertain and women's suffrage came as a shock, has not marked a turning point in either mainstream German history or, more notably, in German gender history. Given the drama of the moment—the collapse of the imperial state, the convening of workers' and soldiers' councils, the negotiation of a major compromise between capital and labor (the Stinnes-Legien agreement of 1918), and the impending bargaining for peace—suffrage appears only fleetingly in the dramaturgy of Weimar history and appeared to have no lasting implications for the doomed republic.

From this perspective the study of citizenship and gender can help us rethink the beginnings of Weimar as marking a rupture in the history of both German civil society and gender relations. In the timeline of German history, in which continuities tend to overwhelm moments of abrupt change, the collapse of democracy usually overshadows the work of imagining and envisioning that shaped its founding. As the framing moment of Weimar, the November Revolution, for example, seldom escapes the categorizations of failure, stillbirth, or betrayal. Similarly, the tangled work of the Nationalversammlung in 1919, which mapped new relationships among the civic, family, and state in the name of democracy and reconstituted the state to make space for the claims of a newly empowered citizenry, has most often been viewed in terms of its fateful compromises, such as Article 48, which Weimar's last stewards implemented to rule by emergency decree. Peter Fritzsche's provocative piece, "Did Weimar Fail?" highlights a new view of Weimar as "strikingly open-ended," "remarkably contingent," and shaped by "eclectic experimentalism" rather than circumscribed by failure.[15] Yet these terms refer mainly to the cultural promise of Weimar in the years of stabilization, rather than to the hopes of political democracy, which were undercut by the trauma of defeat and the unfinished revolution. While some historians have successfully captured the utopian desires and the topsy-turvy sense of displacement unleashed by the republic's recurrent crises, the revolutionary beginnings of Weimar are more often interpreted in terms of the drive to "return to normalcy," to restabilize relations of people and state, women and men.[16]

The widespread perception that gender ideologies and relations were broken in the immediate aftermath of war placed gender at the heart of the project of redefining and reinstating this so-called normalcy. Not only the vast numbers of war dead and injured—the changing landscapes of masculinities and their impingement on the visual and political culture of Weimar—suggest this, but also the transformations of self, state, and society experienced by women in the realms of work, family, and the civic sphere during and after the war. Ute Daniel and Belinda Davis, among others, have drawn attention to the significance of these transformations during the last years of the war, but stopped short of analyzing their implications for the founding of the republic.[17] Thus the end of the war is usually disconnected from the framing moments of Weimar, while the shock of defeat, which lived on in the guise of the Versailles Treaty, serves as the definitive force in galvanizing sentiment against the republic throughout the 1920s.[18]

Another challenge of this study is explaining the relationship between the transformation of the gender order that took place during the war and the citizenship rights that were proclaimed after defeat. Did the wide-scale social protest of women on the home front, including their demands for suffrage, constitute a symptom of new (wartime) fissures in the gender order or did their demands only become thinkable because the gender order was already breaking apart? Did the bestowal of citizenship rights to women in the heat of revolution attest to the recognition of profound differences in the ways men and women experienced or responded to the crisis of total war? Or was the instantiation of women's citizenship rights in the Weimar constitution the first step towards the restoration of a familiar set of gender hierarchies and ideologies? Most German historians would probably accept that some kind of deep change in the relations between the sexes took place during the war as women performed new kinds of labor, gained unprecedented authority in the family and new visibility in public, and learned to wield self-reliance in arenas as diverse as sex, scavenging, rationing, and mourning. But they would scarcely agree about how the profoundly new experiences of men in the trenches and women on the home front influenced the *postwar* gender order.

The debates about whether these changes represented a longer-term (modernizationist) emancipation or one merely "on loan," as Ute Daniel phrased it, were settled some years ago. The war experience of German women has not held up as emancipatory, not least because conditions on the home front and the loss of male family members were so disastrous as to belie most notions of emancipation.[19] In the historical analyses of the aftermath of the First World War, German women's acquisition of new citizenship rights is usually viewed as scarcely resonating into the political culture of Weimar. Feminist historians have also regarded women's acquisition of formal citizenship rights as relatively insignificant, given the massive pressures in other realms of political life towards a restoration of prewar gender roles and ideologies. Women turned away from formal politics as early as 1919, so the argument goes, conceiving of their contribution to the new democracy in terms of "feminine and motherly expertise," practiced most commonly in the expanding realms of the welfare state. The fact that the numbers of women voters and of women elected to public office declined after an intense spurt of politicization between 1918 and 1920 has led many historians to conclude that the vote itself, as the centerpiece of citizenship, was without broader consequences for Weimar politics. In contrast to this view, I contend that the process of defining and delimiting the terms of female citizenship in the National Assembly of Weimar, and the new subjectivities it created, were formative of Weimar political culture, even if its outcome was not equal citizenship for women and men.

Even if more recent scholarship refrains from interpreting women's wartime experiences as emancipatory, a common-sense consensus prevails in much of the historiography that a restoration of gender roles and ideologies did take place after the war. The effects of women's suffrage and the election of women to Germany's first democratic parliament were soon reversed by the recurrent cycles of political turmoil and economic crisis that beset the republic from its founding through the crisis of 1923–24. As women gradually withdrew from the public sphere, traditional gender norms and roles were rapidly reinstated. So one recent text: "Women's willing return to traditional gender roles was ultimately determined by their increased awareness of the limitations placed on their emancipation after the onset of the economic decline in the mid-1920s that brought Weimar's intrinsically patriarchal structures to the fore."[20] In a similar vein, Ute Daniel has argued that "women's forms of spontaneous and unorganized collective action [found] no continuation beyond the world war." Although their sustained protests had a crucial role in dismantling the system of total war, Daniel views them as having no "observable, longer-term consequences for the forms of social relations and women's role in them" after the war because their subversive critique was intrinsic to the particular circumstances of Germany at war.[21] Feminist historians have thus conjured up patriarchal structures that were somehow inherent to German society—despite the dramatic transformations of masculinity and state in the course of the war—and that were quickly resuscitated in the years after the war. On the other hand, historians have drawn a line between the experiences and subjectivities of wartime and its aftermath, thus positing that women's participation in civil society and social protest diminished once the chief object of their discontent—the war itself—had ended and women were thus able to return to their "natural" tasks of family and household, that is, even if families and households were in no sense the same in 1918 as they had been in 1914.

This evocation of closure, of reversal or a return to something preexistent soon after the end of the war raises interesting methodological questions about the different resonances of the categories of women and gender in historical analysis more generally and in the specific task of discerning the "observable consequences" of a moment of rupture like 1918–1920. Confining our observations to the realms of formal politics and the question of women's quantitative participation might make it easy to conclude that women withdrew from or were driven out of public life, while following the lead of scholars in the visual arts and literature affords a rather different sense of the ways in which gender and the apparition of the "new woman" continued to preoccupy the public.[22] The bitter struggles to reestablish familiar gender divisions and hierarchies form important threads of Weimar history, as state and social policy aimed to return men to intact families, to revitalize the family's reproductive function, to restrain and regulate sex, pleasure, birth control, and abortion. Both these positive and negative measures and those aimed to contain women's participation in some of the newly significant publics—from cinema to consumption, parliaments to newly rationalized work places—formed part of a continuous project of restoring a broken patriarchy, one that required renewal and rejuvenation with each dramatic shift and turn of Weimar history. Examination of the arenas of contest over citizenship and gender suggests, however, that this rupture was not repaired in the course of the Weimar Republic and that gender relations never did quite go back to "normal" again. Foregoing this moment of closure at the end of the war might help explain, in part at least, the virulence of Nazi "family policies" that would later drive, uncompromisingly, to institute a revitalized and racialized patriarchy.

Rather than positing a moment of definitive reconstitution of gender, I am interested in probing the contests over gender that ensued in the aftermath of war and revolution and thus in resisting a moment of closure at the end of war in which patriarchy was either destroyed or definitively restored. There is considerable historical evidence that the restoration of the gender order *was* indeed a primary project of Weimar democracy, and feminist historians have delivered much of it: the rapid implementation of the demobilization decrees in 1919, for example, literally stripped women both of their actual jobs and their right to work.[23] The Weimar constitution did institute political rights for women, but left restrictions on their civil rights in marriage and family in place, thus favoring protection of family and reproduction of nation over women's civil rights. Feminist studies of social work and welfare analyze the process by which female social reformers, who envisioned and staffed many branches of the Weimar welfare state, were kept out of the "male-dominated arena of social policy where so-called vital interests of state were being negotiated."[24] My aim is thus not to dispute these efforts to restore familiar gender ideologies and hierarchies, but to probe the ways in which these efforts remained incomplete, to challenge this sense of closure, and to explore the persistence of gender crisis into the later years of the republic. Citizenship figures here then as one transformation—of women's legal status and subject position—that proved irreversible, at least until the Nazis seized power in 1933.

At first glance it appears that citizenship for women in Weimar Germany was confined to those rights which they "earned … in their role as mothers and house-workers," that is, to a highly restricted kind of social citizenship.[25] Indeed, the power and pervasiveness of the German welfare state has meant that most explorations of women's citizenship in German history focus on precisely this arena, the only one in which female citizens were not only clients but also expert visionaries of social reform. In seeking to overcome the limitations of maternalist social citizenship, I probe women's entry into the "specifically political arena" in the last years of the war, during the revolution, and in the struggle for democracy. Following the lead of feminist political theorist Anne Phillips, I consider that political arena one in which people transcend their "more private, localised interests and tackled what should be the community's common concerns."[26] An enormous archive of evidence exists on the manifold ways in which diverse and opposing groups of German women did precisely this during the years under study here, whether from nationalist, Catholic, liberal, or Social Democratic standpoints. Women experienced themselves becoming citizens as they entered debates on matters of indisputably "high" politics, from the consequences of Germany's defeat to the form and foundation of the new state.

Framing Citizenship

Much of the high drama of the Weimar Republic—its initial quest for legitimacy and its anguished struggle to survive—played out on the terrain of citizenship. Mass mobilizations on the home front around food shortages in 1916 spilled into protests against war and annexation and potent calls for full suffrage rights for women and male workers by 1917. This occurred in even more dramatic form by January 1918, when over 1 million workers threw off the last remnants of the *Burgfrieden* in their determined demands for peace without annexations and immediate suffrage reform. The strikes of 1917 and 1918, in which some half of the participants were women, mark a critical turning point in the relationship of women to the state, one that is crucial to the history of the November Revolution and its immediate declaration of female suffrage. Yet police and union reports reveal little about the demands, desires, and actions of female strikers in this volatile moment of transgressive citizenship.[27] We do know that women comprised a significant number of the strike participants and an oddly privileged segment therein, for the reprisals of the military state against striking workers took on highly gendered forms in 1917 and 1918. Male strikers, interpellated at this juncture as citizens by the militarized state, were stripped of their service exemptions and shipped off to the front or to military prisons, while female workers who figured in wartime discourses primarily as (embodied) mothers, war wives or war widows, were able to elude state sanctions. Indeed, already in the case of food protests in 1915–16, authorities had complained about the impossibility of effectively punishing female protesters, many whom were mothers with young children.[28] The participation of women, first in food protests in 1916 and 1917 and then in mass strikes, brought the governability of the cities into question and helped to dismantle military rule over civil society.

This moment of rupture in which the combined ordeals of women on the home front—hunger, cold, poverty, and sickness, next to fears of a prolonged annexationist war—galvanized new and vehement claims of women upon the militarized state. So, for example, war widows—some 533,000 by 1918—were propelled into a wholly new relationship with the state through their struggle for pensions from the state.[29] Police reports attest to the "rage that drove women into public protest," along with the "urge for solidarity that widows felt with their 'sisters,'" and their growing consciousness of themselves "as a distinct group."[30] This distinction sharpened once the veterans returned home and widows recognized "how different [their] situation was from those families which had a husband and a father." Widows became bitterly aware of the inadequacy of their pensions and were forced to compete with men in the labor market. The words of one war widow describe the process by which this group of women embraced a new social identity of citizenship: "The war educated us, and now we begin to place our demands before the state."[31] As their experiences of war propelled them into open confrontation with the state, war victims' pensions would come to represent both a material and symbolic atonement of the state for the violence of war.[32]

While Kaiser Wilhelm II publicly conceded the need for suffrage reform in the spring of 1918, military leaders Hindenburg and Ludendorff vowed that the pending German victory would prevent a dreaded turn towards democracy. At the same time, those who drove Germany onward in a fruitless war identified the protesters on the home front, whose demands for full and participatory citizenship rights were raised with increasing defiance in early 1918, as the very force responsible for the depletion of the German war effort. By implication at least, citizenship's visionaries and advocates, once cast as outside of the nation, would also figure in the formulation of the infamous "stab in the back" legend.[33] The first and perhaps most consequential outcome of the November Revolution was the immediate extension of suffrage rights to women and the abolition of the Prussian three-class franchise system. The subsequent two-year period, through the end of 1920, saw the mass political mobilization of new citizens, including women, as voters, members, even delegates of the new and reconstituted political parties and reinvigorated trade unions. The new political language of republican democracy permeated and recast the prewar political languages of class and estate. This extraordinary moment of politicization coincided with the national humiliation of the Versailles Treaty, with the physical and political remapping of the German nation.

In the early days of November 1918 the war effort collapsed and the Kaiserreich crumbled amidst sailors' mutinies and the sprouting of workers' and soldiers councils from Kiel to Munich. One of the first acts of the revolutionary Council of People's Representatives, which formed between 9 and 12 November, was the proclamation of republican citizenship, including women's suffrage. The issues of women's suffrage and class-restricted suffrage in Prussia had been acutely present in the last two years of the war, in the demands of the mass strikes and the maneuverings of the military authorities in response to civil unrest. Just ten days before this announcement, on 2 November, women's associations of all political hues had called for an audience with the new chancellor, Prince Max von Baden, regarding the question of suffrage rights for women. On 8 November, the day before the revolution, the Social Democrats proposed the formal adoption in the Reichstag of equal suffrage rights for women and men, but it was easily defeated by a coalition of bourgeois parties.[34] Given the refusal of civilian and military authorities, up to the very eve of the revolution, to grant women's demands for suffrage rights, middle-class feminists were stunned when suffrage rights "fell overnight from a storm cloud"[35] on 12 November, making "women into citizens with a dash of a pen, with a mere announcement in the daily paper."[36]

A new electoral law went into effect on 30 November 1918, and the date for the election of the National Assembly was set for 19 January 1919, sparking a month of extraordinary political agitation and mobilization. In the words of one witness:

> Voters were showered with leaflets and every fence, empty shop windows, and street corners were covered with fliers. Political passions of all varieties were reawakened and the party meetings were not the only place they were expressed. Groups assembled on streets and corners, where speeches were held and especially the Spartacus group was everywhere disseminating its viewpoints. Each party, each movement had the instinctive feeling that they were engaged in the final struggle, that this was a decisive moment in the future of German politics and of the German state.[37]

When the National Assembly convened in Weimar in the early winter of 1919, it was clear to those who gathered that the real work of constituting women's citizenship had only begun.[38] The forty-one women delegates comprised 9.7 percent of the assembly and included eighteen Social Democrats and three female representatives of the Independent Social Democrats.[39] Between the months of February and August 1919 legislators deliberated the draft of the constitution, which Hugo Preuss had authored in early January, including three articles that framed and delimited citizenship for women in the new republic. The formal ascription of citizenship rights to women in 1918–19 involved a complex of rights and duties, including active and passive suffrage for women over the age of twenty, protection of the state for marriage and family and constriction of civil rights for women within these "private" institutions, and rights to social protection and social benefits within a refurbished welfare state, defined by men and staffed by women.

It is possible here to offer only a brief overview of the debates surrounding these articles. The centerpiece of the second section of the constitution, *Grundrechte und Grundpflichten der Deutschen* (Basic Rights and Basic Duties of German [Citizens]), Part I, "The Individual," was Article 109, which deemed, "All Germans are equal before the law. Men and women have *in principle* the same rights and duties as citizens."[40] The controversy that ensued over this formulation highlighted the deep apprehension among legislators about the promised equality for women. According to this article, the realization of women's citizenship rights "would depend upon the natural limits" (*naturbedingte Grenzen*) of sexual difference.[41] The qualifying phrase, "in principle," also left open the possibility that local, provincial, or state laws might interpret the law differently, as its critics pointed out.[42] Women in the Independent and Majority Social Democratic delegations led the campaign to strike the term *grundsätzlich* from the constitution. Independent Socialist Luise Zietz asserted passionately that women and men bore equal obligations in relation to the state: women's "*Erfüllung der Mutterpflicht*" (fulfillment of their duties as mothers) was comparable to the sacrifices soldiers made for their fatherland. Zietz contended creatively with the legacy of prewar maternalist feminism when she responded to an apparent barrage of arguments explicating the fundamental differences between the sexes. Equality, she observed somewhat ironically, did not mean that women would have to become soldiers, a prospect that was unlikely in any case, she observed, given the foreseeable abolition of general conscription in Germany under the terms of the peace agreement. *Gleichwertigkeit* (equality), she noted sardonically, had not yet come to mean *Gleichartigkeit* (the same physical essence), particularly with respect to the distinct bodily capacities (*körperliche Veranlagung*) of men and women.[43] Although Zietz's remarks quite explicitly locate citizenships in the real and imagined bodies of soldiers and mothers, the differences between them were not to stand in the way of full civil and political equality. Luise Zietz's much-contested amendment to strike the word *grundsätzlich* from Article 109 was defeated on 15 July 1919 by a vote of 149 to 119.[44]

Under the rubric of "*Gemeinschaftsleben*" (Life in Community), Article 119 placed marriage, "the foundation of family life and the reproduction [*Vermehrung*] of the nation" under the special protection of the constitution. In an intriguing contrast to Article 109, marriage was to be "based on the equality [*Gleichberechtigung*] of both sexes. Reading these two articles in relation to one another reveals the willingness of legislators to locate full equality of the sexes in the private sphere of marriage, an irony that did not escape many of the critics of Article 109.[45] Nor could they overlook the disjuncture between this remarkable declaration of equality and the *Bürgerliches Gesetzbuch* (Civil Code), which favored husbands' dominance over wives with respect to property, employment, and child-rearing. In response feminist legislators moved to overturn the Civil Code, claiming that the two realms of law were inherently contradictory. At the heart of this debate was an issue female activists had pursued in the late 1890s when the women's movement had mobilized to protest the enactment of the new Civil Code, namely, women's right to serve as guardians of their minor children, which the Civil Code prohibited. "Depriving a woman of the right to represent or protect her children is the bitterest injustice that one can do to a mother who has borne her children at the risk of her own life," argued Zietz, once again aligning the sacrifices of motherhood with those of soldiers as citizens in service of the nation.[46] On the grounds that "men and women have the same rights," the Social Democrats proposed an amendment that would revise the Civil Code "in light of the new constitutional equality between the sexes," which was rejected on 15 July 1919 in a relatively close vote of 144 to 128.[47] The National Assembly contemplated not only the relations within families but the meanings of the German family for the state, a question that weighed heavily on those who sought to repair the wounded nation in the aftermath of war. While Article 119 affirmed equality of the sexes as the foundation of the family in its first paragraph, in the next it spelled out the responsibility of state and communes for the preservation of the *"Reinerhaltung, Gesundung und soziale Förderung der Familie,"* (family's purity, health, and social advancement).[48]

The political meanings of the so-called *Frauenüberschuss* (excess of women) also resonated in the debates about women's new constitutional rights. Among these 2 million some "excess" women were thousands of unmarried mothers who were likely to remain single given the high loss of life among men of their cohort. Also at stake were the military benefits for tens of thousands of illegitimate children of soldiers, whose support was terminated by the state at the end of the war. Fitting the fate of single mothers and their children into the new notion of citizenship based in marriage and family proved a challenging task for the assembly.[49] The assertion of Article 121, for example, to establish "the same conditions for physical, spiritual, and social development for both legitimate and illegitimate children"[50] contradicted rather obviously the emphasis on marriage as the "foundation of family life." Thus, feminist delegates' call for the full integration of illegitimate children in the legal entity of family with respect to inheritance and child support failed on the grounds that it would violate the sanctity of marriage, which was at the heart of Article 119.[51] The constitution's extension of state protection of and provision for motherhood, articulated in Article 119, did not draw an explicit distinction between married and unwed mothers. Yet a Social Democratic amendment proposing that unwed mothers be permitted to call themselves "Frau" in their dealings with state bureaucracies, went through a third reading only to be "swept under the table."[52] The restriction of this designation "Frau," of the right to name oneself, to married women makes explicit the inscription of female citizenship in bodies, explicitly in the bodies of mothers and married women. Ultimately, the Weimar constitution's reaffirmation of marriage and delineation of the social and reproductive tasks of the family worked to stabilize a nation at a point of profound crisis. In qualifying women's rights as citizens (in Article 109), the new legislation bound women to families (Article 119) and called upon German women to place their bodies in the service of state and nation.[53]

Swirling through the sources I examined here is a sense that the real work of defining citizenship and making it meaningful had only just begun in 1918: "The break with those who held power until now does not bring our task to an end," noted one contributor to the journal Die Frauenbewegung: "Rather we are standing at the edge of something totally new that we must now create."[54] The density and richness of political vision and debate that fills the pages of journals such as Die Staatsbürgerin, Die Frauenbewegung, Zeitschrift für Frauen-stimmrecht, Die Frau, and Die Frau im Staat, along with the Social Democratic organs Die Gleichheit, its successor paper Die Genossin, and in other remarkable accounts like those from the floor of the Nationalversammlung as it crafted the constitution, makes clear that citizenship became a new imaginary, not least be-cause of the extraordinary engagement of women who, as acting subjects, both intervened in discourses and involved themselves in the realms of citizenship practices.[55] This evidence points to the enormous capacity of new citizenship rights to inspire women's serious and systematic reimaginings of the political.[56] Of course, many of the authors and contributors to this genre of the feminist political tract had written and agitated for the right of women to political par-ticipation for decades before the war. Yet 1918–19 marks a turning point not least because the spaces for citizenship widened within every political milieu and party, and also because feminists were eager to experience citizenship, to prove themselves as citizens at a time when the state had to be rebuilt and the nation had come apart at the seams.[57] Indeed some feminists, disavowing all responsibility for the disastrous war and defeat, defined themselves as citizens who were unencumbered by the past and thus better able to envision a wholly new future than men.[58]

The apparent fact that women did not achieve *equality* or that these explic-itly political arenas would become sites of bitter and violent strife, that many of the most engaged women turned their attention from the political to the social, or were forced to do so, does not lessen the significance of their input and experiences within them. Just as the transformations of the war years lived on in subjectivities well past 1918, so did the new experiences of citizenship resonate in, but also beyond, these very realms of the political where they took shape.

Conclusion: The Subjectivity of Citizenship in Weimar Germany

The arenas of citizenship that were established amidst the refounding of na-tion and state became an important site at which Weimar politics contended with the ruptures in gender ideologies that occurred during the war. Read as an attempt to repair these fractures represented by defeat and revolution, the declaration of women's citizenship can be made to fit the modern narratives of closure that measure short-term gains or losses only to conclude that these moments of transformation had no longer-term consequences for gender, women, or politics during the Weimar Republic. An alternative view is that women's acquisition of citizenship rights opened possibilities for the emergence of new female subjectivities and self-representations, which at the very least made gender a site of continuous contention throughout the history of the republic. The gulf between the official articulations of citizenship and women's own interpretation or experience of this contradictory catalog of rights and duties demarcates the very space in which new subject positions were formed in the early years of the Weimar Republic.

One preliminary conclusion of this study is, then, that the subject position of citizen marked an abrupt and significant change in the volatile landscape of gender in postwar Germany. The work of female activists in fashioning and defending their new rights represents a critical chapter in the delimitation of Weimar democracy, at the level of both political discourses and day-to-day practices. And it is worth noting that despite the array of social and political institutions that worked vigorously to reinstate familiar gender relations and norms throughout the republic, neither citizenship rights nor the subjectivities they produced were reversible. To what extent, then, did the discourses about the "new woman" represent unease and apprehension about women as citizens who, in this one sense at least, could not be reassigned to the private sphere? There are many suggestions that women intellectuals, artists, and novelists played with this very ambiguity in their disparate representations of new women. The coolly critical gazes of the female figures in Marianne Brandt's photo-collages (see essay by Elizabeth Otto in this volume) depict women observing skeptically or bemusedly the marching armies, graveyards, and children playing with toy weapons or bombs exploding, a man boxing, and volcanoes erupting next to the tranquil scenes of boaters rowing across calm waters. As Elizabeth Otto notes, in Brandt's photomontages the apparent "new woman" is the prominent figure who oversees, and thus assembles, the collage of disparate events and people.[59] Or we might consider the brisance of Irmgard Keun's novel, *Gilgi—eine von uns*, which the Social Democratic newspaper *Vorwärts* serialized in 1932 (see essay by Kerstin Barndt in this volume). Gilgi, a single working girl who eschewed identifications with either her job or her class background, also refused the prospect of marrying the man she loved, choosing instead to bear and raise her child alone.[60] The debates about the fate of girls like Gilgi that took place in the pages of *Vorwärts* not only attest to the popularity of this ambiguous figure of the new woman but also delineate arenas of acceptable and dangerous citizenship for women in the late years of the republic.[61] The fact that female flaneurs, who mastered "the art of taking a walk" in the urban spaces of Weimar, or the "little shop girls," who flocked to the movies, were at one and the same time new *citizens* seems worthy of critical reflection, both with respect to the history of women and the history of Weimar's modernity and viability as a site of new democratic publics.[62]

These examples suggest the importance of exploring the ways in which consumption, leisure, and mass culture complicated the terrain of citizenship, which came to involve new "notions of the self, of collective identity and of entitlement associated with the diffusion of mass consumption."[63] So the new legal category of female citizenship might be conceived as forming a stage for the "new woman of the metropolis," whose newness was defined not least by an explicitly embodied representation of self. While the female flaneur, as a specific kind of "new woman," may seem inherently depoliticized and far removed from parliament or political parties, the attention this female figure garnered in the literature and culture of Weimar Germany reveals a deep apprehension, not only about women in public, but more specifically about women in public who were now endowed with the rights of citizenship. Tracing the thread of *gender* through the republic, rather than measuring the losses or gains of *women*, makes clear that the project of healing these ruptures lived on until the republic's collapse.

Notes

This essay took shape in the privileged moments shared with the "Weimar group" at the University of Michigan. It is part of my larger research project, "In the Aftermath of War: Gender and Citizenship in Weimar Germany." This essay first appeared in Kathleen Canning, *Gender History in Practice: Historical Perspectives on Bodies, Class and Citizenship* (Ithaca, NY, 2006), 212–37. It is reprinted here with permission of Cornell University Press.

  1. David Held: "Between State and Civil Society: Citizenship," in *Citizenship*, ed. Geoff Andrews (London, 1991), 19–25.
  2. Rogers Brubaker, *Citizenship and Nationhood in France and Germany* (Cambridge, MA, 1992). Also see Andreas K. Fahrmeir, "Nineteenth-Century German Citizenships: A Reconsideration," *The Historical Journal* 40, no. 3 (1997): 721–52; Dieter Gosewinkel, "Die Staatsangehörigkeit als Institution des Nationalstaats: Zur Entstehung des Reichs- und Staatsangehörigkeitsgesetzes vom 1913," in *Offene Staatlichkeit: Festschrift für Ernst-Wolfgang Böckenförde zum 65. Geburtstag*, ed. Rolf Grawert et al. (Berlin, 1995), 359–78; and the monographs by Dieter Gosewinkel, *Einbürgern und Ausschließen: die Nationalisierung der Staatsangehörigkeit vom Deutschen Bund bis zur Bundesrepublik Deutschland* (Göttingen, 2001) and Andreas Fahrmeir, *Citizens and Aliens: Foreigners and the Law in Britain and the German States, 1789–1870* (New York, 2000).
  3. Bryan Turner, "Contemporary Problems in the Theory of Citizenship," in *Citizenship and Social Theory*, ed. Bryan Turner (London, 1993).
  4. Sociologist Margaret Somers analyzes citizenship as a "narrative identity," constituted "by a person's temporally and spatially variable 'place' in culturally constructed stories … comprised of rules, practices, institutions, and the multiple lots of family, nation, or economic life." See Margaret R. Somers and Gloria D. Gibson, "Reclaiming the Epistemological 'Other:' Narrative and the Social Constitution of Identity, in *From Persons*

to *Nations: The Social Constitution of Identities*, ed. Craig Calhoun (London, 1994), 33. Also see Somers, "Citizenship and the Place of the Public Sphere: Law, Community and Political Culture in the Transition to Democracy," *American Sociological Review* 58, no. 5 (Oct. 1993): 587–620.

5. Ann Taylor Allen, *Feminism and Motherhood in Germany, 1800–1914* (New Brunswick, NJ, 1991), 48, 136–38; Anna Schulz, "Frauenforderungen an die Gesetzgebung," in *Mutterschaft: ein Sammelwerk für die Probleme des Weibes als Mutter*, ed. Adele Schreiber (Munich, 1912), 672–87.

6. See Renate Bridenthal, Atina Grossmann, and Marion Kaplan, eds., *When Biology Became Destiny: Women in Weimar and Nazi Germany* (New York, 1984), which had a field-defining role.

7. Eve Rosenhaft, "Women, Gender and the Limits of Political History," in *Elections, Mass Politics and Social Change in Modern Germany: New Perspectives*, eds. James Retallack and Larry E. Jones (Cambridge, 1992), 148.

8. Charles Maier, *Recasting Bourgeois Europe: Stabilization in France, Germany, and Italy in the Decade after World War I* (Princeton, NJ, 1975).

9. Exceptions here include: Julia Sneeringer, *Winning Women's Votes: Propaganda and Politics in Weimar Germany* (Chapel Hill, NC, 2002), which examines the constructions of female citizenship by party political propaganda; and Heidemarie Lauterer's *Parliamentarierinnen in Deutschland 1918/19–1949* (Königstein, 2002).

10. Thomas Childers, "Languages of Liberalism: Liberal Political Discourse in the Weimar Republic," in *In Search of a Liberal Germany*, eds. Konrad Jarausch and Larry Eugene Jones (London, 1990), 326.

11. Belinda Davis, *Home Fires Burning: Food, Politics and Everyday Life in World War I Berlin* (Chapel Hill, NC, 2000); Robert Weldon Whalen, *Bitter Wounds: German Victims of the Great War, 1914–1939* (Ithaca, NY, 1984); Deborah Cohen, *The War Come Home: Disabled Veterans in Britain and Germany, 1914–39* (Berkeley, CA, 2001); and Sabine Kienitz, *Beschädigte Helden: Kriegsinvalidität und Körperbilder 1914–1923* (Paderborn, 2008). Also see Sabine Kienitz, "'Fleischgewordenes Elend': Kriegsinvalidität und Körperbilder als Teil einer Erfahrungsgeschichte des Ersten Weltkrieges," in *Die Erfahrung des Krieges. Erfahrungsgeschichtliche Perspektiven von der französischen Revolution bis zum zweiten Weltkrieg*, eds. Nikolaus Buschmann and Horst Carl (Paderborn, 2001). For a British comparison, see Joanna Bourke, *Dismembering the Male: Men's Bodies, Britain and the Great War* (Chicago, 1996).

12. Whalen, *Bitter Wounds*, 16.

13. International Institute of Social History (IISH), Amsterdam: Rat des Volksbeauftragten, Protokolle, 14.12.1918–31.12.1918. See especially: "Aufruf des Rates der Volksbeauftragten an das deutsche Volk vom 12. November 1918." Also see Susanne Miller, ed., *Quellen zur Geschichte des Parlamentarismus und der politischen Parteien*, vol. 6: *Die Regierung der Volksbeauftragten 1918/19* (Düsseldorf, 1969).

14. The female membership of the Social Democratic Textile Workers' Union (DTAV), for example, increased 450% (by 260,000 members) between December 1918 and the late fall of 1920. Some 90% of German women voters cast their ballots in the first democratic election in January 1919.

15. Peter Fritzsche, "Did Weimar Fail?" *Journal of Modern History* 68, no. 3 (September 1996): 632–33.

16. Richard Bessel, *Germany after the First World War* (Oxford, 1993); and Elizabeth Domansky, "Militarization and Reproduction in World War I Germany," in *Society,*

Culture and State in Germany, 1870–1930, ed. Geoff Eley (Ann Arbor, MI, 1996), 427–63. Both Bessel and Domansky view much of the early history of Weimar in terms of the desire for a "return for normalcy," even if from very different standpoints. Martin Geyer's *Verkehrte Welt. Revolution, Inflation und Moderne* (München, 1998) is a notable exception to this viewpoint. For the period of the inflation, see Bernd Widdig, *Culture and Inflation in Weimar Germany* (Berkeley, CA, 2001). On the conflicted visions of modernity in Weimar, see Mary Nolan, *Visions of Modernity: American Business and Modernization of Germany* (New York, 1994).

17. Davis, *Home Fires Burning* and Ute Daniel, *The War from Within: German Working-Class Women in the First World War* (Oxford, 1997).

18. Benjamin Ziemann's recent essays on the memory of the war and on masculinity and militarism mark an important exception here. See, for example, his "'Gedanken eines Reichsbannermannes auf Grund von Erlebnissen und Erfahrungen.' Politische Kultur, Flaggensymbolik und Kriegserinnerung in Schmalkalden 1926. Dokumentation," *Zeitschrift des Vereins für Thuringische Geschichte* 53 (1999): 201–32, and the useful essay collection: Benjamin Ziemann and Bernd Ulrich, eds., *Krieg im Frieden: Die umkämpfte Erinnerung an den Ersten Weltkrieg: Quellen und Dokumente* (Frankfurt, 1997). Also see Ziemann, *Front und Heimat. Ländliche Kriegserfahrungen im südlichen Bayern 1914–23* (Essen, 1997).

19. Daniel, *War From Within*.

20. Katharina von Ankum, ed., *Women in the Metropolis: Gender and Modernity in Weimar Culture* (Berkeley, CA, 1997), 6.

21. Daniel, *War From Within*, 293–94.

22. Maria Tatar, *Lustmord. Sexual Murder in Weimar Germany* (Princeton, NJ, 1995); Brigid Doherty, "Figures of the Pseudorevolution," *October* 84 (Spring 1998) and "'We are all Neurasthenics!' or the Trauma of Dada Montage," *Critical Inquiry* 24, no. 1 (Autumn 1997); Dora Apel, "'Heroes' and 'Whores': The Politics of Gender in Weimar Antiwar Imagery," in *Art Bulletin* 79, no. 3 (1997); Patrice Petro, *Joyless Streets: Women and Melodramatic Representation in Weimar Germany* (Princeton, NJ, 1989); Kerstin Barndt, *Sentiment und Sachlichkeit. Der Roman der Neuen Frau in der Weimarer Republik* (Köln, 2003); and Richard McCormick, *Gender and Sexuality in Weimar Modernity: Film, Literature and "New Objectivity"* (New York, 2001).

23. Susanne Rouette, *Sozialpolitik als Geschlechterpolitik: Die Regulierung der Frauenarbeit nach dem Ersten Weltkrieg* (Frankfurt am Main, 1993).

24. Christiane Eifert, "Coming to Terms with the State: Maternalist Politics and the Development of the Welfare State in Germany," *Central European History* 30, no. 1 (1997): 45–46. Also see the path-breaking work of Young-sun Hong: "The Contradictions of Modernization in the German Welfare State: Gender and the Politics of Welfare Reform in First World War Germany," *Social History* 17 (1992): 251–70, and her *Welfare, Modernity and the Weimar State, 1919–1933* (Princeton, NJ, 1998).

25. Hong, "Gender, Citizenship and the Welfare State," 2.

26. Anne Phillips, "Citizenship and Feminist Theory," in Andrews, *Citizenship*, 76–88, see especially 79.

27. Bundesarchiv, Akten der Reichskanzlei (R43, nr. 22a): Streiks 20. November 1918–14. March 1919; Reichskanzlei Akte 548, Filme 12025/12026: Stammakten, 11 Handel & Gewerbe, Nr. 15(9), Ausstände: Streikbewegung 10. Januar 1918–9. März 1918.

28. Daniel, *The War From Within*, 235, 247, 292.

29. Whalen, *Bitter Wounds*, 95–99.

30. Ibid., 76–78, 109.

31. Martha Karnoss, "Organisation der Kriegerwitwen," *Reichsbund* 20 May 1932, 106, as cited in ibid. I am in the process of completing my own evaluation of this valuable periodical.

32. Whalen describes an eerie demonstration of war victims on 22 December 1918, with trucks of paraplegics leading the way, followed by the blind, guided by their dogs, and lastly, the widows and orphans, in *Bitter Wounds*, 124.

33. Gerald D. Feldman, *Army, Industry, and Labor in Germany, 1914–1918* (Providence, RI, 1992 [1966]), 337–41, 446–50; also see Geyer, *Verkehrte Welt*, 48, 100. Feldman does not make a direct connection between calls for suffrage and the formulation of the *Dolchstoßlegende*; his analysis of the strikes of April 1917 and January 1918 suggests, however, that this connection is plausible. Geyer makes a somewhat different point about the implication of women in the "stab in the back" theory: he cites the views of psychologist Emil Kräpelin on the failure of women to endure the long-term deprivation of war that "morally destabilized the home front" and left it unable to hold out.

34. *Die deutsche Nationalversammlung im Jahre 1919 [und 1920] in ihrer Arbeit für den Aufbau des neuen deutschen Volksstaates*, ed. Geh. Justizrat Prof. Dr. Eduard Heilfron, vol. 1, 12. Sitzung, 20. February 1919, 159.

35. The exact citation is: "Über Nacht fiel aus der Gewitterwolke das Frauenstimmrecht hernieder." Marie Bunsen, "Wir Wählerinnen," *Vossische Zeitung* 624, no. 286 (Ausgabe A, 6. Dezember 1918): 2.

36. Helene Lange Archiv, Berlin, Aktenzeichen 1062: Dr. Agnes von Harnack, *Die Frauen und das Wahlrecht*, ed. Ausschuß der Frauenverbände Deutschlands (Vorbereitung der Frauen für die Nationalversammlung. Deutscher Staatsbürgerinnen-Verband e.V.) (n.d.). This pamphlet was likely published in the months between the proclamation of women's suffrage and the January 1919 elections to the National Assembly.

37. Wilhelm Ziegler, *Die deutsche Nationalversammlung 1919/1920 und Ihr Verfassungswerk* (Berlin, 1932), 29–30. Ziegler cites the account by Ferdinand Runkel: *Die deutsche Revolution*.

38. Ziegler, *Die deutsche Nationalversammlung*, 30. Not surprisingly, the Communist Party refused to participate in the election, which delegated and authorized the parties of Weimar to undertake the formation of the republic: the Social Democratic Party (163 delegates), the Democratic Party (75 delegates), and the Catholic Center Party (90 delegates) held 338 of 421 seats in the Assembly, while the Independent Social Democrats (USPD) had 22 seats and the nationalist party (DNVP) 42 seats.

39. Christel Wickert, *Unsere Erwählten: Sozialdemokratische Frauen im Deutschen Reichstag und im Preussischen Landtag 1919 bis 1933*, vol. 2 (Göttingen 1986), 64.

40. Article 109 reads: "Alle Deutsche sind vor dem Gesetz gleich. Männer und Frauen haben *grundsätzlich* dieselben staatsbürgerlichen Rechte und Pflichten." It is worth noting that Hugo Preuss's draft of Part I, "Die Einzelperson" reads: "Alle Deutschen sind vor dem Gesetze gleichberechtigt" without mention of women or men. See *Die Verfassung des Deutschen Reichs vom 11. August 1919* (Stuttgart, n.d.), 36–37. For a comparison of Preuss's draft and the final version of the constitution, see Ziegler, *Die deutsche Nationalversammlung*. Also see the new collection, *Weimar und die deutsche Verfassung: Geschichte und Aktualität von 1919*, ed. Deutsche Nationalstiftung (Stuttgart, 1999).

41. Willibalt Apelt, *Geschichte der Weimarer Verfassung* (Munich, 1946), 306–7.

42. Fritz Stier-Stomlo, "Artikel 109: Gleichheit vor dem Gesetz," in *Die Grundrechte und Grundpflichten der Reichsverfassung: Kommentar zum zweiten Teil der Reichsverfassung,* ed. Hans-Carl Nipperdey (Berlin, 1929), 201–3.
43. For the debates on Article 109, see *Die Nationalversammlung,* vol. 6, 54. Sitzung, 3653; 57. Sitzung, Dienstag, den 15. Juli 1919, 3812–26.
44. *Die Nationalversammlung,* vol. 6, 54. Sitzung, 3653; 57. Sitzung, Dienstag, den 15. Juli 1919, 3812–26.
45. Ziegler, *Die deutsche Nationalversammlung,* 329–30. This article is in Part II of the "Basic Rights and Basic Duties of Germans."
46. *Die Nationalversammlung,* vol. 6, 54. Sitzung, Freitag, den 11. Juli 1919, Sitzung, 3653. For a discussion of this article, see *Gewerkschaftliche Frauenzeitung* 4, no. 2 (29.1.1919): "Die Frau im bürgerlichen Recht"; Gertrud Lodahl, "Die Weimarer Verfassung und die Frauen," *Gewerkschaftliche Frauenzeitung* 4, no. 17 (27 August 1919); and Dr. jur. Anna Mayer, "Neue Rechte-Neue Pflichten," in "Die Frau in der Politik," Beilage der Wochenschrift, *Deutsche Stimmen* (18 January 1920), nr. 2.
47. *Die Nationalversammlung,* vol. 6, 3825.
48. Dr. h.c. Alfred Wieruszowski, "Artikel 119: Ehe, Familie, Mutterschaft," in Nipperdey, *Grundrechte und Grundpflichten,* 72–79.
49. Christian J. Klumker, "Artikel 121: Stellung der unehelichen Kinder," in Nipperdey, *Grundrechte und Grundpflichten,* vol. 2, 107–9.
50. Ziegler, *Die deutsche Nationalversammlung,* 329–30.
51. Wieruszowski, "Artikel 119," 79–80.
52. Lodahl, "Die Weimarer Verfassung und die Frauen."
53. See the interesting commentary on these points in Wieruszowski, 75–78, 89.
54. Elisabeth von Rotten, "Ansprache bei der Kundgebung zum Rechtsfrieden," in *Die Frauenbewegung* 23 (1918): 19.
55. Regine Deutsch, *Die politische Tat der Frau: Aus der Nationalversammlung* (Gotha, 1920); *Frauenstimmen aus der Nationalversammlung. Beiträge der sozialdemokratischen Volksvertreterinnen zu den Zeitfragen,* ed. Buchhandlung Vorwärts (SPD) (Berlin, 1920); Camilla Jellinek, *Die Frau im neuen Deutschland* (Stuttgart, 1920). Selected articles include: Alice Salomon, "Der Ausschuß zur Vorbereitung der Frauen für die Nationalversammlung," *Die Frauenfrage* 21 (1919); Marianne Weber, "Parlamentarische Arbeitsformen," *Die Frau* 26 (1919); "Republik-Demokratie-Nationalversammlung," in *Zeitschrift für Frauenstimmrecht* Nov. 1918; Gertrud Bäumer, "Die deutsche Verfassung und die Frau," in *Die Frau* 26 (1919) and "Die Frauen und die Nationalversammlung," in *Die Frauenfrage* 21 (1919): 3–4.
56. *Die Frauenfrage, Zentralblatt des Bundes deutscher Frauenvereine,* ed. Marie Stritt; *Die Frau,* the "theoretical organ" of the BDF, eds. Helene Lange und G. Bäumer; *Die Staatsbürgerin,* published by the Deutscher Verband für Frauenstimmrecht, ed. Adele Schreiber, later Marie Stritt; *Die Frauenbewegung. Organ für das politische Leben der Frau,* and supplement, *Zeitschrift für Frauenstimmrecht,* published by the Berliner Verein Frauenwohl, ed. Minna Cauer. The women's supplement of the Independent Social Democratic Party was entitled *Aus der Frauenbewegung,* Frauenbeilage der *Freiheit, Berliner Organ der USPD.*
57. Sneeringer, *Winning Women's Votes.*
58. Schreiber, "Revolution und Frauenrecht," 9. Her formulation was: "Wir treten unbelastet in die Politik."

59. See Elizabeth Otto, "Figuring Gender: Photomontage and Cultural Critique in Germany's Weimar Republic" (PhD diss., University of Michigan, Department of the History of Art, 2003).
60. Irmgard Keun, *Gilgi—eine von uns* (1932); Barndt, *Sentiment und Sachlichkeit*, 150–165; Anke Gleber, *The Art of Taking a Walk: Flanerie, Literature and Film in Weimar Culture* (Princeton, NJ, 1999). According to Barndt, the novel appeared in forty-nine installments between 24 August 1932 and 25 October 1932.
61. The novel was so popular that *Vorwärts* called upon its readers to compose essays for prize competitions on "Scenes from Life and Career" with particular consideration of the "The Crisis of Our Time." Barndt, *Sentiment und Sachlichkeit*, 150–52.
62. See, for example, Siegfried Kracauer, "Die kleinen Ladenmädchen gehen ins Kino," in *Das Ornament der Masse* (Frankfurt am Main, 1977), 279–94; Gleber, *The Art of Taking a Walk*; Petro, *Joyless Streets*, esp. 19–21; and Patrice Petro, "Perceptions of Difference: Woman as Spectator and Spectacle," in von Ankum, *Women in the Metropolis*, 41–66.
63. Victoria de Grazia, "Nationalizing Women: The Competition between Fascist and Commercial Cultural Models in Mussolini's Italy," in *The Sex of Things: Gender and Consumption in Historical Perspective*, eds. Victoria de Grazia and Ellen Furlough (Berkeley, CA, 1996), 356. Also see Eve Rosenhaft, "Lesewut, Kinosucht, Radiotismus. Zur (geschlechter-) politischen Relevanz neuer Massenmedien in den 1920er Jahren," in *Amerikanisierung: Traum und Alptraum im Deutschland des 20. Jahrhunderts*, ed. Alf Lüdtke (Stuttgart, 1996), 119–43.

CHAPTER 6

~:~

Feminist Politics
beyond the Reichstag
Helene Stöcker and Visions of Reform

KRISTIN MCGUIRE

Headlines in Berlin dailies in the early months of 1919—and especially in the women's press—were full of calls for women to recognize their privileges and duties as citizens (*Staatsbürgerinnen*) of the new republic. Slogans such as "Women, learn to vote!" "Women in the forefront!" and "Voting rights are voting duties!" called women into the new democratic polity where they were to be equal, voting members. Gaining suffrage and constitutional equality marked a moment of triumph for many women who had been active in suffrage campaigns since the late nineteenth century. The enthusiasm surrounding the vote was reflected in the first elections of 1919, when nearly 80 percent of eligible women cast their vote and thirty-six women were elected to the National Assembly. As one Social Democratic woman exclaimed, "We have voted, we have sent women to all levels of local and state government, and we have helped to write the constitution. … We have created the necessary foundation upon which we can build that equality which alone will make us free."[1]

Although excitement about the vote prevailed among women activists, some disputed the idea that suffrage was the foundation of equality. Helene Stöcker, an activist who had been advocating women's rights in education, work, politics, and sexuality since the 1890s, urged people to think beyond suffrage.[2] She had long viewed universal suffrage as a necessary part of any democratic polity and assumed that with the collapse of the *Kaiserreich*, it would finally be granted. Like other feminists, Stöcker appealed to women to use their vote. Yet she remained skeptical about the long-term significance of the vote as a tool for meaningful social or political change. This skepticism reflected Stöcker's fierce conviction—even more pronounced after the war—that legal and political reform meant nothing without profound cultural change toward a world anchored in new understandings of "love" and what she called motherliness (*Mütterlichkeit*). As director of the Bund für Mutterschutz und Sexualreform (The Association for the Protection of Mothers and Sexual Reform, or the Bund) and editor of its monthly journal, *New Generation*, Stöcker's primary work was to advocate change in how people understood motherhood and sexuality. Historians have often understood Stöcker as a promoter of maternalist politics, which envisioned women gaining access to public and political space specifically because of their essential maternal attributes. Maternalism was a prominent discourse and political strategy among women activists in early twentieth-century Germany. A large body of historical literature on women in the Weimar Republic has considered the tension between essentializing discourses of maternalism on the one hand and visions of political equality on the other. Some scholars have concluded that maternalism and political equality were incompatible, while others have emphasized the gains made in political and social realms through maternalist strategies.[3]

Although *Mütterlichkeit* was at the core of Stöcker's postwar political vision, she did not promote maternalist politics in the classic sense. Stöcker differed radically from feminist leaders such as Helene Lange and Gertrude Bäumer who viewed motherhood itself as women's ticket to citizenship and who, furthermore, believed that inserting women into political life would necessarily improve the moral terrain of politics.[4] Stöcker did not assume that "woman as such will bring about a better era than that which men are capable of achieving."[5] Arguing that the terms of politics had to be changed, Stöcker wrote:

> It is not always the primary fact that is the most essential, such as the fact that woman has come of age politically in the sense that she obtains the suffrage and the right to take part in state affairs. This goes without saying and today is no longer contested even by the middle parties. But the achievement of these formal rights remains useless and unfruitful unless another development proceeds alongside it: perhaps born from the motherly experience of woman, it is the development of that which grants more power to humanity, to the good, and to love.[6]

It fell to both men and women, Stöcker argued, to embody motherliness and thus to create the conditions for a new politics and a new society.

Interpreting Stöcker's activism in terms of maternalism obscures what was a radical vision for postwar political and social change. Stöcker's proposals encompassed an explosive and complex mixture of ideas, including a Romantic ideal of the transformative power of love on the one hand and a belief in eugenic notions of human improvement on the other. Her understanding of women's equality was not based on women as reproducers or as mothers, but rather as evolved individuals committed to a society that nurtured future generations. Stöcker imagined new relations between the individual and the state grounded in a common commitment by everyone to pacifism as the necessary foundation of a solid democracy. She wrote prolifically after the war and engaged passionately in debates that expressed both the apprehensions and the profound hopes of intellectuals and activists as they started to imagine a new society after the war.

In considering Stöcker's portrayal of postwar Germany and her ideas of motherliness as a response to the violence of war, both the radical potential of Stöcker's ideas and also their limits and contradictions become apparent. Stöcker contested standard ideas of gender and politics, but she also set boundaries that defined and prescribed rights and roles. While advocating new possibilities for men and women in both public and in the home, she clearly inscribed women in gender-specific roles (woman's fundamental task, Stöcker wrote, was as educator, protector, and life giver). While exalting democracy and universal participation in the government, Stöcker insisted that only a small group of elite was evolved enough to lead the way. While seeking to forge a connection between personal transformation and political renewal, Stöcker deliberately remained in the realm of utopian and idealist visions that lacked concrete political engagement. Examining how Stöcker wove together core values that now seem paradoxical reveals many of the conflicting ideas that utopian activists and intellectuals embraced in Germany as they tried to make sense of the violence and destruction of the war and the unclear future once the war was over.

The Urgent Stakes in the Wake of War

Throughout the first decade of the twentieth century Stöcker charged full force ahead in her work to promote what she called the *"neue Ethik,"* a philosophy of social change grounded in new understandings of love and sexuality. She and her colleagues at the Bund advocated sexual autonomy and pleasure for women and men, believing that this was the key to personal betterment and ultimately social progress as well. Very much in the spirit of Edward Carpenter's vision of the "new life," Bund members understood themselves as "exploring the interconnections between the transformation of personal life and wider external, radical social change."[7] Stöcker believed that the life-affirming power of spiritual and sensual sexuality led to individual transformation, which in turn maximized and enhanced individual participation in and contribution to society. In her capacity as director of the Bund, Stöcker promoted legislation that offered women choices in the realm of sexuality, including access to birth control and contraception, expanding the rights of single mothers to financial and social support, and revoking the prohibition against marriage for civil servants. Stöcker wrote regularly about birth control and sexual autonomy and lectured throughout Germany and abroad; she was fully engaged in this work when war broke out in 1914. Even though Stöcker frequented international conferences throughout Europe in the years leading up to 1914 and was well aware of heightened tensions in European politics, she described the declaration of war as "striking like a sudden bolt of lightning from the sky."[8]

The enthusiasm Stöcker witnessed among many of her intellectual and activist colleagues when war was announced baffled her. In her war diaries, she described with despair the scene on Unter den Linden, in the middle of Berlin, on 31 July 1914—"crowds, excited people, thoughtless enthusiasm, confused passion."[9] Although recent research suggests that the response in Germany to war in late summer 1914 encompassed more reactions than unified enthusiasm,[10] Stöcker felt surrounded in Berlin by colleagues and friends who unambivalently supported the war. Stöcker expressed particular shock and dismay when her good friend and long-time colleague at the Bund, the SPD Reichstag deputy Eduard David, announced the party's support for the war credits in the Reichstag on 4 August. She reported animated debate with David over his conviction that support of the war effort would garner rewards, such as universal suffrage in Prussia and a package of social reforms. Stöcker saw it as logically impossible to stand for the ideals of the Bund while actively supporting the war. Embracing prominent ideas of social Darwinism, she had always believed that Bund members, such as David, were "evolved" individuals who actively pursued personal and social awareness and sought to achieve higher ideals of community.[11] Support for the "killing machines" of the war was an obvious rejection of these ideals, she claimed.[12] Stöcker had always drawn a firm line in her work between the masses and the vanguard, and her elitism grew more acute during the war. She argued that war nurtured a herd mentality and she questioned what seemed to be a blind acceptance of Germany's politics: "Is this some kind of accommodation to the great masses? I don't understand it. We are scattered, like lost sheep, those of us who do not think and feel as the majority."[13]

Immediately after the outbreak of war, Stöcker increased her activities in the international pacifist movement. She was already a member of the German Peace Society, founded by the well-known pacifist Bertha von Suttner in 1892, but had remained somewhat inactive before the war.[14] In 1914, however, she increased her contacts with active pacifists in Germany, such as Ludwig Quidde, one of Germany's most prominent pacifists of the early twentieth century. Stöcker was a founding member of the League for the New Fatherland (Bund Neues Vaterland), the most visible pacifist organization during the war, and she also participated in the international women's peace conference at The Hague in 1915.[15] She viewed her pacifist activism as a natural outgrowth of her work in the Bund, arguing that sexual reform and the protection of motherhood were meaningless in a society where there was total disregard for human life. She asked what good is it "to deck the main hall of a house whose very foundations have not yet been set?" Thus, in response to the sheer violence and killing of the war, Stöcker melded her efforts for sexual reform and her pacifist activism. She no longer viewed the "new morality" as relevant only to personal relationships.[16] The war made it clear, she argued, that new moral terms were as critical in the arenas of politics as in the realm of sexuality: "We have now learned that not only sexual life, but also the life of the state and of the people will perish in disorder and ruin as long as we tolerate a domain of double morality."[17]

By 1918, Stöcker argued that the demands of total war had drastically changed German society. Militarization had come to dominate the very fabric of social relations, making violence and aggression the new common sense. Individuals had become numb to the horrors of war, accustomed to death and to disfigured bodies hobbling through the streets.[18] Stöcker criticized the state for commending the births of sons as future soldiers and she lamented the intellectuals and artists who extolled the soldiers dying for the homeland. She viewed the general acceptance of brutality during war as obliterating the value of the individual person. In particular to her work in the Bund, Stöcker decried the state's interest in mothers and children during the war; changes in policy that improved conditions for out-of-wedlock children, for example, could not be seen as "successes" when the motivation of the policy was to produce cannon fodder.[19]

Stöcker argued that the war had fundamentally changed the domain of politics as well, again because violence had become an accepted norm. Even as Stöcker welcomed the end of the *Kaiserreich*, she was critical of a revolution based in bloodshed. She saw the street fighting in cities throughout Germany at the end of the war and the revolutionary battles that pitted Germans against each other as evidence that violence was tolerated as political might. In her monthly cover article for the *New Generation* in January 1919, Stöcker argued that violence, hypocrisy, and isolated concentrations of power were defining the young republic. "Is this civil war to be the end of the transformation that we welcomed with great hope; is the old militarized Germany simply becoming a new one?"[20] In the same issue of the journal, Stöcker mourned the brutal murders of Karl Liebknecht and Rosa Luxemburg. She wrote at greater length about political murders when the independent Socialist leader, Kurt Eisner, was killed a month later. In February 1919, just as Eisner lost in the first election of the Bavarian Republic and stepped down from the revolutionary government, the aristocrat Count Arco-Valley assassinated him. Stöcker viewed Eisner's murder as a sinister sign for the republic, as a definitive moment when naïve violence had won out over authentic democratic leadership.

Stöcker described Eisner as embodying a "new spirit" of leadership.[21] Important to Stöcker was that Eisner was an intellectual—he had studied philosophy and published a book on Nietzsche, and had also worked for many years as a journalist. Eisner was also committed to pacifist ideas. He had served time in prison for antiwar agitation and during the revolution he sought alternatives to government by force. Stöcker described Eisner as seeking to "change the souls of men" to instill social values of justice and equality.[22] Stöcker viewed Eisner as a true leader of Socialist and democratic ideals and the kind of individual who could bring Germany into a new future based on his commitment to a "renewal of ideas, an acknowledgement of truth, and an insistence on justice." His death, Stöcker wrote, was "a strike in the very heart of the revolution," referring here to an ideal nonviolent revolution based on the transformation of social values and norms.[23]

Stöcker again expressed her rage and exasperation with German political developments when Gustav Landauer, Eisner's comrade and independent Socialist leader during the short-lived Bavarian "*Räte Republik*," was beaten to death in May 1919. The brutality signaled a reign of terror, she wrote, whether from "the old violence of the right or the new street violence of the left."[24] In the fall of 1919, Stöcker reported on the trials against the murderers of Eisner and Landauer. Although the defendants in both cases were charged and found guilty, Count Arco Valley was sentenced only to five years in prison and the soldier who kicked Landauer to death received five weeks of imprisonment. The unjust court proceedings were a frightening example, Stöcker claimed, of a political double standard that made the founding of a real democracy untenable. She sought to convince people that an "unusually sad and dreary future" lay before Germany in the absence of profound reforms in the critical building blocks of democracy, such as the press, the schools, and the justice system.[25] In an article arguing for the demilitarization of Germany, Stöcker wrote, "We must be relentlessly clear. The old system is not defeated. ... The most heated and terrible battles still stand before us."[26]

In the founding months of the republic, Stöcker identified hypocrisy in the political sphere that she likened to double standards in relations between the sexes. She charged the Majority Socialists and Ebert with pandering to the military leaders of the right because of their own fear of losing power.[27] Ebert talked about new leadership and a renewed German state but maintained the institutions of the old ruling classes, Stöcker argued. Analogously, she claimed, many men and women who pronounced their support for equality between the sexes insisted on upholding "archaic ideas" when it came to sexuality. In making an analogy between political and sexual culture, Stöcker equated the hypocrisies she saw in both arenas. But beyond identifying these double standards, Stöcker asserted that fear of losing control hindered change in both the political and sexual realms. In many years of advocating sexual reform, Stöcker confronted the argument of conservative and moderate commentators that "unleashing" women's sexual pleasure would lead to anarchy in family life. The *neue Ethik* challenge to long-held views about sexual mores seemed to invoke fear that the role of the woman as a pillar of moral standards was at risk.[28] Stöcker argued that after the war, a fear of losing government control led those in power to compromise their own Socialist and democratic ideals and to allow the old officers "to hold the government in the palm of their hand."[29]

The analogy prompted Stöcker to argue that the social and cultural change necessary to reform the meaning of love and sexuality in individual lives was also necessary at the level of state and nation. She urged people to recognize "that moral laws, which we first wanted to bring into play only for both sexes within the realm of love, must also come to unconditional sovereignty in state life and in the life of nations between each other."[30] Stöcker insisted on the importance of a Weltanschauung, arguing that a common commitment to fundamental values and beliefs—in her view, to pacifism and to *neue Ethik* ideas about motherhood, love, and sexuality—was essential for political stability. She even wondered if "the explanation for this inexplicable war might be that so few people have any kind of Weltanschauung at all?"[31] Stöcker understood her ideas about an open, more mutual, and more spiritual sexuality as vital to authentic democratic and pacifist politics because individual transformation would lead to a different *practice* of politics. In order to "reconstruct the vigor of the nation," she argued, activists needed to insist on "the revitalization of sexuality, an awakening and strengthening of the desire for life and procreation, and a 'new morality' based in social needs, rooted in responsible individualities, and free from archaic judgments and erroneous ideas."[32] In Stöcker's analysis, a commitment to communitarian and egalitarian notions of the "new life" was missing from both national and international politics after the war.

In hindsight, Stöcker's appeal to the "evolved" individual and the idealized national collective connected to terms such as *vigor, revitalization,* and *procreation* can be read as signaling an extreme vision of politics because similar themes and terms were later adopted by the National Socialists. For Stöcker, however, her ideas about post-war political and social transformation developed from a tradition of a Romantic utopian and Socialist activism. The life-affirming power of spiritual and sensual sexuality—love, in short, in Stöcker's view—led to individual transformation, which in turn maximized and enhanced individual participation in and contribution to society. This connection between love, sexuality, and the potential for social change was the basis of the *neue Ethik*, and Stöcker aimed to cultivate the awareness of this connection, to "awaken all of those who had been sleeping and unwilling to recognize the bridge that connected their individual lives with society and the development of humanity."[33] The language of connection was familiar to Stöcker's contemporaries and suggests another element in her intellectual commitments: monism, which had been a highly popular movement among modernist intellectuals at the turn of the century, based on the conviction that all phenomena in the world are inherently linked.[34] The monist belief in a fundamental unity between mind, spirit, and body, which posited heightened spiritual meaning in physical and emotional experience, particularly sexual, was a powerful leitmotif in Stöcker's work, as both philosopher and activist.[35] Stöcker's emphasis on a communal politics that brought together evolved individuals was based on these ideal notions of connection and spirituality. Her insistence on disseminating these ideas as broadly as possible was part of a culture of intellectual and activist experimentation after the war.

Mütterlichkeit and a New Political Subject

Stöcker was dismayed about the violence that she believed was reigning in Germany after the war, and yet she expressed tremendous hope about the future. The end of the war and the abdication of the Kaiser had opened politics to redefinition—both who should participate and what kinds of governance structures should be created. This was a moment of opportunity, she claimed: "For the first time in world history, from this defeat on the battlefield, a truly new reconstruction of the world should emerge that is connected with internal politics, as well as a vision of international rights and culture."[36] She called on everyone—women, soldiers, workers, and especially intellectuals and activists—to participate in the reconstruction. "Everyone, even those who are usually not concerned with politics, must finally realize that so-called foreign affairs are no longer solely the concern of 'statesmen' or a few 'people's representatives,' but relentlessly take hold of each individual, in life and in death."[37] Bringing more people into the fray of politics and educating them about political values would create a whole new political landscape, Stöcker argued.

Stöcker did not mean conventional political values; rather, she meant quite specifically the values of motherliness (*Mütterlichkeit*). Indeed *Mütterlichkeit* formed the anchor for Stöcker's vision of a radical post-war politics. Stöcker's descriptions of motherliness differed from other feminists' appeal to the maternal. Unlike leaders in the bourgeois feminist movement, Stöcker unconditionally connected motherliness to pacifism. Valuing human life and defying war at any cost were the most basic characteristics of what Stöcker termed *Mütterlichkeit*. She described motherliness as expressing a powerful human desire for generativity—whether through the physical act of creating the next generation or the spiritual and moral act of fostering it. "Just as physical motherhood is the source of physical life, so is motherliness the principle of the preservation of life," Stöcker emphasized.[38] A second central difference that distanced Stöcker from feminist pacifists such as Anita Augspurg and Lida Gustava Heymann was her insistence that while motherliness was a "female way of being," it was not limited to women nor was it inherent in all women. Stöcker's models of motherliness included Jesus, Plato, and Tolstoy because these were individuals who understood the importance of peace and the concept of the development of the self.[39] Men were theoretically capable of motherliness and should be held to these principles. The important point in Stöcker's view was that both men and women needed to be trained—and should be trained—in these traits of motherliness.

Although Stöcker believed that motherliness was not innate in women, she did contend that women had a greater tendency toward its values. She argued that their *potential* to become physical mothers, whether or not they actually did, made women more inclined toward the values of motherliness. Stöcker believed that this capacity for embodying ideals of pacifism and love toward others would enable women to influence post-war society. Women's formal inclusion in public life gave them the opportunity to create the conditions for a new society not because of the vote itself, but because of the increased possibility to manifest the best of what the feminine spirit had to offer. Women could play a significant role not as reproducers of cannon-fodder, Stöcker claimed, but rather as citizens deeply committed to pacifist politics. She challenged the implication that women had earned citizenship rights through their service to the state as mothers, and instead identified a specific female agency based on her belief about woman's potential relationship to sexuality and to life. She brought to light what she viewed as a female agency that the "modern woman" (that is to say, educated, self-aware, sexually autonomous, and always on the course of personal evolution) epitomized. From this model of female agency, Stöcker urged a radical new political subjectivity for all. As the ideal characteristic of all citizens, motherliness implied a democracy based on a philosophy that elevated love, a politics that respected life, and a state committed to peace and humanity rather than violence and death.

While motherliness was to bring women into political life, it was not a precisely defined concept or political vision. The proposed link between motherliness as a social ideal and political radicalization also remained vague. The formlessness to Stöcker's proposals was intentional. Stöcker's hesitation to propose a more specific plan for Weimar politics is analogous to her position in 1905, when she advocated the new morality as an agenda of social reform. It was impossible to predetermine the future course of the new morality because part of the very definition of the new morality philosophy was an embrace of developing and becoming. "We don't yet know anything definitive or fixed about the essence of the *neue Ethik*; to our good fortune, these demands are not yet set in stone and do not weigh on people with the force of centuries of tradition."[40] By not committing themselves to institutional forms, Stöcker and her colleagues allowed themselves to imagine new possibilities for relationships, roles, and behaviors in intimate and public spheres. In the years after World War I, believing that change was not only imminent but absolutely requisite to create a democratic Germany, Stöcker sought to create a space for a new meaning of politics, and specifically democracy:

> Democracy means a society based on the view that the individual person and spirit are of the highest and most sacred meaning; that assuring the full development of the individual soul is the goal of those who come together to form a state. Such a state can never be complete, but rather must be in constant movement in an uninterrupted development forwards.[41]

In Stöcker's interventions, the details were necessarily always in the process of being defined. She went so far as to say that specific juristic or economic forms were no panacea to social problems; rather, the well-being and productive vitality of society would follow from the ongoing transformation within individuals.[42] "In our movement," she claimed, "we belong to that category of people who believe in the eternal becoming and in the fluidity of all progress."[43]

Stöcker's contributions to discussions about politics at the beginning of the republic—and particularly women's roles in politics—were steeped in contradiction. She was committed to activism and viewed herself as a leader in efforts to change cultural and social norms. She wrote and lectured because, like Eisner, she believed that the work of "changing the souls of men" was the very essence of activism:

> Changes in relations of ownership will remain superficial concerns that can't change the true essence of the matter—people—unless we succeed at changing the very souls of people themselves. *What matters the most are the totally individual, personal changes of attitudes in each individual person, each individual soul.* To influence them—to give a new conviction, a new heart one could say, a new spirit—*that seems to us to be the goal.*[44]

The priority of intellectual, artistic, and political work, Stöcker believed, was to convince as many individuals as possible to commit passionately and resolutely to a pacifist worldview. And yet, hers was an activism rooted in utopian ideals. Stöcker's principled refusal to be more concrete perhaps kept her from participating in a political arena where her ideas may have been forced to be more practically articulated.

Stöcker advocated new possibilities for women in both public life and in home life, particularly promoting women's autonomy and capacity for self-definition. Yet she also increasingly relied on conventional notions of femininity in her arguments for social and political change. She confined women within clearly essentialist terms, arguing for example that "the world is totally lost unless woman learns to be a wife and a mother in a more elevated, proactive sense so that the highest mode of her being can have a maximum effect on the world."[45] Further, while Stöcker sought to free up the experience of women's sexuality, she was a firm advocate of control when it came to the existence and well-being of future generations. She insisted that love and sexuality should be protected from the state as "the most private of private realms," but she advocated state regulation in reproduction. Stöcker embraced the developing science of eugenics as justifying state initiatives for a "healthy" future generation, such as mandatory health tests for engaged couples. In Stöcker's view, these interventions fell short of "state control" and were valuable for mobilizing modern scientific knowledge in the name of progressive social reform.

Stöcker's conviction that scientific advances, particularly in medicine, eugenics, and sexology, would contribute to a more evolved society of happier, healthier individuals was essential to her optimism about Germany's future. She and the Bund radicals advocated individual freedom even as they embraced a social Darwinist, eugenic viewpoint.[46] Seeking to explain this seeming contradiction, historian Edward Dickinson examines the prevailing progressive, scientific worldview at the turn of the century. This included a belief in evolutionary theory and in individualistic social liberalism, which made it possible to imagine, simultaneously, radical individual freedom and "a new set of constraints and repressions, focused not so much on sexuality as on reproductivity."[47] Dickinson rightly emphasizes that scientific languages of evolution and social progress had become hegemonic by the early twentieth century and that new scientific data about human life and the human body grounded the thinking of the *neue Ethik* activists. For those affiliated with the Bund, however, the authority of science only made sense in the context of a new language about love and sexuality that embedded the values of motherliness. Stöcker had a naïve and potentially dangerous notion of the "evolved" individual grounded in a commitment to equality and justice. She wrote passionate articles calling each person to this elevated goal, but she also became ever more convinced that only an elite could govern. Only "a vanguard minority, gathered at the highest level of understanding and intent, could lead the way to a democratic future," she wrote.[48] Stöcker's belief in *Mütterlichkeit* as the core of political values to be taught to all citizens gave way to a narrow view of those who could embody the traits necessary for the democratic society she had in mind.

Conclusion: Utopian Activism in Early Weimar

Stöcker's writings and her passionate pleas in the early Weimar years highlight hope and excitement, as well as doubt and desperation, as intellectuals and activists experimented with rescripting politics and the roles and responsibilities of individuals. The end of the war and the revolution created an atmosphere in which pessimism intermingled with a heady sense of possibility. As Count Harry Kessler noted in his diaries on 6 January 1919, "Today history is in the making and the issue is not only whether Germany shall continue to exist in the shape of the Reich or the democratic Republic, but whether ... an exhilarating vision of utopia or the humdrum everyday world shall have the upper hand."[49] A brand new world seemed possible to Stöcker and her peers when the republic was being founded. Stöcker's view of the future included a vital democracy, embedded in ethics, pacifism, and gender equality. Such alternative visions have often been dismissed in histories of Weimar, and yet they bring into focus the genuine debate about democracy that delineated the founding of the republic.

The contradictions in Stöcker's calls for change remind us that activist ideals—the commitment to change social, political, or cultural norms that by their very nature resist such change—come with inconsistencies and paradoxes. In 1918, Europe was a radically different world from what it had been in the 1890s when Stöcker began to work as an activist for women's rights. Yet each of these moments, the turn of the century and the end of World War I, brought an exhilarating promise of renewal for social and political activists. The exhilaration at the turn of the century reflected an enthusiasm for reform that would create new opportunities and institutions enabling the expression of individual self-realization. In 1918, the exhilaration grew from the promise of democratic self-government and a renewed sense of collective. For most feminists, realizing the national collective included winning equal rights and achieving the recognition and public legitimacy afforded by citizenship. Stöcker remained committed to imagining a better world through a different kind of public participation, namely, citizenship grounded in love toward others and belief in social justice.

Stöcker's understanding of herself as an activist was primarily as a public intellectual whose work was to foster change in people's understanding of social norms. Her imagining of and writing about the future contained both her act of participation in a developing democratic community and her act of defiance against the existing order. Challenging the implication that women had earned citizenship rights through their service to the state as mothers, Stöcker argued that values of motherliness in men *and* women could create a radically transformed state that valued human life. Her strategies for effecting this radical change, couched in a Romantic language of transformation, were often obscure, and one might argue that Stöcker limited the influence of her activist work because of her insistence on a utopian and idealistic vision. And yet, if we understand utopian thinking "as a necessary part of demanding, specifying, and enacting the good life,"[50] taking Stöcker's visions seriously helps us to understand the realm of political possibilities as the republic was being founded. In Stöcker's writings, we glimpse the complexity of the ideas and trends that intellectuals and activists grappled with in early Weimar: from contending with the destruction wreaked by the war, to contemplating a more "healthy" society through technology and science, to debating the possibility of pacifist politics. Stöcker's own emphasis after the war on the value of human life—to the point of ignoring issues of class, and even sometimes of gender—flags the tremendous weight of the experiences of war. Individuals trying to create some sense of order and hope from the chaos in the early years of the new republic were contending both with the legacy of war and with the promise of a future that remained open to definition.

Notes

1. Clara Böhm-Schuch, "Die Politik und die Frauen," *Frauenstimmen aus der National-versammlung,* 1920. Cited in Renate Bridenthal and Claudia Koonz, "Beyond Kinder, Küche, Kirche," in *When Biology Became Destiny,* ed. Renate Bridenthal et al. (New York, 1984), 35.
2. There is a substantial bibliography on Stöcker, including works that range from traditional biography (such as Christl Wickert, *Helene Stöcker. Frauenrechtlerin, Sexualreformerin und Pazifistin* [Bonn, 1991]) to East German criticisms of her as a typical representative of bourgeois tendencies in the early women's movement (Petra Rantzsch), to analyses of her role in the women's movement, the sex reform movement, maternalist discourses, or others. See, for example, Richard Evans, *The Feminist Movement in Germany, 1894–1933* (London, 1976); Amy Hackett, "Helene Stöcker: Left-Wing Intellectual and Sex Reformer," in *When Biology Became Destiny,* 109–130; Ann Taylor Allen, *Feminism and Motherhood in Germany, 1800–1914* (New Brunswick, NJ, 1991); Cornelie Usborne, *The Politics of the Body in Weimar Germany* (Ann Arbor, MI, 1992); Atina Grossman, *Reforming Sex: The German Movement for Birth Control & Abortion Reform* (New York, 1995). More recently, Kevin Repp and Edward Ross Dickinson offer new readings of Stöcker's work in the Bund. Kevin Repp, "'More Corporeal, More Concrete': Liberal Humanism and German Progressives at the Last Fin de Siècle," *Journal of Modern History* 72 (September 2000): 683–703; Edward Ross Dickinson, "Reflections on Feminism and Monism in the Kaiserreich, 1900–1913," *Central European History* 34, no. 2 (June 2001): 191–230.
3. For the former argument, see Geoff Eley, "From Welfare Politics to Welfare States: Women and the Socialist Question," in *Women and Socialism/Socialism and Women,* ed. Helmut Gruber and Pamela Graves (New York, 1998); Geoff Eley and Atina Grossman, "The Gendered Politics of Welfare," *Central European History* 30, no. 1 (1997); Christiane Eifert, "Coming to Terms with the State: Maternalist Politics and the Development of the Welfare State in Weimar Germany," *Central European History* 30, no. 1 (1997). For the latter, see Seth Koven and Sonya Michel, eds., *Mothers of a New World: Maternalist Politics and the Origins of the Welfare State* (New York, 1993); and especially Allen, *Feminism and Motherhood in Germany.* On the question of whether political gains by women during and immediately after the war had any long-term effects on women's equality, see Bridenthal and Koonz, "Beyond *Kinder, Küche, Kirche:* Weimar Women in Politics and Work;" Ute Daniel, who coined the term "a lease on emancipation" in *Arbeiterfrauen in der Kriegsgesellschaft: Beruf, Familie und Politik im Ersten Weltkrieg* (Göttingen: 1989), 259–65; Sabine Hering, *Die Kriegsgewinnlerinnen: Praxis und Ideologie der deutschen Frauenbewegung im Ersten Weltkrieg,* (Pfaffenweiler, 1990), 142–47; Katharina Von Ankum, ed., *Women in the Metropolis. Gender and Modernity in Weimar Culture* (Berkeley, CA, 1997), esp. Introduction, 1–11.
4. On maternalist politics in Germany, see especially Allen, *Feminism and Motherhood in Germany.* Maternalist politics have most often been considered in the context of social reform and the development of the welfare state. See, for example, Koven and Michel,

eds., *Mothers of a New World*; Robert Moeller, "Review Article. The State of Women's Welfare in European Welfare States," *Social History* 19, no. 3 (October 1994): 385–93; Teresa Kulawik, *Wohlfahrtsstaat und Mutterschaft. Schweden und Deutschland 1870–1912* (Frankfurt am Main, 1999); Alex Schäfer, *American Progressives and German Social Reform, 1875–1920* (Stuttgart, 2002). Christoph Sachße, *Mütterlichkeit als Beruf: Sozialarbeit, Sozialreform und Frauenbewegung, 1871–1929* (Opladen, 1994) remains the classic study in Germany.

5. Helene Stöcker, "Mütterlichkeit und Krieg," *Neue Generation* 9 (September 1917): 380.

6. Ibid., 381.

7. Sheila Rowbotham and Jeffrey Weeks, *Socialism and the New Life: The Personal Politics of Edward Carpenter and Havelock Ellis* (London, 1977), 9.

8. Helene Stöcker, "Des Pazifismus Verdächtig," 2. Swarthmore College Peace Collection, Papers of Helene Stöcker, Box 1, Folder 6.

9. Stöcker, "Kriegstagebuch, 1914," 2. Swarthmore College Peace Collection, Papers of Helene Stöcker, Box 1.

10. See for example Wolfgang Kruse, "Die Kriegsbegeisterung im Deutschen Reich zum Beginn des Ersten Weltkrieges: Entsthungszusammenhänge, Grenzen und ideologische Strukturen," in *Kriegsbegeisterung und mentale Kriegsvorbereitung. Interdisziplinäre Studien,* ed. Marcel van der Linden and Gottfried Mergner (Berlin, 1991); in that same volume, Jürgen Rojahn, "Arbeiterbewegung und Kriegsbegeisterung: Die deutsche Sozialdemokratie, 1870–1914;" and Niall Ferguson, *The Pity of War* (New York, 1988), 177–186.

11. See Dickinson, "Reflections on Feminism and Monism in the Kaiserreich."

12. Stöcker, "Kriegstagebuch, 1914," 11 (entry from 30 August 1914). See also "Dr. Eduard David," Box 1, Folder 5.

13. Stöcker, "Kriegstagebuch, 1914," 15 (entry from 7 September 1914).

14. On the Peace Society and the peace movement in Germany, see Roger Chickering, *Imperial Germany and a World without War: The Peace Movement and German Society, 1892–1914* (Princeton, NJ, 1975).

15. See Regina Braker, "Bertha von Suttner's Spiritual Daughters: The Feminist Pacifism of Anita Augspurg, Lida Gustava Heymann, and Helene Stöcker at the International Congress of Women at The Hague, 1915," *Women's International Forum* 18, no 2 (1995): 103–11.

16. Helene Stöcker, "Revolutionskrisen," *Neue Generation* 12 (December 1918): 464.

17. Stöcker, "Mutterschutz und Pazifismus," *Neue Generation* 2 (February, 1919): 66.

18. Helene Stöcker, "Militarisierung der Jugend und Mütterlichkeit," *Das Ziel* 2 (1918): 153–58. On militarization and gender during WWI in Germany, see Elizabeth Domansky, "Militarization and Reproduction in World War I in Germany," in *Society, Culture, and the State in Germany,* ed. Geoff Eley (Ann Arbor, MI, 1997), 427–63.

19. Helene Stöcker, "Mitteilungen: Ortsgruppe Bremen," *Neue Generation* 2 (February 1919): 116.

20. Helene Stöcker, "Zu den Waffen—des Geistes und der Güte!," *Neue Generation* (January 1919): 453.

21. Helene Stöcker, "Ins Herzen der Revolution," *Neue Generation* (March 1919).

22. Stephen Lamb, "Intellectuals and the Challenge of Power: The Case of the Munich 'Räterrepublik,'" in *The Weimar Dilemma: Intellectuals in the Weimar Republic,* ed. Anthony Phelan (Manchester, UK, 1985).

23. Stöcker, "Ins Herzen der Revolution," 123.

24. Stöcker, "Revolutionskrisen," 406.

25. Ibid., 403. Also Stöcker, "Revolution und Gewaltlosigkeit: Zum Jarhestag des 9. November," Neue Generation 11 (November 1919).

26. Helene Stöcker, "Entmilitarisierung," Die Neue Generation 4/5 (April/May 1920): 118.

27. Helene Stöcker, "Neuaufbau," Neue Generation (August 1919): 366–67.

28. See for example Gertrud Bäumer, "Zur Erwiderung" (A response to Meyer-Benfey), Die Frau (February 1908): 308; and Helene Lange, "Feministische Gedankenanarchie," Die neue Rundschau, Heft 3 (March 1908): 401.

29. Stöcker, "Entmilitarisierung," 123.

30. Stöcker, "Mutterschutz und Pazifismus," 62.

31. Helene Stöcker, "Mütterlichkeit und Krieg," Die Neue Generation 9 (September 1917): 373.

32. Summons of the Bund fur Mütterschutz, Die Neue Generation (February 1919): 116.

33. Stöcker, Bund, 7.

34. Dickinson, "Reflections on Feminism and Monism in the Kaiserreich, 1900–1913," 206–07. On monism, see Kurt Bayertz, "Biology and Beauty: Science and Aesthetics in Fin-de-Siècle Germany," in Fin-de-Siècle and Its Legacy, ed. Mikulas Teich and Roy Porter (Cambridge, 1990); Monika Fick, Sinnenwelt und Weltseele: Der Psychophysische Monismus in der Literatur der Jahrhundertwende (Tübingen, 1993); and Gangolf Hübinger, "Die Monistische Bewegung," in Kultur und Kulturwissenschaft, vol. 2, Idealismus und Positivismus, ed. Gangolf Hübinger, Rüdiger vom Bruch, and Friedrich Wilhelm Graff (Stuttgart, 1997).

35. Dickinson, "Reflections on Feminism and Monism in the Kaiserreich, 1900–1913," 207.

36. Helene Stöcker, "Wandlung," Neue Generation 10/11 (October/November 1918): 339.

37. Ibid., 337–38.

38. Stöcker, "Militarisierung der Jugend und Mütterlichkeit," 163.

39. Helene Stöcker, "Aus dem Liebesbrief einer Modernen Frau," Magazin für Literatur, 1897, in Die Liebe und die Frauen (Minden in Westf, 1908), 33.

40. Helene Stöcker, Bund für Mutterschutz, in Moderne Zeitfragen, ed. Hans Landsberg (Berlin, 1905), 5.

41. Stöcker, "Neuaufbau," 363–64.

42. Helene Stöcker, Zehn Jahre Mutterschutz (Berlin: Neue Generation Verlag, 1915), 17.

43. Stöcker, "Mutterschutz und Pazifismus," 65.

44. Stöcker, "Revolution und Gewaltlosigkeit," 528. Italics in the original.

45. Stöcker, "Mütterlichkeit und Krieg," 380.

46. Dickinson, "Reflections on Feminism and Monism," 191. For a discussion of the emerging role of science in political thought and policy, see Greta Jones, Social Darwinism and English Thought: The Interaction between Biological and Social Theory (Sussex, UK, 1980); Donald MacKenzie, Statistics in Britain, 1865–1930: The Social Construction of Scientific Knowledge (Edinburgh, 1981); Paul Weindling, Health, Race and German Politics Between National Unification and Nazism, 1870–1945 (Cambridge, 1989).

47. Dickinson, "Reflections on Feminism and Monism," 191–92.

48. Stöcker, "Neuaufbau," 366–67.

49. Charles Kessler, ed. Berlin in Lights: The Diaries of Count Harry Kessler (1918–1937), trans. Charles Kessler (New York, 1999), 53.

50. Geoff Eley, "What's Left of Utopia? From the New Jerusalem to the Time of Desire," unpublished paper, Humanities Institute, University of Michigan, March 1993, 2.

CHAPTER 7

Producing Jews
Maternity, Eugenics, and the Embodiment of the Jewish Subject

SHARON GILLERMAN

As we consider how to "rethink Weimar" with respect to the history of German Jews, it is useful to reflect upon the ways in which the question of what constituted "Jewish difference" simultaneously fueled the nineteenth-century *Judenfrage* and gave rise to numerous Jewish reconceptualizations of both Judaism and Jewishness. Within contemporary historiography, historians have sometimes approached the issue of "Jewish difference" in conflicting ways. Jewish historians have tended towards overemphasizing Jewish distinctiveness, not only because of their a priori interest in the Jews as a group, but also because of their emphasis on those aspects of Jewish life that distinguished them from non-Jewish Germans. German historians, on the other hand, have tended to underplay difference. This should hardly be surprising, given that the concept of "Jewish difference" is crushed by the weight of German history. Indeed, scholars have been rightfully wary of attributing Jewish identities to historical actors when the Nazi state itself defined the Jewishness of its victims without regard to their own sense of identity. Practically, what this has often meant, however, is that anti-Semitism has come to stand as the prime signifier of Jewish "difference" within narratives of German history.

I would like to argue that historians of both German and Jewish history must begin to find ways of recovering Jews' own representations and experience of their "difference" by exploring both the discursive contexts that produced them and the historically contingent subjectivities they created at given historical moments. As I endeavor to move beyond the often dichotomous historiographical representations that have tended to characterize Weimar Jews as either assimilationists actively seeking to obliterate their "difference" or ideological Zionists committed to cultivating it, I explore how discourses of reproduction within the Jewish community constructed Jewish difference and sought to anchor these differences in a variety of social institutions and policies. In particular, I analyze the overlapping discourses of social hygiene, pronatalism, population policy, and eugenics that sought both to regulate and protect women and make their bodies into sites for ever-increasing medical and social interventions. The work of Atina Grossmann and Cornelie Usborne has clearly demonstrated the centrality of gender, and women's bodies more specifically, for the construction of a distinctly modern society and state in postwar Germany.[1] Building on their work, I want to show how within the Jewish community the idea of reproduction not only placed women at the center of the postwar project of remaking the German nation and Jewish community, but also came to symbolize the continuity of Jewish difference itself. In the postwar context, it was not only German-born Jewish women who were meant to be the vanguard of a new Jewish reproductive hygiene, but Eastern European Jewish immigrant women too, whose generally higher fertility rates underscored their importance for the revitalization of Jewish society. It was precisely their "foreign," "eastern" qualities, their imagined connection to the wellsprings of nation and faith, that would supply a much-needed "blood transfusion" to an ailing community.[2] With a focus on a broad cross-section of leadership within the organized Jewish community, I thus seek to examine how Jewish leaders and policy experts deployed the same medical and social scientific discourses intended to strengthen the German nation in the service of the somewhat different but curiously parallel project of reimagining the Jewish social body. Although the contributions of such prominent Jewish figures in social work, sex reform, and social hygiene as Sidonie Wronsky, Felix Theilhaber, Gustav Tugendreich, and Henriette Fürth are well known, their rendering of German social policy within a specifically Jewish sphere of social life is not. Accordingly, it is my aim to identify how these and other German Jewish experts appropriated these discourses and infused them with altogether new and unanticipated meanings.

In the turbulent years following the war, German proponents of a new biomedical politics sought to make reproductivity a matter of compelling national interest by drawing a powerful linkage between the individual female body and the well-being of the *Volkskörper* (national body). In this context, declining birthrates were viewed by many as a threat both to German national power and the nation's religious and moral condition. Among Jewish leaders specifically, there was broad agreement that, owing to declining Jewish birthrates and battlefield losses, German Jewry faced a potentially catastrophic demographic crisis. In this article, I will trace the processes by which Jewish social reformers situated private decisions about marriage, work, and child bearing at the center of debates about Jewish social policy, and came to diagnose and pathologize the social and reproductive behaviors of men—and to a much greater extent women—in ways that sought to construe the Jewish social body as an organism in significant need of a new and decisive regime of treatment. Insofar as social institutions and policies endow discourses with their social power, I will also outline some of the Jewish institutions that were either created or envisioned for the purpose of managing the potential reproductive resources of the Jewish population. The manner in which religious sources were enlisted and the surprising extent to which traditional religious institutions were transformed as part of an effort to buttress decidedly modern scientific agendas in pursuit of a rationalized population policy suggests the degree to which Judaism itself was being drawn into the project that George Steinmetz has called "the biologization of the social."[3]

Indeed, an examination of the politics of Jewish population programs provides an unusual opportunity for reflecting on the interrelationship of German and German Jewish subject formation. In contrast to the more commonly used category of "identity," the concept of subjectivity forces us to go beyond enlightenment notions of the individual as volitional and autonomous to consider how subjectivities are constituted and produced through language and instances of power. By this I mean to evoke the Foucauldian notion of the subject as a means of discipline and control made all the more effective by discourses of science, hygiene, and individual sovereignty.[4] I thus want to explore at once how the subjectivity of the Jewish policy makers is constituted by the administration of the economy of the Jewish social body as realized through the prudent management of the "wealth" of reproduction/fertility. At the same time I consider how this work positions these policy makers as Jews and Germans who were subordinate to and yet ultimately a part of the regulatory apparatus of the state. To be sure, the group of Weimar Jewish experts I will discuss here were historical actors who exhibited creativity and flexibility in constituting their subjectivities within the historical and cultural constraints of their time. But as subjects of the state, German Jewish subjects' sense of self needed to be constituted at once in relation to state discourses of knowledge and power and those relating to specifically Jewish social practices and discourses.

As an analytical category, subjectivity represents neither a fixed entity nor a static social construction, but rather a process marked by continuous production and transformation. As against a notion of the unitary nature of the subject, subjectivity recognizes the possibility that an individual may occupy multiple subject positions. A study of Weimar Jewish subjectivities, then, proves a fruitful means by which to observe the complex social navigation of this particular group of experts amidst a range of possible subject positions. As representative members of the middle class, individual Jews played a significant role in the development of German social policy and the establishment of the new regimes of social medicine, social work, and eugenics, the ostensible aims of which were the moral and physical improvement of Germans in general and the lower classes in particular. But social policy, especially population policy, also contained an implicit and sometimes explicit racial element in its focus on strengthening the German *Volkskörper* for the relentless struggle against other nationalities.[5] It is precisely the racialized aspect of these discourses that propelled the Jews as a group towards the periphery of the German society. Because Jewish men and women were subjected to classed, racialized, and gendered discourses, the embodied subject thus becomes a central site of contest where notions of nation, class, race, and gender are constantly reworked and reinscribed.[6]

Occupying positions at once at the center and on the margins of German social life, these Jewish experts appropriated medical, social, and population discourses that ultimately produced a new ideal for an embodied Jewish collectivity. But this new collectivity was no longer conceptualized strictly in the liberal sense as an assemblage of autonomous, bounded individual citizens. Its formation instead points to the emergence of a discrete, recognizable Jewish social entity within the framework of the new welfare state. Put in the terminology of the day, this conceptual shift entailed a move away from the nineteenth-century liberal model of *Religionsgemeinschaft* (religious community) to that of *Schicksalsgemeinschaft* (community of fate) or even to the more organicist notion of a Jewish *Volksgemeinschaft*. Accordingly, I want to demonstrate how Jewish medical and social welfare experts transformed these discourses in a manner that subverted their integrative function at once on the level of the individual "embodied" Jewish subjects and on the level of an incarnation of a new Jewish body politic within the boundaries of the state itself. Although these rationalized Jewish bodies were indisputably viewed as molded in the service of the German state, they served simultaneously to strengthen the existence of a distinct Jewish social and, perhaps ultimately, political body. Interestingly, this image of an unassimilable Jewish entity in the heart of the state has historical resonance, hearkening back to eighteenth-century accusations that the Jews constituted a "state within a state."

As the agents of a broadly conceived Jewish social policy, middle-class experts targeted for improvement and reform both middle-class women as well as members of their own proletarian class, which consisted largely of Jewish immigrants from Eastern Europe. Through the regulation and control of the Jewish working-class men and women, community leaders served the interests both of the state and the Jewish community, and, like other confessional groups, received state monies to carry out their work. Although native German Jews often viewed the Eastern Europeans as culturally and religiously backward, the higher birthrates associated with their religious traditionalism were eagerly mobilized in the service of the community and nation. Indeed, in discourses about the reproductive crisis, it is clear that German Jews hoped to harness the vital "premodern" fecundity of this foreign element while simultaneously converting its members into modern liberal subjects. The integration of the "primitive" subject, as a balance to the excessively modern subject, it seems, was viewed as essential for securing the Jewish future.

Beyond the Eastern European working population in particular, it was women who more generally provided the crucial discursive link for the creation of a regenerate social order as envisioned by social policy experts. As "mothers of the race," to use Gertrud Bäumer's phrase, women had a vital role to play in restoring moral and political health to the nation.[7] Indeed, Jewish leaders identified women's bodies as central both for the reproduction of the "race" and for the maintenance of the Jewish social body's distinctive character. If the assimilatory nineteenth century had witnessed "the loss of Jewish uniqueness, helping the Jewish group gain equality but lose its quality," as Sidonie Wronsky argued, then the task for twentieth-century leaders was to save the sick and ailing Jewish *Volkskörper* from the stifling effects of decades of infertility.[8] Creating embodied Jewish subjectivities that could resist the homogenizing power of society and the state became an important aspect of Jewish "women's work" in the 1920s. In the Jewish communal drive to produce a physically and socially distinct Jewish *Volkskörper* that established the bodily boundaries of Jewishness, women were often cast both as the problem and solution, embodying both the threat of a barren future, and the promise of collective renewal.

For most of the nineteenth century German political economists advocated the control of reproduction for the purpose of limiting population growth, but Germany's rapid transformation from a predominantly rural to a highly urban society beginning in the 1880s brought with it a dramatic decline in fertility rates. Virtually overnight, Malthusian warnings of a crisis of overpopulation were superseded by sharp admonitions against the suicidal "one and two-child family system." German birthrates, once the highest in Europe at 40.6 births per 1000, had fallen to as low as 14.7 per 1000 by 1933.[9] By the turn of the century, the "birth decline" seemed to threaten both Germany's national strength and its moral condition. Rapid modernization coincided with a surge of international competition for overseas colonies and imperialist supremacy. As the demand for industrial manpower increased, it was feared that only nations with fast-growing populations would maintain their competitive edge.

Medical and social interventions aimed at the improvement of infant and maternal health were thus incorporated into the drive for national ascendancy, forging a linkage between reproductive practices and German military might. The politicization of human health, as Paul Weindling has shown, marked a shift from the traditional notion of political economy to an emergent "human economy." The terms *child-poor* for small families and *child-rich* for larger ones expressed the growing inclination to view a community's biological resources in economic terms.[10] Although the outbreak of the First World War imparted a new urgency to the issue of German and German Jewish population decline, the war years produced little in the way of actual incentive-based programs.[11]

The establishment of the Weimar welfare state represented a high point in the state's engagement with the question of depopulation. The newly drafted constitution expanded the Wilhelmine policy of state intervention in the private sphere by committing itself to the promotion of population growth and the protection of the family. Although the constitution granted equal rights to male and female citizens, women were especially protected in their role as child bearers. In its encouragement of childbearing, the constitution guaranteed social insurance for all citizens, mothers in particular, and promised housing priority to large families. Although the Weimar state never evolved a comprehensive population policy, the expansion of prenatal and maternity benefits and the establishment of marriage counseling centers to encourage eugenically "responsible" marriages were among the more notable measures undertaken by the state to improve both the quantity and quality of Germany's future progeny.

It was in this context that Jewish anxiety about birthrates focused on the fitness and viability of the Jews as a group. Within the Jewish community, Jewish physicians and social scientists were the first to produce and interpret demographic data warning that the race was physically, mentally, and morally deteriorating.[12] Singularly instrumental in introducing the issue to the Jewish public was the 1911 publication of a slim volume entitled *Der Untergang der deutschen Juden* written by the dermatologist and sexologist Felix Theilhaber.[13] Theilhaber asserted that Jewish moral and physical decline was closely associated with expanding urbanization, unbounded individualism, the growing incidence of chronic diseases, and a reduction in the number of births amongst healthy, productive strata of the population. The drop in the natural growth levels of the Jewish population, which predated general German population developments by at least a decade, meant that Jewish birthrates were significantly lower than the German. By the time the second edition of *Der Untergang* appeared in 1921, Theilhaber's work had achieved near-prophetic status. In 1920, the peak year for Weimar birthrates, non-Jews registered a birthrate of 24 per 1000, while the German Jewish rate peaked at 15 per 1000. By the early 1930s, the Jewish rate had declined to 7.2 compared to the non-Jewish low of 14.7. The decline in Jewish fertility was in fact also much discussed by non-Jewish population policy experts since the Jewish experience was held up as emblematic of the modernization process and as the bellwether for Germany's inevitable future course.

Not surprisingly, the explanations given for the birth decline by both Jews and non-Jews shared several key features. Central to all reproductive discourse, whether Left or Right, was the conflation of private reproductive behaviors with social and national well-being. Accordingly, declining birthrates were most commonly interpreted to signify a deficient commitment to the *Volk*. Opponents of birth control, relatively few in the Jewish community, viewed contraception as a selfish act "that aids and abets the individual's fruitless attainment of sexual pleasure and his disregard for the future of the *Volk*."[14] Both Jewish and non-Jewish advocates of population policy saw such blind self-indulgence and individualism as byproducts of the impersonal social order of the metropolis, and also as being at the root of postwar social breakdown. Contrasting the decadent present with an idealized Jewish past, Jewish leaders across the religious and political spectrum pointed to the premodern era as the embodiment of a strong but fluid bond between family and community, one undisturbed by the artificial divide separating public and private. The essence of this imagined "organic" community was characterized as one in which individuals possessed a "healthy instinct" to sacrifice selfish interests and to act for the sake of the totality.[15]

This inability to sacrifice selfish interests was also manifested in the increasing materialism believed to be characteristic of urban Jewish youth. In accordance with critiques of bourgeois society that rejected materialism and promoted erotic attraction in the service of racial improvement, Jewish social commentators issued scathing indictments of the calculated financial motives that lay behind many Jewish marriages.[16] Citing the existence of a distinct Jewish economy of love, observers noted that, for Jewish men, the income of the female marriage candidate was far more decisive than either her beauty or her figure, whereas for the majority of non-Jews, erotic instincts led them to marriage without regard to economic consequences. "Nowhere do girls from poor or modest backgrounds have such poor prospects for marriage as among Jews," lamented Friedrich Ollendorff, founding member and chairman of the Zentralwohlfahrtsstelle der deutschen Juden, German Jewry's umbrella social welfare organization and the Jewish counterpart to the Catholic Caritas Verband and Protestant Innere Mission. Ollendorff noted that "the increasing value placed on the material side of things has led young men to make even greater demands [of Jewish women]. Any glimmer of a romantic idealism among our boys is quickly stripped away and replaced by cool, rational calculations."[17] Even after the crash of 1923, young men registering with the Frankfurt Jewish marriage bureau reportedly preferred to meet women whose families were still in a position to offer substantial dowries.

The most thoroughgoing critique of social behavior, however, was aimed at the individualism and self-centeredness inscribed on the bodies of childless young women. Increased female employment, together with the social danger embodied in the image of the "New Woman," led social commentators during the Weimar Republic to conclude that the young, emancipated woman was on a "birth strike" that threatened to culminate in women's forsaking of hearth and home for the decadent delights of the city. As a result of modernity in general, and the increased prevalence of birth control in particular, it was believed that the modern woman had lost her desire to bear children and that it was the task of population experts to help her recover it.[18] Jewish women were alleged to be foregoing work experience that would help prepare them for their mothering roles in favor of paid work outside the home.[19] This trend led Theilhaber to conclude that the enticements of the city had led "young Jewish women to become alienated from their calling as housewives and mothers."[20]

Women's employment was thus viewed as the primary reason for the postponement of marriage, a development that accelerated in the postwar period among Jews even more than non-Jews. These late marriages, in turn, were believed to be responsible for the decline in postwar birthrates. According to the results of a 1928–29 Jewish population survey, half of all Jewish women married after the age of twenty-seven, which meant that, according to Theilhaber, "50 percent of female Jews have been excluded from motherhood during the first decade of their child-bearing years."[21] Not only did later marriages mean women would have fewer years in which to bear children, but more years of singlehood also suggested that premarital sex would be much more prevalent. The increased incidence of venereal diseases, was, according to leading eugenic thinkers, responsible not only for bringing on a range of pathological characteristics, and damaging the quality of the nation's hereditary stock, but was also held to be a major cause of sterility.[22] Jewish physicians, such as (Frau) Linna Berg-Platau reported that Jews were contracting sexual diseases more frequently than they had in the past.[23] Thus the prevalent medical view was that late marriages proved the foremost impediment to the continued production of healthy and numerous offspring. Parallel to their non-Jewish counterparts, Jewish physicians, both male and female, identified late marriage as the key not only to German Jewry's quantitative decline but also its qualitative one.

Discourses about Jewish reproduction nevertheless had their distinctive aspects that stemmed from German Jews' status as a minority community. Like late marriage, intermarriage was a social force that undermined the collective vitality of German Jewry. Considered within the community as the ultimate act of social betrayal, it was also viewed as an assault on the reproductivity of the Jewish collective. "Mixed marriage," opined Ernst Kahn, whose book *Der International Geburtenstreik* devoted a chapter to the Jews, "devours that remaining essence of Jewry after [the resulting dimunition from] birth control."[24] Since children born of mixed marriages were excluded from Jewish birth statistics, we might expect the objection to intermarriage to have been based on qualitative considerations, i.e., the consequence of children not being raised as Jews. Interestingly enough, however, interconfessional marriages met with disapproval because they were viewed as largely infertile. "They are almost all childless," noted one observer, "and thus signify no gain for Jewry, even when the women [converts to Judaism] … adhere zealously to their new religion."[25]

If the decline in the number of Jewish births as a result of intermarriage was a function of Jews' status as a minority group, the influx of Jews from Eastern Europe seemed to offer a ready-made antidote. The demographic characteristics of Eastern European Jews were more consistent with traditional patterns of early marriage and high marital fertility, and functioned to significantly off-set the declining birthrates of native German Jews. Their adherence to more traditional religious behaviors was also taken as an expression of a higher level of commitment to the community.[26] Indeed, the Eastern Europeans were often the object of Western fascination, symbolizing the embodiment of a "premodern unfragmented wholeness."[27] But there was a darker side to the "cult of the Ostjuden" that Steven Aschheim describes.[28] The same "difference" that was celebrated by certain population policy advocates and Jewish intellectuals such as, for example, Franz Rosenzweig and Arnold Zweig became, in the hands of the state and Jewish welfare authorities, the basis for designating Eastern European men, women, and children as "asocial" in disproportionate measure. Men who remained jobless fell into the category of "work shy," while women were criticized for the unhygienic households they kept and their inability to create suitable domestic conditions for the proper conduct of family life.

The infusion of younger and more fertile Eastern Europeans into the German Jewish community thus represented an ambivalent bequest to German Jews. While Eastern European Jews brought into modern Germany the fecundity of a premodern social formation, they also constituted an undisciplined mass of bodies in need of modernization. As a result, the Jewish welfare establishment responded to the mixed blessing of the *Ostjuden* by seeking to save Eastern European Jews physically while making them into modern German and modern Jewish subjects. In response to an overwhelming demand for new and expanded forms of social assistance, Jewish welfare workers intensified their activities on behalf of the Eastern Europeans through the creation of job bureaus that offered occupational retraining for young people into the so-called productive professions. Such a transformation of German Jewry's occupational structure, from an overpreponderance of workers in the commercial sector into a labor force with a greater proportion of skilled laborers, was also conceived as a means of enabling workers to start families even at a time of economic uncertainty. In the domestic sphere, women's mothering practices and sexual behaviors were similarly subject to scrutiny during home visits made by social workers. Indeed, within an expanding network of institutions for orphan care and juvenile delinquency, the offspring of Eastern European Jewish mothers were highly overrepresented. My research has shown that while Eastern European Jews made up about one-fifth of the German Jewish population, they made up between 25 to 50 percent of the inmates within Jewish institutions for "wayward youth," although the proportion fluctuated considerably. And it was primarily middle-class women who made up the newly professionalized core of social workers who "reeducated" the Eastern European Jews populating Jewish welfare institutions during the Weimar Republic.

Having identified both the class-specific and the particularly "Jewish" factors impeding Jewish reproduction, population experts next turned to the problem of facilitating its increase. In keeping with their notion of Jewish reproductivity as a resource to be administered and supervised, Jewish population experts sought to harmonize the bionationalist dictates of pronatalism with those of Jewish tradition. In doing so, they also began to recast Jewish difference from its traditional significance as a theological category into an overarching social one that fused together religious and moral teachings with biological imperatives. Having once formed what Theilhaber called Judaism's categorical imperative, the biblical commandment to "be fruitful and multiply" came to be regarded not only as the key to the survival of Judaism and Jewry but, rather paradoxically perhaps, as a measure of the subordination of individual desire to the general good. The very survival of the Jews as a group, once seen to hinge upon religious faith, had become, by the early twentieth century, a biological issue. Through the combined application of social engineering and social control, this new form of Jewish survivalism, one that collapsed biological and moral "truths" into a kind of Jewish biomorality, was a sure sign of a nascent biologically inclined Jewish social imagination.

The "be fruitful and multiply" precept was regularly invoked by advocates of Jewish population policy in support of a "traditionally religious" collectivist ethos that they hoped would reawaken the desire for children, and, ultimately, reinvigorate the community. Theilhaber, himself a leading advocate of sexual reform and birth control, nevertheless mirrored the general conservative and Christian attacks on the "new sexual ethic" and its separation of sexuality from reproduction, when he maintained that Judaism placed erotic life in the service of the higher interests of the nation. "The right to freely determine one's sexual relations," he argued, "had always been subordinated to the aims of a Jewish generative policy."[29] Consistent with his Zionist leanings, Theilhaber stressed the authority of the Jewish *Volksgemeinschaft* over that of religion:

> The [medieval social] system was based upon the correct presupposition that every member of the community participated in a racially most expedient manner with absolutely no regard for his own interests. All aspects of the sex life of Jews accorded with the substantive basis for the overarching conception of the nation whose germ of survival lies within its very being. The fertility and safeguarding of the individual family is but the foundation of the ultimate realization of a nation.[30]

Theilhaber endeavored to shape a secularized, nationalized vision of the once intimate and organic relationship between the Jewish individual and the religious community. But in place of the religious motive, which called upon the individual to subordinate his own will to that of God, Theilhaber viewed the sovereign Jewish people as the greatest good. Just as the family was represented in the rhetoric of population policy as the core unit of the state, the Jewish family was for Theilhaber and other Jewish leaders the foundation of the Jewish nation.

The manner in which theology was yielding to biology also became evident in the ways in which both religious and nonpracticing Jewish commentators subjected Jewish sexual regulations to eugenic scrutiny and evaluated their merit from the standpoint of public health. From such a modern "scientific" perspective, Jewish survival was now presented as being contingent upon the fulfillment of biblically ordained ritual purity laws that imposed the rigid physical separation of a menstruating woman from her husband. Contrasting the survival of the Jews with the disappearance of the nations of antiquity, Theilhaber identified "sexual hygienic institutions and habits of the Jews" as both the moral and biological foundation for Jewish continuity through the ages.[31] Dr. Max Eschelbacher, a liberal rabbi in Düsseldorf, cited a different proof text to make a similar argument. Eschelbacher took the public recitation of the Torah passage enumerating forbidden sexual acts on Yom Kippur to indicate not only that the Torah placed sexual life at the center of its commandments, but that "the entire life of the nation is dependent on its health. When the nation's health is hopelessly degenerate," noted Eschelbacher, "a *Volk* will inevitably decline."[32]

Concurring with his Zionist and liberal colleagues about the relationship between Jewish survival and sexual practices, the Jewish Orthodox physician Dr. Jakob Levy emphasized birth control as the primary source of Jewish moral degeneration. Levy saw marriage as having ceased to fulfill the reproductive needs of the community when it merely served to satisfy individual sexual desires. Once the sexual drive no longer required the marital bond for its fulfillment, wrote Levy, "the downfall of the entire culture is the inescapable result of such degeneration. Greece, Rome, and the German Jews!"[33] Levy also objected to companionate marriage on eugenic grounds, since such marriages were generally characterized by what eugenicists called the "fear of having children." He favored neither quantitative nor qualitative eugenics exclusively, but believed that only their combined application would lead to the production of higher-quality offspring. Levy sought the production of more healthy, genetically untainted Jewish offspring, thereby increasing the number of Jewish geniuses who would uphold Jewish civilization.

Zionists like Theilhaber may have set out most deliberately to shift the focus from Judaism as a God-centered religious system to a form of social organization that invested in the social body the highest authority. But, as we have seen, this tendency was by no means limited to those with Zionist predilections. Liberal, Orthodox, and Zionist conceptions of Jewish sexual hygiene reveal a seamless fusing of physical and spiritual health, of biological and moral truth. They demonstrate that health had indeed become "an ideology of social cohesion."[34] Discourses that emphasized the totality (*Volksganze*) over the sum of its parts resonated compellingly with modernist critiques of individualism shared by proponents of Orthodoxy, Zionism, social-scientific and even liberal viewpoints. By placing reproductivity at the center of a new sociobiological order, otherwise ideologically divided Jews could faithfully maneuver within the Jewish interpretive tradition while remaining true to their own modern scientific sensibilities. Taken together, eugenic health, subordination of the individual will to the communal good, and the restoration of a distinctive Jewish sexual ethic were to be the means by which a regime of rationalized sexuality and reproduction could come to heal the Jewish body social.

Within the short span of the Weimar Republic, the Jewish community won significant praise from non-Jewish advocates of sex reform, eugenics, and pronatalism for "implementing an active population policy."[35] Following the war, Jewish welfare organizations such as the Zentralwohlfahrtsstelle der deutschen Juden had immediately made reproduction a top priority. However, it was not until 1926 that a broader community policy came into being with the creation of German Jewry's first statewide representative body, the Preussischer Landesverband. At the urging of Bertha Pappenheim, the welfare committee of the Landesverband appointed a commission for Jewish population policy, to be presided over by Sidonie Wronsky, a leading social policy expert.[36] During the high holiday season of 1927, the commission published an appeal to its "comrades in faith" in the major Jewish community newspapers. The purpose of the appeal was to generate support for greater communal intervention in the reproductive sphere. It urged Jews to "heed all questions regarding Jewish population policy with increased vigilance … since no issue can be more pressing than raising a new generation strong in body and vigorous in mind."[37]

In February 1929, the committee convened a national conference on Jewish population policy in Berlin. Sponsored jointly by the Preussischer Landesverband and the Zentralwohlfahrtsstelle der deutschen Juden, it was attended by representatives of major Jewish organizations and experts from across the religious and political spectrum. The conferees mapped out a program to stimulate the desire for children on the one hand, while reducing the obstacles impeding early marriages and family formation on the other.[38] The physicians Felix Theilhaber and Arthur Czellitzer championed the most outspoken pronatalist position. Both men were staunch advocates of eugenics and favored the introduction of a Jewish communal *Geburtenpolitik* (birth policy) that would grant subsidies to "child-rich" families. Theilhaber estimated a stipend of 500 Reichsmarks should be paid by the Jewish community to families with more than two children. Insisting that babies rather than buildings represented the more cost-effective investment in the Jewish future, Theilhaber calculated that in "sterile Berlin," as the city was known to pronatalists, such a subsidy would help support the approximately one hundred and twenty families per year that had "third" children.[39] Czellitzer proposed a "child tax" modeled after that of Alfred Grotjahn, according to which "child-poor" families would directly subsidize the "child-rich." On the basis of such a graduated tax, single people were to be assessed in full, childless marrieds three-quarters, while families with three children would be exempt. The resolution passed at the conference endorsed Czellitzer's proposal to link the salaries of Jewish community workers to family status and number of dependents.[40]

But while scarcely anyone at the conference opposed boosting the Jewish birthrate, few regarded pronatalism alone as a sufficient basis for social policy. Skeptics doubted that an annual sum of 500 Reichsmarks could convince families to undertake the sacrifices entailed in supporting an additional child. The pronatalist position on its own received little endorsement from the assembled Jewish social welfare experts. In fact, the conferees passed a resolution anchoring their support for pronatalism within a broader social policy that would extend social, economic, and medical support to families in need. For a community in the midst of acute economic crisis, it was felt, "the imperative for self-preservation through increased propagation can only be permitted if it is prepared to do its utmost to ensure the economic security of those already living."[41]

The proposal to direct funds to promoting early marriage, therefore, won universal support from the delegates. The overwhelming consensus on the virtues of early marriage made the *Frühehekasse* (early marriage fund) an important social policy innovation, not least because it resembled an institution that could claim a long and noble Jewish lineage. Within the early modern Jewish community and through the nineteenth century, the Hachnasat Calah society, or bridal fund, had been a highly esteemed organization with the purpose of providing dowries to poor brides. By the early twentieth century, this traditional institution had been conscripted into the service of eugenic health. Young, modern-minded, socially active women saw themselves implementing "social policy" at the same time as they reinterpreted the traditional offering of mutual aid. Traditionalists could thus continue practicing old-style philanthropy while social welfare professionals dressed up the Hachnasat Calah society as a social institution with eugenic merit.

The German Jewish feminist organization, the Jüdischer Frauenbund, operated the most extensive *Frühehekasse* within the Jewish community. Conceived of as a means to both reverse the population decline and curb the demand for prostitutes and premarital sex, local chapters dispensed cash gifts to enable couples to marry at a young age "before their best energies were spent."[42] Frauenbund clubs also subsidized the furnishing of homes and collected trousseaus, helped arrange loans, and offered free insurance for newly married young couples.[43] The Frauenbund also negotiated a "population-political" agreement with the Phoenix insurance company according to which the company would provide insurance to needy Jewish children in exchange for business referrals by Frauenbund members.[44]

A sufficient supply of quality partners was, however, necessary in order for such early marriage patterns to take hold. At the end of the war, there were calls for the establishment of a network of marriage bureaus to match and screen applicants with references and impeccable qualifications. Some proposed that such bureaus be supported through the donations of satisfied customers.[45] The establishment of marriage bureaus—the modern, impersonal incarnation of the traditional matchmaker—was viewed as an attractive way to rationalize the haphazard process of finding a mate as well as to mitigate some of the social causes of the marriage crisis. Several years later, the Frankfurter Eheanbahnungsstelle became a model for communities across Germany in its attempt to increase the number of "pure" Jewish marriages and births.[46]

Alongside financial incentives to boost the birthrate and the expansion of economic support and social services, the third pillar of a national Jewish population policy called for the provision of medical assistance to Jewish mothers and children. The Jewish community of Berlin was one of many Jewish communities that offered special clinics at neighborhood synagogues for Jewish mothers and their children.[47] Medical assistance was understood broadly to extend to the social sphere, since, according to Dr. Hermann Stahl, a pediatrican at the highly regarded Jüdische Kinderhilfe in Berlin, physicians were executors of social policy and "educators of children and parents in the Jewish sense."[48] In Stahl's view, Jews required special medical services because their physiology differed from that of non-Jews. Specifically, the Jewish nervous system was said to function differently than did its Gentile counterpart. Because Jews' muscular system also reputedly differed from that of non-Jews, physicians like Stahl were avid advocates of Jewish sports organizations. "If we can fulfill this duty [of promoting health]," wrote Stahl, "we shall create a healthy spirit and body that itself will form the basis for a revival of Jewish life."[49]

In their capacity as educators, physicians also dispensed advice to promote an understanding of eugenic considerations in marriage. Both male and female Jewish physicians were called upon to field questions and offer advice on sexual issues. For married couples, these counseling bureaus were to assist couples to resolve martial differences, thereby helping to lessen the likelihood of divorce. During puberty, young people would also have a safe and reliable venue in which to raise questions about sex.[50] For activist physicians such as Stahl and Berg-Platau, this kind of sex counseling represented "the most urgent demand of our time." As Berg-Platau argued,

> Bringing about a clear and urgent understanding of the blessing of a practical reproductive hygiene amongst our self-conscious Jewish youth—hand-in-hand with an awareness of the grave dangers intrinsic to an ill-advised rationalization of sexual life—this is what I hold to be the most important path towards reviving and increasing the desire to reproduce, and in so doing, maintaining our Jewish *Gemeinschaft*.[51]

Though by no means opposed to birth control, Berg-Platau held an ill-advised rationalization of sexual life to consist of any form of birth control, such as abortion, that endangered women's reproductive capacity, or sexual activity that carried with it the danger of contracting sexually transmitted diseases.[52] Since the time when men and women began to separate sexual activity from reproduction, in Berg-Platau's view, the existence of a *Volk* was dependent not only on its reproductive capacity but first and foremost on its will to reproduce. For Berg-Platau as for other of her colleagues, this will to reproduce could best be nurtured through the doctor-patient relationship. In this way, young Jewish "patients" would be guided in their cultivation of an inner spiritual commitment to the community by virtue of their acquisition of, among other things, a practical knowledge of eugenics. Were reproductive-age Jewish individuals to genuinely internalize such a spiritual-biological sense of responsibility towards the community, it would, in paving the way for an auspicious Jewish reproductive hygiene, also demonstrate that the self-policing aspect of Jewish reproductive disciplinary discourses had come to full fruition.

As reproduction came to be regarded as an essential element in the revival of a healthy *Gemeinschaft* during the 1920s, the female body was identified as the crucial vehicle for the continued survival of the national community. A "motherhood-eugenics consensus" that spanned the political spectrum was founded in the assumption that the bearing of healthy children was a crucial social task.[53] The female body had thus come to symbolize in two contradictory but interrelated ways the nation's challenge and its future capacity as a vital and productive organism: the independent New Woman, who by indulging her momentary and bodily desires while disregarding the needs of the community symbolized both the nation's diminished moral fiber and the decline in its birthrate, needed to be transformed into the domesticated, procreative mother, who affirmed her "natural" calling to reproduce, and thus, embodied the true promise of national rebirth.

For these Jewish population experts, the disciplining of the female body thus came to represent the last best hope for securing a viable Jewish future in post-Emancipation Germany. Yet such a development could come about only as Jewish men and women, like non-Jewish Germans, were themselves subjected to bodily forms of social discipline for the purpose of rendering them useful subjects and integrating them into the German state. They, in turn, reproduced the social disciplinary functions of these discourses with respect both to women and Eastern Europeans within the Jewish community just as their non-Jewish colleagues (and many Jews as well) applied them to the working classes in general. But Jews had also increasingly become targets of specifically racial discourses. This was the case particularly towards the end of the 1920s, when a nationalist-exclusivist outlook overtook eugenics and racial hygiene, the two disciplines that had indisputably made race a central category of social analysis but that had not always been explicitly racist themselves.[54]

Yet Jews were more than merely passive subjects of discipline. They also acted as empowered subjects by transforming those discourses that could potentially exclude them. Indeed, the complex interrelationship of German and

Jewish population policy suggests that some Jews in Weimar did not only resist
the potentially exclusionary racial and eugenic measures being promoted by
physicians and the state, they also adapted them to serve their own perceived
interests. Although their work was cut short by economic crises and the ultimate rise of National Socialism, these Jewish experts engaged in the production
of alternative forms of knowledge that, as a consequence, created a discursive
space through which the individual might be empowered to resist dominant
forms of social power. Yet as much as there was a degree of empowerment in
the way these Jews redeployed the discourses and inscribed them with new
meanings, they had also, in the process, become disciplinary agents themselves.
Jewish experts internalized the values of the various disciplines they employed
to order, organize, and productivize the "human material" for the broader
needs of their ethnic-religious community and the German state. These new
regimes of discipline undermined the notion of individual autonomy often associated with the subject even as they executed this through an insistence on
the imperative to maintain corporeal wholeness.

It is the double focus on Jews as active historical agents on the one hand,
and as subjects of the state and social scientific discourses on the other, that
may be of greatest utility in helping to revise contemporary representations of
Jews within Weimar historiography. Viewing Jews as active agents of history
and not merely as the soon-to-be-victims of the Nazi regime permits us to
avoid the distortions and pitfalls of reading Weimar history through the lens
of 1933. At the same time, treating Jewish subjectivities as particular versions
of German subjectivity sheds light on the common set of social forces acting
upon middle-class Jewish and non-Jewish Germans alike. Taken together, both
of these approaches allow us to better comprehend the complexity of Jews who
navigated between and amongst an array of social forces and fields of power.
Following the lead of feminist scholarship, such a focus on Jewish subjectivities
can serve to highlight both the subordination of Jews to non-Jewish Germans
and the diverse ways they maneuvered within a new state that was more inclusive of Jews and within a society that was growing dangerously intolerant of
them.

Ultimately, the inclusion of Jewish representations of their own "difference"
in larger narratives of Weimar history addresses one of the most fraught questions in German and German Jewish history: that of Jewish assimilation. What
these discourses of reproduction tell us is that notions of difference are hardly
monolithic, but are historically specific in that they are constructed and reconstructed in historically specific terms at distinct historical moments. From
the unique application of these discourses within the Jewish social sphere, we
may observe how a new notion of Jewish difference was being forged out of the
very materials of German culture. Rather than viewing assimilation as an ap-
propriation of "external" elements to an internal, autochthonous culture, Amos

Funkenstein reminds us that "Jews expressed their uniqueness and still do, in an idiom always acquired from their environment."[55] This dialectic of assimilation that Funkenstein describes can be brought to light particularly well through the historicization of difference, allowing us to see how some Jews imagined themselves to be the same as non-Jews while also seeking to remain, in a real physical sense, apart from them.

With their emphases on the body, discourses of reproduction thus represent both a continuation and break with the Enlightenment promise of assimilation. At one level, the twentieth-century goal of increasing the Jewish birthrate and bringing about the moral rejuvenation associated with it can be read as a continuation of the regenerationist program of the Jewish Enlightenment, which sought to counter anti-Semitic characterizations of Jews' lack of fitness by demonstrating the moral improvement of the Jews as a group. The eighteenth- and early nineteenth-century emphasis on "civic improvement" led to, among other developments, the wholly unsuccessful attempt by the "enlightened" Jewish leadership to bring about the "productivization" of Jews. This productivization was supposed to be effected via a program of occupational reform that would direct Jews away from the fields of business and finance towards more "respectable" forms of work that included manual labor and the artisan trades. At another level, however, the new emphasis on the body in the twentieth century represents a break with the promise of assimilation and, perhaps, the Enlightenment project as a whole. For the emancipation of the Jews presupposed in one way or another the disappearance of the Jews as a group, either as the result of conversion, or through the gradual falling away of distinctly Jewish social, occupational, linguistic, and national characteristics. The sustained focus on the body as a means of responding to the threat of social annihilation represents, it would seem, a collective reaction against that same social, if not physical, disappearance of Jews that had been so desired just a century earlier, and which now, as a consequence of successful assimilation, threatened to efface Jewish distinctiveness altogether. The embodiment of Weimar Jewish subjectivities may be read, then, as more than a mere deviation from a modern enlightened agenda; it is, in fact, a profoundly counter-Enlightenment move made all the more intriguing by its continued reliance on the authority of science. In the postwar context, the persistence of Jewishness came to be understood by some Jews not simply as the survival of a group bearing distinct religious or cultural characteristics, but as an irrefutable corporeality. Historical-religious notions of Jewish uniqueness were similarly transformed from being viewed primarily as a set of moral-religious attributes to an understanding of Jewishness as a distinct bodily reality.

All this suggests that to recast Weimar historical narratives in a way that will shed light on Jews' complex social position within German society, it is particularly important to figure Jews into Weimar history as a collectivity. As individuals, Jews have been readily included in histories of Weimar politics, culture, social welfare, and the welfare state, but those realms of experience that touch upon Jewish collective existence have been all but excluded from the larger narratives of post–World War I Germany.[56] Such an analysis of Weimar Jewish subjectivities indeed has something important to say about the relationship between the periphery and center in German social life, as well as the unintended consequences of normative discourses when applied by social groups that were situated, at least in some ways, on the margins. The story of Jewish subjectivities then, belongs not to an internalist history of the Jews in Germany, but forms part of the history of *German* self-representation.

Notes

1. Atina Grossmann, *Reforming Sex: The German Movement for Birth Control and Sex Reform 1920–1950* (New York, 1995); Cornelie Usborne, *The Politics of the Body: Women's Reproductive Rights and Duties* (New York, 1992).
2. I borrow this phrase from Elisa Camiscioli, "Producing Citizens, Reproducing the 'French Race': Immigration, Demography, and Pronatalism in Early Twentieth-Century France," *Gender and History* 13, no. 3 (2001): 601.
3. George Steinmetz, *Regulating the Social: Welfare State and Local Politics in Imperial Germany* (Princeton, NJ, 1993), 198–203.
4. Michel Foucault, *Discipline and Punish: the Birth of the Prison* (New York, 1977); "The Politics of Health in the Eighteenth Century," in *Power/Knowledge: Selected Interviews & Other Writings 1972–1977*, ed. Colin Gordon (New York, 1980), 166–82; "Governmentality," in *The Foucault Effect: Studies in Governmentality*, ed. Graham Burchell, Colin Gordon, and Peter Miller (Chicago, 1991), 87–104.
5. Annette Timm, "The Politics of Fertility: Population Politics and Health Care in Berlin, 1919–1972" (PhD diss., University of Chicago, 1999), 3.
6. On "body histories," see Kathleen Canning, "The Body as Method? Reflections on the Place of the Body in Gender History," *Gender and History* 11, no. 3 (1999): 81–95.
7. Usborne, *Politics of the Body*, 25.
8. Sidonie Wronsky, "Die Forderungen der Gegenwart an die jüdische Wohlfahrtspflege" in *Von Jüdischer Wohlfahrtspflege*, ed. Zentralwohlfahrtsstelle der deutschen Juden (Berlin, 1922), 14–15.
9. Usborne, *Politics of the Body*, 3.
10. Paul Weindling, *Health, Race and German Politics between National Unification and Nazism, 1870–1945* (Cambridge, 1989), 10.
11. Usborne, *Politics of the Body*, 17–30.
12. Gustav Tugendreich, "Was für Aufgaben fallen der Sozialhygiene in der jüdischen Gemeinde-Wohlfahrtspflege zu?" *Zeitschrift für Jüdische Wohlfahrtspflege* 1, no. 1 (1929): 42–44.
13. Felix A. Theilhaber, *Der Untergang der deutschen Juden. Eine Volkswirtschaftliche Studie* (Munich, 1911). All further citations are from the second edition published in Berlin by Jüdischer Verlag in 1921.

14. Cited in Dr. Jakob Levy, "'Geburtenstreik'—die Frage der jüdischen Ehe," *Nachalath Z'wi. Eine Monatsschrift für Judentum in Lehre und Tat* 11/12 (1930): 15.

15. Salomon Lehnart (Siegfried Lehmann), "Jüdische Volksarbeit," *Der Jude* 1 (1916–17): 110.

16. Rabbi (Dr.) Max Eschelbacher, "Mischehen," *Ost und West* 17 (March/April 1917): 80–88.

17. Dr. Friedrich Ollendorff, "Einigung der jüdischen Wohlfahrtspflege," August 10 1917, Bundesarchiv Potsdam Deutsch-Israelitischer Gemeindebund 75C Ge1/903 Zentralwohlfahrtsstelle, 10.

18. Zentralwohlfahrtsstelle der deutschen Juden, Preussischer Landesverband Jüdischer Gemeinden, *Jüdische Bevölkerungspolitik. Bericht über die Tagung des Bevölkerungspolitischen Ausschusses des Preussischen Landesverbandes Jüdischer Gemeinden vom 24. Februar 1929*, Schriften der Zentralwohlfahrtsstelle der deutschen Juden/Nr.II, (Berlin, 1929), 21.

19. Ibid., 26.

20. Ibid., 9.

21. Ibid., 77.

22. Weindling, *Health, Race and German Politics*, 246.

23. *Jüdische Bevölkerungspolitik*, 23.

24. Ernst Kahn, *Der International Geburtenstreik. Umfang, Ursachen, Wirkungen Gegenmassnahmen?* (Frankfurt am Main, 1930), 37.

25. Eugen Wolbe, "Selbstmord oder neues Leben? Ein Wort zur Bevölkerungspolitik der deutschen Juden," (Oranienburg, 1918), 17.

26. *Jüdische Bevölkerungspolitik*, 51.

27. Steven Aschheim, *Brothers and Strangers: The East European Jew in German and German Jewish Consciousness, 1800–1923* (Madison, WI, 1982), 187.

28. Ibid., 185–214.

29. Theilhaber, *Der Untergang*, 11.

30. Ibid., 16.

31. Ibid., 7.

32. Rabbi Dr. Eschelbacher, "Jüdische Weltanschauung und Verhütung der Geschlechtskrankheiten," *Zedakah* 3 (July 1928): 46.

33. Levy, "Geburtenstreik," 15.

34. Paul Weindling, "Eugenics and the Welfare State during the Weimar Republic," in *The State and Social Change in Germany, 1880–1980*, ed. W. R. Lee and Eve Rosenhaft (New York, 1990), 155.

35. Dr. Pfeil, "Die Bevölkerungspolitik der deutschen Juden," *Archiv für Bevölkerungspolitik Sexualethik und Familienkunde* (Berlin, 1932), 10.

36. *Jüdische Bevölkerungspolitik*, 4–5.

37. Wohlfahrts-Ausschuss des Preussischen Landesverbandes jüdischen Gemeinden, *Verwaltungsblatt des Preussischen Landesverbandes jüdischer Gemeinden*, 5/6 (15 October 1927): 1.

38. *Jüdische Bevölkerungspolitik*, 83.

39. Ibid., 40–41.

40. Ibid., 59.

41. Ibid., 2.

42. Wolbe, "Selbstmord oder neues Leben?" 7.

43. *Jüdische Bevölkerungspolitik*, 59.

44. Marion Kaplan, *The Jewish Feminist Movement in Germany: The Campaigns of the Jü-discher Frauenbund, 1904–1938* (Westport, CT, 1979), 132.

45. Wolbe, "Selbstmord oder neues Leben?" 19–20.

46. *Jüdische Bevölkerungspolitik,* 38.

47. Bericht über die Sitzung des Bezirkes Schöneberg am 28. 4. 26. Centrum Judaicum, 75A B32 290 #63.

48. *Jüdische Bevölkerungspolitik,* 45.

49. Ibid., 46.

50. *Jüdische Bevölkerungspolitik,* 29.

51. Ibid.

52. Ibid., 21–24.

53. Atina Grossmann's term in *Reforming Sex,* 15.

54. Shela Faith Weiss, "The Race Hygiene Movement in Germany," 27.

55. Amos Funkenstein, "The Dialectics of Assimilation," *Jewish Social Studies* 1/2 (1995): 11.

56. This list is far from exhaustive: David Crew, *Germans on Welfare: From Weimar to Hitler* (New York, 1998); Young-Sun Hong, *Welfare, Modernity, and the Weimar State* (Princeton, NJ, 1988); Grossmann, *Reforming Sex;* Usborne, *The Politics of the Body;* Timm, "Politics of Fertility,"; Christoph Sachße, *Mütterlichkeit als Beruf* (Opladen, 1994); Christoph Sachße and Florian Tennstedt, *Geschichte der Armenfürsorge in Deutschland: Fürsorge und Wohlfahrtspflege 1871 bis 1929* (Stuttgart, 1988); Jürgen Reyer, *Alte Eugenik und Wohlfahrtspflege. Entwertung und Funktionalisierung der Fürsorge vom Ende des 19. Jahrhunderts bis zur Gegenwart* (Freiburg im Breisgau, 1991).

PART III

∼:∼

Symbols, Rituals, and Discourses of Democracy

CHAPTER 8

~:·:~

Reforming the Reich
Democratic Symbols and Rituals in the Weimar Republic

MANUELA ACHILLES

It is a historiographical commonplace that the Weimar Republic lacked the symbolic appeal to bind collective sentiment and win widespread popular support.[1] The historian Detlev Peukert, in an important study of the period, argues that the first German democracy had no founding ritual, and that the absence of such a central symbolic moment in national history contributed to the republic's general lack of legitimacy.[2] His assessment is sustained not at least by major democrats of the period, who testify to the republic's dearth of "propagandistic charisma."[3] Gustav Radbruch, a major representative of the Weimar SPD, for instance, states that the Social Democrats made a mistake when they failed to accompany their republican engagement with the corresponding national music but rather worked "silently" and with "gritted teeth."[4] Since then, so Radbruch laments, "we have learned that the world is not led by reason, but by trifles, or less informally said, that any politics requires symbols and fantasy."[5]

Radbruch's memoirs are typical of recollections deeply affected by the experience of National Socialism. Seen from the perspective of its failure,[6] it is plausible to contend that the republic did not develop a democratic symbolism or culture. In this essay, I wish to brush history against the grain by starting from the contention that despite severe handicaps, the republicans' democratic endeavor—both at its inception and far into the years of relative stabilization—was not without hope of success. However nonrevolutionary the German revolution of 1918–19 may have been, to many contemporaries it still held promise of political change and social mobility, which at the time seemed opportune, if not long overdue. The best-selling Weimar author Vicki Baum, for example, remembers the revolution as being an "immense relief to us, the people, the mothers, wives, families; great hopes and promises for a free, shining future in most quarters. Only a small minority of professional soldiers, die-hards, and inexperienced young hotheads seemed to care about the lost war. Bitter curses followed the Kaiser, the sabre-rattling windbag who had run away and left us in the soup."[7]

The wartime government's failure to ensure an adequate supply of food and other necessities at home, the large numbers of deaths attributable to sense-less military operations and the final defeat, as well as the emperor's flight to Holland all severely eroded confidence in the old regime's legitimacy. The disqualification of the imperial rule translated into a sweeping victory for the democratic parties in the first general elections to the constituent assembly. In turn, this victory provided a window of opportunity for the (legal) constitution of a democratic republic.

The constitution that the constituent assembly voted for on 31 July 1919 and that President Ebert signed on 11 August held two stipulations regarding the republic's national symbolism. Both of those were heavily disputed. Article 3 determined the national colors. Recuperating the tradition of the democratic revolution of 1848, the "new" colors were black, red, and gold. Yet due to pres-sure from the reactionary right and the democratic center, the merchant marine flag kept the imperial black, white, and red with the national colors in the up-per canton of the ensign. Article 109 concerned the equality of all Germans. In a critical demarcation from the flood of honorary medals and titles of empire, it prohibited the state from bestowing orders and honorary titles on its citizens. The constitution held no provision for a national anthem or national holidays.

While the republic broke with the imperial practice of deploying regal splendor and military glory, it still needed to create official symbols in order to project its public image. Key examples included the celebrations of Constitu-tion Day on 11 August, the commemoration and memorialization of particular historical events and persons, as well as the transformations of the national emblems and insignia (such as the federal coat of arms, flags, seals, uniforms, postal stamps, bank notes, coins, medals, boundary stones, etc.). In tracing the design and dissemination of the republican state symbols, as well as their "uses" (Michel de Certeau), I would contend we can approach the *emergence* of an in-clusive democratic culture that transcended the confines of social milieux and political party lines. This essay will explore the state official commemoration of Walther Rathenau's death as one such moment of democratic invention.

Inversions of *Gewalt* in Weimar Germany

The Democratic foreign minister of the republican government was shot on 24 June 1922 by nationalist, antirepublican fanatics.[8] Yet despite the subversive intentions of the assassins, or better, because of them, the murder of Rathenau held great symbolic potential for the republican movement. As Martin Sabrow has shown, millions of Germans across political borders united in mourning, despair, and horror by participating in the mass rallies led by the trade unions, democratic parties, and republican associations.[9] The deceased was praised as a man who for many years had unselfishly put himself in the service of the state, and who had now become a martyr for his country. Rathenau was presented in this way not only in the press but also in the various mourning ceremonies conducted in the federal and state parliaments as well as at workplaces and in schools, universities and churches. Contemporary observers of those events such as Harry Graf Kessler, Georg Bernhard, and Wilhelm Marx all describe the assassination of Rathenau as a "turning point" in German history. Kessler, for example, noted into his diary: "I was thunderstruck. Reflection followed. Now the ... bills have to be settled with the murderers of the Right. ... Helfferich is the murderer, the real, the responsible."[10]

The former vice chancellor of the empire, Karl Theodor Helfferich, of course, did not shoot Rathenau. Yet Kessler's identification of the nationalist politician with Rathenau's actual murderers is comprehensible if seen in light of an extremely polemical attack that Helfferich had launched one day before the murder. In vilifying not only the political actions but also the ethical motivations of his democratic opponent, he employed a strategy quite common to the nationalist rhetoric of the time. Until 1922 nationalist politics quite successfully exploited, and to a large extent monopolized, highly charged ethicopolitical themes. The reproach of a "stab in the back" and "humiliation of Germany" were particularly effective in disqualifying all Social Democratic and liberal democratic attempts to consolidate the republican state. The murder of Rathenau destabilized this discourse. It opened up the opportunity to associate nationalist politics with the murderous actions of its extremist adherents, thus providing the republicans with the rare opportunity to seize the political initiative from the antirepublican Right. In effect, the murder thus became a symbolic coup against socially respected and respectable antirepublicans, for it discredited for a moment their symbols and symbolism. In other words: Rathenau's death marked a historic moment at which a democratic discourse was able to congeal and emerge as a force against certain nationalist truisms about the German republic.

The emergence of a republican discourse and movement as the (indirect) result of a crime raises the question of the intrinsic relationship of violence to power, a problematic that is most prevalent in the German term *Gewalt*, which designates not only "violence," but also "power" and "force." Arno J. Mayer summarizes centuries of theoretical reflection on this issue by arguing that violence is basic to society, especially to its foundation and consolidation. This remark refers to, among others, Thomas Hobbes, Karl Marx, Max Weber, Walter Benjamin, Hannah Arendt, and Paul Ricoeur, who all in one way or another argue that no beginning could be made without violence or without violation. In his "Critique of Violence" published in 1922, Benjamin, for example, discriminates between a violence of foundation, which sets up and anchors a new order of legitimacy (the law); and a violence of conservation, which maintains and enforces it (the police).[11] It would seem, then, that violence is not only normative, but also even normal.

While the murder of Rathenau had great foundational potential, it was also fraught not only with nationalist (if not anti-Semitic) violence but also with republican violations of the public peace. For instance, after the assassination became public, members of the political Left in the Reichstag attacked proponents of the political Right both verbally and physically, addressing them as "gang of murderers."[12] Similar incidents took place in the streets of major cities throughout Germany. In Berlin, a large crowd walking along the Tauentzienstrasse after Rathenau's funeral aggressively assaulted a young man because he wore a high-school student's cap with a black, white, and red ribbon. In Karlsruhe large crowds first destroyed imperial signs and insignia, then wrecked the headquarters of the German National People's Party (DNVP). In Darmstadt, two editorial offices as well as the apartments of two representatives of the German Peoples Party (DVP) were demolished, and the editorial offices of two right-wing newspapers were smashed. In some cases, the antinationalist action of the masses led to confrontations with the police that ended in the death of some protesters. In Darmstadt, the police shot more than twenty people, killing three. In the course of a clash in Hamburg, the police injured several people, one of whom died that very day.[13]

Norbert Elias has stated that a modern nation state needs to pacify its internal social spaces by establishing a monopoly of violence. The murder of Rathenau was a violation of this monopoly. But so was the counterviolence of agitated republican crowds. In this situation, the republicans of state faced both an enormous challenge and a great opportunity. On the one hand, they had to harness the emotions unleashed by the murder. That is, they had to maintain and enforce the state's monopoly of violence. On the other hand, they had to link the republic to the positive political beliefs and symbolic practices of the people. The latter was an important task, which consisted in nothing less than the molding of an inclusive republican symbolism. The *Vossische Zeitung* stated this as follows: "The new Germany demands for *its* institutions, *its* symbols, *its* legal setup, *its* political spirit, faith, and strength."[14] In this context, the symbolic inversion of the Rathenau murder exemplifies how an act of antirepublican violence could be turned to the advantage of the republican cause.[15]

It should be noted that this reversal of terms was not unprecedented. The socialist Left, for instance, adopted the stab-in-the-back motif into the antimilitaristic language of class struggle. An SPD campaign flier, published in 1920, asserted that "the army was not stabbed by the people ... , but by ... those officers who lived comfortably behind the front ... , and sent home boxes and containers, even whole railway carriages of stolen goods."[16] The Left-liberal press, too, gave the antirepublican slur a prorepublican twist. In response to the Erzberger murder in August 1921, the *Ulk*, a satirical supplement of *Berliner Tageblatt*, featured the cartoon *Nationalist Lie and Truth*.[17] The first of two images depicts a soldier in full gear, who faces the eastern front and is stabbed from behind by a worker. The caption comments, "A stab in the back that is a legend." The second image shows a republican politician with briefcase and umbrella, walking through a park. Facing westwards, the unguarded pedestrian is stabbed in the back by an exponent of the antirepublican terrorist organizations. The caption elaborates: "A stab in the back that is no legend." The murder of Rathenau proved to the republican nation that antirepublican propaganda had real effects, thus uniting all supporters of the republic against the ultranationalist Right.

Ein Dolchſtoß, der eine Legende iſt

Ein Dolchſtoß, der keine Legende iſt

Figure 8.1. *Nationalist Lie and Truth:* "A stab in the back that is a legend./ A stab in the back that is no legend." *Ulk. Wochenschrift the Berliner Tageblatts*, 9 September 1921.

Public Mourning and the State

The republican funeral service for Rathenau was the first of its kind, and thus set the stage for the emergence of an official symbolism of mourning. Before exploring the ceremony in more detail, it seems advisable first to consider the public funeral practice of the Second Empire. When in March 1888 Wilhelm I succumbed at the age of ninety after a brief illness, he lay in state in the Berlin Cathedral, where about 200,000 people filed past his body over the course of four days.[18] The imperial protocol also included a solemn procession. The first two sections were composed of the Hohenzollern and their relatives, and a display of the emperor's insignia, which by most accounts were Prussian in origin. Personalities from the arts, sciences, and politics were relegated to the third and last section. Before the eyes of numerous spectators, the march thus demonstrated with imperial splendor that sovereignty resided with the gentry, not with the nation or *Volk*.[19]

Yet at the same time that imperial funerals marked the capital's imperial order, funerals also figured quite prominently in the protest tradition of the working class. In fact, Thomas Lindenberger argues that the public commemoration of the dead was one of the few collective street usages that was democratized in the Wilhelmine Empire.[20] Death, so Lindenberger notes, placed the subjects and their rulers under the same "higher" order of mourning.[21] Since the police had to assign a minimal space to the public expression of grief, there emerged an opportunity for the articulation of oppositional "street politics." This excess space, however, hardly ever produced political confrontations since the commitment to the commemoration's "dignity" tied the energies of the participants to the rituals. Thus public mourning rendered the everyday public order relative, while at the same time preventing its transgression. The liberal middle classes in Berlin, too, frequently turned to funerals in order to dramatize their social solidarity.[22] To the extent that these processions projected an alternative social order, they also challenged the representational authority of the empire. In Wilhelmine times, funerals thus presented highly protean rites of passage. By rendering private grief public, individual loss collective, and social practices political—and vice versa—these ceremonies opened up space for a wide range of oppositional uses of the streets. At the same time access to political honors, in the form of state funerals, for example, remained the de facto privilege of the royal family.[23]

With the founding of the Weimar Republic, the honorary practices of state changed dramatically. At the same time that the constitution prohibited the state from bestowing orders, medals, and titles on its citizens, the government awarded state funerals not only to Walther Rathenau (June 1922), but also to Reich President Friedrich Ebert (March 1925) and Foreign Minister Gustav Stresemann (October 1929). Representatives of the government also attended the Reichstag service for seventeen workers of Krupp Werke shot by French soldiers in Essen (April 1923), as well as the SPD-sponsored funeral of the former Reich Chancellor Hermann Müller (March 1931).[24] The fact that state officials partook in all these funerals indicates that a larger range of citizens became "honorable" in their deaths when compared to the political culture of the *Kaiserreich*. Volker Ackermann rightly asserts that this extension of access to state honors reflects a significant degree of democratization.

How do we read the democratization of a public practice that according to Thomas Lindenberger was already "democratized" in the Wilhelmine Empire? Ackermann argues that the republic developed a new style of representation that for the first time involved rites organized and/or held by the working class.[25] In addition to bestowing posthumous honors on representatives of the people, the republic thus appropriated democratic mourning practices that had been used earlier to challenge the authority of the state. That the oppositional dimensions of those practices were by no means forgotten became evident when their memory precluded the republican government from conducting a full-fledged ritual of state.

Prelude: Spirits of the Past

In the cabinet meeting of 25 June, Vice Chancellor Gustav Bauer of the SPD proposed to have the slain body of Walther Rathenau lay in state in the Reichstag's great hallway with an honor guard.[26] Chancellor Wirth favored the deployment of a bigger military unit, but not for marching in the funeral procession. When it became known that Rathenau's relatives rejected a public burial ceremony, Bauer demanded that the family's wishes give way "in the service of the entirety." Home Secretary Adolf Köster suggested yielding the interment decision to the family, but like his fellow party member, insisted on a "ceremony with the corpse." This concern with Rathenau's dead body indicates that his corpse presented an important vehicle for localizing the republicans' claim to the body politic. Since the deceased represented the assaulted body politic, giving him a proper funeral was critical to the state's passage into a refurbished political order.

New consultations with the family produced a compromise. The graveside service was limited to family and friends,[27] while the government conducted a state official mourning service in the Reichstag. Interestingly, the final program included neither a public viewing of the corpse nor a funeral procession, thus excluding all of the elements that traditionally involved the participation of the masses. It seems fair to assume that the restrictions on public access to the mourning ceremony accommodated fears, especially of Rathenau's family, that a public articulation of grief would give rise to political disturbances.

The government delegated the funeral's orchestration to Edwin Redslob, the Federal Art Expert (*Reichskunstwart*).[28] He started his work with an "ugly dispute." Assuming that the ceremony would take place in the Reichstag's assembly hall, Redslob was stunned when the building's supervising director, seconded by a right-wing member of the Reichstag's Decoration Committee,[29] allotted him the great hallway. On first sight, this assignment seemed plausible enough. After all, Gustav Bauer in the cabinet meeting of 25 June had envisioned a similar scenario. Redslob, however, instantly understood how such a setting served the purposes of the political Right. In the middle of the domed hall stood a larger than life statue of Wilhelm I. Designed and sculpted by Johannes Pfuhl, the imperial monument occupied the hall's optical center. If the mourning service took place here, Rathenau's coffin would have to be placed in the shadow of the emperor. Redslob found such an arrangement unacceptable. He first considered veiling the statue, only to quickly dismiss this option for fear of providing grist to the mill of the reactionary propaganda machine.[30]

When one day before the funeral the location was still undecided, Redslob called on Reichstag President Paul Löbe (SPD), who immediately assigned him the assembly hall.[31] Yet even at the margins of the ceremony the emperor's statue remained problematic. The radical Socialists announced with great embitterment that the USPD would not participate in a mourning service that took place under the symbols of the old regime.[32] The moderate Socialists, too, demanded significant alterations to the Reichstag's imperial ornamentation. For instance, *Vorwärts*, the Social Democratic Party daily, charged that the monarchic memorabilia belonged neither in the Reichstag, nor in the capital's squares and parks, except where they figured as valuable works of art that embellished the city.[33] The reactionary Right, on the other hand, vehemently defended the statue. Rendering the monument "a reminder of the foundation of the German Reich and the Reich constitution of 1871," ultranationalist daily papers such as the *Preußische Zeitung* warned that its removal would "deeply offend wide circles of the nation, thus leading not to the soothing, but to the aggravation of the antagonisms within the people."[34]

Interestingly, the Democrats, in the name of Rathenau, also declined to remove or even veil the imperial statue.[35] Striving to accommodate the nationalist temper, the Democrats found themselves caught in a double bind. Politically, they identified with the republic. Sentimentally, they sided with reaction. They dissolved their dilemma by appealing to ethical, aesthetic, and historical grounds. In a letter to the *Vossische Zeitung*, published after Rathenau's funeral, M. P. Friedrich Fick of the DDP clarified his party's position. First, he branded the Socialists as injudicious, even "almost criminal," for they fed political controversy when "unity and cohesion were more necessary than ever."[36] Second, he depreciated the statue's artistic merits. Third, Fick noted that already in imperial times the idea of a people's house was incompatible with the imperial presence at its center. He then suggested moving the statue to the Reichstag's southern entry hall, which already accommodated several bronze emperors of the first Reich. Fick ended his letter by praising Wilhelm I—"the revered old man"—who together with Bismarck and Moltke laid "the foundations of the second Reich, which in the new form of the free state and after difficult times shall form a mighty protective roof, arching over the German people for another 1,000 years."[37]

Deadlocked by antagonistic political forces, the Reichstag's Decoration Committee recommended enveloping the statue, perhaps in a pyramid of mourning crêpe. Redslob decided to integrated the statue into the mourning decor. Surrounded only by laurel trees, Wilhelm I stood unmoved as the congregation in conclusion of the mourning service escorted Rathenau's coffin to the Reichstag's exit. Did the public notice the monument? Neither *Vorwärts* nor *Berliner Tageblatt* paid it any regard. *Germania* and the *Vossische Zeitung* registered that the statue was unveiled. The latter added that the monument troubled nobody; and that taking political offense at it did not make any sense.[38] The *Preußische Zeitung*, on the other hand, dramatized the emperor's presence in terms of a last-minute rescue from Socialist iconoclasm.[39] The saviors in this plot were female. Katharina von Oheimb of the German Peoples' Party, so the story ran, informed Rathenau's family of the Decoration Committee's veiling decision. Thereupon Rathenau's mother declared that she would abstain from the service under such circumstances, since her son had revered the old emperor.[40] Mobilized by the political Right, Mathilde Rathenau thus safeguarded the emperor's symbolic survival in the name of the slain.

The *Weltbühne*, a major paper of the left-wing intelligentsia in Weimar Germany, retorted by branding the Oheimb initiative as insensitive beyond compare: "In the whole of Germany, there are no proletarian or Jewish women, who would manage to do something like this: to call the old mother of such a victim twenty-four hours after the bloody deed … and to drag her into the fight, which in a republican republic would be unnecessary. It [the republican republic] would have removed both: the statue and this honor [*Zierde*] to the Christian nobility of the German nation."[41] As regards the republic's compliance with the reactionary nationalism, Ignaz Wrobel (alias Kurt Tucholsky) wrote: "When Walther Rathenau lay in state in the Reichstag, his sublime grandfather stood still, as if glazed. A hot quarrel had evolved around him: Should this monarchist statue be removed from this people's house of the republicans or not? Feelings had to be spared. … One surrounded it with laurel trees; it was veiled. Everything here is like this. We crush nothing—we veil it."[42]

Suspended in republican space, the imperial monument was symptomatic of the republic's symbolic economy. Struggling to establish a democratic future, the republicans left the statues and status of the past undetermined. As a result, the tensions between iconoclastic and reactionary desires remained caustic. The

DDP was most affected by this dilemma. Here the attempt to square imperial nostalgia with republican affiliations highlights severe problems with the republican project of reform. Caught in a double bind, the Democrats pursued a double-edged strategy. On the one hand, they engaged in acts of containment, referring the imperial past to the realms of art and history. On the other hand, the displacement of the past from the political onto the aesthetic and historical planes fostered the preservation of imperial, if not monarchic identifications. To study this ambivalence of the republican symbolism in more detail, we must now turn from the ceremony's periphery to its ritual center.

Republican Martyrdom

With the help of theater director Leopold Jeßner and gardening expert Hermann Rothe, Redslob sought an integrative funeral service that represented the new Reich.[43] While its republican symbolism was important, traditional signs of mourning dominated the scene. The assembly hall was lined in black, and decorated with flowers, palms, and laurel trees. Rathenau's coffin took center stage. Draped under the service flag of a federal minister, it stood raised in state on the extended desk of the Reichstag president. Attachés of the Foreign Office kept guard.[44] Closely aligned with the symbolism of state was the symbolism of the Rathenau family. At each side of the coffin lay a large wreath of roses, bearing the clearly legible inscriptions "Mama" and "Edith" respectively. The real eye-catcher, however, was a black, triangular canopy that nearly touched the ceiling. While its construction suggested royal dignity, Greek apotheosis, or Christian resurrection, the canopy also served a dramaturgical purpose. Similar to a theater curtain, it forged into one frame the coffin, flag, and wreaths, thus creating a primary scene of mourning, which it then exposed to the public eye.

Rathenau's links to the German nation at large were represented at the fringes of the stage, in the form of numerous wreaths, positioned in front of the coffin on the speaker's platform, as well as on the front wall of the government tables. Indicating beauty, vitality, hope, as well as the transitory nature of life, the flower arrangements also carried their meaning in a more literal sense. The inscriptions on their ribbons registered Rathenau's diverse affiliations, ranging from the ministries and the diplomatic corps to industrial, bank, and trade associations to art societies and prominent individuals, such as Gerhart Hauptmann, which attested to Rathenau's social rank and political position. Socialist media such as *Vorwärts* emphasized to their audience the black-red-gold colors of the streamers.

At noon, Chancellor Wirth escorted Rathenau's mother to the former imperial box, where she was seated in the place of the emperor. In her privileged location, Mathilde Rathenau occupied a central symbolic position not only *in* the audience, but also *for* it. That is, the fragile, small, old woman lent a human face to the impact of the murder, thus bestowing emotional authority onto the ritual of state. Kessler, for instance, noted that it was the sight of her veiled face, deadly pale and pain ridden, but all self-control, that touched him most.[45] It is important that the maternal image is one of disciplined grief. While this conduct seems consistent with Mathilde's manners,[46] Kessler reports that initially "her one desire was to write and tell Helfferich *he* was the murderer of her son, and then to die herself." In the end, however, she wrote a compassionate letter to Frau Techow, the mother of one of her son's murderers.[47] The note was widely read as a most noble testimony of motherly solidarity. From the republican point of view, Rathenau's mother thus embodied not only the republic's bereavement but also forgiveness and reconciliation.

After Mathilde Rathenau was seated in the former imperial box, a procession led by Reich President Ebert, Reichstag President Löbe, and Chancellor Wirth entered the main hall. The assembly rose to greet them. The program then proceeded along traditional lines, following the standard scheme "music, speech, music."[48] First, the orchestra, which was invisible to the audience, performed Beethoven's Coriolan overture. While this choice of music was quite conventional, it also struck a personal note, since Coriolan was one of Rathenau's favorite compositions.[49] Next came the speeches. At imperial state funerals, the preacher of the court spoke as a member of the Prussian royal house.[50] The denominationally neutral republic lacked an explicitly religious ritual, such as a sermon. Instead three political representatives in the order of their rank delivered secular funeral orations. President Ebert spoke first, followed by Dr. Bell, the Catholic vice president of the Reichstag, and the Protestant Minister Korell of the Democratic Party. In sum, the eulogists thus represented Reich and Reichstag, as well as the parties of the Weimar Coalition and the two predominant churches.

Dramaturgically, the speeches were increasingly political and "politicized."[51] The president's speech was most conciliatory. Situating the assembly next to the family at the site of the coffin, Ebert's leitmotif was the unified nation. The assassins figured as agents of self-exclusion. By murdering a virtuous statesman, they expelled themselves from society, nation, and *Volk*. Bell and Korell struggled more explicitly with the political background of the assassination. Invoking the world history of political murder, Bell asked the republicans to put an end to the antirepublican agitation, while Korell connected the murder to the aftermath of World War I. He was the only speaker who took on the issue of both nationalism and anti-Semitism. All three speakers struggled with the distinction between patriotism and nationalism, claiming the former for the republic and rejecting the latter. Bell designated Rathenau a national martyr, while Ebert and Korell also asserted that the slain minister sacrificed his life for the German nation.

After the final speaker finished, the orchestra commenced the funeral march of Wagner's *Twilight of the Gods* (*Götterdämmerung*). Participants such as Kessler emphasized the emotional impact of the music. Redslob also paid attention to the mourning script. As the funeral march resounded, Rathenau's coffin was taken up as participants formed a double line through which the coffin was carried to the main exit. Then the doors of the Reichstag opened. According to Redslob, "one saw an incredible mass, so that the internal celebration automatically met with the large demonstration of the hundred thousands of people who occupied the Königsplatz."[52] Kessler also described the last encounter of the slain minister with the people as a central symbolic moment of the republic.[53] He then noted into his diaries: "What Lassalle yearned for in his dreams, the entry through the Brandenburg Gate as the president of a German republic... , has been realized by the Jew Rathenau, who has died a martyr's death in the service of the German people."[54]

Rathenau's passage from the inside to the outside of the Reichstag and through the Brandenburg Gate into the heart of the republic invoked the ceremony's integrative appeal. In the democratic imagination, the liberal Jew appeared as the redeemer of the Social Democratic dream, while the numerous spectator-participants attested to the popular acceptance of his sacrifice.[55] On the formal side, the republican media stressed the ceremony's propriety, lauding its "fine artistic sensibility" and "distinguished taste." Interestingly enough, the ultraconservative *Preußische Zeitung* also praised the setting, describing it as "generous" and "tolerant."[56] The nationalist praise might raise concerns about the ceremony's political significance. Was the funeral a republican event? The media of the liberal Left certainly thought so. *Vossische Zeitung*, for instance, wrote:

> The celebration in the Reichstag was the most beautiful homage that anyone could have wished for. The Jew, at whom the shots were aimed, has been elevated to the heroic. ... The death that this man suffered for his work for the fatherland has made him a martyr and has ever more stabilized the republic. That is the usual course of things. A cause for which blood has flowed becomes all the more dear to its supporters; blood witnesses are the pioneers of victory.[57]

While the nationalist public accepted a rite of passing that separated the slain from the living, it rejected integration into a community that canonized the victim of anti-Semitic nationalism as a martyr of the German people. Consensus about the funeral dissolved exactly at the point where the republicans injected meaning into the ceremony. Consequently, the *Preußische Zeitung* attacked the eulogies, labeling them "pedantic" and "embarrassing."[58] Korell with his critique of both nationalism and anti-Semitism received the worst marks. The *Preußische Zeitung* wrote the following about him:

> The irresponsible speech of Vicar Korell provokes opposition. Neither Walther Rathenau nor Friedrich Naumann were precious, great [men] of the German

people. In no way can they be placed next to Frederick the Great—Lessing, Goethe, Schiller, Kleist, Bismarck, Hindenburg. It is totally one-sided to associate the red republic with the ethical principle of the nation. On the legal and constitutional path, we strive for the restoration of the monarchy. Yes, there were also republicans in the imperial Reich. That is, we strive for the monarchy out of the ethical principle of the nation. Our conception of the ethical principle of the nation is certainly different from that of Herr Korell. After the long ugly speech of the Democrat, the march from the *Götterdämmerung* was a salvation.[59]

Belonging to the community of mourners did not forge a political community of republicans. Rather, death suspended all political differences, at least for the moment. It is even an open question as to whether in attending the ceremony the republicans and the nationalists witnessed the same event. While the former focused on the new black-red-gold colors, the latter gave special attention to the hall's glass ceiling, which according to Redslob was covered with mourning crêpe, but in the nationalist mind "radiated" in black-white-red. And where the republicans emphasized the new federal eagle on the national flag, the nationalists saw only its crowned predecessor, looking down at the coffin "from above."[60]

Set to reject the republican attempt to define the nation in memoriam of Rathenau's "sacrifice," the German nationalists still participated in the sacrificial feast. This rendered them part at least of the mourning community. Formally, the ceremony thus transcended the confines of social milieux and political party lines. The integrative effect of the funeral was supported by its orchestration as a familial drama. As we have seen, even the *Preußische Zeitung* rallied behind Rathenau's family, if only strategically to defend the symbolic presence of Wilhelm I in the Reichstag. To some extent, then, one might contend that Rathenau's funeral promoted social solidarity without necessitating political consensus.[61]

Indeed, there are clear indications that in the aftermath of Rathenau's violent death, the symbolic economy of Weimar Germany gained momentum towards the republican cause. Democrats of all stripes now pressed more strongly for the distribution of the black-red-gold national flag. Four weeks after the murder, the national parliament passed the "Law for the Protection of the Republic" with the required two-thirds majority. Promulgated on 18 July 1922, the law was directed against extremism, especially of the antirepublican Right (including its language and its images). On 11 August, President Friedrich Ebert then decreed Hoffmann von Fallersleben's "Deutschlandlied" to be Germany's official national anthem. With this initiative, the Social Democratic president claimed for the republic a liberal democratic tradition that had been appropriated and monopolized by the German nationalists already in imperial times. The date of the proclamation was also highly symbolic. Three years earlier Ebert had signed the Weimar Constitution, thus underwriting the democratic groundwork of the National Assembly. The celebration of this day as "Constitution Day" was a governmental innovation of 1921. Although the extreme political Left and Right opposed the prorepublican initiative, the celebrations expanded in the years of relative stability between 1924 and 1928, culminating in widespread festivities on the occasion of the constitution's tenth anniversary in 1929.

Seen from the perspective of the republic's catastrophic demise in the depression years, it is plausible to contend that the various initiatives in support of Weimar democracy lacked the symbolic appeal necessary to bind collective sentiment and to win widespread popular support. Yet if we brush history against the grain we can identify moments that testify to the republic's enduring capacity for democratic growth and development. As I hope to have shown, the assassination of Walther Rathenau by right-wing fanatics proved counterproductive to the antirepublican cause. Instead of destabilizing the Weimar Republic, the murder carried great symbolic potential, allowing the democrats to seize the ethicopolitical initiative from the political Right, turning the antirepublican action against seemingly respectable nationalist representatives. United in protest and mourning, Weimar republicans reconstituted the shaken community from the body and in memoriam of a German-Jewish martyr. In their view, commitment to the democratic nation was an absolute value that transcended the confines of class, faith, ethnicity, or race. Importantly, this integrative sense of national belonging was no less compatible with German political traditions than Nazi ideology. Quite to the contrary! In combining the ethics of mourning and reconciliation with the works of modern state design, Weimar republicans delineated the contours of a pluralist society in which different ethnic, religious, or cultural groups could coexist peacefully within one democratic nation. While this republican imagined community was not devoid of anti-Semitic stereotypes,[62] the integrative and pluralist thrust of its nationalism clearly marked an alternative route that Weimar Germany might have taken.[63]

Notes

1. For many Alois Friedel, "Die politische Symbolik in der Weimarer Republik" (PhD diss., University of Marburg, 1956), 7; Hagen Schulze, *Otto Braun oder Preussens demokratische Sendung* (Frankfurt am Main, 1977), 753f. More recently Bernd Buchner has offered a more differentiated analysis of the SPD's concern with the symbolic representation and legitimation of the Weimar Republik. Bernd Buchner, *Um nationale und republikanische Identität: Die deutsche Sozialdemokratie und der Kampf um die politischen Symbole in der Weimarer Republik* (Bonn, 2001).

2. Detlev J. K. Peukert, *The Weimar Republic: The Crisis of Classical Modernity* (New York, 1993), 5–6.

3. Wilhelm Keil, *Erlebnisse eines Sozialdemokraten* (Stuttgart, 1948), 2:351. Unless otherwise noted, all translations are my own.

4. Gustav Radbruch, *Der innere Weg: Aufriß meines Lebens* (Stuttgart, 1951), 177. See Friedrich Stampfer, *Die vierzehn Jahre der ersten deutschen Republik* (Hamburg, 1947), 304. Especially bitter, Albert Grzesinski, *Inside Germany* (New York, 1939), 139ff.

5. Radbruch, *Der Innere Weg*, 177.

6. For an excellent discussion of the destination of the Weimar Republic see Peter Fritzsche, "Did Weimar Fail?" *Journal of Modern History* 68, no. 3 (September 1996): 629–56.

7. Vicki Baum, *It Was All Quite Different: Memoirs* (New York, 1964). For an analysis of Weimar democracy in terms of failed expectations, see Thomas Mergel, "High Expectations—Deep Disappointment: Structures of the Public Perception of Politics in the Weimar Republic," in this volume.

8. Between 1919 and 1922 the republic witnessed both a series of upheavals from the Left and the Right and the establishment of numerous antirepublican countermovements, which were often organized as terrorist secret societies. Summarizing the state of affairs in 1922, Emil Gumbel, then a lecturer in statistics at the University of Heidelberg, counted 354 political murders by the political Right, and 22 murders committed by members of the political Left. Emil Julius Gumbel, *Vier Jahre politischer Mord* (Berlin, 1922), 78 and 80. Within this context, the murder of Rathenau appears as just one particular, if extreme, manifestation of a more widespread phenomenon of radical violence. This is indeed the interpretation most general histories of the Weimar Republic have followed. See, for example, Richard Bessel, *Germany after the First World War* (Oxford, 1993), 261; Conan Fischer, *The Rise of the Nazis* (Manchester, UK, 1995), 11.

9. Here and in the following, Martin Sabrow, *Der Rathenaumord: Rekonstruktion einer Verschwörung gegen die Republik von Weimar* (München, 1994), 157. See also, Shulamit Volkow, "Überlegungen zur Ermordung Rathenaus als symbolischem Akt: Kommentar zu dem Vortrag von Gerald D. Feldman," in *Ein Mann vieler Eigenschaften: Walter Rathenau und die Kultur der Moderne*, ed. Thomas P. Hughes (Berlin, 1990), 100, Buchner, *Identität*, 92.

10. Harry Graf Kessler, *Tagebücher 1918–1937* (Frankfurt am Main, 1961), 322 and 385.

11. Arno J. Mayer, *The Furies: Violence and Terror in the French and Russian Revolutions* (Princeton, NJ, 2000), 71 and 84.

12. Similar scenes occurred on the state and municipal levels. *Vossische Zeitung,* 24 June 1922; *Berliner Tageblatt,* 24 June 1922; *Vorwärts,* 24 June 1922.

13. *Hamburger Echo,* 27 June 1922; *Germania,* 28 June 1922; *Germania,* 29 June 1922; *Preußische Zeitung,* 28 June 1922; Sabrow, *Rathenaumord:* 158f.

14. *Vossische Zeitung,* 29 June 1922 (my emphasis).

15. See the cartoon entitled, "A stab in the back that is no legend," in *Ulk: Wochenschrift des Berliner Tageblatts,* 9 September 1921.

16. Cited in Buchner, *Identität,* 200.

17. *Ulk: Wochenschrift des Berliner Tageblatts,* 9 September 1921.

18. Volker Ackermann, *Nationale Totenfeiern in Deutschland: Von Wilhelm I. bis Franz Josef Strauß: Eine Studie zur politischen Semiotik* (Stuttgart, 1990), 48f. and 77.

19. Ibid., 285ff., especially 287 and 339f.

20. Thomas Lindenberger, *Strassenpolitik: Zur Sozialgeschichte der öffentlichen Ordnung in Berlin 1900 bis 1914* (Bonn, 1995), 308.

21. Ibid., 308–13.

22. Ibid., 308 n13.

23. When Bismarck died in 1898, Wilhelm II was prepared to grant him a state funeral. However, the former chancellor had rejected that "honor" before he died. Ackermann, *Totenfeiern*, 25.

24. Here and in the following, ibid., 27ff.

25. Ibid., 284.

26. *Akten der Reichskanzlei: Weimarer Republik: Die Kabinette Wirth I und II*, ed. Ingrid Schulze-Bidlingmaier (Boppard am Rhein, 1973), 2:896–901.

27. This practice was not uncommon in democratic regimes. See Christine Quigley, *The Corpse: A History* (London, 1996), 75.

28. Edwin Redslob, *Von Weimar nach Europa: Erlebtes und Durchdachtes* (Berlin, 1972), 192ff. For a useful descriptive account of the office, see Annegret Heffen, *Der Reichskunstwart: Kunstpolitik in den Jahren 1920–1933: Zu den Bemühungen um eine offizielle Reichskunstpolitik in der Weimarer Republik* (Essen, 1986).

29. See Michael S. Cullen, *Der Reichstag: Parlament Denkmal Symbol* (Berlin-Brandenburg, 1999), 151–209.

30. Redslob, *Von Weimar nach Europa*, 192ff.

31. Ibid., 192.

32. *Vossische Zeitung*, 27 June 1922.

33. Hans Klabautermann, "Patriotismus," *Vorwärts*, 27 June 1922.

34. *Preußische Zeitung*, 27 June 1922.

35. *Vossische Zeitung*, 27 June 1922.

36. Friedrich Fick, "Das Kaiser-Denkmal im Reichstag," *Vossische Zeitung*, 16 July 1922.

37. Ibid.

38. *Vossische Zeitung*, 28 June 1922.

39. *Preußische Zeitung*, 28 June 1922.

40. *Preußische Zeitung*, 27 June 1922.

41. *Die Weltbühne* 18, no. 27 (1922).

42. Ignaz Wrobel, "Die zufällige Republik," *Die Weltbühne*, 13 July 1922.

43. "Die amtliche Graphik des Reichs und ihre Auswirkung auf Kunst und Handwerk," ed. Edwin Redslob, *Gebrauchsgraphik* no. 2 (1925).

44. Harry Graf Kessler, *Walther Rathenau: His Life and Work* (New York, 1930), 359.

45. Ibid., 360f.

46. Stefan Grossmann, "Mathilde Rathenau," *Das Tage-Buch*, 7 August 1926.

47. *Vossische Zeitung*, 30 July 1926. The letter was read to the court at Techow's murder trial—in his defense.

48. Ackermann, *Totenfeiern*, 260–68.

49. Redslob, *Von Weimar nach Europa*, 194.

50. Ackermann, *Totenfeiern*, 17ff.

51. *Dr. Walther Rathenau zum Gedächtnis*, Berlin [o.J]; *Verhandlungen des Reichstages, 1. Wahlperiode*, vol. 356, 8103ff.

52. Redslob, *Gebrauchsgraphik*, 53.

53. Harry Graf Kessler, *Tagebücher 1918–1937* (Frankfurt am Main, 1961), 327.

54. Ibid.

55. See Ackermann, *Totenfeiern*, 280, 284.

56. *Preußische Zeitung*, 27 June 1922.

57. *Vossische Zeitung*, 28 June 1922.

58. *Preußische Zeitung*, 28 June 1922.

59. Ibid.

60. *Preußische Zeitung,* 27 June 1922.
61. David Kertzer asserts that participants in a funeral do not necessarily share the same values, beliefs, or even interpretation of the event. David I. Kertzer, *Ritual, Politics, and Power* (New Haven, CT, 1988), 11f., 69, 76, 96, 100, 118f., 139. Similarly, Katherine Verdery emphasizes that the political life of dead bodies often produces polysemic and even contradictory meanings. Katherine Verdery, *The Political Lives of Dead Bodies: Reburial and Postsocialist Change* (New York, 1999), 3.
62. For an analysis of republican readings of Rathenau's Jewishness, see Manuela Achilles, "Nationalist Violence and Republican Identity in Weimar Germany: The Murder of Walther Rathenau," in *German Literature, History and the Nation.* Papers from the Conference "The Fragile Tradition," Cambridge, 2002, ed. David Midgley and Christian Emden (Oxford, 2004), 305–28.
63. Cf. Karl Dietrich Bracher, *Turning Points in Modern Times: Essays on German and European History* (Cambridge, MA, 1995), 104.

CHAPTER 9

~:~

High Expectations—
Deep Disappointment
Structures of the Public Perception of Politics
in the Weimar Republic

THOMAS MERGEL

The legitimacy and stability of a political system depends not only on its "real" capacities but also on the expectations placed upon it.[1] The higher the expectations, the fewer political options the system has, since disappointment is a constant threat. If there are political alternatives (which, unlike in the US and Great Britain, was generally the case for continental Europe until long after the Second World War), political stability can often be viewed as less the result of a system's effectiveness than of the lower expectations that have been placed upon it. This may, in fact, help explain the stability of France's Third Republic, which long puzzled both contemporaries and historians on account of its structural inadequacies, its opaque decision-making processes, and its widespread nepotism and corruption.[2] However, as far as I can tell, the failure of the Weimar Republic is seldom analyzed in these terms. Instead of probing citizens' expectations of the new system, a backward-looking model combining structures, long-term mentalities, and short-term crisis experiences has dominated explanations of Weimar's failure. Yet similar factors were present in other countries as well without leading necessarily to the rapid collapse of their political systems. Explanations that emphasize the antidemocratic sentiment of the old elites and the experiences of crisis resulting from war, inflation, and the Depression could all be applied to France after 1870. There, too, the Right's rejection of democracy and the need to overcome a lost war were a constant problem.[3] Anyone inquiring into the reasons for the Weimar Republic's instability also needs to know what its citizens expected of it in the first place.

In the following I argue that the instability of the Weimar Republic stemmed largely from the fact that citizens' expectations of both the political system and its politicians were unrealistically high and were thus essentially doomed to be disappointed. Structural problems, such as the systematic overreach of the modern state, do not suffice to explain these expectations.[4] Instead, these high expectations of politics—of all kinds, not only of democratic politics—can also be analyzed historically. In our case, long-term factors, such as the tradition of the authoritarian state or the welfare state, must be viewed in conjunction with short-term factors, for example, the war-induced growth of state action, and the war experience itself—in whichever mythological or ideological guise it may have appeared. The resulting ideology of the *Volksgemeinschaft* or "people's community," which was to be created in political terms, expected politics to achieve the formation of "community," an expectation that, however, exceeded its structural capabilities. Thus citizens' high expectations arose as politics became invested with a compensatory function for the country's failed social integration. In the following I intend to examine the structure of these expectations.

My comments are based on my book, *Parlamentarische Kultur in der Weimarer Republik*, which examines the tension between institutional communication in the Reichstag and public perceptions thereof.[5] By "the public" I am referring mainly to the press and the literary community. My analysis, based on some ten thousand articles from across the entire press spectrum, questions Jürgen Habermas's notion of a (bourgeois) public sphere. His notion assumes a homogeneity that was barely thinkable even in the nineteenth century.[6] At first glance, the public sphere of the Weimar Republic was much more fragmented than its nineteenth-century counterpart, with its disparate publics divided along the lines of the various social and moral milieux. If this were the last word on the matter, then the notion of one public sphere would be out of the question. However, the application of a discourse-oriented theoretical concept of the public sphere makes clear that the Weimar Republic also experienced overlapping discourses, which can best be analyzed through the intersecting webs of communication linking diverse media sites. It is possible to situate these discourses empirically in the reception and discussion of statements from the oppositional press, which was an essential activity of all gazettes. Although the primary function of these discussions was to demean others, they ultimately helped draw attention to key concepts, to the rules of speech, and to the definition of problems. The central point here is not whether these different newspapers agreed, but rather the fact that a shared semantics developed, identifying issues and agendas that could then be discussed publicly. One example is the slogan "partyism" (*Parteiismus*), which the Jungdeutscher Orden introduced in 1927 and which then quickly became a descriptive term for the entire political system. Regardless of whether the notion was shared or not, it was used by the media across the political spectrum.[7] Some of these discourses ran through all camps. They did not lead to a consensus regarding the facts, but they helped to develop common themes, coined turns of phrase, and thus facilitated a shared perception of political reality. Such discourses permit us to draw conclusions regarding collective mentalities. The Social Democrats and German Nationalists may well have offered different answers to the question of whether the Reichstag adequately represented the people; however, a wide range of opinion makers shared the conviction *that* the Reichstag's proper designation was to represent the people in its entirety (and thus that its representative function took priority over the governing function). In particular, discourses on the notions of *Führer* and *Volksgemeinschaft* manifested such "secret agreements" in regard to political expectations. Here the longing for unity and the desire for clarity were most vivid, even if they meant different things to different people. Although *Volksgemeinschaft* could mean a number of things, one could still discuss this utopia with a person from an entirely different ideological background.[8] Thus the following considerations do not assume the existence of harmony, but rather the notion of a concert of contradictory opinions—a network that nevertheless included crossroads of shared interest.

The Promise of the Weimar Republic

The Weimar Republic was a political experiment whose existence was due less to the strength of the republican idea than to the weakness of the regime it succeeded. The revolution of 1918–19 was an upheaval merely in political terms; it changed the parameters of the political system, but not, as in Russia one year earlier, those of the social order. The regime change was largely driven by disappointment with the old system and not so much by hope for the new. As Markus Llanque shows, even those intellectuals who opted for a system change only became acquainted with the ideas of democracy during the war.[9] The high expectations for the republic, which eventually followed, can be explained by the promise with which the republic came into being. In his speech upon the opening of the Weimar National Assembly on 6 February 1919, Friedrich Ebert closed with a quotation from Fichte: "We want to create a Reich of justice and honesty, founded upon the equality of everything that bears a human face."[10] This language entailed high expectations not only in the political system of the "people's state" (*Volksstaat*) but in politics as a whole, which reflected the continuity of the German statist tradition. Despite the abundant scholarship on bourgeois society in the past twenty years, which has firmly rejected the notion of a German deficit of *Bürgerlichkeit*,[11] it is still evident that German bourgeois society gave primacy to state institutions and state organization rather than to the structures and initiatives of civil society. The expectation that politics could solve conflicts and create social harmony was profoundly strengthened by the war experience. During the war, political control attained new dimensions.[12] Social Democrats were not the only ones who believed that the statist-corporatist organization of the wartime economy—which went far beyond anything seen in France—and some form of socialism were the organizational principle of the future. Even Walter Rathenau and Max Weber viewed socialism, or at least the variety embodied in a corporatist system of overall regulation, as inevitable if not wholly desirable.[13]

Of course, the significance of the war experience for such a system of control was by no means restricted to Germany. One can find similar patterns in Great Britain following the Second World War. In Germany after 1918, as in Great Britain after 1945, these ideas combined with sweeping concepts of social harmony. As in the "years of consensus" in Great Britain, which sought to overcome (or sublimate) the traumatic years of interwar class struggle by referring to the shared war experience,[14] in Germany as well the politically induced organization of society appeared to assuage the frictions of the German Empire by transferring the idea of the wartime *Volksgemeinschaft* into peacetime. Thus the republican order of the "people's state" was loaded with social expectations.[15] These were only superficially concerned with what we would describe today as the welfare state. The empire had also been acquainted with the safety nets of the welfare state. No, what was at stake here was a longing for societal unity; the function of politics was to become a model for this unity.

It was precisely the experiences of loss, deprivation, and defeat that supercharged politics with expectation. The Germans were a defeated, impoverished nation caught in a tradition of inner political boundaries. This fragmentation had ostensibly been overcome through the war experience, an event that was promptly transformed into a myth because the desire for unity was so great: This nation exposed itself to competitive democracy, which promised in turn a Reich of beauty and dignity and a new realm of political morality. The fact that most parties bore the word *Volk* in their names was evidence of the promise to unite society through politics.

Expectations of the problem-solving capacities of politics were high after the war in any case, and those placed on the republic were even higher. After all, the republic linked political problem solving and political representation. The Reichstag represented the people and governed it at the same time. This resulted in contradictory expectations. How was parliament, as a representative body of the people that was expected to resemble the actual people, supposed to govern the country? Governing, after all, always means making unpopular decisions. How could a party democracy, which was rooted in conflict, realize the desire for unity? How could a political system that had to be a "machine" and an "operation" (*Betrieb*) in order to function, fulfill the longing for directness and "life?" My argument is that after 1918 at least a portion of the disappointment over politics was due to utopian expectations—utopian because they were contradictory and impossible to fulfill. This was not clear to most contemporaries; to be sure, some perceptive observers, such as Max Weber, were keenly aware of the contradictory nature of some of these expectations. His energetic plea for an illusion-free realism grew from such observations.[16] He could only maintain this perspective because there were certain things that he simply did *not* expect from politics. For example, he rejected the notion that politics could exist without parties, "machines," and "operation." But few of his contemporaries followed his lead. Their contradictions were reflected in the discursive structures in which mutually exclusive notions were the rule rather than the exception.

The Ideal of Representation and the Selection of Leaders

The notion that the Reichstag could be a copy or a mirror of the people was scarcely a new idea. As early as 1867, Bismarck had promised that the Reichstag would be a "photograph" of the German nation.[17] But this expectation assumed a new quality during the Weimar Republic, for the proportional voting system placed new demands on the perfection of this picture. When contemporaries sought to assess the parliament's capacity for accurate representation of the people, they were merely taking the constitution seriously. Furthermore, the notion that fair representation would allow every social group to be represented proportionally in the parliament meant that the limits of representation (the notion, for example, that a minimum percentage of votes was necessary for entry into parliament, exemplified by the federal republic's "5 percent hurdle") failed to convince a majority, even though it certainly was a matter of discussion and debate. In the republican understanding of Weimar, fairness demanded the representation of minorities, no matter how small.[18]

Thus representation had two sides: an objective side, and, increasingly, a more subjective one. On the one hand, "representation" meant a reflection of the people's social structure, conceived as an ensemble of social groups. In the everyday terminology of journalists, this concept suggested that social groups replaced individual citizens as the deputies' electors. So, for example, the newspaper of heavy industry, *Der Tag*, depicted the deputies as the extended arm of their professional interests. In the newspaper's diction, then, it was not the electorate who voted but rather the professions: "The Chambers of Crafts have dispatched a secretary. The commercial community is represented by ten merchants."[19] Consequently, this corporatist notion of social structure was reflected in an election advertisement that was not aimed at the entire people but instead at its social subgroups.[20]

However, the confrontation among organized interests that took place during the 1920s and that favored groups with market power made clear that many parts do not make a whole. The social groups did not blend harmoniously into one nation. As a consequence, a new "subjective" concept of representation began to prevail, from which the Nazis drew vast profit: that of direct and palpable experience. This was not a new idea. Ever since the cultural and class struggles of the nineteenth century, affiliation with the distinct "life-worlds" of various social groups had molded the political landscape and led to the development of a particularistic politics of identity.[21] The category of affiliation based on experience gained a new immediacy in the late 1920s against the background of the war experience. "Having been there" seemed to instill political actors with a higher competence of judgment. Thus it became important to ask whether a person had *really* taken part in the war (and not merely in the wartime bureaucracies), or whether one *really* still worked in a factory (rather than as a union functionary).[22] Even one's age, gender, or status as a homeowner could solidify into political arguments, for only such factors qualified a person to represent others authentically and to defend their interests. Here we see a desire to share "real life" with the people, which implied that only those who lived like the people were able to grasp its problems and find solutions for them.

This collision of the category of experience with professional politics harmed the functionaries. Although the Weimar Republic was characterized by a high level of lobbying and its functionaries had substantial influence—up to 40 percent of Reichstag deputies were salaried lobbyists, not counting the honorary ones[23]—even their own organizations viewed them with mistrust since they represented interests which they themselves "objectively" did not share. For example, the agrarian lobbyist Albrecht Philipp from Saxony, a professional politician since 1912 and a parliamentary representative for the German National People's Party, encountered increasing difficulties with the grass-roots members of his party after 1928. He failed to win their nomination again in 1930, not because he represented his constituency's interests poorly but rather—so it was said "from below"—because he was not a farmer himself, but a high-school teacher. His supporters' argument that as a "professional parliamentarian" he had valuable experiences of a different kind could not prevail against the argument based on his life-world identity.[24] Even in the communist milieu, where the professionalization of politicians was actively promoted, functionaries, and particularly deputies, were continuously suspected of being bourgeois; in this case, the politics of identity also meant control over lifestyles. Thus in 1924 the communist deputy Werner Scholem felt obliged to purchase a coat that was not "the latest in fashion" but was instead more modest, "as befits an attorney of the people."[25] Particularly in the shadow of the new and distressing experience of mobility, which characterized the Weimar era, social mobility aroused suspicion of alienation. Professional politicians were viewed as social climbers, who had abandoned those very life worlds that had originally commissioned these politicians to represent them.

And yet, this discourse about the parliament as a "photograph" of the people, which thought in terms of similarities, was inconsistent with the simultaneous notion that the *best* of the nation should come together in the parliament. Heinrich Triepel, a professor of constitutional law from Berlin, noted in 1923 that the parliamentary arena had become a "world of mediocrity," which hindered "valuable persons" from entering it.[26] Such complaints about the quality of the parliament were essentially nothing other than complaints about the very idea of representation. "One of us" also meant "one like everybody else," or, as the *Vossische Zeitung* stated, if the parliament was supposed to be a "photograph" of the people, then it was "neither better nor worse than the German people in general, without party and class distinctions."[27] This contradiction was persuasive in Weimar politics: the idea of representation stood in a constant tension with the search for the best man, with the search for the Führer.

Inherent in this contradiction was a distinction between regularity and irregularity. Representation included notions of regularity, mirror image, and functionality, which crystallized in the notion of the parliament as a "machine." The constant critical talk of the "operation of the parliament" (*Parlamentsbetrieb*)[28] of "assembly line politics" (*Politik am laufenden Bande*),[29] or of the "master machinist in the parliamentary party" (*Maschinenmeister in der Fraktion*)[30] presented the concept of a standardized, even self-regulating mechanism. This anti-industrial semantic contained within itself the longing for the immediate and the personal. It was not that the Reichstag did *not* function, but rather that it was accused of functioning *too well*. In older political rhetoric, the "machine" described the smooth running of the mechanisms of the state as opposed to the living, organically conceived public sphere of the nineteenth century.[31] The "machine" meant minimizing the influence of the individual and reducing the individual personality to a mere cog in the machine.[32] This rhetoric produced an attitude that viewed political parties not as antagonistic groups but rather as self-serving oligarchies engaged in horse trading that cooperated with one another behind the scenes. From this point of view, the Reichstag prided itself on a representative capacity that had deteriorated into rule by mediocre party functionaries.

The search for the Führer stood in a tense relationship to this machine.[33] This category brought together various quests, ranging from a vague desire for decisive elites who could stand out from an amorphous mass, all the way to a messianic search for a "savior of Germany" who would lead the nation out of its degradation to new glory.[34] Nevertheless, these diverse conceptions of a Führer had one thing in common. In the words of Arthur Moeller van den Bruck: "He is a man who cannot be of a party."[35] For van den Bruck the term *party* manifested not only the disunity of the Germans but also their narrow-mindedness, their adherence to the machine, and their doctrinaire attitudes—in short, their conventional Germanness. In his view, the Führer was a nonconformist, a bolt from the blue, and the very essence of irrationality. This discourse of irregularity and unpredictability was in no way restricted to the political Right, but was widely shared by all sides. Max Weber's notion of charisma included these disparate ideas. In fact, Weber condensed the ongoing discussion and then sharpened it.[36] Whether Left or Right, all sides in Weimar politics contended with the phenomenon of a charismatic leader who could overcome the political paralysis of the republic. Yet, the appearance of the Führer was not amenable to planning; he would simply emerge.[37]

This precept meant a heightened susceptibility to rebellious individualism and also points to those important thematics that rendered Hitler's contingent, narcissistic leadership image acceptable. Stated differently: the emphasis on charisma and incalculability as essential aspects of leadership was a widespread contemporary inclination that helped make Hitler visible in the first place. Precisely those were viewed as Führer who acted in an unforeseen way, who could not be disciplined, and who acted "irrationally." Until Hitler came along, this attribute was rarely applied to the Right. Since the Führer had to be in tune with the people, it was instead applied to politicians who remained close to the "masses," such as Gustav Noske, Carl Severing, Josef Wirth, and even Arthur Mahraun, the leader of the Jungdeutscher Orden (which represented the front generation), who were all accorded this title. If Alfred Hugenberg was also addressed as Führer after 1930, this merely represented the attempt of his entourage to talk charismatic abilities into being. But since Hugenberg was neither a powerful speaker nor had the masses behind him, this title remained restricted to his own small circle of admirers.

The difference between representation, which may have created identity but which also concealed within itself the soullessness of the political machine, and the search for a Führer who bore personal and existential qualities within himself, is one of the characteristics of public political discourse in the Weimar Republic. Anyone who sought to represent the people was faced with an impossible choice: did he want to be like everyone else—part of the "photograph"—or did he want to be a Führer?

Politics as Morality

Carl Schmitt's approach that politics is a profoundly amoral business has informed modern-day conceptions of politics in the Weimar Republic. He believed that effective policies were not cultivated by seeking the common good, but rather by allowing conflicts to sharpen into polar oppositions, parallel to the divisions between enemies in military conflicts.[38] In politics, *good* and *bad* were only conceivable as secondary encodings of distinctions that were essentially political in nature. The intensity of political conflict during the Weimar Republic would seem to confirm this viewpoint.

Still, I believe that Schmitt's view represents a minority position. Rather, the flood of publications on the relationship of politics and morality would suggest that politics was largely conceived in terms of morality already during the war years. In this sense politics figured as a virtuous activity, the main task of which was not to administer reality but to realize visions. Those who conducted politics, then, were supposed to be virtuous, more virtuous in fact than the people themselves. During the interwar period, this conception of an ideal politics gained credence in the face of the shameful social morality that characterized the period of inflation, in particular the black marketeers and the inflation profiteers whose appearance was noticeable in the literature of the 1920s.[39] Politics was to be free of egoism and deal making. Such moral claims echoed as well in the New Year's greetings, which the Reichstag received in 1924 from the Reichslandbund and the *Deutsche Allgemeine Zeitung*. Its authors called for "the will and resolution that can move mountains, the firmness, decency, and above all the selflessness that fundamentally rejects the usual ministerial 'feeding troughs' and other benefits. Clean hands and pure hearts!"[40]

Such expectations fundamentally demanded too much of politics. Where was this kind of purity to begin with? How were politicians in a parliamentary system supposed to do entirely without ministerial perquisites and privileges? The fact that the Reichstag and its representatives failed to embody this ideal was due less to the politics they actually conducted than to the expectations that they were expected to fulfill. The notion of politics as virtue, as a sacrifice for the community, coincided with Weimar society's extraordinary sensitivity to corruption. In the contemporary discussions of political corruption it was always clear that it was a matter of *professionalized*—i.e., "machine"—politicians. Politicians had a reputation for seeking their own advantage and making unsavory deals. The former rector of the Berlin Handelshochschule, Ignaz Jastrow, was probably not even aware of any genuine association with criminals when he termed full-time politicians "professional and habitual parliamentarians" (*Berufs- und Gewohnheitsparlamentarier*) in the democratic *Berliner Tageblatt*.[41]

Corruption is hardly unusual in democratic systems, and it was pervasive in the model democracies of the West. While corruption scandals almost drove the French Third Republic into the ground, British newspaper editors also knew what they were talking about when they spelled Lloyd George as "£loyd George."[42] In the United States corruption had been a hallmark of the political system since the nineteenth century.[43] Denunciations of corruption, then, also entailed an antidemocratic element. There is no doubt that the Weimar Republic was considerably less corrupt than these democracies, and probably also less corrupt than the federal republic later was. In any case, it was not bribes or graft among politicians that preoccupied the public. Nor was it primarily concerned with deputies whose campaigns were financed by industrial lobbies, or those who were employed by trade unions or who received high salaries as members of executive boards. Instead, the German public fretted about the petty benefits that were accorded to politicians—perquisites that the people had to do without. Whether politicians received tailor-made suits for the price of used clothing (as in the Sklarek scandal), or enjoyed hors d'oeuvres and champagne at public expense (as in the Barmat scandal), or spent their holidays in a Swiss hotel (as Matthias Erzberger was falsely accused of do-ing), the outrage and scandal arose from the difference in life-worlds that these symbols of the good life represented in the hunger-worn, austere society of the 1920s. Corruption figured less as an expression of the functional shortcomings of the political system than of the dissonances between the representatives and the represented. Thus one standard topos in the perception of politicians was their well-fed appearance, which cast doubt upon their suitability to represent the people.[44] In the same way, critics challenged the rights of deputies to travel first class on the *Reichsbahn*, a class of service used by only 5 percent of all pas-sengers; this marked yet another separation from the people.[45]

This discourse on corruption, which was actually a politics of identity, is encapsulated in one small example. On 11 February 1923, the Hamburg meat import companies invited female deputies—not their male colleagues—from both the Prussian and the national legislatures to the Reichstag to taste-test frozen meat. The menu was opulent, including steak tartare, cold roast beef, meat broth, and corned beef, along with compote, salad, and mocha for dessert. The ladies were expected to decide which dishes had been prepared from fro-zen meat and which were made from fresh meat. Of course, this "test" was a promotional event designed to improve the prospects for lifting restrictions on the import of frozen meat. The occasion was well chosen, for a debate was sched-uled for the following day on the SPD's proposal to ease the restrictions on frozen meat imports.[46] A large majority approved this measure, although it is un-known whether the banquet of the previous day actually influenced the deputies' opinions. But for the Communist newspaper *Rote Fahne*, which had reported on this "parliamentary corruption dinner" in advance, this was not the crucial point. Rather, in the view of its editors, this episode illustrated "the amenities that par-liamentarism offers loyal bourgeois and Social Democratic deputies." Naturally the female Communist deputies wanted no part of it.[47] Thus it was the good life that corrupted, and politicians could only remain free of this corruption if they practiced dutiful and ethical asceticism—in a word, politics as sacrifice.

Analysis of this enormous excess of expectations prompts a revision of the view of parliament as a reflection of the people: deputies were not supposed to reflect what the *Volk* really *was*, but what it *could potentially become*. Thus the parliament was not a simple mirror; instead, it was to be a utopian kind of concave mirror in which the people could see a vision of itself, not as it actually was, but as it was supposed to be.

Performance Expectations

The expectations the people leveled at the parliament also revealed ideological residues from the past, which as a result of the war years and the new functions the Weimar constitution assigned to the Reichstag took on utopian proportions and became unrealizable in their contradictions. A special double bind existed in the fact that the Reichstag was now expected not only to represent the people but to rule it as well. If questions regarding a given delegate's social location and experience sought to reveal who the delegate was, new questions were now posed as to what the delegate actually *did*. If discussions had already taken place during the *Kaiserreich* about individual deputies' accountability to their voting districts, parliamentarians as a group were now asked what they did for the *Volk*. The question of how to judge a politician's performance was almost exclusively answered numerically, revealing the deep traces that the discourses of economic rationalization and standardization left in politics. In fact, an almost Tayloristic view of political activity was discernible in questions about how many speeches a speaker delivered; about the average length of these speeches;[48] about the numbers of laws passed and the cost of the paper on which they were printed.[49] The way such figures were evaluated was ultimately arbitrary, for any number of laws could just as easily attest to "legislative diligence" as offer evidence of "superfluous legislative activity."[50] This numerical point of view became most obvious in matters involving money: how expensive was a parliamentary enquiry,[51] how expensive was an individual assembly,[52] or even a word uttered in the Reichstag?[53] How much did the average politician cost: how much for an industrious one; how much for a lazy one?[54] Would parliamentarism cost less if the lazy politicians could be sorted out in order to achieve a more favorable cost-benefit ratio?[55] The newspapers decried the empty benches in the plenary sessions, published lists of deputies who had been absent from votes, and calculated the absence rates of the individual parties.[56]

In this way, critics asked how "well" parliamentarians worked. Unlike the meditations on the coming Führer, the question did not focus on extraordinary factors, but rather on matters of function: efficiency is something different than political genius, and attendance did not correlate with charisma. The inflection of this question of performance with the idioms of economic efficiency had the effect of bringing the processes of politics and the machine back into the center of the debate. For only this parliamentary machine was able to distinguish between the industrious and the lazy, between the good and the bad parliamentarians. Yet this same machine, which fostered professionalization—through demands for regular attendance, for the rationalization of parliamentary work, or for a reasonable relationship of costs to benefits—was at the same time a symbol of profound political alienation. Here again an internal contradiction is revealed in these discourses: although politics figured as a sort of customer service, yet which activity is more alienated than that of service provider?

Self-Descriptions

The perspective the public took on the Reichstag and its politicians during the Weimar Republic represents a bundle of mutually contradictory expectations—expectations that demanded far too much of politics. How did politicians respond to these expectations? The fact that the answers they offered sought to fulfill these expectations made the burden of these expectations all the more evident.[57] In the politicians' self-descriptions, which appeared in the handbooks of the German Reichstag, they tried to be all things to all people: they depicted themselves as rooted in the life-worlds of their milieus and also as effective "Führers"; they described themselves as efficient representatives of special interest groups and, at the same time, as attorneys of the common good; they demonstrated their integrity by emphasizing their paths of continuous professional development, their significant achievements, and their cosmopolitanism. Deputies pointed to the ways in which they were anchored in their respective Social Democratic, Catholic, or national milieus, proudly mentioning, for example, that they had shared prison time with August Bebel, or listing the many associations in which they were members. They thus presented themselves as people whose affiliations made them the ideal administrators of their respective world views. They pointed to their organizational achievements as master builders or functionaries, to their wartime military achievements, athletic accomplishments, or to their success as functionaries or in local politics; they told of their travels and listed the firms they had founded or managed.

These sometimes rather immodest reports had much in common with one another. The frequently similar careers they traced were more reminiscent of the "machine" than of the contingency of the Führer—these self-descriptions scarcely presented these deputies as "statesmen." The more the parliament's mediocrity attracted the public's critical eye, the more the myths of social advancement, which the parliamentarians sought to embrace, jarred people's nerves. In 1930, for example, the *Demokratische Zeitungsdienst* mocked the absurdity and vanity of the deputies' accounts in the new Reichstag handbook, in which they sought to acquaint "the world with the details of their career paths and their effectiveness [as deputies]."[58] While the deputies may have seen these reports as honest accounts of their particular achievements, they seemed ridiculous to their readers. Society called for statesmen and instead was faced with braggarts.

Some deputies were clearly aware of the high expectations to which they were subjected and sought to shake off this burden. They told of receiving so many letters that they were unable to afford the postage to reply to all of them,[59] or of their constituents' expectation that delegates help them find jobs.[60] The Center Party deputy Joos characterized these exaggerated expectations in unambiguous terms: "Deputies understand the limits of the effectiveness of legal measures only too well. However, out in the countryside a certain superstition still prevails. People expect salvation and every group imagines that it will come from above. ... The impossibility of realizing the exaggerated hopes which people place in our laws ultimately leads to the collapse of faith and trust in politics, in parties, in the parliament, and finally in the democratic republican state."[61]

The Nazi Response

The National Socialists' opportunity stemmed from the fact that they had nothing to do with all of this. When they entered the Reichstag in large numbers in 1930, a forum was placed at their disposal that would allow them to shape this discourse. They made capital out of the high expectations placed on politics by intensifying these expectations, thus presenting the failure of the current political system in an even more dramatic fashion. This is best illustrated by the Nazis' political language—essentially a language of morality—that denounced those who claimed to have founded a Reich upon beauty and dignity, charging that they had instead created a Reich of corruption, deceit, and oppression. "You, gentlemen, have had eleven years in which to serve the people; but you have also had eleven years in which to swindle the people, and you have made good use of the latter."[62] The current misery, it seemed, was not the result of weakness or failure; on the contrary, it was deliberate sabotage. When the Nazis turned their language against the "system parties," they exploited this moral vision of politics. The hope embodied in the notion of a "people's state," namely, the unification of the fragmented nation through a politics of unity, had been disappointed and now aligned itself with the enemies of the system.

This discourse was intensified by a semantic strategy that the Nazis applied consistently and that was directly aimed at a crucial linguistic agreement of the Reichstag—the reinterpretation of the word *we*. Previously *we* had meant the Reichstag as a whole and also the people, because the Reichstag had described itself as the mirror of the people. The Nazis now set up the dichotomy of *we* (the party, which was simultaneously the people) vs. *you* (the system parties, i.e., the enemies of the people). They accused the government and the Reichstag of having turned away from the people and claimed that instead *they* were the qualified interpreters of the people's soul. "Politics," Gregor Strasser said, "means for us service for the good of the German people and state, and in our view the state is something other than a stage for the essentially irresponsible governments of democracy. ... We embody rights, natural rights, and the right to life of every people's comrade [*Volksgenosse*]. We stand for reason, and for the soul of the German people, which you have denied for so many years."[63] In this rhetoric, the party was the authentic expression of the people and from this perspective even political morality assumed a different face. The NSDAP deputy Jacob Sprenger, who was accused of illegally taking money for attendance at assemblies, casually justified himself by saying that "the difference between your side and ours is that you waste the money, but in our case the money exclusively benefits the party, the popular movement, and thus the people."[64]

The "system parties" were hard pressed to refute the Nazis' claim that they were identical to the German people, for their electoral victories seemed to reflect this increasingly. Indeed, the Nazis also matched the (utopian) *Volk* in their social structure. They were young; they were war veterans; they were not paid by interest groups; they were not professional politicians. In short, they formed a "genuine national community" (interestingly enough, the fact that there were no women in this "national community" was constantly neglected by all discussants). This description, disseminated effectively by Nazi propaganda, made a profound impression on the other parties because it was founded on a shared social idea—that of the "photographic" representation of the people. The search for affiliations and experiences, which had constituted the Reichstag's dignity as a popular representative body, finally ended in the admission that the Nazis indeed represented the people in a much more direct way than did the other parties. Furthermore, they had a genuine Führer who dissolved the contrast between "machine" and contingency by virtue of being a simple man of the people who had experienced war and poverty, but who was also entirely different, as his language, gestures, and "fanaticism" demonstrated. Furthermore, he came from the Austrian irredenta and thus stood for the unity of *all* Germans. In this representation, Adolf Hitler fulfilled the expectation that a Führer had to emerge from the realm of the improbable, a place far from power, but close to the experiences of ordinary people.

Conclusion

In the Weimar Republic a structure of expectations predominated that systematically overburdened politics. This becomes clear when we depart from discourse-analytical level to examine the case of the Reichstag elections, in which—unlike modern-day Bundestag elections—the sitting government did not benefit from an electoral bonus, but was instead penalized. Social Democrat Gustav Radbruch, for example, presumed that wielding government power would automatically mean a loss of votes.[65] In light of this same experience, the DDP glorified its "courage to be unpopular," making it into a "principle that it [the DDP] has the historic task of helping the republic along to victory, even if it must sacrifice itself in the process."[66] This not only described a myth of political sacrifice but was also quite close to the truth. And yet, the disappointment expressed in the voters' tendency to grant and then entirely withdraw their trust in the politicians they had elected was largely homemade. This behavior was not primarily antirepublican; criticism of the political system's lack of problem-solving capacity was aimed at the parliamentary system, since it, after all, existed and had aroused such far-flung expectations. Particularly noticeable is the silence of those voices that aimed to return to the tested—and failed—system of the empire. Even within the political Right, monarchism was largely a dead letter by the second half of the 1920s. Instead, authoritarian models moved increasingly into the foreground and appeared to have been successful: Soviet Russia and Mussolini's Italy. At least they had not disappointed the expectations placed upon them. Both were models that asserted high social claims upon politics. Even if they relied upon violence, they nevertheless held out the prospect of effecting something that German politics had patently failed to achieve: reestablishing the unity of the people, serving as both a "photograph" and as a utopian model at the same time. This vision represented a counterpoint to the analysis of the dismal present, which culminated in the complaint of "partyism," i.e., the disunity of the people. The counter term, *Volksgemeinschaft*, summoned a hunger for harmony, which was intensified by the war experience because it supposedly had been satisfied for a brief period then. The *Volksgemeinschaft* represented a utopia, not only of the Right. Rather, there were other realms of experience in which fragmentation was to be overcome: the unity of the young generation, the experience of the trenches, and not least the experience in the workplace. This assertion of identity in the realm of politics illuminated a transitional problem: coming to terms with the shift from a politics of representation to functioning politics. The concept of a democracy that could achieve this was one marked by homogeneity and here, once again, Carl Schmitt had his finger on the pulse of the times.

The Nazis were also faced with these high expectations after their "seizure of power," and felt compelled to take measures against popular "bellyaching."[67] Their chief instrument against disappointment was movement, i.e., constant surprises in both domestic and foreign policy—with that special quality of the unexpected that was attributed to a genuine Führer. Progressive mobilization and the inclusion of as many people as possible in the Nazi organizational structure avoided the Weimar Republic's problem with everyday politics. And with half a million functionaries active in the NSDAP alone, even this area of activity was no longer conducted at a remove from the people. The "machine" lost its terrors once everyone had become a part of it.

In the early days of the federal republic, the tension between expectation and disappointment was scarcely an issue. No one expected much from politics—in fact, there were no politics. Instead, politics developed over time. The first opinion surveys in the 1950s revealed not only the widespread persistence of authoritarian thought patterns but also a high degree of political alienation and considerable reservations towards politics.[68] Furthermore, the high expectations of the people were now redirected towards the "economic miracle." This undoubtedly took the pressure off politics during the 1950s in the same way that the painful learning process of the 1960s and the development of a civil society took the pressure off of politics during the next decade.[69] I suspect that these two significant developments also cushioned the new expansion of the system's functionary duties, as shown by the Grand Coalition, Keynesianism, and finally the social engineering promises of the social-liberal coalition after 1969. This may explain why Germans in opinion surveys continue to display a high degree of satisfaction with the system, despite constant dissatisfaction with the achievements of the political parties. Today, it would appear, Germans are making a distinction between the system's structure and those who work within it—a distinction that was unthinkable during the Weimar Republic.

Notes

Originally written in German, this article was translated by Alan Nothnagle and edited by Kathleen Canning.

1. My approach here relies loosely on Niklas Luhmann's theory of social structures as structures of expectation. Expectations are restrictions on the free play of possibility—the higher the expectations, the smaller the system's freedom of action since the danger of disappointment rises. Thus a system's performance is actually a result of expectations. Cf. Niklas Luhmann, *Soziale Systeme. Grundriß einer allgemeinen Theorie* (Frankfurt, 1987), esp. 139 f., 391–404.

2. Cf. Jean-Marie Mayeur, *La vie politique sous la Troisième République, 1870–1940* (Paris, 1984), 399 ff.

3. See Wolfgang Schivelbusch, *Die Kultur der Niederlage: Der amerikanische Süden 1865, Frankreich 1871, Deutschland 1918* (Berlin, 2001).

4. Cf. Niklas Luhmann, *Politische Theorie im Wohlfahrtsstaat* (München, 1981); with respect to modern democracies, see *Willibald Steinmetz, Das Sagbare und das Machbare. Zum Wandel politischer Handlungsspielräume, England 1780–1867* (Stuttgart, 1993).

5. Thomas Mergel, *Parlamentarische Kultur in der Weimarer Republik. Politische Kommunikation, symbolische Politik und Öffentlichkeit im Reichstag, 1919–1933* (Düsseldorf, 2002).

6. In his introduction to the 1990 edition of his book, Habermas admitted as much, although not with respect to those public spheres which I analyze. See Jürgen Habermas, *Strukturwandel der Öffentlichkeit* (Frankfurt, 1990). For a similar view see Geoff Eley, "Nations, Publics, and Political Cultures. Placing Habermas in the 19th Century," in *Culture/Power/History: A Reader in Contemporary Social Theory*, ed. Nicholas Dirks et al. (Princeton, NJ, 1994), 297–335. Here Eley also makes a distinction between various public spheres: gender and popular culture, but not Catholicism and the rural milieu.

7. Cf. Mergel, *Parlamentarische Kultur*, 399 ff.

8. Thomas Mergel, "Führer, Volksgemeinschaft und Maschine. Politische Erwartungsstrukturen in der Weimarer Republik und dem Nationalsozialismus 1918–1936," in *Politische Kulturgeschichte der Zwischenkriegszeit 1918–1939*, ed. Wolfgang Hardtwig (Göttingen, 2005), 91–127.

9. Cf. Markus Llanque, *Demokratisches Denken im Krieg. Die deutsche Debatte im Ersten Weltkrieg* (Berlin, 2000).

10. Friedrich Ebert, *Schriften, Aufzeichnungen, Reden II* (Dresden, 1926), 156.

11. Cf. Peter Lundgreen, *Sozial- und Kulturgeschichte des Bürgertums. Eine Bilanz des Bielefelder Sonderforschungsbereichs (1986–1997)* (Göttingen, 2000). For a summary of research see: Thomas Mergel, "Die Bürgertumsforschung nach fünfzehn Jahren," *Archiv für Sozialgeschichte* 41 (2001): 515–38.

12. Cf. Gerald D. Feldman, *Armee, Industrie und Arbeiterschaft in Deutschland 1914–1918* (Princeton, NJ, 1966).

13. Wolfgang Mommsen, *Max Weber und die deutsche Politik 1890–1920* (Tübingen, 1974), 320f.; Walther Rathenau, "Die neue Gesellschaft (1919)," in: *Rathenau, Schriften und Reden*, ed. Hans Werner Richter (Frankfurt, 1964), 278–358.

14. Cf. Arthur Marwick, *British Society Since 1945* (London, 1996), 18–107, esp. 98 ff.

15. It is important to emphasize that one cannot distinguish the republican idea of the *Volksstaat* and the right-wing idea of the *Volksgemeinschaft*, as Markus Llanque (*Demokratisches Denken im Krieg*, 81f.) has attempted to do. The longing for a community-building function of politics was practically universal following World War I. See Gunther Mai, "'Verteidigungskrieg' und 'Volksgemeinschaft.' Staatliche Selbstbehauptung, nationale Solidarität und soziale Befreiung in Deutschland in der Zeit des Ersten Weltkriegs (1900–1925)," in *Der Erste Weltkrieg. Wirkung, Wahrnehmung, Analyse*, ed. Wolfgang Michalka (Munich, 1994), 583–602; and Jeffrey Verhey, *Der "Geist von 1914" und die Erfindung der Volksgemeinschaft* (Hamburg, 2000).

16. Cf. Max Weber, "Parlament und Regierung im neugeordneten Deutschland," in Max Weber, *Gesammelte Politische Schriften* (Tübingen, 1988), 306–443; Weber, "Deutschlands künftige Staatsform," ibid., 448–483.

17. Margaret L. Anderson, *Practicing Democracy: Elections and Political Culture in Imperial Germany* (Princeton, NJ, 2000), 231, 348.

18. Cf. Eberhard Schanbacher, *Parlamentarische Wahlen und Wahlsystem in der Weimarer Republik* (Düsseldorf, 1982), 189–214.

19. *Tag (Nachtausgabe)* 145 (17 June 1924), "Die Berufsgliederung des neuen Reichstages."

20. Thomas Childers, "The Social Language of Politics in Germany: The Sociology of Political Discourse in the Weimar Republic," *American Historical Review* 95 (1990): 331–58.

21. Cf. Anderson, *Practicing Democracy*, 121 f.

22. Cf.: "Die Partei der 'Arbeiter'," *Rote Fahne* 47 (9 May 1924) (aimed at the SPD, whose members included many high officials and functionaries but no "real" workers). On the NSDAP, see "Ist die Sozialdemokratie oder die Nationalsozialistische Partei eine Arbeiterpartei?" *Nationalsozialistischer Pressedienst* (1 July 1932); "Das nennt sich Arbeiterpartei," *Abend* 264 (6 July 1932) (regarding the proportion of workers in the Nazi Reichstag delegation).

23. Heinrich Best, "Challenges, Failures and Final Success: The Winding Path of German Parliamentary Leadership Groups towards a Structurally Integrated Elite, 1848–1999," in *Parliamentary Representatives in Europe, 1848–2000: Legislative Recruitment and Careers in Eleven European Countries*, ed. Heinrich Best and Maurizio Cotta (Oxford, 2000), 138–95, esp. 158, 166ff. The proportion of functionaries had never been nearly so high at any point in German parliamentary history.

24. Mergel, *Parlamentarische Kultur*, 365f.

25. Betty Scholem to Gershom Scholem, 4 April 1924, in *Betty Scholem—Gershom Scholem. Mutter und Sohn im Briefwechsel 1917–1946*, ed. Itta Shedletzky (München,

1989), 102. For the discourse on functionaries in the twentieth century, see Thomas Mergel, "Der Funktionär," in *Der Mensch des 20. Jahrhunderts*, ed. Ute Frevert and Heinz-Gerhard Haupt (Frankfurt, 1999), 278–300.

26. "Die Krisis des Parlamentarismus in der Welt," *Deutsche Allgemeine Zeitung* 186 (22 April 1923).
27. "Parlament oder Diskutierklub?" *Vossische Zeitung* 47 (29 January 1921).
28. "Parlamentsreform. Von Theodor Heuß MdR," *Berliner Börsencourier* 51 (31 January 1931).
29. This is how the former German Nationalist speaker Count Posadowsky described the Reichstag's legislative work. See Arthur von Posadowsky-Wehner, *Volk und Regierung im neuen Reich. Aufsätze zur politischen Gegenwart* (Berlin, 1932), 128.
30. "Notwendige Parlamentsreformen," *Berliner Tageblatt* 393 (21 August 1929).
31. Cf. Barbara Stollberg-Rilinger, *Der Staat als Maschine. Zur politischen Metaphorik des absoluten Fürstenstaats* (Berlin, 1986).
32. Cf. (with further examples) Thomas Mergel, "Gegenbild, Vorbild und Schreckbild. Die amerikanischen Parteien in der Wahrnehmung der deutschen politischen Öffentlichkeit 1890–1920," in *Parteien im Wandel. Vom Kaiserreich zur Weimarer Republik*, ed. Dieter Dowe, et al. (München, 1999), 363–96, esp. 383ff.
33. For an in-depth examination see Mergel, *Führer, Volksgemeinschaft und Maschine*, 110–20.
34. Klaus Schreiner, "'Wann kommt der Retter Deutschlands?' Formen und Funktionen des politischen Messianismus in der Weimarer Republik," *Saeculum* 49 (1998): 107–60.
35. Arthur Moeller van den Bruck, "Der Außenseiter als Weg zum Führer," *Der Tag*, 15 January 1919. Reprint in Moeller van den Bruck, *Der politische Mensch* (Breslau, 1933), 65–75.
36. In Weber's terms: "Aber es gibt nur die Wahl: Führerdemokratie mit 'Maschine,' oder führerlose Demokratie." See Max Weber, "Politik als Beruf" (1920) in his *Gesammelte Politische Schriften*, 506–88, here 544.
37. Cf. this left-wing example from the former USPD Reichstag deputy and (after 1924) editor of *Vorwärts*: Curt Geyer, *Führer und Masse in der Demokratie* (Berlin, 1926).
38. Carl Schmitt, *Der Begriff des Politischen* (Berlin, 1963 [1932]).
39. Hans Fallada, *Wolf unter Wölfen* (Reinbek, 1984 [1937]); Oskar Maria Graf, *Wir sind Gefangene* (München, 1978 [1927]).
40. "Wie muß der neue Reichstag beschaffen sein?" *Deutsche Allgemeine Zeitung* 1 (1 January 1924).
41. "Die 'stärkste Fraktion.' Von J. Jastrow." *Berliner Tageblatt* 299 (25 June 1924).
42. Cf. Geoffrey R. Searle, *Corruption in British Politics, 1895–1930* (Oxford, 1987). On France, cf. the dimensions of the Stavisky Scandal of 1934: Denis Brogan, *France under the Republic. The Development of Modern France (1870–1939)* (Westport, CT, 1974), 652 ff.
43. Mark Summers, *The Era of Good Stealings* (New York, 1993).
44. "The fat liberalists" (Josef Goebbels); Josef Wirth, bloated with alcohol (Harry Graf Kessler); Anton Erkelenz, "impressive with beard and belly" (*Berliner Lokalanzeiger*). Friedrich Ebert's corpulence was frequently mentioned.
45. Mergel, *Parlamentarische Kultur*, 116ff., 388f.
46. Deutscher Reichstag, 331. Sitzung, 12 April 1923. Sten. Ber. 359, 10452–10461. A regulation pertaining to this was proclaimed on 2 November 1923. Cf. Sten. Ber. 380, DS 6315.

47. "Parlamentarisches Korruptionsessen," *Rote Fahne* 30 (6 February 1923).
48. *Deutsche Allgemeine Zeitung* 508 (29 October 1927), 13938, 75 Reden.
49. "Die Flut der 'kleinen Anfragen' im Reichstag," *Freiheit* 288 (1 August 1922).
50. Regarding the first judgment: "Der tote Reichstag ('ungeheure Arbeitsleistung')," *Deutsche Allgemeine Zeitung* 125 (14 February 1925); *Germania* 461 (23 October 1924); , "Reichstagsschluß," *Nationalliberale Korrespondenz* 147 (13 August 1925). Regarding the second: "Statistik der Gesetzgebungsmaschine," *Deutsche Zeitung* 6 (8 January 1927); "Jedem Tag sein Gesetz," *Magdeburger Zeitung* 8 (5 January 1930); "10.600 Gesetze—Wofür wir Diäten bezahlen," *Der Jungdeutsche* 214 (12 September 1928).
51. "Für 500.000 Mark deutschnationale Anfragen," *Vorwärts* 345 (24 July 1922); "Was der Reichstag kostet," *Berliner Morgenpost* 157 (5 July 1921).
52. "Was der letzte Reichstag uns kostete," *8-Uhr-Abendblatt*.
53. "96,95 Mark," *Preuß. Lit. Zeitung* 117 (23 May 1923).
54. "Deutscher Reichstag," *Deutsches Tageblatt* 19 (22 January 1922); "Lex Taschengeld," *Tägliche Rundschau* 169 (9 April 1922).
55. "Verkleinerung der Parlamente," *Deutsche Allgemeine Zeitung* 584 (16 December 1923); "Die Krise des Parlamentarismus," *München-Augsburger Abendzeitung* 18 (20 January 1926); "Deutscher Reichstag," *Deutsches Tageblatt* 19 (22 January 1922). The *8-Uhr-Abendblatt* of 6 January 1925 went the farthest—it recommended reducing the Reichstag to 120 members.
56. "Parlamentarische Pflichterfüllung," *Germania* 322 (4 August 1924); "Abgeordnete, die abwesend sind," *Tag* 186 (5 August 1925); "Die Fehlenden," *Deutsche Tageszeitung* 371 (9 August 1925); "Pflichterfüllung im Reichstag," *Vorwärts* 12 (6 May 1927).
57. For more on the following see Mergel, *Parlamentarische Kultur*, 390–98.
58. "'Autobiographien' der Reichstagsabgeordneten," *Demokratischer Zeitungsdienst*, 23 October 1930.
59. "Ein Uebelstand. Die Portokosten waren vom Abgeordneten selber zu tragen," *Nationalliberale Korrespondenz* 5 (6 January 1922).
60. "Abgeordneter oder Commis. Von Dr. A. Pinkernell MdL," *Berliner Börsencourier* 207 (5 May 1927).
61. "Schwankungen. Von J. Joos MdR," *Germania*, 19 March 1927.
62. Frank II, Deutscher Reichstag, 20./21. Sitzung, (9 February 1931). Sten. Ber. 444, 801f., 807.
63. Deutscher Reichstag, 4. Sitzung, (17 October 1930). Ebd., 57.
64. Deutscher Reichstag, 17. Sitzung, (5 February 1930). Ebd., 707.
65. Gustav Radbruch, *Der innere Weg. Aufriß meines Lebens* (Göttingen, 1961), 178 f.
66. Walter Goetz, "Die demokratischen Fraktionen im Reich, in den Ländern und in den Länderparlamenten," in *Zehn Jahre deutsche Republik. Ein Handbuch für republikanische Politik,* ed. Anton Erkelenz (Berlin, 1928), 148–69, here 154, 169.
67. See Mergel, *Führer, Volksgemeinschaft und Maschine*, 120–26.
68. Forty percent of those surveyed in 1949 were simply "indifferent" to the future West German constitution; in the early 1950s only around a third believed that deputies represented the interests of the population. *Jahrbuch der öffentlichen Meinung 1947–1955,* ed. Elisabeth Noelle-Neumann and Erich-Peter Neumann (Allensbach, 1956), 157, 163.
69. Cf. Ulrich Herbert, ed., *Wandlungsprozesse in Westdeutschland. Belastung. Integration, Liberalisierung 1945–1980* (Göttingen, 2002).

CHAPTER 10

~:~

Contested Narratives of the Weimar Republic
The Case of the "Kutisker-Barmat Scandal"

MARTIN H. GEYER

The so-called Kutisker-Barmat scandal unfolded in the first half of 1925, when Reich President Friedrich Ebert, along with other leading Social Democrats and members of the Center Party, were accused of being corrupted by *Ostjuden* (Jews from Eastern Europe) who supposedly had used their political connections to procure by fraud and bribery large loans from the Prussian State Bank and the Postal Service. The prelude to the affair started at the end of 1924 when it became clear these loans could not be repaid. The arrest of the Lithuanian citizen Iwan Kutisker in mid-December 1924 and of Julius and Henry Barmat, Russian Jews living in Amsterdam and Berlin, on the very last day of the year prompted a highly anti-Semitic campaign in which members of the government were also attacked by an odd coalition of Communists, German Nationalists (DNVP), and members of the radical political Right. There was talk of this scandal being a "Panama" for the Weimar Republic, referring to the Panama Scandal that had rocked the French Republic in the 1890s, in which Jewish financiers were blamed for bribing parliamentarians to sink millions of government funds into the ill-fated canal project in Central America.[1]

In the weeks that followed these initial arrests, the Weimar Republic was immersed in a form of sensationalist politics that appealed to a rather shocked mass audience. Anger mixed with frustration. The memory of the hardship brought about by the war, inflation, and the stabilization of the currency was still painfully vivid. The fact that Jewish foreigners could have received millions at a time when credit was extremely hard to get seemed outrageous, a point the political Right reiterated incessantly to the public, not the least by raising the question of "Jewish influence" in the republic. For their part, the Communists found proof that capitalism had corrupted the Social Democrats and the republic. The conservatives instigated the creation of parliamentary fact-finding committees in both the Reichstag and the Prussian Diet, which initiated hearings as early as January 1925.[2] These public hearings and detailed news reports on the state attorney's investigations, in addition to some leaked confidential information and many rumors, helped to make the Kutisker-Barmat scandal one of the main political events of the year. Indeed, the scandal overshadowed the debate on the complicated process of political coalition building, in the Reichstag, in the Prussia Diet, and in the election for the Reich presidency. In all these cases, efforts were made to discredit the Social Democrats in order to build *Bürgerblock* governments.[3]

The debate focused almost obsessively on the question whether leading Social Democrats—including Reich President Friedrich Ebert, whose son had been employed shortly by the Barmat enterprise—had wielded their influence on behalf of Jews.[4] Derogatorily they were called the *Barmatokratie* or the *Barmatiden*.[5] Such criticism paralleled the vicious attacks on Ebert's purportedly "treasonous" behavior in the January Strike of 1918, all of which was responsible for Ebert's death on 28 February 1925.[6] Politics became a huge spectacle and a vicious struggle amidst the flourishing rumors about political corruption, the influence of *Ostjuden* in German economic and political life, and then, the fatal heart attack suffered by the highly incriminated Center Party member and Reich Post Minister Anton Höfle while he was in pretrial detention. Some contemporaries spoke of a "Barmat psychosis"[7] and that a "pogrom atmosphere" pervaded the public mood.[8]

The case of Kutisker-Barmat is a good example of a modern type of "spectacular politics,"[9] which enables us to analyze the Weimar Republic's contested political culture. The aim of this essay is not primarily to reconstruct and evaluate the case of fraud and bribery. Instead, it examines an almost excessive "surplus" of flourishing narratives and rumors, images and myths that surrounded the case. Embedded in this case were highly contested and politically charged narratives of the political and moral order of the republic, narratives that revolved around war and defeat, money and the decay of economic ethics. As in many other scandals, the multidimensionality of the Kutisker-Barmat affair is comparable to the many layers of an onion. However, these layers are not just trivial incidences to be peeled away in order to get to the "core." Instead they themselves constitute the crux of a modern type of "spectacular politics." Therefore, this essay will explore the stories that revolved around certain people and incidents and thereby blended fact and fiction from the very start. It will be shown how the names Barmat and Kutisker became political and cultural code words that were readily used in the contemporary discourse of both the Left and the Right.[10] The essay starts out by asking how it was possible that these *Ostjuden* epitomized widely circulating images of the "profiteer," the so-called *Kriegs–und Inflationsgewinnler*. Then a closer look is offered of some of the narratives of the Communist Left and the political Right that helped stage the events of 1925. All of these stories revolve around images of luxury and gift-giving, which are examined next. In a final section, it is illustrated how the successful management of the Kutisker-Barmat crisis also could provide a positive narrative for the Weimar Republic, contested as the republic was from the very beginning.

Constructing the Jewish Profiteer

Depending on who was telling the story in the interwar period, the Kutisker–Barmat scandal was either cynical, tragic, or even comical; but it always remained a story of victimization. From the very beginning, the biographies of Julius (or "Judko" as he was called by his friends and enemies alike) Barmat and Iwan Kutisker were lumped together, notwithstanding the fact that they had never known each other personally or professionally. What helped establish this connection was the accusation of credit fraud, the fact that the Kutisker case led to investigations into the business of the Barmats (as well as that of another player, Jacob Michel), and finally the political decision to have two parliamentary fact-finding committees investigate these cases. But there was more to it: from the very beginning, the two main protagonists signified almost archetypically the career of what was decried as the "Jewish profiteer,"[11] and their hyphenated names became a cultural code for exactly that stereotype on which anti-Semitism flourished.[12]

It was difficult to escape this stereotyping, a point exemplified well by Walter Mehring's play *Der Kaufmann von Berlin. Ein historisches Schauspiel aus der deutschen Inflation*, which premiered in September 1929 in an avant-garde but not very successful stage production by Erwin Piscator. The protagonist of this play was—*nomen est omen*—Benjamin Chaim Kaftan, a poor, somewhat naive Jew, who arrives in Berlin from the east with a Yiddish accent, goodwill, and one hundred dollars in his pocket during the inflation. Much to the despair of his dollar-crazy environment, this man does not want to spend his money, but eagerly tries to increase it. He eventually gets his chance when he becomes the puppet of others (one of them being a retired general and clever businessman) who enthrone him with his possession of a mere one hundred dollars as a bank director. In turn, he becomes rich by dealing in scrap metal acquired from the former army, which is, however, full of deployable weapons to be used for the purpose of civil war. With the reputation of a *"Waffenschieber,"* an arms profiteer, our protagonist is given "unlimited credit." To make a long story short, the putsch fails, although angry swastika wearers do destroy the Jewish quarter in the Grenadierstraße (which epitomized Jewish immigration to Berlin from the east). Kaftan thus becomes a victim in a double sense. First he becomes the target of the angry, pauperized masses, who blame him, as a profiteer, for their plight. Mehring refers here to the anti-Semitic riots that occurred in the Berliner Scheunenviertel in November 1923. Second, Kaftan is finally dropped by the very people who had pulled the strings behind the scenes, but only after they squeeze as much money as possible out of him for their military ventures. Once the currency is stabilized, he ends up as poor as he began. In Piscator's interpretation, Kaftan is captured by the police, fights the charges against him in court, has a breakdown, and ends up as a corpse on the autopsy table while students hold a funeral oration. In the original play, Kaftan decides to return to his village, but at the train station Alexanderplatz, he happens to overhear young men from his village who are eager to follow the path of their successful mentor Kaftan and therefore are searching for him in order to reclaim the money the villagers had entrusted to him before he left.

The play was the object of an array of criticisms. For one, Piscator's attempt to reenact the atmosphere of the inflation by fading in pictures, proclamations, and large, rotating telegraphic ticker printouts of dollar exchange rates led some to fault his "mechanical" staging. The play was also said to convey anti-Semitic messages, despite the efforts of both Piscator and Mehring to expose anti-Semitism. In the end, the play pleased no one and was quickly cancelled. Indeed, the stereotype of the profiteer was so powerful and laden with resentments that it was nearly impossible to depict a person like Kaftan as a victim; for anti-Semites this was an absurd proposition to begin with. Finally, the play appeared to exculpate those "pulling the strings" behind the "Kutisker-Barmat scandal."[13]

Others criticized Mehring for having written a "Barmat play without Barmat,"[14] a good point given that Kutisker and Barmat were conflated in the play. Actually, Mehring's plot followed, albeit quite freely, the career of Iwan Kutisker, who allegedly could neither speak nor write German properly, although neither he nor the Barmats spoke Yiddish.[15] After the war, the real Kutisker dealt in German army equipment, a business he continued after he arrived in Berlin in 1919 with several recommendations in his pocket, including some from military contacts. At the end of 1921, Kutisker bought the Stein Bank, which enabled him to enter into transactions with the Prussian State Bank. Later, the court came to the conclusion that he had deliberately deceived officials about the securities put up for the loans; others had been bribed. Among these securities was a huge army depot, the Hanauer Waffenlager, which upon closer inspection was not much more than a huge, highly overvalued pile of scrap metal. This depot had apparently kindled all sorts of fantasies and wishful thinking on the part of those involved in this business, including some officials from the army and the Prussian State Bank. By the time this fraud was finally discovered, the officials had made perfect fools out of themselves. Most everybody agreed that the manner in which the Hanauer depot had been handled "provided delightful material for a comical operetta of the best type,"[16] in part because the Soviet Union and Lithuania were supposed to have shown some interest in it, but even more so because of the appearance of a dubious Romanian "consul" with whom fictitious contracts were signed "in order to milk the state bank like a good dairy cow."[17]

Although there were many good reasons to interpret the Kutisker case as political, not the least because of the army's involvement, most contemporaries dismissed this aspect—it was a case of bribery, fraud, and corruption. The Kutisker case demonstrates that in order for a scandal to be political, it had to involve republican politicians, particularly their alleged connections with Jews. However, it did play an important role in reaffirming clichés of the Jewish profiteer. In almost all accounts of the scandal, Kutisker appeared as the greedy Jew: "In his thoroughly indescribable greed, Kutisker seeks nothing other than acquisition, and therefore he must be labeled as nothing other than an unscrupulous merchant," claimed the Center Party representative in the Prussian parliamentary fact-finding committee, an argument that was heard time and again.[18] Kutisker's story was thus quintessentially one of a man obsessed with money, who acquired loans from the State Bank to rapaciously buy companies, villas, luxury cars, and all the accessories that typified the profiteer and Berlin's newly rich. This was the reason why Goebbels's propaganda ministry later was also interested in the case and commissioned the novelist Hans Fallada to write a novel on the case during the war.[19] In what we know from Fallada's lost manuscript, Barmat und Kutisker were again merged into a single character (although Fallada was mostly interested in Kutisker). He did not want to write a "cheap anti-Semitic novel in the style of Der Stürmer" but wrote instead that it was to be about an "old Jew, a lunatic with a money complex." In Fallada's story there was to be no "skirt-chasing, little bribing, no luxurious intoxications—only money, money, money!"[20] In the end, the editor at the Heyne Verlag was amazed at Fallada's ability to write a "non–anti-Semitic anti-Semitic novel" that fit very well with the Propaganda Ministry's concept of a "belletristic work suitable for anti-Semitic propaganda abroad."[21]

Compared with Kutisker, the five Barmat brothers were far less colorful in both their business ventures and their lifestyles, but they operated on a far bigger scale. Although this scandal also had to do with money, it provided the essentially political twist to the larger story of scandal: in the Barmat story of the political Right, Jews were connected to Socialists, who gave the Jews the opportunity to settle in Germany and to become economically successful at the expense of the German people.

In order to emphasize Julius Barmat's exploitation of Germany, it was necessary to downplay his economic success as a self-made man in Holland before the war and to emphasize his poverty and his supposed Jewish Orthodox upbringing in Eastern Europe instead. Indeed, this was the most common theme in popular descriptions of both German nationalists and the völkisch groups.

Such descriptions alluded to resentful images of *Ostjuden* flooding Germany and other countries especially after the war.[22] Within a short time after his arrival in Amsterdam in 1907, Barmat had married a Dutch woman and had worked his way up from his position as a business correspondent and translator for the police and the courts. He became a millionaire businessman with connections to Germany, Russia, and even Australia by dealing in musical instruments, foodstuffs, and tulip bulbs—the source of some ridicule in Germany—and by investing and speculating in the booming Amsterdam housing and real estate market.[23] Thoroughly ignored was the fact that the Allied powers blacklisted him in the beginning of the war because of his business transactions with Germany and the occupied territories in the East—a pro-German attitude did not fit into the image of a profiteer, just as Barmat's business in the immediate postwar years was not interpreted in the context of desperate efforts to supply foodstuffs to a starving Germany. Instead, it appeared as if the new ruling Social Democrats and the agencies of the Reich fostered Barmat's business with lucrative contracts for food deliveries, representing a boon to Barmat as well as to many others involved in this business.

After 1925, people were greatly obsessed with Barmat's connections to the SPD, specifically with the allegation that Barmat, who had joined the Dutch Social Democrats in 1908, had subsidized a pro-German Socialist newspaper during the war and housed for some time the office of the Second International, exiled from Belgium, in the Keizersgracht, one the most elegant streets of Amsterdam. Moreover, after the war he supposedly became acquainted with high-ranking members of the German Social Democratic Party, such as Friedrich Ebert, Otto Wels (head of the SPD–Reichstagsfraktion since 1919), Otto Gradnauer (minister president of Saxony in 1919 and, after a short interlude as minister of the interior in 1921, representative of Saxony in Berlin), Gustav Bauer (chancellor in 1919–20), the "red king of Prussia" Ernst Heilmann (head of the Prussian SPD fraction since 1921), and Wilhelm Richter (head of the Berlin police since 1920). The latter three were intimate friends of Julius Barmat, and Heilmann and Bauer were even tied loosely to his business.

No doubt the business deals with the agencies of the Reich and the *Länder* responsible for provisioning Germany made Barmat an even richer man than he had been before. Like Kutisker, he was a "profiteer." There were indeed warnings that he was a seedy businessman, someone to be careful of.[24] Hundreds upon hundreds of pages of the fact-finding committee's report addressed the question whether Social Democrats had exerted their influence in securing contracts favorable to Barmat; there are numerous indications that this was the case. In this context, the committee pursued just as intensively the seemingly ridiculous question about who provided visa permits for the *Ostjuden*, namely, for Barmat's brothers Herschel (Henry), Solomon, and Isaac that allowed them not only to enter Germany but also to find housing in a market suffering from a shortage. Conservatives and members of the radical Right had often raised these issues before, thereby invoking images of invading parasites and infectious diseases. The figures of Barmat and Kutisker not only helped personalize the phenomenon of *Ostjuden* "flooding" Germany, but eventually were also presumed to be those responsible for this influx.[25]

During the hyperinflation, Barmat expanded his business, shifting in 1923 from the food trade to the acquisition of industrial enterprises. He acquired most of his eighty-odd enterprises—including machinery, shipping, mining, paper, textiles, and banks—during the winter and spring of 1923–24, that is, in a period of monetary stabilization well after the inflation had ended. Barmat's strategy of purchasing enterprises, most of which were no longer profitable, proved economically devastating, just as it was for Hugo Stinnes, who was bankrupt by April 1925 with debts of more than 150 million marks.[26] The rules of the game had changed: if it was lucrative to go into debt during the inflation, in its aftermath debt threatened to break one's neck.

The issue that excited the public in 1925 was Barmat's seemingly unlimited access to the credit he needed to finance these ventures—a total of 38 million "hard" marks within a year after December 1923[27]—mainly from the Prussian state banks, and later, when that source had dried up, from the Reichspost (National Postal Service). How could men like Kutisker or Barmat obtain credit during an extreme credit crunch when interest rates soared to astronomical heights? Bribery and corruption seemed the answer, with Socialists providing the key to the public coffers. The first accusation was indeed correct. But Barmat pleaded innocent, although they argued that they had become a target of anti-Semitism and that their business was ruined as a result of his incarceration. True as the first argument was, the second was false, for their business failure was immanent by the time of their imprisonment.[28]

Viewed as particularly scandalous was the fact that the Barmat enterprise, like Kutisker, lent the money to private persons as well as to businesses (including banks) during the winter and spring of 1924, and thereby cashed in on the difference between the "cheap" loans it procured and the exorbitant monetary market rate. This occurred at a time when businesses were going bankrupt by the thousands because they lacked credit and when the shortage of money in state coffers even led to layoffs of state officials. Time and again, farmers, artisans, and government officials returned to this image of the archetypical Jewish usurer, usurping the property of producers.[29] In fact, one might argue that the Kutisker-Barmat case perpetuated the tradition of the persecutions of mainly Jewish usurers in the prewar period.[30]

The "Capitalist Corruption of Social Democrats"

Although the political Right thrived on the Kutisker-Barmat affair in 1925, the KPD's *Rote Fahne* had taken the most active role in initiating the political campaign against Barmat and Kutisker in 1924, before the conservative newspapers followed suit.[31] The case evoked vivid memories of war and revolution among the Left, but it also allowed the KPD to draw on earlier events, with anti-Semitic references also looming in the background. If cleavages remained among the old factions of the antiwar Independent Socialists and the Majority Social Democrats even after the two parties reunited in 1922, they were nothing like the unbridgeable gulf that emerged between Social Democrats and the KPD in 1925.

How did the Social Democrats come to work with Barmat, asked the German Comintern expert Karl Radek in his pamphlet, *Barmat und seine Freunde*, which summed up many of the arguments published in the *Rote Fahne*. The answer was clear and obvious: such cooperation was possible because the SPD had aligned itself with both Hindenburg and capitalism during the war, just as Eastern Jewry had done. According to the KPD, Barmat and the entire Kutisker-Barmat scandal were synonyms for the inevitable "capitalist corruption," not only of the SPD but also of the Second International.[32] Barmat was an easy scapegoat because of his close ties to a group of primarily conservative Social Democrats who had enthusiastically supported the war effort, maintaining their allegiance to Imperial Germany until the very end, as was the case with many Social Democrats.[33] In Radek's words, they had misleadingly tried to convince the workers "that they would die for a great cause, that they would die not for the interests of German capital but for the fatherland, for the interests of the working class."[34]

However, there was more to Radek's interpretation of the SPD's downfall than the highly contested responsibility for the war. He built on other stories that were readily available in 1925 among both the Left and the Right. One of these stories connected Barmat with Alexander Helphand, a Jewish Russian political émigré from the 1905 revolution known as Parvus and one of the most colorful figures associated with the German Left. A promising leftist theoretician before the war, Parvus—this "unbelievably fat Socrates" whose "intellect was as broad as his body"[35]—had become a shrewd businessman during the war, artfully mixing money and politics. Parvus viewed a German victory as the precondition for the victory of socialism, so in his view Hindenburg und Ludendorff were nothing other than the executives of the future socialism, first in Germany and then in Europe. He forged links to those Scandinavian Socialists who were friendly to Germany, reaping significant economic benefits from these ties, like the famous coal deliveries to his Danish comrades that the Reich subsidized in order to oust cheaper English coal and influence.[36] Yet one of Parvus's biggest schemes was to bring revolution to Russia, which in 1916–17 would not only relieve Germany of its Eastern Front but also provide him with a new political role. This is in itself a long story that finds Parvus often boasting not only about his great connections to Russian Socialists via Scandinavia but also about his ability to participate actively in revolutionizing Russia.[37] He was successful insofar as he convinced the Foreign Office (which had helped him become a German citizen in 1916) to spend tremendous sums of money to support his "Russian connections." The question whether this money ever arrived in Russia or ended instead in Parvus's pockets or in his Scandinavian ventures is quite another matter. He was also actively involved in arranging safe passage for Lenin from Switzerland to Russia through his clever business companion, Georg Sklarz. Parvus never left any doubt that he disliked the Bolsheviks, particularly Lenin. In fact, soon after the Soviets gained power, Parvus was again in contact with the Foreign Office, attempting to lure officials with his ideas about establishing an anti-Bolshevist organization. At the time of the armistice in late 1918, a fortune's worth of propaganda material, paid for by the Reich, remained stuck in the East. This incident, as well Parvus's earlier involvements in Russia and elsewhere, was first brought up in the fall of 1919 by Maximilian Harden in his journal, *Die Zukunft:* "All of these stories, and a hundred uglier ones have been circulating for months"; copies of official documents were also circulating. Harden compiled these dispersed bits of information into a plausible account, thereby exposing the dubious alliance of Parvus with the Foreign Office and prominent Social Democrats.[38] This in itself constituted a scandal in the view of many observers. Most aggravating for the radical Left was that Parvus's companion Sklarz had received a highly lucrative carte blanche for provisioning the government's troops during the revolutionary turmoil in January of 1918, specifically the Corps Lüttwitz, which had been responsible for killing Rosa Luxemburg, Karl Liebknecht, and other revolutionaries.[39] This was a sore issue on the Left, even more so because everybody knew that Barmat and Parvus were close friends.

These connections also drew attention to the ethics of Social Democratic leaders associated with the worst types of profiteers. A good many functionaries drew additional incomes from the highly subsidized Parvus ventures, such as the Institut zur Erforschung der sozialen Folgen des Krieges (Institute for the Research of the Social Consequences of War) in Copenhagen, the Verlag für soziale Wissenschaft in Germany, and the journal *Die Glocke*. Many of them had written the ominous anti-Bolshevist propaganda material mentioned above that had sparked the "Sklarz scandal." By and large the same group of people, namely, right-wing Social Democrats, came under attack once more in 1925.

Back in 1919–20, the former Reich chancellor Philipp Scheidemann had taken the brunt of the political attacks from the far Left. The man who had warned just a short while before that "Der Feind steht rechts" (the enemy is on our right)[40] was viciously accused of collaborating with "capitalists" and "reactionaries." The issue involved food contracts and his (and his in-law's) personal and business relationships with Sklarz und Parvus, who gladly shared with him the amenities of life, including Parvus's villa in Switzerland and later in Berlin. In order to contain this conflict, a fact-finding committee of the SPD held hearings in 1919–20 to investigate the behavior of Scheidemann and others, leaving Scheidemann with a tarnished reputation.[41] Five years later, another former chancellor, Gustav Bauer, confronted charges very similar to those brought against Scheidemann. In February 1925, Bauer was forced by his party to resign from office as a member of the Reichstag, and a special commission of the SPD excluded him from the party, not the least because of the "incredibly infuriated mood in the factories."[42] For months, the involvement of Social Democrats like Bauer, Wels, and Heilmann in Barmat's business shook the SPD, thereby raising the issues of ethics and politics and posing questions about the future of socialism and capitalism and the path the party had taken since the war and the revolution. All of these issues were debated at the SPD Party congress, held in Heidelberg in September 1925, where the party drafted a new program that represented a marked turn to the left.[43]

The name of Julius Barmat and his dealings with the Reich and the state of Saxony were mentioned in German newspapers for the first time in connection with the controversial activities and business ventures of Sklarz and Parvus. Some of the information revealed then came up time and again in the years that followed.[44] Although no clear connection between Sklarz and Barmat could ever be established, conservative critics argued that the same mishandling of the case "on order from above" that had resulted in the withdrawal of an indictment against Sklarz in 1921 and the transfer of the Berlin state attorney responsible for the case to the Reich Court in Leipzig would repeat itself in the case of Barmat.[45] The activism of the state attorney's office in 1924–25 and the conservatives' outcry over political injustice were rooted in these events.

From Rathenau to Barmat:
Telling the Story of the Jewish "*Rattenkönige*"

By 1920, the radical Right had also taken notice of the information being circulated on Sklarz. An important, widely circulated pamphlet, entitled *Der Rattenkönig und ihre Helfer. Die Wahrheit über den Fall Sklarz (The Rat King and his Helpers: The Truth about the Sklarz Case)*, appeared in 1920 under the pseudonym Sincton Upclaire (a transposition of the name of the American writer Upton Sinclair). The cover of the pamphlet states that the "rat king" reigned over a "society of rats, who are so twisted together and tangled up in their own filth and smut in the nest that they can no longer be separated."[46] Again, this was primarily the story of enrichment of Jewish profiteers and how they were entangled with each other. The pamphlet detailed the efforts to bring about Bolshevism in Russia by sending Lenin there, characterizing Sklarz as the "financier of the special guard of the Reichstag during the unrest" of early 1919—yet omitting the fact that the troops were fighting the Communist Left.[47] The radical Right thus drew a connection between Jews, profiteering, and socialism on the one side, and between Jewish financing and republican combat leagues close to the SPD, on the other.

However, the brunt of the attacks of the political Right was directed against "Jewish war-profiteering" and the *Kriegswirtschaftsgesellschaften*, the semipublic bodies that had organized the war economy, which were depicted as a symbiosis between Jews running the war economy and Socialists. Since the early years of the war, vicious attacks had been made on the Jews, and Walther Rathenau, the head of the department for war supplies (*Kriegsrohstoffabteilung*) was a favorite target of such abuse until his murder in 1922.[48] The argument of the right was simple: the *Kriegswirtschaftsgesellschaften* had exploited the German population and corrupted economic life, thereby causing prices to explode and scarce resources, including food, to be wasted. Rathenau was thus decried as a "rat king of societies that have to mutually support and help each other, where one was always the vendor, customer, or moneylender of the other."[49] The consequences of the "Rathenau system," which had been "born of a Jewish mind," were depicted as the final seed of destruction that brought about Germany's downfall in the war.[50] The Sklarz case fit into this narrative of wartime corruption just as well as did the Kutisker-Barmat affair. Thus it was not far fetched to argue, as did the Zionist *Wiener Morgenzeitung*, that "the Barmat Affair ... represents the climax of agitation against Rathenau."[51] After all, Barmat was vilified as the new "rat king," an image that also proliferated among agrarian groups.[52]

This corresponded with narratives that viewed the "sphere of circulation," meaning the wartime system of trade and distribution, as the primary cause of the impoverishment and misery suffered by the German population. Juxtaposed to this was the sphere of production and men like Hugo Stinnes, an entrepreneur in the field of shipping, manufacturing, and heavy industry and a prominent member of the German Peoples Party (DVP). In 1924, Stinnes's business went bankrupt. In an open letter to Stinnes's widow in 1925, Alfred Rosenberg argued that Hugo Stinnes, like German artisans and farmers, had been financially ruined because he did not understand the "nature of a worldwide Jewish cooperation (*Zusammenspiels*) and had not prepared himself for the battle against ruination." He claimed that the Jewish "*Weltkampf*" (worldwide struggle) would continue until all German enterprises were in Jewish hands.[53] In the novel *Der Kaufmann von Mühlheim* published that same year, Stinnes was portrayed as a national hero—as a fighter against Versailles and for the working class but also as a defender of "productive capital" against the dark forces of finance.[54]

Inspired by conspiracy theories on the "*raffende Kapital*" (hoarding capital), *völkisch* groups spun other stories that circulated widely in the mid-1920s. For example, the anti-Semitic journal *Der Hammer* referred to a "protocol" proving that leading Social Democrats had met with Parvus in Schwanenwerder in 1919, where they had allegedly decided to suspend their calls for socialization and to seek instead to bring about the "confiscation of all property" by way of inflation: "This satanic plan has succeeded. People and princes have been robbed of their cash. Only the money belonging to the Jews has been spared because they rule the international monetary market."[55] In 1925, anti-Semitic radicals argued that "Barmat and Co." offered the best proof that the "Protocols of the Elders of Zion" were real. They especially referred to one passage in the "Protocols": "Just to be on the safe side, we will manipulate the presidential election toward such candidates whose past proves to have a certain situation, a 'Panama' known only to us. This person will then be the obedient executor of our orders, motivated by fear of disclosure and the understandable desire to continue enjoying all the privileges, income, and honors linked to presidential office." Legally, it was tricky to argue like this, especially to suggest concretely that "Ebert possesses a dark point from his past before his election and is therefore committed, come what may, to the Jewish parasites." Having proffered this legal caveat, it was further argued that "the Kutiskers and Barmats have obviously tried everywhere and among all leading personalities to create a 'Panama' in order to have them in their hands. ... So, as always, the Jewish plan matches—how could it be otherwise—Jewish instinct and its effects."[56]

In this sense, the story of Parvus, Sklarz, Kutisker, and Barmat provided powerful clues in a conspiratorial narrative of the political Right and *völkisch* groups particularly in a time of war, revolution, and inflation. Parvus and Sklarz were linked with Lenin's Bolshevist revolution in Russia (an obituary on Parvus referred to him as the "Head of the Nordic Central Committee for Bolshevist Propaganda in Western Europe"),[57] and there was something to the rumor that Barmat sought to align himself with the Ukrainian Bolsheviks in 1917–18. All three of these men allegedly supported the new "Marxist" revolutionary governments in Germany. Not only were they depicted as bribing the new politicians but also as manipulating them so that Parvus, Sklarz, and Barmat—as representatives of "international Jewry"—could gain control of the Prussian State Bank at the expense of the broader German economy and the population at large. The ensuing trial was interpreted as just one more example of a *"Gefesselte Justiz"* (captive law) (Zarnow), a judicial system the hands of which were tied by the "Panama" that was allegedly buried in the résumé of every republican politician. It is the story of the republic in the hands of both Jews and Socialists. Thus it is not astonishing that the military organization of the Social Democrats, the Reichbanner Schwarz–Rot–Gold, was soon referred to as the "Barmat Boys" and the "special guard of the Jews."[58]

Gifts, Luxury, and Schwanenwerder

What enraged the opposition as much as the public was the involvement of money and gifts and the suspicion of dependencies that were created by favors, which made the Social Democrats particularly vulnerable to charges of hypocrisy. Their opponents pointed to an inconsistency between their lofty rhetoric of social justice, imbued with a more or less implicit critique of capitalism, and the behavior of many Social Democrats who seemed to have profited from a close relationship with Barmat. What might be acceptable among bourgeois parties, namely, that money and politics mingled all too easily, should not have been acceptable to Socialists.[59]

The case of Barmat presented a special twist to the relationship between money and morals in 1925 because Barmat, like Kutisker, was not just any businessman or financier. As a profiteer, Barmat evoked memories of the recently experienced "world turned upside down"—the period of inflation in Germany, followed by the time of economic stabilization, when material deprivation, hunger, and the loss of a sense of *"Treu und Glauben"* (good faith) was evident everywhere, while a select but conspicuous few in society indulged themselves in luxurious excess. A dense web of stories and images of such excesses existed in the German collective memory, ready for immediate recall.[60] Indeed, one can interpret the vicious attacks of 1925 as retribution for those who appeared to have pushed the moral destabilization of German society to the extreme in their crazed pursuit for money. The fact that the offenders were Jews, in particular *Ostjuden* who had found their way into German society, implied a strategy of distancing, whereby the "others," strangers, were blamed.

The first chapter of Gottfried Zarnov's book *Gefesselte Justiz*, entitled "the New German Iliad," begins with a subchapter called "The Sybarite Island of Schwanenwerder" in which the rich society of western Berlin was epitomized more than anything else. In early 1923, Barmat moved to this exclusive and reclusive peninsula, with beautiful villas situated in a large park and boat-piers on the Havel River. Rumors had it that Julius Barmat was arrested in the villa of the "big-time profiteer" Parvus, who had settled there only a few years earlier and had died there a few days before Julius Barmat was arrested.[61] Notwithstanding the fact that they lived in different homes, this enabled the personal fates and stories of these two figures to be mingled once again. For Barmat was an equally rich man, who had lived in 1919 in the elegant Hotel Kaiserhof (as did Parvus) and then regularly in the Hotel Bristol. No doubt he spent some of his money engaging in the social life of Berlin, like his brother Henry, who had a large flat on the Kurfürstendamm and was just returning from a hunting party when he was arrested. Since the days of Imperial Germany, Berlin's West Side had had the reputation of being "democratic." Especially to conservative observers, it was painful to see how men like the Barmats invaded the social and political life of Berlin with their contacts to politicians.[62]

Julius Barmat seems to have been a hard-working businessman: a *homo economicus judaicus* (Penslar), yet one who spent his money freely.[63] When his friend Heilmann argued in the fact-finding committee that Barmat was satisfied to eat herring and tripe, he was widely ridiculed (as in a cartoon in the *Rote Fahne*). The public liked more juicy stories, such as the one first uncovered by the *Berliner Börsenzeitung* about an Austrian dancer by the name of Katharina Huber, also known under the pseudonyms of Marga Lundgreen or Kity von Hagen, with whom Barmat was said to have been linked romantically. Pictures of this good-looking showgirl popping out of a cake, dressed up as a barmaid, or dancing scantily clothed in the posh bar Nelson's near the Kurfürstendamm, where Julius Barmat apparently met her after the war, fueled the public's fantasy and the imagination of political conservatives. Such images were nearly primordial with respect to the Berlin of the early 1920s. For the conservative press, Katharina Huber was the Madame de Pompadour of the "Barmat circle" and allegedly bestowed sexual favors upon Heilmann and the head of the Berlin police Richter when Barmat was out of town, that is, until all three of them, as it was rumored, wished to rid themselves of her and forced her to leave Berlin in 1921. This story became confounded with long-standing rumors about Parvus, who was forced to leave Switzerland in 1919, due as much to his reputation as a Russian revolutionary as to his alleged sexual excesses, which were mentioned time and again with respect to his unconventional lifestyle and his utter rejection of "bourgeois mores."[64] These rumors added a risqué touch to the gatherings of leading republican politicians and party functionaries at the homes of both Parvus and Barmat. Indeed, Schwanenwerder had become a social place where conservative Social Democrats like Scheidemann, Otto Wels, Ernst Heilmann, the Prussian minister of education Haenisch, to name just a few, met and talked about politics and business.[65]

It is difficult to say what enraged the general public more: the fact that the State Bank had lost millions to these men or the innumerable stories about little favors, small gifts, food packages, the so-called *Liebesgaben* or sexual favors, and the cash loans, large and small, that Barmat gave away freely—not only to his friends. The stories about Sklarz, Barmat, and Parvus were those imbued with gift giving and favor doing and were interpreted already at the time as illustrations of a strategy of *"Einschmeicheln"* (ingratiation), of securing their acceptance into society and of creating dependencies.[66] Under attack by the KPD for the favors he had bestowed on Social Democrats, Barmat revealed that a member of the KPD who had come to Amsterdam in 1919 during a dockworkers' strike had also received a small personal loan that he had never paid back fully.[67] In the case of Gustav Bauer, it seems that Barmat had indeed tried to foster his dependency or favoritism. One of the officials of the State Bank, who was in good part responsible for the mess, was depicted as victim of the slyness, superior rhetoric, and cosmopolitan appearance of Barmat and particularly Kutisker.[68]

At any rate, contemporaries drew a connection between the favors Barmat dispensed and the favors he received. The fact that stories circulated about "whole barrels of margarine"[69] that had perhaps been given to party officials says more about the deep-seated memories of hunger lingering in the minds of the population than it does about anything else (as does, in a side note, the story widely publicized and handled in the press during the winter of 1924–25 about a mass murderer named Haarmann who sold the human flesh of his victims). In the case of Berlin's police chief Richter, who had risen from the ranks of the metalworkers, such gifts proved to be his downfall. In tears, he admitted to the parliamentary fact-finding committee and also to the state attorney that he had not only received loans totaling 8,100 gold marks and some stocks and bonds, but also a tuxedo, pajamas, a hat, a pair of cufflinks, a lighter, cigars and cigar-clip, expense-paid trips to Holland and Vienna, and two or three free meals at the Hotel Bristol over a long period of time.[70]

Containing the Barmat Affair: A Narrative for the Republic?

As we have seen, the Kutisker-Barmat affair started out as an attack on the Social Democratic political establishment of the Weimar Republic by both the radical Left and the Right, then turned rapidly into a vicious anti-Semitic assault. It ended in 1928 when the court finally handed down convictions in what seemed to defenders of the republic to be a success story for the republic and, not the least, its judicial system: reason had prevailed over emotions and fended off vicious attacks on the republic, thus ran one explanation.[71] Indeed, in order to neutralize the attacks, it was necessary to take "politics" and "political excitement" out of the entire affair and to rationalize it as a case of white-collar crime and grave economic mismanagement. In light of the momentum the case had developed in the political and legal arenas and fueled by an escalating media campaign, this was not easy. By arresting businessmen and even placing the Reich's postal minister in pretrial detention, the state prosecutor's office and especially two young officials, Kußmann and Caspary, created a heightened atmosphere of crisis. Considering how much the DNVP had used the issue of the *Ostjuden* in previous elections, it is fairly impossible to untangle mere political calculations from anti-Semitic motives (although Caspary was Jewish). At any rate, in the eyes of conservatives, the two state attorneys became heroes who promised to expose, once and for all, the *"Barmatsumpf"* (Barmat morass). In fact, the prosecutors inquired into the personal life of Barmat's associates and sought to uncover all sorts of incriminating evidence that went far beyond the case, unraveling earlier cases like Sklarz and other allegations. This would have made perfect sense had they been able to uncover a larger conspiracy. But nothing of this sort materialized, especially no evidence of politically motivated fraud and bribery at the State Bank, despite the fact that the investigative efforts produced over a thousand files.[72] Even weeks after the accused had been arrested and placed in detention, they were not informed of the formal charges leveled against them.[73] Moreover, there was the case of Reich Post Minister Anton Höfle, whose death in police custody threatened to become a real "Panama" of the judicial system. This, together with the allegation that confidential material had been leaked from the prosecutor's office to the press, was the reason that the two abovementioned prosecutors were dismissed from the case and later even subjected to a disciplinary investigation. By no means did the republic act like a cowardly lion; nor did it lack the means and guts to contain the conflict.

These were bold steps to take, but this was part of what one may call the republican success story. The well-known Berlin attorney Siegfried Löwenstein came to the conclusion in 1928 that deposing the two state attorneys was an effort, albeit belated, to "make amends for the damage done by excessive overzealousness." Rather than turning the case over to "youthful, naïve, and overzealous department heads," it was now "placed in the hands of judicious, carefully deliberating men" for further investigation.[74] That there was a need— in the heat of the political contest in 1925—to correct what had gone wrong was soon noted also in the Prussian Diet's summary of its inquiry into the case. For example, the speaker of the German National Party, Deerberg, was astonishingly conciliatory in his summary report for the Prussian fact-finding committee. He argued that no "political influence" had been exerted upon authorities to remove the case from the docket of the two state prosecutors.[75] Despite repeated attacks by conservative groups and individual right-wing politicians on the handling of the case, a broad consensus emerged (excluding the KPD) by the end of the summer that the involvement and the responsibility of individual people had been greatly exaggerated in Barmat's case, especially with respect to the credit policy of the State Bank. Reich President Ebert was taken out of the line of fire altogether, with the argument that he was not implicated in the case and that he had kept his distance from Barmat.[76] The loans granted by the National Post were far more dubious, but Höfle was dead, and it was apparently embarrassing to many conservatives that a member of the Center Party, a potential political ally, had been so deeply involved in the scandal. As the leftist journal *Die Weltbühne* commented sarcastically, the involvement of the Center Party only demonstrated who was really "running the show" in the republic.[77] With respect to the reconciliatory tone of the Prussian fact-finding committee, Communist committee member Bartel fretted that "now all that is missing is a general reconciliation celebration that even Mr. Barmat would be allowed to attend."[78]

There were many other good reasons why such obvious efforts were being made to deescalate the political conflict. The head of the DNVP, Graf Westarp, warned already in February 1925 that "black sheep" were to be found in all parties.[79] Indeed, throughout that entire year, many similar cases surfaced in which industrial and agricultural businesses could no longer meet their credit payments. The case of Hugo Stinnes was merely the most spectacular of these cases. At the final session of the Prussian Diet's committee, the Social Democratic speaker hinted all too obviously at the log rolling taking place behind the scenes when he stressed that his party agreed to be more "accommodating" to agriculture by extending credit where necessary. Furthermore, he continued, the committee members had become "realistic"—he spoke of *Nüchternheit*—so, more than anything else, the scandals of 1924 and 1925 were viewed as part of the general phenomena accompanying stabilization. The president of the Reich Bank, Hjalmar Schacht, had completely supported this view, depicting quite cynically the internal organization and the incompetence of the Prussian officials in running the State Bank.[80]

In 1926, Kutisker was harshly punished; his appeal against the verdict came to naught, and he died in prison a day before his verdict was to be confirmed.[81] The case of Barmat, however, contained a special dimension. No other court trial in German history had ever been staged with such extraordinary effort: five state attorneys, four hundred witnesses, and fifty experts were involved. When the presiding judge fell seriously ill a year into the trial proceedings, his private bedroom was transformed into a courtroom until he could return to the formal courtroom. Both the indictment of the state attorney's office, published in two volumes, and the final verdict of the court were monumental in size.[82] Observers emphasized that the exchanges between defense lawyers and state prosecutors may have been heated at times and that there were "fundamental differences of opinion regarding the actual and the legal assessment of the case," but that the proceedings were fair and had been fought "with chivalry."[83] Justice had prevailed. "Praise the Judges" was the headline of the *Berliner Börsenkurier*, one proudly quoted also in the *Richterzeitung*.[84]

The court concentrated strictly on the issue of the loans of 1923–24, deflecting arguments that only Julius Barmat's arrest had caused the collapse of the Barmat enterprises.[85] The court considered it as proven that Julius and Henry Barmat had bribed officials of the State Bank, sentencing them to eleven and six months in prison, respectively, and slapping each with a heavy fine in addition. Only three people from the State Bank received prison terms and each of them were short. The indictment for fraud was dropped for lack of evidence in accordance with the juridical principle *in dubio pro reo.*

In terms of a narrative of the republic, the court's reasoning is quite interesting und was picked up by all commentators. The court argued that Barmat's business deals occurred during a time of general confusion of values and sentiments that followed the period of war, revolution, and inflation. As a result of the rate of devaluation, at first slow and then quite rapid, "of what had until then been revered as permanent values, individuals had lost their capability to think in terms of stable values." The latter only reemerged when the stabilization of the currency made possible the reinstitution of new standards of value (*Wertbegriffe*). As it was argued, the court had to take into account the deep confusion that had prevailed at the time and had to consider that conditions in 1928 were markedly different from those of a few years earlier.[86] The more or less implicit argument was that the stabilization of the currency had also dispensed with dubious characters like Barmat and paved the way to internal stability of the republic.

National Socialists and the "Gefesselte Justiz"

The efforts to contain the scandals and finally the handing down of the sentences in both cases did not mark the end of the story. One man in particular refused to drop the matter. That man, an accountant named Philipp Lachmann, had been assigned by the state attorney's office the task of inspecting the books of Kutisker's enterprises. Instead of writing a report on financial transactions, he wrote a type of criminal investigation report and indictment that was aimed not so much against Kutisker, but against his famous Berlin lawyer Julius Werthauer and the latter's law partner, who allegedly had known about the fraudulent loans and had advised Kutisker. With the latter dead, the case took a new turn. A private feud emerged between Lachmann and Werthauer, which prompted a series of lawsuits that Lachmann lost; on top of this, Lachmann also lost his standing as a sworn expert in Berlin. All of this spurred him on to write long memoranda and open letters that circulated not only in the newspapers of the political Right. He saw himself not only as a modern Michael Kohlhaas, that archetypical figure in the play of Heinrich von Kleist who wanted to have his personal injustices redeemed; he also saw himself in tradition of Cicero and others who had attacked the corruption of the ancient Roman Republic.[87]

Lachmann's story was tragic, but not only because he was heavily in debt by the early 1930s. Lachmann and the former state attorney Caspary, with whom he had closely collaborated in 1925 (as he already had with the latter's father) were both Jewish, and it was the political Right who was cashing in on this acrimonious campaign of Lachmann. Most people following the case thought the obstinate accountant was simply obsessed or downright crazy, an assessment confirmed by the psychiatric opinions of him solicited by the courts in connection with the trials. In 1930, the journalist Gottfried Zarnow included the Lachmann case in his bestseller *Gefesselte Justiz*, in which the cases of Sklarz, Parvus-Helphand, Barmat, Kutisker, and others were rehashed in a semidocumentary manner.[88] This time the National Socialists were able to take the political initiative. In the winter of 1932–33, the Prussian Diet once more set up a fact-finding committee, the so-called Zarnow Committee, which was to investigate the allegations made in the book, thus unraveling again the earlier cases of Barmat and Kutisker and those allegedly pulling the strings. This committee met the last time at the end of January 1933 under the chairmanship of the NSDAP representative Roland Freisler, the later head of the *Volksgerichtshof*, whose ruthlessness towards his political enemies could already be seen.[89]

The story of Julius Barmat does not end in the seemingly stable years of the late Weimar Republic. In his biography, history did repeat itself, and it is hard to say whether to view this as a tragedy or a rather cynical comedy. After his release from prison in 1930, Julius Barmat and his brothers settled again in Amsterdam. Soon he was linked to what was known as the Stavisky affair in France, a financial scandal similar in nature that deeply rocked the French nation in the first half of the 1930s. New "affairs" involving Barmat came up in Switzerland, Holland, and Belgium, where fascist organizations, apparently aided by Germany, were active to scandalize their business. Starting in 1934, Barmat found himself again involved in several court trials. In Belgium, the highly regarded Catholic minister-president, van Zeeland, had to defend himself against accusations of making allegedly crooked loans to banks close to Barmat during van Zeeland's tenure as vice-president of the Belgian national bank.[90] Under massive public pressure, van Zeeland and all members of his cabinet were finally forced to resign in 1937—Belgium had its Barma scandal. Julius Barmat, who was to be extradited from Holland to Belgium, died on 6 January 1938. When one of his brothers allegedly fled to Russia, the *Völkische Beobachter* wrote sarcastically that he had turned to the red dictator for protection and was now "among his own." Julius Barmat had become the *"Giftblüte der Demokratie"* (poisonous flower of democracy) and the "gravedigger of the democratic system," the man who represented the demise of the republic.[91] With such a reputation, it was no small wonder that the Reich Propaganda Ministry was looking for someone to write Barmat's story—even if the story turned out to really be that of Kutisker. The Barmats and Kutisker came to epitomize in National Socialist propaganda the rats that infested the world—the Eastern Jews who threw off their caftans, shaved their beards, and became cosmopolitan men—in other words, they represented the *"Ewige Jude"* (wandering Jew) as depicted in the 1941 film of the same name.[92] By then, Joseph Goebbels, the profiteer from the "revolution of 1933," had for a long time settled in the elegant villa colony of Schwanenwerder. Roland Freisler was one who advocated *Volksrecht*, people's law, the premises of which diverged from those of the rule of "positive law" that was seen as having protected men like Barmat. Incidentally, his brother Georg Freisler had taken over the law practice of Johannes Werthauer, who had escaped in 1933 to Switzerland.[93] Werthauer had been one of the first thirty people designated in August 1933 not only to lose his German citizenship but also to be expropriated, which started the larger process of Jewish expropriation actively propagated by National Socialists also with respect to "Jewish war and inflation profiteering."[94] Probably in 1934, Philipp Lachmann wrote the last of his lengthy memorandums, this time to Hermann Göring in his function as minister-president of Prussia, arguing for some retribution "for seven years of fighting" and, more urgently employment for himself and Caspary. His efforts were to no avail. Not only was he considered a known complainer, but, now even more importantly, also a Jew, and for the latter there was no place anymore in public service.[95]

Notes

1. It is not clear who made the first reference to a "Panama"; however, it was used equally both by the Left and the Right. For the Panama scandal, see Stephen Wilson, *Ideology and Experience: Antisemitism in France at the Time of the Dreyfus Affair* (London, 1982), chap. 10. There does not exist a comprehensive history of the scandal; see also Cordula Ludwig, *Korruption und Nationalsozialismus in Berlin 1924–1934* (Frankfurt am Main, 1998), 66–75; Stephan Malinowski, "Politische Skandale als Zerrspiegel der Demokratie. Die Fälle Barmat und Sklarek im Kalkül der Weimarer Rechten," *Jahrbuch für Antisemitismusforschung* 5 (1996): 46–65.

2. Winfried Steffani, *Die Untersuchungsausschüsse des preußischen Landtags zur Zeit der Weimarer Republik* (Düsseldorf, 1960), 169–90.

3. Hagen Schulze, *Otto Braun oder Preußens demokratische Sendung. Eine Biographie* (Frankfurt am Main, 1977), 466–74; Heinrich August Winkler, *Der Schein der Normalität. Arbeiter und Arbeiterbewegung in der Weimarer Republik 1924 bis 1930* (Berlin, 1985), 222–28.

4. Joseph Kaufhold, *Der Barmat-Sumpf* (Berlin, 1925); Karlludwig Rintelen, *Ein undemokratischer Demokrat: Gustav Bauer: Gewerkschaftsführer—Freund Friedrich Eberts— Reichskanzler. Eine politische Biographie* (Frankfurt am Main, 1993), 235–48.

5. See also Malinowski, "Politische Skandale," 52.

6. Winkler, *Schein*, 229–31; Walter Mühlhausen, *Friedrich Ebert 1871–1925. Reichspräsident der Weimarer Republik* (Bonn, 2006), 911–980. It is somewhat curious that all of the more recent biographies of Friedrich Ebert, including that of Walter Mühlhausen, mention the *Magdeburger Hochverratsprozeß* but not the Barmat affair.

7. *Sammlung der Drucksachen des preußischen Landtages*, 2. Wahlperiode, 1. Tagung 1925, vol. 7, 2973.

8. Victor Schiff, *Die Höfle-Tragödie. Geschichte eines Justizmordes* (Berlin, 1925), 7, 14, 88.

9. Murray Edelman, *Constructing the Political Spectacle* (Chicago, 1988); Murray Edelman, *The Symbolic Uses of Politics* (Urbana, IL, 1985); Frank Bösch, "Politische Skandale in Deutschland und Großbritannien," *Aus Politik und Zeitgeschichte* 7, no. 13 (February 2006): 25–32.

10. See, i.e., Heinz Reif, "Antisemitismus in den Agrarverbänden Nordostdeutschlands während der Weimarer Republik," in *Ostelbische Agrargesellschaft in Kaiserreich und Republik. Agrarkrise, junkerliche Interessenpolitik, Modernisierungsstrategien*, ed. Heinz Reif (Berlin, 1993), 379–415. Reif stresses the importance of the case (404). However his description on the basis of the agrarian press is a good example of how fact and contemporary fiction are mixed.

11. Martin H. Geyer, *Verkehrte Welt. Revolution, Inflation und Moderne: München 1914–1924* (Munich, 1999), esp. chap. 8.

12. See also the brilliant book by Dietz Bering, *Kampf um Namen. Berhard Weiß gegen Joseph Goebbels* (Stuttgart, 1991). Almost no contemporary photographs remain, yet an abundance of caricatures. For some pictures of the people involved, see Edmund Schulz (mit einer Einleitung von Friedrich Georg Jünger) ed., *Das Gesicht der Demokratie* (Leipzig, 1931), 93–98. No mention of the case is made in Cornelia Hecht, *Deutsche Juden und Antisemitismus in der Weimarer Republik* (Bonn, 2003).

13. See the compilation of critiques in Walter Mehring, "Der Kaufmann von Berlin," in *Drei Jüdische Dramen. Mit Dokumenten zur Rezeption,* ed. Hans J. Weitz (Göttingen, 1995), 297–357, esp. the critique of the *Berliner Tageblatt* journalist Ernst Feder, 325f, and the conversation of the latter with Mehring, who noted that after many fights with Piscator he originally had wanted to stop the play. Ernst Feder, *Tagebücher eines Berliner Publizisten 1926–1932,* ed. Cécile Lowenthal-Hensel and Arnold Paucker (Stuttgart, 1971), 223f. For an analysis see Hans-Peter Bayerdörfer, "Shylock in Berlin. Walter Mehring und das Judenporträt im Zeitstück der Weimarer Republik," in *Conditio Judaica. Judentum, Antisemitismus und deutschsprachige Literatur vom Ersten Weltkrieg bis 1933/1938,* ed. Hans Otto Horch and Horst Denkler (Tübingen, 1993), 307–23; however, the author does not mention the actual case.

14. "Linkskurve," in Mehring, "Kaufmann von Berlin," 306.

15. For a detailed, although not complete description, see the eighty-page verdict handed down by the court on 30 June 1926, Landesarchiv Berlin (LAB) A Rep 358, 62, vol. I. See also the references to Kutisker in the final summaries of the various party representatives in the last session of the Prussian fact-finding committee: *Sammlung der Drucksachen des preußischen Landtages,* vol. 7, 1480.

16. *Sammlung der Drucksachen des preußischen Landtages,* vol. 7, 2966.

17. Verdict against Kutisker (note 15), 76.

18. *Sammlung der Drucksachen des preußischen Landtages,* vol. 7, 2965; see, i.e., "Zum Antrag betreffend den Angeschuldigten Rühe," n.d., Geheimes Staatsarchiv Preußischer Kulturbesitz(GStA PK), I HA Rep 84a no. 56550, fol. 156.

19. The best description (however, without footnotes) is by Günter Casper, "Der Kutisker-Roman," in *Fallada-Studien* (Berlin, 1987), 218–32. See also Cecilia von Studnitz, *Es war wie ein Rausch. Fallada und sein Leben* (Düsseldorf, 1997), chap. 19.

20. Quoted in Casper, "Kutisker-Roman," 325. With respect to Fallada's anti-Semitism and planned novel, see also Ellis Shookman, "Making History in Hans Fallada's *Bauern, Bonzen und Bomben:* Schleswig-Holstein, Nazism, and the *Landvolkbewegung,*" *German Studies Review* 13 (1990): 461–80; Thomas Bredohl, "Some Thoughts on the Political Opinions of Hans Fallada: A Response to Ellis Shookman," *German Studies Review* 15 (1992): esp. 539–41.

21. Casper, "Kutisker-Roman," 229, 220.

22. Trude Maurer, *Ostjuden in Deutschland 1918–1933* (Hamburg, 1986).

23. A very factual business history of the Barmats can be found in the published verdict of the court, which is a remarkable piece of contemporary economic history. *Urteil des Schöffengerichts Berlin-Mitte, Abteilung 206, vom 30. März 1928 in der Strafsache gegen Barmat und Genossen* (Berlin, 1929). Some of the verdict is based on the indictment, which was also published as *Anklageschrift gegen Barmat und Genossen,* 2 vols. (Berlin, 1926).

24. "Barmat und die Auskunfteien," n.d., Politisches Archiv des Auswärtigen Amtes (PA-AA) R 30337 fol. 173–74.

25. Maurer, *Ostjuden*; Shulamit Volkov, "Die Dynamik der Dissimilation. Deutsche Juden und die ostjüdische Einwanderer," in *Zebrochene Geschichte*, ed. Dirk Blasius and Dan Diner (Frankfurt am Main, 1991), 64–78. For example, see "Das Ostjudenproblem," *Neue Preußische (Kreuz-) Zeitung*, 1 February 1925; "Die Ostjuden-Plage," *Neue Preußische (Kreuz-) Zeitung*, 13 February 1925; "Henry Barmats Wohnung," 26 February 1925.

26. Gerald D. Feldman, *Hugo Stinnes. Biographie eines Industriellen 1870–1924* (Munich, 1998), 936.

27. *Urteil des Schöffengerichts Berlin-Mitte*, 11.

28. Verhör Julius Barmats, 12 January 1925, I HA Rep 84a no. 56541, fol. 240–44; Henri Barmat to Ministerialdirektor Huber, 25 January 1925, I HA Rep 84a nr.56544, fol. 102–29.

29. *Urteil des Schöffengerichts Berlin-Mitte*, 15f. This political issue was not part of the trial. This protest, which must be seen also in the context of the firing of government officials and the debates over "revaluation" of former debts, cannot be dealt with here. On the difficulties of agriculture, see Heinrich Becker, *Handlungsspielräume der Agrarpolitik in der Weimarer Republik zwischen 1923 und 1929* (Stuttgart, 1990). A strong critique by the Bavarian Government that referred to a "deep-seated and dangerous excitement" among the population can be found in *Akten der Reichskanzlei. Die Kabinette Luther* (Boppard, 1977), 1:70–80.

30. For the changing debates over "*Wucher*" see Martin H. Geyer, "Defining the Common Good and Social Justice: Popular and Legal Concepts of *Wucher* in Germany from the 1860s to the 1920s," in *Private Law and Social Inequality in the Industrial Age: Comparing Legal Cultures in Britain, France, Germany, and the United States*, ed. Willibald Steinmetz (Oxford, 2000), 457–83.

31. The Communists were well informed when it came to the Barmat scandal, according to the conservative *Kreuz-Zeitung*: "Barmat Verteidigung im Reichstag," *Neue Preußische (Kreuz-) Zeitung* 36, 22 February 1925.

32. Karl Radek, *Die Barmat-Sozialdemokratie* (Berlin, 1925), 43. Next to the articles of the *Rote Fahne*, see also Anonymous, *Barmat und seine Partei* (Berlin, 1925); and the concluding comment by Bartels in the Preußische Untersuchungsausschuß, *Sammlung der Drucksachen des preußischen Landtages*, vol. 7, 2986–3004.

33. Robert Siegel, *Die Lensch-Cunow-Haenisch-Gruppe. Eine Studie zum rechten Flügel der SPD im Weltkriege* (Berlin, 1976).

34. Radek, *Barmat-Sozialdemokratie*, 30. For an account of the SPD during the war, see esp. Susanne Miller, *Burgfrieden und Klassenkampf. Die deutsche Sozialdemokratie im Ersten Weltkrieg* (Düsseldorf, 1974).

35. Harry Graf Kessler, *Tagebücher 1918–1937*, ed. Wolfgang Peiffer-Belli (Berlin, 1961), 203.

36. For the following, see the early, rich account by Maximilian Harden, "Gold oder Weihrauch," *Die Zukunft*. 108 (1920): 1–29; Radek, *Barmat- Sozialdemokratie*, 32–37; Winfried B. Scharlau and Zbynek A. Zeman, *Freibeuter der Revolution: Parvus-Helphand. Eine politische Biographie* (Cologne, 1964); Elisabeth Heresch, *Geheimakte Parvus: Die gekaufte Revolution* (München, 2000).

37. Scharlau and Zeman, *Freibeuter*, 151–243.

38. Maximilian Harden, "Für die Republik," *Die Zukunft* 107 (1919), esp. 276–82; see also Harden, "Gold oder Weihrauch."

39. Harden, "Republik," 279.

40. The Sklarz affair and Scheidemann's involvement is not mentioned in the standard accounts of the SPD; for some aspects of this political scandal, see Niels H. M. Albrecht, "Die Macht einer Verleumdungskampagne. Antidemokratische Agitationen der Presse und Justiz gegen die Weimarer Republik und ihren ersten Reichspräsidenten Friedrich Ebert vom "Badebild" bis zum Magdeburger Prozess" (Phil. Diss., Bremen, 2002), 133–50. In a series of articles reprinted in several conservative newspapers, Eduard Kenkel draws the connection between the Kutisker-Barmat case and that of Sklarz; see "Bilder aus der preußischen Justiz," in *Bergisch-Märkische Zeitung,* 16–23 September 1925.

41. On the establishment of the *Untersuchungsausschuß,* see Protokoll der Sitzung des Parteiausschusses, Berlin, den 13. Dezember 1919, in *Protokolle der Sitzungen des Parteiausschusses der SPD 1912 bis 1921* (repr. Berlin, 1980), 1, 49–55; SPD, *Untersuchungsausschuß zum Fall Sklarz* (Berlin, 1920).

42. For a detailed description of Bauer's involvement, his attempts to cover up his connection to Barmat, and his later exposure, see Rintelen, *Undemokratischer Demokrat,* 235–48, esp. 244–46. In the summer of 1924, he was reinstated due to the efforts by the right wing, but this remained a contested issue.

43. The impact of the Barmat affair is altogether left out by Winkler, *Schein,* 319–27.

44. "Scheidemann gegen Sonnenfeld," *Vorwärts* 305 (17 June 1920). Maximilian Harden, "Das sechste Siegel," *Die Zukunft* 108 (1920): 88f. Otto Armin (Alfred Roth), *Die Juden in den Kriegs-Gesellschaften und in der Kriegs-Wirtschaft* (Munich, 1921), 72f.

45. This aspect of the story cannot be pursued here but was very present in 1925 and led to vicious clashes in the fact-finding committee. See, for example, "Auseinandersetzungen im 'Barmat-Ausschuß,'" *Berliner Tageblatt,* no. 60, 5 February 1925. Schulze, *Otto Braun.* 377–81. Gottfried Zarnow [Ewald Moritz], *Gefesselte Justiz. Poltische Bilder aus Deutscher Gegenwart,* 1 vol.; *Recht und Willkür im politischen Parteienstaat,* 2 vols.; *Politische Bilder aus deutscher Gegenwart* (Munich, 1930–1932), 1:9–12.

46. The distribution of this pamphlet was banned during the year it was published; its antiquarian availability today is a good indication of how widespread it was.

47. Sincton Upclair, *Der Rattenkönig und ihre Helfer. Die Wahrheit über den Fall Sklarz* (Berlin, 1920), 5–10, 12. For the emergence of the anti-Semitic movement, see Uwe Lohalm, *Völkischer Radikalismus. Die Geschichte des Deutsch-Völkischen Schutz- und Trutzbundes 1919–1923* (Hamburg, 1970).

48. Otto Armin (Alfred Roth), *Von Rathenau zu Barmat* (Stuttgart, 1925). In this pamphlet the author uses passages taken from his *Juden in den Kriegs-Gesellschaften.* Werner Jochmann, "Die Ausbreitung des Antisemitismus," in *Deutsches Judentum in Krieg und Revolution,* ed. Werner Mosse (Tübingen, 1971), 409–510; Hecht, *Antisemitismus,* 63–65, 138–52.

49. Otto Armin (Alfred Roth), *Rathenau,* 4. For a good summary of this argument in the agrarian context, see Reif, "Anti-Semitismus."

50. Reif, "Anti-Semitismus," 4, 8.

51. Quoted in Rosenberg, "Offener Brief an Hugo Stinnes," *Der Weltkampf. Halbmonatsschrift für die Judenfrage aller Länder* 2 (1925): 651.

52. So the title in Otto Armin (Alfred Roth), *Rathenau,* 62.

53. Alfred Rosenberg, "Offener Brief an Frau Hugo Stinnes," *Der Weltkampf* 2 (1925): 652.

54. Nathanael Jünger, *Kaufmann von Mühlheim. Ein Hugo-Stinnes-Roman* (Wismar, 1925). See also Bernd Widdig, *Culture and Inflation in Weimar Germany* (Berkeley, CA, 2001), chap. 6.

55. Markwart, "Die Hintermänner," Hammer. Zeitschrift für nationales Leben, no. 25 (1926): 406f.
56. Anonymous, "Barmat und Co. oder der größte Sieg der Demokratie," Der Weltkampf 5 (1925): 193.
57. Anonymous, "Parvus-Helphand-Markus-Klein," Der Weltkampf 2 (1925): 91.
58. Rumpelstilzchen [Adolf Stein], Rumpelstilzchen 1924/25: Haste Worte (Berlin, 1925), 152f. Anonymous, "Barmat und Co."; Karl Rohe, Das Reichsbanner Schwarz-Rot-Gold. Ein Beitrag zur Geschichte und Struktur der politischen Kampfverbände zur Zeit der Weimarer Republik (Düsseldorf, 1966).
59. Rintelen, undemokratischer Demokrat, 243f.
60. Geyer, Verkehrte Welt, chap. 7.
61. Anoynmous, "Barmat und Co.," 22.
62. The newspaper columns of the conservative journalist Adolf Stein are full of such resentments; see Rumpelstilzchen, 1920/21: Berliner Allerlei (Berlin, 1921), 27; for an estimate of the huge expenditures of the Barmats, see Anklageschrift gegen Barmat, 162–66.
63. Derek J. Penslar, Shylock's Children: Economic and Jewish Identity in Modern Europe (Berkeley, CA, 2001), 124–73.
64. See the cartoon published in the Rote Fahne, 25 February 1925; protocols of the interrogation of Wilhelm Richter by the state attorneys, LAB Rep 358 no. 421, vol. 1, fol. 113–26; see Anonymous, "Parvus-Helphand-Markus-Klein," 329, 342.
65. Anonymous, "Parvus-Helphand-Markus-Klein," 340.
66. Space limitations do not permit a detailed discussion here. Unfortunately, we probably know more about gift giving in the early modern period than in the twentieth century.
67. Document without title, GStA PK I. HA Rep 84a, no. 56541, fol. 225–29.
68. See Anklageschrift gegen Barmat, 123, 133; "Zum Antrag betreffend den Angeschuldigten Rühe" (note 18).
69. Radek, Barmat-Sozialdemokratie, 16.
70. "Aus dem Barmat-Sumpf. Nervenzusammenbruch und Geständnis Richters," Bergisch-Märkische Zeitung, 8 July 1925.
71. For a "republican account," see Carl Severing, Mein Lebensweg, vol. 2. (Cologne, 1950), 50–55; Erich Eyck, Geschichte der Weimarer Republik (Erlenbach, 1956), 1:432–36; and Steffani, Untersuchungsausschüsse, 169–90.
72. Siegfried Löwenstein, "Betrachtungen zum Barmat-Prozeß," Deutsche Juristen-Zeitung 33 (1928): 554.
73. Schiff, Höfle-Tragödie, 11.
74. Löwenstein, "Betrachtungen," 554.
75. Sammlung der Drucksachen des preußischen Landtages, 7:2964.
76. The later chancellor, Hermann Müller, would entertain guests at dinner parties with a story about Ebert's reaction to learning that Barmat had made calls from the offices of the Reich president to Amsterdam. On that occasion, Ebert supposedly commented: "Wenn der Saujud noch mal wiederkommt, schmeiß ich ihn hinaus." ("If that Jewish slob comes again, I'll kick him out!"). See Ernst Feder, Tagebücher eines Berliner Publizisten 1926–1932, ed. Cécile Lowenthal-Hensel and Arnold Paucker (Stuttgart, 1971), 102.
77. Anonymous, "Barmat-Urteil," Die Weltbühne 24 (1928): 533. Another member of the Center Party, Lange-Hegermann, a deputy to the Reichstag, was a high official in the Merkurbank of the Barmat-Konzern.

78. *Sammlung der Drucksachen des preußischen Landtages*, 7:2986.
79. "Der Verlauf der Reichstagssitzung," *Berliner Tageblatt*, no. 38, 23 January 1925.
80. *Sammlung der Drucksachen des preußischen Landtages*, 6:2937.
81. For a harsh critique, see Rechtsanwalt F. Nübell, "Der Fall Kutisker," *Das Tagebuch* (1926), 982–87; Ferdinand Nübell, "Kutisker und die Ärzte," *Die Weltbühne* 23, no. 2 (1927): 92–95.
82. Löwenstein, "Betrachtungen," 556.
83. Ibid., 557.
84. Bewer, "Die Lehren des Barmat Prozesses—ein Lob der Richter," *Deutsche Richter Zeitung* 20 (1928): 228–29.
85. *Urteil des Schöffengerichts Berlin-Mitte, Abteilung 206, vom 30. März 1928 in der Strafsache gegen Barmat und Genossen* (Berlin, 1929), 40.
86. Ibid., 40f.
87. Philipp Lachmann an den Ministerpräsidenten [Otto Braun], 12 October 1927, I HA Rep 84a no. 56597, fol. 123–25; in this file there are several of his memoranda. See also Zarnow, *Gefesselte Justiz*, 1:25–29. Next to Werthauer, the Jewish *Staatssekretär* in the office of the minister president Otto Braun, Robert Weismann, was attacked, also for his alleged involvement in the Sklarz case in 1920–21, when Weismann was still the first state attorney in Berlin Mitte.
88. Just a year before, another case in Berlin involving the brothers Sklarek had come up, a case that resembled the Kutisker–Barmat scandal. Christian Engeli, *Gutstav Böß, Oberbürgermeister von Berlin 1921–1930* (Stuttgart, 1971), 226–71. Dagmar Reese, "Skandal und Ressentiment: Das Beispiel des Berliner Sklarek-Skandals," in *Anatomie des politischen Skandals*, ed. Rolf Ebbinghause and Sighart Neckel (Frankfurt am Main, 1989), 374–95; Malinowski, "Politische Skandale."
89. *Niederschriften über die Verhandlungen des 19. Ausschusses—Untersuchungsausschuss zur Prüfung der preußischen Rechtspflege—zum Fall Kutisker-Werthauer*, Preußischer Landtag 4. Wahlperiode, 1 Tagung 1932, I HA Rep 84a 56566 fol. 24–47; "Kuttner wehrt sich," *Vossische Zeitung*, 7 February 1933.
90. Leon Degrelle, *Franck. Barmat. van Zeeland* (Bruxelles, 1937). In 1934, the propaganda ministry arranged that materials from the Barmat trial were given to a correspondent of the Amsterdam newspaper *De Telegraaf*; see "Der Generstaatsanwalt bei dem Kammergericht an den Preußischen Justizminister," 29 September 1934, GStA PK I. HA Rep 84a, no. 56542.
91. "Heimgefunden," *Völkischer Beobachter*, 12 November 1937. "Judko Barmat, Ostjüdische Abenteuer in Belgien: Die Giftblüte der Demokratie," *Völkischer Beobachter*, 8 January 1938.
92. Yizhak Ahren, Stig Hornsjhøh-Møller, and Christoph B. Melchers, "*Der Ewige Jude:*" *Wie Goebbels hetzte. Untersuchungen zum nationalsozialistischen Propagandafilm* (Aachen, 1990).
93. Gert Bucheit, *Richter in roter Robe. Freisler. Präsident des Volksgerichtshofes* (München, 1968), 276f.
94. "Ausgestoßen," no mention of the newspaper, I HA Rep 84a no. 56600, fol 125.
95. Philipp Lachmann to Preußischer Ministerpräsident, General Göring, 20 April 1934, I Ha Rep 84a no. 56603, fol. 10–24.

CHAPTER 11

~:~

Political Violence, Contested Public Space, and Reasserted Masculinity in Weimar Germany

DIRK SCHUMANN

As Richard Bessel has noted, Weimar Germany in many respects remained a postwar society.[1] A shaky economy and deep divisions of opinion about the political system seemed to preclude the reconstruction of peacetime stability. Political violence is often seen as both a symptom and a cause of these divisions. Thus, studies of the Weimar Republic have emphasized the links between those soldiers who joined the *Freikorps* in 1919 because they were unable to readjust to civilian life and the Nazi stormtroopers of the early 1930s.[2] However, as this essay attempts to show, the political violence that ultimately pervaded and helped destroy Weimar Germany was not a direct result of the war but was a product of the political "laboratory" of the early years of the republic. After the brief period of regional civil war came to an end in 1921, militant veterans' associations began to emerge that employed a violence aimed not at killing or maiming but at threatening and intimidating their political opponents. By claiming, conquering, and defending public space, these organizations gradually made limited violence a ubiquitous feature of political culture. In the process, the anti-Republican Right was the driving force while the Left mainly reacted. As all sides centered their public appearances on uniformed men and military rituals, they reasserted a hardened masculinity that further exacerbated political tensions and implicitly challenged the position women had gained in politics and society since the revolution of 1918. As a result of the violence on the streets and the imagery and discourse that accompanied it, the anti-Republican Right managed to unite the *Bürgertum* and some segments of the working classes against the Social Democrats and the Communists.

This essay draws on my recent research on the Prussian province of Saxony[3] (roughly the present *Bundesland* Sachsen-Anhalt, not the Free State of Saxony further south). This was an overwhelmingly Protestant region, comprised of both diverse agricultural and industrial areas. It was, all in all, fairly representative of Protestant Germany. In addition, the province was politically important because the Stahlhelm, the leading right-wing veterans' organization, as well as its left-wing counterparts, the Social Democratic Reichsbanner and the Communist Roter Frontkämpferbund, were all well organized and active there.

To better contextualize my study, I will first explain what I understand by "political violence." The term *violence* has always been contested, not only for the political and moral implications of the term's various definitions, but also for the analytical implications of these definitions. Previously dominant approaches centered on socioeconomic factors of "relative deprivation" and on structures allegedly generating violence; these approaches generally failed to explain the dynamics of violent situations and greatly reduced actors' agency.[4] Recently, there has been a growing tendency to focus on the act of violence itself, on the actors involved, on the symbols and rituals accompanying it, and on its media representation—in other words, on its phenomenology.[5] Drawing inspiration from the "cultural turn" in historiography and relying heavily on "thick description," the phenomenological approach to violence places the human body and its ability to feel pain at center stage. Violence, then, is first and foremost the act of inflicting pain, an act that can be aimed at forcing the victim to give in to specific demands but that can also be an end in itself by providing the perpetrator with pleasure.

While my concept of violence basically follows this new approach, it includes violence against objects as well as violence against persons. This broader concept takes into account that Weimar political violence was often initially directed at symbols of the political enemy and manifested, for example, in stealing or destroying flags and badges. While directed at objects, this violence sometimes spilled over into violence against those carrying and defending these symbols. A clear boundary between the two forms of violence thus cannot be drawn.[6]

What makes violence "political violence?" Under the influence of poststructuralist and feminist approaches, the notion of the political has been expanded considerably beyond parliamentary and party politics. From this perspective, discourses and conflicts about gender roles and cultural values take on political meanings because they strengthen or undermine positions of those who speak and act, widen or narrow room to maneuver, and thus solidify or redistribute societal power, which in turn has an impact on the political system as a whole.[7] More specifically, historians have reconsidered the meaning of collective protest and collective violence within this framework. Belinda Davis has described (violent) subsistence protests in Germany during the First World War as political because they brought into the open and also accelerated the general crisis of the legitimacy of the *Kaiserreich*. Authorities in Berlin and elsewhere could neither ignore these protests, since the shortages of food and other basic items were severe, nor could they put an end to them by resorting to violence, since the protesters were mainly women and, as "women of lesser means," they thus represented the masses of workers whose loyalty was crucial to the war effort. The protests helped trigger large-scale strikes, and the reports about them that the protesting women sent to the soldiers at the front added to the growing alienation from the *Kaiserreich* in the trenches. Thus, the subsistence protest made a crucial contribution to the revolution that brought down the authoritarian regime in November 1918.[8]

Davis's point about the link between subsistence protests, gender, and the revolution is well taken. Moreover, subsistence protests did not stop on 9 November 1918, but occurred in several waves until the end of hyperinflation in late 1923. However, after 1918 the protesters, primarily women, proved unsusceptible to Communist attempts to turn their demonstrations into revolutionary uprisings. As before, their violence was for the most part limited to overturning marketeers' carts and smashing windows. Authorities and the press now made a point of drawing a distinct line between their protests and the violent actions of the radicals on the Right and the Left.[9] When skyrocketing bread prices led to violent local protests in October 1923, the *Magdeburgische Zeitung*, the leading bourgeois newspaper of the province of Saxony, found their cause "purely and exclusively in the economic situation" (*rein und ausschließlich in den wirtschaftlichen Verhältnissen*); "the fact that the more impoverished population is driven to bitter exasperation" (*dass sich der ärmeren Bevölkerung … eine erbitterte Erregung bemächtigen musste*) seemed "self-evident" (*selbstverständlich*).[10] While subsistence protests were viewed with sympathy, the violence of radicals was condemned as a crime against state and society. The *Magdeburgische Zeitung*, for example, denounced the leaders of the right-wing *Kapp-Putsch* in 1920 as "the worst traitors against the state" (*die schlimmsten Staatsverbrecher*), while calling the Communist uprising on the Ruhr that had been triggered by the putsch a "crime" (*Verbrechen*) of similar proportions. In both cases, harsh punishment seemed warranted.[11]

By making this distinction between subsistence protests and political violence and thereby depoliticizing the former, authorities and the press attempted to prevent the subsistence protests from being taken over by the radicals. The protesters themselves apparently neither had lost faith in the new system to the degree they had in the old before 1918 nor did they find that the propaganda of the radicals sufficiently addressed their specific needs. In addition, public discussion underlined the distinction between the subsistence protests and the violence of the radicals by emphasizing the gender difference between the participants. After 1918, women in general were recast in their role as consumers in the public sphere, while men were reascribed their role as producers, both of economic values and of political power.[12] In sum, there were clear differences between the violence of subsistence protests and the violence of partisan street clashes after 1918 both with regard to the respective actors and to the way their actions were publicly discussed. Hence, I am making a distinction here between those acts of violence that had the much more limited goal of securing basic material needs—the violence of subsistence protests—and the violence that was directed against the new state or against competing parties and organizations; only the latter will be defined here as political violence.

The Aftermath of War and Revolution

Political violence did not doom Weimar democracy from the beginning. It was not the unavoidable result of war and revolution that afterwards only varied in form. I am arguing instead that the severe violence of the immediate postwar period was that of a distinct minority and came to a definite close in 1921. Hence, I am critical of the two most common explanations of political violence in Weimar Germany, the so-called brutalization thesis and the thesis that the Bolshevik revolution in Russia was the root of all of the subsequent violence. The brutalization thesis has been put forth, among others, by Eric Hobsbawm, who called the First World War a "machine to brutalize the world," as well as by the late George L. Mosse in even more sweeping terms. Other studies have followed suit.[13] These historians contend that the experience of large-scale violence during the war made soldiers particularly prone to violent behavior even after the war was over, especially when they were attracted by and confronted with radical political movements. To be sure, politics did become much more violent in some European countries after the war, and former front soldiers played a pivotal role in this process. Cases in point are not only the *Freikorps* in Germany and the Fascist *squadristi* in Italy,[14] but also the British Black and Tans, who spared no brutality in their fight against the IRA even though these soldiers had returned from the war neither defeated nor frustrated.[15] It is important to note, however, that these organizations comprised only a minority of the millions of soldiers returning home in 1918. The key question is why the behavior of a minority in some countries helped create a pattern of violence that pervaded the political culture while in others it had little effect. This difference cannot be explained by broadly defining war as a force of long-lasting brutalization.

Equally problematic is the argument that the Bolshevik revolution was the primary reason for the political violence in interwar Europe. Stated most pointedly by Ernst Nolte, the argument describes the threat of Bolshevism as so terrifying to the middle and upper classes that it prompted not only legitimate resistance but also the excessive violence of the Fascist movements.[16] This view not only neglects the continuities between the radical prewar Right and Fascism[17] but it also fails to take into account the actual form and scope of the political violence, which usually was much more limited when exerted by the radical Left than in the case of their right-wing enemies. But even if it is conceded that it was not Communist violence itself but the immense fear of a Communist revolution that triggered the violence of their opponents, the question still remains why this "red scare" played out in very different ways all over Europe: with fairly little violence in England and France, but with substantially more in Germany and Italy.[18]

My main argument against the brutalization and anti-Bolshevism theses is based on a close look at the *Einwohnerwehren* (civil guards). These guards were established nationwide in 1919 by the government and the military in response to demands for protection from cities and counties. Their members typically included farmers, shopkeepers, white-collar workers, and civil servants, many of whom had served in the war. While members continued to lead their normal civilian lives, they were expected to hold regular combat exercises and were provided with vast amounts of weapons and ammunition by the regular army, including machine guns and mortars. Hence, the guards were well prepared for warfare against the perceived enemy of law and order, i.e., the radical Left. The *Einwohnerwehren* have usually been described as an institution that inculcated an aggressive, violence-prone anti-Communism in large parts of the male population all over Germany, especially in the middle classes.[19] In other words, the guards have been seen as a pivotal conduit between the violence of the First World War and the political violence of the later Weimar years; they are thus used to substantiate a continuity that doomed the Weimar Republic from the beginning.

This view is misleading. First, it is important to note that the *Einwohnerwehren* were especially strong in agricultural areas dominated by medium-sized farms, where the number of Communists was very small. The guards were rather weak in the cities, where the number of Communists was substantial and there was accordingly better reason for preparedness. The percentage of self-employed males enrolled in the guards illustrates this difference very well. In the agricultural county of Salzwedel in the north of the province of Saxony, the figure stood at 52.5 percent, while in the industrial and commercial city of Halle it was as low as 8.4 percent.[20] Second, the overwhelming majority of the guards never saw any action at all. In early 1919, when the most severe fighting was taking place in several parts of Germany between forces of the radical Left and the *Freikorps*, the *Einwohnerwehren* were only in the process of being formed. In March 1920, when after the *Kapp-Putsch* parts of the regular army and armed workers clashed in several regions of Germany, including the province of Saxony, the guards were well established but failed to play a significant role. Most of the guards were slow to react or even to assemble, and many were disarmed before firing a shot by groups of workers seeking weapons for resistance against the army.[21]

In sum, if these male *Bürger* had been brutalized by the war with lasting effects and if they had been possessed by a hysterical fear of communism, they would have acted very differently and engaged their left-wing enemies with a vengeance. They failed to do so, however, because they saw themselves mainly as protectors of local community and personal property.[22] This local orientation did not change their deep-seated negative preconceptions of the Left, but it had a restraining influence on how they individually translated these views into action and left open the possibility of solving future conflicts through a democratic political process. Hence, the *Einwohnerwehren* cannot be regarded as catalysts of a general militarization against the Left.

It would therefore be well worth exploring more carefully the chances the Weimar Republic had to build a democratic political culture after its first turbulent years. Political language supplements the evidence of the *Einwohnerwehren*. The hysterical anti-Bolshevism of spring 1919 did not return until the very end of the Weimar Republic as the view of the majority of the *Bürgertum*. In early 1919, the leading middle-class papers of the province had voiced profound fears—the *Saale Zeitung* for instance saw a "Bolshevik wave" engulfing Germany and was afraid it might turn into a "dangerous intoxication" (*gefährlichen Wahnsinnsrausch*).[23] The editorials to welcome the New Year of 1920, however, did not discuss fighting but centered rather on "positive work" as the main task ahead.[24] This change to a sober tone was remarkable and should not be dismissed as pure tactical move. Insisting on "work" as the key political demand, while multifaceted and open to authoritarian interpretations,[25] did suggest common ground and room for cooperation. On the radical Left, a more sober assessment of the political situation gained influence as well. When the Communist Party tried to turn the resistance against a major police deployment in the Halle-Mansfeld region into an armed uprising in March 1921, its appeal fell on deaf ears for the most part. Of its 66,000 members in the region, no more than 3,000 actively participated in the armed actions against the police, and were quickly defeated.[26] As a result of this reckless and disastrous attempt to start a revolution at Moscow's behest, the party lost two-thirds of its members. It thereupon returned to a strategy that gave priority to winning over Social Democrats and trade unionists by patient day-to-day work.[27]

In sum, by mid-1921 overthrowing the government by military means—through a coup d'etat or a large-scale uprising—had ceased to be a viable option for both the radical Right and the radical Left because there was not sufficient popular support for such a course. Attempts to revive this option—with the murders of Erzberger (1921) and Rathenau (1922) and during the turmoil of the hyperinflation of 1923—proved distinctly unsuccessful. Despite (or perhaps because of) the scars that the bloody fighting of the first two Weimar years had left, Germans of opposing political views were not ready to engage in a civil war against each other any more. Germany was not Russia. This absence of massive and large-scale violence created a chance, slim as it may have been, for managing political differences in parliaments and through democratically elected governments. Creating and sustaining a democratic political culture would have been crucial to achieve this aim. As research in the past has mainly and narrowly focused on processes of decision making in parties and cabinets, we now need to focus more on the question of how Weimar political culture evolved over time, how its democratic elements could have been developed further, and why it eventually took a destructive turn, driving masses of voters to parties radically opposed to the republic.[28]

Contested Public Space

Political violence did contribute to the demise of Weimar democracy and the Nazi movement's rise to power. But the violence of the late republic was not uncontrollable; it was not about to plunge the country into another civil war, not even in the turbulent year 1932. Rather, the political violence that characterized the years from 1921 on was low level and fairly spontaneous. It was, as I will show here, the by-product of a new style of politics that sought the control of public space in order to pave the way for and sustain the control of parliaments and governments. Political violence thus helped militarize political culture and divide the political landscape into two opposing camps. This, however, was a gradual process; a slow poisoning of political culture rather than a series of major blows.

During the *Kaiserreich*, public space had a much more limited political function. Streets and squares had served as the staging ground for the representation of the empire in military parades and historical pageants, as the *Bürgertum* looked on appreciatively. The labor movement had tried to use public space to voice its opposition to the political system of the *Kaiserreich*, but for the most part the authorities had prevented it from doing so. Nonetheless, when the Social Democrats did succeed in marching through the streets—such as in the demonstrations against the Prussian three-class suffrage in 1906—middle-class observers were simultaneously impressed and frightened by the large and disciplined masses.

This was the basic model for the right-wing segments of the *Bürgertum* when they started organizing after the turmoil of 1919 and 1920. Perceiving themselves as on the defensive, they claimed a presence in public space as a first step towards regaining political dominance. However, they added a new element that would eventually lead to violence: the militant veterans' associations, represented above all by the Stahlhelm. Founded in Magdeburg as a lobby group with an unspecific political profile, the organization expanded from a dozen members in December 1918 to more than 300,000 nationwide in the late 1920s, moving further and further to the right as it grew.[29] The Stahlhelm's success was not due to its political program—which never got beyond vague nationalist appeals—but to its omnipresence in public space, in big cities as well as in smaller towns and villages. As Peter Fritzsche has shown, Stahlhelm rallies and parades became the focal points of a new political representation of the *Bürgertum* in a public *Festkultur*.[30] By wearing simple, greyish uniforms without signs of rank and greeting each other as "comrade," the members sought to portray an equality not present in the military of the *Kaiserreich*. Thus, on the one hand, the Stahlhelm appealed to sentiments of political nostalgia while, on the other, it presented itself as the embodiment of a new Germany based on military order and discipline that would overcome traditional cleavages, in particular class conflict. This was to be attractive both to the *Bürgertum* and to those parts of the working classes that might be won over from "Marxism"—be it Social Democratic or Communist.

These rallies and parades were deliberately held in towns and villages with heightened tensions between Right and Left. The Stahlhelm sought situations where it was likely to be met with resistance, and this often led to violence. One type of violent incident was the attack on symbols, flags in particular, that took place when the Stahlhelm publicized the establishment of a new local branch by the consecration of a flag in the town square. Its left-wing opponents then tried to gain possession of the flag, and soon both sides were engaged in brawls. Neither side aimed at seriously injuring members of the other, but wanted rather to deny them the physical and symbolic occupation of public space. Yet there was always potential for escalation to even deadly violence. When a number of *Stahlhelmer* and Communists clashed in a village close to the Harz mountain during a flag consecration in August 1921, at least one member of the Stahlhelm opened fire; one man was killed and several others injured.[31] Violence against objects could turn into violence against persons; while there was no necessary escalation, there was no clear-cut boundary, either.

The predominant type of violent incident resulting from the Stahlhelm strategy was the confrontation over the control of public space. In late June of 1923, the Stahlhelm held a *"Deutscher Tag"* in the mining town of Eisleben to celebrate the founding of a local branch. Following a rally with the consecration of a flag, the regional Stahlhelm leader gave a speech and a parade concluded the event. All of this happened on and around the marketplace from morning until noon, the time slot that the police had allocated the organization. After that, the Stahlhelm members, numbering in the thousands, went to local restaurants to have lunch and to enjoy themselves. In the afternoon, the same public space in the middle of the town was occupied by the Left. Several thousand trade union members from Eisleben and neighboring communities gathered in response to a call by the Communists, who dominated the local trade union branch. After their rally and demonstration, the trade union members also went to several local restaurants. Until late afternoon the situation remained quiet, but when the trade unionists began making their way back to the train station they found their way blocked at street intersections by Stahlhelm members. After short exchanges of verbal pleasantries, brawls broke out. Both sides seemed to have prepared themselves by organizing and training groups of five (something that was gleaned from orders heard at the site). The clashes were certainly violent—both *Stahlhelmer* and trade unionists fought with their fists, with sticks, and with pieces of fence—but few shots were fired although some of the participants were armed. All in all, only nineteen people were slightly injured. The police eventually broke up the fight and restored calm.[32]

The pattern of violence that unfolded here was typical, not only for 1923 but for the middle and even the late years of the Weimar Republic as well. A fairly aggressive right-wing organization attempted to claim public space from its opponents on the Left. It used physical force, but only to a clearly limited extent. The same limitation applied to the other side. The weapons used were meant to make this physical force felt but not to cause major harm. The purpose of the violence was not to kill or maim as many opponents as possible. In this respect, there was no civil war raging on Germany's streets and squares in the 1920s.

This was true even for the period between late 1929 and 30 January 1933, the final years of the Weimar Republic. To be sure, when the Nazi stormtroopers entered the fray, the clashes between Right and Left had more serious consequences. Yet even then, the character of the clashes did not change completely. In 1932, when political tensions were running very high and five major electoral campaigns offered plenty of opportunities to clash in the streets, political violence claimed the lives of 155 persons (only seven of them women) in all provinces of Prussia. The victims included fifty-five members of the NSDAP, fifty-four of the KPD, twelve of the Reichsbanner/SPD; thirty-three, among them most of the victims of the "bloody Sunday" in Altona in mid-July, did not have any party affiliation. Most of the deadly encounters had taken place either in Berlin or in the Ruhr area. In the province of Saxony, only nine persons had been killed.[33] This was a definite increase compared to the almost three years from 1929 and the end of July 1931, when in *all* of Germany 155 persons had lost their lives. By contrast, however, 236 persons had died in incidents of political violence in 1923, and street fighting with the *Freikorps* in Berlin had claimed more than one thousand lives in March 1919.[34] Hence, political murder was not "the order of the day" in 1932, as a study on Berlin has claimed.[35] Given that the police had intervened in 234 cases of disruptions of election campaign meetings and other party rallies in the province of Saxony in 1932,[36] nine victims was a fairly low number of casualties. The removal of symbols and the control of public space remained the main goals of political violence even in 1932. Both sides kept certain "rules of the game" that limited the number of fatalities and injuries.[37] It is true that the Nazi SA developed a specific "culture of violence," facilitated by the substantial number of unemployed in its ranks and by its SA residences, where the SA men developed a violence-prone male camaraderie.[38] This, however, was mainly an urban phenomenon and not representative of the SA at large.[39]

Hence, while political violence spread to the most remote places over the course of the 1920s, certain limits remained in place. While the chances of Weimar political culture to reconcile differences dwindled under the impact of violence, they did not completely fade away. Narrowing them more than the violence itself was the language and imagery used to place it in the broader context of political culture.

"Unity" and "Masculinity"

The language of "unity" and the emphasis and display of "masculinity" served more than any other elements of political culture to assign broader meaning to political violence and to legitimize it. From the early 1920s on, politicians and journalists on the Right emphasized the importance of unity—not only the unity of the socially, economically, and politically fragmented *Bürgertum* but also a national unity free of divisive differences of opinions. This concept of unity referred more to the alleged political and emotional unity of August 1914 than to the acceptance of a set of democratic rules, thus putting *Gemeinschaft* in opposition to *Gesellschaft*. As the leading Center-Right paper in the province of Saxony put it after the murder of Walter Rathenau in June 1922, the unity and *Volksgemeinschaft* that was to be established should result in "an indestructible community of feeling" (*eine unzerstörbare Gemeinschaft des Fühlens*) cleansed of "vain pleasure-seeking" (*eitler Genußsucht*) and mammonistic pursuits (*dem Mammonsdienste*).[40] Against the backdrop of previous anti-Communist hysteria, this notion of unity offered an umbrella—the *Volksgemeinschaft*—under which all moderate political forces could unite. But it also threatened exclusion to any who were not willing to forsake their alleged materialism, i.e., to the Socialist labor movement as long as it adhered to the concept of class struggle. When Social Democrats and Communists joined forces in the coalition governments in Saxony and Thuringia in 1923, not only the Communists but also the Social Democrats were accused of preparing a "civil war."[41] Embarking on a course that explicitly put class, not nation, on the center stage, Social Democrats were represented not only as unfit for the *Volksgemeinschaft* but also as its dangerous enemies, and they were indirectly threatened with violence.

This idealization of complete homogeneity and the notion that political opponents were outcasts reappeared in public debates about political violence through the use of the term *Volkskörper* (peoples' body).[42] In March 1920, the *Magdeburgische Zeitung* wrote in a commentary about the Communist uprising in reaction to the Kapp-Putsch that this "affliction of the peoples' body" (*Übel am Volkskörper*) should, if necessary, be removed by an "incisive operation" (*scharfen operativen Eingriff*).[43] The participants in the Communist uprising of March 1921 were called "*Schädlinge*" (a plague)—something that had to be destroyed, not merely punished.[44] In the middle years of the Weimar Republic, this dehumanizing language gave way to a more judicious assessment of communism for a time at least. Even after the street fighting in Berlin at the beginning of May 1929, the *Magdeburgische Zeitung* saw no chance of success for any Communist putsch and hence declared that it was "absolutely wrong to hold up to the citizens the spectre of Bolshevism" (*absolut verkehrt, dem Bürger das Schreckgespenst des Bolschewismus vorzumalen*).[45] But the dehumanizing language returned when the political situation came to a head in July 1932. After there was shooting in the streets of Altona, the same paper defined the Communists as "subhumans in the truest sense of the word" (*Untermenschen im wahrsten Sinn des Wortes*).[46] Arguments such as these, which in essence justified unrestrained violence against the Communists, did not directly translate into such violence until the Nazi takeover in early 1933, but they helped solidify the outsider status of the Communists in the political system.[47] While the assessment of the dangers they presented varied, Communists were portrayed as not eligible for meaningful cooperation and remained locked in the position of absolute outsider.[48]

The hardened masculinity of the front soldier, on which the militarization of political culture centered, was the other key element of political culture that deepened divisions and enhanced the potential for violence. While all sides of the political spectrum participated in this militarization, here again, the Right took the lead. Germany needed "men of steel" (*Männer von Stahl*), as a pastor who frequently spoke at Stahlhelm meetings put it. Franz Seldte, the national leader of the Stahlhelm, declared at the *Frontsoldatentag* in 1924 that only "fighting men and women who are mothers" (*Männer des Kampfes und Frauen, die Mütter sind*) were capable of rebuilding Germany.[49] This rhetoric not only emphasized the extraordinary determination that the organization brought to its activities and made it clear that for the Stahlhelm politics was primarily a fight, not an exchange of ideas. It also showed that the organization aimed at creating a political order that was based not on the fundamental legal equality in gender relations that had been established in 1919, but on their traditional order.[50] Despite the support they gave to the emancipated "new woman" elsewhere, Communists and Social Democrats reacted to the challenge of the Stahlhelm by creating organizations that displayed a very similar militarized masculinity. The Reichsbanner, which the Social Democrats built together with the dwindling number of middle-class supporters of the republic, and the Rote Frontkämpferbund (RFB), both founded in 1924, essentially copied the male-dominated rituals and symbols of the Stahlhelm's public appearances. On all sides there were now big rallies with consecrations of flags, parades, and speeches, during which uniformed men presented themselves as determined fighters.

There were subtle differences, however. The Reichsbanner had its members march in a more relaxed order—they were only a "civil army for the defense of the republic" (*zivile Armee zur Verteidigung der Republik*)[51]—and it avoided hateful language and direct references to its enemies on the Right and the Left when presenting itself in public.[52] Although the Rote Frontkämpferbund did not refer to the virtues of the soldiers of the World War as explicitly as the Stahlhelm, it left no doubt about the spirit the (male) fighters for the revolution should display: "Holy is our struggle, blessed are our weapons. ... We will achieve victory or die. ... Among our women: brothers, weapons! Among our children: weapons! Weapons!" the prominent Communist poet Oskar Kanehl proclaimed in a poem he wrote for the RFB's founding meeting.[53] The virtues of the hardened male warrior were also present in Communist imagery. A 1925 poster advertising a "*Roter Tag*" in the small town of Belgern, for example, shows two men, a worker and a uniformed member of the RFB with a trumpet, holding on to a big red flag in the middle of the picture. Their tall and muscular bodies, clenched fists, and determined faces make them appear as ready for (physical) action, while the bugler, looking as if he were giving a signal, underscores the essential sameness of military and political action. Women are absent, and so are virtues with female connotations.[54] As the Reichsbanner and the Rote Frontkämpferbund were each only one element in a larger network of party suborganizations, the militarized masculinity they displayed did not mean that Social Democrats and Communists had given up on their agenda for women's emancipation. But by taking part in the militarization of political culture, both parties created an unresolved tension between accepting women as equal political subjects and tacitly acknowledging that in certain political arenas they were not equal at all.

This tension is better understood when linked to male anxieties that resulted from the undermining of the male role of breadwinner and protector. Having been shattered by the war and its outcome, this role was called into question again by the high unemployment of 1923–24 and, later on, the Great Depression.[55] Moreover, the expansion of state functions during and after the war, and the public debates about abortion and eugenics in the 1920s, undercut the patriarchal family model (albeit probably not to the point of destroying it).[56] Hence, in addition to helping integrate men in the larger male community of a party organization, getting involved in political violence served to restore a man's bruised self-esteem in the private realm of the family.

In sum, the constant references in political language, verbal and visual, to a masculinity modeled after the hardened soldier helped perpetuate the pattern of violence in contested public space. With every expansive move into new territory, the Stahlhelm also transported images of militarized masculinity, and with the resistance its moves triggered, opportunities were created on all sides to display this very masculinity.

Emotions

Thus far, I have argued that, with regard to weapons and victims, political violence remained clearly limited between 1921 and early 1933. Massive violence only returned when the Nazis came to power and brutally cracked down on their opponents on the Left. At the same time, the language and imagery used to describe political violence, the male camaraderie in the military-style associations, and the street fighting itself created and sustained a set of aggressive emotions towards political enemies. These emotions, however, had to be controlled, given the potential of violence to escalate,[57] and obviously they were, because the Weimar Republic would have otherwise experienced much bloodier confrontations by the late 1920s. This tension between emotionality and rational control so far has largely been left unexplored. I would like to conclude by suggesting some topics and questions for further research in this respect.

In theater, emotions had always had a key role in forming a bond between actors and audience and serving a cathartic function without becoming "real" and disruptive. In Weimar Germany, theater took on increased importance. Well-ordered masses were a prominent feature of popular entertainment as well of the meetings and rallies of the Stahlhelm and its opponents. At major meetings of these organizations, plays written for the occasion were performed.[58] The *Sprechchor* (speaking choir), a new element of the theater of the Left after the revolution, epitomized this close relationship between theater and politics.[59] The lines between the two were blurred. The same applies to the lines between organized religion and politics: people revered *Inflationsheilige*, the Communists invoked the Trinity of "LLL" (Liebknecht, Luxemburg, Lenin) in their celebrations, and the SA commemorated its fallen comrades.[60] These theatrical and religious dimensions of political culture evoked strong emotions: revolutionary enthusiasm, faith in redemption, grief, anger, and hatred.

One way of explaining the boundaries of political violence could thus be to approach the encounters in public space as a form of theater, of ritualized performance (keeping in mind their harmful potential). From this perspective, the street became the stage and the moves on both sides were calculated even though many clashes came about spontaneously, especially during the election campaigns. Since these encounters happened very often, they provided many opportunities to the participants to "rehearse" their "roles" well. It is therefore well worth exploring how the emotions at play here had been created and were reinforced, how strong they actually were and to what extent they were merely theatrical gestures. This may lead to delineating an "economy of emotions" in the Weimar public sphere.

The shaky balance between emotionality and its rational control was also part of the debate about how to (re)construct the subject in response to the traumata of war and defeat. The concept of "new objectivity" played a crucial role here. It combined cool detachment, expressed in its appreciation of technology, with cynicism, sadism, and misogyny, apparent in its fascination with phenomena of violence, *Lustmord* in particular.[61] Despite the ideological fervor spent on discussing political violence, this debate reflected a basic insecurity about how to gauge behavior in the postwar period. In its commentaries after the uprising of March 1921, the *Saale-Zeitung*, the second major bourgeois paper in the Province of Saxony, pointed out that large parts of the population were "physically and spiritually off balance" (*sowohl körperlich als auch seelisch aus dem Gleichgewicht*) and displayed an "excess of nervousness as an outcome of the destructive war" (*Übernervosität als Folge des zerrüttenden Krieges*).[62] Arguments such as these grew out of the prewar and war-time discourse about the importance of strong nerves and remained part of the discourse on violence until the early 1930s. In 1932, the *Magdeburgische Zeitung* expressed the fear that Germany, like a severely ill person, might "succumb to a case of the nerves" (*der Entnervung verfallen*).[63]

The concept of the uniformed male fighter, modeled after the hardened soldier of the war, could be seen as offering a solution to the problem of failing nerves. From this perspective, the restrained political violence I have described in this essay could be viewed as proof that men were capable of fully committing themselves to a cause that entailed great personal risks and yet were able to control their complex and heightened emotions in the process. This hypothesis takes up Klaus Theweleit's dichotomy of the rigid Fascist/male body and the red/female floods threatening it.[64] It includes the Left as well, however, by suggesting that there were general male anxieties about a feminized public sphere in Weimar Germany as opposed to only the class-based anxieties of the (pre-)Fascist male in Theweleit's concept. In this sense, political violence contributed to reasserting masculinity on an individual as well as a collective level. How closely intertwined these levels were, whether there could be conflicts between them, and whether there was a parallel structure for constructing femininity may be questions for future research.

Notes

1. Richard J. Bessel, *Germany After the First World War* (Oxford, 1993), 283.
2. Robert G. L. Waite, *Vanguard of Nazism: The Free Corps Movement in Postwar Germany 1918–1923* (New York, 1952).
3. Dirk Schumann, *Politische Gewalt in der Weimarer Republik, 1918–1933: Kampf um die Straße und Furcht vor dem Bürgerkrieg* (Essen, 2001), English translation, *Political Violence in the Weimar Republic, 1918-1933: Battle for the Streets and Fears of Civil War* (New York, 2009).
4. See e.g., Ted Robert Gurr, *Why Men Rebel* (Princeton, NJ, 1970); Johan Galtung, *Strukturelle Gewalt. Beiträge zur Friedens- und Konfliktforschung* (Reinbek, 1975).
5. Heinrich Popitz, *Phänomene der Macht: Autorität, Herrschaft, Gewalt, Technik* (Tübingen, 1986), 68–108, provides a crucial starting point. Very instructive are the essays in Trutz v. Trotha, ed., *Soziologie der Gewalt* (Cologne, 1997) and in Benjamin Ziemann, ed., *Perspektiven der Historischen Friedensforschung* (Essen, 2002); Wolfgang Sofsky, *Traktat über die Gewalt* (Frankfurt, 1996), English edition, *Violence: Terrorism, Genocide, War*, trans. Anthea Bell (London, 2003) is a most pointed example of this concept.
6. For a detailed discussion of my approach see Schumann, *Gewalt*, 15–22; see also Dirk Schumann, "Gewalt als Grenzüberschreitung. Überlegungen zur Sozialgeschichte der Gewalt im 19. und 20. Jahrhundert," *Archiv für Sozialgeschichte* 37 (1997): 366–86, and "'Gewalt' als Leitbegriff der Historischen Friedensforschung," in Ziemann, ed., *Perspektiven*, 86–100.
7. Cf. Joan W. Scott, *Gender and the Politics of History* (New York, 1988); Kathleen Canning, "Gender and the Politics of Class Formation: Rethinking German Labor History," in Geoff Eley, ed., *Society, Culture, and the State in Germany, 1870–1930* (Ann Arbor, MI, 1996), 105–41.
8. Belinda Davis, *Home Fires Burning: Food, Politics, and Everyday Life in World War I Berlin* (Chapel Hill, NC, 2000).
9. Examples of subsistence protests in Schumann, *Gewalt*, 64–70, 201–2, Davis, *Home Fires*, 80–88, Ute Daniel, *The War From Within*, trans. Margaret Ries (Oxford, 1997), 247f.
10. *Magdeburgische Zeitung*, 24 October 1923.
11. *Magdeburgische Zeitung*, 21 and 27 March 1920.
12. Julia Sneeringer, *Winning Women's Votes: Propaganda and Politics in Weimar Germany* (Chapel Hill, NC, 2002), shows that election campaign propaganda during the Weimar Republic did not address newly enfranchised women as voters equal to men but as representing a specific female sphere.
13. Eric J. Hobsbawm, *The Age of Extremes. A History of the World, 1914–1991* (New York, 1994), 125; George L. Mosse, *Fallen Soldiers: Reshaping the Memory of the World Wars* (Oxford, 1990), 159–81; Andreas Wirsching, *Vom Weltkrieg zum Bürgerkrieg? Politischer Extremismus in Deutschland und Frankreich 1918–1933/39: Berlin und Paris im Vergleich* (Munich, 1999), 546; Klaus-Michael Mallmann, *Kommunisten in der Weimarer Republik. Sozialgeschichte einer revolutionären Bewegung* (Darmstadt, 1996), 109–10.
14. For a detailed analysis of fascist socialization in male peer groups, see Sven Reichardt, *Faschistische Kampfbünde: Gewalt und Gemeinschaft im italienischen Squadrismus und in der deutschen SA* (Cologne, 2002).

15. Richard Bennett, *The Black and Tans* (London, 1976).
16. Ernst Nolte, *Der europäische Bürgerkrieg, 1917–1945: Nationalsozialismus und Bolschewismus* (Frankfurt, 1987).
17. See e.g., Geoff Eley, *Reshaping the German Right: Radical Nationalism and Political Change after Bismarck* (Ann Arbor, MI, 1991); Roger Chickering, *We Men Who Feel Most German: A Cultural Study of the Pan-German League, 1886–1914* (Boston, 1984).
18. For a comparative perspective on postwar political violence in Europe, see Dirk Schumann, "Europa, der Erste Weltkrieg und die Nachkriegszeit: Eine Kontinuität der Gewalt?" in Andreas Wirsching and Dirk Schumann, eds., *Violence and Society After the First World War,* Journal of Modern European History 1, no. 1 (Munich, 2003), 24–43, as well as the contributions by Adrian Gregory (on Britain), Andreas Wirsching (on France and Italy), Piotr Wróbel (on Eastern Europe), and Benjamin Ziemann (on Germany) in that essay collection.
19. See Hans Mommsen, "Militär und zivile Militarisierung in Deutschland 1914 bis 1938," in *Militär und Gesellschaft im 19. und 20. Jahrhundert,* ed. Ute Frevert (Stuttgart, 1997), 265–76; Bernd Weisbrod, "Gewalt in der Politik. Zur politischen Kultur in Deutschland zwischen den beiden Weltkriegen," *Geschichte in Wissenschaft und Unterricht* 43 (1992): 391–404.
20. Schumann, *Gewalt,* 81–82. Even in absolute numbers the difference was huge: 4,998 members in the county of Salzwedel as opposed to only 2,475 in the city of Halle.
21. Examples in ibid., 85–86.
22. This has already been pointed out by Benjamin Ziemann in his *War Experiences in Rural Germany, 1914–1923,* trans. Alex Skinner (Oxford, 2007), 227–40.
23. *Saale-Zeitung* (Halle), 6 March 1919.
24. *Magdeburgische Zeitung,* 1 January 1920; *Saale-Zeitung,* 31 December 1919.
25. For a recent discussion of the terms *work* and *order* in postwar political language in France and Germany see Moritz Föllmer, *Die Verteidigung der bürgerlichen Nation. Industrielle und hohe Beamte in Deutschland und Frankreich 1900–1930* (Göttingen, 2002), 195–214.
26. Schumann, *Gewalt,* 115–42.
27. Sigrid Koch-Baumgarten, *Aufstand der Avantgarde. Die Märzaktion der KPD 1921* (Frankfurt, 1986), 323, 328–29.
28. In his study *Parlamentarische Kultur in der Weimarer Republik. Politische Kommunikation, symbolische Politik und Öffentlichkeit im Reichstag* (Düsseldorf, 2002), Thomas Mergel has shown how the political culture of the Reichstag provided chances for cooperation that even partially included the Communists. See also his contribution in this volume.
29. Volker Berghahn, *Der Stahlhelm: Bund der Frontsoldaten, 1918–1935* (Düsseldorf, 1966).
30. Peter Fritzsche, *Rehearsals for Fascism: Populism and Political Mobilization in Weimar Germany* (New York, 1990); cf. his intriguing book, *Germans into Nazis* (Cambridge, MA, 1998).
31. *Landeshauptarchiv Magdeburg* (LHAM) C 20 Ib 4613, fol. 92–93.
32. LHAM C 20 Ib 4665/II, fol. 37–39, 41–45, 52–53; *Stiftung Archiv der Parteien und Massenorganisationen der DDR im Bundesarchiv* (SAPMO) Ry 1/I 3/11/18, fol. 150–54.
33. *Geheimes Staatsarchiv Preußischer Kulturbesitz* (GSTA PK) I. HA Rep. 77 Tit. 4043 Nr. 122, fol. 325–28.

34. The figures for 1929–1931 and 1923 in *Welt am Montag*, 12 October 1931 (based on official statistics and newspaper reports) in GSTA PK I. HA Rep. 77 Tit. 4043 Nr. 120, fol. 301; the figure for Berlin in Wirsching, *Weltkrieg*, 130.

35. Christian Striefler, *Kampf um die Macht. Kommunisten und Nationalsozialisten am Ende der Weimarer Republik* (Berlin, 1993), 9. Dirk Blasius also overstates the extent of political violence in his *Weimars Ende: Bürgerkrieg und Politik 1930–1933* (Göttingen 2005).

36. LHAM C 20 Ib 1859/VI, fol. 1–2.

37. Richard Bessel, *Political Violence and the Rise of Nazism: The Storm Troopers in Eastern Germany, 1925–1934* (New Haven, CT, 1984), 96.

38. Reichardt, *Kampfbünde*, 406–505.

39. Bessel, *Political Violence*, 52–53; Schumann, *Gewalt*, 285–86. The argument of Pamela Swett's study *Neighbors and Enemies: The Culture of Radicalism in Berlin, 1929–1933* (New York, 2004) that what seemed to be political violence was rather an attempt to defend the autonomy of proletarian neighborhoods (in which political affiliations were of only secondary importance) is not convincing.

40. *Magdeburgische Zeitung*, 25 and 29 June 1922. Cf. Dirk Schumann, "Einheitssehnsucht und Gewaltakzeptanz. Politische Grundpositionen des deutschen Bürgertums nach 1918 (mit vergleichenden Überlegungen zu den britischen 'middle classes')," in *Der Erste Krieg und die europäische Nachkriegsordnung: Sozialer Wandel und die Formveränderung der Politik*, ed. Hans Mommsen (Cologne, 2000), 83–105, and now the comprehensive study by Thomas Rohrkrämer, *A Single Communal Faith? The German Right from Conservatism to National Socialism* (New York, 2007).

41. *Saale-Zeitung*, 27 June 1923; *Magdeburgische Zeitung*, 9 November 1923.

42. Cf. the thorough analysis by Moritz Föllmer, "Der 'kranke Volkskörper'. Industrielle, hohe Beamte und der Diskurs der nationalen Regeneration in der Weimarer Republik," *Geschichte und Gesellschaft* 27 (2001): 41–67.

43. *Madgeburgische Zeitung*, 22 March 1920.

44. *Saale-Zeitung*, 24 March 1921.

45. *Magdeburgische Zeitung*, 5 May 1929.

46. *Magdeburgische Zeitung*, 20 July 1932.

47. In this context, a brief note on anti-Semitism: It did not play a major role either in the right-wing arguments (except for its extreme fringe) or in the actual violence—the "other" clearly were the Communists.

48. It goes without saying that this position was not only forced upon the Communists but also self-imposed.

49. *Magdeburgische Zeitung*, 18 January 1922 and 21 January 1924.

50. As recent studies have shown, women's organizations and leading female representatives of the moderate and extreme Right themselves, while sharing the view that men and women were essentially different, insisted that women should play a public role in Weimar Germany to bring to bear their "maternal" qualities and thus help restore a strong and unified nation. See e.g., Raffael Scheck, *Mothers of the Nation: Right-wing Women in Weimar Germany* (New York, 2003) and Christiane Streubel, *Radikale Nationalistinnen: Agitation und Programmatik rechter Frauen in der Weimarer Republik* (Frankfurt, 2006).

51. *Volksstimme*, 15 May 1924.

52. Cf. Benjamin Ziemann, "Republikanische Kriegserinnerung in einer polarisierten Öffentlichkeit. Das Reichsbanner Schwarz-Rot-Gold als Veteranenverband der sozialistischen Arbeiterschaft," *Historische Zeitschrift* 267 (1998): 357–98.

53. LHAM C 20 Ib 1960/I, fol. 21. "Geheiligt ist unser Krieg, Gesegnet sind unsere Waffen ... Wir werden siegen oder sterben ... Bei unseren Weibern: Brüder, Waffen! Bei unseren Kindern: Waffen, Waffen!"

54. *Landesarchiv Merseburg* C 48 Ie 948, fol. 46. For the "male" character of the political culture of the KPD, see also Eric D. Weitz, *Creating German Communism, 1890–1990: From Popular Protests to Socialist State* (Princeton, NJ, 1997), 188–270.

55. Cf. Eve Rosenhaft, "Links gleich rechts? Militante Straßengewalt um 1930," in *Physische Gewalt: Studien zur Geschichte der Neuzeit,* ed. Thomas Lindenberger and Alf Lüdtke (Frankfurt, 1995), 238–75.

56. Elisabeth Domansky, "Militarization and Reproduction in World War I Germany," in *Society, Culture, and the State in Germany, 1870–1930,* ed. Geoff Eley (Ann Arbor, MI, 1996), 427–63.

57. Cf. Popitz, *Phänomene,* 73.

58. Examples in Schumann, *Gewalt,* 247–53.

59. Richard Bodek, *Proletarian Performances in Weimar Berlin: Agitprop, Chorus, and Brecht* (Columbia, SC, 1997).

60. Cf. Sabine Behrenbeck, *Der Kult um die toten Helden. Nationalsozialistische Mythen, Riten und Symbole* (Cologne, 1996); Mallmann, *Kommunisten,* 220–30.

61. See Helmuth Lethen, *Cool Conduct: The Culture of Distance in Weimar Germany* (Berkeley, CA, 2002); Maria Tatar, *Lustmord: Sexual Murder in Weimar Germany* (Princeton, NJ, 1995).

62. *Saale-Zeitung,* 29 March and 3 April 1921.

63. *Magdeburgische Zeitung,* 1 January 1932.

64. Klaus Theweleit, *Männerphantasien,* 2 vols (Frankfurt, 1977–78).

PART IV

Publics, Publicity,
and Mass Culture

CHAPTER 12

~:·~

"A Self-Representation
of the Masses"
Siegfried Kracauer's Curious Americanism

MIRIAM HANSEN

In his review of a Berlin operetta production in February of 1933, Siegfried
Kracauer contrasts the small chorus lines of "Girls" and "Boys" with their
American prototype and refers to the latter as "a self-representation of the
masses subject to the process of mechanization."[1] At first glance, this formulation seems untouched by the critical ambivalence that marks Kracauer's famous essay on "The Mass Ornament" (1927), not to mention his disillusioned
indictment of American chorus lines in "Girls and Crisis" (1931). However,
as I will try to show, the idea that mass culture might harbor the possibility of
an aesthetic and public self-representation is an important facet of Kracauer's
complex engagement with the discourse of Americanism that catalyzed debates on modernity and modernization in Weimar Germany and elsewhere. It
is significant that he reiterates this idea as late as 1933, when it was more than
obvious that a non- and antidemocratic type of mass (self-)representation had
won out.

As has been well documented by historians of Weimar culture, the metaphor
of "Amerika" encompassed a wide range of ideas and images: Fordist-Taylorist
principles of production—mechanization, standardization, rationalization, efficiency and speed, the assembly line—and attendant promises of mass consumption; mass democracy and civil society, that is, freedom from tradition
and hierarchy, egalitarian forms of interaction, and social as well as sexual and
gender mobility (the "new woman" and the alleged threat of a "new matriarchy");
and not least the cultural symbols of the new era—skyscrapers, jazz ("*Neger-
musik*"), boxing, revues, radio, cinema. Whatever its particular articulation
(to say nothing of its reference to the actual United States), the discourse of
Americanism crystallized positions on modernity, from cultural-conservative

jeremiads to euphoric hymns to technological progress. Within pro-American discourse, the political fault lines are usually drawn between those who found a solution to the ills of capitalism and a harmonious path to democracy in the Fordist gospel ("white socialism") and those who believed that modern technology, and technologically based modes of production and consumption, furnished the conditions, but only the conditions, for a truly proletarian revolution ("Left Fordism").[2]

The discourse of Americanism should not be conflated with the more specific historical process of "Americanization," that is, the transfer of American-style business practices to Germany (and other parts of Europe).[3] Still, with the introduction of Fordist-Taylorist principles of production in both industry and the service sector, along with the accompanying spread of cultural forms of mass consumption, the very categories developed to comprehend the logics of modernity—mechanization, rationalization, standardization, reification—assumed a more concrete, and more complex and contradictory, face. To be sure, Germany had seen experiments in and debates on rationalization earlier, in fact before World War I.[4] And while there was a distinct push for Fordist-Taylorist methods in the mid-1920s, they were not implemented everywhere, or at the same pace, and thorough rationalization largely remained an aspiration.[5] But to the extent that it had become a very real possibility, the American system of mass production and mass consumption signaled a paradigmatically distinct set of values and visions—not simply modern civilization threatening traditional culture but, more specifically, a new material and social regime of modernization that competed with European versions of modernity.

I am less interested here in situating Kracauer within canonical Weimar debates on modernity than in tracing his engagement with American-style mass and media culture as it evolved between roughly 1924 and 1933—not only as a response to the mounting political crisis and the failure of bourgeois culture to address it but also as an elaboration of issues that point beyond both the historical moment and the national reference point. During the brief period leading up to the end of the Weimar Republic, Kracauer turned "Amerika" from a metaphysically grounded metaphor of disenchanted modernity into a more empirically oriented diagnostic framework for exploring the possibility of democratic mass culture under the conditions of advanced capitalism. This is hardly to say that he uncritically embraced capitalism as an economic and social system. But the Soviet "experiment" did not present a realistic alternative to him, as much as he admired individual filmmakers and writers such as Eisenstein, Vertov, and Tretyakov. Rather, in the face of rising Nazism, Kracauer sought to describe the particular logics by which capitalist mass culture, entwined with the new technological media, seemed both to furnish the conditions of self-reflection, self-determination, and self-organization on a mass scale and to restrict, neutralize, and undermine those very principles.

In the first years of the republic, the connection between Americanism qua industrial rationalization and the new mass-mediated culture, in particular cinema, was by no means established, at least not until the implementation of the Dawes Plan in 1924, which ushered in both a large-scale campaign of rationalization and the consolidation of Hollywood's hegemony on the German market.[6] In a report for the *Frankfurter Zeitung* on a conference of the Deutsche Werkbund in July 1924, Kracauer presents this gathering of designers, industrialists, educators, and politicians as a site of missed connections. The conference was devoted to two main topics, "the fact of Americanism which seems to advance like a natural force," and the "artistic significance of the fiction film."[7] Kracauer observes a major failure to see connections in the speakers' basic approach to Americanism: they went all out to explore its "total spiritual disposition," but, true to the Werkbund's professed status as an "apolitical organization," they left the "economic and political pre-conditions upon which rationalization ... is based substantially untouched." While both proponents and critics of rationalization seemed to articulate their positions with great conviction and ostensible clarity, the second topic of the conference remained shrouded in confusion. "Curiously, perhaps due to deep-seated prejudices, the problem of film was dealt with in a much more biased and impressionistic way than the fact of mechanization, even though both phenomena, Americanism and film composition after all belong to the same sphere of surface life."

A few months later, Kracauer would begin his own "turn to the surface," shifting from the largely lapsarian stance of his early writings that resonated with the period's pessimistic discourse on modernity to a programmatic exploration of the ephemeral and marginalized realities of contemporary life. This involved a transvaluation of the term "surface" (*Oberfläche*) from a locus of sheer negativity—the atomized world of mere appearances disassociated from truth—to a site of fascination where contemporary reality manifests itself in an iridescent multiplicity of phenomena.[8] Beginning in 1925, his articles increasingly revolve around quotidian objects (the typewriter, inkwells, umbrellas, pianellas); spaces (metropolitan streets, squares and architecture, arcades, bars, department stores, train stations, subways, homeless shelters, unemployment offices); and the media (photography, illustrated magazines, film), rituals, and institutions of an expanding leisure culture (tourism, dance, sports, cinema, circus, variety shows, amusement parks).[9] Although the trope of the surface still implies the vertical topography of idealist philosophy, in Kracauer's critical practice the *Oberfläche* increasingly loses its prefix and becomes a *Fläche*, an epistemological plane that allowed him to trace new configurations (such as the one he famously dubbed the "mass ornament"), and read them as indices of the possible direction(s) the historical process might take; hence the shift in focus from the great metaphysical questions of the age to the phenomena of daily life and the culturally low-ranking practices of an emerging culture of mass consumption.

Yet, as I have argued elsewhere, Kracauer's theoretical interest in popular genres such as the detective novel, film, and the circus precedes this shift in tone and attitude; it has rather specific roots in Kracauer's philosophy—or theology—of history, (antagonistically) indebted to secular Jewish messianism and literary gnosticism, and the peculiar form of modernist materialism he derived from this mode of thinking.[10] From 1923 on, his reviews in the *Frankfurter Zeitung* begin to outline an aesthetics of fragmentation, distortion, reification, and externality across various films and film genres, as well as other products of entertainment culture. In holding up a distorted mirror to a distorted reality, such products both registered the historical process—the "disintegration of the world" (*Weltzerfall*)—in all its negativity and provided it with an aesthetic discourse that Kracauer considered more truthful than ongoing efforts in bourgeois culture to restore an irretrievably lost unity.

Kracauer's so-called turn to the surface in 1925, no doubt fueled by his reading of Marx and Marxist theory, radicalized these earlier observations into a critical program. Paradoxically, the materialist impulse to register, transcribe, and archive the surface manifestations of modernity was still motivated—as well as licensed—by the eschatologically tinged hope that modernity could and would be overcome: "America will disappear only when it completely discovers itself."[11] The enigmatically self-reflexive construction of this phrase suggests, for one thing, that the discovering subject cannot not remain outside or above the terrain explored; for another, that the subject of discovery harbors its own means and media of self-understanding. Accordingly, the more Kracauer immersed himself in this project, the less sanguine he became about the possibility of transcending modernity, and the more passionately he engaged in immanent critique. More "realistic" than either "a radical cult of progress" or a pessimistic lament that evades responsibility, he endorsed an "uncertain, hesitant affirmation of the civilizing impulse," a stance that "awaits the promises without foregoing"—the right to, the task of—"critical observation; it views the phenomena that have freed themselves from their foundation not just categorically as deformations and distorted reflections, but accords them their own, after all positive possibilities."[12]

Which particular possibilities did Kracauer perceive in the cultural manifestations of American-style rationalization? One line of argument builds dialectically on the widespread critique of mechanization (in the vein of *Lebensphilosophie*) according to which Taylorist methods of production, the regime of the assembly line, epitomize the logic by which human beings have become henchmen of a seemingly autonomous technology and, instead of becoming its masters, have themselves become machine-like. From his earliest reviews on, Kracauer endorsed slapstick comedy (*Groteske*) as a cultural form in which Americanism supplied a popular and public antidote to its own regime. Slapstick comedy seemed to subvert the economically imposed discipline in well-improvised orgies of destruction, confusion, and parody like no other genre:

One has to hand this to the Americans: with slapstick films they have created a form that offers a counterweight to their reality: if in that reality they subject the world to an often unbearable discipline, the film in turn dismantles this self-imposed order quite forcefully.[13]

More specifically, slapstick films brought into play the imbrication of the living and the mechanical, the "revolt of the slaves" (Simmel) that animates material objects and puts them on a par with human agents.[14] These in turn assume a thing-like physiognomy (Keaton's deadpan face serving as a case in point); lacking the authority and interiority of a sovereign ego, they are vulnerable to the push and pull, the malice of objects and people alike.[15]

To the extent that Kracauer's theorizing of slapstick turns on the imbrication of people and things, living and mechanical, it could be said to hark back to Bergson's famous essay on laughter (1900). But there is another side to his effort to understand the cultural manifestations of Americanism from technology, which points forward (partly verbatim) to Benjamin's notion of film as "second technology," as a medium capable of engaging the effects of capitalist-industrial technology in the mode of play.[16] In an essay that begins with a culturally pessimistic critique of tourism and social dancing ("and other outgrowths of rational fantasy" like radio and "telephotography"), Kracauer shifts to an immanent account of "what one expects and gets from travel and dance— a liberation from gravity [*Erdenschwere*], the possibility of an aesthetic relation [*Verhalten*] to organized drudgery" (S 5.2:292, 294; MO 70, 72). Switching to first person plural, he ends on a redemptive, almost techno-utopian note:

> We are like children when we travel, playfully excited about the new velocity, the relaxed roaming about, the synoptic view of geographical complexes that previously could not be grasped. We have fallen for the ability to have these spaces at our disposal; we are like conquistadors who have not yet had the leisure to reflect on the meaning of their acquisition. ... Technology has taken us by surprise, and the regions it has opened up are still glaringly empty. [S 2:296; MO 73]

The enthusiasm in this passage is tempered by the sense of lack of, and need for, a reflexive and public discourse on technology—a discourse whose contours Kracauer discerned in the new forms and media of leisure and entertainment.

The second line of argument vis-à-vis Americanism that complements and increasingly comes to frame Kracauer's reflections on technology concerns the mass, or masses, as a distinct social and cultural formation that he saw crystallize in and around American and American-style entertainment forms. Since this is the line of argument that I will trace in the following sections, I refrain from offering any general definition of Kracauer's concept of the mass, or masses, not least because the concept is subject to significant fluctuation and ambiguity. Suffice it for now to note that, explicitly and implicitly, Kracauer's exploration of this particular aspect of America sets itself, on the conservative side, not only against the longstanding lament about mass-marketed culture, but also against late nineteenth-century elitist-pessimistic theories of the crowd (as synthesized by Gustave Le Bon) that essentialized, psychologized, pathologized, and demonized the crowd, or mass in the singular, as an atavistic force that required a leader.[17] On the other hand, as we shall see, Kracauer also tries to complicate leftist conceptions of the masses predicated on the working class and the idea of a revolutionary proletariat. The rhetoric of "discovering America," after all, refers not simply to object of exploration, but to a heuristic strategy for discovering whatever might be qualitatively and historically distinct, as yet unrecognized and undefined, in an area so overdetermined by competing discourses.[18] Accordingly, rather than engaging directly with sociological, psychological, or political debates on the nature of the modern mass, Kracauer takes the detour through the ephemeral phenomena of the burgeoning entertainment culture—as aesthetic configurations that at once spawn and respond to a new type of collective.

The Mass as Ornament and Public

In 1925, Kracauer began to review the American- (that is, Ziegfeld-) style live revues that were increasingly sweeping across German vaudeville stages. These reviews, which in key motifs read like sketches for "The Mass Ornament," are still experimental in stance and tone. While he treats the revues broadly as cultural symptoms of mechanization and industrial rationalization, the implications of this trajectory are far from determined.[19]

Recognizing the marked departure of American-style revues from the military prototype of their European counterparts, Kracauer reports on the Frankfurt performance of the Tiller Girls (actually a British troupe), whose tour inaugurated the "American age" in Germany:

> What they accomplish is an unprecedented labor of precision, a delightful Taylorism of the arms and legs, mechanized charm. They shake the tambourine, they drill to the rhythms of jazz, they come on as the boys in blue: all at once, pure duodeci-unity [*Zwölfeinigkeit*]. Technology whose grace is seductive, grace that is genderless because it rests on joy of precision. A representation of American virtues, a flirt by the stopwatch.[20]

Kracauer's pleasure in such precision does not rest with an aesthetics of technology; rather, it turns on the aesthetic transformation of the technological regime into an expression of alternative social relations. It is significant that he does not conflate mechanization and rationalization with an a priori negative concept of standardization. He feels threatened neither by the flaunted loss of individuality, nor by the fragmentation of the individual body. In the stylized economy of the revue—its fragmentary, serial, incessantly metamorphing compositions—standardization translates into a sensual celebration of collectivity, a vision, perhaps a mirage, of equality, cooperation, and solidarity. This demo-cratic ethos includes a vision of gender mobility and androgyny (girls dressed up as sailors), a mark of Americanism to both its proponents and enemies. Thus Kracauer's account conveys a glimpse of a different organization of social and gender relations—different at least from the patriarchal order of the Wilhelmine family and norms of sexual behavior that clashed with both the reality of working women and the critic's own sensibility.[21]

Kracauer's valorization of Taylorist revue aesthetics and the "American influence" on the genre serves not least to excoriate the retrograde style of the show's German numbers, with their bad melange of monarchism ("Queen Luise descending from a perron in historical costume"), militarism, mother love, and Viennese *Gemüt*. However, when he returns to these examples in an all-round polemic against the genre a few months later, the Tiller Girls fall prey to the same sarcastic condemnation ("mindless automata produced by Ford"), along with the weekly newsreels that are supposed to lend the program a sheen of actuality.[22] The refrain that punctuates the essay, "in the age of technology," not only highlights the gap between technological modernization and a culture not up to its challenges ("the cars travel through geographical space, the soul is cultivated in the parlor"),[23] but also suggests a lack of consciousness in the very cultural products that flaunt their synchronicity and presentness, a point that anticipates the concern about the "muteness" of the mass ornament.

In the essay on "The Mass Ornament," Kracauer's shifting assessments of American-style chorus lines are theorized as an ambivalence that characterizes the phenomenon itself. The Tiller Girls have evolved into a historicophilosophical allegory that, as is often pointed out, anticipates key arguments of Horkheimer and Adorno's *Dialectic of Enlightenment* (1947). The once exuberantly portrayed dance troupe now figures as a critical emblem of displays that proliferate internationally in cabarets, stadiums, and newsreels, patterns formed by thousands of anonymous, uniform, de-eroticized bodies ("sexless bodies in bathing suits").[24] The abstraction of the individual body into elements or building blocks for the composition of larger geometrical figures corresponds, as an "aesthetic reflex," to the Taylorist principle of breaking down human labor into calculable units and refunctioning them in the form of working masses that can be globally deployed. As a figure of capitalist rationality, Kracauer argues, the mass ornament is as profoundly ambivalent or ambiguous (*zweideutig*) as the historical process that brought it forth—a process of demythologization that emancipates humanity from the forces of nature or, in Kracauer's words, "effects a radical demolition of the positions of the natural" (in particular the powers of the church, monarchy, and feudalism), but does so only to reestablish the natural in ever new forms. By perpetuating socioeconomic relations "that do not encompass the human being," capitalist development reproduces these relations as natural—as given, unquestioned, immutable, rather than historical and political—and thus reverts to myth; rationality itself has become the dominant myth of modern society (S 5.2:61–62; MO 80–81).

Unlike his fellow critical theorists, however, Kracauer does not locate the problem in the concept of enlightenment as such (which at any rate he associated less with German idealism than with the utopian reason—justice and happiness—of fairy tales canonized in the French eighteenth century). Rather, he argues that the permeation of nature by reason has actually not advanced far enough—the problem with capitalism is not that "it rationalizes too much," but that it rationalizes "too little." This hyperbole implies the distinction, key to subsequent debates within the Frankfurt School, between instrumental rationality—the unleashed Ratio that "denies its origins and no longer recognizes any limits"—as opposed to reason as *Vernunft* that reflects upon its own contingency, goals, and procedures.[25] The mass ornament embodies the incomplete advance of rationalization, that is, one without self-reflexive reason, by stopping halfway through the process of demythologization, remaining stuck between the abstractness endemic to capitalist rationality and the false concreteness of myth. Yet, just as he knows that the emergence of humanist reason is inseparable from the development of capitalism, Kracauer rejects any thought that this development could be reversed: "The process leads right through the middle of the mass ornament, not back from it" (S 5.2:67; MO 86).

The essay on the mass ornament has been criticized for its reductionist analogy between cultural forms and the capitalist-industrial production process ("to the legs of the Tiller Girls correspond the hands in the factory" [S 5.2: 60; MO 79]), an analogy that allegedly ignores the aesthetic specificity of the revues, their playful negation of the abstract regime they reflect.[26] Such criticism fails to see that the relationship Kracauer delineates is neither literal nor obvious, but instead heuristic and symptomatic. Since he first reviewed the Tiller Girls in 1925, the connection between the new dance form and Fordist-Taylorist rationalization, between chorus line and assembly line, had more or less become a topos, notably with Fritz Giese's illustrated paean to "girl culture" published the same year.[27] This topos, however, remained stuck in the binary discourse of Americanism, which either welcomed the revues as a "new culture of training" (*Trainingskultur*) or decried them as a yet another manifestation of mechanization and standardization, the "growing drive toward uniformity" and "complete end of individuality."[28] In contrast to either euphoric or lapsarian accounts, Kracauer's essay assumes a more dialectical stance toward the phenomenon, reading it as an index of a contradictory historical development. Above all, where the Americanist discourse extols technical rationality or, respectively, laments mechanization, Kracauer develops his argument from within a Marxist critique of capitalism.

If Kracauer at this point shares the Marxist (more specifically Lukácsian) assumption of the totality of capitalism, this does not mean that he subscribes to a determinist model of base and superstructure. Methodologically, he instead borrows from the language of psychoanalysis, extending it into the political and social realm, in particular the ideological mechanisms of public consciousness. The simultaneous omnipresence and occlusion of capitalism takes the form of a paradox: "The production process runs its secret course in public [*läuft öffentlich im Verborgenen ab*]" (S 5.2: 60; MO 78). In other words, it manifests itself in public, yet remains concealed, unseen, unconscious. In his study of employee culture written two and a half years later, Kracauer invokes the "purloined letter" in Poe's well-known story (later famously analyzed by Lacan) to describe a similar paradox—that of the salaried masses who increasingly dominate the appearance of Berlin's cityscape but whose life eludes consciousness, both their own and that of the bourgeois public. "Hundreds of thousands of salaried employees daily throng the streets of Berlin, yet their life is more unknown than that of the primitive tribes at whose customs those same employees marvel in the films."[29] Like Poe's letter, the salaried masses remain unnoticed "because [they are] out on display."[30] The cover of unconsciousness, Kracauer ventures in the often-cited epigraph to "The Mass Ornament," actually offers a cognitive gain. "The inconspicuous surface-level expressions" of an epoch yield more substantial insights about "the position [this] epoch occupies in the historical process" than the "epoch's judgments about itself" (MO 75). But they do not do so on their own. Like the image configurations of dreams, they require a conscious work of "deciphering." Accordingly, echoing Freud's *Interpretation of Dreams*, Kracauer links this work in other texts to the metaphor of hieroglyphics, a figure that, like the mass ornament, combines abstract, graphic lines with visual concreteness and ostensible self-evidence.[31]

The mass ornament requires critical deciphering for two reasons. One, because the educated public fails to recognize the cultural, aesthetic significance of these displays that, Kracauer asserts, capture contemporary reality more aptly than older forms predicated on concepts of community such as folk and nation, to say nothing of obsolete bourgeois notions of individual personality. Two, the work of deciphering is needed because the mass ornament itself remains "mute," unpermeated by reason, and therefore lacks the ability, as it were, to read itself. "The Ratio that gives rise to the ornament is strong enough to mobilize the mass and to expunge [organic] life from the figures constituting it. Yet it [the Ratio] is too weak to find the human beings in the mass and to render the figures transparent to cognition" (S 5.2:65; MO 84)—cognition, that is, of the social and economic conditions that they inhabit and signify. Instead, the modernizing impulse is deflected into the mere physicality of *Körperkultur* or body culture (gymnastics, eurhythmics, nudism, fresh air), much as that movement may dress itself up in neospiritual ideologies.[32]

Obviously, Kracauer tries to distinguish between a bourgeois humanism to which the mass ornament gives the lie and a modernist humanism that would combine the anonymous, precarious, and decentered subjectivity of mass existence with the principles of equality, justice, and solidarity, a humanism grounded in self-reflexive reason. It is no coincidence that he invokes the example of Chinese landscape paintings, a representational space from which "the organic center has been removed" (S 5.2:64; MO 83).[33] This comparison, however, begs the question of who reoccupies the empty space in front of, or, in the case of the mass ornament, above the representation—specifically, which invisible hand or eye organizes its patterns, and to which purposes and effects.

Whether the mass ornament is merely an "end in itself" (a parodistic consummation of Kantian aesthetic autonomy) or organized by the "invisible hand" of the capitalist system (which also appears as an "end in itself"), Kracauer seems to leave the answer deliberately vague. Since his concept of the mass ornament is transnational, if not emphatically internationalist (and implicitly opposed to LeBonian crowd theory), he does not at this point consider the fusion of mass ornament aesthetics with an extreme nationalist ideology focused on a fascist leader.[34] When he returns to the term *mass ornament* in *From Caligari to Hitler* (1947), referring to *Triumph of the Will* (1935), he suggests a genealogy linking the Nazi regime's "ornamental inclinations," as choreographed and eternalized by Leni Riefenstahl, with Fritz Lang's *Die Nibelungen* (1924), without mentioning his earlier analysis of American-style mass displays.[35]

Even in "The Mass Ornament," however, one can already discern the contours of Benjamin's analysis, in the epilogue to his Artwork essay, of fascism as a politics that aestheticizes the masses, instead of giving them their right (that is, to change property relations).[36] Kracauer's distress over the "muteness" of the mass ornament relates to a particular structure of miscognition and denial that he would soon focus on in his study on salaried employees. Benjamin was to observe a similar structure at work in the success of fascist mass politics, in particular the aesthetic pleasure in spectacles amounting to total (including self-) destruction, which he theorized as a splitting of experience into agency, object, and observer.[37] (A further trajectory could be drawn from the mass ornament to Adorno's analysis of mass culture as hieroglyphic writing—as a modern form of pictographic script that facilitates the internalization of domination by keeping its author (monopoly capitalism) invisible: "no shepherd but a herd."[38]

Still, Kracauer is reluctant to name the transcendental subject of the mass ornament in any unequivocally pessimistic way. Despite his no doubt growing ambivalence, I would argue that he still wants to leave the empty space of the author and ideal beholder open for the empirical subjects who are present at these displays and to whom they are addressed. For the mass in the mass ornament is not just the one on display. In Kracauer's rhetorical design, the "ornament of the mass" (as the German title translates literally) includes not only the abstract patterns of moving bodies qua spectacle but also the spectating mass "which relates to [the ornament] aesthetically and which represents nobody"—nobody, that is, other than itself, a heterogeneous crowd drawn "from offices and factories" (S 5.2:59, 60; MO 77, 79). While the mass ornament itself remains "mute," it acquires meaning under the "gaze" of the masses, "who have adopted it spontaneously" (S 5.2:66; MO 85). Against its detractors among the educated (who have themselves unwittingly become an appendix of the dominant economic system while pretending to stand outside or above it), Kracauer maintains that the audience's "aesthetic pleasure in the ornamental mass movements is legitimate" (S 5.2:60; MO 79); it is superior to an anachronistic assertion of high-cultural values because at the very least it acknowledges "the facts" of contemporary reality. And even though the spectating masses are, in tendency, just as unaware of their situation and similarly stuck in mindless physicality, there is no question for Kracauer that the subject of critical self-encounter has to be, and can only be, the masses themselves.[39] Whether such self-representation will have a chance to prevail is as much a matter of the "go-for-broke game" of the historical process as the turn to the technological media that, as he argues in his essay "Photography," could either advance or defeat the liberatory impulses of modernity.[40]

Already in his 1926 essay on the Berlin picture palaces, "Cult of Distraction," Kracauer's argument revolves around the possibility that something like a self-articulation of the masses might be taking place in these metropolitan temples of distraction—the possibility, quoted at the beginning of this essay, of a "self-representation of the masses subject to the process of mechanization." Bracketing both cultural disdain and critique of ideology (though not without characteristic deadpan irony), he observes that in Berlin, as opposed to his native Frankfurt and other provincial cities, "the more people perceive themselves as a mass, the sooner the masses will also develop creative powers in the spiritual domain that are worth financing." As a result, the so-called educated classes are losing their provincial elite status and cultural monopoly. "This gives rise to the homogeneous cosmopolitan audience [*das homogene Weltstadt-Publikum*] in which everyone is of one mind, from the bank director to the sales clerk, from the diva to the stenographer."[41] That they are "of one mind" (*eines Sinnes*) means no more and no less than that they have the same taste for sensual attractions, diversions, or distractions. The concept of *Zerstreuung*, diversion or distraction, in the radical twist that Kracauer gives the originally cultural-conservative concept, combines the mirage of social homogeneity with an aesthetics that is profoundly decentering and disunifying, at least as long as it does not succumb entirely to industrial strategies of high-art aspirations and gentrification.[42] In "the discontinuous sequence of splendid sense impressions" (which likely refers to an already elevated version of the variety format that early cinema had adapted from live popular entertainment), the audience encounters "its own reality," that is, a social process marked by an increased heterogeneity and instability. Here Kracauer locates the political significance of distraction as a structurally distinct mode of perception: "The fact that these shows convey precisely and openly to thousands of eyes and ears the disorder of society—this is precisely what would enable them to evoke and keep awake that tension which must precede the inevitable radical change [*Umschlag*]" (W 6.1:211; MO 327).

It should be noted that Kracauer does not (at least not yet) assume an analogical relation between the industrial standardization of cultural commodities and the behavior and identity of the mass audience that consumes them—an assumption derived from Lukács's theory of reification that would become axiomatic in both Adorno's critique of the culture industry and, with a different valorization, even in Benjamin's theses on art and industrial re/production. For one thing, Kracauer did not condemn commodification, serial production, and standardization as such, as can be seen in his many positive reviews of popular fiction, especially detective and adventure novels, as well as in his repeated, if sometimes grudging, statements of admiration for Hollywood over UFA products.[43] For another, Kracauer would not have presumed that people who watched the same thing were necessarily thinking the same way; and if they did pattern their behavior and appearance on the figures and fables of the screen, the problem was primarily with the direction taken by the German film industry, its circulation of escapist ideology on screen and compensatory gentrification of exhibition. Again and again, in daily reviews as well as in the series reprinted under the titles "The Little Shopgirls Go to the Movies" and "Film 1928," Kracauer castigated films that advanced their audience's denial of growing economic uncertainty and social volatility.[44] In other words, his critique was aimed less against the lure of cinematic identification in general than against the economic and political conditions responsible for the unrealistic tendency of such identification.

The cinema is a signature of modernity for Kracauer not simply because it attracts and represents the masses, but because it is the most advanced cultural institution in which the masses, as a relatively heterogeneous, undefined, and as yet little-understood form of collectivity, constitute a new form of public. This is to say that the cinema audience, while lacking the coherence and familiarity of a traditional community, represents more than the sum of randomly assembled individuals. For they gather at the motion picture shows as spectators, that is, in collective acts of reception and aesthetic judgment, and in so doing might find their own experience reflected in others, both on and in front of the screen. As Heide Schlüpmann has argued, Kracauer sketches a theory of a specifically modern public sphere that resists thinking of the masses and the idea of the public as an opposition (one still upheld by Jürgen Habermas in his 1962 study, *The Structural Transformation of the Public Sphere*). Kracauer "neither asserts the idea of the public against its [actual or putative] disintegration and decline," Schlüpmann points out, "nor does he resort to a concept of an oppositional public sphere" (à la Oskar Negt and Alexander Kluge). Rather, Kracauer sees in the cinema a blueprint of an alternative public that "can realize itself only through the destruction of the dominant public sphere," that is, bourgeois institutions of high art, education, and culture that have lost all touch with reality.[45]

Alternative, too, I would add, because, unlike the partial publics of the traditional labor movement, the cinema offers a public sphere of a different kind. Culminating the multiplication of spaces already advanced by other media of urban commercial culture (shop windows, billboards, etc.), the cinema systematically intersects two different types of space, namely, the local space of the theater and the deterritorialized space of the film projected on the screen. It thus represents an instance of what Michel Foucault has dubbed "heterotopias": places that "are absolutely different from all the sites that they reflect and speak about." Sites of transportation like trains and planes, sites of temporary relaxation like cafés, beaches, and movie theaters function, in Foucault's words, as "something like counter-sites, a kind of effectively enacted utopia in which … all the other real sites that can be found within the culture are simultaneously represented, contested, and inverted."[46] Taking our cue from Foucault, we could read Kracauer's insight into the specifically modern type of publicness of cinema not just as a sociological observation but also as a structural one, in the sense that he recognized early on the significance of the cinema's intersection of a semianonymous, semicollective theater experience with a product whose simultaneous mass circulation exceeded the local, national, and temporal boundaries of live events.[47]

As can be expected, Kracauer's leap of faith into a commercially based collectivity has made him vulnerable to the charge that he naively tries to resurrect the liberal public sphere, thus unwittingly subscribing to the ideology of the marketplace.[48] To be sure, he adheres to political principles of general access, equality, justice, and, perhaps more steadfastly than some of his more staunchly Marxist contemporaries, the right to and necessity of self-determination, that is, democratic forms of living and interaction. Yet Kracauer is materialist enough to know that these principles do not miraculously emerge from the rational discourse of communicatively competent, inner-directed subjects, let alone from efforts to restore the authority of a literary public sphere. Rather, cognition has to be grounded in the very sphere of experience in which modernization is most palpable and most destructive—in a sensual, perceptual, aesthetic discourse allowing for "a self-representation of the masses subject to the process of mechanization."

As I suggested above, Kracauer's concept of the masses developed within a force field defined, on the on hand, by elitist-pessimistic crowd theory (popularized by Le Bon and adapted by thinkers as disparate as Spengler and Freud) and, on the other, by Socialist and Communist conceptions of the masses as the traditional or revolutionary working class (corresponding, in turn, to negative and phobic usages of the term by the former).[49] If Kracauer shared with crowd theory the emphasis on the class-blurring character of the modern mass, he aligned that assumption with his inquiry into the conditions of possibility of mass democracy. Where conservative crowd theory turns on the bourgeois intellectual's fear of the mass as powerful other, Kracauer displays an amazing lack of fear—fear of touch, violence, or contagion—toward a social formation that, after all, he knew himself to be part of, whose experience he shared in a number of respects. His nonphobic relation to the modern mass made him a seismograph, a critical one to be sure, attuned to the historical and political mutability of the phenomenon as much as its conceptualization.

The specifically modern mass that Kracauer was to track began to enter public awareness in Germany with World War I. Industrialized warfare, mass killing and death, mass starvation, and epidemics brought into view the masses as an object of violence and disease (rather than, as in crowd theory, their putative subject and source). While social privilege protected to some extent against these ravages, the sheer scale made suffering a statistical probability as much as a matter of class. Following the revolution of 1919, which mobilized the image of the masses as a powerful agent (whether heroic or vilified), mass existence continued to be associated with the stigma of misery, culminating in the 1923 inflation that spread the experience of destitution and loss far beyond the industrial working class. During the short-lived phase of economic recovery, however, the masses began to appear less as a suffering and more as a consuming mass—a mass that came into visibility as a social formation in collective acts of consumption.[50] And since consumer goods that might have helped improve living conditions (for instance, refrigerators) were still considerably less affordable than in the United States,[51] the main objects of consumption were the fantasy productions, including images of consumer goods, and environments of the new leisure culture. In these fantasy productions, Kracauer discerned the contours of an emerging mass society, which, for better or for worse, was productive in its very need and acts of consumption.

Conclusion

I have traced Kracauer's reflections on mass culture from his welcoming of Americanist entertainment forms as surface phenomena more truthful to the upheavals of modernity than efforts to restore bourgeois cultural values, but also as playful relief from tradition, hierarchy, and identical subjecthood; through his perception of the mass as public and of mass culture as a form of collective self-representation, enabling an aesthetic engagement with the experience of rationalized labor and its psychosocial effects.[52]

After the 1929 stock market crash and a sharp rise in unemployment internationally, American cultural imports such as jazz and chorus lines could only seem inadequate and posthumous. As Kracauer writes in "Girls and Crisis" (FZ 26 May 1931), "as much as they may enthusiastically swing their legs, they come as a procession of phantoms out of a dead past."[53] Devoid of promises of abundance and equality, Fordist-Taylorist technology assumed a more sinister face; as Bloch put it regarding James Whale's *Frankenstein* (1931), the "golem" represents "technology with false consciousness, the fear of an America, without prosperity, of itself."[54]

The onset of the depression reinforced Kracauer's critical stance toward technological modernization unaccompanied by changes in the relations of production and a public reflection on its psychosocial effects. Resuming his earlier pessimistic critique of rationalization as a regime that seizes all domains of experience and reduces them to spatiotemporal coordinates, he increasingly assails the destruction of memory advanced as much by modern architecture and urban planning as by illustrated magazines and the entertainment business. The site and symbol of contemporaneity, simultaneity (*Gleichzeitigkeit*), and presentness—the "frontier" of America in Europe—is the city of Berlin, a city that "has a magical means of wiping out all memories."[55] Many houses on the Kurfürstendamm, which Kracauer dubs a "street without memory," have "had their ornaments knocked off," which still provided a "bridge to yesterday"; the deprived facades "now stand without a foothold in time, a symbol of the ahistorical change that takes place behind them."[56]

This critique implicates not least the functionalist school of modern architecture (Le Corbusier, Mies, Gropius, and the Bauhaus), with its crusade against the ornament (inaugurated by Adolf Loos) and idealization of a new "culture of glass" (so desperately welcomed by Benjamin).[57] An architect by training, Kracauer had acknowledged such asceticism as an "honest" if ambiguous response to the ruling economic system, wishing that the "scurrilous grief" that clings to the glass surfaces would inspire a form of architecture that allowed "the human being to emerge from the glass" (S 5.2:74). By 1929, he indicts the vernacular profusion of architectural modernism qua Neue Sachlichkeit for its secret complicity with the business of distraction: "like denial of old age, it arises from dread of confronting death" (SM 92). By a similar logic, as he had shown, the repressed ornament returned with a vengeance—in the very aesthetics of technology that ordained the mass spectacles of chorus lines and sports events.

By 1929, the margin of ambivalence that Kracauer had granted the "mass ornament" has all but disappeared from his writings. Mass formations, whether in the circus or the reopened Berlin Lunapark, appear as unequivocally determined by, and excessively mirroring, the regime of rationalization: "Which is more rationalized, a factory or the circus?" The playful and parodistic tone of Kracauer's earlier accounts of Taylorist choreography gives way to grim analysis: the stopwatch timing of the presentation may turn "hours into years," but it does not leave "the slightest gap." With the "elimination of the clowns," who earlier had offered an anarchic supplement to rationalization (in both circus and slapstick comedy), there is no more space for improvisation, nor time for parody.[58]

In such accounts, the "muteness" of the mass ornament seems absolute, irredeemable. As rationalized entertainment eliminates any alterity from the performance or displays, the consuming collective loses whatever degree or kind of agency and self-determination they might have been granted before. "An invisible organization sees to it that the amusements push themselves onto the masses in prescribed sequence," he writes in an analysis of a form of "organized happiness" that anticipates Adorno as much as Disney World.[59] With the disappearance of ambivalence in both Kracauer's stance and the phenomena he analyzes, mass culture loses the dimension of critical self-reflection he had discerned in the best of Hollywood films (such as Frank Urson's remarkable social drama *Chicago* [1927], which he had celebrated for its relentless indictment of "girldom").[60] He had located this reflexive dimension not only in mass-cultural products, at the level of representation, but more importantly in the sphere of reception—in the possibility that people "subject to the process of mechanization" might themselves see and feel the "double face" of modernity (emblematic in the roller-coaster of the pre-remodeled Berlin Lunapark that took the riders first to the top of its landmark facade—a painted skyline of Manhattan—and then behind that facade, allowing them to be "enchanted and disenchanted at the same time"[61]). In the measure that this possibility recedes in Kracauer's writings, the critic himself returns to a position outside and above the masses.

Without American-style mass entertainments providing a reflexive supplement to rationalization, the chances that America would "completely discover itself" ("completely" less in an extensive than in an intensive, radical sense) were dwindling. In his own discovery of "Amerika," Kracauer had hoped for a German version of mass-mediated modernity that would be capable of enduring the tensions between a capitalist economy in permanent crisis and the principles and practices of a democratic society. Crucial to this modernity would have been the ability of cinema and mass culture to function as an intersubjective horizon in which a wide variety of groups—a heterogeneous mass public—could negotiate and reflect upon the contradictions they were experiencing, and in which they could confront otherness and mortality instead of repressing or aestheticizing it.

Kracauer, like Benjamin, found a counterimage to Americanized Berlin in Paris—a city whose streets inspired memory, fantasies, and dreams (to say nothing of films); whose crowds were constantly circulating and in flux, allowing for a process of mingling that did not suppress gradations and differences; whose luminous advertisements (*Lichtreklame*) far exceeded their economic function by projecting undecipherable hieroglyphs into the sky.[62] But, unlike

Benjamin, Kracauer kept returning to Berlin as long as he could—because, with its juxtaposition of "harshness, openness, … and glamour," that city, not Paris, was the "center of struggles in which the human future is at stake."[63]

The more relentlessly Kracauer criticized the pathologies of mass-mediated modernity, the less he seems to have subscribed to his earlier utopian thought that, some day, "America will disappear." In fact, the more German film production cluttered the cinemas with costume dramas and operettas reviving nationalist and military myths, and the more the industry accommodated to and promoted the political drift to the Right, the more it became evident that America must not disappear, however mediocre, superficial, and inadequate its current mass-cultural output might be. The constellation that is vital to Kracauer's understanding of cinema and modernity is therefore not that between Paris and Berlin, but that between a modernity that can reflect upon, revise, and regroup itself, albeit at the expense of (a certain kind of) memory, and a modernity that parlays technological presentness into the timelessness of a new megamyth: monumental nature, the heroic body, the re-armored mass ornament—in short, the modernism exemplified by Albert Speer and Leni Riefenstahl. When the Nazi regime perfected this form of modernism into the millennial modernity of total domination and mass annihilation, America had to become real, for better or for worse, for Kracauer and others to survive.

Notes

This article is an excerpt from Chapter 2 of my book *Kracauer, Benjamin, Adorno on Cinema, Mass Culture, and Modernity*, forthcoming University of California Press. It also substantially revises my earlier essay, "America, Paris, the Alps: Kracauer (and Benjamin) on Cinema and Modernity," in *Cinema and the Invention of Modern Life*, ed. Leo Charney and Vanessa Schwartz (Berkeley, CA, 1995), 362–402. I am grateful to Dan Morgan for careful readings and critical suggestions.

1. "[E]ine Selbstdarstellung der dem Mechanisierungsprozeß unterworfenen Massen." S. Kracauer, "Berliner Nebeneinander: Kara-Iki—Scala-Ball im Savoy—Menschen im Hotel," *Frankfurter Zeitung* (hereafter abbreviated as *FZ*) 17 February 1933, rpt. in Kracauer, *Berliner Nebeneinander: Ausgewählte Feuilletons 1930–33*, ed. Andreas Volk (Zürich, 1996), 29–35; 32. Unless an English source is cited, all translations of Kracauer's writings are my own. Hereafter, the inclusion of the German source in references indicates that the translation has been modified.

2. For a sample of Weimar texts on Americanism, see *The Weimar Republic Sourcebook*, ed. Anton Kaes, Martin Jay and Edward Dimendberg (Berkeley, 1994), chap. 15. Also see Frank Trommler, "The Rise and Fall of Americanism in Germany," in *America and the Germans: An Assessment of a Three-Hundred-Year History*, ed. Frank Trommler and Joseph McVeigh (Philadelphia, 1985), 2:332–42; Kniesche and Brockmann, eds, *Dancing on the Volcano*, part II: "American Influences in Weimar"; Mary Nolan, *Visions of Modernity: American Business and the Modernization of Germany* (New York, 1994); Thomas J. Saunders, *Hollywood in Berlin: American Cinema and Weimar Ger-*

many (Berkeley, CA, 1994), chaps. 4 and 5; Alf Lüdtke, Inge Marßolek, and Adelheid von Saldern, eds, *Amerikanisierung: Traum und Alptraum im Deutschland des 20. Jahrhunderts* (Stuttgart, 1996). My approach to Americanism is indebted to Victoria de Grazia, in particular "Americanism for Export," *Wedge* 7–8 (Winter–Spring 1985): 74–81, and her magisterial study, *Irresistible Empire: America's Advance through Twentieth Century Europe* (Cambridge, MA, 2005).

3. On the distinction and relation between "Americanization" and "Americanism," see de Grazia, *Irresistible Empire*, 552–56 and passim.

4. Maier, "Between Taylorism and Technocracy," 44–54; Nolan, *Visions of Modernity*, 42–50.

5. See Alf Lüdtke, *Eigen-Sinn: Fabrikalltag, Arbeitererfahrung und Politik vom Kaiserreich bis in den Faschismus* (Hamburg, 1993), 244–54.

6. On the juncture of cinema and Americanism, see Saunders, *Hollywood in Berlin*; also Kristin Thompson, *Exporting Entertainment* (London, 1985); Ian Jarvie, *Hollywood's Overseas Campaign: The North Atlantic Movie Trade, 1920–1950* (Cambridge, 1992); David W. Ellwood and Rob Kroes, eds, *Hollywood in Europe: Experiences of a Cultural Hegemony* (Amsterdam, 1994); and Ruth Vasey, *The World According to Hollywood, 1918–1939* (Madison, WI, 1997).

7. Kr. [Kracauer], "Die Tagung des Deutschen Werkbunds," *FZ* 29 July 1924. On the Werkbund, see Frederic J. Schwartz, *The Werkbund: Design Theory and Mass Culture before the First World War* (New Haven, CT, 1996).

8. Inka Mülder-Bach, "Der Umschlag der Negativität: Zur Verschränkung von Phänomenologie, Geschichtsphilosophie und Filmästhetik in Siegfried Kracauers Metaphorik der 'Oberfläche,'" *Deutsche Vierteljahresschrift* 61, no. 2 (1987): 359–73; Gertrud Koch, *Kracauer zur Einführung* (Hamburg, 1996), 42–46.

9. Kracauer's micrological and phenomenological approach to the historic experience of modernity appears prescient in view of similar pursuits in academic historiography decades later; see, most recently, Alexa Geisthövel and Habbo Knoch, eds, *Orte der Moderne: Erfahrungswelten des 19. und 20. Jahrhunderts* (Frankfurt, 2005).

10. On Kracauer's relation to Jewish messianism and literary gnosticism, see my essay "Decentric Perspectives: Kracauer's Early Writings on Film and Mass Culture," *New German Critique* 54 (Fall 1991): 47–76.

11. Kracauer, "Der Künstler in dieser Zeit," *Der Morgen* 1, no. 1 (April 1925); *Schriften* (hereafter abbreviated as *S*) 5, ed. Inka Mülder-Bach (Frankfurt am Main, 1990), 1, 305; also see "Gestalt und Zerfall," 21 August 1925, rpt. *S* 5.1:324–29.

12. Kracauer, "Reise und Tanz," *FZ* 15 March 1925, *S* 5.1: 295; "Travel and Dance," in Kracauer, *The Mass Ornament: Weimar Essays* (hereafter abbreviated as *MO*), trans. and ed. Thomas Y. Levin (Cambridge, MA, 1995), 65–73.

13. Raca [Kracauer], "Artistisches und Amerikanisches," *FZ* 29 January 1926, rpt. *Werke* (hereafter abbreviated as *W*), 6.1, ed. Inka Mülder-Bach (Frankfurt a.M., 2004): 198–99.

14. Georg Simmel, *The Philosophy of Money*, trans. Tom Bottomore and David Frisby, ed. D. Frisby (London, 1990 [1907]), 483.

15. See, for instance, Kracauer's review of *The General*, "Buster Keaton im Krieg," *FZ* 5 May 1927, *W* 6.1:338–40.

16. Walter Benjamin, "The Work of Art in the Age of Its Technological Reproducibility, Second Version," trans. Edmund Jephcott and Harry Zohn, in Benjamin, *Selected Writings* [hereafter *SW*]: *Vol. 3, 1935–1938*, ed. Michael W. Jennings et al. (Cam-

bridge, 2002), 117f., 124n10. Also see my essay, "Room-for-Play: Benjamin's Gamble with Cinema," *October* 109 (Summer 2004): 3–45.

17. Le Bon conflates the terms *mass* and *crowd*; see J. S. McClelland, *The Crowd and the Mob: From Plato to Canetti* (London, 1989), chap. 7, "Crowd Theory Makes its Way in the World: The Le Bon Phenomenon," esp. 196–215.

18. Kracauer returns to the metaphor of "discovering America" in his semiautobiographical novel *Ginster: Von ihm selbst geschrieben, Schriften* 7, ed. Karsten Witte (Frankfurt am Main, 1973 [1928]), where he has the protagonist and his friend Otto debate questions of scientific methodology. While Otto proposes a method that emphasizes "secondary matters" (*Nebensachen*) and "hidden" or "secret paths" (*Schleichwege*) so as to arrive at "scientifically cogent hypotheses," Ginster does not believe that the point is even to reconstruct an "original reality": "According to his theory, Columbus had to land in India; he discovered America. ... A hypothesis is valid only under the condition that it misses its intended goal, so as to reach another, unknown goal" (34).

19. In an earlier review he still reads revue aesthetics in Bergsonian terms, that is, as a chiastic relation between people and things: "The living approximates the mechanical, and the mechanical behaves like the living." rac [Kracauer], "Schumann-Theater," *FZ, Stadt-Blatt* 5 March 1925, rpt. in Kracauer, *Frankfurter Turmhäuser: Ausgewählte Feuilletons 1906–30*, ed. Andreas Volk (Zürich, 1997), 93–95; 93.

20. raca [Kracauer], "Die Revue im Schumann-Theater," *FZ Stadt-Blatt* 19 May 1925, rpt. in *Frankfurter Turmhäuser* 95–98; 97.

21. Among the numerous discussions of Kracauer's gender politics, see Heide Schlüpmann, "Die nebensächliche Frau: Geschlechterdifferenz in Siegfried Kracauers Essayistik der zwanziger Jahre," *Feministische Studien* 11, no.1 (May 1993): 38–47; Patrice Petro, *Joyless Streets: Women and Melodramatic Representation in Weimar Germany* (Princeton, NJ, 1989), 63–70; E. S. Goodstein, "'The Most Mendacious Prototypes Have Been Stolen From Life'—Femininity and Spectacle in Siegfried Kracauer's Reading of Weimar Mass Culture," *Faultline: Interdisciplinary Approaches to German Studies* 1 (1992): 49–67. On the Tiller Girls in the context of Weimar androgyny and sexual politics, see Maud Lavin, *Cut with a Kitchen Knife: The Weimar Photomontages of Hannah Höch* (New Haven, CT, 1993); Kirsten Beuth, "Die wilde Zeit der schönen Beine: Die inszenierte Frau als Körper-Masse," and other essays in *Die Neue Frau: Herausforderung für die Bildmedien der Zwanziger Jahre*, ed. Katharina Sykora et al. (Marburg, 1993). Helmut Lethen stresses the antipatriarchal implications of Americanism in his study of modernist "codes of conduct," *Cool Conduct: The Culture of Distance in Weimar Germany* (1994), trans. Don Reneau (Berkeley, CA, 2002); see, for instance, his discussion of Carl Schmitt's rejection of Americanism as the worst form of "father devouring [*Vaterfraß*]"(186).

22. "Die Revuen," *FZ* 11 December 1925, S 5.1: 338–42.

23. Kracauer, "Die Jupiterlampen brennen weiter: Zum Potemkin-Film," *FZ* 16 May 1926, W 6.1:236.

24. "Mass Ornament," *MO* 76, also see 77. In the following, references appear parenthetically in the text. Among the many commentaries on this essay, see Karsten Witte, "Introduction to Siegfried Kracauer's 'The Mass Ornament,'" *New German Critique* 5 (Spring 1975): 59–66; Levin, "Introduction," *MO* 15–20; and Koch, *Kracauer*, chap. 3.

25. Kracauer, "The Revolt of the Middle Classes: An Examination of the *Tat* Circle," *FZ* 10 and 11 December 1931, *MO* 112.

26. See, for instance, Klooss and Reuter, *Körperbilder Menschenornament im Revuetheater und Revuefilm* (Frankfurt 1980): 71–2; and Sabine Hake, "Girls and Crisis: The Other Side of Diversion," *New German Critique* 40 (Winter 1987): 147–64, 156.

27. Fritz Giese, *Girlkultur: Vergleiche zwischen amerikanischem und europäischem Rhythmus und Lebensgefühl* (Munich, 1925).

28. Giese, *Girlkultur*, 35; Stefan Zweig, "The Monotonization of the World" (1925), *Weimar Republic Sourcebook*, 398. For an anti-American(ist), antifeminist critique of Giese's book, see Richard Huelsenbeck, "Girlkultur," *Die Literarische Welt* 2, no. 16 (1926): 3.

29. Kracauer, *Die Angestellten: Aus dem neuesten Deutschland* (1929), *Schriften* 1, ed. Karsten Witte (Frankfurt am Main, 1978), 212; *The Salaried Masses: Duty and Distraction in Weimar Germany* (hereafter abbreviated. as *SM*), trans. Quintin Hoare (London, 1998), 29.

30. Ibid. (emphasis added).

31. See Kracauer, "Berliner Landschaft," *FZ* 8 November 1931, reprinted under the title "Aus dem Fenster gesehen," *S* 5.2: 401: "The knowledge of cities hinges upon the deciphering of images uttered as if in a dream" (*ihrer traumhaft hingesagten Bilder*). The term *hieroglyph* appears, among other places, in "Über Arbeitsnachweise: Konstruktion eines Raumes," a material analysis of the social reality of unemployment, *FZ* 17 June 1930, *S* 5.2:185–92.

32. For Kracauer's polemics against "body culture" and sports see, for example, "Sie sporten," *FZ* 13 January 1927, *S* 5.2:14–18; also his review of *Wege zu Kraft und Schönheit* (revised version, 1926), *FZ* 5 August 1926, *W* 6.1: 253–55; "Mass Ornament," section 5; and *SM* 78–80.

33. The decentered space of Chinese landscape painting has figured as a (mythical) topos in the modernist critique of representational systems based on Renaissance perspective from Brecht through Barthes, in particular the alleged challenge of Chinese painting to the centrality of the beholder and his or her perceptual identification with the transcendental subject of the representation. See, for instance, Stephen Heath, "Lessons from Brecht," *Screen* 15, no. 2 (Summer 1974):103–28.

34. McClelland, *Crowd and Mob*, 231–32, 238–40, 297, and passim.

35. Kracauer, *From Caligari to Hitler: A Psychological History of the German Film*, intro. Leonardo Quaresima (Princeton, NJ, 2004 [1947]), 302f., 94f.

36. Walter Benjamin, "The Work of Art in the Age of Its Technological Reproducibility, Third Version," trans. Harry Zohn and Edmund Jephcott, in Benjamin, *Selected Writings, Volume 4: 1938–1940*, ed. Michael Jennings et al. (Cambridge, 2003), 269–70. The parallel is further developed in Kracauer's exposé for a "study on fascist propaganda solicited by Adorno for the Institute for Social Research in New York: "Masse und Propaganda (Eine Untersuchung über die fascistische Propaganda)," December 1936, unpublished manuscript, printed in *Siegfried Kracauer 1889–1966*, ed. Ingrid Belke and Irina Renz, *Marbacher Magazin* 47 (1988): 85–90, especially section 4, "Ansatz der fascistischen Scheinlösung."

37. See Susan Buck-Morss, "Aesthetics and Anaesthetics: Walter Benjamin's Artwork Essay Reconsidered," *October* 62 (Fall 1992): 3–41.

38. Max Horkheimer and Theodor W. Adorno, "Das Schema der Massenkultur: Kulturindustrie (Fortsetzung)" (1942), in Adorno, *Gesammelte Schriften*, vol. 3, ed. Rolf Tiedemann (Frankfurt am Main, 1981), 299–335.

39. See, for instance, Kracauer's discussion of the gap between mass formations (as object of organization and surveillance) and mass democracy (as the condition of social and economic justice) in his essay on unemployment agencies, "Über Arbeitsnachweise," 190–91.

40. Kracauer, "Photography," *FZ* 28 October 1927, *MO*, 47–63, 61.

41. Kracauer, "Cult of Distraction: On Berlin's Picture Palaces," *FZ* 4 March 1926, *W* 6.1: 208–13; *MO* 323–28.

42. On the genealogy of the concept of distraction, see Leo Lowenthal, "Historical Perspectives on Popular Culture," in *Mass Culture*, ed. Bernard Rosenberg and David Manning White (New York, 1957); for a longer account in German, see Leo Löwenthal, *Schriften 1: Literatur und Massenkultur*, ed. Helmut Dubiehl (Frankfurt am Main, 1980), chap. 1.

43. See, for instance, Kracauer's obituary, "Edgar Wallace," *FZ* 13 February 1932; "'Berlin-Alexanderplatz' als Film" (comparison with Sternberg, *An American Tragedy*), *FZ* 13 October 1931, *W* 6.2:546–50; "Der heutige Film und sein Publikum," *FZ* 30 November and 1 December 1928, rpt. as "Film 1928": "It is not the standardization [*Typisierung*] of film that is reprehensible. On the contrary." (*W* 6.2:152, *MO* 308). For a similar stance, see Benjamin, "This Space for Rent," *One-Way Street* (1928), in Benjamin, *Selected Writings: Volume 1, 1913–1926*, ed. Marcus Bullock and Michael W. Jennings (Cambridge, 1997), 476.

44. Anonymous, series of eight articles, *FZ* 11–19 March 1927, rpt. as "Die kleinen Ladenmädchen gehen ins Kino," *W* 6.1: 308–22, *MO* 291–304; "Film 1928"; "Not und Zerstreuung: Zur Ufa-Produktion 1931/32," *FZ* 15 July 1931, *W* 6.2: 519–23; "Gepflegte Zerstreuung: Eine grundsätzliche Erwägung," *FZ* 3 August 1931, *W* 6.2: 528–30; "Ablenkung oder Aufbau? Zum neuen Ufa-Programm," *FZ* 28 July 1932, *W* 6:3:90–94. Also see Kracauer's programmatic statement "on the task of the film critic," "Über die Aufgabe des Filmkritikers," *FZ* 23 May 1932, *W* 6.3:61–63.

45. Heide Schlüpmann, "Der Gang ins Kino—ein Ausgang aus selbstverschuldeter Unmündigkeit: Zum Begriff des Publikums in Kracauers Essayistik der Zwanziger Jahre," in *Siegfried Kracauer*, ed. Kessler and Levin, 267–84.

46. Michel Foucault, "Of Other Spaces," *Diacritics* 16 no. 1 (Spring 1986): 22–27.

47. See Hansen, *Babel and Babylon: Spectatorship in American Silent Film* (Cambridge, MA, 1991), chap. 3.

48. See, for instance, Lethen, *Neue Sachlichkeit, 1924–1932: Studien zur Literatur des "Weissen Sozialismus"* (Stuttgart, 1970), 102–4.

49. For a discussion of Kracauer's concept of the mass(es) in relation to Freud, see Koch, *Kracauer*, 39–42.

50. See Alon Confino and Rudy Koshar, "Regimes of Consumer Culture: New Narratives in Twentieth-Century German History," *German History* 19, no. 2 (2001): 135–61, and Konrad H. Jarausch and Michael Geyer, *Shattered Past: Reconstructing German Histories* (Princeton, NJ, 2003), chap. 10, "In Pursuit of Happiness: Consumption, Mass Culture, and Consumerism."

51. Detlef J.K. Peukert, *Weimar Republic: The Crisis of Classical Modernity* (New York, 1992), 174–77.

52. In my chapter from which this essay is drawn, I go on to also trace a more pessimistic (to some extent protopoststructuralist) assessment of mass-cultural self-representation as an ideological matrix that gives presence to an imaginary social identity. While these

shifts do not necessarily mark an evolution toward a more "mature," realistic stance that would cancel out the earlier positions, they do respond to acute political and economic developments.

53. Kracauer, "Girls and Crisis," trans. Courtney Federle, *Qui Parle* 5 no. 2 (Spring/Summer 1992): 51–52. See also Kracauer, "Renovierter Jazz," *FZ* 25 October 1931, S 5.2: 390–92.

54. Ernst Bloch, "Bezeichnender Wandel in Kinofabeln" (1932), *Gesamtausgabe g* 9 (Frankfurt am Main, 1965): 77; "prosperity" in the original.

55. Kracauer, "Die Wiederholung: Auf der Durchreise in München," *FZ* 29 May 1932, S 5.3: 71–72.

56. Kracauer, "Straße ohne Erinnerung," *FZ* 16 December 1932, S 5.3: 173.

57. Kr [Kracauer], "Das neue Bauen: Zur Stuttgarter Werkbundausstellung: 'Die Wohnung,'" *FZ* 31 July 1927, S 5.2:68–74. For Benjamin's endorsement of "*Glaskultur*," see "Experience and Poverty" (1933), trans. Rodney Livingstone, *SW* 2:731–36.

58. Raca [Kracauer], "Zirkus Sarrasani," *FZ* 13 November 1929, rpt. in *Frankfurter Turmhäuser*, ed. Volk, 126–28.

59. Kracauer, "Organisiertes Glück: Zur Wiedereröffnung des Lunapark," *FZ* 8 May 1930, rpt. in *Siegfried Kracauer*, ed. Volk, 233–35.

60. Raca. [Kracauer], "Girldämmerung," *FZ* 22 June 1928, W 6.2:95–97. This review, which betrays the writer's own ambivalence toward (New) women, concludes with the statement, "American miracles happen in Hollywood."

61. "Roller Coaster," *FZ* 14 July 1928, trans. Thomas Y. Levin, *Qui Parle* 5, no. 2 (1992): 59.

62. On Kracauer's city images, in particular the differential figuring of Paris and Berlin, see Inka Mülder-Bach, "'Mancherlei Fremde': Paris, Berlin und die Extraterritorialität Siegfried Kracauers," *Juni: Magazin für Kultur und Politik* 3 no. 1 (1989): 61–72; Eckhardt Köhn, *Straßenrausch: Flanerie und kleine Form: Versuch zur Literaturgeschichte des Flaneurs bis 1933* (Berlin, 1989), 225–48; David Frisby, "Deciphering the Hieroglyphics of Weimar Berlin: Siegfried Kracauer," in *Berlin: Culture and Metropolis*, ed. Charles W. Haxthausen and Heidrun Suhr (Minneapolis, 1991), 152–65; Anthony Vidler, "Agoraphobia: Spatial Estrangement in Simmel and Kracauer," *New German Critique* 54 (Fall 1991): 31–45; and Anke Gleber, *The Art of Taking a Walk: Flanerie, Literature, and Film in Weimar Culture* (Princeton, NJ, 1999).

63. Kracauer, "Berliner Landschaft," *FZ* 8 November 1931, S 5.2:401; also see "Unfertig in Berlin," *FZ* 13 September 1931, S 5.2: 375.

~:~

CHAPTER 13

Neither Masses nor Individuals
Representations of the Collective
in Interwar German Culture

STEFAN JONSSON

The image was made by the Hungarian artist László Moholy-Nagy in 1927, entitled *Massenpsychose* or, alternatively, *In the Name of the Law* (Figure 13.1). It is one of Moholy-Nagy's photoplastics, a mixed-media form that he experimented with during his years as a Bauhaus teacher. Moholy-Nagy emphasized that the photoplastic image portrays "concentrated situations" that can be developed instantaneously through associations.[1] An Eskimo would be unable to understand a photoplastic sheet, he claimed, because the image speaks only to viewers accustomed to an urban world characterized by the compression and simultaneity of objects and events. The photoplastic image teaches such viewers to perceive the relationships structuring their world. The image, Moholy-Nagy said, "is directed towards a target: the representation of ideas." To this end, the title is crucial. "By means of a good title a picture's grotesque or absurd entirety may become a sensible, 'persuasive truth.'"[2] What, then, we may ask, is the truth revealed by the title of this image, *Massenpsychose*, or, alternatively, *In the Name of the Law*?

According to Moholy-Nagy, the photoplastic scene is a condensation of an idea. I want to follow up on this hint. The image, I suggest, may be seen as an ironic diagram of the influential theory of mass psychology. By implication, the image also addresses the general discourse on "the masses" that was prevalent in Europe in this period. I am not arguing that the artist necessarily intended such an interpretation, only that it is the best way of showing how it resonates with the conflicts of Weimar culture.

Let's look at the picture. The relationships in the image are hierarchical. The pool player masters the female swimmers. The female gunslinger controls the Africans in her own cylinder and the male figure in the adjacent one. The general stands at the peak of the pyramidal structure, thus governing the field as

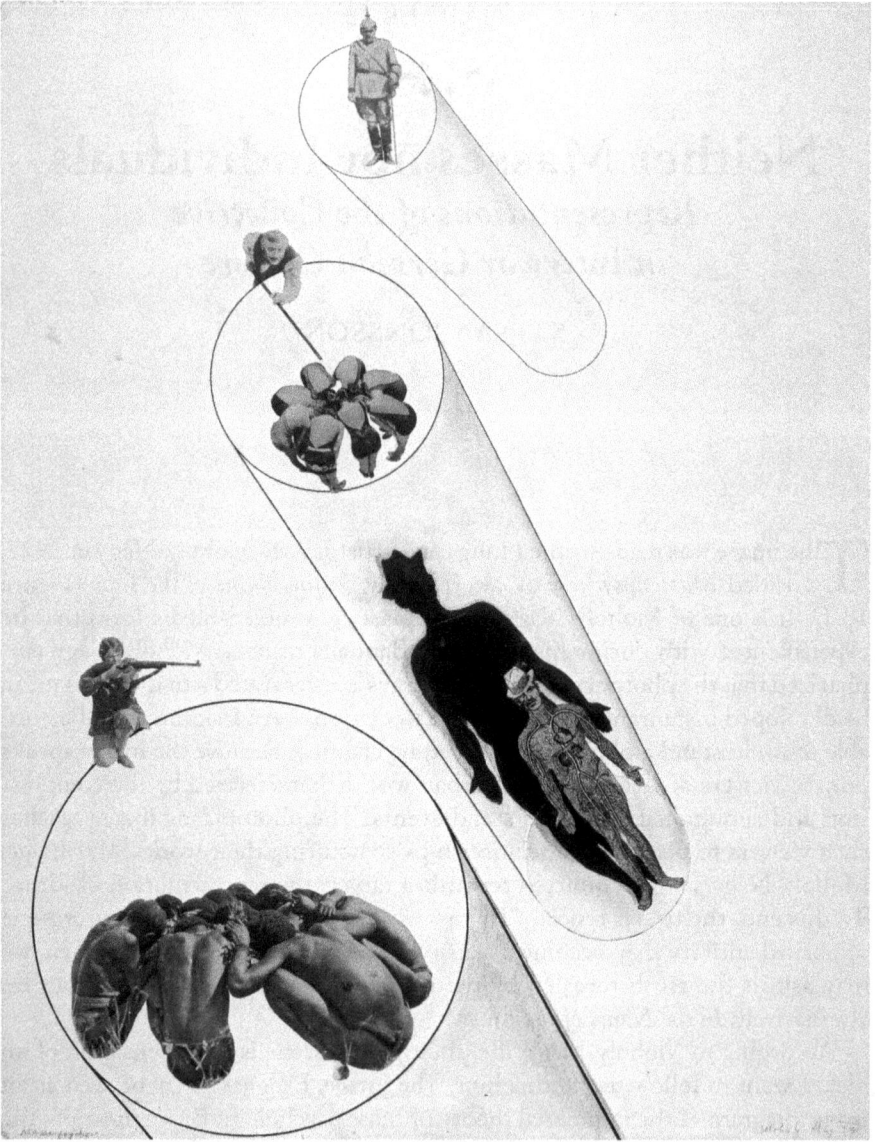

Figure 13.1. László Moholy-Nagy, *Massenpsychose/In the Name of the Law*, 1927.

a whole. In *Massenpsychose*, individuals with recognizable faces hold the positions of dominance. Faceless females and Africans, by contrast, occupy the positions of subordination. Moholy-Nagy portrays the latter in accordance with the principles of mass psychology: human subjects who form a crowd lose their individual identities, claimed Gustave Le Bon and Gabriel Tarde, the founders of mass psychology. This is because they are eager to conform, obeying the laws of "imitation," as Tarde argued, or "contagion," which was Le Bon's term for the same concept. What results from this psychic chain reaction is a collective agent behaving like a "decapitated animal," as Henry Fournial argued, or, as Tarde expressed it, like a "wild beast without a name."[3]

In Moholy-Nagy's image, the individuals in the position of dominance carry phallic objects. These objects would then signify the traits that, according to Tarde and Le Bon, characterize a leader. Metonymically linked to the king's scepter and the magical wand, the cue, the bayonet, and the rifle are signs of the leader's charismatic power, the instrument of suggestion with which he manipulates the sentiments of the masses. "A crowd is at the mercy of all external exciting causes," Le Bon states. The crowd is "the slave of the impulses it receives."[4]

The affective influences that govern a crowd, Tarde and Le Bon argued, scrape off the individual's layer of cultivation and reason, making him or her conform to the lowest common denominator of the group, the base instincts of his unconscious. This process is also captured by Moholy-Nagy's photoplastic. Consider the man with the giant shadow at the bottom of the second cylinder, locked at the intersection of the trajectories of the bullet, the billiard ball, and the thrust of the bayonet. What remains of his civilized being is just the hat. The rest—his entire body—has lost the skin of cultivation that shelters individuality. A shadow is a conventional symbol of the subject's unconscious passions. I think this is an accurate reading here, for it conforms to another central thesis of mass psychology: in the crowd, the subject is subdued by his impersonal instincts. His individual identity is overshadowed, and he merges with the faceless *bête humaine* represented by the females and the Africans.

Finally, the transparent cylinders, resembling the test tubes of a chemical laboratory, suggest that *Massenpsychose* also portrays the methodology of mass psychology.[5] The French historians and sociologists who inaugurated the analysis of the crowd modeled their studies on the natural sciences, branding their newly parceled-out domains with names such as "social physics," "social statics," and "social dynamics." They understood the social field in terms of psychological charges of interacting social atoms that could be measured by a neutral scientist. Hippolyte Taine, the first true historian of the crowd, wanted to explain the evolution of French society through such a chemistry of passions. Just as the chemist analyzed the contents of his test tubes, so Taine examined society. In this spirit he concluded, famously, that the psychological forces manifested in history are comparable to chemical compounds: "Vice and virtue are products like vitriol and sugar."[6]

The photoplastic image, said Moholy-Nagy, is a representation of ideas. Indeed, *Massenpsychose* manages, with a few carefully organized images and lines, to represent the idea of the masses that was deeply embedded in interwar European society and that attained scholarly credentials in the disciplines of mass psychology and mass sociology. However, in representing the way in which the discourse of mass psychology represents society, *Massenpsychose* exhibits the ideological message of this discourse, and invites the observer to pass judgment on it. Lacanian before Lacan, the image reveals the oppressive agency operating "in the name of the law." On this reading, then, Moholy-Nagy's *Massenpsychose* is *not* a representation of the psychology of the masses. Rather, it is a representation of mass psychology as a discipline of knowledge and power. To be precise, it is a visual representation of mass psychology's theoretical representation of the psychology of the masses.

Now, if a certain discourse, which once structured the prevailing perception of society, is itself transformed into an object of perception, or revealed as an ideology, this would seem to indicate that the discourse in question has lost some of its legitimacy. Or else it would not be possible to think outside it, much less turn it into an object of critique. Evidently, Moholy-Nagy's image records such a transformation in the dominant conception of the masses. In the following pages, it is precisely this transformation that I want to examine.

Crises of Representation

Writers, thinkers, artists, and filmmakers of the Weimar Republic were preoccupied by the masses. Several of them elaborated full-blown social theories and aesthetic programs, not to speak of political organizations and ideologies, on the basis of the social agent that they designated by that term. For instance, the masses are at the core of the research projects of the Institut für Sozialforschung, of the influential Cologne school of sociology, and of the Bauhaus school. The theme also dominates the writings of Elias Canetti, Robert Musil, Hermann Broch, Bertolt Brecht, Siegfried Kracauer, Ernst Jünger, and Oswald Spengler, to mention just a few. Here I will discuss only a fraction of this giant corpus. For lack of space I will not be able to develop a full analysis even of the few works that I have selected, which should be thought of as illustrations of a more general argument. This argument concerns the perspectives from which the Weimar ideas of the masses were produced.

My basic proposition is that the masses should not be seen as a social *fact*, but as a recurrent *theme* of a political and cultural discourse that essentially concerns the problem as to how society ought to be represented, and by whom. In general terms, I am arguing that the object that mass psychology purports to analyze, the masses, is a fantasy that the discourse in question projects onto the social landscape. How can this be? The masses, I want to submit, is a product of the specific ways in which society, or, more properly, the social, has been represented—politically and intellectually—throughout the modern period.

The act of representing the social field structures this field by instituting a distinction between representatives and represented. This distinction also effects a distribution of power and of knowledge between social agents, determining which human beings will be excluded from cultural and political institutions and hence subsumed under the notion of "the people," and which will be included in those institutions and hence able to ascend to the position of society's political and cultural representatives.

In Europe at the end of the nineteenth century and the first decades of the twentieth, this distribution tended to assume the form of a distinction between individual citizens and masses, the latter defined, typically, as a social matter characterized by its passions, the former by a mind characterized by its reason and hence capable of executing power by rationally representing the passions of the masses.[7] It follows from this presupposition that the appearance of masses in art, in literature, in the cultural consciousness more generally, or, indeed, in the street, is an index of a crisis of representation. This could be a crisis of *aesthetic* representation, in the sense that there are no longer any generally accepted ways of depicting society. But it could also be a crisis of *political* representation, a crisis of democracy, in the sense that there is no longer any consensus as to who are the rightful political representatives of the social body.

Even a hasty glimpse at the history of the Weimar Republic proves that it was beset by crises of the above-mentioned kind. It is against this background, then, that we may explain why the masses formed a focal point of interest in Weimar culture. Conversely, in order to know what the masses signified in Weimar society, we would be well advised to relate the term to the crises of cultural and political representation that characterized this society.

This analytic task remains to be carried out, however. Existing accounts of the Weimar discourses on the masses, and indeed of the concept of the masses in general, are flawed in at least two ways. The first weakness has to do with the construction of an allegedly continuous "discipline" called mass psychology, with its own genealogy of founders, traditions, branches, subdepartments, and intrinsic preoccupations. When Weimar ideas on the masses are analyzed in relation to this diachronic construct, the historical specificity and contextual references of the Weimar discussion is often occluded.

A second weakness derives from a theoretical one-sidedness. Accounts of the Weimar discourses on the masses are often framed by the theoretical and ideological ambiguities that marked the concept of the masses as it was defined in mainstream German cultural philosophy and social science. Weimar social scientists, including mass theorists such as Wilhelm Vleugels, Gerhard Colm, Alfred Vierkandt, Leopold von Wiese, and Theodor Geiger, typically defined the masses either as the opposite term of an idealized norm of individuality, or as the opposite of an equally normative notion of "organization" and "community."[8] Hence, the emergence of the masses was automatically judged as a threat to cherished ideals of *Geist, Bildung*, Reason, Order, Authority, Community, and Cohesion. Later scholars have not always accepted this definition, to be sure. Indeed, most of them have rejected it as unscientific.[9] Yet, such critiques have addressed only the particular *individualistic* notion of the masses, that is, the masses as the opposite of individuality and social organization, While this approach is understandable—after all, it was this notion that dominated the scholarly and political jargon of the period—it fails to register that the Weimar discourse on the masses also connotes a more multiple, malleable, and contra-dictory phenomenon than the one that the social scientists tried to circum-scribe in their conceptual systems. As I will show, the Weimar "mass" was far more than an ideological projection or a flawed sociological concept. Indeed, to treat the masses as an ideological figure or as a concept yields predictable if not meaningless results. But there is another way to approach this name of the nameless: as a pseudoconcept, that is, as a fiction disguised in the high jargon of social theory, or as a social theory ever predestined to crash land in ideologi-cal terrain. As a concept, then, *the masses* is a meaningless term. As a historical sign, however, it is loaded with meaning.

Limitations of Crowd Psychology

The scholarly discourse of mass psychology emerged as a result of the ongoing effort to understand the agency of "the people" that had begun to play a po-litical role with the French Revolution and emerged as an immediate political threat with the Paris Commune. Le Bon's enormously successful *La Psychologie des foules* (1895) is usually regarded as the discourse's doxa.[10] Surveys of crowd psychology tend to dwell first on its French and Italian origins. They then jump to Sigmund Freud's reinterpretation of Le Bon in *Massenpsychologie und Ich-Analyse* (1921). Freud's essay is typically seen both as a continuation of Le Bon's theory and as a new departure, out of which comes the various theories of the masses of the 1920s and onward.[11] These surveys tell a continuous story where very little happens between Le Bon and Freud.

This story is not only incomplete but also skewed. Late nineteenth-century mass psychology was a limited interdisciplinary field, situated between positiv-ist sociology, clinical psychology, and public policy. The Weimar discourse on the masses, by contrast, concerns society in its totality: it addresses the future of humankind and it often unfolds entire metaphysical systems, as is the case with the theories of Sigmund Freud and Elias Canetti. The most extreme case, Her-mann Broch's unfinished *Massenwahntheorie*, encompassed virtually all branches of knowledge from criminology and pedagogics to demography and theology.

A crucial chapter is missing here. Between the turn of the century and 1921 lie at least three events that shattered inherited assumptions about society and politics: first, the establishment of universal suffrage in most Western countries, brought about by the dual force of the labor movement and the women's movement; second, World War I, with its patriotic frenzy; third, the Russian Revolution, which many Europeans perceived as the ultimate "revolt of the masses," especially so in Germany, which experienced its own Socialist revolutions in 1918–19, when the proletariat for a brief moment sought to organize society without any of its traditional authorities. Of course, such events had to have a tremendous impact on both the intellectual and the popular view of the masses.

Georg Simmel's Mass Sociology

Georg Simmel's works bridge the years exactly between the codifications of mass psychology around 1890 and the end of World War I. His writings also show how the conception of the masses that Weimar intellectuals operated with differs from French mass psychology. Simmel's name is seldom mentioned in the discourse of mass psychology. I believe few have cared to extract his theory of the masses from the general sociology in which it is embedded. In fact, it was Simmel who presented for the German-speaking public the two books that exerted the greatest influence on the formation of crowd psychology, Le Bon's *La Psychologie des foules* (1895) and Scipio Sighele's *La folla criminale* (1892).[12]

In his 1895 article on Le Bon, Simmel immediately questions the notion of the autonomous individual. Is it not true, he asks, that the method of the *Geisteswissenchaften* and the inheritance theory of the natural sciences (i.e., Darwinism) have demonstrated that the individual is a mere cross section (*Schnittpunkt*) of social tendencies? "Thus, society is everything, and what the individual can add to its properties is a *quantité négligeable*." Yet, this proposition, too, is problematized. For is it not also true, Simmel asks, that all things that we value in life, everything exceptional and elevated, are "the products of individuals who have raised themselves above the social average?"[13] It is impossible, Simmel concludes, to determine whether society is prior to the individual, or vice versa.[14]

Having thus refused to privilege either individual or society, Simmel goes on to refute many of the assumptions of both Le Bon and Sighele. He rejects their definition of the crowd as a single being governed by a "mass soul."[15] He also rejects the idea that the crowd can be defined by suggestibility. In Simmel's view, the psychological processes of an individual within a crowd are no different than those of an individual by himself.[16] In refuting the idea of a mass soul and that of suggestibility, Simmel in fact rejects two major criteria that until then had been used to define the crowd, to the effect that he dissolves the foundation of French and Italian crowd psychology and removes the frightening qualities that it attributes to the masses. Yet, in limiting the substance of the definition of the masses, Simmel at the same time extends the concept's applicability. No longer an entity following its own psychological laws, and no longer a simple ideological projection of the bourgeoisie, the mass is retained as a category for a certain type of sociation, or *Vergesellschaftung*, that encompasses modern society in its totality.

It should be remembered that, in Simmel's view, sociological inquiry concerned not the contents of human activity, but the *social forms* under which this activity is pursued. Basically, this entailed the formal study of human interaction, including the ways in which this interaction generates institutions, hierarchies, and structures of subjectivity, in a word, various forms of sociation. Like Max Weber and Ferdinand Tönnies, the other two great founders of German sociology, Simmel inserted these forms of sociation in a historical trajectory whose guiding thread is rationalization, differentiation, and individualization. For the human subject, these processes appear to be liberating. Yet, the emancipatory thrust ends in unprecedented forms of unfreedom, as the subject becomes entangled in a network of functions and abstractions that deprives it of individuality. If we follow Tönnies's analysis, we encounter, at history's end, the instrumentalized aggregate that he called *Gesellschaft*. If we follow Weber's analysis, we encounter a person locked inside the infamous iron cage. If we follow Simmel, we are faced with the mass.

In my view, Simmel's definition of the mass may be summarized as follows: the mass is the concrete form in which the relation of human subject and society is made manifest in modern society. In presenting this notion of the masses, Simmel reiterates one crucial feature of Le Bon's and Sighele's analyses, although he casts it in a theoretical frame that he had developed independently already in *Über sociale Differenzierung* of 1890. The issue concerns the leveling impact of the masses. A crowd, Simmel argues, must base its actions on qualities that all its members have in common, and "what everyone has in common can only be the property of the one with the least property."[17]

Simmel founds this argument on a theory about the relation between "the individual level" and "the social level" that is central to his sociology.[18] He argues that the smaller and more homogeneous a society is, the lesser the difference between the level of the individual and that of the social group. As society grows larger and more heterogeneous, the individual has greater possibilities to differentiate himself. The diversification of labor allows anyone to perfect his or her mastery of a limited task. As a consequence, however, the common ground shared with others is greatly reduced; it can consist only of the simple needs and generic traits of the entire species. Whenever a human being wants to interact with others, or wants to influence them, he or she must descend to this level, for this is the only ground that he or she shares with those fellow humans.[19] The form of sociation in modernity thus allows everyone to become a genius in his or her own *Gebiet*, at the cost of becoming an idiot in everything else. Simmel calls it a "sociological tragedy."[20]

The consequences of the sociological tragedy are manifested in the mass, Simmel argues. An individual that attempts to assert his or her individuality socially finds that he or she can effectively do this only by descending to the lowest common denominator of the members of his society. It is in this context that Simmel produces a clear definition of the mass. He discusses the questionable virtue of journalists, actors, and demagogues who "seek the favor of the masses." This would not be so bad, he states, if these persons really served the mass as a sum of individuals. Yet, the mass they serve is no such sum:

> It is a new phenomenon made up, not of the total individualities of its members, but only of those fragments of each of them in which he coincides with all others. These fragments, therefore, can be nothing but the lowest and most primitive. It is this *mass*, and the level that must always remain accessible to each of its members that these intellectually and morally endangered persons serve—and not each of its members in its entirety.[21]

This sociological tragedy is accentuated by a related dilemma that Simmel calls "the tragedy of culture," or the conflict between "subjective culture" and "objective culture."[22] He argues that modern culture is more tormented than any other era by the conflict between individuals, whose urge to express their individuality freely is stronger than ever, and a life world that has grown so dense, so rigid, and so intrusive, that it effectively prevents everyone from expressing his or her individuality. In his famous essay "The Metropolis and Mental Life" (1903), Simmel thus contends that the growing division of labor reduces the individual "to a *quantité négligeable*, to a grain of dust as against the vast overwhelming organization of things and forces that gradually take out of his hands all progress, spirituality, and value."[23]

As we have seen, in his article on Le Bon's mass psychology, Simmel stated that the mass reduces the individual to a *quantité négligeable*, a negligible quantity. Here, using the same figure of speech, he claims that modern society as such reduces the individual to a negligible quantity. Evidently, the same form of sociation is at work in both cases. Simmel argues, in short, that in modern society, the mass constitutes the relation—the point of mediation—between the human subject and society. The mass is the objective culture and the structure of sociation, in opposition to which the subject tries to express his or her individuality. In Simmel's theory, everything external to the mass is also external to the social; it is individual. The mass is the social essence of the human subject.

When Simmel speaks of the mass, he does not imply a concrete social phenomenon, as the French crowd psychologists did. For him, the crowd is a sociological structure, always construed in dialectical tension with another abstract structure, individuality. In Simmel's *Lebensphilosophie*, these structures are eventually assimilated into a metaphysics, as two forms of appearance of the eternal dialectic between life and form. Just as life seeks to appear in its naked immediacy, but can only do so by producing forms that betray this immediacy, so does individuality seek to realize itself by raising above the level of the masses, but only to find itself pulled down to the common level from which the project of self-realization must begin anew. This is what Hegel would have called a bad dialectic, for it has no telos or synthesis. For Simmel, however, the problem is not so much that the dialectic is infinite, but that it has come to a standstill in modernity. The institutional forms that once kept individuality elevated above the dull level of normality have been dismantled. Therefore, the dialectical tension between individuality and mass has collapsed. The two will henceforth ceaselessly pass over into each other.

The Individual or the Masses

"My legacy," Simmel wrote shortly before his death, "will be like cash, distributed to many heirs, each transforming his part into use according to *his* nature."[24] I believe Simmel's theory of the masses provides such a supreme articulation of the ideological dilemmas in the Weimar Republic that it fuses with the general cultural horizon of that society. And, as Simmel predicted, the dilemmas that he formulated were inherited by many, and resolved in several different ways.

On one hand, the traditional principle of individuality was reinforced and magnified as a response to the alleged leveling of the human condition in modernity. This tendency became the dominant one. German sociologists and intellectuals constantly rehashed Simmel's dialectic between the principles of individuality and massification. "The contempt for the masses is a typical characteristic of most intellectuals of the Weimar Republic," Helmuth Berking observes.[25] Their contempt of the masses was a defensive reaction, he explains.[26] It mirrored a historical situation in which the privileges of opinion that the intellectual elite had learned to take for granted were undermined by media technology, urban forms of life, and ideas of democracy and equality. Indeed, for the Weimar mandarins whose worldview was organized in terms of *Bildung* (education), *Geist* (intellect), *Kultur* (culture), *Persönlichkeit* (personality), *Seele* (soul), *Innerlichkeit* (inwardness), and *Individualität* (individuality), the masses could not but appear as a symptom of decline. Hence the frequent appeals to the necessity of personal cultivation and aesthetic education of all citizens, hence the calls for *Führung* (leadership), and hence the reminders of the responsibility of the elite in the life of the nation.[27]

This is the Weimar discourse on the masses that is best known, the one that was institutionalized under fascism. Theoretically, this version is as sterile as it is simple: given the definition of the masses as opposed to individuality, and given the view of individuality as the support of culture and knowledge, the conclusion follows automatically: a representation of the masses as disorderly and destructive, as an agent of leveling passions that must either be raised by education, struck down by suppression, or cleansed by fascist pedagogics.

But once the notion of the masses is uncoupled from idealized individuality, it takes on more interesting meanings. It is well known that modernist culture, and Weimar modernism in particular, articulates radically new ideas about the human subject.[28] In twentieth-century art, we witness a decomposition and asymmetric reconstruction of the human face and body. In architecture, the idea of the interior as the padded case of the individual's essence gives way to the utopian living spaces of Gropius or Mies van der Rohe. Numerous novels chronicle how the separate space of individuality, materialized in the *intérieur*, is invaded by external forces, to the extent that the self appears as a random mass of impersonal elements. Where there was once a sovereign individual, there is now, as Robert Musil stated, "a big, vacuous, round O." The result of this process is not only a postindividualistic idea of human subjectivity, but also a postindividualistic notion of the masses.

Siegfried Kracauer and the Postindividualistic Mass

In his early essay "Die Gruppe als Ideenträger" (1922), Siegfried Kracauer follows Simmel as he lists the characteristics of the individual that becomes part of a group. Such a person undergoes a leveling process: "The subject's unique totality is thus banned from the newly emerging group-self, and only those traits common to all the various subjects belonging to the group can contribute to the construction of a group individuality."[29]

Kracauer argues that *das Vollindividuum* (the full individual) disappears in the group. What emerges instead is a reduced being, fixated only on the narrow goal that the group members have in common. Like Simmel, Kracauer speaks of "fragments of individuals":

> The people united in a group are no longer full individuals [*sind keine Vollindividuen mehr*], but only fragments of individuals whose very right to exist is exclusively a function of the group's goal. The subject as an individual self [*Einzel-Ich*] linked to other individual selves [*Einzel-Ichen*]: a being whose resources must be conceived as endless and who, incapable of being completely ruled by the idea, still lives in realms located outside the idea's sphere of influence. The subject as a group member: a *partial self* [*Teil-Ich*] that is cut off from its full being and cannot stray from the path which the idea prescribes for it.[30]

Outside the collective, Kracauer states, there exists something called *das Vollindividuum*; within the collective, this being becomes a partial self, a *Teil-Ich*. The mass is thus defined as a corruption of authentic individuality.

Compare this analysis to the more canonical one in "The Mass Ornament" of 1927. In the analytic framework that Kracauer employs in this essay, the masses are not measured against an idealized notion of individuality. A notion such as *das Vollindividuum* has no role to play. As Kracauer makes clear, the complete individual is only conceivable either in the fully mythologized world, where each being is independently meaningful as a natural sign of the divine creation, or in the fully enlightened world, where each being is independently meaningful by virtue of a reason that has liberated humankind from the constraints of myth and nature. In the historical existence proper to men and women, however, they are always entangled in various kinds of collectives. The actually existing human being is never more than a partial self, a *Teil-Ich*, for whom the notion of a nonalienated individuality appears as a utopian condition that can be realized only through the protean effort of the collective to raise itself above nature and institute a kingdom of reason, or through the complete subjection of the collective under some kind of new myth.

In Kracauer's view, the mass ornament is a cultural form typical of an intermediary stage in a long historical cycle moving between the extreme poles of myth and reason. The choreographed ornaments formed by dancers or athletes are thus on the one hand a result of a reorganization of human relationships according to the principles of reason. Human activity is liberated and asserted as an end in itself, independent of nature and tradition. On the other hand, the end to which the activity is directed bears no relationship to the men or women who are actually participating in the mass ornament. The patterns they form in the stadium or on the stage are not offered to their senses but can be seen only by spectators placed at a distance, like an aerial photograph. In sum, the mass ornament represents an unprecedented rationalization and coordination of human activity, but this reorganization does not benefit those who literally build the ornament with their own bodies and movements. On the contrary, they find themselves subjected to a new form of mythological totality, beyond their control.

Kracauer explains that the subjection of the dancer or actor to the mass ornament mirrors the human condition under capitalism. Like the mass ornament, the capitalist division of labor liberates human activity from older forms of bondage. And, as is the case with the mass ornament, the liberation offered by the capitalist system fails to encompass the human subject, but serves to subordinate him or her under the reign of an abstract law. What Kracauer calls *the mass*, then, is precisely the effect of this social contradiction: people are liberated from old oppressive communities but at the same time enslaved under a new set of abstract social relationships.

Crucially, Kracauer, in "The Mass Ornament," rejects the presupposition of individuality—the *Vollindividuum*—that made "The Group as Bearer of Ideas" a somewhat predictable sociological exercise in the wake of Simmel and Tönnies. As a result, he is able to paint a more intriguing picture of the social drama. The mass ornament, along with capitalism itself, emerges as a transient way of representing society as such. This society is no longer a society of individuals, but of partial selves—swinging legs, heads, and arms without bodies, a mass of passions and interests. No longer a simple sign of cultural decline, the masses signify a reservoir of ambiguous social, political, and aesthetic energies that are not yet fully fixed in the order of power and knowledge, not yet represented.

Reorganization of Social Passions

"Our concept of the mass is derived from the standpoint of the individual," Bertolt Brecht wrote in the late 1920s. "The bourgeoisie has no understanding of the mass. It always just separates the individual and the mass."[31] The section of Brecht's notes that is published as "Marxistische Studien" contains not only a critique of the individualistic definition of the masses that dominated Weimar culture, but also an attempt to conceptualize the relation of mass and individual that takes Kracauer's analysis one step forward. According to Brecht, the individual is a "dividual," a being that can be divided into smaller components. The reason for the dividable nature of the individual is that he or she is part of different collectives, each of which offers the subject a different identity. The term *individual* is thus an abstraction, concealing the fact that the human subject really is a superimposition of many different characters, or, as our contemporary vocabulary would say, subject positions. As Brecht states concisely, "What should be stressed about the individual is precisely his divisibility (as he belongs to several Collectives)."[32]

Brecht's perspective has wide-ranging consequences. First, the individual, in his or her dividable nature, appears as a mass: "The individual appears to us ever more as a contradictory complex in continuous development, similar to the mass."[33] Second, the individual now emerges as a secondary phenomenon in relation to a more basic social reality consisting of masses, collectives, classes, and groups. Instead of seeing the mass as an eclipse of individuality, Brecht regards the mass as the condition of possibility for the emergence of individuality. To be sure, Brecht acknowledges that a society dominated by large collectives entails the destruction of what he calls "the person." But this destruction only reveals that the person was never but a social construction in the first place. The fundamental and originary element of humanity, culture, or society is not, to use Kracauer's terms, *das Vollindividuum*, but rather *das Teil-Ich*. Or as Brecht states:

> The expanding collectives entail the destruction of the person. The suspicions of the old philosophers concerning the fragmentation of the human being are realized: thought and being are mirrored in the person as a terrible disease. He

falls apart, he loses his breath. He turns into something else, he is nameless, he no longer has any face, he escapes from his overstretched state into his smallest proportion—from his dispensability into nothingness—yet having made the passage into his smallest proportion he recognizes, deeply breathing, his new and true indispensability within the whole.[34]

The mass thus comes across as a social medium in which a false notion of individuality is first decomposed into its constituent parts, after which these subindividual components rearrange themselves, as it were, constituting new subjects according to available mechanisms of collective identifications. What Brecht has in mind when developing his constructivist aesthetics and his ideas about the epic theater is precisely such a reconstitution of humanity. "We will start from the mass-character to seek the individual and thus construct him," he states in his notes. The same task is frequently announced in his writings on theater, or in the plays themselves, the canonical statement being the "intermission speech" in *Mann ist Mann:* "Here tonight, a man will be reassembled like a car / Without losing anything in the process."[35]

What Brecht calls "the destruction of the person," after which the subject is rebuilt, also organizes two remarkable novelistic projects of Weimar culture: Alfred Döblin's *Berlin Alexanderplatz* and Robert Musil's *The Man Without Qualities.* In both we encounter a hero, Franz Biberkopf and Ulrich, respectively, who at the beginning tries rather desperately to establish a firm sense of self. In both cases, the effort fails, and the hero descends to a state of insanity. Brecht's description of the fate of the person may be read as a note on Döblin's and Musil's heroes as well: they fall apart, they lose their breath. They go over into something else, they are nameless, they no longer have any faces, they escape from a situation in which they are superfluous by becoming mad and by confronting their own nothingness—just like Kafka's heroes, incidentally, escape from their tormenting human condition by becoming animals. At the same time, both novels, like Brecht, affirm this descent into nothingness as a step towards a more truthful relationship to the social totality. And in both novels, this process of individual decomposition and rebirth is mediated by the experience of the masses. Ulrich's experiences of the urban crowd are thus rendered as epiphanies that dilute individuality in an ocean of sensory stimuli. Note the affinity between the following passage and Kracauer's description of the mass ornament:

For whenever his travels took him to cities to which he was not connected by business of any kind, he particularly enjoyed the feeling of solitude this gave him, and he rarely felt this so keenly as he did now. He noticed the colors of the streetcars, the automobiles, shop windows, and archways, the shapes of church towers, the faces and the facades. ... Such aimless, purposeless strolling through a town vitally absorbed in itself, the keenness of perception increasing in proportion as the strangeness of the surroundings intensifies, heightened still further by the connection that it is not oneself that matters but only this mass of faces, these movements wrenched loose from the body to become armies of arms, legs, or teeth, to all of which the future belongs—all this can evoke the feeling that being a whole and inviolate strolling human being is positively antisocial and criminal. But if one lets oneself go even further in this fashion, this feeling may also unexpectedly produce a physical well-being and irresponsibility amounting to folly, as if the body were no longer part of a world where the sensual self is enclosed in strands of nerves and blood vessels but belongs to a world bathed in somnolent sweetness.[36]

The last pages of *Berlin Alexanderplatz*, on the other hand, evoke what Brecht would have called the rebuilding of the subject through his or her unification with the collective. Döblin's final lesson is not that a subject that is embedded in the collective is diminished or fragmented, but, on the contrary, that his or her powers are multiplied:

One is stronger than I. If there are two of us, it grows harder to be stronger than I. If there are ten of us, it's harder still. And if there are a thousand of us and a million, then it's very hard, indeed.

But it is also nicer and better to be with others. Then I feel and I know everything twice as well. A ship cannot lie in safety without a big anchor, and a man cannot exist without many other men.[37]

Though these examples are crude, they give an idea of the possibilities for representing society that are opened up once the masses are no longer predefined as a negation of a normative individuality. Kracauer, Brecht, Döblin, and Musil all agree that the mass negates individuality, but the work of negativity is for them a work of reason that discloses a layer of social life far deeper than the individual. It is this substance of sociality that they attempt to represent, as they seek new ways of conceptualizing, narrating, or depicting the masses.

Of course, *the masses* is not the correct term to employ here. For what they refer to is the social body before it crystallizes into individuals, classes, groups or whatever other designation we may choose. What we see in the postindividualistic conceptualizations of the masses, of which Weimar culture offers so many brilliant examples, is thus neither individuals nor masses. What we see, rather, is the social in the most elementary sense, as it exists before being interrupted by those forms of *Vergesellschaftung* and those systems of representation that divide society into individuals and masses.[38]

If we continue to use *the masses* as a term to describe these postindividualistic images of society, we must thus qualify our usage of that word. The importance of the masses represented here is not that they destroy a person's individual identity, but that they present a social situation in which the human subject reexperiences the entire course of its concurrent socialization and individuation, sensing both what it is like to lose one's individuality by becoming

part of the swarm and what it is like to shape one's individual identity by adapting to, or deviating from, the norms and forms offered by the collective. In this
view, the masses signify not a fall from social organization to disorder, but an
ongoing reorganization of social passions.

A graphic illustration of this condition is offered by George Grosz's work,
especially the prints and drawings (Figure 13.2). The unity of the pictorial
plane is exploded by a dissonant play of horizontal, vertical, or diagonal lines
that appear to extend beyond the frames of the image. No individual is so autonomous that he or she may be set apart from his or her fellows by means
of an unbroken line of contour. Instead, the outlines of one person intersect
with those of his or her neighbor, and both of them are dissected by or merge
with the jagged lines of the tilting cityscape. Shapes are superimposed upon
one another. Forms interconnect in one great social chain. Neither individuals
nor masses: what Grosz presents is an agglomeration of subindividuals—*Teil-
Ichen*—in the process of splitting away from or fusing with other similar subjects. Grosz's work presents a visual diagram of the dividable nature of the
human subject, and the agglomerative nature of the collective. Small wonder
that Grosz is often identified with the spirit of Weimar culture itself. What
we see in his drawings is not the mass as ornament but the multitude as move-
able montage: a society in permanent crisis that continually reconstitutes itself
without reference to any stable positions of sovereignty.

Johanna in the Revolution

In its early versions, for example in Le Bon, mass psychology asserted that the
masses are of feminine nature, a subservient and malleable matter, in relation
to which the leader exercises his powers.[39] By rejecting the conception of individuality as a subject-position that is external to the masses, the writers I have
discussed also refuted the sexual ontology that ascribed masculine qualities
to the leader-individual and feminine ones to the masses. This transformation
may be related to the consolidation of the women's movements in the interwar
period, as "*die neue Frau*" (the new woman) symbolized a constituency that
could not be reduced to either of the conflicting classes in the social struggle.[40]

Yet, while the women's movements pressed for a more multilayered interpretation of society than conventional class analysis offered, the notion of
femininity could also operate as an ideological and aesthetic fantasy that transcended the dualistic framework that split the social body in individual citizens
and proletarian masses. Interestingly, two emblematic Weimar dramas, Ernst
Toller's *Masse-Mensch* (1919) and Brecht's *Die heilige Johanna der Schlachthöfe*
(1927), follow this pattern. Both stage a violent antagonism between the anonymous masses and a group of capitalist individuals. Both posit a female hero as

Figure 13.2. George Grosz, *Ecce Homo*, 1922–1923, plate 68.

a mediatory figure in this struggle: in Toller's play she is called "*Die Frau*," (The Woman), in Brecht, Johanna. The heroines are personifications of the dehumanized collective. Their solidarity is without limits. In her prophetic dream, Johanna sees herself at the head of all the protest marches and uprisings of human history.[41]

Yet, Johanna and The Woman are somehow too good for this world, as Brecht would have said. They are utopian figures, symbols of a social democratic reformism or a humanist universalism that bear no relation to the fractured political reality of Weimar Germany. Moreover, both dramas allude to the nineteenth-century practice of allegorizing the nation and the people as a feminine figure. Like Marianne, the allegory of the French people, or Germania, her German equivalent, Johanna and The Woman appear as the *corpus mysticum* of the people, redeeming the antagonisms that destroy the *corpus politicum* of male society. On a structural level, then, Brecht's and Toller's heroines, notwithstanding their Socialist convictions, are akin to "the great German mother," the allegorical mother of the nation through which conservative segments of the women's movement and fascism itself sought to represent the German tribe.

Unlike the Fascist figure of femininity, however, Brecht's and Toller's heroines fail to represent the collective. By foregrounding these failures, both dramas problematize the inherited principle of representation, according to which the masses is a force of potentiality that must be mobilized by the leader or the vanguard party. Brecht's Johanna and Toller's Woman shift positions as the revolution unfolds—now assuming the role of the individualized leader, now embracing the anonymity of the movement, now emerging as negotiators between the struggling classes. Yet, they always end up betraying the collective they wish to serve. Such is the tragic kernel of these dramas: although The Woman and Johanna are virtual embodiments of the people, neither dispose of the forms—that is, the rhetoric, the organization, the revolutionary strategy, the institution—by which they could represent the people politically. If we read these texts as efforts to address the crisis that haunted Weimar society—how to represent society politically and culturally?—we must conclude that they fail to project an image of democracy, that is, a form of representation that does not define itself in opposition to an excluded majority branded as "the masses." But precisely in this failure, there emerge their truths as political dramas, in the sense once summarized by Heiner Müller: the task of political theater is not to invent new possibilities but to demonstrate the impossibility of reality.[42]

Mass Media and Collective Culture

Masse-Mensch and *Die heilige Johanna der Schlachthöfe* each stages a collective that blurs the distinction between individual and mass, at the same time questioning the gendering of society in terms of masculine and feminine qualities. Placing a woman at the head of the revolution, the dramas illustrate the postindividualistic figuration of the masses that characterized a crucial part of Weimar culture. Interestingly, this process may also be traced in the image of Moholy-Nagy I opened with. Moholy-Nagy's photoplastic situates the figure of femininity at both sides of an opposition: it is linked both to the subdued masses (the faceless female swimmers huddling together in their circular collective) and to the sovereign leader (the armed woman is a picture as good as any of the potency of the new woman).

This is not the only aspect where *Massenpsychose* elaborates contradictory codes. Indeed, by consistently employing a double focus, Moholy-Nagy's image encompasses the whole trajectory of the discourse on the masses, from its inception in France in the 1880s and 1890s to the transformations it underwent in the Weimar Republic. In Moholy-Nagy's image, we see the discourse on the masses from two different historical points at once. On the one hand, we stare at the content of the image: a social hierarchy with firm boundaries between individual leaders and the masses. To be sure, such is the image of society presented by mass psychology and mass sociology, from Tarde to Freud, from Le Bon to Hitler.

On the other hand, we may reflect upon the image's public mode of address, which encourages an egalitarian posture. Contrary to the implied audience of the mass ornament, the implied spectator of the photoplastic has acquired such a high level of "literacy" in mass psychological matters that he or she can be counted on to decode, almost instinctively, the meaning of the photoplastic constellation. The image invites its public to reflect on mechanisms of power, on the relation between leaders and subjects, between individuals and masses. Indeed, Moholy-Nagy argued that photoplastic images constituted a new visual language, suitable for all kinds of public uses, from commercial advertising to propaganda. The photoplastic thus perfectly matches his constructivist program. As he argued in his article "Constructivism and the Proletariat," constructivism "is the socialism of vision—the common property of all men."[43] From this perspective, the image becomes a critique of the dominant, individualistic notion of the masses, and it suggests an alternative way of representing society.

In sum, the public that the image addresses is a negation of the society depicted in the image itself. *Massenpsychose* thus activates a social contradiction. It provides a visual representation of a society divided between leaders and masses, while at the same time, through its mode of interpellation, realizing a public culture without either individuals or masses. The image trusts the viewers' ability to undo the dichotomy of individuals and masses and to project itself in a utopian direction, beyond those mechanisms of power that split the social field into a set of individual leaders and a faceless mass.

In so doing, Moholy-Nagy also demonstrates a more general feature of Weimar modernism. For it seems that the deconstruction of the dichotomy of individuals and masses presupposes a cultural medium that dissolves the opposition between aesthetics and politics, or aesthetics and public culture. This new medium is of course the photoplastic technique itself, which is hard to locate in any conventional system of aesthetic genres. Evidently, the negation of the distinction between individual and mass leads to an interrogation or transgression of the distinction between art and its other—whether we call it mass culture, primitive culture, folk culture, propaganda, proletkult, or constructivism. All dominant views of art have presupposed a conception of the authentic and creative individual. By thinking through the phenomenon of the masses, Moholy-Nagy undercut this individualist foundation of aesthetics and robbed art of its conceptual and institutional autonomy. No longer anchored in the private sphere or the bourgeois interior, art and literature were redefined as forms of social production, the artist and author as producers. It is symptomatic that Döblin's *Berlin Alexanderplatz* appeared not only as a novel, in 1929, but also as a *Hörspiel* (radio play) in 1930, and then as film, in 1931; that Brecht's *Three-Penny Opera* was produced as opera, novel, and film, and then as a book documentation that addressed precisely the tensions between these media; that, finally, Kracauer published most of his analyses as newspaper articles. In these cases, the presence and pressure of the masses determined the very forms of artistic and intellectual labor. And for us, who have no stake in the political crises of the Weimar Republic, the crucial legacy of its discussion about the masses may lie precisely in this cultural-aesthetic realm rather than in the political one. Erasing the distinction between art and mass culture in their intellectual and artistic practice, the Weimar modernists I have discussed in this essay invented an aesthetics founded on a notion of the public and the collective.

Notes

1. Lázsló Moholy-Nagy, "Photography Is Creation with Light," in Krisztina Passuth, *Moholy-Nagy* (London, 1985), 304. Originally published as "Fotografie ist Lichtgestaltung," *Bauhaus: Zeitschrift für Bau und Gestaltung* 2, no. 1 (1928): 2–9.
2. Ibid., 305.
3. Cited in Susanna Barrows, *Distorting Mirrors: Visions of the Crowd in Late-Nineteenth-Century France* (New Haven, CT, 1981), 132, 141.
4. Gustave Le Bon, *The Crowd: A Study of the Popular Mind* (Marietta, GA, 1982), 17. Originally published as *La Psychologie des foules* (Paris, 1895).
5. I am indebted to Heinrich Dilly, who has pointed out this parallel to me.
6. Hippolyte Taine, *Histoire de la littérature anglaise*, 4 vols. (Paris, 1902–1907), 1: viii.
7. I develop this argument in greater detail in an ongoing two-volume project on the history of the idea of masses in European culture. The first volume discusses the general

political and aesthetic problematics of this idea from the French Revolution to the present: *A Brief History of the Masses: Three Revolutions* (New York: 2008); the second volume, forthcoming as *Cultures of the Crowd*, deals with the culmination of this history in interwar German and Austrian culture.

8. Gerhard Colm, "Die Masse: Ein Beitrag zur Systematik der Gruppen," *Archiv für Sozialwissenschaft und Sozialpolitik* 52 (Tübingen, 1924), 680–94; Theodor Geiger, *Die Masse und ihre Aktion: Ein Beitrag zur Soziologie der Revolution* (Stuttgart, 1926); Wilhelm Vleugels, *Die Masse. Ein Beitrag zur Lehre von den sozialen Gebilden* (Munich, 1930); Leopold von Wiese, *System der Allgemeinen Soziologie*, 2nd ed. (Munich, 1933), 407–46.

9. See Helmuth Berking, *Masse und Geist: Studien zur Soziologie in der Weimarer Republik* (Berlin, 1984); Manfred Franke, "Der Begriff der Masse in der Sozialwissenschaft: Darstellung eines Phänomens und seine Bedeutung in der Kulturkritik des 20. Jahrhunderts" (Diss., Johannes Gutenberg-Universität, Mainz, 1985). Helmut König, *Zivilisation und Leidenschaften: Die Masse im bürgerlichen Zeitalter* (Reinbek bei Hamburg, 1992); Nori Möding, *Die Angst der Bürgers vor der Masse: Zur politischen Verführbarkeit des deutschen Geistes im Ausgang seiner bürgerlichen Epoche* (Berlin, 1984).

10. On the origins of mass psychology, see Barrows, *Distorting Mirrors*; Robert A. Nye, *The Origins of Crowd Psychology: Gustave Le Bon and the Crisis of Mass Democracy in the Third Republic* (London, 1975).

11. In addition to the numerous entries on "masses" and "mass psychology" in encyclopedias of philosophy and the social sciences, which are all governed by this perspective, see Serge Moscovici, *The Age of the Crowd: A Historical Treatise on Mass Psychology*, trans. J. C. Whitehouse (Cambridge, 1985); Peter Sloterdijk, *Die Verachtung der Massen: Versuch über Kulturkämpfe in der modernen Gesellschaft* (Frankfurt am Main, 2000); Stanley J. Tambiah, *Leveling Crowds: Ethnonationalist Conflicts and Collective Violence in South Asia* (Berkeley, CA, 1996); Leon Bramson, *The Political Context of Sociology* (Princeton, NJ, 1961); Paul Reiwald, *Vom Geist der Massen: Handbuch der Massenpsychologie* (Zürich, 1946).

12. In November 1895 Simmel reviewed Gustave Le Bon's *La Psychologie des foules*, published in France the same year: Georg Simmel, "Massenpsychologie," *Die Zeit. Wiener Wochenschrift für Politik, Volkswirtschaft, Wissenschaft und Kunst* 5, no. 60 (23 November 1895): 119f. In 1897 he reviewed the German translation of Scipio Sighele's *La folla criminale*, originally published in 1892 and translated into French the same year: Georg Simmel, "Über Massenverbrechen," *Die Zeit. Wiener Wochenschrift für Politik, Volkswirtschaft, Wissenschaft und Kunst* 13, no. 157 (2 October 1897): 4–6. Simmel also introduced Gabriel Tarde and reviewed his *Les lois de l'imitation* in *Zeitschrift für Psychologie und Physiologie der Sinnesorgane*, vol. 2 (1891), 141f. These articles are republished in Simmel, *Gesamtausgabe*, ed. Otthein Rammstedt (Frankfurt, 2000), 1, 248–51, 353–61, 388–400.

13. Simmel, "Massenpsychologie," 119.

14. Ibid. Cf. his *Soziologie: Untersuchungen über die Formen der Vergesellschaftung* (Munich, 1922 [1908]), 366.

15. Simmel objects that this definition stems from a confusion of cause and effect. While it is true that collective action often results in one massive effect—the destruction of a certain building, the roar that emerges as if from one throat—this does not mean that collective action is the result of one common cause, a collective soul ("Über Massenverbrechen," 5).

16. As Simmel argues, the emotional impact of a mountain view is not qualitatively different from the impact of a surrounding crowd (ibid.).

17. Georg Simmel, *Über sociale Differenzierung* [1890], in *Gesamtausgabe*, 2: 210. See also "Massenpsychologie," 119.

18. Simmel, *Über sociale Differenzierung*, 199–236. The analysis of mass behavior formulated here thus returns in his article on Le Bon, "Massenpsychologie" of 1895, in his majestic *Soziologie* of 1908, and in *Grundfragen der Soziologie (Individuum und Gesellschaft)* of 1917. The remarkable constancy of Simmel's analysis of the masses is signalled by the fact that certain formulations are repeated in all four publications.

19. Georg Simmel, "Group Expansion and the Development of Individuality," in *On Individuality and Social Forms*, 251–93; original in *Soziologie*, 527–73; cf. *Über sociale Differenzierung*, cf. 169–98.

20. Georg Simmel, *Fundamental Problems of Sociology: Individual and Society*, in *The Sociology of Georg Simmel*, ed. and trans. Kurt H. Wolff (New York, 1964 [1950]), 32; *Grundfragen der Soziologie*, 94.

21. Simmel, *Fundamental Problems*, 33; *Grundfragen der Soziologie*, 96.

22. Simmel, "Subjective Culture," in *On Individuality and Social Forms: Selected Writings*, ed. Donald N. Levine (Chicago, 1971), 227–34; "Vom Wesen der Kultur," in *Brücke und Tür: Essays des Philosophen zur Geschichte, Religion, Kunst und Gesellschaft*, ed. Margarete Sussman and Michael Landmann (Stuttgart, 1957), 86–94.

23. Georg Simmel, "The Metropolis and Mental Life," in *On Individuality and Social Forms*, 337. Translation modified. "Die Grossstädte und das Geistesleben," 240f.

24. Levine, "Introduction," xiii.

25. Berking, *Masse und Geist*, 65, 66–68.

26. Ibid., 66–68. See Fritz K. Ringer, *The Decline of the German Mandarins: The German Academic Community, 1890–1933* (Cambridge, 1969).

27. See Ringer, *Decline of the German Mandarins*.

28. See my *Subject Without Nation: Robert Musil and the History of Modern Identity* (Durham, NC, 2001), chapter 1. Siegfried Kracauer, "The Group as Bearer of Ideas," in *The Mass Ornament: Weimar Essays*, trans. and ed. Thomas Y. Levin (Cambridge, 1995), 152; "Die Gruppe als Ideenträger," in *Schriften*, ed. Inka Mülder-Bach (Frankfurt am Main, 1990), vol. 5, bk. 1, 179.

29. Kracauer, "The Group as Bearer of Ideas," 152; "Die Gruppe als Ideenträger," 179.

30. Kracauer, "The Group as Bearer of Ideas," 151; "Die Gruppe als Ideenträger," 177. Translation modified.

31. Bertolt Brecht, "[Notizen über] Individuum und Masse," in *Gesammelte Werke* (Frankfurt am Main, 1967), 60.

32. Ibid.

33. Ibid., 62.

34. Ibid., 60.

35. Bertolt Brecht, *Mann ist Mann*, in *Gesammelte Werke*, 1, 336.

36. Robert Musil, *The Man Without Qualities*, trans. Sophie Wilkins and Burton Pike (New York, 1995), 785f; *Der Mann ohne Eigenschaften*, ed. Adolf Frisé (Reinbek bei Hamburg, 1978), 723.

37. Alfred Döblin, *Berlin Alexanderplatz: The Story of Franz Biberkopf*, trans. Eugene Jolas (New York, 1997), 633.

38. It remains to be explored to what extent this definition of "the social" corresponds to ancient and recent notions of "the multitude," in Spinoza's or Hardt and Negris's sense.

See the latter's *Multitude: War and Democracy in the Age of Empire* (Cambridge, MA, 2004).

39. In interwar Germany, fascism associated the masses with feminine qualities that needed to be purged or subdued in order to transform the masses into the organized body of the army, the nation, and *das Volk*. See Klaus Theweleit, *Male Fantasies*, vol. 2: *Male Bodies: Psychoanalyzing the White Terror*, trans. Erica Carter and Chris Turner (Minneapolis, 1989), 3f, also published as *Männerphantasien*, vol. 2: *Männerkörper: zur psychoanalyse des weißen Terrors* (Frankfurt am Main, 1978), 9f.

40. For an overview, see Katharina von Ankum, ed., *Women in the Metropolis: Gender and Modernity in Weimar Culture* (Berkeley, CA, 1997).

41. Bertolt Brecht, *Die heilige Johanna der Schlachthöfe*, in *Ausgewählte Werke (Jubileums-ausgabe)* (Frankfurt am Main, 1999), 1, 406.

42. Quoted by Hans-Thies Lehmann, *Das Politische Schreiben: Essays zu Theatertexten* (Berlin, 2002), 8.

43. Lázsló Moholy-Nagy, "Constructivism and the Proletariat," in *Moholy-Nagy*, ed. Richard Kostelanetz, Documentary Monographs in Modern Art (London, 1971), 185. Originally published in *MA* (Budapest), May 1922.

CHAPTER 14

❧ ⋮ ☙

Cultural Capital in Decline
Inflation and the Distress of Intellectuals

BERND WIDDIG

The German Hyperinflation

For many Germans, inflation was one of the most decisive and traumatic experiences of the twentieth century, an experience that had repercussions far beyond the economic sphere. The ever faster-swelling stream of money betrayed long-held persuasions, swept away livelihoods, and destroyed the trust and confidence of a whole generation.

At the root of the inflation was the German government's attempt to finance the First World War and the reconstruction of the postwar society largely through loans and excessive printing of new money. Political and financial leaders—some willfully—disregarded the monetary consequences, and Germany underwent an inflationary process during and immediately after the war, culminating dramatically in the hyperinflation of 1923. Prices rose in that year by an astronomical 75 billion percent. In 1914 the exchange value of the mark stood at 4.20 marks for one dollar. By the end of 1923 the value of the German mark had deteriorated to 4.2 trillion marks for one dollar.

Table 14.1. Percentage increases in internal prices

Year	Percentage Increase
1914–1918	140%
1919	223%
1920	67%
1921	144%
1922	5,470%
1923	75,000,000,000% (75×10^9)

Source: Charles Maier, *In Search of Stability. Explorations in historical political economy* (Cambridge: Cambridge UP, 1987) 198.

At the height of the hyperinflation, workers were paid daily. They rushed to the next store to buy something before the bundles of banknotes they had just received became worthless. When the inflation was finally over in 1924 with the introduction of the *Rentenmark,* it had resulted in a tremendous redistribution of income and wealth. While speculators and some industrialists profited from the inflation, many others, especially the middle class and retired people, lost their savings and suffered severe economic and social hardship. Especially hard hit was a group of people that is at the center of this article: German intellectuals, or, as they were often called in the 1920s, "*die geistigen Arbeiter.*" As members of the middle class and largely unprotected by trade unions or other powerful professional organizations, writers, artists, journalists, professors, and scientists saw their economic status drastically deteriorating during the inflation.

I will first illustrate this dire economic situation of intellectuals during the inflation, which is necessary to understand the urgency and desperation of the discussions that ensued around the general status of intellectual work during the early 1920s. The overwhelming centrality of money, the predominance of the economic, the radical changes in the social structure that characterize the period of inflation caused many intellectuals to ask fundamental questions about the worth of their work. To put this in Pierre Bourdieu's terms, intellectuals asked what real value did their "cultural capital" still have during the period of inflation. The devaluation of *Geld* was about to destroy their economic status; was the inflation thus also destroying the foundations of German *Geist* and high culture? I will take up this question in the third and fourth parts of the essay. If we understand inflation as a rapid process of massification, with a single entity simultaneously losing its value, when we add to this the frightening experience of the centrality of money, which makes everything quantifiable and exchangeable, then a strong analogy comes to mind: that between inflation and a conservative, highly critical concept of mass culture; a modern mass culture that was seen as invading and threatening the spheres of high culture. I will address this link between culture and inflation in part five of the essay.

The Distress of the *Geistige Arbeiter*

In his brief essay "Intellektuellendämmerung" (Intellectuals' Twilight) of 1920, the critic Michael Charol stresses a distinction among intellectuals that became of great economic importance during the inflation: "Economically, intellectual workers [*geistige Arbeiter*] can be divided into two groups: those with salaried positions [*Festbesoldete*] and those with freelancing positions [*Freie*]."[1] The first group consists of scholars, professors, teachers, and artists who had salaried positions with the state and of those who received a regular monthly income from private businesses, such as journalists, theater directors, or editors at publishing houses. While the economic situation of intellectuals with salaried income became increasingly difficult, those who made a living as freelance authors, artists, or actors were often hit even harder during the inflation. All freelancers and many professionals such as lawyers and doctors suffered especially because they received payments for their goods or services often with considerable delay, which resulted in an even further devaluation of their income.[2] The distress of many independent authors was highlighted by a spectacular trial in February of 1921 when the well-known expressionist writer Georg Kaiser was sentenced to one year in prison for burglary. Kaiser defended himself during his trial by claiming that sheer physical survival had necessitated his act.[3] Yet it is very difficult to make generalizations about the experiences of the various members of this group, because their position as freelancers allowed them to react more flexibly to the inflation. It is somewhat easier to draw a picture of those intellectuals who received their main income through a salaried position. To give some specific examples, I would like to look here briefly at the situation of professors in German universities.

In 1923, Dr. Georg Schreiber, a delegate of the Center Party in the Reichstag and himself a professor, published the detailed survey *Die Not der deutschen Wissenschaft und der geistigen Arbeiter* (The Distress of German Science and Intellectual Workers) to steer public attention to "the alarming decline of our intellectual culture."[4] Schreiber focuses especially on the situation of German universities and research laboratories. He provides ample evidence of how seriously the work of researchers and scholars in both the sciences and the humanities was threatened by rising prices, which could no longer be covered by the budgets of their academic institutions. For example, the price for a microscope that had cost 1,000 marks before the war had risen to 400,000 marks in December of 1922. The price for a liter of pure alcohol had risen over the same period from 50 Pfennig to 1,500 marks, making it difficult to undertake even basic experiments.[5] Budget amendments usually came too late to account for the rising costs of maintaining a laboratory.

The conditions in the social sciences and humanities were equally dire. The library of the Department of Canonical Law at the University of Munich had a budget of 2,000 marks in 1922. Yet the subscription price for a single scholarly journal was already 10,000 marks.[6] The purchase of foreign journals had become nearly impossible for any German library. But even the purchase of German books and journals was hampered, primarily as a result of the exorbitant price rise of paper. In 1920, leading German scientists and scholars founded the *Notgemeinschaft der deutschen Wissenschaft* (Emergency Society for German Science and Scholarship) with the hope that sponsorship from German industry and business would help to alleviate the situation. Unfortunately, these efforts were only of very limited success.[7]

At the same time, German universities experienced a flood of new students when tens of thousands of demobilized soldiers enrolled after the war. During the summer semester of 1918, 80,000 students were studying at German universities, by 1923 this number had increased to 112,000.[8] Many of them worked while studying to ensure a most rudimentary standard of living. Their prospects for a future career in academia or education looked dim. There were far too few positions available for university graduates. For the first time, a kind of academic proletariat grew up in Germany.

The hardest blow for professors and researchers during the inflation was the rapid devaluation of their income. The total compensation of a professor in Wilhelmine and Weimar Germany consisted of two parts: his basic salary as a higher civil servant (*höherer Beamter*) and a fee students had to pay for attending lectures, seminars, or to take exams. In addition, some added income resulted from scholarly publications or consultations. As many of the students were already impoverished, fees were held at a relatively constant level after the war. In addition, the higher civil servant salaries increased only slowly during the inflation. The effect was not only that a professor's income in 1922 had shriveled to one-third of his real prewar income. What often proved to be the greatest humiliation was the decline of the salary in comparison to other social groups. In 1913, the salary of a higher civil servant was seven times that of an unskilled worker. In 1922, a professor earned only 1.8 times more than an unskilled worker.[9]

For some left-wing intellectuals, the economic destruction of the intellectual classes was the logical consequence of the crisis of capitalism. The economist Emil Lederer argued: "We cannot solve the crisis of intellectual work without at the same time opening up the question of how social labor is at all possible at higher levels. We have to deal with the crisis of capitalism if we want to do away with the crisis of intellectual labor."[10]

Yet for the majority of intellectuals, especially members of German academia, the frightening compression of income differences between salaried intellectuals and workers was not greeted as a call for solidarity with the working masses against capital, but rather as an "immoral perversion of conditions," as a contributor wrote in *Die Weltbühne* of 21 June 1923. He complained that a school director was now earning less than a janitor and that engineers and architects made less money than locksmiths and bricklayers. This position in *Die Weltbühne* is symptomatic of a basic discussion that emerged from the concrete economic circumstances of intellectuals during the early 1920s. The inflation fundamentally rearranged social relationships, and almost all participants in the discussion realized that even after a currency reform, things would never be the same. It was thus all the more urgent for intellectuals to reflect on their role and their work in this newly emerging society.

Cultural Capital and the Dynamics of Inflation

On 21 September 1922 the sociologist Alfred Weber (1868–1958) gave the keynote address at the yearly general convention of the *Verein für Sozialpolitik in Eisenach*. Founded in 1872 and celebrating its fiftieth anniversary at this convention, the *Verein für Sozialpolitik* was the most important and respected scholarly association for social scientists in Wilhelmine and Weimar Germany. Alfred Weber, the brother of Max Weber, had long been an active member in the *Verein* and was well known not only as a cultural sociologist but also as a political figure, being one of the founders of the left-liberal *Deutsche Demokratische Partei*. His convention address *Die Not des Geistigen Arbeiters* (The Distress of the Intellectual Worker) was the most widely discussed document on the inflation's impact on German intellectuals at the time. I have chosen Weber's keynote address because of its representative character. It captures the self-understanding and the fears of many mainstream bourgeois professors, scientists, and writers of the time. Reading this text of 1922, I was struck by the many echoes and similarities it has with the cultural sociology of Pierre Bourdieu. Thus, interpreting *Die Not des Geistigen Arbeiters* through a dialogue with Bourdieu's work will link this text to modern cultural studies and at the same time elucidate the historical specificity of Weber's reflection on the changing status of intellectuals as a result of the inflation.

Just like Alfred Weber in *Die Not des Geistigen Arbeiters*, Bourdieu is concerned with the social and economic parameters that shape cultural production. Bourdieu's most influential analytic term is probably that of *cultural capital*, which he defines as "a form of knowledge, an internalized code or a cognitive acquisition for or a competence in deciphering cultural relations and cultural artifacts."[11] Like economic capital, cultural capital is not equally distributed throughout society, yet most important is the fact that the possession of economic capital does not necessarily imply possession of cultural or symbolic capital, and vice versa.[12]

Important to my analysis of Alfred Weber's speech is the specific relationship between cultural production and its surrounding society that Bourdieu developed in his 1983 article "The Field of Cultural Production: The Economic World Reversed." While he refers in this article mainly to artistic production (paintings, poetry, novels), the same principles hold also largely true for the works of scholars and scientists. For Bourdieu, the field of cultural production in general is structured by the opposition between two subfields. The first one is the field of "restricted production" and is largely synonymous with "high culture." Bourdieu characterizes this field as "production for producers": poets who write largely for an audience that consists mostly of connoisseurs and other poets, scholars who usually address their specialized works to a small audience of other scholars. The goal is not economic profit but rather different forms of "symbolic profit" such as prestige and artistic or scholarly celebrity that results paradoxically from, as Bourdieu writes, "the profit one has on seeing oneself (or being seen) as one who is not searching for profit."[13] A whole network of cultural institutions such as museums, libraries, and the educational system sustain the existence of this field. The other subfield is defined by "large-scale production." It contains popular culture, the world of television, of large-scale cinematic productions, of lifestyle magazines, of the bestseller book market. Here economic capital and monetary profits play a dominant role, products are geared towards a wide audience, and while formal experimentation is rare, this field does sometimes borrow from avant-garde concepts that are developed in the field of restricted cultural production.[14]

Bourdieu regards these subfields as the result of two principles of hierarchization that struggle with each other: "the heteronomous principle, favorable to those who dominate the field economically and politically and the autonomous principle which those who advocate it identify with [a] degree of independence from the economy, seeing temporal failure as a sign of election and success as a sign of compromise."[15] However, the heteronomous and the autonomous principles are both ideal types. At one extreme, a cultural product that would be completely submitted to external economic forces would eventually become unrecognizable as a cultural product. At the other extreme, a radically autonomous work or art that disregards any institutional setting or response by an audience would run the risk of being denied any reception at all and would soon be forgotten. In reality, each cultural product contains a unique mixture of both principles. Bourdieu points out that the field of "restricted cultural production" is marked by the constant effort of its members to exclude those whose work is considered to be compromised by economic profits. Yet as much autonomy and critical distance the producers of "restricted cultural productions" may claim from the dominant, economically and politically powerful class, Bourdieu nevertheless considers them as members of the dominant class because of their possession of symbolic capital. Thus, he refers to intellectuals and artists as a "dominated fraction of the dominant class."[16]

Let me now link Pierre Bourdieu's work to Alfred Weber's speech and the situation of the intellectuals in the early 1920s. It is remarkable how Weber's speech of 1922 unintentionally employs many of Bourdieu's theoretical parameters. The speech "The Distress of the Intellectual Worker" is a spirited defense of "restricted cultural production," and at the same time a tacit avowal that the effects of the inflation on social conditions radically called into question the possibility of intellectual independence. At the beginning of his address, Weber tries to define "intellectual work." Is all work that requires intellectual means therefore "intellectual work?" Are white-collar workers such as insurance agents, salesmen, and lower-level civil servants "intellectual workers?" Obviously not, and he legitimizes the special status of real "intellectual workers" by invoking the same principles of "cultural capital" that Bourdieu describes. Intellectual work for Weber is not entangled in any kind of functional relationship towards an economic goal. "The intellectual and artistic endeavor is … first and foremost a mental unloading [*seelische Entladung*] of productive intellects whose thinking is naturally anchored in the general public [*im Allgemeinen*]."[17] And foreshadowing Bourdieu's principle of autonomy, Weber writes:

> Such work, as much as it comes in contact with ruling social forces, may not be directed towards money. … Economic matters may only provide a provisional footstool on which such work can rest in a moment of exhaustion. Intellectual work is distorted and devalued, when it is being done for monetary gain [*ein Geldberuf wird*]. The artist or the scholar who strives for money becomes a scoundrel; and even the writer, the journalist, the physician, and the lawyer—all those for whom money plays an important role are, in my opinion, jeopardized. … The value of intellectual work for the society as a whole cannot be calculated, it is not quantifiable, not measurable.

> Most of art, literature, and basic science may appear as not essential to life, something that one could demolish or let deteriorate without being disturbed in one's comfort.[18]

Weber establishes here a strong demarcation line defending pure cultural production against the intrusion of those heteronomous forces that would submit intellectual work to economic factors. He vehemently disavows that such intellectual work has any measurable economic value, thus defining it as part of what Bourdieu calls "restricted cultural production."

Furthermore, Bourdieu stresses that despite the lack of economic capital, intellectual work creates a strong cohesion among the dominant class in a given society. Weber is equally aware of this mechanism. He identifies the dominant class as the main consumers of intellectual work and the main providers for the next generation of "intellectual workers." Most importantly, Weber shares with Bourdieu the same understanding of the paradoxical position of critical high culture within capitalism. In the course of two or three generations, economically successful bourgeois families had amassed so much capital that the next generation could to some degree live off this capital. A new group emerged that Alfred Weber calls *Rentenintellektuelle*, rentier intellectuals.

Weber considers this group as a "last independent island outside strict class interests, an asylum for ideas and arguments that were not linked to the economic." And he continues: "The social-reformist and socialist critique of capitalism … during the second half of the nineteenth-century would not have been possible without their existence; the proletariat would probably have been without leaders."[19] Like Bourdieu, Weber places the position of the critical intellectual not at the margins of capitalist society, but rather at its very core.

Yet all of this describes a world that in June of 1922 had largely vanished. The inflation, Alfred Weber points out, had destroyed the capital savings of the rentier intellectuals, had led to the rapid decline of salaried incomes for intellectual workers, and had caused the decline of universities, museums, libraries, and theaters. Weber warns his audience not to naively believe that things would return back to the old situation after the inflation. "These changes have been too deep, and they have affected the fundamental relationship between the intellectual sphere and the rest of life, especially the economic sphere."[20] Weber foresees that as a result of the inflation, with its trend towards industrial concentration, Germany will enter an era of a "limitless reign of the economic" in which all intellectual life will be swallowed up by business interests.[21] Cultural life will simply become an "appendage" of the economic sphere.[22] In other words, the traditional economic base for the field of "restricted cultural production" had been largely destroyed by the inflation.

Nevertheless, Weber's thoughts on how to rescue intellectual life imply an embrace of the economic realities. He predicts that a new type of intellectual will replace the rentier intellectual. The *Arbeitsintellektuelle* (worker intellectual) will combine his intellectual education with a practical training that will allow him to earn a steady income. He will be part of the newly emerging class of educated white-collar workers who will take over the role of the disappearing *Bildungsbürgertum* and become his main audience. Weber also advises intellectuals to organize themselves in unions, even though he realizes that the very nature of their product would make it difficult to fight for such goals as common wage structures. In his speech, Weber indicates that he himself doubts whether he had the strength to become such an *Arbeitsintellektueller*, combining practical work and intellectual pursuits. The discussion that followed his address raised indeed serious questions about the feasibility of his concept.

Weber's desperate attempt to give some practical advice to his audience indicates how helpless he and many other intellectuals were in the face of the unfolding inflation. As an economic force, it destroyed their material livelihood, yet there is an additional, partially hidden aspect to this traumatic experience that needs to be further analyzed. The specific and unique dynamics of inflation called the very worth of restricted cultural production into question. This aspect has not so much to do with the status of writers, artists, and scholars, but rather with the status of their products, with the status of high culture and "restricted cultural production" under the conditions of a rapid devaluation of money.

The Value of Art and Intellectual Work

First of all, inflation resulted in an overwhelming sense that the out-of-control circulation of money would engulf every aspect of people's life, that everything would become quantifiable in an unpredictable, often senseless maelstrom of devaluation. In that sense, monetary inflation exposed, attacked, and devalued a core principle of restricted cultural production. As Alfred Weber puts it, "The value of intellectual work ... cannot be calculated, is not quantifiable, and cannot be measured."[23] This definition declares intellectual work to be incommensurable with the basic functions of money: it appears as the complete opposite of money. It implies that intellectual and also artistic work possesses an immunity against the forces of monetary circulation. In short, intellectual and artistic work is "invaluable." On the one hand, this "invaluable" quality of intellectual work, according to the paradoxical principle of an "economic world reversed" predestines it as a source of cultural capital. On the other hand, with the destruction of a class that once needed this cultural capital for its cohesion and identity, the term *invaluable* unveils its other, ugly meaning: because it cannot be measured in monetary terms, it suddenly, under the condition of inflation, loses its worth rapidly. The following cartoon plays on this difference of meaning.

The scene takes place against the distant backdrop of the Brandenburg Gate in Berlin. A shabbily dressed German, most probably a member of the *Bildungsbürgertum*, holds a truly "invaluable" piece of art under his arm: Rembrandt's *The Man with the Helmet*. The scene echoes an all too familiar and traumatic situation during the inflation: the impoverished middle class, having lost all of its savings, has to sell its most cherished possessions such as art, books, and jewelry in order to survive. In the illustration, the impoverished *Bürger* is approached by a stereotypical American who brings with him a barrel labeled "American bacon."[24] The cartoon's shock effect lies only partially in the suggestion that anybody in his right mind would ever trade this Rembrandt painting at all. It is heightened by the crudeness of the barter situation. By claiming that the main quality of the painting is its age, the American legitimizes his offer of trading an old painting for old lard. It is interesting how the illustration plays here with the principle of a "reversed economy" inherent in the field of high culture. As a work of art, the painting is in part so valuable because of its age. The age of *The Man with the Helmet* proves that it harbors an immaterial, a timeless, almost spiritual value that has survived throughout the centuries. Within the sphere of economic production, age indicates just the opposite: the older an object, the less value it has—old lard being a quite drastic example. Obviously, the illustration allows for a further interpretation: the viewer may decide that the American knows all too well that the age of a painting cannot be compared to the age of lard, that he is just pretending to be an "uncultured American" in order to strike a great deal.

The scene exposes a brutal invasion and annexation; it depicts the dominance of the "heterogeneous principle" of economic capital with the goal of profit over the "principle of autonomy" embodied in the priceless work of art. In that sense, the Rembrandt painting stands for all other products of "restricted cultural production": the work of avant-garde artists, of writers as well as scholars. In a culture of inflation in which everything is drawn into circula-

Figure 14.1.
Eduard Thöny,
Starving Germany:
"Well, you give me
your old painting,
and I give you
my old lard,"
Simplicissimus 24.
(12 November
1919): 456.

tion and exchange, be it monetary or barter exchange, everything becomes calculable and exchangeable, even an "invaluable" painting turns into just another object to be bought, sold, or bartered. Repudiating its artistic, "intellectual" value, the worth of the painting is determined by the crudest form of materialism: it is old, therefore, it's not worth more than old lard.

Inflation and Mass Culture

While Alfred Weber's speech is an in-depth analysis of the fate of "restricted cultural production," he remains strangely silent about the sphere of "large-scale cultural production," although the period of inflation was accompanied by an unprecedented rise of a new mass culture, with its dance revues, sporting events, and, above all, the new medium of film. Could it be that this emerging mass culture that exemplifies Bourdieu's "heteronomous principle" of economic profit was conceived by Weber and his audience as part of the problem, as simply an extension of the economic forces, even as a "cultural inflation"?

Bourdieu's quite complex analysis of cultural production starts from a simple insight: the creation and existence of a cultural good is fundamentally shaped by the triangle of production, circulation, and consumption. The three parts of this triangle relate to each other in varying and historically unique ways. Bourdieu is careful not to introduce any kind of economic determinism into his investigations; literature, art, and intellectual life do not "reflect" the economic situation of a certain group or society, but rather constitute a field that "is relatively autonomous from the demands of politics and economics."[25]

Using Bourdieu's differentiation between "large-scale cultural production" and "restricted cultural production," we can conclude that both fields represent quite different models of a "cultural economy." In general, high culture tends to idolize the producer and his/her product, especially within the tradition of the Romantic artist/genius, while downplaying the distributive and consumptive side that involves the censoring or supportive force of publishers and gallerists, audience reception, the role of critics, etc. Popular culture, on the other hand, tends to be more concerned with the distributive and consumptive sides of cultural products.

It is significant that in the critical discourse of the 1920s, two very different concepts of consumption were applied to high culture and to mass culture. The enjoyment of high culture was believed to leave the consumer with an asset of lasting value. The two operative terms here are *Sammlung* (collecting, saving) and *Bildung* (formation, education, accumulation, growth). The very concept of high culture was organized around these principles; it was regarded as a savings account of (national) culture that would accrue a steady amount of interest over time. Popular culture, on the other hand, was believed to be consumed without any savings accumulating. Here the operative terms are *Zerstreuung* (entertainment, dissemination, distraction) and what I may call, for lack of a better term, *Vergessen* (forgetting, escape from reality). Within these two cultural economies, money had a very different status and function. Mass culture fully integrated money through its reliance on wide circulation and consumption. High culture, as we have seen, tended to suppress or even deny its ultimate reliance on money.

While the inflation attacked the principles of *Sammlung* and *Bildung*, the cultural economy of large-scale production was much better suited to react to the onslaught of the inflation. Because its consumption was instantaneous, because it did not rely on the investment of cultural capital, because it was not related to an idea of formation and saving, and because it did not deny the centrality of money for its formation, mass culture provided, in a sense, the most suitable cultural economy for the period of inflation. One can push this point even further. From the perspective of a defensive, critical position of high culture, it can be easily argued that mass culture was so eminently suitable for the times of inflation because it presented in itself an "inflation of culture." It was closely intertwined with monetary circulation; it "devalued" cultural goods by orienting itself towards quantity rather than quality; its operative elements were the massification and circulation of cultural products. Its sense of time was *here* and *now*, its relationship to cultural tradition eclectic. Like the young speculators on the stock exchange, mass culture's producers and heroes often came socially out of nowhere and reached almost instantaneous fame overnight or were forgotten within a few months. My point is that the heated debate about the power and the dangers of mass culture during the 1920s received some of its intensity from the strong analogies between inflation and popular culture. For a member of the traditional *Bildungsbürgertum*, the attempt to integrate popular culture as a legitimate part of the overall spectrum of German cultural life was hampered by the simultaneous experience of inflation and the emergence of modern mass culture. The following caricature presents a fitting visual representation of this remarkable amalgamation between the dynamics of mass culture and inflation.

This illustration from *Simplicissimus* encapsulates the three dynamics of inflation that apply both to the cultural as well as the economic nature of the

Figure 14.2. G. Oelkranz, *Gutenberg and the Billion-Printing Press:* "I didn't intend this," *Simplicissimus* 27 (15 November 1922): 469.

currency devaluation. The ongoing massification is strikingly apparent as the printing machine is spewing out an uncontrolled stream of paper money. Closely related to the dynamic of massification is the aspect of devaluation that is captured in the way the paper money flows out of the machine. The rapid circulation that characterizes inflation is encoded both in the greedy hands that grip the money and in the big transmission wheels of the printing press.

The overriding thematic tension in this picture is created by the contrast between the running money-printing press and Johannes Gutenberg, who stands next to the machine holding his head and moaning in a mixture of consternation and panic: "I didn't intend this." The illustration depicts the two different kinds of cultural economies. The figure of Gutenberg holding a single, valuable book (possibly a copy of the Gutenberg Bible) in his hand symbolizes the field of restricted cultural production and the domain of high culture. What makes this illustration so insightful is the fact that the printing press contains two layers of meaning: it symbolizes both the inflation and the field of large-scale cultural production, for we can easily imagine that the next printing job of this machine will be another artifact of mass circulation, some pulp fiction or an entertainment magazine.

It is important to realize that the two different domains of cultural production are, nevertheless, linked by certain commonalities. These commonalities ensure that the Gutenberg figure is not just a perplexed bystander from a different century, but rather is thematically related to the unfolding mass production on the right side of the illustration. First of all, both domains share paper as a common material base. The big rolls of paper on the machine can be used to print books, paper money, or a mass-circulating magazine. Second, they share a common production technology, the printing press. Third, the illustration depicts Gutenberg as an inventor with doubts and self-accusations, and the picture poses the question to what extent he and his technology can be held responsible for the inflationary printing of money.

The question is framed within an interesting historical constellation by placing a fifteenth-century figure next to a modern printing press. This historical and cultural discontinuity urges the viewer to reflect on a common parameter that may bridge the apparent gap. What I see at the core of Gutenberg's seemingly shocked recognition concerns the fundamental character of reproduction and is closely related to Walter Benjamin's arguments about the effect of reproduction technologies in modern societies that he describes in his *Das Kunstwerk im Zeitalter seiner technischen Reproduzierbarkeit* (The Work of Art in the Age of Mechanical Reproduction).

Benjamin argues that the social and cultural effects of reproduction technology become especially apparent in the artwork's loss of aura, in its loss of authenticity. The reproduction of a work of art "detaches the reproduced object from the domain of tradition. By making many reproductions it substitutes a plurality of copies for a unique existence."[26] It is important to mention that "aura" is not just an attribute of a work of art. Modern mass societies in general, Benjamin argues, are characterized by a decay of aura that is caused by the desire of modern masses "to bring things 'closer' spatially and humanly, which is just as ardent as their bent toward overcoming the uniqueness of every reality by accepting its reproduction."[27]

The book that Gutenberg holds in his hand still seems to radiate an "aura." Within the context of this picture, it appears to be an almost sacred object. And yet the illustration forces us to partake in Gutenberg's belated and painful recognition: by inventing the technology of printing he has started a process of reproduction that invariably destroys the auratic qualities of the reproduced products, as the right side of the picture strikingly indicates. Benjamin registers this loss of aura, but he has also great hope in the formative power of reproduction technologies. For him, they create the potential for a new alignment between art and progressive social change, especially with the increasing importance of film in modern society.

In our context, however, a different scenario emerges. The illustration establishes a powerful link between reproduction and the creation of money that Benjamin does not mention in his essay. In many ways, we can understand the medium of money as the most anti-auratic force in modern society. Money, as Simmel observed, takes away the uniqueness of all objects; it functions as a powerful agent that indeed brings things closer, but also rips them out of a context of tradition. It is equally important to realize that money in its very essence is always a reproduced entity.[28] New money must be printed constantly within a functioning monetary system, yet this process of reproduction has to take place under strict control. Thus, money always embodies both the potential and the danger of reproduction. Walter Benjamin rightly states that modern societies communicate largely through symbolic and cultural forms that emerge from techniques of reproduction. What he fails to acknowledge is the hidden inflationary aspect that lurks within any process of reproduction: the fact that, as inflation shows, reproduction can become a limitless, out-of-control process that utterly devalues the product.

The enormous economic and social decline that many intellectual workers experienced during the inflation resulted in a fundamental discussion about their economic and social role in postwar Germany. I presented Alfred Weber's speech *Die Not des geistigen Arbeiters* as a representative text that in my mind captures the self-understanding and the fears of many German intellectuals during the inflation. Weber's speech is indicative of their status insecurity. With the demise of the *Rentenintellekuellen*, the cultural dominance of the *Bildungsbürgertum* had certainly ended, yet the question about the role and function of the *geistige Arbeiter* in the emerging, more economically oriented modern mass and media culture of the Weimar Republic remains largely unresolved.

In the second part of this essay, I argued that the specific dynamics of inflation called into question the worth and value of restricted cultural production, of those works of art and intellectual pursuit that were seen as incommensurable with economic exchange. In addition, inflation as a process of rapid massification and reproduction required a break with tradition and urged a sense of presentness into the everyday life of people. I argued that inflation stands in an analogous relationship with the different phenomena of mass culture such a film, dance revues, and sporting events that gained rapid popularity during the early 1920s.

The inflation came to a sudden end with the introduction of the *Rentenmark* in December of 1923. Its long-term cultural and sociopsychological effects are much more difficult to weigh than its economic consequences. What we can do, however, is try to uncover the different aspects of an experience that remains in the collective memory of Germans as one of the great traumas of the twentieth century.

Notes

This essay is based on chapter seven of my book *Culture and Inflation in Weimar Germany* (Berkeley 2001). It is reprinted here with permission of University of California Press.

1. Michael Charol, "Intellektuellendämmerung," *Der Kritiker* 2, no. 49/50 (1920): 6.
2. See Reinhard Wittmann, *Geschichte des deutschen Buchhandels: Ein Überblick* (München, 1991), 316.
3. See Anton Kaes, "Die ökonomische Dimension der Literatur: Zum Strukturwandel der Institution Literatur in der Inflationszeit (1918–1923)," in *Consequences of Inflation*, ed. Gerald Feldman et al. (Berlin, 1989), 309–10.
4. Georg Schreiber, *Die Not der deutschen Wissenschaft und der geistigen Arbeiter. Geschehnisse und Gedanken zur Kulturpolitik des Deutschen Reiches* (Leipzig, 1923), 5.
5. Schreiber, 18–19.
6. Schreiber, 22.
7. See Gerald D. Feldman, *The Great Disorder: Politics, Economics, and Society in the German Inflation, 1914–1924* (New York, 1993), 542–44.
8. See Fritz K. Ringer, *The Decline of the German Mandarins: The German Academic Community 1890–1933* (Cambridge, 1969), 65.
9. See Alfred Weber, *Die Not der Geistigen Arbeiter* (München, 1923), 42.
10. Quoted in Feldman, *The Great Disorder*, 551.
11. Randal Johnson, "Editor's Introduction: Pierre Bourdieu on Art, Literature and Culture," in Pierre Bourdieu, *The Field of Cultural Production: Essays on Art and Literature*, ed. Randal Johnson (Oxford, 1993), 7.
12. Symbolic capital is closely related to cultural capital and refers to the degree "of accumulated prestige, celebrity, consecration or honor and is founded on a dialectic of knowledge (connaissance) and recognition (reconnaissance)." See ibid.
13. Ibid., 15.
14. Ibid., 16.

15. Bourdieu, *The Field of Cultural Production,* 40.
16. Johnson, "Editor's Introduction," 15.
17. Weber, *Not der Geistigen Arbeiter,* 7.
18. Ibid.
19. Ibid., 14.
20. Ibid., 26.
21. Ibid., 27.
22. See ibid., 23.
23. Ibid., 7.
24. The dichotomy between American "materialism" and the German "pursuit of higher values" is a subtheme that accompanies the discussion about the role of intellectual. Georg Schreiber in his survey *Die Not der deutschen Wissenschaft und der geistigen Arbeiter,* for example, writes: "The intellectual worker is the administrator and producer of the intellectual capital [*geistiges Kapital*]. ... It has always been an advantage of German intellectual work that in contrast to the American and Asian intellectual life it could boast with intellectual billionaires [*Milliardäre des Geistes*]—even now despite the fact that these billionaires have become economically part of the proletariat" (110).
25. Johnson, "Editor's Introduction," 12.
26. Walter Benjamin, "The Work of Art in the Age of Mechanical Reproduction" in *Illuminations,* ed. Hannah Arendt, trans. Harry Zohn (New York, 1969), 221.
27. Ibid., 223.
28. It is noteworthy that money itself contains a certain auratic quality. The value of authenticity, of *Echtheit,* that marks the auratic work of art, is disseminated onto each paper bill. Different from the work of art, however, paper money knows no original. The insistence on authenticity is absolutely essential for the functioning of money because it draws a line between "real" money and counterfeit money.

PART V

Weimar Topographies

~:~

CHAPTER 15

Defining the Nation in Crisis
Citizenship Policy in the Early Weimar Republic

ANNEMARIE SAMMARTINO

Between 1918 and 1922, revolution and postwar settlements radically altered the political map of Europe. Postwar treaties did not simply redistribute territory in Central and Eastern Europe; rather, by allowing the principle of national self-determination to govern the territorial arrangements of the postwar world, these settlements legitimated nationalism as the most important organizing principle of the region. Self-determination meant different things to Ukrainian peasants, the Czech proletariat, and Polish intellectuals, but the slogan's power allowed it to capture the imagination of men and women across Central and Eastern Europe. New boundaries shaped national identities throughout the region, and at the same time, no state perfectly conformed to the abstract principle regarding the ideal congruence of nations and states. Instead, the ethnographic realities of Central and Eastern Europe meant that each state had a highly ambivalent relationship to national borders, and a series of overlapping territorial claims destabilized these settlements as soon as they were drawn up.[1] Revolution, war, postwar settlements, and migration joined forces to create a situation of fluidity and a sense of crisis across the region. Nationalism was enshrined as an organizing principle at the very same time that its meaning was thrown into crisis. What did nationality mean in countries contending with huge shifts of territory and population? How would the new postwar states, riven by deep political divisions, handle the nationality question in comparison to the empires they replaced?

The contentious debates inspired by the Weimar Republic's citizenship policy and practice in the first years after the republic's birth reflected the still unsettled meaning of the nation in postwar Germany. On the one hand, the new naturalization regulations of 1921 were defined more loosely, due to the newfound political clout of the Socialists, particularly in Prussia and Saxony. On the other, a newfound interest in *Auslandsdeutsche*, or foreigners of German descent, and concerns about the immigration of "undesirables" from Eastern Europe drove conservatives in Bavaria and elsewhere to emphasize ethnicity as the primary basis for citizenship claims. This debate tested the fragile equation of ethnicity and culture that formed the basis of the 1913 German citizenship law, which defined citizenship in terms of "ethnocultural" identity. The 1913 law itself had represented a delicate consensus, but even this was shattered in the wake of the war and postwar upheavals. In this essay, I examine how disparate cultural and ethnic definitions of the German nation competed with one another on both the national level and within individual German states in the years 1919 through 1922. The virulence of these disagreements in the early Weimar Republic reflected the symbolic weight of stabilizing German identity in the midst of such crisis. Their insolubility spoke to the deep and bitter lack of consensus about the meaning and boundaries of the German nation in the first years of the fledgling Weimar Republic.

Refugee Crisis

During the nineteenth century, Germany was a country of both immigration and emigration. Prior to World War I, the majority of foreigners in Germany were Polish migrant workers who entered Germany to work in mining or on Junker estates. The German state developed an extensive system of measures to keep track of these workers.[2] Additionally, the late nineteenth century bore witness to a wave of immigration of Eastern European Jews. At one time, as much as 10 percent of all Prussian gendarmes were stationed on the German-Russian frontier, rules were established requiring identity cards for all immigrants, and 1,000-mark fines were imposed on smugglers who helped immigrants cross the border. Yet even such drastic measures failed to halt the immigration of Eastern European Jews to Germany.[3] Mass expulsions of Jews took place in Prussia in 1884–85 and 1904–1906, but restrictionist campaigns foundered on fears that harsh treatment of Jewish immigrants could negatively affect Germany's image in the world.[4] The Wilhelmine state proved itself incapable of limiting migration to those categories of immigrants it found necessary, namely, Polish seasonal workers imported to work on the large Prussian estates. Although xenophobic rhetoric waxed and waned during the *Kaiserreich* depending largely on economic imperatives, public discourse generally presented Jews and Poles alike as "products of the backward East, speakers of inferior languages and elements of subversion."[5]

The war and postwar period brought another wave of immigrants to Germany, in particular refugees displaced by the dislocations of these conflicts. John Hope Simpson has counted nearly 10 million refugees on the European continent in the mid-1920s.[6] Whether they were fleeing revolution or border revisions, it is exceedingly difficult to determine definitively the number of refugees in Germany during and after World War I.[7] Those refugees comprised approximately four groups: Germans who lived in territories lost as a result of the redrawing of German borders according to the Treaty of Versailles; Germans who had lived elsewhere in Eastern Europe before the war, including Russia; Eastern European Jews; and finally, non-Jewish, non-German refugees from Czarist Russia. This fourth category is the most difficult to define, but encompasses refugees from various ethnic backgrounds who had lived in the Russian empire before the peace settlements of 1918. According to Claudena Skran, the majority of the refugees arrived in Germany in 1919 as Russia plunged into full-scale civil war and the territorial revisions mandated by the Treaty of Versailles went into effect.[8] Scholars estimate that the border shifts that took place in Eastern Europe in the course of the postwar settlements displaced between 1 and 1.3 million "Germans."[9] Inclusion of the Russian Germans (*Rußlanddeutsche*) increases the number of refugees by approximately another 120,000.[10] There were approximately 70,000 Eastern European Jews.[11] Finally, historians estimate that a half-million non-Jewish, non-German Russians sought refuge in Germany between 1917 and 1922.[12]

The massive number of refugees inspired widespread fears about an inundation of the Reich with foreigners during the first few years of the Weimar Republic. In February 1920, police in Frankfurt an der Oder appealed to the Prussian border police, calling for a more vigorous defense of the border and listing the hardships that migrants from the East "inflicted" on the German people, including housing shortages, increased pressure on the food supply, and the importation of Bolshevik ideas.[13] Echoing these complaints, the German Society for Population Politics (Deutsche Gesellschaft für Bevölkerungspolitik) warned the Reich interior ministry about the deleterious effects of this migration: "Since the end of the war, a great migration [*Abwanderung*] from Russia and the former Russian section of Poland to Germany has begun. From month to month, this migration is becoming culturally and economically more dangerous for the German people."[14]

In establishing new citizenship policies and practices for the Weimar Republic, both national and local state officials rarely dealt with the practical challenges of immigration and the refugee crisis. Indeed in the early years of the Republic, even Social Democratic Prussia approved only slightly more than half of the citizenship applications it received. Between 1921 and 1923 the numbers of citizenship applications that Prussia approved increased by 250 percent— from 6,953 to 17,848. In those same years the number of approved applications from "foreigners from the East of non-German descent" (*fremdstämmige Ostausländer*) decreased from 757 to 309.[15] According to these figures, no more than 30,000 people applied for citizenship in Prussia in any given year, most of whom were ethnic Germans from Eastern Europe. Yet in those same years, hundreds of thousands of foreigners arrived on German soil. Thus, few of these new immigrants—and especially the Eastern European Jews who inspired the most fear in German officialdom—actually applied for German citizenship.[16]

However, although few of these new migrants were actually applying for citizenship, the migration crisis increased pressure on the state to define the symbolic limits of the German national community. The national citizenship regulations that were drawn up in 1920 and implemented in 1921 justified their limitations on new naturalizations through references to the influx of foreigners and the demands that they placed upon Germany.[17] In 1923, the Bavarian interior minister referred to difficulties created by the "flood of immigrants" to explain the necessity of a restrictive naturalization policy:

> I need to constantly stress the economic difficulties created by the flood of immigrants of foreign descent, in particular, the ways in which they create pressure on the market for jobs and apartments. The danger is even greater since a large portion of these foreigners have built their existence on the destruction of the economic life of Germany and would not be able to advance if Germany were a healthy nation. It is tempting to think that granting citizenship only to those foreigners from the East who have been in Germany for years and have "adapted themselves to German culture" is without great consequence. However, we must not forget that the renewed immigration of Eastern elements has provided fresh blood to this community and so the cases of foreigners from the East must be dealt with even more carefully.[18]

Interestingly, the tangible benefits that citizenship would confer upon foreigners, such as state unemployment benefits or voting rights, and the reasons why these might increase the danger posed by foreigners residing in Germany did not play a role in the official discussion of naturalization. Instead, debates about citizenship often emphasized the competition for scarce resources within Germany, even though immigrants—who, for the most part, could or would not be deported—would continue to compete for these resources regardless of whether they were citizens.[19] Citizenship policies and practices could not and were not designed to actually control the numbers or types of foreigners within Germany. Rather, citizenship policy functioned as a battleground upon which German officials debated the meaning of the German nation. The opening salvos in this conflict began almost immediately after the republic's foundation.

Citizenship Policy and Practice

The citizenship law of 22 July 1913 governed citizenship policy during the Weimar Republic. Rogers Brubaker has argued that the 1913 law represented the triumph of the principle of *jus sanguinis* (law of blood) over *jus soli* (law of the soil, i.e., residency), defining Germany as a community of descent and thus marking "the nationalization, even the ethnicization, of German citizenship."[20] According to Dietmar Schirmer, "The effect [of the 1913 law] was the decoupling of German-ness and the German nation-state. Of course, if German-ness is deterritorialized, so that those in possession of it cannot lose it regardless of their conditions, the reverse must also be true. Whoever does not have German blood cannot acquire German-ness, no matter how hard he or she tries."[21] According to this law, candidates for naturalization submitted their applications to local offices, where they were reviewed and then forwarded for approval to the Interior Ministries of the various German states. Each federal state was then required to submit a list of potential citizenship applicants for review by the other federal states, which were allowed to raise objections to those they considered undeserving of citizenship in the Reich. In cases of disagreement, a committee of the *Reichsrat*, the upper house of parliament comprised of representatives from each of the federal states, decided applicants' citizenship status by a majority vote.[22]

In 1919, Wolfgang Heine, the interior minister for the Social Democratic Prussian government, articulated some guiding principles for the adjudication of citizenship applications in the new republic. Heine negotiated a fine line between statist and ethnic definitions of German citizenship. On the one hand, he stated that it was a national duty to repatriate those former Germans who immigrated to Germany, without exception. With regard to foreigners seeking naturalization, he noted that they surely did not do so for their own personal gain, since there was little a weakened Germany could give them; therefore, they must be motivated by "a firm inner connection to the German state."[23] Heine thus called for the naturalization of all applicants who had served in the war or had sons who had served, including Jews and Poles.[24] The nationalist government in Bavaria, which took power after the crushing of the Communist *Räterepublik* in spring 1919, opposed Heine's proposed naturalization policy. Fearing that the Reich might be overwhelmed with Eastern European Jews, the Bavarian government framed its objections in terms of the impact of mass immigration on Germany's national and economic interests.[25]

This conflict between the two largest states in the republic led to a conference in 1920 and the drafting of national guidelines for determining the citizenship of those immigrants who arrived in Germany after the end of the war.[26] In light of the growing numbers of migrants from the East, the guidelines of the Reich's Interior Ministry took a cautious approach to the granting of citizenship.[27] Keeping in mind the shortages of housing, food, and work that plagued the new republic, they instructed local governments "only to accept people that demonstrate a positive population growth in a political, cultural, and economic respect." The most important criterion of suitability for citizenship was a foreigner's "way of life, namely, in Germany itself, that expresses a sufficient understanding for the German way of life and for his public-legal responsibilities in the federal state and the community."[28] Positive indicators included: "birth in Germany and an upbringing according to German methods and in a German environment, having a German mother, or marriage to a German in combination with a long-term, trouble-free life in Germany."[29]

German ancestry was an important test of an applicant's suitability for German citizenship. But the ministry guidelines also listed other factors, such as residence in Germany, exposure to German methods of child rearing and education, etc., implying that ancestry alone was not a sufficient basis for a citizenship claim and that culture had an important role in forging this connection to Germany. The guidelines further specified that an applicant should be able to "prove that he possesses a German character [*Eigenart*] and the ability to fit into the German cultural community. Here too, it is certain that foreigners of German descent are more likely to fulfill this standard than others."[30] The phrase "more likely" reflected a certain ambivalence on the part of those who drafted the guidelines. They recognized the importance of descent while not deeming it the sole determinative of German character. Rather, German descent was important mainly insofar as it made one "more likely" to have internalized German culture.

While the specific criteria of the Interior Ministry's guidelines are interesting, so too are what these guidelines omitted. A draft circulated among the German states a year earlier contained two clauses that did not appear in the final document; the first strictly forbade granting citizenship to foreigners from the East of non-German descent, while the second would have bestowed citizenship on the second generation of this group of foreigners, thus continuing prewar policy. These two clauses foundered in the face of opposition from the Prussians, whose representative objected that "such clauses would signal a return to Prussia's earlier Poland policy and must be avoided. The applications of *fremdstämmige Ostausländer* must be reviewed along the same principles applied to other applications."[31] Interesting as well is the fact that in their final version, the policy guidelines did not reflect Heine's willingness to grant citizenship to men who had fought in the German army. As it was, the citizenship guidelines so painstakingly argued over in late 1920 had little effect on naturalization policy in the individual states. Despite its absence from these citizenship guidelines, service, including but not limited to military service, and cultural assimilation both played a role in the adjudication of citizenship cases.[32] Rather, after the guidelines went into effect, conflicts about the worthiness of *fremdstämmige Ostausländer* for citizenship continued, pitting the principles of cultural assimilation and ethnic determinism against one another as before. There was no marked difference between the handling of citizenship cases before and after the release of the guidelines in 1921.

Social Democrats controlled the Prussian state, which also had the largest number of foreigners in the Reich throughout the early Weimar period. As noted above, Prussian naturalization practice tended to recognize the potential for the assimilation of foreigners to a greater degree than that of Bavaria, which insisted upon longer residency periods than Prussia. Yet to say that Prussia was more accepting of nonethnic Germans does not mean that its representatives entirely ignored ethnicity in adjudicating naturalization applications. Indeed, Prussian officials turned to the Fürsorgeverein für deutsche Rückwanderer (Aid Association for Returning German Migrants), an organization founded in 1909 to encourage the migration of *Auslandsdeutsche* to Germany and to verify applicants' German descent. The Prussian state often denied applications of recent immigrants who were not of German descent.[33] Officials routinely assumed that non-German applicants were trying to get German citizenship solely for reasons of expediency. For example, the police president of Berlin accused the "Russian-Polish factory worker, Abraham Halpern, Jewish religion" of only wishing to keep his job to avoid deportation and separation from his German wife."[34] The police president was doubtful that Halpern had demonstrated a sufficient "firm inner connection" to Germany despite marrying a German woman. He did not sympathize with Halpern's desire to maintain his livelihood and family. Halpern's familial obligations were deemed to be entirely personal and were looked upon with suspicion.

Nonetheless, non-Germans (even Jews) could receive the approval of the Prussian state for their citizenship applications. In 1920, Württemberg forwarded to the Prussians the application of Aisik Borodowisch, a Jewish factory owner who had resided in Germany since 1903 and had unsuccessfully applied for citizenship in 1908, 1909, 1911, and 1916. Citing his military service and the fact that he did not signify a danger to the public order, the Württemberg minister of the interior recommended that Borodowisch be granted citizenship, a recommendation accepted by the Prussian Interior Ministry.[35] The police president of Berlin forwarded the application of the Jewish doctor Helene Eliasberg to the Prussian Interior Ministry after she submitted recommendations from the Charité Hospital and the Ministry for Science, Art, and Public Education.[36] Yet even applicants who, on the basis of their names at least, appeared to be of German descent were sometimes denied citizenship because they were considered to be "alien [*Wesensfremd*] to Germandom." In December 1921, a local official recommended that the Prussian Interior Ministry reject the application of the miner Johann Müller, because he was barely competent in the German language, despite his long-term residence in Germany. Moreover, this official presumed that Müller only applied for citizenship in order to avoid the regulations that applied to foreigners and was actually considering returning to Russia for work.[37] Much like Halpern, his desire to secure his livelihood was a factor against recommending Müller's application. In several cases, various federal states contested the citizenship applications of suspected Communists even though they were of undisputed German descent.[38]

At the same time, those who were of German descent could surmount obstacles that a non-German could not hope to overcome. In 1919 the Prussian interior minister approved the naturalization of a Russian citizen of German descent, Johann Bergerack, despite his robbery conviction and ten-day jail sentence in December 1914. The local official who sent the application to the Prussian Interior Ministry wrote: "As a German returnee, Bergerack is to be considered a desirable addition to the population. I am approving his application considering his unobjectionable conduct since he was punished." With this recommendation, the Prussian Interior Ministry approved his application.[39] Similarly, the unemployed factory worker Anna Donat, another person of German descent from Russia, was judged a desirable addition to the population although she had only been in Germany since 1916 and was unemployed at the time of her application.[40] Finally, the Berlin police president recommended an applicant named Milsch even though he was a "known homosexual," because he was both of German descent and had served honorably in the war, receiving the Iron Cross and behaving, to the knowledge of the police president at least, "morally" during the time of his service.[41]

Although Prussia was more willing to grant citizenship to applicants of German descent, descent was only one criterion, albeit an important one. In general, it appears that Prussian officials followed Heine's dual citizenship policy that viewed citizenship as a privilege based on German descent and public utility. They favored those who had performed military service, or, as in the case of Eliasberg, the doctor, other publicly useful tasks. At the same time, Prussian Interior Ministry officials were wary of applicants whose applications for citizenship appeared to be motivated by personal gain. A lofty and "firm inner connection" to Germany was to become a crucial criterion for the award of citizenship rather than more limited personal goals of improving one's own life or that of one's family.

The case of Moritz Estersohn, a Russian citizen who applied for Prussian citizenship in 1919, after over twenty years of residence in Germany, represents one intriguing instance in which the Prussian Interior Ministry challenged local officials' rejection of an applicant for German citizenship. Precisely because it was not a clear-cut case, the Estersohn case illustrates some of the tensions that underlay citizenship policy in the early Weimar Republic. Estersohn first submitted his application for naturalization in 1919. After the local government in Arnsberg rejected his application in August of that year, the Prussian Interior Ministry inquired as to the reasons for the rejection, noting that, according to his name and religion, he appeared to be of "*German* nationality."[42] The mayor of Hagen, where Estersohn was living, responded that Estersohn had been punished for insubordination and the theft of some potatoes while serving in the army. Furthermore, the mayor emphasized that *Freikorps* units had arrested Estersohn and used this as proof that he "belonged to political circles that wanted to destroy the peace of the population." The mayor added that Estersohn was originally Jewish and had only converted in 1898.[43] Even in the face of these seemingly damning allegations, the Prussian government still considered forwarding Estersohn's application to the other German states for approval. The Prussian commissioner for public order challenged this apparent leniency towards Estersohn, reiterating the objections initially raised by the mayor of Hagen that Estersohn was a Communist, Jew, and thief, and adding that he was a profiteer besides.[44] Estersohn was rich enough to hire his own lawyer, who responded to these accusations by noting that his client had served two and a half years in the army although he was a Russian citizen at the time. Furthermore, the lawyer denied that Estersohn was a Communist, affirming that he belonged instead to the SPD.[45] The records do not indicate if the Prussian government ultimately awarded citizenship to Estersohn, and even if it had, it is highly doubtful that Bavaria or other more conservative states would have approved his application. Nonetheless, the bureaucratic exchanges over Estersohn's citizenship case continued through at least mid-1921. Estersohn's citizenship case became entangled in two seeming irreconcilable images. The Prussian Interior Ministry could not decide if he was a successful businessman, long-term resident, and war veteran, or if he was a Jewish, Communist war profiteer and thief.[46] Caught between these two potential Estersohns, the ministry seemed unable or unwilling to decide between them.

In the case of conflict, naturalization decisions were forwarded to a committee in the *Reichsrat*, in which each state had a vote and the majority's decision carried. In the *Reichsrat*, the German states tended to split between those that held to the Bavarians' more conservative line, such as Württemberg, and others that followed a more liberal policy, such as Prussia and Saxony.[47] Indeed, the Bavarians, who were firmly committed to a *jus sanguinis* or ethnic approach to citizenship, proactively used their veto power to force votes in the *Reichsrat* on applicants they considered unacceptable.[48] Although the Reich's guidelines set a ten-year residency minimum for the acceptance of citizenship applications from those of non-German descent, the Bavarians applied their own standard of a twenty-year waiting period to the applications of *fremdstämmige Ostausländer*, routinely rejecting applications from other federal states that did not fulfill this criterion.[49] The Saxons and Prussians repeatedly complained to the national Interior Ministry that Bavaria prevented them from exercising their own citizenship policy by using its veto power to enforce its more restrictive guidelines.[50]

Saxony in particular objected to the Bavarians' heavy-handed use of their veto power in the *Reichsrat*. The Interior Ministry of the SPD/USPD coalition that governed Saxony during the first years of the republic repeatedly submitted citizenship applications to the other German states for approval, even when the applicants had been in the country fewer than twenty years or were otherwise likely to provoke a Bavarian veto. Opinion was divided in Saxony about this strategy. While the Dresden District Office complained about the Bavarian veto policy, some within the ministry argued that Saxony should not recommend the naturalization of foreigners who were inevitably destined for a Bavarian veto.[51]

The case of Johann Goluchowski demonstrates the lengths to which the Saxon interior minister, Robert Lipinski, was willing to go to protest Bavarian intransigence.[52] Goluchowski served in the German army for a little more than a year during the war, but otherwise appeared ill suited for German citizenship, especially according to Bavaria's strict standards. Goluchowski was an illiterate and unemployed Russian-Pole who had only lived in Germany since 1910. When the Leipzig authorities forwarded his case to the Interior Ministry for approval in November 1919, they noted their reservations regarding his naturalization.[53] Nonetheless, in a letter to the Leipzig District Office from May 1922, Lipinski stated that he saw no reason to deny Goluchowski citizenship. Lipinski regarded Goluchowski's lack of employment as temporary and he countered accusations that Goluchowski did not speak German by stating that he had spoken enough German to serve in the army. Lipinski even explained Goluchowski's criminal conviction from early 1922 as a minor setback, one that was more than offset by his otherwise unblemished record.[54] Lipinski's promotion of Goluchowski's application reflects his resolute refusal to accept the citizenship criteria that Bavaria sought to impose on the other German states. Furthermore, since by 1922 it was more than clear that Goluchowski had no hope of approval from Bavaria, Lipinski's insistence on Goluchowski's candidacy for naturalization can also be seen as an attempt to test the patience of the Bavarians.[55]

It is important to keep in mind that even the Bavarian state did not deny Jews access to German citizenship. At least in theory, an Eastern European Jew could apply for citizenship after a twenty-year residency period. The Bavarians claimed that this time frame represented the minimum time necessary for an Eastern Jew to acquire German cultural values.[56] In practice, this policy did not necessarily mean that the Bavarian government would actually grant citizenship to those Jews who fulfilled this residency period. Yet it does make clear the importance in the political climate of the early Weimar Republic of phrasing its opposition in terms of a residency requirement, rather than a total ban on citizenship for Eastern European Jews. Even the Bavarian twenty-year waiting period was itself a departure from prewar practice, in which immigrant Jews were not usually able to gain citizenship until the third generation of residence in Germany. Put another way, had the Bavarian state proposed a twenty-year residency requirement in 1913, this would have been a very progressive stance, but seven years later, the twenty-year requirement represented the extreme nationalist position.

When faced with a non-German citizen who had lived for a long period of time in Germany, the Bavarians occasionally relented and allowed this person to be naturalized. For example, David Linick, a prosperous Jewish businessman who had resided in Germany for eighteen years and "had an understanding for the German way of life and German customs" (*deutsches Wesen und deutsche Sitten*) was awarded citizenship in 1921, despite Bavaria's initial objections.[57] Similarly, in 1921, even Bavaria was willing to approve Hermann Rieder's citizenship application when Baden, his state of residence, offered his son's already approved application for German citizenship and his daughter's marriage to a German citizen, and Rieder's own active involvement in Jewish aid organizations as evidence of his commitment to Germany.[58] If involvement in Jewish aid organizations could even be considered a positive criterion for citizenship, then the meaning of a commitment to the German cultural community was clearly more complicated than it appears at first glance.

Tensions between cultural and ethnic definitions of German citizenship continued to play a role throughout the remainder of the Weimar Republic. This was most clearly the case in the relatively liberal state of Prussia. In 1925, the Prussian government agreed to the Bavarian demand that foreigners from the East be subject to a twenty-year waiting period before being considered for citizenship.[59] Two years later, a new Prussian minister of the interior, Albert Grzesinksi, sought to replace the category of *"Deutschstämmigkeit"* (German descent) with *"Kulturdeutscher"* (cultural German). In so doing, he explicitly sought to remove the barriers to the naturalization of Jews, and as such his definition of *Kulturdeutscher* included connections to family members residing in Germany, birth or upbringing in German-speaking regions or settlements, attendance at German schools, German names, and adherence to "German customs and language."[60] Against the opposition of most of the other German states and most national ministries, Grzesinski also rejected a fifteen- or twenty-year waiting period, and sought to reinstate Prussia's ten-year waiting period for citizenship applicants from the East that had prevailed at the outset of the Weimar Republic.[61]

Conclusion

In the aftermath of World War I, national belonging became a rallying cry for men and women across Central Europe as the meaning of the nation was thrown into question by territorial, ideological, and population shifts. While officials of the new republic agreed that German citizenship should be limited to those who could prove their German identity, the criteria for assessing this identity were less clear. The highly contentious debates surrounding naturalization reflected a lack of unanimity regarding the combination of ethnic and cultural factors that constituted what it meant to be German. If von Spreti and other Bavarians were committed to an ethnically defined vision of the German nation, the Saxon interior minister, Lipinski, insisted on the possibility of assimilation, even for a Russian-Pole with little command of the German language and a criminal record. Nonetheless, few officials adhered to either of these extreme positions. Even Bavarian advocates of an ethnic standard still allowed for the possibility of assimilation after twenty years of residence, and even Saxon Socialists accepted the standard ten-year residency requirement. Attitudes towards ethnicity and culture existed along a spectrum, rather than representing hard and fast extremes.

Yet if the Saxons and the Bavarians shared more than they often admitted, the very virulence of this debate was also instructive. Conservative nationalists in particular insisted that these questions of naturalization were so central to the future of the German nation and the German state that no compromise was possible. In this way, citizenship policy became caught in the same dynamic of extremism and paralysis that so poisoned the political life of the republic. Meanwhile, regardless of the particular standard they applied, German officials were reluctant to grant citizenship to all but the most "deserving" applicants. Even if some officials believed in the possibility of assimilation, few foreigners could actually meet this high burden of proof in practice. Foreigners might be able to remain in Germany, but entry to the German national community was limited to a small minority. Yet restrictive citizenship policies did little to counteract the influx of immigrants. Ironically, as a result of their parsimonious citizenship policy, Germans would find themselves confronted with exactly what they most feared—a huge population of foreigners on German soil.

Notes

This essay follows an argument originally published as "Culture, Belonging, and the Law: Naturalization in the Weimar Republic," in *Citizenship and National Identity in Twentieth Century Germany*, edited by Geoff Eley and Jan Palmoski (Stanford, 2008). The author thanks Stanford University Press for permission to reprint.

  1. On the paroxysms of this nation-making moment in general, see Arno J. Mayer, *Wilson vs. Lenin: Political Origins of the New Diplomacy, 1917–1918* (New Haven, CT, 1959); Alfred Cobban, *The Nation State and National Self-Determination* (New York, 1969); Hugh Seton-Watson, *Nations and States* (London, 1982); and Hugh Seton-Watson, *Eastern Europe between the Wars, 1918–1941* (New York, 1946). Joseph Rothschild's *East Central Europe between the Two World Wars* (Seattle, 1974) provides a useful synthetic overview of the period. The question of national minorities is addressed by C. A. Macartney, *National States and National Minorities* (New York, 1968) and Raymond Pearson, *National Minorities in Eastern Europe, 1848–1945* (London, 1983). More re-

cently, see Aviel Roshwald, *Ethnic Nationalism and the Fall of Empires: Central Europe, Russia, and the Middle East, 1914–1923* (London, 2001). Unlike these earlier works, Roshwald pays attention not only to the rise of state systems but also to the role of popular nationalism in driving political developments. In a new and highly readable account of the Paris peace conference, Margaret Macmillan, *Paris 1919: Six Months that Changed the World* (New York, 2002) makes clear how little of the postwar order was determined by the great powers themselves. The literature on revolution and nation-state formation in each of these countries is too extensive to enumerate here.

2. Klaus J. Bade, *Europa in Bewegung: Migration vom späten 18. Jahrhundert bis zur Gegenwart* (München, 2000), 222–31. Bade discusses in some detail the system of incentives and restrictions surrounding Polish seasonal labor in Prussia. For more on the Polish migrant workers, see: John J. Kulczycki, *The Foreign Worker and the German Labor Movement: Xenophobia and Solidarity in the Coal Fields of the Ruhr, 1871–1914* (Oxford, 1994); John J. Kulczycki, *The Polish Coal Miner's Union and the German Labor Movement in the Ruhr, 1902–1934: National and Social Solidarity* (Oxford, 1997); Richard Charles Murphy, *Guestworkers in the German Reich: A Polish community in Wilhelmian Germany* (New York, 1983); Krystyna Murzynowska, *Die polnischen Erwerbsauswanderer im Ruhrgebiet während der Jahre 1880–1914* (Dortmund, 1979); Valentina-Maria Stefanski, *Zwangsarbeit in Leverkusen: polnische Jugendliche im I.G. Farbenwerk* (Osnabrück, 2000); Christoph Klessmann, *Polnische Bergarbeiter im Ruhrgebiet, 1870–1945* (Göttingen, 1978); Hans-Ulrich Wehler, "Die Polen in Ruhrgebiet bis 1918," *Vierteljahresschrift für Sozial- und Wirtschaftsgeschichte* 48 (1961): 20–235.

3. Jack Wertheimer, *Unwelcome Strangers: East European Jews in Imperial Germany* (Oxford, 1987), 14–15.

4. Ibid., 36, 40. For more on the Polish expulsions in the 1880s, see Richard Blanke, "Bismarck and the Prussian Polish Policies of 1886," *Journal of Modern History* 45, no. 2 (1972): 211–29; Richard Blanke, *Prussian Poland in the German Empire (1871–1900)* (New York, 1981); Joachim Mai, *Die preussisch-deutsche Polenpolitik, 1885/87; eine Studie zur Herausbildung des Imperialismus in Deutschland* (Berlin, 1962); Lech Trzeciakowski, *The Kulturkampf in Prussian Poland* (New York, 1990); Hans-Ulrich Wehler, "Polenpolitik im Deutschen Kaiserreich," in *Krisenherde des Kaiserreichs 1871–1918* (Göttingen, 1972).

5. Wertheimer, *Unwelcome Strangers*, 27. Nonetheless, it is important to keep in mind that even if Poles did make up a large percentage of at least the Prussian population, the 1910 census counted only 70,000 Jews, or one-tenth of 1 percent of Germany's total population, living in the Reich. Although this census surely missed many immigrants who sought to avoid the German authorities, the majority of Eastern European Jews, unlike the Poles, used Germany as a way-station in their attempt to migrate further westward.

6. John Hope Simpson, cited in Michael Marrus, *The Unwanted: European Refugees in the Twentieth Century* (New York, 1985), 51.

7. Looking at census figures, Dieter Gosewinkel states that the percentage of people with foreign citizenship and speaking foreign languages in 1925 was 2.1 percent, compared to 7.5 percent in 1900. Gosewinkel, *Einbürgern und Ausschliessen: die Nationalisierug der Staatsangehörigkeit vom Deutschen Bund bis zur Bundesrepublik Deutschland* (Göttingen, 2001), 339.

8. Claudena Skran, *Refugees in Inter-War Europe: The Emergence of a Regime* (Oxford, 1995), 34.

9. Marrus, *The Unwanted*, 52; Bade, *Europa in Bewegung*, 278. As even officials were often unclear whether they were talking about German citizens displaced from territories that used to belong to the Reich or ethnic Germans from elsewhere in Eastern Europe, it is hard to determine exactly what these numbers are referring to. Marrus simply cites the 1 million figure as the number of "German" refugees, and it is unclear if he is referring to just those Germans displaced from territory that had once been German or also to those of German descent spread out across Eastern Europe. Because of the similarity of this 1 million figure to Bade's, which he makes clear is the number of Germans displaced from formerly German territory, I am assuming that he is referring to this. Jochen Oltmer also assumes approximately 1 million refugees from the territories ceded as a result of the treaty of Versailles, 120,000 people from Alsace-Lorraine and 850,000 from the Polish territories. Jochen Oltmer, "Migration and Public Policy in Germany, 1918–199," in *Crossing Boundaries: The Exclusion and Inclusion of Minorities in Germany and the United States*, ed. Larry Eugene Jones (New York, 2001), 59. The 1.3 million figure is provided by Rainer Münz and Heinz Fassman, "Geschichte und Gegenwart europäischer Ost-West-Wanderung," in *Internationale Wanderungen*, Demographie aktuell Nr. 5, ed. Rainer Münz, Hermann Korte, and Gert Wagner (Berlin, 1994), 22.
10. Oltmer, "Migration and Public Policy in Germany, 1918–199," 60.
11. Trude Maurer, *Ostjuden in Deutschland: 1918–1933* (Hamburg, 1986), 65.
12. John Hope Simpson claims that, as of January 1922, there was a maximum of 250,000 Russians living in Germany. Robert H. Johnston, *New Mecca, New Babylon: Paris and the Russian Exiles, 1920–1945* (Kingston, ON, 1988), 13. Articles from the far-right *Deutsche Allgemeine Zeitung* and the Republican *Vossische Zeitung* from the same month also estimated between 250,000 and 300,000 Russian émigrés in Germany. "Die russischen Emigranten in Deutschland," *Deutsche Allgemeine Zeitung*, 5 January 1922; J. E. "Die neue Völkerwanderung/Russischer Flüchtlinge," *Vossische Zeitung*, 3 January 1922. This figure is on the low side; most other estimates start at a half-million total population of Russians living on German soil during this period, of whom the vast majority arrived as refugees or immigrants in the aftermath of the revolution. According to American Red Cross figures, there were approximately 560,000 Russians in Germany in 1920. Frederic Nansen's League of Nation's High Commission for Refugees stated that there were 600,000 Russians in Germany as of 1923. Bettina Dodenhoeft, "*Laßt mich nach Rußland heim*": *russische Emigranten in Deutschland von 1918 bis 1945* (Frankfurt am Main, 1999), 9. In 1922, the Interior Ministry reported that the International Red Cross estimated that 600,000 Russians currently lived in Germany (B Arch R 1501/114140, Bd. 2, 48. Letter from the Reichsminister des Innern to the Auswärtiges Amt, 6 March 1922). Karl Schlögel has argued that there were approximately 500,000 Russians living in Germany between 1921–1923, half of whom were resident in the capital. Karl Schlögel, "Das Domicil eines Schattenbereichs: Russische Emigranten in Berlin in der 20er Jahre," in *Die Russen in Berlin 1910–1930* (Berlin, 1995), 16. I find this somewhat hard to believe, however; since there was no other city with anything like a comparable number of Russians, I am not sure where this quarter of a million Russians who were not living in Berlin were supposed to be living.
13. This letter from the Zentral-Polizeistelle Osten, Frankfurt (Oder) to the Landesgrenzpolizei on 5 February 1920 provides one representative list (BA R 1501/114049, 13). These stories ranged from the seemingly banal to the ridiculous. One story circulated in the right-wing press that Jewish immigrants running a factory were using cats, dogs, and garbage to create aspic. Maurer, *Ostjuden in Deutschland*, 134.

14. Letter from the Deutsche Gesellschaft für Bevölkerungspolitik to the RMdI, 9 April 1920, BA R 1501/114049, 135. Although I do not have the space to discuss this in greater detail here, it should be clear that these accusations against immigrants from Eastern Europe recycled familiar anti-Semitic stereotypes that long predated the Weimar era.

15. Gosewinkel, *Einbürgern und Ausschliessen*, 359. As I will discuss, the relatively liberal policies of the first years after the war became stricter very quickly. Gosewinkel does not note what percentage of applications by *fremdstämmige Ostausländer* were approved and if (or how) this changed over this period.

16. Donald Niewyk writes that the obstacles Eastern European Jews faced in gaining citizenship meant that only a small minority ever submitted naturalization applications. Donald L. Niewyk, *The Jews in Weimar Germany* (Baton Rouge, LA, 1980), 16.

17. Guidelines sent from the RMdI to the *Länder*, BA R 1501/112384, 237 and 239.

18. Letter from the Bavarian Interior Minister to the Bavarian Representative to the *Reichsrat*, 15 September 1923. BayHStA, MA 100317.

19. For more on the inability or unwillingness to deport foreigners during the early Weimar Republic, see Annemarie Sammartino, "Migration and Crisis in Germany, 1914–1922," (PhD diss., University of Michigan, 2004), chapters 5, 8, and 9. While the Socialists insisted that Germany should provide a haven for Eastern European Jews fleeing persecution, the Conservatives and Liberals (DDP) believed that Germany should protect anti-Bolshevik Russians who had sought refuge in Germany.

20. Ibid., 114. See also: Markus Lang, *Grundkonzeption und Entwicklung des deutschen Staatsangehörigkeitsrechts* (Frankfurt am Main, 1990), 47–49.

21. Dietmar Schirmer, "Closing the Nation: Nationalism and Statism in Nineteenth- and Twentieth-Century Germany," in *The Shifting Foundations of Modern Nation-States: Realignments of Belonging*, ed. Sima Godfrey and Frank Unger (Toronto, ON, 2004), 24.

22. This process was laid out in § 9 of the *Reichs- und Staatsangehörigkeitsgesetz* of 1913 and was essentially left unchanged after World War I.

23. Letter from Heine to the Staatsrat für Anhalt in Dessau, 31 May 1919. SächsHStA, Staatsministerium des Innern 9725, 14.

24. Ibid. See also: Gosewinkel, *Einbürgern und Ausschliessen*, 353.

25. Gosewinkel, *Einbürgern und Ausschliessen*, 354.

26. Guidelines sent from the RMdI to the Länder, 1 June 1921. BA R 1501/112384, 237–40.

27. Ibid., 237.

28. Ibid., 239.

29. Ibid.

30. Ibid., 240.

31. Report on the results of a meeting at the RMdI about many questions regarding the law for citizenship in the Reich and the states, 3 September 1920. BayHStA, MA 100317.

32. Gosewinkel, *Einbürgern und Ausschliessen*, 356.

33. See the case of Frommert for an instance where the Fürsorgeverein für deutsche Rückwanderer was called in to attest to an applicant's German descent. GStA PK, Rep. 77, Tit. 226b, Nr. 1F, Bd. 2.

34. Letter from the Polizeipräsident to the Oberpräsident zu Charlottenburg, 28 February 1919. GStA PK, Rep. 77, Tit. 226b, Nr. 1H, Bd. 2. It appears that Halpern had married a German woman whose parents "would not have understood if he had been deported" and had to take their daughter with him.

35. Letter from the Württemburg Ministry of the Interior to the Prussian Ministry of the Interior, 20 September 1920. Letter from the Prussian Ministry of the Interior to the Würrtemburg Ministry of the Interior, 9 November 1920. GStA PK, I. HA., Rep. 77, Tit. 226b, Nr. 1B, Bd. 3.

36. Application sent from the Polizeipräsident in Berlin to the Prussian Interior Ministry, 17 February 1919. The Interior Ministry's response is not recorded. GStA PK, 1. HA., Rep. 77, Tit. 226b, Nr. 1E, Bd. 1.

37. These reasons were actually used to describe an application from Syllies, but the letter from the Regierungspräsident in Munster to the Prussian Interior Ministry from 21 December 1921 describing the case states that the same factors applied for the case of Müller. GStA PK, 1. HA, Rep. 77, Tit. 226b, Nr. 1, Bd. 41.

38. See, for example, the case of Alfred Schoft, a Communist of German descent, who was denied citizenship by the Bavarians on the grounds that his citizenship would create a danger to public order. Letter from the Bavarian representative to the *Reichsrat* (Nüßlein) to the Bavarian Minister of Justice, 22 October 1922. BayHStA, MA 100317. See also: Letter from the PMI to the SMI, 19 May 1921, regarding the citizenship of Paul and Reinhard Richter. SächsHStA, MInnen, 9816, 20. The Saxons' response to this letter, specifically their contention that membership in the Communist Party was not sufficient grounds for the denial of a citizenship application, is also interesting in this regard. Letter from the SMI to the PMI, 6 June 1921. SächsHStA, MInnen, 9816, 23. See also the multiple objections to the citizenship application of Johann Werner, who participated in the March 1921 Communist uprising. Letter from the PMI to the SMI, 29 June 1921. SächsHStA, MInnen, 9816, 39. Letter from the Württemburgische Ministerium des Innern to the SMI, 31 May 1921. SächsHStA, MInnen, 9816, 40. Letter from the Lübeck Stadt und Landamt to the SMI, 28 May 1921. SächsHStA, MInnen, 9816, 41.

39. Letter from the Cöpenick Regierunspräsident to the Prussian Ministry of the Interior, 9 July 1919. According to a date stamp, the application was approved on 22 August 1919. GStA PK, 1. HA., Rep. 77, Tit. 226b, Nr. 1B, Bd. 3.

40. Letter from the Regierungspräsident in Potsdam to the Preussisches Ministerium des Innerns, 21 May 1919. Application was approved according to a date stamp on 16 August 1919. GStA PK, 1. HA., Rep. 77, Tit. 226b, Nr. 1D, Bd. 2. It is unclear from this letter if Ms. Donat was married or single, but as special mention was made by the Potsdam Regierungspräsident of her lack of employment, I tend to think that she was single.

41. Letter from the Police President to the Prussian Ministry of the Interior, 29 July 1918. GStA PK, 1. HA., Rep. 77, Tit. 226b, Nr. 1M, Bd. 3.

42. Letter from the Prussian Interior Ministry to the Regierungspräsident in Arnsberg, 31 August 1919. GStA PK, 1. HA., Rep. 77, Tit. 226b, Nr. 1E, Bd. 1. Emphasis in original.

43. Letter from the Mayor of Hagen to the Regierungspräsident in Arnsberg, 6 October 1919. GStA PK, 1. HA., Rep. 77, Tit. 226b, Nr. 1E, Bd. 1.

44. See, for example, the letter from the Staatskommision für die öffentliche Ordnung to the Prussian Interior Ministry on 28 September 1920. GStA PK, 1. HA., Rep. 77, Tit. 226b, Nr. 1E, Bd. 1.

45. Letter from Ellinghaus to the Prussian Interior Ministry, 14 December 1920. GStA PK, 1. HA., Rep. 77, Tit. 226b, Nr. 1E, Bd. 1.

46. Estersohn's business success is not explicitly discussed, but I am assuming that he was successful enough to afford a lawyer, something that most applicants did not seem to have.

47. See, for example, the heated debate between Saxony and Bavaria in 1922–23. BayH-StA, MA 100317.

48. Letter from the Bavarian Interior Ministry to the Bavarian Foreign Ministry, 9 December 1921. In this letter, the official also writes that one needed to be careful because even some with German names were not necessarily Germans. Thus, it was necessary to check what schools the applicant had gone to, whether he spoke German, and "seemed German," etc. This official's own last name, by the way, was von Spreti. BayH-StA, MA 100317.

49. Letter from the Mecklenburg-Strelitzisches Ministerium to the Bavarian Ministry of the Interior. The Mecklenburg-Strelitz minister acknowledges the Bavarian twenty-year requirement. BayHStA, MA 100317. This requirement was established by the Bavarians at least as early as 1922, as a letter from the Bavarian Interior Minister, von Spreti, to the Badische Staatsministerium, Ministerial Abteilung für Präsidialische, Reiche- und auswärtige Angelegenheiten from that year references this. BA R 1501/108045, 12. The Prussians raised their minimum residency requirement to fifteen years in 1921 and to twenty in 1925. Gosewinkel, *Einbürgern und Ausschliessen*, 356.

50. Letter from the Prussian Minister of the Interior to the RMdI, February 17, 1923. Letter from the Saxon Minister of the Interior to the RMdI, May 17, 1922. BayHStA, MA 100317.

51. For the Dresden district office's position, see a letter from the Dresden Kreishauptmannschaft to the Ministerium des Innern, 23 January 1922. SächsHStA Ministerium des Innern 9725, 56. Internal memo from 27 October 1920. SächsHStA Ministerium des Innern 9710, 249.

52. Lipinski was a member of the USPD until that party disbanded in late 1920, after which he joined the SPD. Lipinski was minister of the interior for the first few months of the republic, and then again between July 1920 and February 1923. See http://www.sachsen.de/de/11/geschichte/regenten/1918–1924/inhalt_re.html.

53. Kreishauptmannschaft Leipzig to Sächsisches Minister des Innern, 28 November 1919. SächsHStA Ministerium des Innern 9710, 255. The Kreishauptmannschaft Leipzig sent a later warning about Goluchowski, n.d. SächsHStA MdInnern 9710, 348.

54. Sächsisches Minister des Innern to the Kreishauptmannschaft Leipzig, 17 May 1922. SächsHStA MdInnern 9711, 19.

55. Lipinski's own skepticism regarding Goluchowski's chances at naturalization may be guessed at by the way that he ends his letter: "The Ministry of the Interior has no objections to including him in the monthly list [of people sent to the other *Länder*] for the goal of naturalization." Lipinski surely had no illusions that Goluchowski would actually be granted citizenship, merely that he was worthy of inclusion on the monthly list. (Ibid.) For other examples along the same lines, see the handling of the cases of Haber and Gewürz. Letter from the Sächsisches Innenministerium to the Kreishauptmannschaft Chemnitz, 8 November 1921. SächsHStA MdInnern, 9710, 356. See also the case of the widow Tumpowsky and her daughter. Tumpowsky had moved to Germany before 1870 and her daughter had been born in Germany. Tumpowsky's two sons had served in the military and been naturalized. Although the local authorities

feared that both Tumpowsky and her daughter could become burdens on the state, the ministry recommended their naturalization, claiming that this sort of potential burden was not sufficient grounds for denying their applications. Letter from the SächsMdI to the Kreishauptmannschaft Leipzig, 17 January 1923. SächsHStA MdI, 9711, 83.

56. Letter from the Bavarian Interior Minister to the Bavarian Representative to the *Reichsrat*, 15 September 1923. BayHStA, MA 100317.
57. After a letter from Baden describing the situation, the Bavarian minister of the interior relented in a letter dated 4 May 1921. BayHStA, MA 100317.
58. Letter from the Bavarian minister of the interior 24 June 1921. BayHStA, MA 100317.
59. Gosewinkel, *Einbürgern und Ausschliessen*, 356.
60. Ibid., 361.
61. Ibid., 362.

CHAPTER 16

~:~

Gender and Colonial Politics after the Versailles Treaty

LORA WILDENTHAL

In November 1918, the revolutionary government of republican Germany proclaimed the political enfranchisement of women. In June 1919, Article 119 of the Versailles Treaty announced the disenfranchisement of German men and women as colonizers. These were tremendous changes for German women and for the colonialist movement. Yet colonialist women's activism changed surprisingly little, and the Weimar Republic proved to be a time of vitality for the colonialist movement.

The specific manner in which German decolonization took place profoundly shaped interwar colonialist activism. It took place at the hands of other colonial powers and at the end of the first "total" war. The fact that other imperial metropoles forced Germany to relinquish its colonies, and not colonial subjects (many of whom had tried and failed to drive Germans from their lands in previous years), meant that German colonialists focused their criticisms on those powers. When German colonialists demanded that the Versailles Treaty be revised so that they could once again rule over Africans and others, they were expressing not only a racist claim to rule over supposed inferiors but also a reproach to the Entente powers for betraying fellow white colonizers.

The specific German experience of decolonization affected how Germans viewed their former colonial subjects. In other cases of decolonization, bitter wars of national liberation dismantled fantasies of affection between colonizer and colonized. In the German case, the absence of an all-out confrontation with colonial subjects nourished colonialists' fantasy that Africans, Pacific Islanders, and Chinese had never wanted them to leave. This fantasy was expressed in the titles of interwar colonialist books such as *Master, Come Back* and *When Will the Germans Finally Return?* and through the frequent invocation of individual Africans' statements of loyalty.[1] After 1919, then, colonialists thoroughly sentimentalized and romanticized the relationship of German colonizer to colonized.

Germany's specific manner of decolonization also affected gender relations among German colonialists. German men could no longer claim the colonies as quintessentially male space. Now the combat front of the First World War, as direct or vicarious experience, took the place of the colonies as a key site of "male fantasies." And, as in the earliest years of colonial conquest, nurses were the only women allowed into that male space.[2] Colonialist women no longer criticized German men for excluding them from a colonial paradise, but rather joined with the men in criticizing the Entente powers. Colonialist women's fantasies of colonial freedom and independence, as well as their organizational efforts, still sometimes conflicted with men's. Yet colonialist women most often expressed their relationship to German men as one of maternal solicitude and comradeship in the face of a common victimization.

The new, post-1919 German colonialist identity, which was inflected with a profound sense of victimhood, turned out to be well suited to colonialist women. In the pre–First World War colonialist movement, women had to emphasize their uniquely feminine expertise in order to preserve their niche. While the Weimar Republic ended the political inequality of women that had produced those strategies, the strategies themselves persisted. Colonialist women used their new formal political voice to perpetuate their claim to feminine expertise, especially through maternalism.[3] While their rhetoric of unique feminine tasks was a sign of weakness and constrained choices before the war, now that same rhetoric found new salience under conditions of imposed decolonization.

Colonialist women were well suited in several respects to mount agitation in the 1920s and 1930s. Colonialist men's channels of high politics and big business, from which women had always been excluded, had become less important. Diplomatic protests to the Entente powers were fruitless. Business between Germany and its former colonies was at first forbidden, then struggled in the mid-1920s before receiving another blow in 1929. Colonialist women, who had developed their projects at a time when women lacked a formal political voice or recognized expertise in statecraft, science, or large-scale business, were less seriously hampered by these new restrictions. The loss of formal political authority over Africans and Pacific Islanders did not affect their programs as much as it did many colonialist men's because secular colonialist women had always directed most of their efforts at other Germans. Several thousand Germans lived in the former colonies, and colonialist women were able to continue their femininely "unpolitical" work in nursing, schools, settlement of unmarried women, and aid to needy German families.[4]

The Women's League of the German Colonial Society (Frauenbund der Deutschen Kolonialgesellschaft) and the Women's Red Cross Association for

Nursing in the Colonies (Frauenverein vom Roten Kreuz für Krankenpflege in den Kolonien), the two main prewar organizations run by and for colonialist women, argued that the best way to overcome the decolonization imposed by the Entente was a gradual, informal retaking of the former colonies household by household, community by community. Colonialist women's focus on feminine essence and the household, rather than formal political boundaries, was now a positive advantage, for after the First World War the household was the only territory that many Germans felt they could still control. Hedwig Heyl, the home economics expert who served as chairwoman of the Women's League from 1910 until 1920, responded to the Versailles Treaty article that removed the colonies from German rule with the motto, "Wherever Germans are abroad, colonization is taking place, regardless of the territory that may be disputed them."[5] Like much revisionist and antirepublican rhetoric of the interwar years, this motto was both vacuous and extreme. By conflating Germans' mere existence with the power ambitions of colonization, it politicized everyday existence and deformalized the rules and procedures of colonial rule, citizenship, and borders. It also made new alliances possible: older distinctions and rivalries dissolved among advocates of colonial Germans, Germans living in East Central Europe, and Germans in places such as Brazil or Canada. Members of all these groups joined organizations such as the German Protection League for Borderlands Germans and Germans Abroad (Deutscher Schutzbund für das Grenz- und Auslandsdeutschtum). Legal citizenship was no longer the main criterion of Germanness for Germans whose homes were now located in Poland and Czechoslovakia, or for Germans in the Southwest African mandate who accepted South African citizenship in 1925 in exchange for the right to remain there undisturbed. The definition of who was a German shifted to "cultural" public enactments such as church attendance.[6] Colonialist women's existing formulas for conjuring feminine and German essence were tailor-made for anti-republican and *völkisch*, or racialized German, agitation.

As historians of German feminism have noted, women who had opposed feminism and suffrage rights before the war were as quick as Left-liberal and socialist women to seize their new political rights in 1918.[7] Politically active conservative women in organizations such as the housewives' associations used women's new basic political rights to oppose the republic itself.[8] The rapid prominence of these nationalist and right-wing women is less surprising when seen in the context of their political mobilization in nationalist associations already before the First World War. Women gained experience in committee work, agitation materials, and public speaking in the Patriotic Women's Leagues (Vaterländische Frauenvereine), the German-Evangelical Women's League (Deutsch-Evangelischer Frauenbund), the German League against Women's Emancipation (Deutscher Bund zur Bekämpfung der Frauenemanzipation, and women's nationalist and colonialist pressure groups.[9] The First World War intensified that training, with its National Women's Service (Nationaler Frauendienst).[10] Else Frobenius (1875–1952), for example, gained journalistic and public speaking skills as general secretary of the Women's League of the German Colonial Society between 1913 and 1922, then discovered after 1919 that party, state, and voluntary association posts "fell into her lap."[11]

At the moment when key feminist demands had been realized or seemed within reach, and when increased numbers of women were entering universities and even studying the "colonial sciences,"[12] the older ideology of feminine expertise continued to shape women's colonialist activism. Colonialist women and men reiterated the anti-intellectual, professionalized housewifeliness that Heyl had done so much to promote across the women's movement.[13] A pamphlet from during the First World War, for example, sought to gain women's support for the colonial empire by presenting economic problems in terms of a fictional housewife's everyday use of leather, cooking oil, cotton, and chocolate.[14] The pamphlet conflated "household" with "economy" (both *Wirtschaft*). Colonialists offered the female citizen of the Weimar Republic similar fare after the war. For example, during the 1925 "Colonial Week," the colonialist and feminist politician Else Lüders addressed "the housewives of Berlin" on the importance of tropical products for running a household.[15] The conflation of "household" and "economy" connected German women's new political role, which required them to be aware of economic issues, with traditional gender roles.

Both the Women's League and the Women's Red Cross Association came to define Germanness and its propagation in terms of individuals and households, not by state territory. They saw the individual Germans or German families they supported as outposts of German culture. The Women's Red Cross Association expressed this shift in 1922 when it changed the rest of its name from "for Nursing in the Colonies" to "for Germans Overseas" (Frauenverein vom Roten Kreuz für Deutsche über See). The organization continued its work among Germans who remained or settled anew in the former colonies (including Qingdao and a new post in Tianjin), but added Germans living in Peru, Argentina, Brazil, Chile, Curaçao, Lithuania, Paraguay, Spain, and the United States.[16] The women's organizations no longer claimed to operate throughout various territories, but rather only among German persons and families in those territories. Before the war the Women's Red Cross Association had never completely excluded colonial subjects from its services; now, it announced that colonial subjects would have to do without their help.[17] For the Women's League, the shift in focus from territory to individual persons meant the end of its attempts to change the sexual behavior of the entire population in a colony. If the Women's League or Women's Red Cross Association decided that recipients were deficient in racial or national virtue, they could easily cut off funds and repudiate them as representatives of German culture. Discarding Germans found unworthy had never been so simple under formal colonial rule, as colonialists' fretting over the difficulty of deporting "white proletarians" indicated. Because the former colonies were no longer the legal responsibility of the German state, Weimar- and Nazi-era heirs of radical nationalism were more untrammeled than ever in their selective representation of the former colonies as a pure German space and refuge from the realities of postwar Germany. Colonialist women, as female citizens of the Weimar Republic, now had the same formal access to the state as men—but at a moment when the state had lost importance among colonialists of both sexes.

Colonial Revision in Weimar

Because colonial revisionism eventually became the property of the far right and especially the Nazi party, it is easy to overlook its appeal across the political spectrum in the early years of the Weimar Republic. Many Germans referred to Article 231 of the treaty, which placed complete responsibility for the war on Germany, as the "war guilt lie" (*Kriegsschuldlüge*). Colonialists adapted that slogan to refer to Article 119 and the Entente's accusations of cruelty as the "colonial guilt lie" (*koloniale Schuldlüge*). As the Left-liberal colonial expert Moritz Julius Bonn recalled, the manner of German decolonization "made many Germans colonial-minded who before had been in the habit of decrying colonies."[18] Anger at the "war guilt lie" and "colonial guilt lie" smothered domestic discussion of Germany's own annexationist war aims, which had included extensive Western and Eastern European lands as well as *Mittelafrika*, a swathe of the continent intended to connect Cameroon with German East Africa.[19]

In 1925, a procolonial caucus formed in the Reichstag. This Inter-Party Colonial Union (Interfraktionelle Koloniale Vereinigung) spanned, from Right to Left, the German National People's Party (DNVP), the German People's Party (DVP), the Catholic Center Party (Z), the German Democratic Party (DDP), and the Social Democratic Party (SPD). The SPD, originally an entirely anticolonial party, had developed a wing in favor of "reformed" colonialism in the last years before the First World War. Now that wing gained the support of leading SPD women: Marie Juchacz, Wally Zepler, and Clara Bohm-Schuch proclaimed their opposition to Article 119.[20] Even the Independent Social Democratic Party (USPD), which had broken away from the SPD during the First World War out of principled opposition to annexations, briefly joined the revisionists: in March 1919 it voted in favor of a National Assembly resolution that called the anticipated Article 119 "unbearable, unfulfillable, and unacceptable."[21] That was the last time the USPD supported colonial revision, however. The new and small German Communist Party (KPD) rejected all procolonial statements.

Likewise, only a few nonparliamentary political associations spoke out against colonial revision. One was the German branch of the International Women's League for Peace and Freedom (Internationale Frauenliga für Frieden und Freiheit), to which several important German feminists, including the lawyer Anita Augspurg, belonged.[22] The colonialist movement followed its public speeches with intense irritation. After a speech in favor of self-determination by peoples of color by Magda Hoppstock-Huth, a male colonialist reporter fulminated: "The 'modern' woman is as barren as this chatter. Women without children and nations without colonies—those are the results of free self-determination!"[23] Helene Stöcker, an important radical feminist and pacifist, participated in the League against Colonial Oppression and Imperialism's famous 1927 congress in Brussels.[24] Opposition to colonial revision could be dangerous in the first years after the war; the colonial soldier turned pacifist and anticolonial journalist Hans Paasche was murdered for his views in 1920.[25] Support for colonial revision, by contrast, posed neither physical nor political risks—which helps explain its ubiquity, including among women's organizations. The Federation of German Women's Associations (Bund Deutscher Frauenvereine, BDF) actively supported colonial revision. In 1920 its general manager, Dorothee von Velsen, and Else Frobenius organized a coalition of women's organizations to agitate on behalf of borderlands Germans and Germans abroad, including colonial Germans, which numbered, Frobenius claimed, 3 million members. And in 1921, Frobenius and the DVP Reichstag delegate Clara Mende organized a "Women's Committee against the Guilt Lie" (Frauenauschuss zur Bekämpfung der Schuldlüge).[26] These responses to Article 119 were far more common than those of Hoppstock-Huth, Stöcker, or Paasche.

Outrage over the "colonial guilt lie" served to unite Germans more effectively than real existing colonialism had ever done.[27] But new divisions soon arose. Alongside pure colonial revision—the demand for restoration of the colonies in exactly the same form as before the war—proposals for new forms of colonial power emerged. These proposals arose out of pragmatism in the face of the Entente's intransigence rather than from a principled turn away from formal empire. In 1920 former governor of Samoa and colonial secretary Wilhelm Solf suggested that international (white) oversight was appropriate for all colonies, not just the formerly German ones, in order to protect colonial subjects from abuses that had taken place in every modern colonial empire.[28] Reichsbank president Hjalmar Schacht (DDP) proposed in the early 1920s that the European states and the United States form a chartered company for the joint exploitation of lands extending from Africa to Russia.[29] Former colonial secretary Bernhard Dernburg (DDP) suggested in 1926 that Germans should work to increase their trade in tropical products and to improve conditions for German settlers abroad, but that formal political rule now looked too expensive and difficult due to "the race problem that has arisen in Africa" (he apparently meant pan-Africanism).[30] Wilhelm Külz, now minister of the interior (DDP), favored Schacht's and Dernburg's ideas.

These proposals infuriated other, more rigid colonialists. Former governor of German East Africa Heinrich Schnee (DVP), the radical nationalist publicist Wilhelm Föllmer, and Franz Ritter von Epp, a *Freikorps* leader and Nazi Party member since 1928, called proposals such as Schacht's a "colonial policy stab in the back" and proclaimed their unswerving insistence that the former colonies be restored to full German control.[31] In the Reich Working Group on the Colonies (Koloniale Reichsarbeitsgemeinschaft, KORAG), a coalition of colonialist organizations founded in 1922, they claimed the right to speak for genuine colonial revision. These extreme revisionists, who resisted the stabilization of the Weimar Republic, narrowed the political range of the colonialist movement and, from the mid-1920s, moved it toward the far right.

In the mid-1920s, the colonialist movement still included people whom the Nazis rejected, such as the Reich League of Jewish Front Soldiers member Theodor Freudenberger. He lectured in 1927 on his experiences as one of General Paul von Lettow-Vorbeck's army in German East Africa. Lettow-Vorbeck was colonialists' idol because he led the only German force that was undefeated in the field at the time of the armistice.[32] Freudenberger wished to disprove both the "colonial guilt lie" and also two "prejudices": that Jews did not do their share of fighting during the First World War, and that Lettow-Vorbeck had been able to hold out so long because there were no Jews among his colonial force (in fact, Freudenberg noted, there were seventeen, some of whom died in action).[33] The notice of Freudenberger's lecture in *Der Kolonialdeutsche*, a periodical that served at various times in the 1920s as the official organ of the German Colonial Society, Women's League, Women's Red Cross Association, and several colonial veterans' associations, shows us that the myth of Jewish underrepresentation on the front in the First World War, exemplified by a census of Jews in the military in 1916, was alive and well.[34] It also shows that while colonial revision was important to Freudenberger, Freudenberger's concerns about anti-Semitism were not important to other colonialists. The notice of his lecture did not comment on how he disproved the "prejudices," but rather only on how well Freudenberger had argued against the "colonial guilt lie."

As for Lettow-Vorbeck, he took active part in armed counterrevolutionary activity since the first weeks of the Weimar Republic. The colonialist movement as a whole exhibited a clear antirepublican tendency by 1928.[35] The stock market crash of 1929 brought more support for far-Right positions. Under Schnee and Epp, the colonialist movement moved ever closer to the Nazi Party between 1928 and 1933. It was not necessarily an obvious partnership, for the Nazi Party had shown almost no interest in overseas colonial issues between 1919 and 1927, while the Right-liberal DVP had established itself as both the most strongly procolonial party and a prorepublican one.[36] The colonialists' motive for joining forces with the Nazis was to escape their upper-bourgeois reputation and become a true movement of the common people (*Volksbewegung*). The Nazis, meanwhile, wanted to establish an alliance with traditional conservatives. In 1932, Schnee resigned from the DVP; by then he took for granted that the NSDAP was necessary to any solution to the crisis of the republic. He joined the Nazi Party in 1933, by which time the colonialist-Nazi alliance was already in place.[37] The Women's League and the Women's Red Cross Association enjoyed unbroken success across the political divide of 1933. The Women's League expanded from a 1925 membership of 6,500 to 20,560 in 1930, 24,000 in 1932, 25,000 in 1933, and 30,000 in 1936.[38] The Women's Red Cross Association also expanded from the latter half of the 1920s onward, regaining 14,000 members by 1928; in 1935 it reached a longtime goal of founding its own nursing mother house.[39]

The German Woman as Victim

Throughout the Weimar Republic and into the Nazi era, colonialist women's writings continued to pour forth. Writers of the 1920s portrayed women in the colonies as victims and, as we will see below, also as mothers, and as emancipated comrades. Germany was defeated in 1918, and mobilized Africans were among the soldiers victorious over it. Germans experienced Africans in military authority over them in two episodes: the French, Belgian, and British occupation of the German colonies, and the French occupation of the Rhineland. France's militarization of colonial subjects, already controversial before the war, now became associated with rumors of sexual violence; imperial defeat was associated with sexual violence.[40] This was new: the German colonial empire had not seen any racialized rape scares like the intermittent "Black Perils" in South Africa between 1893 and 1913, or the rape scare that led to the White Women's Protection Ordinance in British-controlled Papua New Guinea in 1926.[41]

As the Entente powers invaded and occupied the various German colonies, they interned and usually deported German civilians there. Only in Southwest Africa were Germans generally allowed to remain, except for male officials, who were deported mostly to South Africa.[42] Government officials who interviewed deported colonists upon arrival in Germany asked them leading questions with respect to race, in order to assemble evidence of Entente atrocities. "How rapid was the expulsion or escort out of the colony? Who carried it out (colored soldiers?) and how?" asked the official questionnaire. In cases of "maltreatment," the questionnaire asked: "By whom? (perhaps by colored soldiers?)"[43] Over the years, stock phrases of purple prose emerged for describing the deportations. A colonialist man recalled in 1931 the experiences of Ada Schnee, wife of the German East African governor Heinrich Schnee, during the Belgian occupation of the town of Tabora: "The Belgians swept in with wild hordes from the

Congo. The occupation of Tabora was indescribable … perhaps never before in the world [*sic*] had white women been subjected to such persecution. In the middle of the night the women suddenly found savages in their bedrooms; with shaggy hair, protruding lips and red eyes they stood there with knife in hand before a delicate European woman and demanded everything."[44] The author of this passage had not been present at these events, nor even in Tabora; he was imagining them. In this case we can compare his statement directly with Ada Schnee's own. In her memoir, which by no means sought to minimize the violence and injustice of the Belgian occupation, Schnee described in comparatively sober terms how "many women found themselves suddenly facing a guard of *askari*, with arms at the ready, in their bedrooms."[45] Ada Schnee did mention elsewhere instances of rape during the occupation of Tabora—but the rape victims were African, not German women.[46]

Ada Schnee and Elly Proempeler, the deported widow of the district officer of Tabora killed in the war, did repeatedly mention sexual fear. Unlike the Rhineland protesters, however, they made a point of differentiating among Africans. Proempeler wrote, "I have been asked here at home so often, did not the blacks act very shamelessly toward us women as soon as we were alone," and made a point of contradicting this assumption.[47] She devoted an entire chapter to recording the aid that Africans and Afro-Arabs who had been under German rule rendered her. Here Proempeler was mobilizing the revisionist insistence on mutual affection between colonizer and colonized against a metropolitan racist sexual paranoia. Proempeler and Schnee reserved their language of sexual paranoia for the Congolese and other African soldiers under Entente rule. Even so, none of the memoirs by women deportees records any rape or lesser sexual molestation of a German woman by an African man.[48] Likewise, the deportees' responses to the government interviewers showed that German colonists suffered many serious hardships, such as being forced to march long distances while ill and underfed, arbitrary measures at the hands of local officials, and even stonings by hostile European colonists in French or Belgian colonies. They also indicated outrage and fear at being placed under the guard of African soldiers.[49] But no women among the interview respondents were able to confirm any instances of sexual violence.

Women deportees intended their published diaries to document Entente outrages, and they interpreted the shame of military defeat in terms of women's sexual vulnerability. Yet what these memoirs mainly conveyed was a record of German women's patriotic fortitude and ability to protect themselves, even in the absence of their husbands. Schnee, for example, referred repeatedly to how she faced down British and Belgian officials by simply refusing to follow their orders. They were victims, but without the stigma of sexual defeat.

Depictions of the second episode of rape scares about colonial soldiers, the so-called black shame on the Rhine (*schwarze Schmach am Rhein*), stand in marked contrast to the expulsion of German settlers from the colonies. Between 1919 and 1925, France occupied the Rhineland with a military force that included soldiers from French colonies in Africa and Indochina. The occupation elicited outrage from German men and women of all political persuasions.[50] In letters, petitions, and assemblies they expressed their fury at African and other non-European soldiers' exercising military authority over Germans and at purported occasions of violence toward civilians, especially women. Very few of these claims of assaults were substantiated; most were utter invention.[51] The campaign against the "black shame on the Rhine" was fed by the imagination—a quite pornographic imagination, as agitation materials from the campaign show—rather than facts.[52] Both women and men participated. In her pamphlet *Men Unarmed, Women Unprotected*, one agitator, Luise Paasche, asserted that women had to take up the struggle against the war guilt lie and the "black shame on the Rhine" because male political leaders had failed them.[53] Rape symbolized not only defeat at the hands of the uncivilized, but also the weakness of German men, especially those who were in charge of the new Weimar Republic. Black people's presence in Germany was associated with defeat, humiliation, and powerlessness. Interracial desire, which had been admitted and sometimes even praised before the First World War, was now denied and reinterpreted as rape. The 600–800 children born to colonial soldiers and German women were stigmatized as "Rhineland bastards" and subjected to sterilization in 1937.[54]

Both episodes show that racial and sexual fears could overwhelm empirical facts in narratives of the end of German colonial rule. But while a reworking of reality into a symbolic narration took place in both the campaign against the "black shame on the Rhine" and in accounts of the colonial deportations, the stakes for German women were not the same in both. Sexual victimhood inside Germany was additional evidence of the injustice of the Versailles Treaty; indeed, the more extreme the sexual predation, the sounder the case revisionists could launch. Sexual victimhood in the former German colonies had another meaning that made it difficult for colonialist women to express. White women's sexual vulnerability was one of the oldest arguments for excluding them from the African colonies—but colonialist women during and after the First World War wanted to forge ahead with colonial projects, even in the absence of formal colonies. They had no intention of disqualifying themselves from active roles in the former colonies.

The German Woman as Mother

The Women's League posed as an organization that stood above politics. With the loss of formal empire, this depoliticized notion of female colonialist activism took on even more importance. It was achieved primarily through images of maternal solicitude. Adda von Liliencron, the first chairwoman of the Women's League, played the role of mother for "sons" (colonial soldiers); Hedwig Heyl did the same for "daughters" (women entering professionalized housework and other new or reformed women's careers); and Hedwig von Bredow, chairwoman between 1920 and 1932, presented herself as a mother to both sexes and all ages. Bredow was the first Women's League chairwoman to see a German colony firsthand (she traveled to Southwest Africa in 1927–28 when she was 75 years old, and to Tanganyika and Southwest Africa in 1931), and gained the nickname of "Mother of the Germans in Africa" (*Mutter der Afrikaner*).[55] The Women's League represented itself as a caring and providing mother of colonial Germans: it offered loans to colonists' family members who happened to be visiting Germany in summer 1914 and were stranded there, it placed colonists' children with families in Germany as "colonial godchildren" (*Kolonialpatenschaften*), and it welcomed the deportees back to Germany, receiving them with food and clothing.[56]

The mothers of Germans abroad continued their pre–First World War efforts to maintain German culture in communities abroad. They focused especially on youth and on schools, as institutions both close to home and ostensibly beyond politics.[57] They quickly complained that the mandate administrations were neglecting the needs of German communities. Now other Europeans or whites, not "natives," were the greatest threat to German culture. Meanwhile, the Women's League saw African youth not as the object of German colonizing efforts but as rivals for the resources of the mandate administration.[58] Frobenius's successor as general secretary of the Women's League, Nora von Steinmeister, complained in 1933: "For negro children in today's Southwest and East Africa, the best has been provided, the mandate government and the missions have built beautiful schools for them. Even high schools are available for negro children—but *German* parents for the most part *lack the means* to provide even only a primary school education for their children."[59] They demanded accommodation for white German students in the colonies.

The mandate administrations at first rejected German colonists' requests for special German schools or for German programs within existing white children's schools. Southwest Africa was the first to yield on the issue, and in late 1922 the Women's League began to reconstruct and expand German kindergartens, pupils' dormitories, and schools in Lüderitzbucht, Gibeon, Keetmanshoop, Karibib, and Swakopmund.[60] In 1932, the Women's League established a dormitory, the "Hedwig von Bredow House," for German children from all over the mandate who were attending school in the capital, Windhoek. In April 1933, the Women's League opened the Hedwig Heyl Housekeeping School (Hedwig-Heyl-Haushaltungsschule) in Windhoek. The Women's League also shipped books and periodicals, as long as they were not "too modern," for the edification of youth and families in the mandate.[61]

After 1925, when Germans were allowed to reenter Tanganyika, as many as two thousand Germans settled there, mostly as coffee planters.[62] In contrast to Southwest Africa, German East Africa had offered hardly any schools for white German pupils before the war. The Women's League created new schools during the 1920s in Lupembe, Sunga, and Oldeani.[63] The Women's League also sent governesses to isolated farmsteads in Tanganyika, Southwest Africa, and Angola, where Portugal allowed a number of German colonists to relocate. The Women's League also made an effort to complete children's sentimental education as Germans by bringing them to Germany for apprenticeships or university education.[64] It gave scholarships and operated dormitories for them in Bad Harzburg (1936), and in Wuppertal and Blankenburg (1939). Meanwhile, to sustain the interest of Germany-born youth in the former colonies, the Women's League carried out procolonial agitation in the schools, helped organize "colonial youth groups" (which had to join the Hitler Youth in 1933), and contributed to a colonialist periodical for youth created in 1924, *Jambo*.

The Women's Red Cross Association concentrated on that other primary task of German mothers, nursing, declaring that "there can be no more beautiful task for the German woman than to see to it that Germans abroad do not have to do without German nursing care in case of need or illness."[65] It managed to retain one hospital in the former colonies during the war, the Princess Rupprecht Convalescent Home in Swakopmund, Southwest Africa; all others were seized. But it was permitted to resume activities in Tanganyika in 1925 and Cameroon in 1927, and it regained or founded anew several hospitals and clinics during the Weimar Republic.[66] It also continued its prewar efforts to sustain kindergartens. It took on one new project: to "promote the image of Germandom in Turkey" by training "young Turkish women from good families" as nurses.[67] Like the Women's League, the Women's Red Cross Association sought to provide for the cultural needs of German youth, forming its own youth groups in Germany in 1926.[68]

In 1926, the Women's League resumed what had been its main prewar effort: the sponsorship of unmarried women's emigration. The first women emigrants to be sponsored after the war went to Southwest Africa and Tanganyika; in 1929 the Women's League began to send women to South Africa, Angola, Mozambique, Kenya, South America, and Mexico as well.[69] The numbers of women sponsored soon surpassed those of the prewar years.[70] Colonialist women and men still disputed which was the best sort of women to sponsor.[71] The Women's League's continuing interest in women with certification led to the founding of a third colonial housekeeping school in Germany in 1926. A cooperative venture of the Women's League, the Holstein town of Rendsburg, and the Reich Ministry of Education (the Women's Red Cross Association had dropped out after showing early interest), its first students enrolled in 1927.[72] Unlike the earlier schools at Bad Weilbach and Witzenhausen, the school in

Rendsburg was a resounding success. Enrolled at full capacity from 1930 on-
wards, it grew in size continuously and remained in operation far longer—until
1945—than its predecessors had during the era of actual colonial empire.[73]
Also unlike the earlier women's schools, the Rendsburg school was intended
not only to train "girls and women" (between seventeen and thirty-four years of
age) from Germany for Africa, but also to train colonists' daughters in the ways
of metropolitan Germanness. Its first pupils included young women from the
Southwest African mandate.[74] Its curriculum taught skills such as houseclean-
ing, cooking, butchering, cheesemaking, woodworking, and livestock care, as
well as basic medical skills and "colonial sciences," especially foreign languages,
politics and, beginning in 1930, genetics (*Vererbungslehre*).[75]

Agnes von Boemcken described in 1930 how the domestic tasks, such as
cooking, sewing, and nursing, were not necessarily the most important thing
the school offered:

> The deeper, more beautiful part of this school is this: that all who were united
> in a joyful year of youth should enter into life with the consciousness: We are
> German women, called upon to contribute in the smallest daily realms of life
> to keeping German that which is German. ... We women, we German women
> want to prove that it is not governments and peoples who can take or give colo-
> nies as they see fit, but rather that they are built up and preserved through quiet,
> unobtrusive work; that the German wife and mother will be victorious in spite
> of all treaties and international agreements.[76]

In Boemcken's rendition of Hedwig Heyl's decade-old motto, women were inherently revisionist because, as mothers, they lived and worked in a realm that
was beyond politics and more powerful than politics.

The German Woman as Emancipated Comrade

During and after the First World War, *comradeship* became a ubiquitous term
for both sexual and nonsexual relationships between women and men.[77] Men
emerged from the war more vulnerable than before; women experienced new
powers. Gender relations no longer presumed to the same extent women's dependency on men. Instead, women represented themselves working alongside
men or even supplanting them. Yet while the prewar legal and social subordination of women changed in the 1920s and 1930s, equality did not take its place.
The interwar period was a time of men's ambivalence about women and of
women's ambivalence about emancipation.[78]

Across Europe, the "reconstruction of gender" and reordering of women's
lives, appearances, and aspirations in the wake of the First World War was fundamental to the reconstruction of national identity.[79] At a time when masculine
identity was extremely vulnerable, women emerged as symbols of a coherent

culture and society, helping to limit, or at the very least provide a framework for, political change. Germans vented their fascination and irritation with the new possibilities of women through the image of the "New Woman." The dream of some and nightmare of others, the New Woman was politically enfranchised and economically and sexually independent. Free of family responsibilities, she embraced consumerism and entertainment and lived for herself. Both contemporaries and historians have been skeptical of the image of the New Woman, seeing it as a mask obscuring women's actual circumstances of continued low pay and family burdens. Indeed, the New Woman was more image than reality, given that few women really possessed much of their own economic security and autonomy from family responsibilities. Even if women did enjoy new freedoms, those freedoms were linked to new limitations and expectations: to be a cheerful, sexy, and tireless rationalized worker at home and in the workplace.[80]

Although the Right and far Right excoriated the New Woman, there were some women of those political views who evinced a New Woman-like independence. One was the anti-Semitic publicist Lenore Kühn (1878–1955), who was twice divorced, received a doctorate in philosophy in 1908, and joined many far-Right causes during Weimar, including the neopagan and anti-Semitic German Faith Movement (*Deutsche Glaubensbewegung*). She edited a women's supplement to the DNVP's official journal, and briefly published her own monthly, *Woman and Nation (Frau und Nation)* in the mid-1920s. She also penned a sex manual, *Diotima, The School of Love*, at the suggestion of Eugen Diederichs, a noted publisher close to the youth movement. She intended *Diotima* to be a "natural history of love" that avoided the "usual conflations of the social-ethical and the purely erotic."[81] After 1933 Kühn was quite close to Nazism without ever joining the party. Other, similarly independent-minded far-Right women did become active in the NSDAP, such as Lydia Gottschewski and Elsbeth Zander.[82] Some colonialist women also displayed a New Woman-like independence, such as Else Frobenius (1875–1952), who, twice-divorced and childless, was continuously immersed in her career as a journalist, book author, and expert on political matters affecting borderlands Germans and Germans abroad from before the First World War through the end of the Second World War.

Some interwar colonialist women undertook journeys alone to the former colonies for purposes quite apart from marriage and motherhood, and so may be seen as colonialist exemplars of the New Woman. While such journeys were not unprecedented, their completely positive and serious reception in the colonialist movement was. Suspicion or sarcasm no longer inevitably greeted single women who were not intent on marriage, as it had before the war.[83] In 1928, a naturalist Gulla Pfeffer became the first German woman to carry out a research expedition in Africa "*without aid or accompaniment* by other Europeans."[84] Several women produced political travelogues after journeys around the former colonies by automobile and airplane. They visited scattered German settlers and reported on political and economic conditions. In the late 1930s, Ilse Steinhoff toured Southwest Africa, South Africa, and Tanganyika by herself, briskly dismissing the notion that her trip required any special bravery, and published a book of her photographs.[85] Another photojournalist, Eva MacLean, published an account of a trip she undertook alone to Cameroon.[86] Women like Steinhoff and MacLean needed no husband or family to take them to the colonies. They presented themselves as independent advocates of revisionism who were fully capable of judging Germans' political future and Africans' attitudes, much as Paul Rohrbach and Wilhelm Külz had done before the war. Indeed, they claimed to be able to do everything men did, and some things—such as adhering to rules of hygiene while on safari—better.[87]

Interwar colonialist women's writings often depicted a comradeship with German men that permitted independence for women without feminist critique of existing social relations. A 1937 colonialist novel by Christine Holstein, for example, portrays a wife whose husband's physical frailty serves as a plot device for her guilt-free emancipation.[88] The two are struggling farmers, in part because of the lasting effects of her husband's injuries sustained in the First World War. After her husband's death, she becomes a skillful farmer and proudly surveys her fields, "with sharp eyes sweeping across the wide open spaces, satisfied with her herds, her cornfields, her bank account."[89] Even though Southwest Africa was so far from Germany, and not even officially German any longer, it remained a colonial setting where women could weave together feminine independence, German chauvinism, deference to a (dead) husband, and economic success. As these writings suggest, the image of the emancipated woman from the early years of the Weimar Republic persisted among colonialist women in the Nazi period, even as the meaning of that emancipation was hollowed out.

Notes

This essay was originally published as a chapter in my book *German Women for Empire* (Durham 2001). It is reprinted here with permission of Duke University Press.
1. Ida Schuffenhauer, *Komm wieder Bwana. Ein deutsches Schicksal* (Berlin, 1940), and Senta Dinglreiter, *Wann kommen die Deutschen endlich wieder? Eine Reise durch unsere Kolonien in Afrika* (Leipzig, 1935). On loyalists see, e.g., Johanna Rosenkranz, "Eine Hamburger Schule zeigt ihre Kolonialschau," *Die Frau und die Kolonien*, no. 12 (December 1937): 184, and "Brief eines Kamerun-Negers," *Übersee- und Kolonialzeitung* 8, no. 19 (1 October 1928): 327. Colonialists frequently invoked the colony Togo and the East African soldiers (*Askari*) who fought under General Paul von Lettow-Vorbeck in the First World War as collectively loyal. E.g., Heinrich Schnee's *German Colonization Past and Future: The Truth About the German Colonies* (London, 1926), esp. 167–68; and Adjaï Oloukpona-Yinnon, *Unter deutschen Palmen. Die "Musterkolonie" Togo im Spiegel deutscher Kolonialliteratur (1884–1944)* (Frankfurt am Main, 1998).

2. Klaus Theweleit, *Male Fantasies. Volume 1: Women, Floods, Bodies, History* (Minneapolis, 1987), and Regina Schulte, "The Sick Warrior's Sister: Nursing During the First World War," in *Gender Relations in German History. Power, Agency and Experience from the Sixteenth to the Twentieth Century* (London, 1996), 121–41.

3. On maternalist rhetoric after 1918, see Raffael Scheck, "Women against Versailles: Maternalism and Nationalism of Female Bourgeois Politicians in the Early Weimar Republic," *German Studies Review* 22 (1999): 21–42.

4. There had been 14,830 Germans in German Southwest Africa in 1914; colonialists counted about 12,000 in the mandate by 1930. In German East Africa before the war, there had been 5,336 German colonists; by 1930 there were 2,000 in postwar Tanganyika. Wilhelm Arning, "Die Stellung des Frauenbundes in der Kolonialpolitik von heute," in *Koloniale Frauenarbeit*, ed. Frauenbund der Deutschen Kolonialgesellschaft (Berlin, 1930), 39.

5. Cited in Else Frobenius, *30 Jahre koloniale Frauenarbeit* (Berlin, 1936), 17.

6. Arning, "Die Stellung des Frauenbundes," 39.

7. Raffael Scheck, "German Conservatism and Female Political Activism in the Early Weimar Republic," *German History* 15 (1997): 34–55, and Ute Planert, *Antifeminismus im Kaiserreich. Diskurs, soziale Formation und politische Mentalität* (Göttingen, 1998), 241–45.

8. Renate Bridenthal, "Professional Housewives: Stepsisters of the Feminist Movement," in *When Biology Became Destiny: Women in Weimar and Nazi Germany*, ed. Atina Grossmann, Marion Kaplan, and Renate Bridenthal (New York, 1984), 153–73.

9. Doris Kaufmann, *Frauen zwischen Aufbruch und Reaktion. Protestantische Frauenbewegung in der ersten Hälfte des 20. Jahrhunderts* (Munich, 1988), and Planert, *Antifeminismus im Kaiserreich*, esp. 130–51.

10. Sabine Hering, *Die Kriegsgewinnlerinnen. Praxis und Ideologie der deutschen Frauenbewegung im Ersten Weltkrieg* (Pfaffenweiler, 1990), 47–80.

11. Else Frobenius, "Der goldene Schlüssel. Erinnerungen aus meinem Leben," 132. This is a typescript written in 1942–1944 and now published as *Erinnerungen einer Journalistin zwischen Kaiserreich und Zweitem Weltkrieg*, ed. Lora Wildenthal (Weimar, 2005).

12. Weimar-era women in the colonial sciences included the linguist Elise Kootz-Kretschmer and anthropologist Hilde Thurnwald.

13. Heyl responded to the war with even greater determination to "promote and uplift the calling of the housewife and mother in all strata of the population." Frobenius, "Der goldene Schlüssel," 103.

14. Kolonial-Wirtschaftliches Komitee, ed., *Die deutsche Hausfrau und die Kolonien* (Berlin, n.d.), 9.

15. *Der Kolonialdeutsche* 5, no. 5 (1 May 1925): 99.

16. *Der Kolonialdeutsche* 5, no. 1 (31 December 1924): 15 and 6, no. 17 (1 September 1926): 294–95, and *Die Brücke zur Heimat* (1928): 170 and (1929): 60.

17. *Der Kolonialdeutsche* 4, no. 11 (29 October 1924): 195.

18. Moritz J. Bonn, *Wandering Scholar* (New York, 1948), 149.

19. Fritz Fischer, *Germany's Aims in the First World War* (New York, 1967), 102–3, 317–19, 359–60, 596.

20. Adolf Rüger, "Das Streben nach kolonialer Restitution in den ersten Nachkriegsjahren," in *Drang nach Afrika. Die deutsche koloniale Expansionpolitik und Herrschaft in*

Afrika von den Anfängen bis zum Verlust der Kolonien, ed. Helmuth Stoecker (Berlin, 1991), 265; and Alfred Mansfeld, ed., *Sozialdemokratie und Kolonieen* (Münster, 1987).

21. Mary E. Townsend, *The Rise and Fall of Germany's Colonial Empire 1884–1918* (New York, 1966), 387.

22. Bundesarchiv Berlin-Lichterfelde, hereafter BA DKG 158, Bl. 56–58 ("Nie wieder Kolonien!" flier).

23. *Der Kolonialdeutsche* 8, no. 5 (1 March 1928): 77, 78 (quote). On Hoppstock-Huth, see Ute Gerhard, *Unerhört. Die Geschichte der deutschen Frauenbewegung* (Reinbek bei Hamburg, 1991), 352, 384.

24. Hans Zache, "Deutschland und der Kongress der 'unterdrückten Völker,'" *Koloniale Rundschau,* no. 4 (1927): 99.

25. Hans Paasche, *Die Forschungsreise des Afrikaners Lukanga Mukara ins innerste Deutschland,* ed. Franziskus Hähnel (Munich, 1988), 117.

26. Frobenius, "Der goldene Schlüssel," 122, 125.

27. Woodruff D. Smith, *The Ideological Origins of Nazi Imperialism* (New York, 1986), 196–230, and Rüger, "Das Streben nach kolonialer Restitution."

28. Wilhelm Solf, *Afrika für Europa. Der koloniale Gedanke des XX. Jahrhunderts* (Neumünster i.H., 1920).

29. Adolf Rüger, "Richtlinien und Richtungen deutscher Kolonialpolitik 1923–1926," in *Studien zur Geschichte des deutschen Kolonialismus in Afrika. Festschrift zum 60. Geburtstag von Peter Sebald,* ed. Peter Heine and Ulrich van der Heyden (Pfaffenweiler, 1995), 454, 461; and Franz Ansprenger, *The Dissolution of the Colonial Empires* (New York, 1989), 125–26.

30. Rüger, "Richtlinien," 461. Külz's position is also documented there.

31. Ibid., 460–61. Föllmer was editor of the populist and race purity-oriented *Koloniale Zeitschrift* before the war.

32. Although British and Belgian forces had occupied most of German East Africa by late 1916, Lettow-Vorbeck's force did not surrender until after Germany itself did in November 1918. On Lettow-Vorbeck, see Theweleit, *Male Fantasies.*

33. "Kolonialpropaganda beim jüdischen Frontsoldatenbund," *Der Kolonialdeutsche* 7, no. 5 (1 March 1927): 75.

34. Friedländer, *Nazi Germany and the Jews,* 73–75.

35. Hildebrand, *Vom Reich zum Weltreich,* 89–100.

36. Ibid., 100, 219, 437.

37. Ibid., 100–247, esp. 185–87 on Schnee.

38. Frobenius, *30 Jahre,* 27; and Steinmeister, "Jahresbericht ... 1929/30," 7. Its rapid expansion in the latter half of the 1920s reawakened the old conflict with the German Colonial Society over men who joined the former but not the latter. DKG 158, Bl. 18 (Steinmeister to DKG, 24 July 1929); Bl. 27 (DKG to Women's League, 10 June 1929); Bl. 191–92 (letter fragment), and the lists of men's names in BA DKG 158, Bl. 103–58, 177–90, which included Dernburg, Kuhn, Lindequist, Meyer-Gerhard, and Ramsay (Bl. 108, 184).

39. *Der Kolonialdeutsche* 8, no. 9 (1 May 1928): 147, and Hildegard von Lekow, "50 Jahre Rotkreuzarbeit," in Heinrich Schnee et al., *Das Buch der deutschen Kolonien* (Leipzig, 1937), 290.

40. Pascal Grosse, *Kolonialismus, Eugenik und bürgerliche Gesellschaft in Deutschland 1850–1918* (Frankfurt am Main, 2000), 193–238, and Melvin E. Page, "Introduction: Black

Men in a White Men's War," 2–3, in Melvin E. Page, ed., *Africa and the First World War* (New York), 1987.

41. Margaret Strobel, *European Women and the Second British Empire* (Bloomington, IN, 1991), 5–6.

42. Henderson, *The German Colonial Empire*, 125.

43. BA RKA 1895, Bl. 4 (questionnaire).

44. Hans Draeger, "Ada Schnee, die Gattin," in Hans Draeger, ed., *Gouverneur Schnee. Ein Künder und Mehrer deutscher Geltung. Zu seinem 60. Geburtstag* (Berlin, 1931), 125–26.

45. Ada Schnee, *Meine Erlebnisse während der Kriegszeit in Deutsch-Ostafrika* (Leipzig, 1918), 110.

46. Ibid., 109.

47. Elly Proempeler, *Kriegsgefangen quer durch Afrika. Erlebnisse einer deutschen Frau im Weltkriege* (Berlin, 1918), 33.

48. These are Schnee, *Meine Erlebnisse*; Proempeler, *Kriegsgefangen quer durch Afrika*; Maria Roscher, *Zwei Jahre Kriegsgefangen in West- und Nord-Afrika. Erlebnisse einer deutschen Frau* (Zurich, 1918); and Maria Matuschka, *Meine Erinnerungen aus Deutsch-Ostafrika von 1911–1919* (Leipzig, n.d.[1919]).

49. Reichskolonialamt, ed., *Die Kolonialdeutschen aus Kamerun und Togo in französischer Gefangenschaft* (Berlin, 1917); on African soldiers as guards, see 2, 160, and throughout the cited memoirs.

50. Some smaller number of Africans and other non-Europeans may have remained part of the occupation force until the end of the occupation in 1930. Gisela Lebzelter, "Die 'schwarze Schmach.' Vorurteile—Propaganda—Mythos," *Geschichte und Gesellschaft* 11 (1985): 37–58; Robert C. Reinders, "Racialism on the Left. E. D. Morel and the 'Black Horror on the Rhine,'" *International Review of Social History* 13 (1968): 1–28; and Tina Campt, Pascal Grosse, and Yara-Colette Lemke-Muniz de Faria, "Blacks, Germans, and the Politics of Imperial Imagination, 1920–60," in *The Imperial Imagination: German Colonialism and Its Legacy*, ed. Sara Friedrichsmeyer, Sara Lennox, and Susaane Zantop (Ann Arbor, MI, 1998), 208–14.

51. Sally Marks, "Black Watch on the Rhine: A Study in Propaganda, Prejudice and Prurience," *European Studies Review* 13 (1983): 297–334, and Reiner Pommerin, *Sterilisierung der Rheinlandbastarde: Das Schicksal einer farbigen deutschen Minderheit 1918–1937* (Düsseldorf, 1979), 23.

52. See the images reproduced in May Opitz, Katharina Oguntoye, and Dagmar Schultz, eds., *Showing Our Colors: Afro-German Women Speak Out*, trans. Anne V. Adams (Amherst, MA, 1992), 46–47, and Pommerin, *Sterilisierung der Rheinlandbastarde*, 14, 31.

53. Luise Paasche, *Männer wehrlos, Frauen schutzlos. Unsere Propagandareise gegen die Schuldlüge* (Neckargemünd, 1927), esp. 17–18; see also 20–28.

54. Campt, Grosse, and Lemke-Muniz de Faria, "Blacks, Germans, and the Politics of Imperial Imagination, 1920–60," 208 (statistic), and Pommerin, *Sterilisierung der Rheinlandbastarde*.

55. Frobenius, *30 Jahre*, 18 (see also 27); and Else Frobenius, "'Und wenn sie gleich alt werden …' Dem Gedächtnis von Hedwig von Bredow," *Die Frau* 40 (1932–33): 93.

56. Frobenius, *30 Jahre*, 13–14. Some twenty years later, when the first German deportees from Tanganyika began to arrive in Germany in 1940, the Women's League (then Division IV of the Reich Colonial League) repeated these tasks. Agnes von Boemcken, "Deutsche Rückkehrer aus Ostafrika in der Heimat," *Die Frau und die Kolonien*, no. 3 (March 1940): 17–21.

57. While its statutes were not officially changed, the Women's League did publish a revised set of organizational goals that placed youth and education at the top. See, e.g., endpapers of *Koloniale Frauenarbeit* [1930]. See also Gertrud Schröder, "Frauenaufgaben in Südwestafrika," *Der Kolonialdeutsche* 8, no. 1 (1 January 1928): 7.

58. Karl Körner, "Vom deutschen Schulwesen in Südwest," in *Koloniale Frauenarbeit* [1930]: 14.

59. Nora von Steinmeister, "Aus dem Leben der Kolonialdeutschen," in *Das Buch der deutschen Kolonien*, ed. Anton Mayer (Potsdam, 1933), 304. See also RKA 995, Bl. 224 (flier, n.d.).

60. Körner, "Vom deutschen Schulwesen in Südwest," 13.

61. Anne Maag, "Einrichtung von Lesemappen und Büchereien in Südwestafrika," in *Koloniale Frauenarbeit* (1930): 20–21.

62. The reentry dates for Germans in other former colonies varied according to each territory's administrative decision. Germans managed to repurchase expropriated plantations in Cameroon from 1925; in 1928, Germans were allowed to reenter New Guinea. Frobenius, *30 Jahre*, 26.

63. Theodor Gunzert, "Deutsches Schulwesen in Ostafrika," in *Koloniale Frauenarbeit* (1930): 9–10. See also BA RKA 995 passim, and Marcia Wright, *German Missions in Tanganyika 1891–1941: Lutherans and Moravians in the Southern Highlands* (Oxford, 1971), 162, 188.

64. Margarete von Zastrow, "Fortbildung afrikanischer Jugend in Deutschland," *Koloniale Frauenarbeit* (1930): 31–34.

65. *Der Kolonialdeutsche* 8 (1928): 58.

66. Hildegard von Lekow, "Rotkreuzarbeit in den Kolonien," in *Das Buch der deutschen Kolonien*, ed. Anton Mayer (Potsdam, 1933), 289–291, and Hintrager, "Unsere Frauenauswanderung," in *Koloniale Frauenarbeit*, ed. Frauenbund der Deutschen Kolonialgesellschaft (Berlin, 1930), 26–27.

67. *Der Kolonialdeutsche* 6, no. 12 (15 June 1926): 214; 6, no. 15 (1 August 1926): 261; and 7 (1927): 411 (quote).

68. *Der Kolonialdeutsche* 6, no. 4 (1 March 1926): 62; and no. 8 (15 April 1926): 134.

69. Nora von Steinmeister, "Jahresbericht des Frauenbundes der Deutschen Kolonialgesellschaft 1929/30," in *Koloniale Frauenarbeit* (1930): 5. On Tanganyika, see BA RKA 72 passim.

70. In 1929–30, for example, the Women's League dispatched eighty-eight women and girls to Southwest Africa and Tanganyika, including sixty-four unmarried women. Steinmeister, "Jahresbericht … 1929/30," 4.

71. Men still saw marriage and motherhood as the main goals. Hintrager, "Unsere Frauenauswanderung," 30; and Paul Rohrbach, *Afrika. Beiträge zu einer praktischen Kolonialkunde* (Berlin, 1943), 289. Hintrager, one of the authors of the German Southwest African ban on intermarriage, now directed the Reich Office for Emigration Affairs (*Reichstelle für das Auswanderungswesen*). See also BA RKA 72, Bl. 94 (Gunzert to Women's League, 20 August 1928); and Bl. 240 (Gunzert to Women's League, 28 March 1931). The new consensus that emerged is apparent in Nora von Steinmeister, "Jahresbericht … ," 5 and Hintrager, "Unsere Frauenauswanderung," 30; see also "Die Akademikerin ist die beste Kolonistin," *Die Frau und die Kolonien* 1, no. 11 (November 1932): 145. An article encouraging women to study at university appeared in the Women's League organ in 1937: Susi Teubner, "Mädel mit 'Kopf fürs Studium,'" *Die Frau und die Kolonien*, no. 12 (December 1937): 179–80.

72. Frobenius, *30 Jahre*, 24, and Mechtild Rommel and Hulda Rautenberg, *Die kolonialen Frauenschulen von 1908–1945* (Witzenhausen, 1983), esp. 31, 33, 35.
73. Rommel and Rautenberg, *Die kolonialen Frauenschulen*, 87.
74. Frobenius, *30 Jahre*, 24; Rommel and Rautenberg, 52; and BA RdI 27215, Bl. 3 (Körner, "Bericht," n.d. [1934]).
75. Rommel and Rautenberg, *Die kolonialen Frauenschulen*, 40, 67. Its curriculum, like that of the Bad Weilbach school, was based on the Reifenstein school run by Ida von Kortzfleisch.
76. Agnes von Boemcken, "Koloniale Frauenschule Rendsburg," in *Koloniale Frauenarbeit* (1930): 18–19. See also 17.
77. One of countless examples, in this case from the pen of a colonialist woman, may be found in Else Frobenius, "Eine Frauenfahrt an die Front," *Die Frau* 24 (1916–17): 541. See Elisabeth Domansky, "Militarization and Reproduction in World War I Germany," in *Society, Culture, and the State in Germany 1870–1930*, ed. Geoff Eley (Ann Arbor, MI, 1996), 461–62.
78. Renate Bridenthal, "Something Old, Something New: Women Between the Two World Wars," in *Becoming Visible*, ed. Renate Bridenthal, Claudia Koonz, and Susan Stuar (Boston, 1987), 473–97.
79. Mary Louise Roberts, *Civilization without Sexes: Reconstructing Gender in Postwar France, 1917–1927* (Chicago, 1994); Susan Kingsley Kent, *Making Peace: The Reconstruction of Gender in Interwar Britain* (Princeton, NJ, 1993); and Victoria de Grazia, *How Fascism Ruled Women: Italy 1922–1945* (Berkeley, CA, 1992).
80. Else Hermann, Siegfried Kracauer, and Hilde Walter, as excerpted in *The Weimar Republic Sourcebook*, ed. Anton Kaes, Martin Jay, and Edward Dimendberg (Berkeley, CA, 1994), 207–8, 216–18, 210–11; Friedrun Bastkowski, Christa Lindner, and Ulrike Prokop, eds., *Frauenalltag und Frauenbewegung im 20. Jahrhundert. Bd. 2: Frauenbewegung und die "Neue Frau" 1890–1933* (Frankfurt am Main, 1980); and Renate Bridenthal and Claudia Koonz, "Beyond *Kinder, Küche, Kirche*: Weimar Women in Politics and Work," in *When Biology Became Destiny*, ed. Grossmann, Kaplan, and Bridenthal, 33–65.
81. Detlev Kühn, "Lenore Kühn—eine nationale Mitstreiterin der Frauenbewegung," *Nordost-Archiv*, no. 61–62 (1981): 39–56, and no. 63–64 (1981): 31–54 (quote on 32–33). See *Diotima. Die Schule der Liebe* (Jena, 1930), which was published anonymously and ran into several editions up to 1965.
82. On Gottschewski and Zander, see Claudia Koonz, "The Competition for a Women's *Lebensraum*, 1928–1934" in *When Biology Became Destiny*, ed. Grossmann, Kaplan, and Bridenthal, 199–236; and Koonz, *Mothers in the Fatherland: Women, the Family and Nazi Politics* (New York, 1987).
83. Lene Haase satirized that prewar response to a German woman traveling alone for pleasure to German Southwest Africa in her book *Raggys Fahrt nach Südwest. Roman* (Berlin, 1910); see also Clara Brockmann, *Die deutsche Frau in Südwestafrika: Ein Beitrag zur Frauenfrage in unseren Kolonien* (Berlin, 1910).
84. Gulla Pfeffer, "Meine Kamerun-Nigeria-Expedition," *Der Kolonialdeutsche* 8, no. 18 (15 September 1928): 304. See also Gulla Pfeffer, *Die weisse Mah. Allein bei Urvölkern und Menschenfressern*, Minden i.W., 1929.
85. Ilse Steinhoff, *Deutsche Heimat in Afrika. Ein Bildbuch aus unseren Kolonien* (Berlin, 1939), unpaginated. During the Second World War, Steinhoff worked as a reporter in

Croatia. See her article "Ein neuer Staat entsteht" in the *Berliner Illustrierte Zeitung* of 15 May 1941, 550–51, repr. in *Konkret* (January 1992): 36–37.

86. Eva MacLean, *Unser Kamerun von heute. Ein Fahrtenbuch* (Munich, 1940). An example of her short journalism is Eva MacLean, "Shopping in Sansibar," *Die Frau und die Kolonien*, (1932): 139–43. See also Dinglreiter, *Wann kommen die Deutschen endlich wieder?* and Louise Diel, *Die Kolonien warten! Afrika im Umbruch* (Leipzig, 1939).

87. Inge Wild, "Der andere Blick. Reisende Frauen in Afrika," *Etudes Germano-Africaines*, no. 10 (1992): 125.

88. Christine Holstein, *Deutsche Frau in Südwest. Den Erlebnissen einer Farmersfrau im heutigen Afrika nacherzählt* (Leipzig, 1937). Holstein was the pseudonym of Margarete Jähne.

89. Ibid., 139.

CHAPTER 17

The Economy of Experience in Weimar Germany

PETER FRITZSCHE

One of the defining features of political culture in the Weimar era was the conviction that Germany's future depended on a fundamental replenishment of experience that would then be available for conversion into political and social capital. There was no agreement on just where these experiences might lie, but contemporaries repeatedly cast themselves as intrepid explorers of new dimensions of time and space to seek them out. They endeavored to open up unrealized sources of politically sustainable time to carry Germans forward or else attempted to divest themselves of outmoded practices and assumptions in order to finally maximize their ability to adapt to changing times; they excavated depth or played on surface. Although the testimonies of social observers in the 1920s are not accurate in any verifiable way, they reveal how widespread was the premise that the postwar world needed to be remapped. It is this effort, first at casting aside older cognitive templates, then at retooling and recalibrating new ones, that characterizes much of the diverse cultural work of the Weimar period. This revamped economy of experience structures autobiographical scenes like the one Ernst von Salomon (born in 1902) recollects in 1930 in his semiautobiographical novel, *Die Geächteten* (*The Outlaws*, *1930*) about the new year 1918–19.

A young man at the end of World War I—someone who had not fought on the battlefront, but did encounter first-hand in Berlin the hardships of the homefront—Salomon sets the scene carefully. He is reading Walther Rathenau's recently published essay, *Von kommenden Dingen* (*In Days to Come*, 1917), although "the thin hope for the spiritualization of the mechanical seemed to me to be a meager answer." Throughout the night he read and read, and then he looked out the window of his room.

> The candle flickered and died, and the bulky profile of the tenement building, filled to the roof with people, the tangle of flues and chimneys, the crum-

bling rooflines dissolved like ghosts against the velvet background. I stood up and leaned out the window, peering into the canyons of courtyards in which the racket of the coming day could already be heard. I felt seventeen years enough to know that this had to be subdued rather then ensouled.[1]

Not only are Rathenau's answers inadequate, but the hard social facts seen from the window are unsatisfactory because they do not contain spiritual substance. Salomon ultimately abandons the city for a journey of discovery, joining the *Freikorps* in the Baltic and eventually conspiring in the 1922 assassination of Rathenau himself—all stations in his search for a new nation to be founded in the future.

The scene recreates an exemplary cartography of Weimar Germany. In the first place, Salomon admits to the solidity of the metropolis. The tenement building has sufficient visual and aural presence—"*Gewirr*" (tangle), "*Lärm*" (racket)—to defy Salomon's effort to imagine its spirituality. With its "*klobige Umrisse*" (bulky profile) and "*brüchigen Linien*" (crumbling lines), the city he sees is also strongly disorienting. While Salomon is unmistakably repelled by the metropolitan spectacle, he also recognizes its overwhelming power. At the same time, however, Salomon makes sure readers do not mistake the spectacle for the real. Not only is he, in the retrospective account of 1930, searching for ways of making sense of the things outside his window in 1918, in this case by reading Rathenau's essay, but twelve years later he is writing his own manuscript to appeal to an as yet unrealized *völkisch* community. This literary activity introduces the subjunctive tense that does not take the appearances of the city or the situation of postwar Germany for granted, one that realizes the possibility of persuasion, mobilization, and conversion. The message of Salomon's reading and writing is that there can be movement from the apparent to the possible. For all its sensory distinctiveness, the city's layout is not permanent and might vanish in an instant to be replaced with another kind of living community, which in this case belongs to the nation.

Salomon maps out two very different versions of the contemporary, which rehearse the longings and vexations of Germans in the years after World War I. He contrasts the disenchanted business of civilization with the enchanted possibilities of community, the ahistorical surface of the metropolitan present with the historical depth of the imagined nation. He connects the two locations, one behind the other, by the most tenuous means, a ghostly vision. The two worlds Salomon identifies in *Die Geächteten* are difficult to map on to each other. The one cannot be seen clearly or readily from the vantage of the other, and travel between the two places depends on idiosyncratic conviction. This lack of calibration foregrounds an epistemological crisis that is resolved by the strenuous, always unfinished work of tearing up old maps and redrawing new ones. Of course, while Salomon searched for the hidden nation, there were many other observers, also in Berlin, who used the material culture of the city to dispel the illusions of German grandeur and to build more modest, streamlined lifeways. Both efforts of reconstruction in the present, however, rested on a massive invalidation of the past, and on a sharp differentiation between surface, which was the evidence of the new, profane organization of social life, and depth, the potential affiliations with political and cultural communities more or less desirable.

The two registers of "surface" and "depth" appear again and again in contemporary texts, and they have been picked up by scholars to make sense of the cultural innovation of the Weimar period. Janet Ward, for example, argues that "New Objectivity" (*neue Sachlichkeit*) "constitutes this century's most concentrated systematization of surface, and has become one of European modernism's best-known visual codes ... to describe the modern urban, commercial experience."[2] Although she is fully aware of the overfunctionalization of social relations embedded in Weimar *Sachlichkeit*, Ward holds out for a partial recuperation of the emancipatory aspects of the new urban formations envisioned in the 1920s. At the same time, it was precisely the overwhelming presence of the mass media and "the cult of distraction" that spurred counterpunctual searches for more durable communities of belief. As Martin Lindner and Ulrike Hass have argued, Weimar cultural projects on both the Left and the Right operated in the subjunctive mode in an attempt to recreate social intimacy and historical depth.[3] Each register implied the other, and even if contemporaries valorized the utility of depth in radically different ways, they upheld a common vision of recent history in which the constant iteration of the new had severed lines of historical continuity and valorized the radical possibilities of the present. In the end, the "delinquency of history" served as a predicate for wholesale social and political reconfiguration.[4] The past was transformed more and more into something that once was, "*Einst,*" a categorical otherness that obscured its own internal temporal differentiations or its long-term evolutionary aspects and thus its potential pertinence to the here and now.[5] The present was no longer the familiar place where the trends of the past culminated, but the unknowable site where the new and unexpected were encountered.

That it was Weimar Germans and not their wartime foes who imagined both the invalidation of the past and the possibilities of new life is not surprising given the unprecedented collective nature of the war effort and, more pertinently, the collapse of the social and political order that had made that effort possible. *Zusammenbruch* (collapse) was an extremely democratic experience. Reinhart Koselleck has pointed to the new knowledge that military defeat made possible. Historical thought, he argues, is a mix of *extrapolation*, which systematically imposes order onto the diachronic according to broad, discernible patterns, and *interpolation*, which introduces new material and new perspectives to account for surprise. For Koselleck, methodological innovation is the product of interpretive interpolation. To ask the question why events happened the unexpected way they did is to privilege interpolation over extrapolation. For that reason, Koselleck concludes, it is losers rather than winners who are most likely to introduce innovation into historical perspectives. Insofar as they reflect on what has passed, it is the losers who face the more serious "scarcity of answers" (*Beweisnot*) and who search for new causes that can explain the occasion of disaster.[6] Without explicitly saying so, Koselleck suggests what the role of history writing might be: to create or maintain an active subject in acknowledged conditions of displacement. If the surprise of defeat is to be explained at all, and the defeated subject is to be rebuilt and reactivated, a new economy of experience needs to be put in place in order to revise ideas that had been taken for granted and to revaluate notions of contingency, possibility, and necessity. This revisionist labor is the precondition for renewed historical activity. For the winners, however, revisionism is not nearly so urgent because victory privileged the extrapolation of the seemingly self-evident lessons of the historical process rather than the interpolation of new, worrisome elements. In contrast to the almost obsessive inquests into the state of the new that characterizes Weimar, cultural production in interwar France and Britain was much more affirmative, conservationist, and even nostalgic, faithful to the idea that the postwar world could be righted to its prewar state.[7] There was little of this faith in Weimar Germany.

Koselleck's notion of *Beweisnot* is a useful way to make sense of the cultural activity of the Weimar period. It captures both the suspicion that previous systems of apprehension had become invalid and also the effort to uncover new materials and new methods. These are two distinct operations, but they are both premised on the proximity of danger and surprise and on the malleability of the material world so that it is possible for the report on *Not* or scarcity to open up imaginative space to discover the treasures of newly authoritative *Beweise*. Much of this ground has been surveyed by Helmut Lethen in his rich literary account of *Neue Sachlichkeit, Cool Conduct: The Culture of Distance in Weimar Germany*.[8] But Lethen's emphasis on the whirlwind of dispersion obscures other motions, particularly the extensive search for means to reinsert innovation into the stream of history. The evidence summoned up to describe the loss of history was always an attempt to rebuild the subject in a new regime of necessity and possibility.

Surface

Ernst von Salomon's apprehension of the dark shapes and uneven lines of the tenement, and his shock at its profane, material immediacy, was commonplace in the 1920s. Beginning after the war and over the course of the inflation, social commentators described German society in relentlessly urban terms. The contemporary city stood for a sometimes mournful, sometimes appreciative invalidation of the national past. "The war began with enthusiastic, völkisch, dynastic and self-conscious ideas," commented Eugen Diesel, and "it ended in the world of machines and masses, of organizations unleashed, of uncontrollable abstractions" from which there was no escaping.[9] Although Georg Simmel died in 1918, his 1904 analysis of "mental life" in the metropolis proved exemplary, and it was Weimar-era critics who developed his initial inquiries into the purely functional social relations that came with the intense circulation of goods and people in the city and the invasive extension of money as the measure of all things. Indeed, the postwar city, and particularly Berlin, provided the most vivid evidence for the abrading, dispersive forces of modern life that seemed to shatter the social bonds of community and obstruct the transmission of cultural and historical tradition. While much of this commentary took up conventional antiurban themes that would have been familiar to Wilhelmine audiences, the point was not so much to argue for or against the city, but to dramatize the utterly new situation in which Germany found itself and to insist on the profound force of technological change and on the reach of mass culture. Commenting that "the construction of life is at present in the power of facts far more than of convictions," Walter Benjamin took the measure of the power of city views in the 1920s.[10] Reports from the city, themselves a distinctive Weimar-era genre developed by Joseph Roth, Bernhard von Brentano, and Siegfried Kracauer, as well as Benjamin, were attempts to reconsider the power of material facts, the organization of society, and the nature of historical change.[11] The typical caricatures of *"Einst und Jetzt"* (then and now) in the mass media, the zeal among authors to identify and classify new phenomena, and the introduction again and again of unprecedented social types to illustrate the contemporary moment indicates just how compelling the idea of the new was in the 1920s.

What is striking about the reports on the crisis of inheritance is the epochal nature of the break that observers believed they were seeing. They rendered the specific aspects of Germany's military defeat, political revolution, and economic disarray in extremely hypostatized terms in order to reveal the brand new historical ground encompassed by the city. Siegfried Kracauer provides one of the most evocative accounts of this modern condition, in which he links total mobilization with the oblivion of history. In his acclaimed 1932 essay, "Street Without Memory," Kracauer described the Kurfürstendamm as a new place because it incorporated "emptily flowing time in which nothing endures." A continuous train of new shops, new fashions, and new facades effaced any memory of what had been: "The new enterprises are absolutely new and those that have been displaced by them are totally extinguished." The prewar sandstone ornaments, themselves once completely up-to-date, now already "a bridge to yesterday," were simply knocked down.[12] Amidst ceaseless renovation, the Kurfürstendamm stood for a city that lived entirely without the past. As a sandstone city, both literally and imaginatively, Berlin was not so much newly modern as eternally new.

Although prewar feuilletonists had already grabbed at the image of the sandstone facades to indicate the transitory nature of metropolitan Berlin, Kracauer read into the mundane facelifts on the Kurfürstendamm a much more general concept of modern time, characterized by emptiness. "I know of no other city that is capable of so promptly shaking off what has just occurred," he concluded.[13] As a result, city space was filled with a fortuitous, unconnected success of events. Events gave the city a luminous, spectatorial quality, but tore away at its history. It is true that Kracauer recoiled from the idea of a present that lacked any traction to move into the future, but he acknowledged the fundamental importance of the process of the desacralization of the past, one that had relentlessly stripped away the false virtues of Wilhelmine Germany's elite culture and depleted the reservoirs of its class-based experience. There was no turning back: "The process leads directly through the mass ornament and not backward."[14] This was the significance of the pervasive popular culture of the city.

First in the tawdry terms of the inflation economy in the first postwar years and later amidst the functionalist operations of the stabilization in the mid-1920s, Kracauer's notions were widely retailed throughout the Weimar period. Again and again, observers dramatized the break with the past in terms of the animation of mass entertainments and the utter ahistoricity of a deliberately urbanized present. In his 1931 survey of the inflation, Hans Ostwald regarded main streets reduced to little more than "money streets" in which a "ground-floor architecture" of "juice bars," "gin shops," and "cigarette and tobacco stands" flourished against a transitional backdrop of "posters and paper scraps."[15] Exchange (money, shops) corresponded to ephemerality (scraps) to deny the accumulation of meaning or the orientation of history. The inflation had cheapened life not only by forcing people to sell their keepsakes and heirlooms but by turning treasures into junk as a result of curbside exchanges. Moreover, the war allegedly reduced countless city people to salesmen, who lived buying and selling in the most public and unadorned way. Memories of the war were repeatedly debased into the terms of the market. The widespread belief that veterans in fact constituted the great majority of postwar street vendors and that war cripples were simply hustlers and fakes, a familiar theme in Weimar film and theater, indicated how the national effort of the Great War had steadily been drained of social meaning.[16] Heroism was reduced to hucksterism, history to a hoax. All that was left was ceaseless, profane exchange.

The onset of monetary stabilization in 1924 cleared the streets of itinerant vendors and paper scraps, but images of circulation and traffic persisted to characterize the new sobriety as it had the great inflation.[17] The now voluminous literature on the so-called Golden Twenties remains conspicuously centered on the city. Guided by the flat, functionalist representations of New Objectivity and the arguments of critics such as Kracauer, scholars emphasize the extension of mass culture that was relentlessly "modern, ahistorical, [and] respectless" and the calibration of everyday life to a regime of constant movement.[18] Texts and images in Weimar's mass media themselves reported on the profound impact of the new metropolitan world throughout the 1920s, gaining their authority not so much by virtue of their verisimilitude but through the fact that they were so widely consumed. The very habit of reading the paper, something almost every Berliner did each day, confirmed the "the coproduction in this enormous process."[19]

The cumulative "reality effect" of newspapers, illustrated weeklies, and films was to give an imposing face to the non-stop production of the new. Readers were presented with the seemingly self-evident facts of "*das neue Leben*," (new life) "*das Leben von morgen*," (life of tomorrow) and "*die neue Zeit*" (new times) by a generation of media-savvy experts, including science-fiction writer Hans Dominick, architect Adolf Behne, and Eugen Diesel, son of the engineer. The unconditional form of the future tense they deployed is astonishing. However fantastic their visions of the future appear in retrospect, they portrayed a totally reconstructed contemporary landscape dominated by huge cities, busy thoroughfares, and disciplined, serried masses all enlarged on a vertiginous scale by the huge magnifying lens of Americanization. In an early version of the "International Style" of the 1950s, the specter of Americanization in the 1920s indicated that the future would be governed by transformations in technology in ways that owed little to past traditions or to the separate cultural developments of individual nations: the new subjects were masses, not *Völker*; their places were cities, not nations; and they composed lifestyles rather than cultures. The "new life forms are entirely independent of party affiliations," informed Eugen Diesel in 1931; "a life-style emerges from the spirit of technology to which we are all beholden, whether Communist or National Socialist."[20] The implication was clear to Hannes Meyer: "The fatherland fades away. We learn Esperanto. *We become citizens of the world.*"[21]

What gave the representation of the technological future particular authority was its colonization of the private sphere, a space previously considered traditional and timeless. Throughout the 1920s, the new world was consumed as fashion. *Bubiköpfe* (bobbed hair) and sheer, trim dresses, the form and arrangement of furniture, the management of social relations with the opposite sex, and urban lifestyle in general were inscribed with the signs of historical difference.[22] The prominent place given over to women in these images is important: the feminine sphere no longer marked the persistence of natural or timeless formations, but rather the wholesale transformation of all aspects of life. Moreover, proponents of "*das neue Wohnen*" (the new home) quite self-consciously promoted the destruction of the keepsakes of the past. Appalled by what he called "ein Fetischismus mit den Gegenständen" (a fetishism for objects) Bruno Taut called for an enormous house-cleaning that would rid the homes not only of old-fashioned "Vorhängen … Teppichen, Vorlegern" (curtains, carpets … rugs) but also commemorative "Photos und Souvenirs" and other "Erinnerungsreste" (memory scraps) (memories had become scraps).[23] It was clear that "*die neue Wohnung*," the title of Taut's 1924 book that sold twenty-six thousand copies in four years, "is first, not an attic; second, not a trinket store; and third, not a museum."[24] The new architects worked energetically to create "spaces in which it is not easy to leave behind a trace," as Walter Benjamin noted.[25]

There was something liberating about living without traces of the past. "After so many years of dying and grieving, of hatred and worry, today the masses of people in all countries have the opposite slogan: live well and forget everything else," reported the *Berliner Illustrirte Zeitung* in a revealing 1930 article entitled "Modern Comfort:" "People are happy with their bodies, made healthy with dance and sport." Even without economic security or political stability, observers believed that the young generation had found individual ways to manage the crisis. "They are able to adapt and to adjust," commented Viktor Dohna; "having come of age during the war and inflation," "they are utterly unspoiled." In the very acts of casting off the inheritance of the past, "young people" had found a refreshing self-reliance: "A few terms are missing in their dictionary of life," Dohna discovered: "to postpone something," "to think about later," to consider "something beneath them," "but we have to," and "we simply can't do that."[26] Novelists Irgmard Keun and Vicki Baum incarnated just this independence in their breezy, likable characters. For the sociologist Hellmuth Plessner, the improvised lifestyles of the 1920s provided a glimpse onto a new, rehabilitative individualism. He argued that the solvent potentials and restless mobility of modern life had withdrawn the conditions for returning home. To attempt such a return would result in a fixation on a single identity, refurbish reactionary politics, and inhibit the development of the individual person, who could live fully only as a traveler, an explorer, or, in other words, a metropolitan. Here Plessner anticipated the figure of the postmodern fugitive, whose terrain is the brand-new, completely mobilized global cityscape.[27]

The imaginative finish to Weimar's surface is intellectual labor of an impressive sort because it poses so insistently the possibility of the loss of history in the administration of things. Putting aside the question of how accurate was the media simulation of the present, the authority invested in the "now" and the "new" in these years is remarkable. The description itself is less revealing than the act of description. The representation of surface put into question the self-evident nature of historical, national, and other collective meanings. In many ways, surface mirrors the *Beweisnot* to which Koselleck refers; the invalidation of once-authoritative historical narratives. It was this work of invalidation that Kracauer, for one, found to be the most positive consequence of the spread of

mass culture. However Kracauer was alarmed at the nontransformative nature of constant motion. The big-city public of clerks and employees, whom he
studied with care, remained entirely distracted by the present moment, their
interests and commitments pressed into the same sandstone forms as the city's
facades. For Kracauer this meant that metropolitans were not able to take their
bearings or understand their historical condition, and thus could not act in
politically liberating ways.[28] By the onset of the depression, the glamour of the
surface had little connection with the misery of people's lives: the *Lebenskünstler*
(hedonist) of the 1920s had run out of tricks as Hans Fallada shows in *Little
Man, What Now?* Suddenly, the new person, apparently freed from the ballast
of the past and invited to take pleasure in her new nakedness, stood isolated
and defenseless. It is at this point that Kracauer's analysis is brought up short
because he cannot detect the means by which the masses might move beyond
the "cult of distraction." The rehabilitative aspects of the loss of the inheritance
of prewar German history are thus unwittingly submerged in a much more
vexing problem of the loss of historical memory and historical subjectivity.

The Subjunctive Tense

Although the main thrust of Siegfried Kracauer's essays was to report on the
annihilation of history in the economic and technical rhythms of the city, he left
some clues of new life at the scene of devastation. In his 1930 essay, "Screams
of the Street," Kracauer surveyed the "terror that is without an object" permeat-
ing the prosperous "streets in the west" precincts of Berlin: "their populace do
not belong together and the atmosphere in which communal actions emerge
is completely lacking in them." "Without content," "screaming out their emptiness," streets and buildings expressed the ahistorical and solitary aspect to the
city. And yet Kracauer sensed the existence of other places: he makes out the
noise of a "National Socialist gang" and the "penetrating odor" of Communist
riots in a proletarian district, "Neukölln perhaps or Wedding."[29] However, Kracauer stays put on the Kurfürstendamm and ends up missing the gang and the
riot and does not make sensible different registers of noise or different kinds
of smell.

Kracauer does not turn the corner because for him the presence of the new
was manifest in the overpowering forms of mass culture in the contemporary
city. Focused as he was on the metropolis, Kracauer had surprisingly little to
say about the vividness of the body of the nation, the trauma of defeat, or the
experience of the war. His shop girls crowded Potsdamer Platz and flocked to
Haus Vaterland, but did not seem connected to larger political or social enti-
ties. Indeed, one of the reasons why Kracauer is on Potsdamer Platz is to stage
just this sort of escape from the oppressive political hierarchies of recent Ger-

man history. Yet on streets perpendicular to the Kürfurstendamm there is evidence of other ways of thinking about *Jetztzeit* (the present time). Kracauer's offhand references to political gangs and proletarian riots stand in for a much broader effort in the Weimar period to search for new sources of collective power, which is the point of departure for Ernst von Salomon when he leaves Berlin.

Weimar echoed with the "tap, tap, tap" of the surveyor on uncertain ground: the effort to take bearings and discover historical potential. Ernst Jünger, for one, was thrilled by the seemingly unexplored terrain that lay at his feet: "After laying dry for a long time, the once-secure precincts of order explode like gunpowder, and the unknown, the extraordinary, the dangerous become not only familiar but also permanent features."[30] It was precisely the vast evidence of the detonations of the present that made the effort to insert innovation into the stream of history and to rebuild the social body of the nation conceivable. Jünger dramatized the present as a moment completely disconnected from the past in order to search for hitherto unacknowledged techniques of mobility— Koselleck's *Beweise*. This was the work of interpretive innovation, or interpolation, designed to create for Germany a new, active historical subjectivity.

It was the World War that provided the most usable resources for recreating the national subject. The war was at once the site of the invalidation of the past and the point of departure for the future, a point of view that made Germany so different from France or Britain; to paraphrase Kracauer, "The process leads directly through the war and not backward." With its new social and political formations and vast technological productions, and given the perilous state in which it had left the world, the war was, along with the city, the primary form that the present took in Weimar Germany. Insofar as it was experienced as the extreme and violent intrusion of the new, the war offered the nation what I call *techniques of mobility*, the means to imagine and propose new historical itineraries. Three aspects stand out. In the first place, the war released a wave of historical revisionism. History lessons were turned over and over again as contemporaries tried to figure out the direction to history. The war also introduced the *Volk* as the proper subject of German history. And finally, the jeopardy of war and the rigors of technological change prompted an often anguished quest for experience to endow the new historical subject with comparative advantages of capacity and expertise. The achievement of what Wolfgang Schivelbusch refers to as the "culture of defeat" was to think through the alterity of the present in order to envision and initiate radical social and political departures.[31]

To discern an alternative social reality beneath the surface of the city was to take an energetic interest in the work of history. The "task" of searching for the "sources of the new" had the potential for realizing new contours of individual freedom, as Gerhart Pohl, editor of the Leftist journal *Neue Bücherschau*, indicated,[32] and the intensive scrutiny of city life was an effort to find new modes of sociability, but historical revisionism itself remained largely contained by the idea of the nation and the goal of rehabilitating the *Volk*. Not only had the war drawn people out of parochial life-worlds and personal time zones, but it had placed them into a shared time of the German nation. Ernst Jünger somewhat melodramatically conjured up "'farmers' boys who slipped from the country-side into world history's chamber of horrors" in the years 1914–1918.[33] This does not mean that there was a single, authoritative version of the experience of the war, but rather a common effort to remember the war and to tease out its significance, which was why Salomon found himself reading Rathenau.

"Right after the end of the great war," wrote Hermann Hesse in 1932, "our country was filled with saviors, prophets, and disciples, echoed with premoni-tions of apocalypse or hopes for the advent of the Third Reich."[34] What Ulrich Linse refers to as "barefoot prophets" grabbed repeatedly at the collars of post-war passersby to provide complete answers to the national destiny. The Treaty of Versailles, more than any other event, was endlessly discussed. To America's best reporter, H. R. Knickerbocker, who traveled across Germany in 1930 and 1931, Weimar's citizens talked constantly about the World War, the Treaty of Versailles, and the aggression of France.[35] Versailles provided "one of the most general formulas of a popular political science" summarizes Martin Geyer in a study that extended well beyond the resentments of the nationalist Right.[36] Itinerant lecturers repeatedly spoke on topics of economic, political, and his-torical interest in the "*Deutsche Abende*" sponsored by local patriotic societies across Germany.

The anti-Semitism of hundreds of racial associations had dramatic success capturing at least the attention of middle-class readers; followers of the notori-ous racist Theodor Fritsch handed out as many as 2 million leaflets between November 1918 and March 1919, and in just the single year 1920, the Ger-man Völkisch Defense and Combat League claimed it had distributed a total of 7,642,000 pieces of propaganda.[37] Social Democrats also acquired a large, if evanescent readership in the first years after the war. The independent study of the political parameters of the postwar years is conspicuous and suggests the ways in which the individual dramatized itself in terms of a new study of history.

One way of getting a sense of how the fate of the German people became the object of anguished personal concern is to consider the autobiographical recol-lections of old Nazi fighters gathered up by the American sociologist Theodor Abel in 1936. To be sure, the authority of Nazi narratives since 1933 con-taminates the recollections of what had happened before, and Nazi statements are hardly representative of German autobiographies generally. Nonetheless, they provide some illustration of the popular effort to rethink history. These activists strained to discern itineraries of history in the years after 1918 and de-scribed the profound unsettlement of their individual lives in the light of new social relations and new collective commitments. Again and again, history was visualized in terms of catastrophic endings, violent beginnings, and explosive uprisings. To account for his journey to National Socialism, an East Prussian farmer began his memoirs with the day "exactly twenty years ago, when I was only five years old. I first saw field-grey-clad soldiers with sabres and guns, and my own father dressed the same way. My mother watched, serious and worried. War! I heard this word then for the first time, but I soon understood it."[38] A sense that a previous life had been left behind prevailed: "My old world broke asunder in my experiences" in the war, recalled one Catholic National Social-ist.[39] By the fall of 1918, another Nazi reported, "everything in the fatherland had begun to stagger."[40] "Soon thereafter came the revolution," explained an activist in a breathless, telegraphic style for which the medium is the message: "it was something new, incomprehensible. For me, something unknown."[41]

Future party members remembered themselves as ravenous readers, fasci-nated with history already in school, as was Hitler,[42] and later browsing among newspapers until they reported finally picking up a Nazi edition, or visiting political meetings until they found themselves in agreement with one or an-other Nazi orator. This stock taking is evidence of a remarkable visualization of the indeterminate but sensible forces of history, which were alternatively imagined in Marxist, nationalist, or racial terms. Quite a few autobiographers had seriously considered Marxism, or at least articulated its alleged shortcom-ings. "Having thrown aside the Marxist idea long ago, I thought and thought," recalled one miner who eventually "in 1928–1929 ... read and heard about Adolf Hitler," whose "words went right to my marrow."[43] One future member of the Nazi Party, a teacher from Vorsfelde, explained that in the 1920s two books stood on his desk: "Adolf Hitler's *Mein Kampf* and Karl Marx. *Jawohl* Karl Marx! ... Learning, reading, comparing." Eventually, the teacher admitted that "Karl Marx disappeared" from his desk; Hitler did not.[44]

The image of books on desks should draw attention to the vast new popular history literature that was consumed in the 1920s. Oswald Spengler's *The De-cline of the West*, which insistently questioned the self-sufficiency of European and especially French and British historical narratives, was a runaway best-seller in the 1920s and spawned a historiographical controversy that worked itself into everyday speech. And it was not only Spengler; a shelf of popular books appeared between 1918 and 1933, self-consciously seeking to diagnose the "crisis of the times" that had resisted the application of conventional his-toriographical paradigms: in addition to Rathenau's essay, *Von kommenden Dingen*; Moeller van den Bruck's *Das Dritte Reich* (1926); Hermann Graf Key-serling's *Die neuentstehende Welt* (1926); Adolf Behne's *Neues Wohnen, Neues Bauen* (1927); Frank Matzke's *Jugend bekennt: so sind wir!* (1930); Karl Jaspers' *Die geistige Situation der Zeit* (1931); Ernst Günther Gründel's *Die Sendung der jungen Generation* (1932); and Ernst Jünger's *Der Arbeiter* (1932). Salomon, for one, took note of his reading frenzy in the early 1920s: "For a time I was interested in national economy … my pockets were full of broschures and graphs … Then I took up religion," and then "literature," "from Edda to Spengler, one after another," so that on his shelf "Rathenau and Nietzsche, Stendhal and Dostoevsky, Langbehn and Marx stood unordered side by side."[45] Simply the effort to read the signs of the times indicates the viability of popular historical revisionism, a genre premised on an acknowledgement of the instability of authoritative readings, a willingness to think in terms of discontinuity, and an insistence on the open-endedness of the future.

The effort to discern the directions of history corresponded to the effort to envision and enable a new historical subject. Without overstating the argument, the hidden, imperiled, or incapacitated *Volk* was the central object of desire in German politics in the interwar years. The common effort of fighting the war and the distinctly national terms of military defeat and the political and economic ordeals that followed all worked to make the case for the nation. Whatever the political viewpoint of Germans, war snatched and killed and mutilated bodies because those bodies were German and therefore gave a living reality to the notion of the *Volkskörper*. Germany had changed profoundly since August 1914, testified Wilhelm Stapel at the end of the war: "The entire people had been cast in a new radiance."[46] For him, as for many others, the *Volk* had come to life and finally recognized itself as the proper subject of German history. However nebulous concepts as the "*Volksstaat*" (peoples' state) or "*Volksgemeinschaft*" (peoples' community) were, they had popular resonance that cannot be overlooked. However incomplete and unsatisfactory the "peace of the fortress" (*Burgfrieden*) had been in the years 1914–1918, the ideal of national solidarity and the claims of collective social responsibility structured postwar political expectations. Social Democratic workers and nationalist burghers certainly collided in fundamental ways, but they claimed entitlements on the basis of the *Volksgemeinschaft*.[47] The more populist connotations of nation, as opposed to state or Reich, also guided criticism of Wilhelmine Germany, which was widely condemned for its codes of deference and ranks of hierarchy, and for its inability to create a genuine German patriotism. The wartime icons of generic heroes—the soldier, the worker, the peasant—remained in place throughout the Weimar period, confirming the authority of ordinary "*Volkstümlichkeit*" (ethnicity) in political culture. Indeed, no Weimar politician, except for the Communists, dared approach the electorate without using the address of "*Volk*."

What emerges during Weimar is a new sense of national space in which citizens actively sought to find or identify Germany. As a consequence, national events were staged in local arenas in a process of theatricalization, and local destinations were regarded as parts of the nation in a metaphorical or synecdochical operation. Some of the biggest rallies held in local places during the

Weimar Republic were those that assembled Germans of all political convictions onto market squares to protest of the terms of the Treaty of Versailles in spring 1919 and again to demonstrate against the plebiscites in Silesia two years later. These brought together on a single dais German Nationalists and Social Democrats and even Independent Socialists. But the breadth of political coalitions should not be taken as the prime indicator of the depth of national feeling. Throughout the 1920s, new patriotic and paramilitary formations choreographed the nation in homespun ceremonies, parades, and rallies that owed little to the conventions of Wilhelmine patriotic festivity, the initiatives of the republican state, or even the fraternal class culture of prewar Social Democracy. From Münich, one official observed, no Sunday passes "when one does not see bands roaming the streets, already in the morning, banners hauled out of the army museum, and people running around in old uniforms or at least wearing their medals and decorations."[48] Throughout Germany, local sociability became more dense, more inclusive, and more politically salient. "To line up the numerous large and small political demonstrations and gatherings that had taken place since the end of the war is to take stock of a remarkable picture of patriotic mass culture," concludes Martin Geyer. At larger rallies such as the 1923 Deutsches Turnfest in Munich or the 1927 Stahlhelm rally in Berlin, film producers arrived on scene with cameras to screen the patriotic spectacle to moviegoers across the nation. Focusing on the serried ranks of marchers, the camera eye provided compelling images of the power of mass movement. Long before Leni Riefenstahl and her 1934 propaganda classic, *Triumph of the Will*, the mass media invited consumers to imagine the evidence of the *Volk* and to insert themselves in its body.[49]

Travel to other German places identified the vividness of the nation as well. At least until the depression, when tourist activity declined significantly, Germans moved about as they had never before. "All of Germany is on the move," the *Frankfurter Zeitung* reported as early as 1921, a comment that gained credibility as the culture of the weekend and reduction of the work week to forty-eight hours facilitated excursions to out-of-town attractions or the seashore: the "German railways recorded a more than sixfold rise in Sunday return tickets from the prewar period to 1929," notes Rudy Koshar. New expectations about leisure and entertainment certainly encouraged travel, but an underlying desire to "Get to Know Germany," the motto of a popular series of picture books, the *Deutschland-Bildhefte*, mobilized citizens as well. A desire to experience the unity of the nation by exploring local customs and physical contrasts filled German youth hostels, which registered 4 million overnight stays in the late 1920s, up from 60,000 immediately after the war.[50] And there was also considerable interest in the particular places that had been scarred by recent German history. In a remarkable trend, dozens of German associations held annual meetings in the borderlands, especially in East Prussian Königsberg, and offered their members guided tours of the border itself to view "severed railways and blocked roads," the violence done to the German nation. According to one estimate, 400,000 young people crossed the Polish Corridor to travel to East Prussia in just one year, 1930.[51] Travel in Germany was increasingly travel to a neglected, but recoverable Germany.

Remapping the nation was always more a journey than a destination. Long gone were the timeless rural landscapes the *Heimatbewegung* (homeland movement) had cherished at the turn of the century. The intervening war years had fashioned a more dynamic, restless environment in which new affiliations and new loyalties were taking shape in a decidedly national rather than regional context. National feeling involved a quest for something still half hidden away, not an invocation of particular tradition and custom.

Techniques of Mobility

In the end, remapping the nation implied the identification of new methods and power sources that would endow the national subject with comparative advantages of capacity and expertise. The fact of military defeat, the loss of colonies, and thus the diminishment of Germany's engagement with foreign cultures and geographic trials prompted an often anguished search for new experience. In what might be called an "economy of experience," critics repeatedly observed, classified, and diagnosed Germans and their activities in an effort to dramatize or relieve the national crisis of energy. They at once projected the outlines of a dangerous but highly resourceful era that had emerged from the war, and looked for signs that Germans had the opportunities, skills, and strength to exploit it to their advantage. By replenishing German politics with strong-armed verbs, the imagined zone of danger made the reinviogration of the nation both necessary *and* possible.

Germany's sense of jeopardy was never so acute as it was at the end of World War I, which cost the nation-state more than 1 million men killed and threatened the integrity of its territory. International relations remained perilous for the new republic and Carl Schmitt even wondered if countries would be exterminated for not paying their global debts, a plain reference to Germany's reparation obligations.[52] But the postwar era was also magical and resourceful. For Jünger the war had opened up an immense realm of possibility. Military technology had evolved into a "second nature" that had fundamentally reshaped Europe. "A new ardour, a new energy inspires life," Jünger asserted; "the men who today are behind the machine guns will tomorrow be in industry, carrying their tempo into the markets and the large towns, creating the political situation and giving the world a new face."[53] These men made plausible a whole new order of active verbs to describe the assault and seizure of the planet.

By dramatizing Germany's technological proficiency, Jünger argued for Germany's unrealized political freedom. Indeed, I would argue that modern technology in the 1920s served as a vast metonym for war itself. The constant iterations of the "New Man" or the "new type"—the athlete, the race-car driver, the aviator, and the expert—to which popular magazines introduced readers can be seen as civilian versions of the new warrior. The circulation of big-city traffic, the new practices of rationalization, and the fine calibration of larger and more powerful machines retold the storyline of wartime innovation and wartime necessity again and again. In many ways, the map of the technologically capable nation corresponded to visions of the totally mobilized city discussed above. Images of war and urban life were frequently paired in the mass-circulation press: the technological capacities of the city insured that future war would be more fearsome, and the high-tech war of the future leaving cities more vulnerable to aerial bombardment and civilian panic. It is often forgotten that fear of massive air attack was as deeply rooted among Europeans in the 1920s and 1930s as the terror of all-out nuclear war was during the Cold War. In one of the most influential books published after World War I, *The Outline of History* (1920), H. G. Wells left no doubt that a future conflict would leave Europe ravaged by air attacks, making the "bombing of those 'prentice days," 1914–1918, look like mere "child's play."[54] Interestingly enough, the proliferate images of gas war and gas masks, which civilians, particularly women and children, were shown using, demonstrated the reach of this militarized new time into the household goods and private lives of contemporaries, just as had the descriptions of "the new life" (*das neue Leben*) and "the new times" (*die neue Zeit*).[55] The mutual reinforcement between war and the city, between danger and capacity, and between the jeopardy of the nation-state and its ability to master the most perilous challenges, could be browsed in the pages of the *Berliner Illustrirte Zeitung*. The 6 June 1926 issue, for example, included photographs of street battles in Poland, of an ocean liner against the backdrop of the New York City skyline, and of the explosion of a munitions factory in Wertheim; another issue in October 1930 juxtaposed stories about record achievements in sports, gas attacks on Paris, and a Swiss aviator over Africa; a year later the combination was racing cars, Germany's zeppelin over the pyramids, and revolution in Spain.[56] These were combinations of the wholly "altered world" (*veränderte Welt*) that Ernst Jünger, H. G. Wells, and many others claimed that war, technology, and urban life had in fact fashioned.

What were the requirements of this seemingly self-evident new era? In an almost obsessive practice of self-observation, Germans scanned the resources of the country and the make-up of the population, building up a vast archive of items and types that would be needed to master this "altered world," and comparing the archive to the capacities of other states. Germany pitted itself in relentless competition with its neighbors. It is no surprise that the United States, as the most technologically marvelous nation, fascinated Weimar Germany, not only because it offered such an authoritative version of a totally reconstructed environment but because its exuberant liberation from tradition corresponded most closely to Germany's revisionist ambitions in the 1920s.[57] The *Berliner Illustrirte* reflected on "technological progress:" "this catch phrase has become an unrelenting directive." With far fewer automobiles per capita, and thus fewer trained drivers than the United States, Britain, or France, for example, Germany was "determined to catch up with them."[58] Although Germany did not have New York, *Reclams Universum* located the place it which it might emerge: "The world city is taking shape right here in the Ruhr."[59] However, the nation did excel in aviation; was there any issue of *Die Woche* or the *Berliner Illustrirte* that did not publish photographs of aviators, airplanes, and especially zeppelins, which were so often shown in menacing geopolitical angles over New York, the pyramids, or the high seas? There was extraordinary value in Germany's record of aeronautical experience: aviation was widely regarded in the 1920s as the most sophisticated machinery of its time, requiring intricate knowledge, demanding superlative abilities from airmen, and beckoning a prosperous, if dangerous "air age." Since it was theoretically possible to reach any point by air, aviation privileged those "young" nations such as Germany or Italy that mobilized technology and marginalized formerly prosperous naval powers such as Britain and France. Aviation thus had the potential to rearrange the balance of military and political power. It also offered Germany the opportunity to extend its interests around the globe, "to think in terms of continents again," despite the Reich's defeat in the world war. The globe-trotting adventures of German fliers such as Günther Plüschow and Marga von Etzdorf, the first east-to-west crossing of the Atlantic by a German flight team, and the crew of the "Graf Zeppelin," which transnavigated the globe in 1929, all depicted the acquisition of crucial technical and political skills that were cosmopolitan and frankly imperialist. In decisive ways, aviation allowed Germany to be at home in the postwar world.[60] In a more general way, the Weimar fascination with geopolitics further rewrote terms of possibility and necessity to Germany's advantage, revealing a "heroic earth" in which previously unrecognized features promised the nation and the *Volk* dynamic political opportunities.[61]

However, the most valuable achievement of German technology was the potential to produce new, more capable men and women. It enabled not simply technical competence but unparalleled moral accomplishment, and the image of the solitary aviator with his "cool, clear-reckoning head" and "hot-burning forward-striving heart" was quite familiar to Weimar readers. Scholars have emphasized the ways in which physiognomical typologies added up to a defense endeavor to give knowable contours to a "society in disarray" by providing the "means for differentiating and discriminating" and "for drawing new boundaries and putting up barriers for security."[62] But the proliferation of physiognomical readings should also be regarded as an effort to *re*-classify, to retrieve, and reach beneath the surface or behind appearances in order to find sites of traction and movement, to identify the techniques of mobility. A classic reading of the new warrior comes from Friedrich Georg Jünger:

> The transformation of war corresponds to a transformation of the warriors. This becomes obvious when you compare the vivacious, carefree, enthusiastic faces of the soldiers in August 1914 with the dead-exhausted, haggard, totally tensed faces of the soldier of the war of attrrition from the year 1918. Behind the arc of this struggle, wound ever more tightly until it snaps, appears the face of war, formed and moved by a violent, mental shock, from the stations of a road of great suffering, from battle to battle, which are the hieroglyphic signs of the relentless, strenuous work of destruction. Here we see the type of soldier who has been shaped by the hard, sober, bloodly never-ending confrontation of men and materiél. He is characterized by the hardened nerves of the born warrior.[63]

Strength was associated with pitilessness and relentlessness, virtues appropriate to the new technological and political challenges of the present moment, and the passage from 1914 to 1918 signaled the accumulation of the kind of experience necessary to reactivate German energies. Although infinitely more capable than his prewar counterpart, thanks to the experiences of the front, the envisioned new man plainly showed the strain of adapting to the rigors of the age; he required hardening and steeling and exposure to emotional extremes of heat and coldness. This was the self-appointed task of the paramilitary associations, especially the nationalist Stahlhelm but also the leftist Reichsbanner, in which veterans explicitly sought to toughen the adversarial physical body of the soldier and to train brothers and sons who had been too young to fight in the war. As many as 1 million German men passed through paramilitary groups in the 1920s and early 1930s, and they provided observers with reliable indicators of national regeneration that promised to overhaul the "*Volkskörper*" weakened by defeat, revolution, and economic crisis

The soldier was the basic model by which other highly mobilized types were introduced: athletes, workers, technicians, and the "new woman." "People will allow themselves to become harder and more sober," ascertained Walter Schönbrunn in "Life tomorrow." Athletes attracted particular attention because their commitment to rebuild their bodies, steel their nerves, and train their reflexes seemed to enhance the collective national body.[64] So too did German women, who were prominently profiled and carefully distinguished from purely domestic types still prevalent in Eastern Europe and the frivolous "Sportgirl" or "*Luft-Girl, ein neuer Modetyp*" (air-girl, a new fashion type). Strong, independent, and whole, the projected new woman combined athletic capability and technical knowledge, but retained her femininity. That it was not only men but also women who possessed "*Stählungsmöglichkeiten*" (the ability to steel oneself) dramatizes how the imagined imperatives of the technological present and the renovatory possibilities of the future nation revised even familiar categories of gender.[65]

If the rigors of the war made it possible to envision a more self-reliant and capable person, disciplined in body and spirit, the war also exposed the vulnerability of the population as a whole. Food scarcities and disease had left Germans weaker and sicker, while the enormous costs of fighting the war cast the expenses of attending to allegedly unfit physical or mental groups in a new light. The medicalization of social policy during the 1920s was in part a result of the recognition among medical experts and welfare officials that the nation needed not only to invest additional resources to insure the health of the German people but to make distinctions about who could and could not be sustained by national policy. Biology, in particular, seemed to offer the techniques to radically remake the community in conditions of danger. Given its pseudoscientific claims to nurture healthy bodies and weed out deleterious influences and inheritances, biology offered nationalist thinkers a ready-made vocabulary for social revolution. It recast politics in an exceptionally vivid and active way, promising to provide the nation with highly useful technologies of mobility in the self-designated conditions of extreme technological stress and fierce international competition in which World War I had been only the first installment.[66]

Detlev Peukert has outlined the "crisis of classical modernity" during the Weimar Republic, a strenuous period in which neither political democracy, social reform, nor economic recovery could establish conditions of stability. As a result, the past looked more rosy. "Memories of the Wilhemine past grew fonder as the realities of life under the Republic grew more austere," he writes. It was only as the national crisis worsened in the early 1930s that "the mirage of racial 'renewal' and a re-created 'national community' became increasingly attractive."[67] For all the synthetic virtues of Peukert's analysis, however, he neglects the degree to which crisis was not simply a condition that happened, but one that was imagined, embellished upon, and distorted in ways that were culturally revealing and politically combustible and not always pessimistic. There was an elective affinity between the diagnosis of crisis and the conviction of the malleability and potentiality of the national form. The war, in particular, was conceived as a wholly new historical condition in ways that did not characterize Britain or France. It was the effort in Germany to upend historical continuities, to dramatize the new, propitious moment, and to invoke the national peril that gave Weimar culture its radical subjunctive quality and made it the privileged terrain for an industrious and often menacing design of the future.

Notes

1. Ernst von Salomon, *Die Geächteten* (Berlin, 1930), 196–98.
2. Janet Ward, *Weimar Surfaces: Urban Visual Culture in 1920s Germany* (Berkeley, CA, 2001), 9.

3. Martin Lindner, *Leben in der Krise: Zeitromane der neuen Sachlichkeit und die intellektu-elle Mentalität der klassischen Moderne* (Stuttgart, 1994); Ulrike Hass, *Militante Pastorale: Zur Literatur der antimodernen Bewegungen im früheren 20. Jahrhundert* (Münich, 1993).

4. On the "delinquency of history," Peter Fritzsche, "Landscape of Danger, Landscape of Design: Crisis and Modernism in Weimar Germany," in *Dancing on the Volcano: Essays on the Culture of the Weimar Republic*, ed. Thomas W. Kniesche and Stephen Brockmann (Columbia, SC, 1994), 29–46.

5. See Reinhart Koselleck, *Futures Past: On the Semantics of Historical Time* (Cambridge, MA, 1985).

6. Reinhard Koselleck, "Erfahrungswandel und Methodenwechsel. Eine historisch-anthropologische Skizze," in *Historische Methode*, ed. Christian Meier and Jörn Rüsen (Münich, 1988), 42, 52.

7. Charles L. Mowat, *Britain between the Wars, 1918–1940* (Chicago, 1955); Christoper Shaw and Malcolm Chase, eds., *The Imagined Past: History and Nostalgia* (Manchester, UK, 1989); Patrick Wright *On Living in an Old Country: The National Past in Contemporary Britain* (London, 1985); Romy Golan, *Modernity and Nostalgia: Art and Politics in France Between the Wars* (New Haven, CT, 1995); and more generally Modris Eksteins, *Rites of Spring: The Great War and the Birth of the Modern Age* (Boston, 1989).

8. Helmut Lethen, *Verhaltenslehren der Kälte: Lebensversuche zwischen den Kriegen* (Frankfurt, 1994). In English translation: *Cool Conduct: The Culture of Distance in Weimar Germany*, transl. Don Reneau.(Berkeley, 2002).

9. Eugen Diesel, *Der Weg durch das Wirrsal* (Stuttgart, 1932), 182.

10. Walter Benjamin, *One Way Street and Other Writings.* (London, 1979), 45.

11. Joseph Roth, *Berliner Saisonbericht. Unbekannte Reportagen und journalistische Arbeiten 1920–39*, ed. Klaus Westermann (Cologne, 1984); Bernhard von Brentano, *Wo in Europa ist Berlin? Bilder aus den zwanziger Jahren* (Frankfurt, 1981); Siegfried Kracauer, *Strassen in Berlin und anderswo* (Berlin, 1987).

12. Siegfried Kracauer, "Strasse ohne Erinnerung," *Frankfurter Zeitung*, 16 December 1932, reprinted in *Strassen in Berlin*, 19–24. Bernhard von Brentano, Kracauer's predecessor at the *Frankfurter Zeitung*, made the same observation earlier. See his "Berlin—von Süddeutschland aus gesehen," in *Wo in Europa ist Berlin?* 96–97.

13. Siegfried Kracauer, "Photography," in Kracauer, *The Mass Ornament: Weimar Essays*, ed. Thomas Y. Levin (Cambridge, 1995), 57–58.

14. Henri Band, *Mittelschichten und Massenkultur: Siegfried Kracauers publizistische Auseinandersetzung mit der populären Kultur und der Kultur der Mittelschichten in der Weimarer Republik* (Berlin, 1999), 60.

15. Hans Ostwald, *Sittengeschichte der Inflation* (Berlin, 1931), 231.

16. The cynical conviction that war cripples were mostly hustlers still circulated in Hans Fallada's 1937 account of the inflation, *Wolf unter Wölfen* (Berlin, 2001 [1937]), 62.

17. Lethen, *Verhaltenslehren der Kälte*, 44–45.

18. Anton Kaes, "Die ökonomische Dimension der Literatur: Zum Strukturwandel der Institution Literatur in der Inflationszeit (1918–1923)," in *Konsequenzen der Inflation—Consequences of Inflation*, ed. Gerald D. Feldman et al. (Berlin, 1989), 318.

19. Walter Schönbrunn, "Das Leben von morgen," in *Reclams Universum*, no. 36 (6 June 1929): 788.

20. Eugen Diesel, *Das Land der Deutschen* (Leipzig, 1931), 222. The original quote in German: "Die neuen Lebensformen sind ganz unabhängig von der Parteirichtung; aus dem

Geiste der Technik heraus marschiert ein … Lebenstil, dem wir alle verfahren sind, ob wir nun Kommunisten sind oder Nationalsozialisten." See also Kurt Pinthus, "Die Überfülle des Erlebens. 10 Jahre ununterbrochener Sensationen," *Berliner Illustrirte Zeitung,* no. 9, 28 Feb. 1925; and Karl Jaspers, *Die geistige Situation der Zeit* (Berlin, 1949 [1931]), 79–84.

21. Hannes Meyer, "The New World," in Anton Kaes et al., eds., *The Weimar Republic Sourcebook* (Berkeley, CA, 1994), 446.

22. The theme of the household as a site of historical differentiation is developed by James Chandler, *England in 1819: The Politics of Literary Culture and the Case of Romantic Historicism* (Chicago, 1998), 148–50.

23 Bruno Taut, *Die neue Wohnung: Die Frau als Schöpferin* (Leipzig, 1924), 10–11. See also Adolf Behne, *Neues Wohnen—neues Bauen* (Leipzig, 1927); and Ward, *Weimar Surfaces,* 76–80.

24. Taut, *Die neue Wohnung,* 60.

25. Quoted in Ward, *Weimar Surfaces,* 73.

26. Viktor Dohne, "Bei den jungen Leuten," *Berliner Illustrirte Zeitung,* no. 12, 23 March 1930.

27. Irmgard Keun, *Gilgi—eine von uns* (Berlin, 1931), and *Das kunstseidene Mädchen* (Berlin, 1932); Vicki Baum, *Stud. Chem. Helene Willfüer* (Berlin, 1928); and Helmuth Plessner, *Grenzen der Gemeinschaft: Eine Kritik des sozialen Radikalismus* (Bonn, 1924).

28. See Kracauer, *Die Angestellten: Aus dem neuesten Deutschland* (Frankfurt am Main, 1930); and Band, *Mittelschichten und Massenkultur.*

29. Kracauer, "Schreie auf der Strasse," *Frankfurter Zeitung,* 19 July 1930, reprinted in *Strassen in Berlin,* 27–29.

30. Cited in Martin Meyer, *Ernst Jünger* (Munich, 1990), 165. See also Stefan Breuer, *Anatomie der Konservativen Revolution* (Darmstadt, 1992), 14, 45–47.

31. Wolfgang Schivelbusch, *Die Kultur der Niederlage: Der amerikanische Süden 1865, Frankreich 1871, Deutschland 1918* (Berlin, 2001).

32. Quoted in Lindner, *Leben in der Krise,* 164.

33. Hass, *Militante Pastorale,* 80.

34. Quoted in Hass, *Militante Pastorale,* 163. See also Salomon, *Geächteten,* 210–11.

35. H. R. Knickerbocker, *The German Crisis* (New York, 1932), 42–43, 76, 94, 97, 206–9.

36. Martin Geyer, *Verkehrte Welt: Revolution, Inflation, und Moderne, München 1914–1924* (Göttingen, 1998), 288.

37. Peter Fritzsche, *Germans into Nazis* (Cambridge, 1998), 131.

38. "The Story of a Farmer," in Theodore Abel, *The Nazi Movement: Why Hitler Came to Power* (New York, 1966), 289.

39. Peter H. Merkl, *Political Violence under the Swastika* (Princeton, NJ, 1975), 53.

40. Ibid., 160. See also Heinrich Potz, folder 50, Box 1, Theodore Abel Papers, Hoover Institution Archives, Stanford, CA; Martin Dries, "Aus Meiner Kampfzeit," 31 December 1936, Bundesarchiv, NS26/529; and Josef Schimmel, "Meine Kampferlebnisse," n.d. [1937], Bundesarchiv, NS26/532.

41. Hans Müller, folder 99, Box 2, Theodore Abel Papers, Hoover Institution Archives, Stanford, California. See also Fritz Schuck, folder 172, Box 3, ibid.

42. Hans Plath, folder 96, Box 2; Ernst Schmitt, folder 265, Box 5; Oskar Klinkusch, folder 349, Box 5, Theodore Abel Papers, Hoover Institution Archives, Stanford, CA; Heinrich Wilkenloh, "Meine Kampferlebnisse," 31 December 1936, Bundesarchiv, NS 26/531. See also William Stern, ed., *Jugendliches Seelenleben und Krieg* (Leip-

zig, 1915), 12. Beiheft zur *Zeitschrift für angewandte Psychologie und psychologische Sammelforschung.*

43. Merkl, *Political Violence*, 89.
44. Rudolf Kahn, folder 31, Box 1, Theodore Abel Papers, Hoover Institution Archives, Stanford, CA; see also Fritz Junghanss, folder 526, Box 7.
45. Salomon, *Geächteten*, 208, 214–15.
46. St. [Stapel], "Wohin geht die Fahrt?" *Deutsches Volkstum* 12, no. 1 (January 1919): 1–3. See also Moeller van den Bruck, "Der Revolutionsgewinn," *Gewissen*, 11 November 1919, no. 31.
47. Belinda Davis, *Home Fires Burning: Food, Politics, and Everyday Life in World War I* (Chapel Hill, NC, 2000); Anne Roerkohl, *Hungerblockade und Heimatfront: Die kommunale Lebensmittelversorgung in Westfalen während des Ersten Weltkrieges* (Stuttgart, 1991).
48. Württemberg's ambassador to Bavaria quoted in Geyer, *Verkehrte Welt*, 123.
49. Geyer, *Verkehrte Welt*, 267, 127. See also "Aufmärsche," *Berliner Illustrirte Zeitung*, no. 23, 6 June 1926; "Die Welt im politischen Fieber," *Berliner Illustrirte Zeitung*, no. 42, 19 October 1930.
50. Rudy Koshar, *German Travel Cultures* (New York, 2000), 71, 73, 75.
51. Elizabeth Harvey, "Pilgrimages to the 'Bleeding Border': Gender and the Rituals of Nationalist Protest in Germany, 1919–39," *Women's History Review* 9 (2000): 213.
52. Carl Schmitt, *The Concept of the Political*, trans. George Schwab (Chicago, 1996 [1932]), 55n23.
53. Ernst Jünger, *Copse 125: A Chronicle from the Trench Warfare of 1918*, trans. Basil Creighton (London, 1930), 106.
54. H. G. Wells, *The Outline of History* (New York, 1920), 1084–85, quoting the Royal United Service Institution's Sir Louis Jackson.
55. "Ingenieurkrieg," *Berliner Illustrirte Zeitung*, no. 40, 4 October 1925; "Die Grösste Gefahr für die Menschheit: Die Gaskrieg-Rüstungen," *Berliner Illustrirte Zeitung*, 19 January 1930; "Manöver zum Schutz gegen Gasangriffe," *Berliner Illustrirte Zeitung*, no. 21, 25 May 1930; "Wie eine französische Zeitschrift der Zukunftskrieg schildert" [*Vu*], *Berliner Illustrirte Zeitung*, no. 43, 26 October 1930; and "Ein Grossstadtbild wie es in Europa jetzt immer häufiger zu sehen ist," *Berliner Illustrirte Zeitung*, no. 16, 19 April 1931.
56. *Berliner Illustrirte Zeitung*, no. 23, 6 June 1926; no. 43, 26 October 1930; no. 17, 26 April 1931.
57. Mary Nolan, *Visions of Modernity: American Business and the Modernization of Germany* (New York, 1994).
58. "Fortschritt der Technik," *Berliner Illustrirte Zeitung*, no. 44, 31 October 1925.
59. *Reclams Universum*, no. 9, 26 November 1931.
60. Peter Fritzsche, *A Nation of Fliers: German Aviation and the Popular Imagination* (Cambridge, 1992), chapter 4.
61. David Murphy, *The Heroic Earth: Geopolitical Thought in Weimar Germany, 1918–1933* (Kent, UK, 1997); and Ewald Banse, *Expressionismus und Geographie* (Braunschweig, 1920).
62. Lynne-Mare Hoskins Frame, "Forming and Reforming the New Woman in Weimar Germany," (Diss. University of California, Berkeley, 1997), 3.
63. Friedrich Georg Jünger, "Krieg und Krieger," in *Krieg und Krieger*, ed. Ernst Jünger (Berlin, 1930), 65. See also Bernd Hüppauf, "Langemarck, Verdun, and the Myth of a *New Man* in Germany after the First World War," *War and Society* 6 (1988): 70–103.

64. "Weshalb boxen wir?" *BZ am Mittag,* no. 131, 15 May 1927; "Fussball ist das Spiel unserer Zeit," *Berliner Illustrirte Zeitung,* no. 40, 4 October 1925; Eduard Ritter von Schlech, "Rekorde im Skisport und ihr nutzen," *Berliner Illustrirte Zeitung,* no. 43, 30 October 1930.

65. See Frame, "Forming and Reforming the New Woman in Weimar Germany," 94, 135, 137–38, 191.

66. Paul Weindling, *Health, Race and German Politics between National Unification and Nazism, 1870–1945* (Cambridge, 1989); Cornelie Usborne, *The Politics of the Body in Weimar Germany: Women's Reproductive Rights and Duties* (Ann Arbor, MI, 1992); Bernd Ulrich, "Die Kriegspsychologie der zwanziger Jahre und ihre geschichtspolitische Instrumentalisierung," in *Modernität und Trauma: Beiträge zum Zeitenbruch des Ersten Weltkrieges,* ed. Inka Mülder-Bach (Vienna, 2000); and Moritz Föllmer, "Der 'kranke Volkskörper.' Industrielle, hohe Beamte und der Diskurs der nationale Regeneration in der Weimarer Republik," *Geschichte und Gesellschaft* 27 (2001): 41–67.

67. Detlev Peukert, *The Weimar Republic: The Crisis of Classical Modernity,* trans. Richard Deveson (New York, 1989), 13–14.

~: BIBLIOGRAPHY :~

Weimar History and Culture (General)

Balderston, Theo. *Economics and Politics in the Weimar Republic.* Cambridge, 2002.

Berghahn, Volker R. *Imperial Germany 1871–1918: Economy, Society, Culture and Politics.* New York, 2005.

Bessel, Richard, and E. J. Feuchtwanger. *Social Change and Political Development in the Weimar Republic.* London, 1981.

Bookbinder, Paul. *Weimar Germany: The Republic of the Reasonable.* Manchester, UK, 1996.

Crew, David F. "The Pathologies of Modernity: Detlev Peukert on Germany's Twentieth Century." *Social History* 17, no. 2 (May 1992): 319–28.

Durst, David. *Weimar Modernism: Philosophy, Politics and Culture, 1918–1933.* Oxford, 2004.

Eley, Geoff, ed. *Society, Culture and the State in Germany, 1870–1930.* Ann Arbor, MI, 1996.

Evans, Richard J. *The Coming of the Third Reich.* Harmondsworth, UK, 2003.

Eyck, Erich. *A History of the Weimar Republic,* 2 vols., translated by Harlan Hanson and Robert G. L. Waite. New York, 1970.

Feldman, Gerald D. "The Weimar Republic: A Problem of Modernization?" *Archiv für Sozialgeschichte* 26 (1986): 1–26.

Feuchtwanger, E. J. *From Weimar to Hitler. Germany 1918–33.* New York, 1993.

Föllmer, Moritz, and Rüdiger Graf, eds. *Die "Krise" der Weimarer Republik. Zur Kritik eines Deutungsmusters.* Frankfurt, 2005.

Fritzsche, Peter. "Landscape of Danger, Landscape of Design: Crisis and Modernism in Weimar Germany." In *Dancing on the Volcano: Essays on the Culture of the Weimar Republic,* edited by Thomas W. Kniesche and Stephen Brockmann, 29–46. Columbia, SC, 1994.

———. "Did Weimar Fail?" *Journal of Modern History* 68, no. 3 (September 1996): 632–33.

———. *Germans into Nazis.* Cambridge, 1998.

Fröhlich, Michael, ed. *Die Weimarer Republik. Portrait einer Epoche in Biographien.* Darmstadt, 2002.

Fulbrook, Mary. *Germany Since 1918.* London, 1997.

Gay, Peter. *Weimar Culture: The Outsider as Insider.* New York, 2001 [1968].

Geyer, Michael, and Konrad Jarausch. *Shattered Past: Reconstructing German Histories.* Princeton, NJ, 2003.

Graf, Rüdiger. *Die Zukunft der Weimarer Republik: Krisen und Zukunftsaneignungen in Deutschland 1918–1933.* Munich, 2008.

Hardtwig, Wolfgang, ed. *Ordnungen in der Krise: Zur politischen Kulturgeschichte Deutschlands 1900–1933.* Oldenbourg, 2007.

———, ed. *Politische Kulturgeschichte der Zwischenkriegszeit 1918–1939*. Göttingen, 2005.

Heiber, Helmut. *Die Republik von Weimar*. Munich, 1996 [1968].

Herf, Jeffrey. *Reactionary Modernism: Technology, Culture and Politics in Weimar and the Third Reich*. Cambridge, 1984.

Hobsbawm, Eric J. *The Age of Extremes: A History of the World, 1914–1991*. New York, 1994.

Kolb, Eberhard. *The Weimar Republic*. London, 1988.

Laqueur, Walter. *Weimar: A Cultural History*. London, 1974.

Lehnert, Detlef. *Die Weimarer Republik*. Stuttgart, 1999.

Lethen, Helmut. *Cool Conduct: The Culture of Distance in Weimar Germany*, translated by Don Reneau. Berkeley, CA, 2002.

Lieberman, Ben. "Testing Peukert's Paradigm: The 'Crisis of Classical Modernity' in the New Frankfurt, 1925–1930." *German Studies Review* 17, no. 2 (May 1994): 287–303.

Mai, Gunther. *Europa 1918–1939: Mentalitäten, Lebensweisen, Politik zwischen den Weltkriegen*. Stuttgart, 2001.

McElligott, Anthony, ed. *Weimar Germany*. Oxford Short History of Germany. Oxford, 2009.

Möller, Horst. *Weimar. Die unvollendete Demokratie*. Munich, 1985.

Mommsen, Hans. *From Weimar to Auschwitz: Essays in German History*, translated by Philip O"Connor. Oxford, 1990.

———. *The Rise and Fall of Weimar Democracy*, translated by Elborg Forster and Larry Eugene Jones. Chapel Hill, NC, 1996.

Nicholls, Anthony James. *Weimar and the Rise of Hitler*. New York, 2000 [1968].

Peukert, Detlev J. K. *The Weimar Republic: The Crisis of Classical Modernity*, translated by Richard Deveson. New York, 1992.

Rosenberg, Arthur. *Entstehung der Weimarer Republik*. Frankfurt, 1955.

———. *Geschichte der Weimarer Republik*. Frankfurt am Main, 1955.

Schulze, Hagen. *Weimar. Deutschland, 1917–1933*. Berlin, 1998 [1982].

Weitz, Eric D. *Weimar Germany: Promise and Tragedy*. Princeton, NJ, 2007.

Winkler, Heinrich August. *Weimar, 1918–1933: die Geschichte der ersten deutschen Demokratie*. Munich, 1993.

———. *Weimar im Widerstreit: Deutungen der ersten deutschen Republik im geteilten Deutschland*. Munich, 2002.

Wirsching, Andreas, and Jürgen Eder, eds. *Vernunftrepublikanismus in der Weimarer Republik: Politik, Literatur, Wissenschaft*. Stuttgart, 2008.

The Legacy of World War I for the Weimar Republic

Baumeister, Martin. *Kriegstheater. Großstadt, Front und Massenkultur, 1914–1918*. Essen, 2005.

Behrenbeck, Sabine. *Der Kult um die toten Helden. Nationalsozialistische Mythen, Riten und Symbole*. Cologne, 1996.

Bessel, Richard. *Germany after the First World War*. Oxford, 1993.

———. "The 'Front Generation' and the Politics of Weimar Germany." In *Generations in Conflict: Youth Revolt and Generation Formation in Germany, 1770–1968*, edited by Mark Roseman, 121–36. Cambridge, 1995.

Barth, Boris. *Dolchstoßlegenden und politische Desintegration. Das Trauma der deutschen Niederlage im Ersten Weltkrieg, 1914–1933*. Düsseldorf, 2003.

Buschmann, Nikolaus, and Horst Carl, eds. *Die Erfahrung des Krieges. Erfahrungsgeschichtliche Perspektiven von der französischen Revolution bis zum zweiten Weltkrieg*. Paderborn, 2001.

Chickering, Roger. *Imperial Germany and the Great War, 1914–1918*. Cambridge, 1998.

———. *The Great War and Urban Life in Germany. Freiburg 1914–1918*. Cambridge, 2007.

Cohen, Deborah. *The War Come Home: Disabled Veterans in Britain and Germany, 1914–1939*. Berkeley, CA, 2001.

Daniel, Ute. *Arbeiterfrauen in der Kriegsgesellschaft: Beruf, Familie und Politik im Ersten Weltkrieg*. Göttingen, 1989.

———. *The War from Within: German Working–Class Women in the First World War*, translated by Margaret Ries. Oxford, 1997.

Davis, Belinda. *Home Fires Burning: Food, Politics and Everyday Life in World War I Berlin*. Chapel Hill, NC, 2000.

Domansky, Elizabeth. "Militarization and Reproduction in World War I Germany." In *Society, Culture and State in Germany, 1870–1930*, edited by Geoff Eley. Ann Arbor, MI, 1996. 427–63.

Düffler, Jost, and Gerd Krumeich, eds. *Der verlorene Frieden. Politik und Kriegskultur nach 1918*. Essen, 2002.

Duppler, Jörg, and Gerhard P. Groß, eds. *Kriegsende 1918. Ereignis, Wirkung, Nachwirkung*. Munich, 1999.

Ecksteins, Modris. *Rites of Spring: The Great War and the Birth of the Modern Age*. London, 1989.

Feldman, Gerald D. *Army, Industry, and Labor in Germany, 1914–1918*. Oxford, 1992.

Ferguson, Niall. *The Pity of War*. New York, 1988.

Geyer, Michael. "Insurrectionary Warfare: The German Debate about a Levee en Masse in October, 1918." *Journal of Modern History* 73 (September 2001): 462–63.

Hagemann, Karen, and Stefanie Schuler–Springorum. *Home/Front: The Military, War and Gender in Twentieth–Century Germany*. New York, 2003.

Hering, Sabine. *Die Kriegsgewinnlerinnen: Praxis und Ideologie der deutschen Frauenbewegung im Ersten Weltkrieg*. Pfaffenweiler, 1990.

Hirschfeld, Gerhard, Gerd Krumeich, Dieter Langewiesche, and Hans–Peter Ullmann, eds. *Kriegserfahrungen. Studien zur Sozial– und Mentalitätsgeschichte des Ersten Weltkriegs*. Essen, 1997.

Horne, John, and Alan Kramer. *German Atrocities 1914: A History of Denial*. New Haven, CT, 2001.

Kienitz, Sabine. "'Fleischgewordenes Elend': Kriegsinvalidität und Körperbilder als Teil einer Erfahrungsgeschichte des Ersten Weltkrieges." In *Die Erfahrung des Krieges*, edited by Nikolaus Buschmann and Horst Carl. Paderborn, 2001.

———. *Beschädigte Helden. Kriegsinvalidität und Körperbilder 1914–1923*. Paderborn, 2008.

Kocka, Jürgen. *Facing Total War: German Society 1914–1918*. Cambridge, MA, 1984.

Kramer, Alan. *Dynamic of Destruction: Culture and Mass Killing in the First World War*. Oxford, 2007.

Kundrus, Birthe. *Kriegerfrauen. Familienpolitik und Geschlechterverhältnisse im Ersten und Zweiten Weltkrieg*. Hamburg, 1995.

Leed, Eric J. *No Man's Land Combat and Identity in World War I*. Cambridge, 1979.

Lerner, Paul. *Hysterical Men: War, Psychiatry, and the Politics of Trauma in Germany, 1890–1930.* Ithaca, NY, 2003.

Liulevicius, Vejas G. *War Land on the Eastern Front: Culture, National Identity and German Occupation in World War I.* Cambridge, 2000.

Llanque, Markus. *Demokratisches Denken im Krieg. Die deutsche Debatte im Ersten Weltkrieg.* Berlin, 2000.

Mai, Gunther. *Das Ende des Kaiserreichs. Politik und Kriegführung im Ersten Weltkrieg.* Munich, 1997.

Michalka, Wolfgang, ed. *Der Erste Weltkrieg. Wirkung, Wahrnehmung, Analyse.* Munich, 1994.

Mommsen, Hans, ed. *Der Erste Krieg und die europäische Nachkriegsordnung: Sozialer Wandel und die Formveränderung der Politik.* Cologne, 2000.

Mosse, George L. *Fallen Soldiers: Reshaping the Memory of the World Wars.* Oxford, 1990.

Roerkohl, Anne. *Hungerblockade und Heimatfront: Die kommunale Lebensmittelversorgung in Westfalen während des Ersten Weltkrieges.* Stuttgart, 1991.

Ullrich, Volker. *Vom Augusterlebnis zur Novemberrevolution. Beiträge zur Sozialgeschichte Hamburgs und Norddeutschlands im Ersten Weltkrieg.* Bremen 1999.

Ulrich, Bernd. "Die Kriegspsychologie der zwanziger Jahre und ihre geschichtspolitische Instrumentalisierung." *Modernität und Trauma: Beiträge zum Zeitenbruch des Ersten Weltkrieges,* edited by Inka Mülder–Bach. Vienna, 2000.

Whalen, Robert. *Bitter Wounds: German Victims of the Great War, 1914–1919.* Ithaca, NY, 1984.

Winter, Jay, and Jean–Louis Robert, eds. *Capital Cities at War: Paris, London, Berlin 1914–1919.* Cambridge, 1997.

Ziemann, Benjamin. *Front und Heimat. Ländliche Kriegserfahrungen im südlichen Bayern, 1914–1923.* Essen, 1997.

———. "Republikanische Kriegserinnerung in einer polarisierten Öffentlichkeit. Das Reichsbanner Schwarz–Rot–Gold als Veteranenverband der sozialistischen Arbeiterschaft." *Historische Zeitschrift* 267 (1998): 357–98.

———. "Die Erinnerung an den Ersten Weltkrieg in den Milieukulturen der Weimarer Republik." In *Kriegserlebnis und Legendenbildung. Das Bild der 'modernen' Krieges in Literatur, Theater, Photographie und Film,* vol. 1: *Krieg und Literatur, Internationales Jahrbuch zum Kriegs– und Antikriegsliteraturforschung,* 249–70. Osnabrück, 1999.

———. *War Experiences in Rural Germany, 1914–1923.* Oxford, 2007 (abridged version of *Front und Heimat*).

Revolution, Crisis and the Founding of Democracy

Broué, Pierre. *The German Revolution, 1917–1923.* Translated by John Archer, edited by Ian Birchall and Brian Pearce. Chicago, 2006 [1971].

Caldwell, Peter C. *Popular Sovereignty and the Crisis of German Constitutional Law: The Theory & Practice of Weimar Constitutionalism.* Durham, NC, 1997.

Carsten, F. L. *Revolution in Central Europe, 1918–1919.* Berkeley, CA, 1972.

Dobson, Sean. *Authority and Upheaval in Leipzig, 1910–1920.* New York, 2001.

Geyer, Martin. *Verkehrte Welt. Revolution, Inflation und Moderne.* München, 1998.

Gietinger, Klaus. *Eine Leiche im Landwehrkanal. Die Ermordung der Rosa L.* Berlin, 1995.

Heilfron, E., ed. *Die deutsche Nationalversammlung im Jahre 1919 in ihrer Arbeit für den Aufbau des neuen deutschen Volksstaates*. Berlin, 1919.

Hucko, Elmar M., ed. *The Democratic Tradition: Four German Constitutions*. Oxford, 1987.

Rödder, Andreas. *Weimar und die deutsche Verfassung. Geschichte und Aktualität von 1919*. Stuttgart, 1999.

Rurüp, Reinhard, "Problems of the German Revolution 1918–19." *Journal of Contemporary History* 3, no. 4 (October 1968): 109–35.

Schivelbusch, Wolfgang. *The Culture of Defeat: On National Trauma, Mourning and Recovery*, translated by Jefferson Chase. New York, 2003.

Sternsdorf–Hauck, Christiane. *Brotmarken und rote Fahnen. Frauen in der bayerischen Revolution und Räterepublik 1918/19*. Frankfurt, 1989.

Ulrich, Bernd, and Benjamin Ziemann, eds. *Krieg im Frieden: Die umkämpfte Erinnerung an den Ersten Weltkrieg: Quellen und Dokumente*. Frankfurt, 1997.

Weberling, Anja. *Zwischen Räten und Parteien. Frauenbewegung in Deutschland 1918/19*. Pfaffenweiler, 1994 .

Winkler, Heinrich August. *Die Sozialdemokratie und die Revolution von 1918/19: ein Rückblick nach sechzig Jahren*. Berlin, 1979.

———. *Von der Revolution zur Stabilisierung: Arbeiter und Arbeiterbewegung in der Weimarer Republik, 1918 bis 1924*. Berlin, 1984.

Gender, Sexuality, Bodies

Abrams, Lynn and Elizabeth Harvey, eds. *Gender Relations in German History: Power, Agency and Experience from the Sixteenth to the Twentieth Century*. Durham, NC, 1996.

von Ankum, Katharina, ed. *Women in the Metropolis: Gender and Modernity in Weimar Culture*. Berkeley, CA, 1997.

Apel, Dora. "'Heroes' and 'Whores': The Politics of Gender in Weimar Antiwar Imagery." *Art Bulletin* 79, no. 3 (September 1997): 375–92.

Bastkowski, Friedrun, Christa Lindner, and Ulrike Prokop, eds. *Frauenalltag und Frauenbewegung im 20. Jahrhundert. Bd. 2: Frauenbewegung und die "Neue Frau" 1890–1933*. Frankfurt am Main, 1980.

Benninghaus, Christine. "Das Geschlecht der Generation. Zum Zusammenhang von Generationalität und Männlichkeit um 1930." In *Generationen. Zur Relevanz eines wissenschaftlichen Grundbegriffs*, edited by Ulrike Jureit and Michael Wildt, 127–59. Hamburg, 2005.

Berghaus, Günther. "'Girlkultur': Feminism, Americanism, and Popular Entertainment in Weimar." *Journal of Design History* 1, no. 3–4 (1988): 193–219.

Bessel, Richard. "Was bleibt vom Krieg? Deutsche Nachkriegsgeschichte(n) aus geschlechtergeschichtlicher Perspektive." *Militärgeschichtliche Mitteilungen* 60, no. 2 (2001): 297–305.

Boak, Helen. "Women in Weimar Germany: The 'Frauenfrage' and the Female Vote." In *Social Change and Political Development in Weimar Germany*, edited by Richard Bessel and E. J. Feuchtwanger. London, 1981.

———. "Women in Weimar Politics." *European History Quarterly* 20, no. 3 (1990): 369–99.

Bridenthal, Renate. "Something Old, Something New: Women Between the Two World Wars." In *Becoming Visible*, edited by Renate Bridenthal, Claudia Koonz, and Susan Stuard, 473–97. Boston, 1987.

Bridenthal, Renate, Atina Grossmann, and Marion Kaplan, eds. *When Biology Became Destiny: Women in Weimar and Nazi Germany*. New York, 1984.

Canning, Kathleen. "Gender and Sexuality in Weimar Germany." In *Weimar Germany*, Short Oxford History of Germany, edited by Anthony McElligott. Oxford, 2009.

———. *Gender History in Practice: Historical Perspectives on Bodies, Class and Citizenship*. Ithaca, NY, 2006.

Frame, Lynne. "Gretchen, Girl, Garçonne? Weimar Science and Popular Culture in Search of the Ideal New Woman." *Women in the Metropolis*, edited by Katherina von Ankum. Berkeley, CA, 1997.

Ganeva, Mila. *Women in Weimar Fashion: Discourses and Displays in German Culture, 1918–1933*, Rochester, NY, 2008.

Gerhard, Ute. *Unerhört. Die Geschichte der deutschen Frauenbewegung*. Reinbek bei Hamburg, 1991.

Graf, Rüdiger. "Anticipating the Future in the Present—'New Women' and Other Beings of the Future in Weimar Germany." *Central European History* 42, no. 4 (2009): 647–73.

———. "Girlkultur or Thoroughly Rationalized Female: A New Woman in Weimar Germany?" in *Women in Culture and Politics: A Century of Change*, edited by Judith Friedlander, Blanche W. Cook, Alice Kessler-Harris, and Carroll Smith-Rosenberg, 62–80. Bloomington, IN, 1986.

———. "The New Woman and the Rationalization of Sexuality in Weimar Germany," in *Powers of Desire: The Politics of Sexuality*, edited by Ann Snitow, Christine Stansell and Sharon Thompsn, 153–76. New York, 1983.

Grossmann, Atina. *Reforming Sex: The German Movement for Birth Control and Sex Reform 1920–1950*. New York, 1995.

Hagemann, Karen. *Frauenalltag und Männerpolitik. Alltagsleben und gesellschaftliches Handeln von Arbeiterfrauen in der Weimarer Republik*. Bonn, 1990.

———. "Men's Demonstrations and Women's Protest: Gender and Collective Action in Urban Working Class Milieus During the Weimar Republic." *Gender & History* 5, no. 1 (1993): 101–19.

Hake, Sabine. "Girls and Crisis: The Other Side of Diversion." *New German Critique* 40 (Winter 1987). 147–64.

Harvey, Elizabeth. "Gender, Generation and Politics: Young Protestant Women in the Final Years of the Weimar Republic." *Generations in Conflict: Youth Revolt and Generation Formation in Germany, 1770–1968*, edited by Mark Roseman, 184–210. Cambridge, 1995.

———. *Women and the Nazi East: Agents and Witnesses of Germanization*. New Haven, CT, 2003.

Hau, Michael. *The Cult of Health and Beauty in Germany: A Social History, 1890–1930*. Chicago, 2003.

Kaplan, Marion. *The Jewish Feminist Movement in Germany: The Campaigns of the Jüdischer Frauenbund, 1904–1938*. Westport, CT, 1979.

Lauterer. Heidemarie. *Parlamentarierinnen in Deutschland 1918/19–1949*. Königstein, 2002.

McCormick, Richard. *Gender and Sexuality in Weimar Modernity: Film, Literature and "New Objectivity."* New York, 2001.

McGuire, Kristin. "Helene Stöcker"s "*Neue Ethik*" and the Contested Realm of Sexuality." In *Sisters of Subversion: Histories of Women, Tales of Gender,* 142–51. Amsterdam, 2008.

Meskimmon, Marsha, and Shearer West, eds. *Visions of the "Neue Frau": Women and the Visual Arts in Weimar Germany.* Aldershot, UK, 1995.

Meyer-Büser, Susanne. *Bubikopf und Gretchenzopf—Die Frau der zwanziger Jahre.* Exhibition Catalogue, Hamburg, 1995.

Nolan, Mary. "Housework Made Easy: The Taylorized Housewife in Weimar Germany." *Feminist Studies* 16, no. 3 (1990): 549–77.

Petersen, Vibeke Rützou. *Women and Modernity in Weimar Germany.* New York, 2001.

Petro, Patrice. *Joyless Streets: Women and Melodramatic Representation in Weimar Germany.* Princeton, NJ, 1989.

Reese, Dagmar, Eve Rosenhaft, Carola Sachse, and Tilla Siegel, eds. *Rationale Beziehungen? Geschlechterverhältnisse im Rationalisierungsprozess.* Frankfurt am Main, 1993.

Roos, Julia. "Prostitutes, Civil Society and the State in Weimar Germany." In *Paradoxes of Civil Society: New Perspectives on Modern Germa and British History,* edited by Frank Trentmann, 263–80. New York, 2000.

Rosenhaft, Eve. "Women, Gender and the Limits of Political History." In *Elections, Mass Politics and Social Change in Modern Germany: New Perspectives,* edited by James Retallack and Larry E. Jones, 148–69. Cambridge, 1992.

———. "Lesewut, Kinosucht, Radiotismus: Zur (geschlechter)politischen Relevanz neuer Massenmedien in den 1920er Jahren." In *Amerikanisierung: Traum und Alptraum im Deutschland des 20. Jahrhunderts,* edited by Alf Lüdtke, Inge Marßolek, and Adelheid von Saldern, 126–27. Stuttgart, 1996.

Rouette, Susanne. *Sozialpolitik als Geschlechterpolitik: Die Regulierung der Frauenarbeit nach dem Ersten Weltkrieg.* Frankfurt am Main, 1993.

Sachße, Christoph. *Mütterlichkeit als Beruf: Sozialarbeit, Sozialreform und Frauenbewegung, 1871–1929.* Opladen, 1994.

Scheck, Raffael. "German Conservatism and Female Political Activism in the Early Weimar Republic." *German History* 15 (1997): 34–55.

———. "Women against Versailles: Maternalism and Nationalism of Female Bourgeois Politicians in the Early Weimar Republic." *German Studies Review* 22 (1999): 21–42.

———. *Mothers of the Nation: Right-Wing Women in Weimar Germany.* New York 2003.

Schlüpmann, Heide. "Die nebensächliche Frau: Geschlechterdifferenz in Siegfried Kracauers Essayistik der zwanziger Jahre." *Feministische Studien* 11, no. 1 (May 1993): 38–47.

Smith, Jill Suzanne. "Working Girls: White–Collar Workers and Prostitutes in Late Weimar Fiction." *The German Quarterly* (Fall 2008): 449–72.

Sneeringer, Julia. *Winning Women's Votes: Propaganda and Politics in Weimar Germany.* Chapel Hill, NC, 2002.

von Soden, Kristine. *Die Sexualberatungsstellen der Weimarer Republik, 1919–1933.* Berlin, 1988.

Stoehr, Irene. "Housework and Motherhood: Debates and Policies in the Women's Movement in Imperial Germany and the Weimar Republic." In *Maternity and Gender Policies: Women and the Rise of the European Welfare States,* edited by Gisela Bock and Pat Thane, 213–32. London, 1991.

———. "Staatsfeminismus und Lebensform. Frauenpolitik im Generationenkonflikt der Weimarer Republik." In *Rationale Beziehungen? Geschlechterverhältnisse im Rationalisierungsprozeß,* edited by Dagmar Reese, Eve Rosenhaft, Carola Sachße, and Tilla Siegel, 105–41. Frankfurt am Main, 1993.

Streubel, Christiane. *Radikale Nationalistinnen: Agitation und Programmatik rechter Frauen in der Weimarer Republik*. Frankfurt, 2006.

Sykora, Katharina, et al., eds. *Die Neue Frau: Herausforderung für die Bildmedien der Zwanziger Jahre*. Marburg, 1993.

Tatar, Maria. *Lustmord: Sexual Murder in Weimar Germany*. Princeton, NJ, 1995.

Theweleit, Klaus. *Male Fantasies*, vol. 1: *Women, Floods, Bodies, History*, translated by Erica Carter. Minneapolis, 1987.

———. *Male Fantasies*, vol. 2: *Male Bodies: Psychoanalyzing the White Terror*, translated by Erica Carter and Chris Turner. Minneapolis, 1989.

Usborne, Cornelie. *The Politics of the Body in Weimar Germany*. Ann Arbor, MI, 1992.

———. "The New Woman and Generation Conflict: Perceptions of Young Women's Sexual Mores in the Weimar Republic." *Generations in Conflict: Youth Revolt and Generation Formation in Germany 1770–1968*, edited by Mark Roseman, 137–64. Cambridge, 1995.

———. *Cultures of Abortion in Weimar Germany*. New York, 2007.

Wickert, Christel. *Unsere Erwählten: Sozialdemokratische Frauen im Deutschen Reichstag und im Preussischen Landtag 1919 bis 1933*, vol. 2. Göttingen, 1986.

Wildenthal, Lora. *German Women for Empire, 1884–1945*. Durham, NC, 2001.

Jews and Anti-Semitism in Weimar Germany

Aschheim, Steven. *Brothers and Strangers: The East European Jew in German and German Jewish Consciousness, 1800–1923*. Madison, WI, 1982.

Baranowski, Shelly. "Conservative Elite Anti-Semitism from the Weimar Republic to the Third Reich." *German Studies Review* 19, no. 3 (1996): 525–37.

Bayerdörfer, Hans–Peter. "Shylock in Berlin. Walter Mehring und das Judenporträt im Zeitstück der Weimarer Republik." In *Conditio Judaica. Judentum, Antisemitismus und deutschsprachige Literatur vom Ersten Weltkrieg bis 1933/1938*, edited by Hans Otto Horch and Horst Denkler, 307–23. Tübingen, 1993.

Benz, Wolfgang, Arnold Paucker, and Peter Pulzer, eds. *Jüdisches Leben in der Weimarer Republik*. Tübingen 1998.

Brenner, Michael. *The Renaissance of Jewish Culture in Weimar Germany*. New Haven, CT, 1996.

Brenner, Michael, and Derek Penslar. *In Search of Jewish Community: Jewish Identities in Germany and Austria 1918–1933*. Bloomington, IN, 1998.

Funkenstein, Amos. "The Dialectics of Assimilation." *Jewish Social Studies* 1, no. 2(1995): 11–28.

Gillerman, Sharon. *German into Jews. Remaking the Jewish Social Body in the Weimar Republic*, Stanford, CA, 2009.

Goldberg, Ann. "The Black Jew with the Blond Heart: Friedrich Gundolf, Elisabeth Salomon, and Conservative Bohemianism in Weimar Germany." *Journal of Modern History* 79 (June 2007): 306–34.

Hecht, Cornelia. *Deutsche Juden und der Antisemitismus in der Weimarer Republik*. Bonn, 2003.

Judd, Robin. *Contested Rituals: Circumcision, Kosher Butchering, and Jewish Political Life in Germany, 1843–1933*. Ithaca, NY, 2007.

Large, David Clay. "'Out with the Ostjuden': The Scheunenviertel Riots in Berlin, November 1923." In *Exclusionary Violence: Antisemitic Riots in Modern German History*, edited by Christhard Hoffmann, Werner Bergmann, and Helmut Walser Smith, 57–76. Ann Arbor, MI, 2002.

Maurer, Trude. *Ostjuden in Deutschland 1918–1933*. Hamburg, 1986.

Niewyk, Donald L. *The Jews in Weimar Germany*. Baton Rouge, LA, 1980.

Penslar, Derek J. *Shylock's Children: Economic and Jewish Identity in Modern Europe*. Berkeley, CA, 2001.

Pulzer, Peter. *Jews and the German State: The Political History of a Minority, 1848–1933*. Detroit, 2003.

Rothschild, Joseph. *East Central Europe between the Two World Wars*. Seattle, 1974.

Sieg, Ulrich. *Jüdische Intellektuelle im Ersten Weltkrieg: Kriegserfahrungen, weltanschauliche Debatten und kulturelle Neuentwürfe*. Berlin, 2001.

Skran, Claudena. *Refugees in Inter-War Europe: The Emergence of a Regime*. Oxford, 1995.

Van Rahden, Till. *Jews and Other Germans: Civil Society, Religious Diversity, and Urban Politics in Breslau, 1860–1925*, translated by Marcus Brainard. Madison, WI, 2008.

Walter, Dirk. *Antisemitische Kriminalität und Gewalt. Judenfeindschaft in der Weimarer Republik*. Bonn, 1999.

Wertheimer, Jack. *Unwelcome Strangers: East European Jews in Imperial Germany*. Oxford, 1987.

Literature, Society and Mass Culture

Barndt, Kerstin. "'Engel oder Megäre.' Figurationen einer 'Neuen Frau' bei Marieluise Fleißer und Irmgard Keun." In *Reflexive Naivität. Zum Werk Marieluise Fleißers*, edited by Maria E. Müller and Ulrike Vedder, 16–34. Berlin, 2000.

———. *Sentiment und Sachlichkeit. Der Roman der Neuen Frau in der Weimarer Republik*. Köln, 2002.

———. "Aesthetics of Crisis: Motherhood, Abortion, and Melodrama in Irmgard Keun and Friedrich Wolf." *Women in German Yearbook* 24 (2008): 71–95.

Bathrick, David, and Eric Rentschler, eds. Special issue of *New German Critique* on *Weimar Mass Culture*, no. 51 (Autumn 1990).

Berking, Helmuth. *Masse und Geist: Studien zur Soziologie in der Weimarer Republik*. Berlin, 1984.

Bodek, Richard. *Proletarian Performances in Weimar Berlin: Agitprop, Chorus, and Brecht*. Columbia, SC, 1997.

Bullivant, Keith, ed. *Culture and Society in the Weimar Republic*. Manchester, UK, 1977.

Confino, Alon, and Rudy Koshar. "Regimes of Consumer Culture: New Narratives in Twentieth–Century German History." *German History* 19 no. 2 (2001): 135–61.

Dalton, Margaret Stieg. *Catholicism, Popular Culture, and the Arts in Germany, 1880–1933*. Notre Dame, IN, 2005.

Fore, Devin, "Döblin's Epic: Sense, Document, and the Verbal World Picture." *New German Critique* 99 (Fall 2006). 171–207.

Führer, Karl-Christian. "Auf dem Weg zur 'Massenkultur'? Kino und Rundfunk in der Weimarer Republik." *Historische Zeitschrift* 262 (1996): 739–81.

———. "German Cultural Life and the Crisis of National Identity during the Depression, 1929–1933." *German Studies Review* 24 (2001): 461–86.

Goodstein, E. S. "'The Most Mendacious Prototypes Have Been Stolen From Life'—Femininity and Spectacle in Siegfried Kracauer"s Reading of Weimar Mass Culture." *Faultline: Interdisciplinary Approaches to German Studies* 1 (1992): 49–67.

Harvey, Elizabeth. "Culture and Society in Weimar Germany: The Impact of Modernism and Mass Culture." In *German History since 1800*, edited by Mary Fulbrook. London, 1997.

Hass, Ulrike. *Militante Pastorale: Zur Literatur der antimodernen Bewegungen im frühren 20. Jahrhundert.* Munich, 1993.

Haxthausen, Charles W., and Heidrun Suhr, eds. *Berlin: Culture and Metropolis.* Minneapolis, 1990.

Horkheimer, Max, and Theodor Adorno. *Dialectic of Enlightenment.* Amsterdam, 1947.

Huyssen, Andreas. "Mass Culture as Woman: Modernism"s Other." In *After the Great Divide: Modernism, Mass Culture, Postmodernism*, 44–62. Bloomington, IN, 1986.

———. "Modernist Miniatures. Literary Snapshots of Urban Space." *PMLA* 122 (January 2007): 27–42.

Jelavich, Peter. *Berlin Alexanderplatz: Radio, Film and the Death of Weimar Culture.* Berkeley, CA, 2006.

Jelavich, Peter. *Berlin Cabaret.* Cambridge, 1993.

Jonsson, Stefan. "Masses, Mind, Matter: Political Passions and Collective Violence in Post–Imperial Austria." In *Representing the Passions: Histories, Bodies, Visions*, edited by Richard Meyer, 69–102. Los Angeles, 2003.

———. *A Brief History of the Masses: Three Revolutions.* New York, 2008.

Kaes, Anton. "Schreiben und Lesen in der Weimarer Republik." *Literatur der Weimarer Republik 1918–1933*, edited by Bernhard Weyergraf, 38–64. München, 1995.

Kniesche, Thomas W. and Stephen Brockmann, eds., *Dancing on the Volcano: Essays on the Culture of the Weimar Republic.* Columbia, SC, 1994.

König, Helmut. *Zivilisation und Leidenschaften: Die Masse im bürgerlichen Zeitalter.* Reinbek bei Hamburg, 1992.

Lacey, Kate. *Feminine Frequencies: Gender, German Radio, and the Public Sphere, 1923–1945.* Ann Arbor, MI, 1996.

Lamb, Stephan, and Anthony Phelan, "Weimar Culture. The Birth of Modernism." In *German Cultural Studies*, edited by Rob Burns. Oxford, 1996.

Lehmann, Hans–Thies. *Das Politische Schreiben: Essays zu Theatertexten.* Berlin, 2002.

Leydecker, Karl, ed. *German Novelists of the Weimar Republic: Intersections of Literature and Politics.* Rochester, NY, 2006.

Lindner, Martin. *Leben in der Krise: Zeitromane der neuen Sachlichkeit und die intellektuelle Mentalität der klassischen Moderne.* Stuttgart, 1994.

Lüdtke, Alf, Inge Marßolek, and Adelheid von Saldern, eds. *Amerikanisierung: Traum und Alptraum im Deutschland des 20. Jahrhunderts.* Stuttgart, 1996.

Möding, Nori. *Die Angst der Bürgers vor der Masse: Zur politischen Verführbarkeit des deutschen Geistes im Ausgang seiner bürgerlichen Epoche.* Berlin, 1984.

Nolan, Mary. *Visions of Modernity: American Business and the Modernization of Germany.* Oxford, 1994.

Phelan, Anthony, ed. *The Weimar Dilemma: Intellectuals in the Weimar Republic.* Manchester, UK, 1985.

Plessner, Helmuth. *Die Einheit der Sinne. Grundlinien einer Ästhesiologie des Geistes.* Bonn, 1923.

———. *Grenzen der Gemeinschaft. Eine Kritik des sozialen Radikalismus.* Bonn, 1924.

———. *Gesammelte Schriften,* vol. 5. Frankfurt am Main, 1980–85.

Reinhardt, Stephan. *Lesebuch Weimarer Republik. Deutsche Schriftsteller und ihr Staat von 1918 bis 1933.* Berlin, 1982.

Reuveni, Gideon. *Reading Germany: Literature and Consumer Culture in Germany before 1933.* London, 2006.

Ringer, Fritz K. *The Decline of the German Mandarins: The German Academic Community, 1890–1933.* Cambridge, 1969.

Rosenhaft, Eve. "Brecht's Germany, 1898–1933." In *The Cambridge Companion to Brecht,* edited by Peter Thomson and Glendyr Sacks. Cambridge, 1994.

von Saldern, Adelheid. "Massenfreizeit im Visier. Ein Beitrag zu den Deutungs- und Einwirkungsversuchen während der Weimarer Republik." *Archiv für Sozialgeschichte* 33 (1993): 21–58.

Schräder, Bärbel, and Jürgen Schebera. *The Golden Twenties: Art and Literature in the Weimar Republic.* New Haven, CT, 1990.

Schütz, Erhard. *Romane der Weimarer Republik.* München, 1986.

Weyergraf, Bernhard, ed. *Literatur der Weimarer Republik 1918–1933.* München, 1995.

Visual Culture and Film

Adkins, Helen. "Erste Internationale Dada–Messe." *Stationen der Moderne: Die bedeutenden Kunstaustellungen des 20. Jahrhunderts in Deutschland.* Berlin, 1988.

Baumhoff, Anja. *The Gendered World of the Bauhaus: The Politics of Power at the Weimar Republic's Premier Art Institute, 1919–1932.* Frankfurt am Main, 2001.

Bergius, Hanne. "Fotomontage im Vergleich: Hannah Höch, Marianne Brandt, Alice Lex–Nerlinger." In *Fotografieren hieß teilnehmen: Fotografinnen der Weimarer Republik,* edited by Ute Eskildsen, 42–50. Düsseldorf, 1994.

Bürger, Peter. *Theory of the Avant–Garde.* Translated by Michael Schaw. Minneapolis, 1984.

Dada: Zurich, Berlin, Hannover, Cologne, New York, Paris, edited by Leah Dickerman with essays by Brigid Doherty et al. Exhibition Catalogue. Washington, DC, 2005.

Doherty, Brigid. "'We are all Neurasthenics!' or The Trauma of Dada Montage." *Critical Inquiry* 24 (Fall 1997): 104–18.

———. "Figures of the Pseudorevolution." *October* 84 (Spring 1998): 64–89.

Finney, Gail, ed. *Visual Culture in Twentieth Germany: Text as Spectacle.* Bloomington, IN, 2006.

Frieden, Sandra, Richard W. McCormick, Vibeke R. Petersen, and Laurie M. Vogelsang, eds. *Gender and German Cinema,* vol. 2. London, 1993.

Frisby, David. *Cityscapes of Modernity: Critical Explorations.* Cambridge, 2001.

———. *Fragments of Modernity: Theories of Modernity in the Work of Simmel, Kracauer, and Benjamin.* Cambridge, 1986.

Gleber, Anke. *The Art of Taking a Walk: Flanerie, Literature and Film in Weimar Culture.* Princeton, NJ, 1999.

Hake, Sabine. *Topographies of Class: Modern Architecture and Mass Society in Weimar Berlin.* Ann Arbor, MI, 2008.

Hansen, Miriam. "Decentric Perspectives: Kracauer's Early Writings on Film and Mass Culture." *New German Critique* 54 (Fall 1991): 47–76.

Heffen, Annegret. *Der Reichskunstwart: Kunstpolitik in den Jahren 1920–1933: Zu den Bemühungen um eine offizielle Reichskunstpolitik in der Weimarer Republik.* Essen, 1986.

Isenberg, Noah, ed. *Weimar Cinema: An Essential Guide to Classic Films of the Era.* New York 2008.

Kaes, Anton. *Kino–Debatte. Texte zum Verhältnis von Literatur und Film 1909–1929.* Munich, 1978.

———. *Shell Shock Cinema: Weimar Culture and the Persistence of War.* Princeton, NJ, 2009.

von Keitz, Ursula. *Im Schatten des Gesetzes. Schwangerschaftskonflikt und Reproduktion im deutschsprachigen Film 1918–1933.* Zürich, 2005.

Köhn, Eckhardt. *Straßenrausch: Flanerie und kleine Form: Versuch zur Literaturgeschichte des Flaneurs bis 1933.* Berlin, 1989.

Lane, Barbara Miller. *Architecture and Politics in Germany 1918–1945.* Cambridge, 1995 [1968].

Lavin, Maud. *Cut with a Kitchen Knife: The Weimar Photomontages of Hannah Höch.* New Haven, CT, 1993.

Lewis, Beth Irwin. *George Grosz: Art and Politics in the Weimar Republic.* Princeton, NJ, 1991.

Makela, Maria, and Peter Boswell, eds. *The Photomontages of Hannah Höch.* Minneapolis, 1996.

McCloskey, Barbara. *George Grosz and the Communist Party: Art and Radicalism in Crisis.* Princeton, NJ, 1997.

Minden, Michael, and Holger Bachmann, eds. *Fritz Lang's Metropolis: Cinematic Visions of Technology and Fear.* Rochester, NY, 2000.

Müller, Jürgen. "Der Vampir als Volksfeind: F. W. Murnau's 'Nosferatu': ein Beitrag zur politischen Ikonografie der Weimarer Zeit." *Fotogeschichte* 72 (1999): 39–58.

Otto, Elizabeth. "Medium und Körper in Marianne Brandts Fotomontage *me*." In *Marianne Brandt – Fotografien am Bauhaus,* edited by Elisabeth Wynhoff, translated by Axel Hase, 32–40. Stuttgart, 2003.

———. "Uniform: On Constructions of Soldierly Masculinity in Early Twentieth–Century Visual Culture." In *Künstlermythen und Männlichkeitsbilder: Geschlechterentwürfe in der Kunst des Kaiserreiches und der Weimarer Republik,* edited by Martina Kessel, 17–42. Cologne, 2005.

———. *Tempo, Tempo! The Bauhaus Photomontages of Marianne Brandt.* Berlin, 2005.

Petro, Patrice. *Joyless Streets: Women and Melodramatic Representation in Weimar Germany.* Princeton, NJ, 1989.

Rentschler, Eric, ed. *The Films of G. W. Pabst: An Existential Cinema.* New Brunswick, NJ, 1990.

Saunders, Thomas J. *Hollywood in Berlin: American Cinema and Weimar Germany.* Berkeley, CA, 1994.

Schlüpmann, Heide. *Unheimlichkeit des Blicks. Das Drama des frühen deutschen Kinos.* Basel, 1990.

Schmölders, Claudia, and Sander Gilman, eds. *Gesichter der Weimarer Republik. Eine physiognomische Kulturgeschichte.* Bonn, 1999.

Sekula, Allan. "The Body and the Archive." In *The Contest of Meaning: Critical Histories of Photography*, edited by Richard Bolton, 343–89. Cambridge, MA, 1990.

Ward, Janet. *Weimar Surfaces: Urban Visual Culture in 1920s Germany*. Berkeley, CA, 2001.

Weinstein, Joan. *The End of Expressionism: Art and the November Revolution in Germany*. Chicago, 1985.

Willett, John. *Art and Politics in the Weimar Period: The New Sobriety 1917–1933*. New York, 1978.

Citizenship, Migration, Boundaries of the Nation

Brubaker, Rogers, "Homeland Nationalism in Weimar Germany and Weimar Russia." In *Nationalism Reframed: Nationhood and the National Question in the New Europe*, 107–47. Cambridge, 1996.

Caldwell, Peter C. "The Citizen and the Republic in Germany, 1918–1935." In *Citizenship and National Identity in Twentieth–Century Germany*, edited by Geoff Eley and Jan Palmowski, 40–57. Stanford, CA, 2008.

Campt, Tina, Pascal Grosse, and Yara-Colette Lemke-Muniz de Faria. "Blacks, Germans, and the Politics of Imperial Imagination, 1920–60." In *The Imperial Imagination: German Colonialism and Its Legacy*, edited by Sara Friedrichsmeyer, Sara Lennox, and Susanne Zantop, 205–29. Ann Arbor, MI, 1998.

Eder, Klaus, and Bernhard Giesen, eds. *European Citizenship between National Legacies and Postnational Projects*. Oxford, 2001.

Fahrmeir, Andreas. *Citizenship: The Rise and Fall of a Modern Concept*. New Haven, CT, 2007.

Gosewinkel, Dieter. *Einbürgern und Ausschließen: die Nationalisierung der Staatsangehörigkeit vom Deutschen Bund bis zur Bundesrepublik Deutschland*. Göttingen, 2001.

Held, David. "Between State and Civil Society: Citizenship." In *Citizenship*, edited by Geoff Andrews, 19–25. London, 1991.

Marrus, Michael. *The Unwanted: European Refugees in the Twentieth Century*. New York, 1985.

Murphy, David. *The Heroic Earth: Geopolitical Thought in Weimar Germany, 1918–1933*. Kent, UK, 1997.

Nathans, Eli. *The Politics of Citizenship in Germany: Ethnicity, Utility and Nationalism*. Oxford 2004.

Oltmer, Jochen. "Migration and Public Policy in Germany, 1918–199." In *Crossing Boundaries: The Exclusion and Inclusion of Minorities in Germany and the United States*, edited by Larry Eugene Jones. New York, 2001.

Sammartino, Annemarie. "Culture, Belonging and the Law. Naturalization in the Weimar Republic." In *Citizenship and National Identity in Twentieth–Century Germany*, edited by Geoff Eley and Jan Palmowski, 57–72. Stanford, CA, 2008.

Schirmer, Dietmar. "Closing the Nation: Nationalism and Statism in Nineteenth- and Twentieth-Century Germany." In *The Shifting Foundations of Modern Nation-States: Realignments of Belonging*, edited by Sima Godfrey and Frank Unger, 35–58. Toronto, ON, 2004.

Schlögel, Karl. "Das Domicil eines Schattenbereichs: Russische Emigranten in Berlin in der 20er Jahre." In *Die Russen in Berlin 1910–1930*. Berlin, 1995.

Politics, Parties, and Political Mobilizations

Achilles, Manuela. "Nationalist Violence and Republican Identity in Weimar Germany: The Murder of Walther Rathenau." *German Literature, History and the Nation*. Papers from the Conference "The Fragile Tradition," Cambridge, 2002, edited by David Midgley and Christian Emden, 305–28. Oxford, 2004.

Breitman, Richard. *German Socialism and Weimar Democracy*. Chapel Hill, NC, 1981.

Buchner, Bernd. *Um nationale und republikanische Identität: Die deutsche Sozialdemokratie und der Kampf um die politischen Symbole in der Weimarer Republik*. Bonn, 2001.

Carsten, F. C. L. *The Reichswehr and Politics, 1918–1933*. Oxford, 1966.

Childers, Thomas. "Languages of Liberalism: Liberal Political Discourse in the Weimar Republic." In *In Search of a Liberal Germany*, edited by Konrad Jarausch and Larry Eugene Jones. London, 1990.

———. "The Social Language of Politics in Germany: The Sociology of Political Discourse in the Weimar Republic." *American Historical Review* 95 (1990): 331–58.

Diehl, James M. *Paramilitary Politics in Weimar Germany*. Bloomington, IN, 1977.

Föllmer, Moritz. *Die Verteidigung der bürgerlichen Nation. Industrielle und hohe Beamte in Deutschland und Frankreich 1900–1930*. Göttingen, 2002.

Fritzsche, Peter. *Rehearsals for Fascism: Populism and Political Mobilization in Weimar Germany*. New York, 1990.

Hunt, Richard N. *German Social Democracy, 1918–1933*. New Haven, CT, 1964.

Jones, Larry Eugene. *German Liberalism and the Dissolution of the Weimar Party System, 1918–1933*. Chapel Hill, NC, 1988.

Kaufmann, Doris. *Katholisches Milieu in Münster 1928–1933: Politische Aktionsformen und geschlechtsspezifische Verhaltensräume*. Düsseldorf, 1984.

Lieberman, Ben. "The Meanings and Function of Anti-System Ideology in the Weimar Republic." *Journal of the History of Ideas* 59, no. 2 (1998): 355–75.

———. *From Recovery to Catastrophe: Municipal Stabilization and Political Crisis in Weimar Germany*. Oxford, 1998.

Maier, Charles S. *Recasting Bourgeois Europe: Stabilization in France, Germany and Italy in the Decade after World War I*. Princeton, NJ, 1975/1988.

Mallmann, Klaus–Michael. *Kommunisten in der Weimarer Republik. Sozialgeschichte einer revolutionären Bewegung*. Darmstadt, 1996.

McElligott, Anthony. *Contested City: Municipal Politics and the Rise of Nazism in Altona, 1917–1937*. Ann Arbor, MI, 1998.

Mergel, Thomas. *Parlamentarische Kultur in der Weimarer Republik. Politische Kommunikation, symbolische Politik und Öffentlichkeit im Reichstag*. Düsseldorf, 2002.

———. "Führer, Volksgemeinschaft und Maschine. Politische Erwartungsstrukturen in der Weimarer Republik und dem Nationalsozialismus 1918–1936." In *Politische Kulturgeschichte der Zwischenkriegszeit 1918–1939*, edited by Wolfgang Hardtwig, 91–127. Göttingen, 2005.

Mommsen, Hans. "Militär und zivile Militarisierung in Deutschland 1914 bis 1938." In *Militär und Gesellschaft im 19. und 20. Jahrhundert*, edited by Ute Frevert, 265–76. Stuttgart, 1997.

Mühlhausen, Walter. *Friedrich Ebert 1871–1925. Reichspräsident der Weimarer Republik*. Bonn, 2006.

Nolte, Ernst. *Der europäische Bürgerkrieg, 1917–1945: Nationalsozialismus und Bolschewismus*. Frankfurt, 1987.

Pore, Renate. *A Conflict of Interest: Women in German Social Democracy, 1919–1933.* Westport, CT, 1981.

Rohrkrämer, Thomas. *A Single Communal Faith? The German Right from Conservatism to National Socialism.* New York, 2007.

Rüger, Adolf. "Richtlinien und Richtungen deutscher Kolonialpolitik 1923–1926." In *Studien zur Geschichte des deutschen Kolonialismus in Afrika. Festschrift zum 60. Geburtstag von Peter Sebald,* edited by Peter Heine and Ulrich van der Heyden. Pfaffenweiler, 1995.

Sabrow, Martin. *Der Rathenaumord: Rekonstruktion einer Verschwörung gegen die Republik von Weimar.* München, 1994.

Schanbacher, Eberhard. *Parlamentarische Wahlen und Wahlsystem in der Weimarer Republik.* Düsseldorf, 1982.

Schumann, Dirk. "Gewalt als Grenzüberschreitung. Überlegungen zur Sozialgeschichte der Gewalt im 19. und 20. Jahrhundert." *Archiv für Sozialgeschichte* 37 (1997): 366–86.

———. "Einheitssehnsucht und Gewaltakzeptanz. Politische Grundpositionen des deutschen Bürgertums nach 1918 (mit vergleichenden Überlegungen zu den britischen "middle classes")." In *Der Große Krieg und die Nachkriegsordnung: Politischer und kultureller Wandel in Europa 1914–1924,* edited by Hans Mommsen, 83–105. Stuttgart, 2000.

———. *Political Violence in the Weimar Republic, 1918–1933: Battle for the Streets and Fears of Civil War,* translated by Thomas Dunlap. New York, 2009.

Ward, William R. *Theology, Sociology, and Politics: The German Protestant Social Conscience 1890–1933.* Bern, 1979.

Weisbrod, Bernd. "Gewalt in der Politik. Zur politischen Kultur in Deutschland zwischen den beiden Weltkriegen." *Geschichte in Wissenschaft und Unterricht* 43 (1992): 391–404.

Weitz, Eric D. *Creating German Communism, 1890–1990: From Popular Protests to Socialist State.* Princeton, NJ, 1997.

Winkler, Heinrich August. *Der Schein der Normalität: Arbeiter und Arbeiterbewegung in der Weimarer Republik 1924–1930.* Berlin, 1988.

Wirsching, Andreas. *Vom Weltkrieg zum Bürgerkrieg? Politischer Extremismus in Deutschland und Frankreich 1918–1933/39: Berlin und Paris im Vergleich.* Munich, 1999.

———. *Herausforderungen der parlamentarischen Demokratie: die Weimarer Republik im europäischen Vergleich.* Munich, 2007.

Wirsching, Andreas and Dirk Schumann, eds. *Violence and Society After the First World War.* Munich, 2003.

Woods, Roger. *The Conservative Revolution in the Weimar Republic.* London, 1996.

Wright, Jonathan. *Above Parties: The Political Attitudes of the German Protestant Church Leadership 1918–1933.* Oxford, 1974.

Inflation, Occupation and Crisis 1923-24

Balderston, Theo. *The Origins and Course of the German Economic Crisis: November 1923 to May 1932.* Berlin, 1993.

Campt, Tina. "The Rhineland Campaign and Converging Specters of Racial Mixture." In *Black Germans and the Politics of Race, Gender and Memory in the Third Reich,* 31–62. Ann Arbor, MI, 2004.

Feldman, Gerald D. *The Great Disorder: Politics, Economics, and Society in the German Infla-tion, 1914–1924.* New York, 1993.

Fischer, Conan. *The Ruhr Crisis, 1923–24.* Oxford, 2003.

Holtferich, Carl. *The German Inflation 1914–1923: Causes and Effects in International Per-spective.* Berlin, 1986.

James, Harold. *The German Slump: Politics and Economics, 1924–1936.* Oxford, 1987.

Kaes, Anton. "Die ökonomische Dimension der Literatur: Zum Strukturwandel der Insti-tution Literatur in der Inflationszeit (1918–1923)." *Konsequenzen der Inflation–Conse-quences of Inflation,* edited by Gerald D. Feldman et al., 307–29 Berlin, 1989.

Koller, Christian. "*Von Wilden aller Rassen niedergemetzelt.*" *Die Diskussion um die Ver-wendung von Kolonialtruppen in Europa zwischen Rassismus, Kolonial– und Militärpolitik (1914–1930).* Stuttgart, 2001.

Maß, Sandra. *Weiße Helden, schwarze Krieger. Zur Geschichte kolonialer Männlichkeit in Deutschland 1918–1964.* Köln, 2006.

Nelson, Keith L. "The 'Black Horror on the Rhine': Race as a Factor in Post–World War I Diplomacy." *Journal of Modern History* 42, no. 4 (December 1970): 606–27.

Ostwald, Hans. *Sittengeschichte der Inflation. Ein Kulturdokument aus den Jahren des Markt-sturzes, mit Abbildungen.* Berlin, 1931.

Webb, Steven B. *Hyperinflation and Stabilization in Weimar Germany.* New York, 1989.

Widdig, Bernd. *Culture and Inflation in Weimar Germany.* Berkeley, CA, 2001.

The Weimar Social Body/Social Welfare

Crew, David. *Germans on Welfare: From Weimar to Hitler.* New York, 1998.

Eghigian, Greg. *Making Security Social: Disability, Insurance and the Birth of the Social En-titlement State in Germany.* Ann Arbor, MI, 2000.

Eifert, Christiane. *Frauenpolitik und Wohlfahrtspflege. Zur Geschichte der sozialdemokratischen "Arbeiterwohlfahrt."* Frankfurt, 1993.

———. "Coming to Terms with the State: Maternalist Politics and the Development of the Welfare State in Germany." *Central European History* 30, no. 1 (1997): 45–46.

Eley, Geoff. "From Welfare Politics to Welfare States: Women and the Socialist Question." In *Women and Socialism/Socialism and Women,* edited by Helmut Gruber and Pamela Graves. New York, 1998.

Eley, Geoff, and Atina Grossman. "The Gendered Politics of Welfare." *Central European History* 30, no. 1 (1997): 67–75.

Flemming, Jens, Klaus Saul, and Peter–Christian Witt. *Familienleben im Schatten der Krise. Dokumente und Analysen zur Sozialgeschichte der Weimarer Republik, 1918–1933.* Düs-seldorf, 1988.

Föllmer, Moritz. "Der 'kranke Volkskörper.' Industrielle, hohe Beamte und der Diskurs der nationale Regeneration in der Weimarer Republik." *Geschichte und Gesellschaft* 27 (2001): 41–67.

Frohman, Larry. "Prevention, Welfare, and Citizenship: The War on Tuberculosis and In-fant Mortality in Germany, 1900–1930." *Central European History* 39, no. 3 (9/2006): 431–81.

Harvey, Elizabeth. *Youth and the Welfare State in Weimar Germany.* Oxford, 1993.

Hong, Young–Sun. *Welfare, Modernity and the Weimar State, 1919–1933,* Princeton, NJ, 1998.

Lüdtke, Alf. *Eigen–Sinn: Fabrikalltag, Arbeitererfahrung und Politik vom Kaiserreich bis in den Faschismus*. Hamburg, 1993.

Mackensen, Rainer, ed. *Bevölkerungslehre und Bevölkerungspolitik vor 1933*. Opladen, 2002.

Mouton, Michelle. *From Nurturing the German Nation to Purifying the Volk: Weimar and Nazi Family Policy, 1918–1945*. Cambridge, 2007.

Petersen, Klaus. "The Harmful Publications (Young Persons) Act of 1926: Literary Censorship and the Politics of Morality in the Weimar Republic." *German Studies Review* 15, no. 3 (1992): 505–23.

Pörtner, Rainer, ed. *Alltag in der Weimarer Republik. Erinnerungen an eine unruhige Zeit*. Düsseldorf, 1990.

Reyer, Jürgen. *Alte Eugenik und Wohlfahrtspflege. Entwertung und Funktionalisierung der Fürsorge vom Ende des 19. Jahrhunderts bis zur Gegenwart*. Freiburg im Breisgau, 1991.

Ross, Chad. *Naked Germany: Health, Race and Nation*. Oxford, 2005.

Sachße, Christoph, and Florian Tennstedt. *Geschichte der Armenfürsorge in Deutschland: Fürsorge und Wohlfahrtspflege 1871 bis 1929*. Stuttgart, 1988.

Schwartz, Michael. *Sozialistische Eugenik: eugenische Sozialtechnologien in Debatten und Politik der deutschen Sozialdemokratie 1890–1933*. Bonn, 1995.

Toepfer, Karl. *Empire of Ecstasy: Nudity and Movement in German Body Culture, 1910–1935*. Berkeley, CA, 1997.

Weindling, Paul. *Health, Race and German Politics between National Unification and Nazism, 1870–1945*. Cambridge, 1989.

———. "Eugenics and the Welfare State during the Weimar Republic." In *The State and Social Change in Germany, 1880–1980*, edited by W. R. Lee and Eve Rosenhaft. New York, 1990.

Williams, John Alexander. *Turning to Nature in Germany: Hiking, Nudism, and Conservation, 1900–1940*. Stanford, CA, 2007.

From the End of Democracy to the Rise of the Nazis

Bessel, Richard. *Political Violence and the Rise of Nazism: The Storm Troopers in Eastern Germany, 1925–1934*. New Haven, CT, 1984.

Blasius, Dirk. *Weimars Ende: Bürgerkrieg und Politik*. Göttingen, 2005.

Broszat, Martin. *Hitler and the Collapse of Weimar Germany*. Translated and with a foreword by Volker Berghahn. London, 1987.

Fischer, Conan. *The Rise of National Socialism and the Working Classes in Germany*. New York, 1996.

———. *The Rise of the Nazis*. Manchester, UK, 1995.

Harsch, Donna. *German Social Democracy and the Rise of Nazism*. Chapel Hill, NC, 1993.

Kershaw, Ian. *Weimar: Why Did German Democracy Fail?* New York, 1990.

Lüdtke, Alf, Inge Marßolek, and Adelheid von Saldern, eds. *Amerikanisierung: Traum und Alptraum im Deutschland des 20. Jahrhunderts*. Stuttgart, 1996.

Ludwig, Cordula. *Korruption und Nationalsozialismus in Berlin 1924–1934*. Frankfurt am Main, 1998.

Panayi, Panikos, ed. *Weimar and Nazi Germany: Continuities and Discontinuities*. London, 2001.

Patch, William L. *Heinrich Brüning and the Dissolution of the Weimar Republic.* Cambridge, 1998.

Rosenhaft, Eve. *Beating the Fascists: German Communists and Political Violence 1929–1933.* Cambridge, 1983.

———. "Links gleich rechts? Militante Straßengewalt um 1930." In *Physische Gewalt: Studien zur Geschichte der Neuzeit,* edited by Thomas Lindenberger and Alf Lüdtke, 238–75. Frankfurt, 1995.

Smith, Woodruff D. *The Ideological Origins of Nazi Imperialism.* New York, 1986.

Striefler, Christian. *Kampf um die Macht. Kommunisten und Nationalsozialisten am Ende der Weimarer Republik.* Berlin, 1993.

Swett, Pamela. *Neighbors and Enemies: The Culture of Radicalism in Berlin, 1929–1933.* New York, 2004.

Winkler, Heinrich August. *Der Weg in die Katastrophe: Arbeiter und Arbeiterbewegung in der Weimarer Republik 1930–1933.* Berlin, 1987.

Witnesses of a Time/Zeitzeugen/Memoirs

Baum, Vicki. *Es war alles ganz anders. Erinnerungen.* Köln, 1987.

Brecht, Arnold. *The Political Education of Arnold Brecht. An Autobiography, 1884–1970.* Princeton, NJ, 1970.

Canetti, Elias. *Memoirs.* New York, 1999.

Frobenius, Else. *Erinnerungen einer Journalistin. Zwischen Kaiserreich und Zweiten Weltkrieg,* edited by Lora Wildenthal. Köln, 2005.

Göll, Claire. *Ich verzeihe keinem. Eine literarische Chronique scandaleuse unserer Zeit,* translated by Ava Belcampo. Bern, 1976.

Heymann, Lida Gustava (im Zusammenarbeit mit Dr. jur. Anita Augspurg). *Erlebtes–Erschautes Deutsche Frauen kämpfen für Freiheit, Recht und Frieden, 1850–1940.* Meisenheim am Glan, 1972.

Isherwood, Christopher. *Berlin Stories: The Last of Mr. Norris and Goodbye to Berlin.* New York, 1963.

Kessler, Harry Graf. *The Diaries of a Cosmopolitan: Count Harry Kessler, 1918–1937,* translated and edited by Charles Kessler. London, 1991.

Price, Morgan Philips. *Dispatches from the Weimar Republic: Versailles and German Fascism.* London, 1999.

Roth, Joseph. *Berliner Saisonbericht. Unbekannte Reportagen und journalistische Arbeiten 1920–39,* edited by Klaus Westermann. Cologne, 1984.

———. *What I Saw: Reports from Berlin 1920–1938,* translated with an introduction by Michael Hofmann. New York, 2003.

Scheidemann, Philip. *The Making of a New Germany: Memoirs of a Social Democrat,* translated by J. E. Michell. Freeport, NY, 1970.

Document Collections

Brinkler–Gabler, Gisela, ed. *Frauen gegen den Krieg. Mit Texten von Glaire Goll, Helene Stöcker, Bertha von Suttner, Clara Zetkin et al.* Frankfurt, 1980.

Jacobson, Arthur J., and Bernhard Schlink, eds. *Weimar: A Jurisprudence of Crisis*, translated by Belinda Cooper et al. Berkeley, CA, 2000.

Kaes, Anton, Martin Jay, and Edward Dimendberg, eds. *Weimarer Republik. Manifeste und Dokumente zur deutschen Literatur 1918–1933*. Stuttgart, 1983.

———. *The Weimar Republic Sourcebook*. Berkeley, CA, 1994.

Kolb, Eberhard, and Reinhard Rürup, eds. *Quellen zur Geschichte der Rätebewegung in Deutschland*, 3 vols. Bonn, 1968.

McElligott, Anthony. *The German Urban Experience 1900–1945: Modernity and Crisis*. London, 2001.

Noakes, Jeremy, and G. Pridham, *Nazism 1919–1945: The Rise to Power: A Documentary Reader*. Exeter Studies in History No. 6. Exeter, UK, 1998.

Ritter, G. A., and Susanne Miller, eds. *Die deutsche Revolution 1918/19: Dokumente*. Hamburg, 1975.

~: INDEX :~

www.ingramcontent.com/pod-product-compliance
Lightning Source LLC
Chambersburg PA
CBHW060019030426
42334CB00019B/2107